ECSTATIC

"*Bacchus*"

Hendrik Goltzius (c. 1558 – 1617)

ECSTATIC

For Dionysos

H. Jeremiah Lewis

Nysa Press

Copyright © 2011 by H. Jeremiah Lewis

All rights reserved. No part of this book may be reproduced by any means or in any form whatsoever without written permission from the author, except for brief quotations embodied in literary articles or reviews.

This book is humbly dedicated to my Lord Dionysos
and to all those who belong to the god:
the ones who were there before me,
as well as the ones who will come after.

May we all one day dance together in Nysa!

LENAIA
by Sarah Kate Istra Winter

In the swirling madness of the dance, your presence is visceral.
I close my eyes but do not see some vision of your face
No, you are in my sweat, and my breath carries your scent
as I shout your name, and fall heavily to the ground.

Here, you are a warm, thick skin around mine
The fur and musk of an animal, with a lover's tender touch.
You cradle me as the fury pours out, and I cry,
knowing this is not the end of it.

Again, the wine slips down my throat – you are inside me.
My legs want to collapse, but you push me forward
All the maddened people are sweeping past me, cups in hand.
I must follow, for your pleasure, I must join them.

All night, I give you all I have to give
My surrender palpable, and tasting of blood.
For all the pain that rends me like a sacrifice,
I love you – my destroyer, you softly brutal god.

ACKNOWLEDGEMENT

I would like to thank my beloved *paredros*, Sarah Kate Istra Winter. How much do I owe you and how much do you mean to me? My answer is simple: everything.

CONTENTS

Introduction xiii

SECTION I: ESSAYS

Intoxicated By Dionysos 3
How I See Dionysos 5
What's In A Name? 7
The Paths To Dionysos 10
Why Dionysos? 19
Meditations On The Dionysian Life 22
Don't You Forget About Dionysos 24
Choice 27
The Mystery Of Meilikhios And Bakchios 31
So You Want To Get To Know Dionysos, Eh? 33
The Other Side Of Religion 34
It Hurts To Set You Free: Reasons Why Not Everyone Should Be A
    Dionysian 37
Beyond Patrons 41
Finding Dionysos 45
A Fertile Faith 48
The True Dionysian 52
Speaking About The Unspeakable 54
Dionysian Worship In 5 Easy Steps 58
The Feast Of The Senses 60
Devotional Activities For Dionysians 70
The Miracles Of Dionysos 84
A Wine-Fueled Rant 88
Can A Dionysian Drink Beer? 91
Lampteria 93
Anthesteria For The Lonely Soul 95
The Lasting Value Of The Goat Song 110
Dancing With Dionysos 113
Not Always An Orgiastic God 116
The Queerness Of Dionysos 118
Stronger Than Dirt 124
The Land Of The Free And The Home Of Dionysos 127
Nympholepsy On The Mckenzie 132
The Geese And The God 134

Cleansing The Doors Of Perception 136
This God Is A Prophet.. 141
The Oracle Of The Leaves 143
Dionysos The Magical God... 154
Nothing To Do With Dionysos?... 157
The Symbols Of Dionysos... 161
On The Ritual Cry 169
He Makes Me Wet 171
That's Hot 176
The Pussy-Loving God... 178
Foxes In The Vineyard 180
Bacchus And Dionysos: More Than Just Good Drinking Buddies 182
The Gods Seen Through The Eyes Of Dionysos 185
Wild Child Full Of Grace.. 195
Much Ado About Nothing 199
Lacunae 203
A Neo-Orphic Interpretation Of The Myth Of Ariadne 206
Some Thoughts On Arakhne And Erigone 208
Thoughts On Orestes And Anthesteria.. 211
Nonnos Of Panopolis: Last Of The Greek Epic Poets 213
The Lusiads.. 216
The Ivy-Covered Cross: A Comparison Of Dionysos And The Judeo-
    Christian God.. 218
The Bull-Loving Kings: A Brief Study Of The Ptolemaic Patronage Of
    The Apis Cult.. 244
The Mighty Bull Of The Two Lands... 253
A Strange God In A Strange Land: The Changing Face Of Dionysos In
    Hellenistic Egypt 309
Praises Of The Strong Fruitful One.. 344
Quid Me Nutrit Me Destruit.. 347
I Value My God's Cock 349
Do You Remember When We Were In Africa?.. 357
Experiencing Greco-Egyptian Dionysos 361

SECTION II: POETRY

To Dionysos... 367
Preliminary Prayer... 368
Invocation Of Dionysos 369
Hymn To Dionysos Meilikhios... 370
Lenaia... 371
Hymn For The Worthy Bull And His Mother... 372
To Dionysos II 373
Hymn To Egyptian Dionysos 374
Hymn To Dionysos Petempamenti 375
A Prayer... 376
Invocation Of Passion 377
A Hymn To The Lord Of The Western Lands.. 379

To Dionysos At Delphi	380
To Dionysos Of The Desert	381
To The Holy Bull	382
Fragments Of Lenaia	383
Acrostic Lenaia Poem For Dionysos	385
A Garland For Dionysos On Anthesteria	387
The Thyia	393
Fragments Of An Initiate	395
Dionysos Mainómenos	396
To Dionysos Khoreios	397
To Dionysos Orthos	398
Epiphany	399
Possessed	400
Confession Of A Dionysian Mummer	402
Entheos	404
Tarantella	406
Chthonic	407
A Modern Dionysia	409
Bursts Of Drunken Poetry	410
Lusios	411
Memories	412
Written In Wine	413
Longing For Dionysos	414
My Life In The Labyrinth	416
To My Beloved	417
Omophagia	418
The Song Of The Fire-Born	419
Ecstasy By Midnight	420
Dionysos To His Mainad	421
The Mask	422
The Crown	423
Pentheiad	424
Anamnesis	425
Arakhneiad	426
Althaía	428
A Lament For Ampelos	429
Da-Pu-Ri-To-Jo Po-Ti-Ni-Ja	432
The Marriage Of Dionysos And Ariadne	434
Ariadne And Dionysos In Egypt	436
Peacock Bacchus	438
Hymn To Dionysos, Father Of The Ptolemies	439
A Feast Of Flagons	442
The Oracles Of Ptolemy Philopator	444
Alexandria, 1910	452
A Hymn To Hermes Dionysodotos	454
Hermes And Dionysos	456
Golden Verses	457
A Poem For Dionysos	459

The Satyr's Life For Me 461
Sotadean Verse 464
Hymn To Priapos 465
The Prophet Of Dionysos 466
I Could Never Love A Woman Who Wasn't A Mainad 469
The Call Of The Mainad 470
The Dancers On The Hill 471
Mainades Invoking The God 472
After The Revel 474
Experiencing Dionysos 475
After 476
Questions From Dionysos 477

SECTION III: STORIES

Running With The Apis 481
The Sign 489
The Initiation Of Ivy 491
A Translation Of Oinomaos Of Alexandria's *Philopseudes* 5.23 Ff. ... 493
Worship Of The Gods Is Not In Vain 496
On Whether It Is Acceptable To Discuss Sacred Things 498
The *Hieros Logos* Of Isidoros 500
The True Account Of The Death Of Dionysos 511
Ariadne's Story 516
Justice 526
A Dialogue Of The Gods 534
Remorse 537
Love Among The Vines 538
The Bacchae 2005 546
The Satyr Of New Orleans 560

Appendix I: Select List Of Dionysian Epithets 563
Appendix II: A List Of Gods With Whom Dionysos Is Syncretized ... 566
Bibliography 567
About The Author 570
Also From Nysa Press 571

INTRODUCTION

Most temples in ancient Greece had a *thesauros*. Not a book full of uncommon words – though this is where our thesaurus comes from – but a place to store all of a god's wealth and offerings left by thankful visitors over the centuries. Here you could find silver tripods and drinking vessels inlaid with precious stones, gold and ivory statues of ornate craftsmanship, trophies from the battlefield and numerous *stelai* extolling the unsurpassed virtues of the deity and the marvelous things they had done on behalf of their votaries. Interspersed with these treasures one could also find humbler gifts left by the common folk: images made of clay and wood, knucklebones, bits of pottery or unadorned plaques with little more than the name of the god and who had left it scratched on the surface. Over time this chamber could grow too crowded with offerings. The more valuable and impressive items were put out on display in the temple's courtyard or along the processional route. Other things were buried in large pits, recycled or sold off to finance the activities of the cult. Many pilgrims came just to see the fabulous wealth of the god since these items could have important historical value in addition to their material and spiritual worth. Guides made a brisk business showing the curious around, though at times they were no better informed than their modern-day counterparts at archaeological sites across the globe.

There is no temple of Dionysos in this land where I can leave offerings for my god. Nor am I a rich man or skilled with my hands. But one thing that I do have is words, and a great many of them at that. I like to think of this book as my Dionysian *thesauros*, filled with so many offerings that it's starting to get a little crowded around here.

I've been writing about the god for a large portion of my life now. The earliest piece in this collection was penned around 1993. The latest, about a week before we went to press. This collection doesn't contain every single thing I've ever written about or for Dionysos, though it's awfully close. A good deal of it has seen print elsewhere – in magazines and newsletters, blogs and websites, anthologies and my other Nysa Press books. That's actually what inspired me to put this volume together. Until now this material has been scattered all over the place and much of it hasn't been read – by me or anyone else – for the better part of a decade. This body of work, however, represents my history with Dionysos. In it you can see reflected my developing relationship with him, my deepening understanding of his nature and ways, the incredible experiences I've had worshiping him and countless other details of my life over the last twenty years. But this story only fully emerges when all of the pieces are united and displayed side by side.

Some will no doubt feel that I could have been a little more discriminating in what I chose to include here without doing damage to the whole. Undoubtedly they are correct. There is a fair amount of repetition throughout these pieces, themes I returned to several times over the years and even whole passages that got recycled now and again. Some of the material, particularly in the poetry section, may be lacking in polish and technical skill. Some of it may be rambling, disjointed, trivial and overly personal. I do not deny these charges, though I do hope that the rest of it makes for interesting and informative reading. I have certainly tried to provide as broad a picture of Dionysos and his worship in both its ancient and contemporary expressions as possible. To do so I have drawn on the best scholarship available to me, supplemented by my own insights, experiences and creativity. As a result I think it's safe to say that this book is not like anything else on the market today. It can't be, since fundamentally this is the story of my life with the god up to this point. Perhaps in another twenty years I'll bring out a sequel to *Ecstatic*. Undoubtedly it will be a very different book from the one you are currently holding in your hands, for I am likely to be a very different person by then.

But no matter how much I change one thing remains certain: I will always be madly, passionately in love with this strange, confusing and beautiful god Dionysos. He's been the central focus of my life since adolescence and I am proud to offer him this commemoration of our time together. It's been a wild and at times challenging ride but I feel confident in saying that the best is yet to come. May Dionysos look upon this collection and smile!

– H. Jeremiah Lewis,
who serves the god as Sannion,
in the great city of Eugene, Oregon,
on the 5th of April, 2011 by the common reckoning,
which is the Festival of Dionysos Triumphant!

SECTION I
Essays

"This stranger, this new god whom you ridicule –
it is impossible for me to tell you just how great he is
and how highly he'll be regarded one day
throughout the whole of Hellas."
– Euripides, *The Bakchai* 341 ff

INTOXICATED BY DIONYSOS

Dionysos is one of the most popular of the Greek gods and also one of the most addictive. He seeps into your consciousness, slowly and subtly at first. Perhaps you read something about him in a book that catches your attention, or you have a strange encounter late one night that takes your breath away. And at first you think that's just going to be it. After all, he's not really your kind of god, and you're certainly not his kind of person. But somehow you keep coming back to him (that incident plays over and over again in your mind; random phenomena spill into your life with such frequency that they begin to feel not-so-random after all; his dark and powerful myths intoxicate your soul, though you may find it embarrassing to admit as much) and no matter how hard you try to resist or ignore him he just won't go away. And then one day you stop resisting. You admit that Dionysos' ivy has firmly wrapped itself around you and you're as good as stuck: he's become your god, and you wouldn't have it any other way.

Amusingly, it's not just religiously-inclined people that this happens to. The scholar Jane Ellen Harrison started out writing her masterpiece *Prolegomena to the Study of Greek Religion* as an exploration of the Keres or spirits of the dead, and about half-way through found that it had taken on a life of its own, becoming a full-fledged treatise on Dionysian worship with the Keres as a parenthetical afterthought, a fact she bewilderingly confessed to a friend in a personal letter quoted in the book's introduction. Walter Otto, who penned the seminal *Dionysus: Myth and Cult* (which many Dionysians consider to be their Bible) wrote so rapturously of the god that many of his colleagues accused him of being a closet Pagan. And then there is Friedrich Nietzsche, who started off as an atheist and respected philologist, but came to identify so strongly with the god that in his waning days in a sanitarium he signed all of his letters 'Dionysos Zagreus.' Such is the powerful intoxication of the god, impossible to shake!

So who is this god Dionysos? It's a question that's been asked repeatedly over the centuries, beginning with Pentheus in Euripides' *Bakchai*. As the young king eventually found out (to his great misfortune) it is not an easy question to answer.

Dionysos wears many masks. He is a maddeningly complex god to pin down. Every time we think we've got him figured out he slips our bonds and laughs as we throw our hands up in frustration. He is a god of joyous celebration – and the most frightening destructive madness. He is a soft, feminine god – and the embodiment of masculine virility, honored with unapologetically phallic rites. He is a wild god of vegetation, haunting the forest and mountain with his nymph companions, causing the earth to bloom with a riot of colorful flowers and thick green foliage – and also the bringer of civilization and the patron of the highly refined dramatic arts. He is a god of the crowd, bringing an orgiastic, collective frenzy – who nevertheless can touch the heart of the individual, coaxing them through fear and self-imposed limitations into a life of freedom and authentic self-expression. He is many things to many people – and sometimes that changes over time, as our relationship and the personal needs that shape it change themselves.

Above all, though, Dionysos is alive! We Dionysians feel him and know him and continue to be inspired by him today. He is not a dusty relic of a bygone age, carefully locked away in a museum somewhere – but a powerful, authentic, living GOD. He is just as vital and relevant to our lives today as he was over 3,200 years ago when the Mycenaeans first etched the name Di-wo-nu-so onto clay. Dionysos is as old as time, and yet continually reborn and new. His nature and the stories told about him will never be exhausted.

HOW I SEE DIONYSOS

In the Museo Archaeolgica Nazionale in Naples, Italy there is an Attic stamnos which has always struck me as a perfect expression of the essence of Dionysos. It depicts a ritual dance in the Lenaion, Dionysos' oldest temple in Athens, where the epiphany of the god amid the new vintage was celebrated.

At the center of the scene stands an idol of Dionysos – a bearded mask on a pillar draped in colorful robes, with ivy tendrils growing out of it where one would expect to see arms. Before the idol an altar with pitchers of wine has been erected and two priestesses are ladling out the wine and offering a libation, while their sisters dance around in a flourish of erotic ecstasy – their lithe limbs, disheveled hair, flowing skirts, thyrsoi, and torches so real and full of energy you expect them to leap off the stamnos at any moment.

Dionysos breathes through every inch of the stamnos. He is the god of exuberant life, of fullness, of joy and all that overflows its bounds. His presence is intoxicating, inspiring, causing our spirits to rise up and break free of the fetters that bind them. Without even thinking about it, our bodies respond to the music that always accompanies his epiphany – the deep, primal rhythms of life – and we dance and sing and laugh and play, seeming drunk and mad to those who do not hear the music. Yet there is nothing foolish in the dance, for it is the most sublime form of worship, our bodies becoming vessels through which the god manifests. The dance is also a celebration of the primal powers of creation, the same process of renewal depicted in the rising ivy and the pouring of the wine. The whole world becomes intoxicated with his spirit, participates in his great cosmic dance: sap courses through trees and they sprout with fresh young buds; the earth grows moist and black and decks herself with flowers of the loveliest hues; animals feel the heat of his presence and begin coupling, and we humans flee our homes and cities and our socially-constructed roles to revel in the mountains with the mythic followers of the god, discovering our true natures in the process.

Dionysos' ecstasy is contagious, epidemic, spreading from person to person until there is a mighty throng, a swarm, a mass of bodies moving as one. Yet in the midst of all this noise, motion and excitement stands Dionysos – still, calm, serenely aloof as the mask from whose sightless eyes he peers out. This is Dionysos the Other, the Paradox, encompassing all, uniting every opposite, yet who always has more to show every time we think we've got him figured out. He is the effeminate, long-haired foreigner in soft, flowing robes and the ferocious, bellowing, bull-headed lord of battles who brandishes a flaming sword; he is the tender consoler who came to heal Ariadne when her grief was so great she was on the brink of death, and the pitiless instrument of vengeance which made the daughters of Minyas consume the roasted flesh of their own children. His nature is that of a mystery which cannot be solved by the mind. Our bodies know the truth, however, and once we submit to the spirit, understanding dawns and we know both who we are and who he is. The answer is EUOI!

WHAT'S IN A NAME?

The *Kratylos* has always been one of my favorite dialogues by Plato. At heart it is a meditation on the power of language and the relationship between objects and the names by which we know them. Sokrates maintained that this relationship was neither casual nor accidental – even when it comes to the gods, about whom men of sense must ultimately admit that they know nothing. Only the gods know their own true names and characters. But it's still worth examining what names the wise men of ages past have ascribed to them, for these names often reveal important things about the activities of the gods in the world and in relation to mankind.

What does it say about Dionysos, then, that he was never given a proper name? It was just as apparent to the ancients as it is to us that what we call the god is merely a title. Granted, we have been calling him by this title for a very long time. The earliest instance of it – Linear B *di-wo-nu-so* – comes from an inscription found at the Palace of Nestor on Pylos dated to the 12th or 13th century BCE. Eventually it spread throughout the Greek world with a variety of regional variations. For instance in Boiotia we find "*Dionūsos/Diōnūsos*," in Thessaly "*Dienūsos/Diennūsos*," in Ionia "*Deonūsos/Deunūsos*," in Aeolia "*Dinnūsos*" and so on.

The precise meaning of this title has always remained something of a mystery. It's apparent that it is comprised of two separate elements and most people have assumed that the first part derives from *dios*, the genitive form of Zeus. It's the *-nysos* part that's a bit trickier to unravel since it appears to be of non-Greek derivation. This didn't stop the ancients from coming up with a great many conflicting etymologies, however.

The philosopher Pherekydes of Syros, for instance, held that *nũsa* was an obscure word for trees (*FGrH* 3.178) while others felt that it meant "mountain" or referred to the mythical Mount Nysa of the god's infancy:

> "Zeus removed the child from the body of his mother and handed him over to Hermes, ordering him to take the babe to a cave in Nysa which lay between Phoenicia and the Nile river, and deliver him into the care of the Nymphai who would rear him and with great solicitude bestow upon him the best of care. Consequently, since Dionysos was reared in Nysa he received the name he bears from Zeus and Nysa." – Diodoros Sikeliotes, *Library of History* 4.2.3

Nonnos seems to be having a bit of light-hearted fun when he writes:

> "Hermes the son of Maia received him near the birthplace hill of Dracanon and holding him in the crook of his arm flew through the air. He gave the newborn Lyaios a surname to suit his birth, and called him Dionysos, or Zeus-limp because Zeus, while he carried his burden, lifted his foot with a limp from the weight of his thigh, and *nysos* in the Syracusan language means limping." (*Dionysiaka*, 9.16-24)

While Macrobius in the *Saturnalia* (1:18) recorded a more lofty interpretation:

> "The physical philosophers claim that he is the Material Mind or better yet *Nous* itself, which is easily discernable from the god's name since Dionysos comes from the Mind of Zeus (*Dios nous*)."

Although it's common to derive the first part of the title from Zeus, that was not the only possibility that the ancients considered. Sokrates provided the following playful etymology:

> "There is both a serious and a facetious account of the form of the name of this god. You will have to ask others for the serious one; but there is nothing to hinder my giving you the facetious account, for the gods also have a sense of humor. Dionysos, the giver (*didous*) of wine (*oinos*) might be called in jest Didoinysos; and wine, because it makes most drinkers think (*oiesthai*) they have wit (*nous*) when they have not, might very justly be called *Oionous*." – Plato, *Kratylos* 406b

While in the Suidas (s.v. *Dionysos*) we find:

> "The son of Semele. So named from accomplishing (*dianuein*) for each of those who live the wild life; or from providing (*dianoein*) everything for those who live the wild life."

Likewise some contemporary scholars have rejected the traditional Zeus-sprung form. Michael Janda (*Die Musik nach dem Chaos*) held that it came from the verbal stem *diemai* "to chase, hurry, impel" and agreed with Pherekydes that *nūsa* referred to trees, making the title of the god "he who runs among the trees" or "runner in the woods." He also considered the possibility that it had cosmological significance, proposing Dionysos as "he who impels the (world-)tree."

I suppose at this point you are expecting me to come out decisively in favor of one of these theories. Well, I'm not going to do it. I don't think any of them explain who the god is, at least not completely, because in the end the god is too vast and paradoxical to be confined by our labels and puny thoughts. That's why he doesn't have a proper name, since what can be named can be understood, and yet the only way to even begin to understand Dionysos is to accept that you never will. He does, however, have a title and that title expresses valuable information about his personality and the things associated with him. As such it must remain flexible, fluid, capable of being read on multiple levels simultaneously. And that's why all these different people over the centuries have seen such different things reflected in it: mountains and trees and distant lands and nymphs and rushing motion and intoxication and gifts and wisdom and Zeus – are not these the things of Dionysos? How wonderful that his name should contain all of them and countless other mysteries as well! So look and see what is revealed to you – but do not cling to that alone, assuming that it is all there is no matter how wonderful it is, for there is always more where Dionysos is concerned.

THE PATHS TO DIONYSOS

Quintus Aurelius Symmachus, one of the last defenders of Classical Paganism, remarked: "What matters the path by which one seeks the truth? One road alone does not suffice to attain so great a mystery!" Although his wisdom could be applied to many things, it holds especially true when we are approaching the god Dionysos, who is the mystery of all mysteries. I cannot tell you the number of times I've received e-mails from people who have begun to feel a call from Dionysos but stop dead in their tracks because they are afraid of what heeding such a call might do to them, or feel that they could never be a true Dionysian. By which they usually mean either a drunken mystic sensualist or a wild woman who leaves behind her home and family to rave with the god on the mountain-top and consume the raw flesh of freshly killed animals. And these people are probably right: it isn't within their nature to act in such a way or to radically commit themselves to tearing down the walls of fear and inhibition that they have spent a lifetime building up. But that doesn't mean that there is no place for the god within their lives, or that they can't benefit in even a small way from having a relationship with him.

In Euripides' famous play *The Bakchai*, the headstrong young king Pentheus believed that there was only one way to worship Dionysos and that was through drunken debauchery and madness. The wise Teiresias, who was a blind seer dedicated to Apollon, advised him that there was more to the god than what one might at first surmise. In addition to being the lord of the vine he is a god of all vegetative life. A kindly benefactor to humankind, he brings joy and merriment to care-worn hearts; he is a strong god, and warlike, who was able to conquer large parts of the world; and while he enjoys festive celebration and sensuality, that wasn't the only way that he could be honored. In fact, he goes on to say:

> "Dionysos does not, I admit, compel a woman to be chaste. Always and in every case it is her character and her nature that keeps a woman chaste. But even in the rites of Dionysos the chaste woman will not be corrupted." (*Bakchai* 315)

That is an important line. It shows that what matters lies in the heart of each individual. Dionysos helps us find our authentic self, the part of us which too often becomes dulled and corrupted and hidden under layers of fear and social respectability. Dionysos is the god who awakens us, who brings us fully to life, and the means of accomplishing that, and the form that it will take when manifested, differs from person to person. For some, intoxication and revelry are the doors through which we pass into wholeness; others find a quieter, more contemplative approach works best for them. Dionysos doesn't want us to pretend to be something we're not, to offer him false worship because we think this, and only this will be pleasing to him. He wants us to unfold the truth within us, to strip away the lies and false exterior and revel in wholeness with him. And he won't force us to do something we don't want to or aren't ready to; a chaste woman will remain chaste within his rites.

When we look at the mythology connected with Dionysos we find the truth that there are many paths which lead to him amply reflected. The way of the mainad and the way of the mystic may stand out most prominently, but there are others of equal importance.

For instance, we find the way of Teiresias himself, which I call the path of *philia* or friendship. For such a person Dionysos must always remain on the periphery. They are devoted primarily to another god, whose demands on them are of central importance. To embrace Dionysos completely would be to forsake the relationship they already have with their god, to violate their principles, to go against their own innate psychology. Dionysos does not want this. He respects his family and their territorial claims, and he would not cross that boundary even if he could.

Instead what he offers to such people is temporary release. A time of license and celebration which, once completed, reverts back to normal life. Such a person may have fond feelings for Dionysos, but nothing more. No intense devotion, no strong commitment. They may do a lot to contribute to the work of the god, for instance by helping to put on festivals for him, by writing poetry in his honor, by telling others about Dionysos, by helping those who are truly devoted to the god – but all their efforts are those of an outsider.

And Dionysos looks fondly upon this sort of work. They have much to contribute, for he is a social god, the god of the throng and crowd, the god whose mania spreads among large groups of people, the god who, according to Euripides, wishes to receive honors from all. If his worship was reserved for only the few who are intensely devoted to him, none of this would be possible. In fact, the really good rituals that he so enjoys would never come to be, for there are all sorts of details that need to be taken care of which the diehard mystics would probably overlook. Stuff such as organization, acquiring goods, setting up things, getting people together, etc. Other gods inspire the sort of people that are good at handling these little details, but Dionysos benefits from their presence at his ceremonies.

And Dionysos, in turn, can help these people strengthen their relationship to their own gods. Many times people have described Dionysos as a gateway god. He may be the first one that catches their interest, that starts them along the path of Hellenismos, that helps them deal with certain issues and tears down mental blockages, but after that they don't feel any deep connection to him. Instead, another god rises up in prominence for them, someone who more properly fills their spiritual needs, someone who inspires that deep, committed devotion on their part. They often become confused and saddened: where did Dionysos go? Did I do something wrong and that's why he disappeared? Since he was the first, why do I feel so much more for ____?

Although these thoughts are natural, and may be important steps on the introspective path, it is also important to remember that Dionysos is a fluid god who comes and goes at will, and who has a very strong working relationship with the other gods. They will often do things for each other when one of them is better suited to the task than the others. So it's quite possible that that's what lies behind this: you were never meant to be a Dionysian, but rather a friend of Dionysos.

Related to this path, but different from it, is the way of the satyr. For these people, Dionysos is first, foremost, and in the end, a god of exuberance, joy, celebration, sex, drunkenness, and reveling. Although they may be aware that there's more to the god, it doesn't really matter. They need to unwind and let go, and he's there to help them. This is the face of the god that is seen most prominently in our wider culture. In fact, most people know Dionysos only as the drunken frat-boy party god.

At first this bothered me because I was aware of the deeper complexity of the god – I saw him, in fact, primarily as a dark, dangerous, mysterious force of liberation and spiritual ecstasy. I thought they were ignorant and had only the shallowest of relationships with him. But then I came to realize that perhaps this was exactly the thing that they most needed and therefore it is what the god provides them with.

We live in a society that thrives on control and repression. From birth we are bombarded with messages that tell us our bodies are bad and that everything we do with them is sinful, that we can't trust our instincts, that to let go is weak and disgusting, that we will never be good enough, thin enough, pretty enough, and that the only value lies in transcendence, in controlling our every thought and action, in lifting ourselves out of the muck and looking up to heaven for our redemption.

The satyr stands in direct and radical opposition to this. In the face of seriousness he bellows with laughter. To those who would hold up an idealized, impossible image of beauty, he flaunts his grotesque obesity and says this flesh, too, is beautiful. He affirms that there is nothing wrong with enjoying yourself, in experiencing the pleasures of life to their fullest, that man is an animal and he shouldn't try to hide that or pretend otherwise. That sex, food, and drink are good things in and of themselves, that they don't need to be given a polite spiritualizing coat of whitewash to be tolerated.

True, such a path may not be fulfilling to all, but it has its value and its place within the Dionysian realm. Sometimes it can lead into a deeper understanding of the god, but plenty of times it doesn't. And I don't think Dionysos is bothered by that. He comes to people where they are, as they are, and he gives them as much of his blessings as they are ready and able to accept. Maybe these people will never feel sublime spiritual union or behold the mysteries of death and rebirth which are his provenance, but at his hands they have felt joy and release, and who can say what good this will end up doing for them in the long run?

The polar opposite of this path would have to be the way of Orpheus. To some this may seem paradoxical. What has asceticism and restraint to do with Dionysos? Isn't he the wild, sensual god of liberation? He is. But his ecstasy can also be felt in other ways. It can lead to an awareness that there is something more to us than just our bodies, and that this intangible principle is the most important part of us. He is a god of liberation, and sometimes we need to be freed from a gross, dense materialism, to let our souls fly free, to elevate our minds, to transcend our limitations.

Dionysos has nothing to do with addiction. Addiction is bondage, and Dionysos is all about freedom. Indulgence taken too far is slavery. And so Dionysos is there to help those who are battling against the invisible chains that keep them from living an authentic and self-governed life. Dionysos is the one who invented the custom of watering wine and who taught the ancients to drink temperately. As the god says in a comedy by the playwright Euboulos:

> "Three kraters only do I propose for sensible men; one for health, the second for love and pleasure and the third for sleep. When this has been drunk up, wise guests depart for home. The fourth krater is mine no longer, but belongs to hubris; the fifth to shouting; the sixth to revel; the seventh to black eyes; the eighth to summonses; the ninth to bile; and the tenth to madness and people tossing furniture about."

He is also a very sensual god, and when a behavior becomes conditioned, automatic and addictive, so that you have to keep doing it in order to function, how are you truly enjoying it? When you drink to the point of oblivion every night, you don't get the positive benefits of alcohol. When you have to have a cigarette every twenty minutes or you go insane, you're a slave, and all those harmful chemicals in your body, choking on phlegm when you wake in the morning, and emphysema or cancer, stop you from feeling the goodness and pleasure of life and enjoying other activities besides.

Dionysos can help us pare down these things, open us to a more expansive vision of life, feel all that it has in store for us. Also, by restraining ourselves, and indulging in an act infrequently, the pleasures become magnified many times over when we finally permit ourselves to enjoy them. Take sex, for instance. If you copulate every single night, several times a night, over a prolonged period, it becomes dull, boring, and eventually you may start to lose sensation. But go for a period without it and see what a difference there is. Your desire will grow stronger, and start to bleed through into other aspects of your life. You may start to become so sensitive that the slightest touch drives you wild. And when you do finally have sex, the intensity of your orgasm after the build-up will be mind-blowing.

Dionysian asceticism isn't about denying our pleasures or the world – it's about reshaping them, intensifying them, redirecting them into other avenues. There are of course other ways to do this, but the path of discipline and denial can be a powerful tool towards that end.

A path which benefits from Orphic discipline and asceticism, but which differs widely from it in aims and methodology, is that of the mainad. The mainades were the wild-women who followed Dionysos. They were his companions, his hunting-pack, his nurses and protectors. The path of the mainad is one that is only open to women (or those who possess the souls of women). And not every woman who is a devoted follower of Dionysos is actually a mainad. There is something special about this role and what it actually signifies.

To begin with, the mainad is a mad-woman. She is one who is filled with the spirit of the god, who has given complete control of her mind and body over to him to use as he will. Her consciousness recedes before the divine presence, and he guides her every step. Through him she is able to perform miraculous physical feats like touching fire without being burned, enduring other types of pain, lifting impossible weights, running for great lengths, possessing an elasticity in her movement which is not normally possible, consuming harmful substances without any negative effects and other related activities. Many stories said that the mainades could draw milk, oil and wine from the ground, and while I haven't actually seen this myself I've seen enough not to discount it outright.

But a mainad is more than just a 'horse' for the god (to borrow the terminology of Afro-Caribbean religions which have a very similar phenomenon in their entranceddevotees). A mainad is also the one who rouses the god, who calls him up from the depths, awakens him from sleep and death, and brings him forth into this world. She is the mortal double of the nymphs and goddesses who performed this function in the myths: she is at once his mother, his lover, his protector and hunting-companion. And that is why I say that only a woman can be a mainad, because there is something that happens when the masculine spirit of the god comes into contact with the receptive feminine vessel. It is very different from when the god's spirit fills a masculine vessel, as we shall discuss later.

A mainad is also a woman apart. She doesn't truly come into her own until she is in the wild, be that the dark forests of her mind or the physical mountain far from her home and her ordinary life as mother, wife, daughter, etc. To do so, she must forsake her normal obligations, must challenge the assumptions of what a good woman is and does, must strip away her inhibitions, her doubts and fears, must purify herself in the god's madness so that she may emerge whole and wild and fiercely independent and free.

And she must do the same for the god. She first coaxes his spirit up and nurtures it, as we see in accounts of the mainades taking young beasts to the breast or performing their secret rites to awaken Liknites, the infant god in the basket. Then she arouses him through her songs and dances, which are performed before the masked idol. She draws him out of it and excites him to dance, to come into his fullness as the wild and raving god of ecstasy. Sometimes this has an overtly sensual nature, as in the case of the Bridal Mysticism that we will soon be discussing, but other times it doesn't and can be simply the intoxication of life, the liberation of the dance, the pulse and thrum of all creation. When the god is ready, they rush down the mountain together, howling, mad, until they come upon their victim and tear it apart.

They are hunters. Fierce. Terrible. Hungry for flesh, aching to feel the warm spray of blood across their lips. And if the god should grow weak and tired in the revels, it is the duty of the mainad to hunt him, to slay her lord and tear him to pieces, so that he may emerge reborn and whole at another time.

This is powerful stuff. And as I said, not every woman is capable of it, however devoted to her god she may be, however strongly she has felt his ecstasy before. Only in the meeting of this constellation of practices does the actual mainad emerge. Without it, she is simply a devotee, possibly his priestess, possibly his lover, but not a mainad.

What of the lover? The best image of this is Ariadne, the bride of Dionysos, or her mortal counterpart during Anthesteria, the wife of the Arkhon Basileos. But it would be a mistake to assume that only a woman can be the lover of the god, for we also have accounts of Ampelios, of Prosymnos, of countless men who over the centuries have met the god in lust and found that transformed into the sublimest of spiritual unions with Dionysos.

The story of Ariadne is worth recounting, for it serves as the model of this type of relationship. She was a mortal princess of Crete who had fallen in love with Theseus, and for that love had turned her back on her family and her land, betraying them so that her beloved could live. Escaping, they stopped on Naxos where Theseus abandoned her because he didn't really love her. She ran after his departing ship, but collapsed on the rocks at the shore. Overcome with grief at what she had done, and agony at being spurned, she fell asleep wishing that she would die. It was at that point that Dionysos came to her, awakening her with his kiss and claiming her as his bride.

In a way this serves as an allegory of the human soul. So many of us are caught in misery, guilt and pain. We feel trapped and abandoned, rejected by the world and infinitely far from our homes. And so we go to sleep. We let our souls die, overcome by the hardship of existence. And it takes the hand of a lover to draw us back to the waking world. We respond to his touch with a deep longing that rouses our souls until we are fully awake, fully alive, and free of all the impurities that caused us to go to sleep. We embrace him, join with him in a union that is at once spiritual and sensual, and from that we experience the deepest, profoundest joy of our lives, which burns as brightly as the stars at night.

Others may not have such an intensely redemptive experience, but they respond to the god as a lover. They seek him out in the darkness, through the labyrinth they follow his laughing voice, and as they draw nearer their hearts leap with ecstasy, their steps are sprightly with dance, they burn and ache and love and create. He visits them in dreams and visions, teasingly revealing himself, reveling with them, seducing and making love to them. He fills them with joy and pleasure and his full abundance. And when he is not near, they ache for him with an intensity undreamed of, and only that union can make them whole. They belong to him, body and soul, like a wife to her husband and a husband to his wife.

For such people the language of love, of sexuality, of Bridal Mysticism which can be found running through the Abrahamic faiths, Tantra, Saivite Hinduism and numerous Pagan paths as well, is their preferred vocabulary to describe this unique religious experience. Often such people will not readily admit to it. They are embarrassed, uncomfortable, fearful of what others might say. And so they will only hesitantly reveal the depths of their feelings for the god to others who have undergone the same sort of thing. But I have come across a number of people for whom this is a reality, whatever others might think of it.

Another path which lies open for some is that of the vessel or avatar, which is perhaps best represented by Akoites. Akoites was the helmsman on the ship of Tyrrhenian pirates that captured Dionysos, who at that time was disguised as a young prince. The pirates sought to ransom him off, but unlike the others Akoites saw through the disguise and recognized the god for what he was. He pleaded with his fellows to let the god go, but they refused and eventually were punished for their acts. Akoites, however, was saved, and he spent the rest of his life serving the god and carrying his message to distant lands. According to Ovid it was Akoites, serving as mortal vessel for the god, who came to Thebes and confronted Pentheus.

This sort of thing was common in the Dionysian mysteries. A male priest – and in the accounts it is always a man who fills this role of *Bakchos*, at once god and the priest of the god, like the women who alone are mainades – would become filled with the spirit of the god, a process called *enthousiasmos* which meant literally "he has a god in him," and then throughout the ritual would represent the god in all his actions, speak with the god's voice, work wonders at his behest, and in short, allow him to be manifest in the physical world.

Nor was this sort of thing limited simply to a religious setting. There were a number of people from antiquity who came to deeply identify with the god, so much so that this shaped their behavior and how people perceived them. Their whole being became suffused with his presence, so that it was as if the god peered out of their eyes and acted through their body. Their lives were a mortal reflection of the god, and whether consciously or unconsciously, they came to act out and manifest his mythology through their existence. Alexander the Great, Ptolemy Philopator and Marcus Antonius are prime examples of this from the ancient world, but many have seen this same pattern reflected in the lives of Friedrich Nietzsche, Arthur Rimbaud, Elvis Presley, and perhaps most famous of all, Jim Morrison.

These people serve as a lightning-rod for which the forces of liberation, inspiration, madness, sensuality, joyousness and destruction may collect. They represent everything about the god: his fluidness, his sexual ambiguity, his love of pleasure, his rebelliousness, his desire to tear down walls and destroy the old social order in order to create something new – but also his self-destructive excesses, his inconsistency, his uncontrollable emotion. Unless they learn moderate self-control they are prone to burning out fast and furiously, and to grand self-absorbed dysfunctional displays that ruin both their own lives and those of everyone around them. But before that happens they are beautiful and prophetic, they show the way to liberation, to connection with wild nature and our truest selves. They transform everything they touch and make it shine just as brightly as their own souls which are lit with the fire of the god himself. And that is why people draw near to them, unconsciously desiring contact with the divine source of that light and power.

Such a person's life need not end in tragedy. Nor is it always the case that they will become a famous, charismatic artist or political figure. Many more people simply act out the myths of the god in their own lives, undergoing powerful, painful transformations, traveling widely, blurring the lines and challenging social conventions and common assumptions, inspiring creativity, connection, and liberation in those they encounter, and sometimes serving as a vehicle by which the god can touch lives and awaken people to his presence. They are following, then, in the footsteps of Akoites just as surely as Alexander or Jim Morrison.

The last path that we will consider (though there are certainly others) is one that a lot of people might not actually consider under the heading of 'ways to Dionysos,' and that is the path of *theomachia*, or the one who fights against the god.

There are numerous examples of this from mythology – Pentheus is of course the most famous, but there is also Lykourgos, the Minyades, the Proitides, and Desderides the Indian king. Although the details of their stories differ in many regards, they often follow a similar pattern. The god calls to them, and they resist. He makes other attempts to get their attention, and they either ignore him, spurn him, or actively try to suppress the activities of his followers. Finally, he confronts them. He inflicts madness on them, and draws out their failings and self-destructive tendencies, exploiting these to teach them a lesson. Finally they are forced to confront themselves and the god, and either relent and accept him, or are punished in a most cruel and creative manner.

Now, obviously this is not a very desirable path, but it is one that exists. And it is one in which the god is most intimately felt. When one capitulates at the first attempt of Dionysos to reach them and immediately rushes off to follow him, there is no need for pain and unpleasantness, for tearing down the barriers and the destruction of their personality. Such people have it easy, and the god needn't spend much time working on them. They experience him solely as a force for good and joy, scarcely intuiting that there's more to him. But the more we resist, the more he has to push his way into our lives. He will bring up our anxieties and inhibitions, he will push against our walls and masks until they crumble and break altogether. He will force us to confront what we fear the most, and he won't let up until we finally succumb to his greater power. This is a path of pain and suffering, a path in which we have to fight hard, with everything we have, to resist him. In so doing, however, we often come to a much greater understanding of ourselves than those who never resist, because the god holds us down and forces that introspection upon us. When we finally do give into his call, it means something. It has completely changed our lives and we have a level of intimacy with him which others will never experience. We also get to see depths of the god concealed to others: his darkness and terribleness, his awesome power, his true divinity. And once one finally embraces the Dionysian life, they will never let go of it, they will hold it as the dearest thing because he has ensured that they have nothing left, and they will be steadfast and vigilant, lest they slip back into his disfavor. So for that reason I have no problem counting this as among the ways to Dionysos, though it's certainly not one that I would recommend to others!

Now, in considering these different paths it has been necessary to discuss them in isolation and emphasize their differences. But the truth is nothing is ever so simple or clear-cut with the god. And while there are those who follow one path and one only, the vast majority of people blur the line and step foot equally on many of them. There are also paths which I have not felt it necessary to discuss, since these are either too general or too specific. And anyway, the point isn't to blindly follow what another has set down for you, but to find the path that leads you best into the heart of Dionysos. For that, you are the final and sole arbiter, and the only one who can determine whether you are a true Dionysian or not is the god himself.

WHY DIONYSOS?

That's really the thousand-*drachma* question, now isn't it? "Why Dionysos" is something I've asked myself more times than I can count over the years. What is it about this god that inspires such an intense attraction in me? Why him and not one of the many other gods out there, each of whom are equally wonderful and worthy of passionate devotion in their own way? How did he come to have such a strong hold on me?

You'd think the last question would be easy enough to answer, even if the others are a little harder to put into words. But I can't really pinpoint the exact moment when my infatuation with him began.

I remember having a series of dreams and strange encounters with a shadowy figure in early adolescence that I eventually came to realize was Dionysos. At the time I had no idea who he was and spent the next several years chasing his shadow through a number of different religious systems. But the fact that I did this shows that the desire for him was already in me even if I didn't know enough at the time to look in the right place for him. All the gods that interested me during this seeker phase shared certain qualities with Dionysos – but not enough to serve as a substitute for him. It was only him, always only him that could meet my spiritual needs and so I wandered until I found him. And having found him I can't imagine my life without him at its center. I have strong, important relationships with other divinities but they always take a back seat to Dionysos. The ones I honor the most, such as Hermes and Spider, are the ones who help me draw closer to Dionysos and make it possible for me to do the work that he asks of me. If they don't fit into that pattern then they are irrelevant to me, however much I might otherwise like and respect them. It's why it never went anywhere between me and Apollon, Artemis, Kybele, Isis, Thoth and a host of others. What they asked of me was often too much or too unrelated to the realm of Dionysos for me to be comfortable with it. Likewise, although I felt an attraction to them, there was no blossoming of a relationship with Osiris, Serapis, Antinous, Zeus, Pan and a couple deities outside the Greco-Egyptian fold. They were so similar to Dionysos in certain ways that there just wasn't room in my life for them in anything more than a casual fashion – and often not even that. The reasons that others approach these gods and the experiences people have with them were already being fulfilled for me by Dionysos. Sometimes I had a hard time even seeing these gods because all I'd pick up on was their Dionysian qualities and then my mind inevitably drifted back to him. Things are different with Hermes and the other primary gods and spirits I honor. They are compatible enough that there is no dissonance or territorial issues – but they're also unique enough that Dionysos doesn't eclipse them.

So what is it about Dionysos that does it for me? Fuck, what isn't there? I mean, everything about him makes me all squishy inside and feeling like I've got a school-girl crush on him. Everything I love about life, about the world, about being human has got Dionysos' hands all over it. It doesn't matter what interest I develop – sooner or later I'm bound to discover a previously unknown Dionysian connection to it. And honestly, that's kind of cool. I mean, he's this immense god with all these different sides and yet there's nothing random or hodge-podge about it. All these different aspects fit together smoothly, forming a cohesive and easily discernable whole. Even when you'd think they'd be contradictory I've discovered that if you just look hard enough, long enough, and go deep enough, it becomes obvious why they're associated with him and equally obvious why certain other things are never listed as part of his divine repertoire. All of this shows that he's real, that there's a genuine personality behind it. He's not an archetype, a collection of assorted qualities and concepts. If he was he'd be a lot less complicated, a lot less contradictory – and a lot less interesting. Let's start with the sound-bite description that everyone uses for him.

Dionysos is the vine-god, the wine-god. Okay, and by extension he could also be a god of the wider vegetative realm – of trees and flowers and all that. Maybe even a god of fertility because that's what fuels the growth of grapes and by extension also a god of animal life because they're all about fertility too. Makes perfect sense, right? Then why is he the god of actors and of drama? Alright, maybe tragedy grew out of primitive rites enacted as part of the harvest celebration – but why is he the god of women, the god of foreigners, the god of madness and the inversion of social order? None of these things are especially connected with wine or fertility – there are plenty of other vegetation gods around the world who lack this particular constellation of associations. And yet we've just scratched the surface. He's also the god of healing, of purification, of liberation, of poetic inspiration, of battle-frenzy, of kingship, of the dead, of newborn babies and teens going through transitional rites, of cross-dressing effeminate males, of manly men renowned for their sexual prowess, of sailing, of mountain-climbing and a list of other things that goes on and on and on.

And yet he's not the god of everything. There's not the cold, calculating reason of Athene, the humble domestic tranquility of Hestia or the delicate craftsmanship of Hephaistos. The list of things that Dionysos isn't is nearly as long as the list of things he is – and that helps us to better understand Dionysos-qua-Dionysos. Because both the things that belong to him and those that don't are a natural outgrowth of his distinctive personality. Even if it seems odd that a wine-god would also be a god of the dead or the god of puberty rites, it makes sense when you think of who Dionysos is and consider the totality of his attributes in relation to each other. Sure, there's no direct link between Quality A and Quality N, but there is between M, N and O and if you trace the thread back far enough you'll eventually arrive at A.

And that just blows my mind because there's *so much to him* and it all fits together and it's all deeply fascinating and you could spend a lifetime exploring all these nuanced bits and pieces and never really make a dent. There's always so much more to learn, so much more to explore and experience and realize what it really means as opposed to what you've just conceptualized in your head. I mean, "madness" and "liberation" and "fertility" are just words, empty sounds we repeat to ourselves until we've actually felt them and lived them and come to understand them. It's only by way of this process that we ever come to know the real Dionysos and not just this mental construct that has been created for us. And the more you do that the more you want to do it, need to do it – and that, I guess, is how I got wrapped up in all this and why he is my god in a way that no other is. Once you start chasing him it's impossible to find your way out of the labyrinth – especially when you have no desire to leave anyway.

MEDITATIONS ON THE DIONYSIAN LIFE

What is it like to have a relationship with Dionysos? Well, to begin with he is a very intense god whose presence intensifies everything, often to a fever pitch. He comes into our lives like a whirlwind – frenzied, ecstatic and beautiful, melting, changing, heightening everything he touches. Those walls we built up, those masks we carefully constructed to shield us from the painful and frightening things in our past and in the world dissolve before him like brittle clay submerged in water. He coaxes us out of the shadows into the light of day, unfolding us gently like a flower to behold the beauty and warmth of a world enchanted and infused with his radiance and life-nourishing essence. He drives off our sorrows and fears, leaving us free and alive, a whole vista of unexplored sensations and emotions now open to us. He holds out a cup full of the wine of life and bids us drink deeply from it, then courses through our bodies: a dizzying, maddening, blessed fire which drives us to dance and shout and laugh in a state of unparalleled bliss. This is what it means to touch the god and be touched by him in return – and having felt the ecstasy of an encounter with Dionysos you will never forget it.

But sometimes that's the problem. We are mortals. It's not possible for us to maintain that peak of pure experience and divine joy indefinitely. Some try and manage an intimacy with him which most can only dream of – but even the greatest mystic must eventually come down from the mountain and walk amid the mortal world. And for some this can be a sad and disheartening experience. But it needn't be – in fact, it shouldn't be. Because Dionysos is no world-denying, body-hating ascetic contemptuous of the commonplace, dreaming of a fantasy land that doesn't exist. His world is here, now, and he recognizes no dichotomy and in fact tears down all barriers which might impede the flow of life and spirit.

The goal of the Dionysian is not to have great mind-blowing trips, to cultivate strange powers and unique experiences like notches on a belt, with all the time between as this dull, dismal interlude to real existence. Rather, the purpose of the true Dionysian is to resist such spiritual dilettantism and to work a much more subtle and powerful form of magic than the mainades of old did when they drew fountains of wine from the earth or tore apart wild bulls with their bare hands. Our task is to gradually transform consciousness, to awaken ourselves to an awareness of the world as it truly is, to its beauty and complexity and contradictory nature, the inherent rhythm of creation and destruction which beats through the hearts of all living things. This pulse is so omnipresent that we often cannot hear it, since it has been with us from the moment we drew our first breath, and even before that. It sounds in even the humblest of circumstances, in the cadence of our footfalls as we walk through the hallway at work, in the splash of water as we do the dishes after dinner. It is with us always, and so we never hear it; but Dionysos urges us to open our ears and listen, for that song is his song, the song of life which he performs for all creation. Such a simple thing, really, this mindfulness, this being present in the world around you – and yet for many in our fast-paced, hectic society it's next to impossible to accomplish. And so they feel disconnected, alien, cut-off from the source of life. But how much of that is just in their heads?

The biggest barrier to a rewarding spiritual life is usually one's own self. Not the true self, the primal core of our being whose fiery essence is composed of the same essential stuff as the stars in heaven and Dionysos himself – no, not our true self, but the illusionary self that we create for ourselves, composed of fears and self-doubt and the internalized criticism of our family, friends, and society. Our wants and petty aspirations, our material desires, that part of us which is defined by the work we do during the day, the clubs we belong to, our political, racial and even familial identity – all the things that we take to us and wrap around our true selves, weaving a cocoon of illusionary identity in order to fit in with other people who have a similar identity. But none of this is who we truly are, as we find when those strands are cut and fall away. It may be painful to lose them, since we can grow attached to our carefully constructed ego, but we will not cease to be if they are lost. And that is an important distinction to keep in mind. Because if we should begin to lose part of our true selves, a process of death begins. And sometimes the weight of all these masks, all these layers of ego can begin to smother our true selves, snuff out the flame of our immortal being.

And when Dionysos senses that happening he intervenes. He comes to us and challenges us to remember who we truly are, to loosen the threads that bind us, to lift the masks and stare out at the world with our own true eyes once more. And when gently coaxing and subtle reminders are not enough, Dionysos will put on a frightening visage and he will begin to tear all of that stuff away from us, devouring it with his sharp and vicious teeth, and that can be the most painful experience imaginable if you are deeply attached to the false layers. It can feel like you are being torn apart alive, the flesh peeled from your body to reveal muscle and blood and raw nerve endings. And if you resist, if your fear gets the better of you and you fight to stay trapped in ego-snares, you can even die. But if you trust him, if you let him dissolve the falseness, you will find him to be gentle and kind and full of greater love than you could ever have imagined. Not a soft, sentimental, indulgent love – for Dionysos' love is a challenge which we must always strive to meet. His love is freedom and truth, an erotic attraction to our primal being and the transcendent unity of all creation. With that love blazing in our hearts we flee from our homes, our settled, conventional existence, to run free through the forested mountain heights, proclaiming our adoration of him through ecstatic song and dance. Io euoi! Io Dionysos the liberator!

DON'T YOU FORGET ABOUT DIONYSOS

One of the greatest devotional hymns ever written about the god Dionysos is no doubt Simple Minds' 80's classic "Don't You (Forget About Me)." Granted, most people probably haven't quite thought of this song in that context before. In fact, it's a pretty safe bet that many of you (or at least those of you who are of a certain age) find it difficult to hear this song and think of anything other than the seminal John Hughes teen comedy for which it was composed. Of course, that needn't be as big of a stumbling block as one might assume, since *The Breakfast Club* is full of Dionysian themes (rebellion against authority, transgression of social norms, breaking down artificial boundaries, dissolution of identity and discovery of a deeper, more authentic self; hell, there's even ingestion of mind-altering substances).

But the song goes much deeper than that. The lyrics are full of allusions to Dionysos and the experience of being initiated into his mysteries. At least, that's how it comes across to me, though I confess that I don't really know *what* the author intended. But with lines like this, you've got to wonder.

Won't you come see about me?

Ah, the Great Invitation of Dionysos, calling the mad ones out of their homes and ordinary lives to revel with him in the wild places. This comes to each of us at different times and different ways. How will you respond to the call? What will you give up to follow him?

I'll be alone, dancing you know it baby

Dionysos, of course, is the dancer, *khoreios*, and the leader of the dance. Often, however, there is a solitariness to him, a stillness amid the flurry and frenzy of the throng.

Tell me your troubles and doubts

Dionysos is Meilikhios, the Gentle One, he who brings forgetfulness of cares, he who frees the soul from its constraints, he who, in the words of Nonnos, wept to stop the tears of mortal man from flowing.

Giving me everything inside and out

There are those who come to the celebrations of Dionysos. They want to have fun, get drunk, and feel, for a few moments at least, the blessed liberation of the god. These are the wand-bearers that Plato spoke of. But there's another group as well, the Bakchoi. They're in it for the long-haul. They're committed to living the Dionysian life, to being free. But you know what freedom costs? Everything. Your fears, your doubts, your inhibitions, your desire to lead a normal life: all of these must be sacrificed on the altar of the god if you would be a true *mystai*. And that's just the start. The real work of liberation takes place inside you, within your soul. It is messy, and painful, and challenging in ways you never could have expected going into it. But once you've started, you can't turn back. Having tasted the freedom he offers, you'll never be satisfied with anything less.

Love's strange
To the Orphics Dionysos was the Primordial Eros and love the path that leads back to the divine. Love changes the way we think and relate to the world; it makes us strangers to our mundane selves.

so real in the dark
The world by night is a different place than it is during the day. Mysterious, magical, frightening, playing tricks on our perception: this is the realm that the god inhabits, the time when he and his holy band revel in the hills. This is where initiation takes place, where we come to learn of the real things.

Think of the tender things that we were working on
We are the tender things, once the god has begun working on us, stripping back the layers, releasing what has lain hidden for so long. We are vulnerable in this state, like Marsyas with his flesh flayed. And so we must do our part to speed the process along; the more we struggle, the greater the pain we feel. But if we submit it passes quickly. Thus our spiritual transformation is a collaborative effort between us and the god.

Slow change may pull us apart / Going to take you apart / I'll put us back together at heart, baby
The ancient poets tell us that before Dionysos there was Zagreus, and that Zagreus was torn apart by the Titans and all of his flesh was consumed save his heart. Though this dismemberment was horrible, out of the remnants our god Dionysos was formed, created with the heart of Zagreus. This is the process of initiation, which we all must go through. First we are dismembered, our shattered limbs and consciousness scattered to the winds. Then, through the agency of the god, we are brought back together, made anew in his image, healed and restored. First dismemberment, then remembering.

I won't harm you or touch your defenses / Vanity and security
Though Dionysos wishes for us to be whole and free, he will not force this upon us. We must make the choice on our own. If we feel the need for boundaries, he will respect them. He may push against them, up to that point, but he won't cross it, not unless we ask him to. Of course, we may miss out on a great many things because of that, and often the defenses we cling to the strongest are the most harmful to us, born of fear and dysfunction. But the sacrifice must be a willing one.

Will you stand above me? / Look my way, never love me / Will you recognize me? / Call my name or walk on by

These lines remind us that Dionysos is singing a beautiful love-song to humanity. We humans are like Ariadne, abandoned and desolate on the beach of Naxos; we are in danger of succumbing to the slumber of the senses. But he seeks to rouse us, to stir within us a memory of who we are and who he is and what the world is truly like – divine and full of enchantment, as in the glorious prose hymn of Nietzsche. He wants us to recognize him, like Akoites alone among the Tyrrhenian pirates; he wants us to follow him into the forest and revel in freedom, to call out his name in joyous celebration.

Well, will you?

CHOICE

We often talk about Dionysos as the god of freedom, the one who comes to liberate us from our chains whether they are personal inhibitions, psychological addictions, societal convention or even physical bondage.

There are many ways that he works his wonders in our lives, but one of the most important is also, in some respects, the simplest: he reminds us that we've got a choice. Think back on the bulk of his myths: what's he usually doing? Trying to get people to seriously think about their lives and what they want out of them, to show them that they don't have to settle for what's been given to them or follow certain predetermined roles just because that's what everyone expects them to do. He urges people to take responsibility for their actions, to realize that they've got the power to change things, to look at things in a different light.

King Midas couldn't conceive of anything more valuable than gold until Dionysos showed him otherwise. Akoites couldn't imagine any way out of violence and thievery until Dionysos revealed to him the power of dreams. Hephaistos and Hera were trapped in a cycle of violence and recrimination until Dionysos intervened. Ariadne thought herself worthy of death for the crimes of her past until Dionysos woke her up on Naxos. Countless women believed that they could be nothing more than wives and mothers until Dionysos got ahold of them. And he even tried to reason with his bitterest enemies. How many times does Dionysos come before Pentheus, humbling himself and pleading with him to turn aside, to let go of his wrath and delusions and choose the path of peace instead? The same course of action was taken with Lykourgos and the daughters of Minyas, though it didn't do them any more good than it did Pentheus.

That's because we humans are stubborn, stupid and blind, and cling to our misery even as it destroys us. We do this because although misery isn't exactly comfortable, it is familiar and unchallenging. Freedom is scary because it opens the doors of possibility into realms full of strangeness and uncertainty. Maybe something worse lies in store for us if we walk through those doors. Maybe we'll be confronted with trials greater than we can handle. Maybe it'll take us far from home and everything we've ever known. Maybe it'll end up transforming us into people we'd hardly recognize any more – or like. Maybe we'll see that there's nothing to all the excuses and empty stories we've told ourselves to justify our stagnation and unhappiness and then we'll actually have to start taking responsibility for our actions and the contents of our lives. Maybe...but is all of that necessarily such a bad thing? Don't you want to be in charge of your life? Don't you want to know that if you fail or succeed it's because of what's in you and not a result of what others have done to you in the past or because of all those nebulous, intangible forces stacked against you?

When it comes down to it most people don't have any idea how truly free they are. Unless someone's keeping you locked away in a basement somewhere there's not a damned thing stopping you from picking up and starting your life over from scratch somewhere else. Seriously. Tomorrow you could decide to move all the way across the country to Florida, change your name, change your hair, get a bunch of tattoos and become an exotic dancer, leaving your job, your life up to this point, your family and everyone who's ever known you behind for good. There's nothing stopping you from doing that or anything else you could dream of – except yourself. I know because I've already done it twice in my life and for all I know I may end up doing it again.

Granted, that sort of radical transformation may not be for everyone and even my own re-creations weren't quite on that level. And I'm not saying it'd be easy, by any means. In fact, for most of us it'd be damn hard, full of unimaginable sacrifices and pain, with only a slim chance of genuine success. (Besides, no sensible person actually *wants* to live in Florida.) But the fact remains, it *can* be done. And if there's nothing stopping a person from making a change of that magnitude, then there's nothing stopping you from making the changes in your own life that you feel are necessary. You don't like the career you've got? Start over. So what if you're fifty? Aiskhylos wrote his best plays when he was eighty. Sure, the economy's tough and there may not be a whole lot of money or security in making artisan furniture or illustrating children's books or whatever your calling happens to be, but do you really want to spend the rest of your life chained to a desk performing tedious, mind-numbing work that eats away at your soul? The sooner you get started the more time you'll have to grow yourself a new career and even if it's not exactly what you dreamed of, certainly you can find *something* more in keeping with your goals and personal values. In the end, it's your life – what are you going to do with it?

Or take another situation. There are a lot of folks who feel bound to the people in their past, even though those people are cruel, indifferent or toxic to them. There's nothing in the world that forces you to keep talking with them if you don't really want to. But they're co-workers! Then talk to them as much as the conditions of your employment require and ignore and avoid them the rest of the time. But they're friends of friends! A true friend will understand and not force you to socialize with someone whom you don't get along with. If it's unavoidable, then find new friends and social environments to hang out in. But they're the only friends I've got and I don't want to be alone! What's so scary about being alone? We're born that way, we leave the world that way, each night when we sleep we enter the world of dreams alone. If you aren't comfortable with your own company, can't find ways to entertain yourself and meaningfully fill your time on your own, then you aren't going to be happy anyway, even if you're constantly surrounded by a crowd. But they're family! So what? We all share blood if you go far enough back, and otherwise "family" is just a concept. It's an important one, to be sure, but if they're actively harming you in some way you're not obligated to remain in touch with them. Your own health and happiness have to come first. And you can always create a new family of people you like, people who nourish you, support your interests and enrich your life. They may not have your DNA but they're family in every way that matters.

And even more importantly we must take full responsibility for our actions. How often have you seen a person caught in a vicious cycle of escalating violence and blame? Person A did something shitty to Person B so B retaliates by doing something even worse and so on and so forth until they've dragged everyone else into it and no one is entirely sure why they're fighting any longer, just that their side is in the right and it won't be stopping any time soon. It's easy to laugh at this sort of madness – and weep when we see it played out on the geopolitical stage every night on the news – but the truth is many of us are ensnared in this sort of thing without even realizing it. It's imperative that we do, however, and that we take personal responsibility in this and all such situations. Hate and violence are choices. So are love and peace. You choose to keep the old wounds fresh and create new ones – or you choose not to. Any time you find yourself thinking "I *have* to feel or act this way," or "this is what I was taught, it's all I've ever known" or "if I don't do ___, someone else will do ___ to me" it should give you profound pause. You're not thinking at that point, you're just following the programming in your brain, *re*acting instead of acting. And if you're okay with being a robot, that's fine. But Dionysos expects something bigger and better of us. Maybe you can't stop the cycle. You definitely can't control how another thinks or acts. But you do have control over yourself and the choices you make and that's all that you'll be held accountable for in the end. You have the choice to end your part of it here and now – or to keep it going. And no one else can take that away from you.

Related to this, of course, are the choices we make about what we do with our bodies and what we put into them. Every time that you take a swig of alcohol, every time you take another drag of that cigarette, every time you eat something you know is bad for you, every time you put off exercising, or get into bed with someone you don't really care for, you are making a choice. Maybe you've got a bad past or shitty genetics that predispose you to these behaviors and cloud your judgment, but each and every time you do it you're consciously making a decision. Your past isn't some tangible person holding a gun to your head saying, "Do this or I'll splatter your brains all over the wall!" The people who fucked you over before aren't pouring the glass down your throat. It's just you, alone with your choices and the consequences of those choices.

I could go on and on but I'm sure you get the point. Nothing ever has more power over us than we're willing to give it. There will always be consequences for our choices, and sometimes those consequences can be greater than we're prepared to deal with. But the flip side of the coin is that when we realize that we are making a choice and taking responsibility for our decisions, we know what we're getting into and that it's our choice, something we can endure if we feel it's worth it – or not, if we don't feel it adds up. I may not follow every dream I've got. Living as a mad poet on the streets is romantic but I'm not interested in the realities of poverty, hunger, danger and disease that come with it. So instead I've chosen to pursue other dreams, dreams that are more realistic and attainable and won't inevitably lead to my destruction. Dreams that are a balance between freedom and security. I also do other things I know I probably shouldn't – but I do them because I *choose* to, not because I *have* to. I own my choices and take full responsibility for what happens as a result of them. It never comes as a surprise when the consequences catch up with me. I may not like it, but I knew going in it was at least a possible outcome. I don't blame other people or my history for the decisions I make. I know that I'm not just sleep-walking through life, doing only what's programmed into me. I'm living the way I've decided to and accepting everything that naturally follows from those choices. And if I don't like the consequences, I change my actions or I live with them, intentionally. And that, to me, is the heart of having a Dionysian lifestyle. The only victim he tolerates is a sacrificial one – the bloodier the better!

THE MYSTERY OF MEILIKHIOS AND BAKCHIOS

The face that Dionysos presents to us under the name of Meilikhios is one of joy and gentleness, one of languid pleasure and soothing comfort. He is the god of release, of healing from anxieties, emotional distress, and dysmania or unhealthy madness. Athenaios tells us (3.78c) that on Naxos the people worshiped the god through two masks, reflecting his dual and contradictory nature. The first mask was made out of grapevine and represented Dionysos as Bakchios, the Raving, a dark, destructive god of madness, of intense, uncontrollable passions, of tension held to the point of breaking. The other mask, made of fig-wood, represented Meilikhios, the Gentle, who was the kind and soothing deliverer from madness, the quiet after the storm, the warm, glowing, post-orgasmic bliss, the tender affection that people feel upon coming together at communal meals.

A key to understanding the nature of the god under this name lies in the wood from which his cult mask was crafted. Figs have always been a staple food in the Mediterranean diet. They are sweet and go well with other foods and in their red, juicy pulp the Greek saw certain obvious parallels to the sexual organs, which provide not just pleasure but the continuance of our species. For this reason the sacred phalloi carried in Dionysos' processions were made out of this wood.

Clement of Alexandria reports (*Protr.* 30) an Argive story about how the first phallos came to be. They said that even though Dionysos had accomplished many wonderful things in the world, his heart was still saddened by the fact that the soul of his mother languished in the gloomy depths of Haides. So he traveled to Lerna where there was a bottomless lake that was said to lead to the Underworld. But before Dionysos could proceed he was stopped by the Guardian of the Lake who barred his path. Prosymnos, the sentry, had been placed there by Haides himself and threatened with dire punishments should he ever let anyone pass. But upon seeing Dionysos Prosymnos' heart warmed with the memory of what it had been like to be alive and he longed to feel the pleasures of the flesh one last time. Overcome with love for Dionysos he agreed to guide him through the Abyss, even knowing it would cost him dearly, whereupon Dionysos confronted the Lord of the Dead and won the soul of his mother. Dionysos did not forget the pledge he had made to the sentry, and so he returned to the shores of Lerna to lay with him – but Haides had already enacted his terrible vengeance and turned Prosymnos into a fig tree. Dionysos cut off a branch and whittled out an exact replica of his member and adopted the passive role in the sex act that he might grant Prosymnos his final wish and give him the pleasure of his body. Afterwards, phalloi were used in Dionysos' worship and a lamb was submerged into the depths of the lake to commemorate the kindness Prosymnos had shown to Dionysos.

Even in such an odd little story, which Clement presents in the most mocking of tones, we can see how Dionysos longs for us to be happy and joyful, how his presence banishes sorrow and transforms suffering into something beautiful and eternal.

When you hear the name of Dionysos Meilikhios, he who is most gentle, most kind, and most beautiful of all the blessed immortals, let your mind fall to your own life and how the god has touched you, those times when you felt serene and content, when you felt confident and successful, when you felt loved and in love, when you had good food to eat and fine friends to share it with, when you were saturated with the simple joy of existence. Remember these things and give thanks to the god who bestows all of these blessings upon us, these and others beyond counting. And think also about the subtle paradoxical message which lies at the heart of the story of Prosymnos and in the two masks at Naxos – namely that we have Meilikhios only through Bakchios, that joy is the transformation and purification of suffering.

We Dionysians, perhaps more than other people because of our closeness to it, are keenly aware that life does not contain only unmixed joy, but that it can be filled with great suffering and immeasurable pains. Often it can be difficult to perceive the joy and bliss of life through our depression, anxiety, pain and the obstacles that get thrown in our path. Sometimes these things can be so overwhelming that it is difficult to remember a time when we felt otherwise. But we don't have to face these things alone. Dionysos is always there for us – and he is greater than all of our suffering. He who was torn apart by the Titans, he who was driven mad by Hera, he who was rejected in his own home by Pentheus and mocked by the daughters of Minyas – he who as the grapevine is pruned until it seems dead, who as the grape is cut and pressed and stomped upon. None suffers such as he, and yet through it all he continues, persists, and thrives. And what's more, his greatest triumph and gift to man – wine – comes only through that suffering he so directly experiences. There is something of Dionysos within each of us, and like him we shall find glory through the transformation of our suffering. No matter what you are facing, Dionysos can help you get through it, help you weave that suffering into something beautiful and eternal, reshape its nature from sadness into joy, from meaninglessness into value, from hardship into triumph. For this is Dionysos' true gift to man, symbolized by the wine and the phallos made of fig-wood, by the two masks named Bakchios and Meilikhios, Dionysos dismembered and then remembered through our lives.

SO YOU WANT TO GET TO KNOW DIONYSOS, EH?

First thing you need to understand about Dionysos: no matter what you are expecting from him he's going to surprise you. He is the Other; he appears in diametrical opposition to our expectations; he is the canvas upon which we paint our fears and hopes, our dreams and our prejudices, so that we might then confront them, integrate them, and transform them.

To those who are repressed, he appears as wild and dissolving because that's what they most need. But imagine a person who is already 'free,' who lives a dangerous and hard life? If Dionysos appears like that it's not going to have much of an effect because they're used to it and jaded in a sense. Instead, to such a person, he may appear soft and comforting and offer them tenderness, because that tenderness is the hardest thing in the world to accept for them.

Dionysos is *constantly* challenging us. His whole existence is a challenge to the status quo, to the natural order and our acceptance of things as they are, even if in our heart of hearts we know that isn't how they *should* be.

For the Greeks, who could be very chauvinistic, who felt a sense of superiority to the rest of the world, to women, to the natural world – how did Dionysos appear? Dressed as a foreigner, effeminate, and surrounded by the vibrant forces of nature.

Our society has a very unwholesome attitude to sex, to the body, to rigid gender roles. And so Dionysos manifests himself now as a very sensual deity who can be very, very masculine without denigrating the feminine (because it seems that most men these days are either assholes or eunuchs), offering a path to wholeness.

Partying, drunkenness, lewd conduct – these might not be the ways that you approach Dionysos. He may have nothing to teach you through them; there may be something else deep inside you that needs healing, that needs to be inverted, transformed, and released.

You want to know how Dionysos is going to manifest in your life? Find the thing that's the hardest for you to do, that you absolutely can't stand or could never imagine yourself doing, find what you hate the most – and you'll discover Dionysos there, pushing at it, pushing you to walk through it.

THE OTHER SIDE OF RELIGION

I believe that it is good to worship Dionysos. That's probably fairly obvious by this point (why else would I have put together a book of this size) but it bears stating anyway. And though I could argue at length for the personal benefits that come about as a result of this worship (and have numerous times elsewhere) the primary reason why I feel this way is because Dionysos desires our worship.

I'm sure this statement will probably come as a surprise to a lot of people. We are conditioned in our society to think about religion predominantly from the human side of the equation. For a lot of folks religion has become little more than a form of cheap therapy, a way to work through their issues, to find peace, contentment, happiness, enlightenment, etc. In short it's a way to make us better people. For others it's a way to gain material or spiritual benefits. Worship is seen as a kind of business transaction or divine vending machine. You put in your prayers, offerings, good deeds, etc., and the gods will then dispense health, wealth, wisdom and similar blessings in equivalent measure. On the other extreme are those who espouse the view that worship is entirely one-sided. The gods are not moved by our piety and in fact require nothing at all from us, being perfect and all-powerful. We benefit from our worship of them because it allows us to draw closer to them and experience their awesomeness and the blessings that emanate from them as a result of their benevolence. At best our offerings and actions are a symbolic expression of gratitude; assuming they are anything more is rankest superstition and hubris.

I find all of these approaches to be deeply flawed and terribly presumptive, shaped as they are by limited human understanding and an unwillingness to consider things from another perspective – though I find the last view far more egregious. How do advocates of this view know that it is the truth? Did the gods come down from Olympos and communicate this "fact" about themselves directly? Did every god in existence do so? After all, something that may hold true for one of them or even a handful of them may not apply equally to the whole divine chorus, especially when you have divinities of an entirely different order of being – daimones, nymphai, heroes, elder gods, etc. – included in the pantheon. Or rather, might this not be the conclusion that certain individuals have reached based on assumptions they were making about what constitutes the nature of divinity?

Now I'm not suggesting that they are wrong. In fact even if this knowledge wasn't directly communicated by the gods to mankind it's entirely possible that the adherents of this view managed to hit upon the truth entirely on their own, through good human reasoning. But without possessing absolute certainty I'm just not willing to assert that the gods get nothing out of worship.

Especially when there are perfectly sound reasons for thinking it may have been otherwise, at least as far as Dionysos is concerned. After all there are numerous myths that show Dionysos concerned with receiving proper cultus and divine honors. He is said to have traveled beyond the boundaries of the known world instructing people in his mysteries and the art of viticulture. In a number of places the introduction of his cult was opposed, resulting in a confrontation between the god and representatives of the community, with Dionysos often forced to visit madness and savage vengeance upon those who reject him and especially those who would deny others the right to worship as they see fit. Clearly this suggests that such things were not a matter of indifference for Dionysos.

But myths are just stories, the fanciful invention of poets and old women, some readers are now no doubt insisting; there's no reason to assume that they are accurate reflections of things that actually happened! And perhaps that's true. Of course, none of us were around back then and for all we know something very like that could have happened. Even if none of these events took place I think it's significant that people said that they did. The stories had to make some sort of sense to the ancients based on what they themselves had experienced and understood about the nature of Dionysos. If these stories did not resonate with the people on at least some level then why did they continue telling them over the span of centuries, and why do we find similar stories told in widely different locales, including places that had no direct contact with each other?

But let us assume, against all probability, that these accounts have no basis in reality, either as distorted history or a reflection of what people felt was possible because of what they had experienced or intuited about Dionysos. Are we similarly to discard all of the records of mankind's interaction with Dionysos? Things like:

Plagues sent when his temple or rites were defiled.
Signs given to reorganize his cult when it had deteriorated.
Oracles commending his worship.
Miracles.
Prophetic dreams, visions and visitations.

These aren't just the stuff of a distant age of myth. Many of them took place during well-documented historical periods, the Classical era through the Hellenistic and Roman up to the decline of Paganism in Europe. We have a wealth of inscriptions, private correspondence, passages in respected historians and philosophers, etc., recording things of this nature. Are we to assume that it was all entertaining folk-tales, delusions or propaganda? And if you reject all of this material then how are we to know anything about the god at all? To do so calls into doubt Dionysos' very existence, which is something that I'm just not willing to do. I don't know that I'd say every tradition, every scrap of evidence that's come down to us is absolutely true but some of it very likely is. And the sheer volume of it suggests something important about the god, namely that he is especially concerned with us humans and that he desires to be worshiped in a specific manner. If he doesn't then why would he bother communicating with us in such a direct fashion?

I can't really answer these questions since I am not privy to the thoughts of the god – nor is anyone else, beyond what Dionysos chooses to reveal to them – but we can surmise that he gets *something* out of these interactions and that he has his own reasons for making them happen.

Perhaps on some level Dionysos actually needs us. Perhaps we do something for him which he cannot do on his own. After all the grapevine, which is deeply connected with him, requires human effort and ingenuity to reach maturity in a way that no other plant does, nor can wine be made without our assistance. We take the raw stuff of nature and transform it into a miraculous beverage, man and god collaborating in the process. Perhaps on another level he requires us to arouse his spirit at times, to set him free just as he sets us free at other times. Or in the act of possession perhaps Dionysos is given the opportunity to experience existence and the world through a physical form, with flesh and blood and mortal eyes, a perspective that a spiritual being might not otherwise have ready access to. Or perhaps he just finds us amusing. For all we know eternity is awfully boring and our capricious, foolish and tragic humanity provides him with an opportunity for rare amusement. Or maybe we're some sort of pet project of his, Dionysos having long ago recognized the raw potential in our race. He has devoted himself since to cultivating us, evolving us, shaping us in his image just as the vintner toils in the field with his prized vines. Or maybe he's using us for self-aggrandizement, a way to make his awesomeness manifest in the world for the other gods to behold. I could think of a thousand other possibilities and yet, in truth, I have no idea why Dionysos does what he does with us or what he gets out of it. But I do know that he's got his reasons and it's a terrible mistake to assume that worship is a one-sided thing. Likewise I believe that Dionysos may desire different things from different people and that it is important for each individual to ask him what that is and to do their best to accomplish it should Dionysos choose to make that apparent.

IT HURTS TO SET YOU FREE: REASONS WHY NOT EVERYONE SHOULD BE A DIONYSIAN

Although Dionysos and Jesus Christ share a great deal in common, as I have discussed at length elsewhere, one of the biggest, and in some respects the most important difference between them is exclusivity. Jesus himself is reported to have said, "I am the way, the truth and the life; none shall come to the Father except through me." Not content with depriving others of a relationship with his Heavenly Father, Jesus advocated shunning, violence, murder and eternal torment and hellfire for all who held ideas contrary to his own.

While Dionysos was eager to receive divine honors as well – so much so that he gathered a large army and led them to the far corners of the earth in order to spread his glad tidings – at no point did he attempt to deprive other gods of their own proper worship. Indeed, Dionysos appears to have been uniquely concerned with the promotion of cultus for other gods. He is credited with founding the Oracle of Zeus-Ammon, the construction of Atargatis' temple and instructing people in the mysteries of the Great Mother Rheia-Kybele. An impressive number of deities were connected to him through myth and cult, including Zeus, Hera, Demeter, Persephone, Hephaistos, Poseidon, Apollon, Artemis, Ares, Hermes, Aphrodite, the Kharites, the Horai, Pan, Priapos, Isis, Osiris, Horus, Apis, Serapis and countless gods with whom he was syncretized at various times. To be a Dionysian, even an especially devoted one, is to be a polytheist.

But even more significant is how Dionysos treats those who disagree with him. It takes more than expressing doubt about his divinity or even outright mockery to bring on the wrath of Dionysos. Although there are a great many myths in which Dionysos punishes mortals – often in a truly horrific fashion – it is always in retaliation for exceptional deeds of violence and cruelty and usually in response for something done to one of his votaries. The Minyades forbade their slaves from participating in the festival of Dionysos; Lykourgos chased the god's nurses into the sea; the Athenians murdered Ikarios and dumped his body in a well; Pentheus sent his men to disrupt the celebrations of the mainades; Agave and her sisters mocked Dionysos' dead mother; the Tyrrhenian pirates threatened to torture and slay Akoites; and so on and so forth. Dionysos will placidly suffer indignities when they are directed solely at him – as his interrogation by Pentheus in Euripides' masterful play *The Bakchai* demonstrates – but he is ferocious on behalf of others, especially when they are powerless to defend themselves.

The supreme virtue of Dionysos is personal liberty – a concept named after him in his Roman guise, no less – which is the right of the individual to believe and act in the manner that seems most fitting to them. This is especially true in the realm of religion, even when one's personal choices are in conflict with the general themes of Dionysian worship, as Euripides wrote:

> "Dionysos does not, I admit, compel a woman to be chaste. Always and in every case it is her character and her nature that keeps a woman chaste. But even in the rites of Dionysos the chaste woman will not be corrupted." (*Bakchai* 315)

Had things gone in another direction and the cult of Dionysos retained its supremacy in the Western world, our history would have likely ended up very, very differently. No religious persecution, destruction of other gods' holy sites, heresy trials or the Inquisition. Perhaps the greatest controversy of our day (leading to schisms within the *thiasos katholikos*) would be between those arguing that wine must be mixed with water in the ancient fashion and those who prefer to drink theirs neat. Or maybe we'd see clashes over the proper size of the *phalloi* carried in the god's procession or whether Dionysos ought to be depicted bearded or youthful. Whatever the hot button issue, however, I just can't imagine folks getting worked up over it enough to torture and kill each other. Though I suppose the nature of humanity being what it is, we would find a way to screw it up.

Now, as delightful as it may be to imagine a world in which Dionysos is the supreme god and his cult the dominant force shaping modern society, that's not really where I was headed with this. Indeed, I'm much more concerned with the world as it is and specifically Dionysos' place in that world. Even more to the point I do not believe that Dionysos is or should ever be considered the supreme god. He may very well be such for me – my whole life revolves around him – but there are very sound reasons why this shouldn't be the case for everyone, beyond even the existence of a multitude of other deities which the cult of Dionysos fundamentally affirms, each with their own unique virtues, blessings and preferred methods of worship. Though this is certainly an important point – since Dionysos can only truly be understood within a polytheistic context, as some of his greatest boons are entirely dependent on his relationship with other deities – it is certainly not the only reason why I feel this way. Even limiting ourselves just to Dionysos and what he is and does, it's safe to say that his worship just isn't for everybody.

To begin with, Dionysos demands much of his devotees, especially those who have a more than casual relationship with him. Most people, of course, never go beyond the surface. They see him as a fun, light-hearted party god and his worship an opportunity to get drunk, let down their hair and blow off a little steam. This is a perfectly valid way to approach him and serves a supremely important social function. Even in ancient times there were those who sought nothing more from the god than this and he was quite happy to give them precisely what they wanted. His gifts are free to all, and we are free to take as much from him as we desire or can handle. But there is a great deal more to the god than just this and alongside the *narthekophoroi* or "wand-bearers" were the Bakchoi, those devoted to him on a much deeper level. The ones who didn't return to their homes and ordinary lives once the revel was over, the ones who allowed the god to tear them apart and remake them in his image, the ones who gave up everything to follow him in his travels to distant lands, the ones who went mad and were never the same again.

It can seem glamorous to describe the *bios Dionusou* or "Dionysian life" that way, though the reality is often anything but. The further out you go with the god the harder it can be to function in ordinary society. Sometimes, a lot of the time actually, the things he shows us aren't pleasant, aren't the sort of things a sane person wants in their head. And even before you get to that point you've got to go through purification, got to confront all of the dark, primal and frankly terrifying things that lurk within the subconscious. Before these can be brought to the surface and released through *ekstasis* there's a shitload of stuff you've got to work through. All those fears and doubts and insecurities, all your addictions and inhibitions and mental hang-ups, all the societal conditioning that's been drummed into you from birth. Most of the time we're not even aware how deeply this stuff runs, how much it's been ingrained into us and shapes our whole conception of who we are and how the world works. You strip a few layers back and think you're done – but there's always more of them and Dionysos is good at revealing them, even when we wish he wouldn't. But once you've started down this path and are truly committed to it you can't stop. No matter how painful it is, how much you don't want to deal with certain things, how much you seem to be losing in the process. Once you cross a certain threshold you've got to be willing to give it all over to him, no matter what.

In fact, once you get to that point it can be really fucking dangerous to stop. Because once you've started stripping away the layers you're going to be raw and vulnerable. That societal conditioning is there for a reason, after all. It keeps all the other stuff locked away, safely in check. Makes us functional and able to deal with other people. Granted, we'll only ever be a mere shadow of our true selves that way, our full potential unrealized, and if the mask is on too tight it can lead to all sorts of problems of its own. But you start taking that off and don't follow through to the end, shit's going to bubble up to the surface and cause you all sorts of trouble. This is when you see people with serious psychological disorders, people with addictions to sex and drugs and power, people that can't deal with the intensity of emotion and spirit that fills them. It gets to be too much for a lot of people and they simply break under the pressure. They fall victim to their own excesses and weaknesses, to madness and things far worse. It destroys their lives and very often the lives of everyone around them.

Of course, even if you stick with it there's no guarantee that you'll escape that fate. Even the best among us may prove incapable of holding up under the stress. Even when you're doing it right, even if you're clearly listening to Dionysos and doing everything he tells you, it can get really bad before it gets better – and it may never get perfect. We Dionysians don't exactly have the best success rate. Just look at the ones who fully embraced his calling and lifestyle: Alexander, Ptolemy Philopator and Auletes, Mark Antony, Friedrich Nietzsche, Jim Morrison. All of them were exceptional men who did incredible things, who reflected the god as fully as a mortal can. And yet all of them were also broken, self-destructive, dangerous and in some sense, ultimately failures. Of course they were on a fairly unique path which most Dionysians will never tread, but even the rest of us face great adversity and rarely transcend our own limitations.

I say this not to be all doom and gloom or to suggest that it's not worth pursuing this path – because, for me at least, it absolutely is and I can't imagine anything else that would be even remotely as rewarding and fulfilling as this has been. But one should be aware that there are very real dangers and consequences associated with this path before diving head first into it. And perhaps the true Dionysian won't care anyway, driven to pursue the extreme regardless of consequences and dire warnings, out of a desire to embrace all that life holds in store for them, the good and the bad alike. But it bears stating anyway, and there's no shame in recognizing that this path isn't for you, especially before you've gotten too deeply into it to turn back.

BEYOND PATRONS

The thing that brings people to Hellenismos is usually the gods. Sure, there's the occasional person who comes to the religion through a fascination with ancient Greek history and culture, or because of their great admiration for her literature (and who doesn't feel their soul stir upon reading the opening lines of the *Iliad*) but I rather suspect that these individuals are in the minority. For most it is the gods who lead us here – and who keep us around long after we find out what an opinionated, argumentative, and cantankerous bunch Hellenists can be.

And while there are those people who are drawn equally to the whole pantheon, and to the gods precisely *as* a pantheon, again, I don't think this is terribly common. Most people, when they describe what brought them to Hellenismos, will cite a strong attraction to a particular deity, or perhaps to a small group of them. While this attraction may change over time, blossoming to include other gods or passing from one deity to another, for many this attraction holds a singular power in their life. They may feel especially devoted to this divinity who inspires their greatest aspirations and most praiseworthy efforts, and they often feel that in some respects the divinity reciprocates by showing interest in their development and a certain measure of protectiveness for them. This type of relationship is usually called patronage, which borrows as its model the client system of ancient Rome, and has precedent in the relationships between Odysseus and Athene (*Iliad* 2.279), Aristeas and Apollon (Herodotos 4.20), Marcus Antonius and Dionysos (Plutarch's *Life of Antony*), and perhaps most famous of all, Socrates and his *daimonion* (Plato's *Apology*).

Plato has voiced what many in a patron relationship intuitively feel – namely that every human soul is under the control and guidance of a particular divinity: "The Demiurge divided the whole mixture into souls equal in number to the stars, and assigned each soul to a star....and when he had sown them, he committed to the younger gods the fashioning of their mortal bodies." (*Timaios* 41-2) And in the *Phaidros* he adds, "He who follows in the train of any god honors him, and imitates him as far as he is able; and this is his way of life and the manner of his behavior. Everyone chooses the object of his affections according to his character." (252c)

This is, clearly, a very important relationship. Even if one's patron is not directly responsible for the creation of their soul and body, our proximity to the divinity will certainly have an effect on our life. This may be on the subtlest of levels, for instance by influencing our thoughts, whether that be simply by making us think about something in a totally different light or by exerting a kind of gravitational force which constantly draws us back to a particular network of associations, images, and concepts. And yet, even this seemingly simple thing can have a profound effect on our lives, for our thoughts, to a large extent, shape who we are and how we react to the world around us. If we are aligned to a particular world-view, which is under the domain of a single deity and which exists in counter-distinction to other divinities, we are going to make different decisions than if we were aligned to the world-view of someone else. For instance, the Dionysian world-view is one of freedom, and abundance, and the transgression of boundaries resulting in an orgiastic loss of distinctions. How different that is from the law and order and rational remoteness of Athene's world-view. (Of course it is important to remember that the gods are not simply ideas or archetypes, but distinct beings, and further, as true divinities they represent a totality which embraces both a particular point as well as its polar opposite: thus, healing gods also bring plague, rationality contains an element of ecstasy, and there is a speck of light at the center of even the vastest darkness.)

I can personally attest that having this world-view, this cluster of ideas in the back of my head, has caused me to make decisions I might not have otherwise. Dionysos is always there inspiring me to boldly take life by the throat, to experience things to their fullest, to be aware of the sensual beauty which surrounds me, and to root out within myself whatever threatens to hold me back or diminish my experiences of the world. He is the enemy of fear, of stasis, of empty formality. I have had to make hard choices, to give up things I thought important to me because in the end they were really strangling me and keeping me enslaved, and he is constantly urging me to open myself up to a deeper awareness and acceptance of frightening and challenging ideas. The *bios Dionusou* (Dionysian life) is an unfolding process, and one that I am constantly striving to live. Thus, I am who I am today largely because of my devotion to this god. I suspect a follower of Demeter or Apollon or Poseidon feels exactly the same way about their god and the impact which that deity has had in their life.

And that's really the point that I want to make. No matter how great a god is, no matter how fully they may fulfill the desires of the individual devotee, no god in a polytheistic system exhausts the totality of existence, nor claims the whole of the world as theirs alone, nor monopolizes the ways of being and worship. All of the gods exist in relationship to each other. This may be through diametrical opposition or through a certain affinity or even a similarity of essence. They are friends, enemies, lovers, relatives, and more – a plurality of beings relating to each other and creation in every conceivable manner, their relationships forming a wonderful, complex tapestry which animates the cosmos and our lives within it. This is the fundamental, beautiful truth of polytheism – and unfortunately, there are times when the patron relationship can endanger that.

Because of my close identification with Dionysos and his world-view other relationships have been closed off to me. I have almost nothing to do with Athene, Apollon, and Artemis. Sometimes this is a result of the decisions I have made in life, sometimes it's because there is a spiritual repulsion that takes effect like when you place two magnets together and they push away from each other, and much more commonly I am simply so preoccupied with Dionysos, so conditioned to find his presence in the world, that I either don't think to look for the others or miss them entirely when they are present. I don't think that this is necessarily a bad thing, but it is certainly limiting. There is so much out there that it would be a real shame if I never had the opportunity to see and experience it. Sometimes this intense focus can actually be harmful, in the way that if you only eat one food, no matter how tasty it may be, you are depriving yourself of complex nutrients that you can get only through a diverse and well-balanced diet. Each of the gods have certain blessings to bestow on us, lessons to teach us, experiences to share with us. If we are locked into only one pattern there's going to come a time when that pattern leads us into conflict and pain. Dionysian exuberance and abundance can easily become addiction and fatal excess. Just look at Jim Morrison or Baudelaire if you have any doubt. These men led life to its fullest – and burnt out in a very short span of time. That may make for a Romantic ideal (it's better to be consumed by fire than to fade away) but realistically, they couldn't sustain that level of intensity, and their art – especially in the case of Morrison – suffered for it. In the beginning, his work was brilliant and prophetic; towards the end, sad, self-obsessed, and pathetic. Imagine if he had acquired some Apollonian restraint and discipline, if he had learned to temper his spirit just a bit, to curb his addictions, to find real freedom instead of nihilistic renunciation. His craft could have gone on for years, allowed to grow and mature and reach its full potential. Perhaps he could have changed the world with his words – instead he ended up a miserable, bloated drunk choking to death on his own vomit in a bathtub in Paris.

My relationship with Dionysos is unquestionably the most important in my life – the one constant in a world of Protean transformation. No other god can hold a candle to that, or come close to the affections I have for him. And yet, sometimes those secondary and tertiary relationships have radically altered the course of my life. They have opened me up to new experiences and taught me lessons Dionysos either couldn't or felt needed to be done by someone else in order to bring the point home more forcefully.

Sometimes those relationships have lasted for a long time. Hermes, for instance, has been present in my life for a number of years. He has refined my writing, encouraged me to undertake strange journeys, revealed things about certain parts of my personality that didn't fit into the Dionysian mold, and nudged me to take on a more magical practice. He has also been a doorway through which I was able to make contact with other gods. As a consequence, I consider him to be a second patron, only slightly below Dionysos in my own personal divine hierarchy. But there are other gods who have come into my life for only very brief periods, whose presences have focused on one particular area or idea, and once that issue has been resolved, have passed back out of my life. Horus came in seemingly only to inaugurate an interest in Egyptian religion; after about a week or two of intense epiphanies I've had very little to do with him since. Zeus came to teach me about power and its responsibility. Aphrodite to lend beauty and refinement to my life. Sobek to protect me during a difficult transition. Hekate made it possible for me to attend Pantheacon in 2007. If I had turned my back on them, refused to have anything to do with them because Dionysos is my all and everything, think how much smaller my life would be as a result of that.

I've also noticed, unfortunately, that some people feel inadequate spiritually because they do not have a strong attachment to a single god. They feel like they aren't good enough, that they're doing something wrong, that maybe this isn't the religion for them since everyone else has a patron and they don't. This is nonsense. The patron relationship is not the *de facto* form in Greek religion. It is a unique experience, one that has special benefits but also comes with heavy duty responsibilities, and which is not the norm, now or back in antiquity. In ancient times the average person tended to pray to a wide variety of gods. At different times in their lives different gods would have had different levels of importance to them. Artemis was said to watch over young girls, but once they reached maturity and marriage she became remote until they were pregnant and gave birth. Hestia or Demeter would likely have held more sway over them while they were concerned with the domestic sphere. If they were sailing, they may have made offerings to Poseidon, a god they otherwise would have had no contact with unless they lived on the coast. Others would have been prominent only at festival time or if they entered a particular career, and so forth. Taken as a totality over time, this created a possibility for an abundance of minor relationships – which is by far the norm, both today and in antiquity, however common the patron relationship may be.

So people shouldn't be worried if they don't have a patron – maybe they just haven't found one yet but the god is still out there waiting for them, or maybe they don't have one, and instead are meant to cultivate a number of these other relationships. There is no one right way – the religious life of each person is as unique and individual as a snowflake, to make use of that insipid metaphor. Instead of trying to conform to the pattern of someone else, they should be seeking what works the best for them. That may involve recognizing the existence of a patron relationship – or moving beyond the concept altogether.

FINDING DIONYSOS

Every so often I'll get an e-mail from someone who says that they're really attracted to Dionysos but no matter what they do they can't seem to feel his presence. Doesn't matter how much they drink, what type of music they listen to, whether they perform elaborate rituals or something spontaneous and on the fly. My question at that point is "So, where do you normally try to connect with Dionysos?" to which they usually respond, "Well, in my home. In front of his shrine." It doesn't even occur to them to call upon him anywhere else, which is why it's hardly surprising that they're running into this sort of difficulty.

Dionysos isn't like other gods. Many of the things that work perfectly fine for them just aren't going to cut it when he's involved. Now I do think that it's important to maintain a shrine in his honor. It's a way to give over a part of your home and thus a part of your life to him and it can be a powerful thing to surround yourself with tangible reminders of Dionysos. Each of the components that make up my shrine for him have been chosen with the utmost care. Many of them found their way onto his shrine because they played an important role in previous ritual experiences. So, for instance, I've got a medallion on his offering tray that I wore during the first major public ritual I helped lead for him. There's the cup I use to pour all of my libations. A bull figurine that reminds me of one of the initiations I underwent. A snake and phallos that were crafted by my partner and once graced her own shrine. A little plastic gecko I coincidentally found while listening to The Doors and pondering the similarities between Jim as Lizard King and Mark Antony as Neos Dionysos. And so on and so forth. Each item has its own story and all I've got to do is glance at them to have a wealth of memories and associations come flooding back into my mind. Plus I've got a crazy amount of statues, posters, paintings and other representations of Dionysos hanging around the shrine and he's a pretty god to look at. I love my shrine. I've had some pretty powerful experiences in front of it. But not all of them and by no means the most important of the bunch.

In fact, as much as I enjoy tending that shrine I'd say that the majority of the work I do with him takes place far away from it. And appropriately so. Dionysos isn't just the wild god – he's the god of wild places. This is something that the ancient Greeks were keenly aware of. Pause for a moment and reflect on the places where they sought him. Up on the mountain top or deep in some primordial forest. In the swamp or the desert, along the coastal shore or far beneath the earth in a cave. Even when they built temporary, artificial structures to worship him in, they fashioned them in the likeness of nature, whether it was a tent made of leaves and branches or a grotto with running water and vegetation. The pillars of his temples were twined with ivy or carved with representations of trees and flowers. Wherever Dionysos was present nature was close at hand. Hell, even his name suggests the mystical mountain of his youth.

So anyone who wishes to honor the god would do well to remember this. Just as the mad-women fled their homes to be close to him, so must all those seeking a deeper connection with the god. Of course that doesn't mean that the only way you're going to connect with Dionysos is by going out on an extended camping trip in the heart of a forest far away from civilization. That sort of thing is wonderful if you can manage it, but Dionysos' spirit can be found closer to home as well. Most cities have parks or tree-lined paths and these are excellent places to go hunting for Dionysos, especially if you go for a walk at night. The world is a different place once the sun goes down. Everything becomes strange and magical and wild things lurk in the shadows. Open yourself up to those unfamiliar energies and you'll be a lot closer to discovering the god. Being out when others seek the safety of their homes, doing things that are peculiar and unexpected and perhaps even socially frowned upon, putting yourself in situations that feel a little dangerous – whether it's justified or all in your head – helps the transition into altered states of conscious which are essential for an authentic Dionysian experience.

And when you're out there, be as open as you can to random possibility. When you're in your home there's only so much that you can see or do. But when you're out in the wild a whole world of communication becomes possible. You can see messages on billboards or bumper-stickers, catch meaningful scraps of song from a passing car or someone's home, strangers can approach you and say exactly what you needed to hear at precisely that moment, you can stumble upon a bed of ivy or some wild creature or any of a host of other important things. One of the reasons why it seems as if the gods are speaking to mystic types so regularly is because they often spend a great deal of time out in the world listening for them. If they only stayed in front of their shrines, the gods and spirits would only have the things in the mystics' abodes and minds with which to communicate to them. And sure, that may be more than enough to work with – but why make it harder than it has to be?

But more than that I feel that certain aspects of Dionysos manifest themselves only in the wild and surrounded by nature. All the intellectual understanding in the world can't replace actually touching the ivy that clings to a tree, the moist soil or soft moss against your bare feet, the smell of flowers in bloom or the breeze off of a river. These are not just the things we associate with the god, symbolic tokens that convey certain facts about him – they *are* him. I can tell you that Dionysos lives in trees but until you've wrapped your arms around a massive trunk, felt the bark scratch your flesh, smelled the fragrance and heard the slow, ancient pulse within…well, you're never truly going to understand what that means.

So the next time you want to get to know Dionysos better pack up some incense, wine and candles and head out into nature, wherever you can find it.

You don't need anything more complex than that. Pray to him with the words you find in your heart. Look for his image manifest in nature. Listen for what he's got to tell you. Open yourself up to the wildness that surrounds you – and is within you. That is where you'll find the god.

A FERTILE FAITH

It's pretty clear that my religious focus is, well, a little lop-sided. Of the forty-plus festivals that make up my calendar, something along the lines of twenty-five of them involve Dionysos in one way or another. In many instances he's the sole recipient of honors. Other times he's worshiped alongside someone else or the nature of the festival is such that there's a pretty good chance he'll put in an appearance.

After Dionysos, the various land-spirits are best represented, with around twenty festivals to their credit, while the dead – both collectively and certain special individuals honored on their own – get something like eighteen. Hermes comes in right behind them with sixteen, while Spider gets a respectable (and numerically appropriate, though I didn't plan it out that way) eight. Aphrodite gets three or four, as does Demeter (though most of hers are shared with Dionysos) and Bast, Persephone and Poseidon each get one. The remainder of the festivals are thematic or seasonal, and may be occasions to honor all the gods and spirits collectively or just times to mark what's going on around here.

That alone tells you a lot about where my priorities lie and what sort of religion I practice. Looking through the festivals you can see a lot of repetitive themes. Fertility is probably the biggest, although it's a very particular kind of fertility. It's the fertility of the earth and the things that come from the earth: grain and fruit and trees and plants and of course the dead who rise up out of the ground with all the rest. It isn't a human-centric fertility that concerns me, except insofar as our life depends on the nourishment we receive from the things that grow in the earth. There are no festivals to help make babies or promote the growth of other animal life. (Though that animal life is honored in several of them.) The way I see it, the folks around here are doing a fine enough job reproducing on their own. In fact, most of the problems we're facing as a species are directly related to over-breeding. I consider this such a plague to the planet that I've taken steps to ensure that I won't be contributing to the problem.

When I had the surgery I was a little concerned, to be honest, since fertility plays such an important role in my spiritual life, especially as a priest of Dionysos who is, well, a highly phallic deity (in case you hadn't noticed). How could I serve such a potent being when I planned to render myself infertile? (And yeah, vasectomies don't actually make you infertile – they just ensure you can't do anything with it. But that's quibbling over split hairs. Or *vasa deferentia*, as the case may be.) Even if I never planned to have children – gods forbid! – shouldn't I at least be capable of doing so?

But then I came to realize that there need be no conflict between my politics and my beliefs. While Dionysos' abundant fertility certainly encompasses human reproduction it is by no means exhausted by it. In fact, there's a great deal more to it than just hard cocks and good, old fashioned orgiastic baby-making. He is first and foremost the god of vegetative life. In fact most people know him only as the lord of the vine and the sacred drink made of its fruit. His potency extends over the whole of creation – including the realm of the human soul. Where does our creativity come from – our art and dreams and all the best and noblest aspects of human culture and civilization – if not from the dark and fertile recesses of our minds? Through him these things can be brought forth and made to live – and that's a fertility I can get behind. Many of my festivals, in fact, work with fertility in this way, as a means of exploring the further reaches of human consciousness, cultivating ecstatic states, channeling inspiration, celebrating artistry, beauty and the awesome accomplishments of our race.

As is fitting for one who is so dedicated to Dionysos and Hermes, a great deal of the festivals on my calendar involve practices that could be regarded as magical. Of course it is a very different sort of magic than most people are used to and some might even question whether these practices fall under that rubric at all. I am thinking specifically of rites whose purpose is the alteration of consciousness, whether to induce ecstatic states, commune with gods and spirits, learn the future, receive visions and dreams or acquire power to accomplish certain goals. I have no interest in debating terminology – whether one considers such things magic or not, they're the heart of my religious practice and have been from the beginning. Almost as soon as I discovered the gods I realized that such ways of interacting with them were possible and that I wanted to devote my life to doing this sort of thing.

Almost every one of my festivals involves worship of this sort. Obviously it isn't the reason why I celebrate these festivals. My religion has a solidly devotional focus. It's about honoring the gods and spirits, thanking them for their manifold blessings, cultivating that sense of joyous wonder that comes from being in their presence, celebrating all that they are and do and how the world around me changes through the cycle of the seasons. Mine is a religion of love and service to the divine – but a big part of that service involves these sorts of practices.

Often I can't even help it. I'll be going through the normal worship routine and something will take hold of me. Images flood my mind, concepts coalesce, shapes appear before my eyes, sounds and voices come from everywhere and nowhere at once – the presence of the divine is made manifest to me. Since I appear to have some propensity for this sort of thing I have begun taking advantage of it and consciously cultivating practices that make it even more likely to happen. So, for instance, a lot of my rituals involve music, dance, singing and chanting, mask-wearing, processions, all-night vigils, fasting and feasting, the consumption of alcohol and other strange substances and paying a close attention to my surroundings. In fact the vast majority of my rituals are conducted outdoors, in the midst of nature or the heart of the city. Many of them take place at night or during dusk when the world becomes a different place – stranger, wilder, more beautiful and primitive. I don't think I could do a lot of the things I do if I remained safely behind doors, in front of my shrines. For one thing I wouldn't be able to honor many of the spirits that I do, since they only dwell in those wild places. To worship them I must go where they are – and make myself a little wild as well.

It is only when I began doing so that I really got to know them. Before, such beings were only on my periphery and I hardly had any dealings with them at all. Now they are the primary focus of my religion after Dionysos and Hermes and my whole way of worshiping has changed to accommodate their needs. It's the biggest reason why I no longer consider myself purely Hellenic or Greco-Egyptian. How could I when the largest portion of my pantheon is comprised of local land-spirits and related beings?

One of the biggest changes that have come about with the alteration of my focus is how I view sacrifice. A lot of people only look at it from our perspective, what we get out of it and why we do it. Some go so far as to maintain that it is merely a symbolic act, that the gods don't get anything out of it other than a feeling of appreciation from their devotees. In fact many even say that the gods require nothing at all from us, certainly not any sort of material or spiritual sustenance and that to believe otherwise is rankest superstition and hubris to boot. Maybe this is true of such elevated beings as gods – though many cultures throughout the world, both ancient and modern, would beg to differ – but I don't think that's true for most land-spirits and the dead.

In my experience offerings make them stronger, more powerful, more capable of acting in the world – especially when it comes to the dead. I don't know why this seems to be the case, and I don't think they're entirely dependent on these offerings, otherwise they would have been rendered completely impotent during the long centuries of Christian dominion. But I also don't think that it's necessary to fully understand such profound mysteries in order to witness the results of our actions.

Therefore a fundamental part of my religious practice involves feeding the spirits. This takes a multitude of different forms ranging from leaving offerings of food and drink to more intangible gifts of time, attention and my own spiritual power. Sometimes it's as simple as cleaning up the litter left by the riverbank or writing a poem for them or just listening to what they've got to say. Sometimes it involves more important things like temporarily bringing them through into this world and giving them a body to inhabit. And sometimes it's much, much more complicated than all of that. But always there is an exchange, a transferal of energy of one sort or another, and I feel afterwards that I've left them a little better off than they were before. This, in turn, makes me happier since I am directly involved in the life of my land. They have given me so much – a beautiful place to live, good food to nourish my body, inspiration for my writing, help when I most needed it – it seems only proper to give something back to them in return, to make it a relationship built on mutual assistance, an exchange of resources tangible and intangible, instead of the mindless consumption so prevalent in our wider society today. I don't believe that what I do will ever be enough to balance the scales – there are far too many who think only 'gimme, gimme,

gimme' – but I can at least do what I am able to. And if I'm deluded and what I do for the spirits has no effect whatsoever because they don't really need anything anyway, then so be it. It does me no harm, and I can think of far worse ways to spend one's time. But if I'm right and they do receive some benefit from this, then it's all the more important that it be done.

THE TRUE DIONYSIAN

The only rock upon which a Dionysian life can be firmly established is regular worship and devotional activity. It's not enough to think fondly about the god, to get drunk every now and again, to be free and liberated and show how little societal conventions have a hold on you. These things alone do not make you a Dionysian. Alone they more often than not just make you an ass.

Dionysos is a *god* and as such he is due proper cultus. This means a routine of worship involving prayers, libations, offerings and other things like dance and *ekstasis*. Beyond this it is also important to mark certain times as holy to him and to celebrate these through elaborate rituals, feasts, processions, etc. I don't think it necessarily matters what festivals one keeps for Dionysos — and indeed these ought to be determined by one's geographical location and prior history with the god anyway — but one really should have a calendar of festivals for Dionysos and stick to it as much as humanly possible. If you aren't willing to put in even that minimal amount of effort on his behalf then why would you expect him to show any concern for you?

Unfortunately I've seen far too many people express the idea that once you get to a certain point in your relationship with Dionysos all that stuff becomes unnecessary. "That sort of thing is fine for the average wand-bearer but I'm a Bakchos, an initiate. I've seen things ordinary people can only dream of. So why bother?" one person actually had the audacity to say.

I was, as you can imagine, completely floored by this hubris. First off, nobody reaches a point where these things become superfluous. *Nobody.* You don't get closer in your relationship with Dionysos than Alexander the Great, Ptolemy Philopator or Marcus Antonius, all of whom were Dionysos incarnate, the god made flesh on earth. And yet each of these men assiduously kept the festivals of the god and used their wealth and power to ensure that others were able to as well. Even if you, personally, no longer benefit from doing such things you ought to be committed to helping others draw closer to the god.

And I just don't buy that anyone can reach a point where they stop benefiting from these activities. I, too, am an initiate of the god. I've undergone things that would blow people's minds. I've experienced the god as intimately as it's possible for a mortal to do, and you know what? All that just left me with an even stronger desire to draw closer to him. In my experience the best possible way to do that is through regular worship. By setting aside time for him weekly, monthly and annually I fill my life with the spirit of the god, I create opportunities to encounter him and I do things that are both pleasing to him and necessary.

Peak experiences with a god do not last. No matter how great they are, we always come back to ordinary awareness. They have to be rekindled through continuous encounters, encounters that remind us of what came before and create the opportunity for new blessings and insights to manifest. I benefit immensely every time I stand in the presence of Dionysos, even when those benefits are not immediately apparent or even something tangible that I can point to. And even if I, personally, don't get anything out of it (which isn't the point anyway) I have the knowledge that I am doing something for my god and there is nothing that I'd rather devote my time and energy to than serving him.

Furthermore, initiations are just preparation for the real work which is carried out through our worship and festivals. I have experienced no mystery greater than what happens at Lampteria, Turbe, Lenaia or Anthesteria. When properly celebrated these are all mysteries in their own right – and mysteries that recur year in and year out, not just on a single special occasion.

It is not enough to claim the title of "Dionysian" – one must continually prove themselves worthy of it through their thoughts, actions and priorities. If you've gone more than a couple months without engaging in an act of worship for the god then you are no Dionysian, simple as that. I don't care what great things you've done in the past or how well you think you know him – right now is all that matters. So let your lips always taste of wine, your head always be crowned with ivy and the god's name rapturously and perpetually on your tongue if you would be counted among the blessed followers of our Lord Dionysos!

SPEAKING ABOUT THE UNSPEAKABLE

I'm just going to come out and say this: the old mysteries are dead and it's pointless to even try and reconstruct them. It's not because we're completely ignorant of what happened during them. Actually, we've got a lot more evidence than most people realize, especially for the mysteries celebrated outside Eleusis. Even there we're on pretty solid footing, at least when it comes to the overall themes and procedures involved.

The central experience of the initiates eludes us and would even if someone had violated the oath of secrecy and left us a first-hand account of all the things said and done. A mystery isn't something you can learn or know. By definition it's something experienced, something that takes place deep in the individual's soul. Unless you've gone through that experience yourself you're never going to understand it. Without the experience it's just words and concepts, meaningless gibberish mixed with our preconceived notions. That's why the initiates vowed never to speak of it. Not because exposing the secret would have damaged the mystery, but because it was pointless to share such things with someone who had not undergone it themselves. It would only confuse them and make it impossible for them to have that authentic experience because it wouldn't mean the same thing to them any longer.

We lack the proper frame of reference, the cultural identity and cosmology that brought to life the mystery-experience for the ancients. As long as the identity of the gods is shaped for us by the writings of long-dead men and the religion is something of the past that we are studying, imitating and trying to reconstruct, the mysteries will remain forever closed off to us. The mysteries were an outgrowth of a living faith, a living culture. They developed over time, through the accumulated shared experiences of a people. They were bound by time and space, by culture and language. That's why you had to be a fluent speaker of Greek in order to be initiated. It wasn't that foreigners were inherently inferior – the Greeks actually had a great reverence for the antiquity and wisdom of their neighbors – it's that the underlying concepts that fed the mystery-experience and brought it to life in the heart and soul of the initiate remained unintelligible to anyone who didn't properly understand Greek. These mysteries were inseparable from Greekness and once that Greekness passed from the world, so did the mysteries.

That's why we'll never have the ancient mysteries back. Even if we gather together all of the fragmented pieces and add our best guesses and inspiration to fill in the blanks, the end product just isn't going to be the same. The act of reconstruction, as well as our modern additions and above all the lack of a proper cultural context, means that we're going to end up with something else entirely, a hodge-podge worthy of Dr. Victor Frankenstein.

Does that mean that we are doomed to live in a world without mysteries? No! Absolutely, unequivocally not!

The mysteries came from the gods – and they're not just a divine gift but an experience of them that is direct and incontrovertible. As long as the gods exist – and they'll still be here long after the last human passes from this world – there will be mysteries.

But the thing we've got to get through our heads is that they're not going to be the ancient mysteries. They can't be, not if they're a true mystery. You see, a mystery is rooted in the experiences and understanding, the culture and language of the initiate. We don't live in 5th century Athens and no matter how much we read or how much we pretend we'll never understand what it was like back then. It will never be *our* living culture. And in fact, the more we build up the sanctity of the past, the greater the distance that separates us becomes. So the first thing we've got to do is let all of that go, get rid of our veneration of antiquity and the belief that the ancestors knew the gods better than we'll ever be able to. The gods are alive and a part of the living world. That means that we've got to look for them in the here and now, in our own land, in our own lives, in the fabric of our consciousness and culture.

There's nothing wrong with looking back to the past for inspiration and information, especially in regard to cult practice and the ways that the gods once revealed themselves to man. This is vital information that has changed little over the intervening centuries. But that should never stand in the way of having a direct and personal relationship with those gods who are just as much *our* gods as they once were *their* gods. And a big part of acknowledging that they are living gods is accepting that they are capable of change, that we can discover in them things that our ancestors may only have been dimly aware of. More to the point we must be open to what the gods wish to share with us today, in these new lands that we find ourselves in. Maybe it will be the same as what they revealed back then – maybe it'll be something radically different. But whatever it is we must be open to it and not just what we expect to find.

Mysteries, if they come, will arise out of our collective experiences of the gods today, where we are. When the mysteries come they will be the mysteries of Eugene, the mysteries of Las Vegas, the mysteries of San Francisco, the mysteries of Boston, the mysteries of Miami. The mysteries of Eleusis could be celebrated nowhere else. Demeter had different cult centers throughout Greece, including places that had their own mysteries just as ancient and esteemed as those at Eleusis. But there was only one Eleusis and one set of rites carried out there. This is why all attempts at transplanting them to other locations have been doomed to failure. It was there and only there that she finally settled after her long and painful search (hence the site's name); only there where she was received by the king whom she instructed in gratitude for his kindness; only there where she adopted

Triptolemos and sent him out to teach the world agriculture; there where she was reconciled with her daughter and all the rest that formed the backdrop of the mysteries. This happened nowhere else in all the world, so these mysteries could take place nowhere else. In those other places different things had happened, such as her transformation into a mare or her seduction of a mortal man. As a result those places had their own unique mysteries.

The mysteries that we will celebrate here are likewise going to be shaped by time, place and culture. A shaft of harvested grain simply cannot mean to us what it once did to our ancestors, not unless we entirely reject the modern world and return to a more primitive agrarian society. Even then it will have different connotations for us for at least the first few generations and probably long after that. How could it not, for won't it symbolize the turning away from industrial society and those who made the big, brave leap, something our ancestors never had to do? Whole new myths could be spun off of that scenario and that's what future generations would be responding to. Even without such a monumental break there's a whole body of myths and symbols that form our current cultural identity and it's through these that the gods manifest themselves to us. Even when the symbols remain constant their meaning changes for us and we should accept it, embrace it instead of pretending otherwise.

I do not speak of this matter purely in the abstract. I am one of the *mystai*. I have been initiated into the mysteries of my god Dionysos. In fact I've undergone initiation into several of his mysteries, each slightly different from the others and all of them powerful, life-changing experiences. I recognized many of the details from accounts I had read of the ancient Dionysian mysteries, but there were also differences, things unique to my situation and relationship with him. Had that not been a component I don't think it would have been as powerfully transformative an experience as it turned out to be. In fact, some of the most idiosyncratic elements were also some of the most traditional, the elements I found running through those past accounts. It's just that the form these themes took were novel and shaped by my experiences and insights, which is what allowed it to speak to me and thus made it a mystery. It wasn't at all what I had been expecting, which allowed it to catch me off guard and do the necessary transformative work. Repeatedly while this was happening I found myself going, "Holy shit! This is what was meant by X, this is what it really feels like to have Y happen." There was an odd sense of overlap, of timelessness, of variations on a central theme running through my life and the lives of those who had stood in this position before me. I wish that I could be more precise, share more of what happened and what it felt like – but it wouldn't do any good. You wouldn't understand until it was your time to stand there and go through it, and even then I couldn't predict exactly what form that experience would take or what it would mean to you while it was happening and afterwards. But it left me a changed man and closer to my god than I ever could have anticipated and that's what the mysteries are all about in the end.

But it's important to remember that initiation isn't an end unto itself; it's only the beginning of a process that is continually ongoing. You never leave the *telesterion*, you just gain deeper and deeper awareness through ever more nuanced experiences. And though it changes everything about who you are and how you relate to the gods and the world, it doesn't change your need to seek them and worship them.

That's the thing that a lot of people don't seem to get. They think that once you've gone through initiation you don't have to do anything except sit back and bask in the continuous presence of the gods. Bullshit. You're still going to struggle and still going to have to work at it. That perfect understanding you get during the mysteries fades back into everyday consciousness. And sometimes – hell, in my experience it's pretty much all the time – you've got to try even harder afterwards because the stuff that worked before doesn't cut it post-initiation. Yeah, I'm a *mystes* now, but I still keep a shrine, go through the regular routine of ritual practice, observe festivals and do all the work that's necessary to have an active and fulfilling spiritual life. And sometimes it doesn't get me anywhere. I struggle with doubt, with my own weaknesses and shortcoming, with the distance I sometimes feel from my gods and spirits, with the fear that maybe I've gone crazy or I'm just wasting my time with all this stuff. The fact that I once felt that intensity, that certainty, that powerful and awesome direct connection to my god can make everything a lot harder because it looms over me, reminding me that I no longer have it and making me wonder if there's something wrong with me because of that. How could I go from **that** to *this*?

The only solution I've found is to keep going, keep trying, to claw my way through the resistance until I get back there or somewhere like it. It's long, difficult, unglamorous and many times unrewarding on the surface of it. But I will say this much: having experienced what I've experienced, I know what's possible and can never settle for less. It's as much an inspiration as it can sometimes be an obstacle. But I wouldn't have had the beautiful experience without the regular practice that led up to it, nor would I ever find my way back without the practice. It's sort of like that old famous Zen saying, "Before enlightenment: chop wood, carry water. After enlightenment: chop wood, carry water." If you think initiation into the mysteries is a shortcut you're deluding yourself and that delusion is going to keep you from ever experiencing the mysteries to begin with. It's only possible through a living religious tradition centered on living gods. If you don't make the path your own, you'll never be able to follow it to them.

DIONYSIAN WORSHIP IN 5 EASY STEPS

Step 1

Worship Dionysos. There is no better way to deepen your relationship with the god than by approaching him in ritual. It really doesn't matter what you do at this stage, just that you do something. When people are first starting off they get intimidated because they don't know all the right steps, any of the right words, very much about who the god is, and they're so afraid of messing up that they end up not doing anything at all. Dionysos is a very approachable god – he's not going to bite your head off because you flub something. You will, however, miss out on a great deal if you never actually approach him. So start doing something for him, even if it's just pouring a simple libation, spending some time in meditation, reciting a hymn, or having a heart-to-heart with him each night. Whatever you decide on doing, do it regularly, because this helps build up a relationship and gives your actions added power, and don't change what you do every single time. For ritual to be effective it needs to be repeated and regular.

Step 2

Read about Dionysos. If you want to understand who Dionysos is, it's important to know who he was, specifically how the ancients saw, understood, and interacted with him. There are numerous excellently written books out there dealing with Dionysos (he seems to be a favorite subject for scholars). The best of these are *Dionysos: Archetypal Image of Indestructible Life* by Carl Kerenyi and *Dionysus: Myth and Cult* by Walter Otto. In addition to all of the scholarly works on him, go back to the ancient sources and immerse yourself in his myths. Many of these can be found online (especially at Theoi.com) if you don't feel like spending a fortune on building up your own private library. Read the websites that have been written about him by modern followers of the god. Speak to the authors of the sites and other followers of the god.

Step 3

Process the information you've acquired. A good way to do this is to get several journals and begin writing down any notes or interesting information you come upon or thoughts you have while reading. Map out his epithets, associations, and myths, and try to see which ones go together. Figure out what the myths and historical information mean to you, personally, and how they might affect your practice. Keep a record of any rituals you do, dreams that come to you, or strange experiences you have. Don't think that you'll be able to keep all of this information straight in your head. Even some of the most important moments in our lives fade with time or disappear altogether. It's an invaluable resource to be able to look back over this information at a later date.

Step 4

Try to find ways to deepen your relationship with Dionysos and see his presence in your life at times other than just during ritual. Spend time in wild places, such as mountains, forests, swamps, etc. where he was traditionally felt to reside. Start dancing for him. Dancing can lead to a greater awareness of your body, and trigger altered states of consciousness – but more than that, it's fun, and he likes to see his worshipers dance. Even if you only do it in private, in front of your shrine, and never let anyone else see you it can be a powerful and rewarding exercise. You will learn things about him through your body that you never could through intellectual activity alone. You may also choose to take up yoga or a martial art to get in touch with your body. See lots of movies and plays, as drama and comedy were considered sacred to him in antiquity. Challenge yourself. Try to break habits and personal barriers. Many of these are the result of societal conditioning, which serves to hinder our spirits and stifle our creativity and connection to the vital powers of nature which are Dionysos' preserve. Get in touch with the darker parts of your personality, those parts of yourself which are uncomfortable and socially unacceptable. The more we repress this side of ourselves, the stronger it becomes, until it finally finds a way to burst forth, degraded and deformed. Dionysos can help us express this in a safe and healthy manner before it does that. See what other points of contact exist between yourself and the god.

Step 5

Explore more traditionally Hellenic methods of worshiping the god. There has to be something to a practice that's over 4,000 years old! There are many excellent websites that cover every aspect of Hellenic worship. Read over these, compare them (because there can be great disagreement and some false information out there) and try to figure out what was done and the reasoning behind why it was done. Implement those things that you like in your practice. Set up a shrine for Dionysos if you can, and perform regular worship there. This should be an expression of your personal relationship with the god, and contain images associated with him such as his animals, his colors, his plants, and so forth. Research the ancient festivals held in his honor. Consider observing modern festivals as well – ones that other people have come up with, or something you create to honor a particular aspect of the god or to commemorate an important event in your relationship with him. (Information on modern and ancient festivals – including non-Athenian, lesser-known ones – can be found at wildivine.org/dionysos_festivals.htm.)

THE FEAST OF THE SENSES

From time to time people write to me and say something along the lines of, "I've felt Dionysos' call and accepted it. Okay, *now* what do I do?"

I've done my best to provide some of those answers through the various websites that I've maintained, because back when I was first starting out there just wasn't a whole lot of information available for cultivating the kind of deep, personal relationship I wanted with the god. Even the basics of Hellenic ritual were hard to come by, and a lot of us had to piece this stuff together through trial and error and plenty of false starts along the way.

In a way you can see the evolution of my spiritual life and practice through the essays that first appeared on my Sannion's Sanctuary website many years ago. My first attempts at ritual and articulating the theology that shaped it was still very much indebted to Wiccan-influenced neo-paganism. Then came the ultra conservative "do things exactly as the ancients did; innovation is nothing but creeping incipient fluffyism" reconstructionist phase. Then, slowly, as I gained more experience and my relationship with Dionysos deepened and matured, the lines started to blur, my stances grew softer, I became more interested in free-flowing ecstatic types of ritual, and the yardstick by which I felt things ought to be judged was first whether an action was pleasing to the gods, and secondly whether it contributed to effective worship on the part of the individual. Today I maintain that those two points are what matter most; the rest, while important in their own way, are just window-dressing that adds to the experience.

So, to bring it back to the original question, what would I suggest to someone who is just getting started? After all, 'do what the gods find pleasing and what works for you' is hardly very helpful when you haven't figured that out yet and are actually taking your first steps down this path. The best recommendation that I have at the moment is something that I have taken to calling the Feast of the Senses. By now you're probably asking, "What is this Feast of the Senses thing that he keeps mentioning? I've never heard of it before. Is it something ancient?"

The answer to that is twofold: yes, you have heard of it before, I just gave it a swanky new name – and no, it is completely modern and this is the first time that I have written about it. A contradiction, you say? Why yes, indeed it is – and you'd better get used to that kind of thing if you're going to have any kind of relationship with Dithyrambos.

You see, the Feast of the Senses is pretty much your average devotional ritual – just stripped down to its barest essentials. While in its present form it is geared towards initiating a relationship with Dionysos, it's the sort of thing that can be used for pretty much any deity, with only slight modifications. In fact, I have been using it in my devotions for quite some time without realizing that that's what I was doing – nor was I alone in this. I have seen a number of other folks from traditions as diverse as Heathenry, Wicca, Thelema, Feri, Saivitism, and Hellenismos perform very similar types of ritual. And it makes sense – although our gods and the core practices of our traditions may differ, the human brain is pretty much hard-wired the same way for most people, and the point of this exercise is to use that wiring to apprehend divinity around us. The Feast of the Senses is precisely that: a celebration of the divine through our various senses, using our thoughts, taste, touch, scent, sight, hearing, and more numinous faculties to perceive the divine and draw us into its mysterious presence.

Too many people these days approach ritual through Protestant Christian eyes. (Thankfully Catholic and Orthodox rituals usually contain an element of theatricality and a sense of the holiness embedded in actions and words, something that tends to make Protestants very uncomfortable.) Many – both Christians and Neopagans – believe that it is sufficient to recite a couple phrases, go through rote actions, and the whole time remain as passive spectators, their minds and spirits entirely untouched by what they're doing. It's all in the head, mechanical and intellectual. They're bored most of the time – and what's worse, they're probably boring the gods to tears with their worship. As a Dionysian, you should never settle for this kind of thing. Your worship of the god should be awful, meaning something that stirs your deepest emotions and culminates in a sense of profound awe before divinity. You should worship him with your whole being – mind, spirit, and body. Your worship should engage all of your senses. In the words of Abramelin the Mage, you should enflame your spirit with prayer. Think about that for a moment.

If you're just reading something off of a script and doing these robotic actions, you're not really there; you're trapped in ego-awareness, and your soul cannot commune with the divine. Our senses are like the bridge which allows us to cross over to other worlds, to move from here to *there*, to close the distance between ourselves, our mind on the one hand, and our soul and the divine on the other. These are tools which broaden our awareness and ground us in a true sense of being. They flip the switch in our brains which triggers ecstatic states.

There is so much going on all the time that we're totally oblivious to. Right now you're reading this text – and that's probably all that exists for you. But what about the feel of the paper in your hand, or the chair beneath your butt, or the floor beneath your feet? What about the way your clothes rub against your skin as you move? Or the temperature of the air on your exposed skin? Can you still taste the remnant of your last meal or the drink you just took on your tongue? Is there music playing in the background, or the sound of your neighbors walking down the hall outside your room? Can you smell the faint, lingering scent of detergent on your clothes? Can you feel the blood flowing through your veins or the beating of your heart in your chest?

If you're like most people, until I pointed these things out the answer was probably no. And in some situations that's okay. If you were perfectly aware of everything going on at all levels while you were on a crowded bus you'd go insane from stimulation overload. But there are situations where this deepening of awareness is of paramount importance, and one of those situations is unquestionably when we stand before our god in worship.

Good ritual should awaken you on all of these levels and stimulate your whole being. That's why we use the props of ritual in the first place. The Neoplatonists believed that certain divine sympathies existed between physical things and the divinities, and that different things were connected to different divinities. Thus each god had certain scents, certain words, certain images, certain sounds, and certain mental associations which they did not necessarily share with other divinities. These were the ways that spiritual beings manifested within the material realm. And by focusing their awareness on them and manipulating these subtle connections – the divine imprint of the gods in material substances – the theurgist could affect deeper communication with the gods.

That is the key to the Feast of the Senses. It is attuning ourselves to the spirit of Dionysos by focusing on the material items which possess a divine sympathy with the god and are the vehicles through which his spirit manifests itself in the material or mundane world. Just as these items allow Dionysos to descend into this world, by following the threads back to their source we can experience a deep communion or mingling of our souls with his through the height of religious ecstasy which the Greeks called *enthousiasmos*.

(For more on the theoretical principles that this practice is based on, I would direct the reader to consult Porphyry's *On Images* and Iamblikhos' *On the Mysteries*.)

Preparation

Before one celebrates the Feast of the Senses a good deal of preparation is called for.

To begin with, one must cultivate a proper mindset. True, the point of the Feast is the full engagement of the senses and an outward focusing of them. There are very little to no spoken parts; no active memorization or recitation. The point is to feel and sense and explore the presence of divinity through material substances. The intellect takes a backseat position and is subordinated to the bodily senses. But it has its role to play within the Feast – it is brought into harmony or alignment with the other senses and used to heighten their power and direct them towards divinity. The intellect associates things, drawing parallels between objects that it considers similar. Thus when we smell a familiar perfume, an image of a long-forgotten loved one may instantly arise within our mind, conjured by the intellect because of the association it has fabricated between the two. This is the primary function of the mind and intellect within the Feast. And to ensure that it can perform this role in the optimal manner, it must be properly fed and programmed before the Feast begins.

Think of the mind as a sponge which absorbs all of the information that passes through it, fed by our senses. It stores that information as memories until the will calls upon it and seeks to access those memories or draw parallels. In order to have an effective Feast, one must make sure that the mind is full of Dionysian information.

Thus, in the time leading up to your celebration of the Feast immerse yourself as fully in the world of Dionysos as possible. Read everything that you can find on his mythology, history, cult, symbols, and the experiences of his modern followers. It doesn't matter if you've read this stuff before – throw yourself into it with complete gusto, cramming your brain with the information until it's ready to burst. Don't worry about retaining the information or making sense of it. In fact, it's better if you don't – because then it isn't being filtered by the ego-intellect, but bypasses those cognitive centers and heads straight for the memory banks of your brain, which will make it easier for you to form random associations during the Feast. Read every chance you get: on your way into work, on your lunch break, during any leisure hours you may have, and especially right before you turn in for the night, since in your tired state there will be more of a chance that the information will sink in.

When you're not reading, reflect on what you've read. Think about his myths and the various levels of interpretation that they afford. Map out all of his epithets and associations and figure out which ones go with which – and try to determine why these things are associated with him. Try to follow the threads of his cults and associations as they develop over time and across wide geographical distribution. Figure out which of the conclusions in the books or articles you've read are just the speculations of the assorted authors and which are supported by actual historical fact and your own past experiences with the god. Personalize all of this by figuring out what this random information means to you, what it says about the god and how he might conceivably act in your life based on that. See if any patterns emerge about a consistent Dionysian *ethos*. (Are there certain behaviors which seem to find favor with the god and others which might incur his displeasure? Are there certain activities that recur which you should begin implementing in your life?) Above all think about who Dionysos is, what all these stories, ideas, and images can tell you about his nature – and how he may have revealed himself to you in the past, whether you were aware of it or not.

Next, think about the things associated with him. Track them down and set them up in a shrine for the god. Pile up as many representations as you can: his animals, his plants, certain stones, or colors, or just random items that remind you of him. A cheap way to acquire these (especially when you're just starting off) is to print pictures found online. Spend some time doing image searches for relevant keywords: all of the items related to him, all of the variant spellings of his name, anything you can think of linked to the god, however small, remote or improbable. Either set these up on their own, or else turn them into a collage or use them in some other art project.

Also, start compiling a playlist of Dionysian music. Consider ambient, darkwave music such as Vas, Dead Can Dance, Natacha Atlas, and Juno Reactor. Consider rock music like the Doors, Faith No More, System of a Down, and even Prince. Consider Classical music, world music (especially Greek, Armenian, Middle Eastern, and Sufi chants), or techno music. Include songs about freedom, wine, sex, and the other things associated with him. It doesn't have to make sense or even be something that another person would equate with the god – it just has to remind you of him, for whatever reason. Hell, if Country and Western or Polka reminds you of Dionysos, make a collection of those songs! Put all of this music together and listen to it often, so that it soaks into your brain and begins to have strong Dionysian associations for you, even when you hear those songs in completely random settings.

Another thing that you can do in preparation for your celebration of the Feast is to go where the god is. Spend time outdoors: in your garden, in a park, out in the woods or a nearby hill or mountain. Go to theaters, movie houses, and clubs, or stroll abandoned city streets late at night. Go for long walks, letting your mind wander and keeping an eye out for signs of the god's presence around you. Maybe you'll run across one of his sacred images, or see a random poster or billboard that has something relevant to say to you, or maybe you'll feel the god's numinous presence stirring in the trees around you or causing the fruit to ripen and the flowers to unfold. Remember, as Thales said, all things are full of gods – and sometimes the gods like to play hide and seek with us. As you go about your journeys, think about why people associate these places with Dionysos. What special qualities do they possess that suggest his epiphanies and *parousia* or presence? Do you feel his presence more fully in one place over another – and if so, why do you think this is the case?

At this point your mind should be properly prepared to celebrate the Feast of the Senses. Now, a word is in order before we proceed to describe it. The Feast is not intended to replace regular formal devotional or religious rituals. Those things have a power all their own, and there is great utility in their outward focus. The Feast is meant to supplement that kind of practice, to deepen it and help one more fully experience the presence of the god. But if this is the only type of ritual you perform, you'll be missing out on a great deal. For one thing, there is a danger of it becoming too internalized, your relationship one of thoughts and feelings as opposed to concrete actions. The gifts that the gods bestow on us are material – as should be the acts of thanksgiving that we return to them. Those traditional methods have also been proven to work effectively over the millennia of Greek religious practice. To ignore that successful track record seems hardly desirable, besides which, their long duration show that the gods clearly find these forms pleasing – and isn't that the whole purpose of religious ritual in the first place, to make the gods happy? But innovation is not a bad thing, and there is nothing antithetical within the Feast to traditional practice. In fact, when the two forms are united they can be incredibly powerful.

The Feast itself

One needs very few props to perform this ritual. Certainly no script of rehearsed lines, no elaborate costume, no ceremonial tools or complex offerings. The absolute requirements are very simple: yourself, your senses, and the god. Nothing else is needed, though there are a bunch of items that contribute to a more effective celebration of the Feast. Here are some suggested items:

> Music
> Fruit
> Wine
> Two glasses, one for you and one for the god
> Incense or perfume
> A candle
> Representations or symbols of the god
> A quiet, secluded place where you won't be interrupted for the duration of your ritual

And that's pretty much it! Of course, you can add whatever else you'd like to the mix – especially substituting different foods for the fruit or dressing in specific attire worn solely for him – but the point is, this is a very easy ritual to perform, and requires very little to do it.

So, to begin the ritual, set up your items. If you feel like doing some kind of purification or consecration of yourself and the space beforehand, you can – but it's not necessary, especially if you're doing this in a temple room or before your shrine for the god, which should already be properly dedicated to holy service. Make sure that you have a decent amount of time to perform the Feast in – at least 20 to 30 minutes, though it can take an hour or longer to perform it if you really get into the spirit of the ritual. You should be able to play music and make noise without fear of disturbing the people around you or being disturbed by them. This ritual can require intense concentration and focus so make sure the people you live with understand that and won't be barging in on you in the middle of it. You will also need to be in near total darkness – the only light coming from the candle – and want to have space to dance and move about in.

Once all of these preliminary considerations have been taken care of and the space set up as you want it, take several deep breaths and center yourself. Relax as completely as you can, letting all mundane thoughts depart from your mind. Stand for a few moments, with your arms raised and stretched out. Let yourself just *be* in this receptive posture. Feel your legs holding you up. Feel your arms extended. Feel the breath circulating through your body. Feel yourself relaxing, but also aware that you are about to experience communion with Dionysos through your senses. Feel the desire for his presence stir within your soul. Call up from your memory any past experiences you've had with him. Try to remember exactly what that felt like. Conjure an image of the god within your mind, however you see him. Let other images flood your consciousness, his different faces and forms, the various objects and ideas associated with him, until you can almost feel him standing there beside you. Let the desire for him deepen within you, until you ache to reach out and touch him.

Then, call to him. Ask him to be there with you, to share this moment, this Feast with you, to reveal himself to you in all of his forms. Put all of the desire and longing that you possess for the god into your voice. Speak, confident that he can hear you. Feel the voice as it rises up from your chest, vibrating through your throat, caressing your lips as it leaves your mouth and spills out into the air surrounding you. Say whatever comes to your mind. It can be a full invocation, with as many of his epithets and the formulaic phrases of ritual as you can remember – or just his name, spoken aloud. A formal declaration of invitation or the inarticulate plea of a lover long separated, aching for union. It doesn't matter *what* you say – only that you speak aloud.

Then light the incense or apply the perfume. Make sure that you have chosen a scent that is connected with him somehow, be it something that others recognize as belonging to him or just something that has always reminded you of the god personally. Pause. Breathe deeply. Be in the moment. Focus entirely on the scent wafting up and enfolding you. Really smell it. All of the subtle nuances. Does the scent have a shape and texture for you? What memories does it stir within your mind? Why do you think this scent is connected with him – and what does that say about who the god is? Remind yourself, over and over again, *this is how the god smells*. Feel him draw closer to you through this scent.

Now light the candle. Turn off all other lights. Explore the darkness around you. Can you see shapes through the shadows – or is everything pitch black? Is this the darkness of a cave, of night, the darkness out of which life emerged, and to which it must return; the darkness which lies like a shroud over the mysteries? Call to mind all of the epithets and associations that Dionysos has with darkness, night, shadows and concealment. Feel the darkness as deeply as you can. Plumb the depths of the great unknown. Is it comforting – or does it cause fear to rise up within you? Why? Remember *this is where Dionysos is*.

Now turn to the candle, a pool of light in the darkness. Draw close to it. Place your hand over the flame, as close as you can without getting burned. Feel the heat licking against your skin. Remember that Dionysos is in the light, just as much as he is in the darkness. Think about the warmth of the sun on your skin, the sun that gives life, coaxing the young buds to blossom on the branch. Feel Dionysos in the heat and warmth, as the source of life that moves through all the plants and animals. Let your mind wander back to a time when you felt flushed with that heat of life, full to bursting, intoxicated and *alive*. Let the heat stir within your body, spreading up from your loins, down from your cheeks, meeting at your heart which has begun to race with excitement at the dawning presence of the god. Lower your hand closer and closer to the flame, until it seems almost unbearable. Remember: *this is what it feels like to be in the presence of the god* – white hot, brilliantly intense, life ratcheted up to such a feverish pitch that any moment now it's going to burst into an inferno...but it doesn't. It holds its place, maintains its form, kept going at the peak of perfection, a dwarf star dancing in the infinite abyss.

Now, raise your eyes a little and take in the images on your shrine. Look at them as if you are seeing them for the very first time. Focus on each item individually, reflecting on its connection to the god, the role it has within his myths, his cult, his realm of influence. Then take a step back and see all of them together, forming an intricate collective whole, a tapestry or collage depicting the god. See the connections between the items, how the mask and the phallos, or the bull and the grapevine go together. Take in their contours, the colors that you can see in the shimmering glow of the candlelight. Watch the play of the flickering shadows upon their form. Focus on them with such deep concentration that the items appear almost alive to you. Can you see the panther's chest heaving, its fur slick with sweat? Can you see the empty eye sockets of the silent mask gazing back at you, looking deep into your soul? Can you smell the grass and snow depicted in the picture of Mount Parnassos, hear the lilting pipes of the satyrs as they play their music for the dancing mainades? Can you see the spirit of Dionysos coursing through all of these things, moving gently beneath the surface? Remember: *this is what the god looks like.*

Now start the music you have prepared. You can either stand or sit comfortably while you listen. Let the sound wash over you, surrounding you, enfolding you in its rhythm, carrying you off to another world, a land of the imagination. Allow your thoughts to unfold as they will, seduced by the sounds of the music. How does this make you feel? What emotions does it unleash? What images does it conjure? Let the words dissolve into random sounds, without meaning or association, the human voice become just another instrument contributing to the melody and rhythm. Then, in time, listen for what the words have to say to you. They will come as disjointed messages, in promiscuous phrases taken out of context but meaningful for their randomness. You will hear things in them that you never have before, even though you've listened to the song a thousand times. You will understand things hidden in the song, things perhaps even its composer was not aware of. Feel the bass vibrate through your whole body. Feel the melody and rhythm move you, change you, draw hidden things out of you. Remember: *this is what the god sounds like.*

As you see fit, permit yourself to respond to the music with your body. Let it guide you, direct you, cause you to move as it wills. The sound corresponds to physical motion, it has its own movement and dance, and all of that lies trapped within you. Bring yourself into alignment with the music: give the invisible expression through your body. Sway gently to the music, as if you are being buffeted by a strong breeze. Let your head roll lazily about, your body swaying back and forth, your arms rising and falling of their own volition. At first do not be cognizant of dancing: simply *move*.

Feel the life stirring within you. All life possesses motion of some kind. All life, from the tiniest atom to the unfathomably large cosmos, is caught in perpetual motion, united in a single dance, the dance of creation, destruction and transformation, the dance of life in its countless forms. Join in that dance. Give expression to the movement within you, the motion of your soul, the motion of the music, the motion of life. Do not worry about moving properly. Do not concern yourself with whether you are a good dancer, whether your steps are elegant, beautiful, sexy. No one is there to judge you. No one is going to think you are a clumsy oaf. Dionysos demands only that we dance, not that we dance well. So just dance. Move. Be alive. Praise the god through your body. Celebrate your existence by participating in the dance. Let it take you where it will. Let your rational mind recede into the background. Have no thoughts except for movement, except for being one with your body and using it as a tool to give thanks to the god. Dance fast, dance slow, shake your head about wildly, stomp your feet, slide gracefully around the room, stay in one spot and spin, spin, spin until you're ready to collapse in a dizzy pile of limbs. Go down on all fours and crawl about like a leopard or panther stalking its prey; slither on your belly like a serpent; thrust your pelvis out and hop around like a joyously lustful satyr; toss your head back wildly and contort your body however the god wills you to, giving yourself completely to him in the frenzy of mainadic dancing. Remember: *this is how the god moves.*

When you are done dancing, pour yourself a glass of wine. Then pour a glass for Dionysos. Pause for a moment. Drink in the heady aroma of the wine. Let the smell surround you, intoxicate you, rouse your desire to drink it. Remember *that this is how the god smells.* Take a moment to look at the wine, dark like blood in the shadows, reflecting the light of the flickering candle flame. Think about what the wine symbolizes. That this is the blood and tears of the god, that his spirit dwells in it. Reflect on the myths of its invention, the stories of how he brought it to mankind. Contemplate its dual nature: a remedy for our sorrows, inspiring joy, light-heartedness, freedom and exuberant intoxication – but also that it is a dangerous poison, a madness-inducer that unlocks the chambers of the soul and unleashes whatever lies hidden within our hearts, be that a ferocious beast or a glorious angel. Remember that above all else, this is the thing most intimately connected with the god. He is the grape and the juice that is poured from it, after it is stomped and pressed and has undergone its manifold transformations. Remember that *Dionysos is the wine* and you are about to consume him. Thank him for his gift and then drink the wine.

Take a sip. Hold it in your mouth, letting it coat your tongue, tease your throat. What does it feel like? What does it taste like? Is it sweet, tart, warm, heady? Hold it there, fully in the moment, experiencing everything that this mouthful of wine has to teach you. Then swallow it, and feel the wine as it passes through your throat, as it enters your body, its warmth spreading out as it passes through you. Drink more, taking bigger, deeper sips. Have no thoughts except for those connected with the consumption of the wine. Can you feel the wine begin to take effect? Its heat spreading, your vision going clear or hazy, your limbs starting to feel loose, your head going fuzzy, your pulse quickening, sounds distorting, shadows deepening. Remember: *this is what the god feels like inside you.*

When you are ready, take up the fruit. Grapes. Pomegranates. Figs. Apples. Oranges. Whatever you have chosen; all fruit belongs to him, but each has its own qualities, and those qualities suggest different things about the god. Hold the fruit in your hands. Feel its weight, the texture of its skin, its hardness or softness in your palm. Roll it around, enjoying the touch of it against your skin. What color does it have in the darkness? In the candlelight? Explore everything about it without yet tasting it. Think about how this fruit is connected with the god, and what it can tell you about him. Then taste it. Hold it in your mouth, without yet chewing. Feel the texture against your tongue, the nuances of its taste. Then bite down, mindful of what it is like to feel your teeth tear into it, ripping it apart, releasing the juices to spill out over your lips. Does it feel good, primal, animalistic to consume its flesh? Relish the taste of it, the nourishment that it will bring to your body, the strengthening of your own life-force by partaking of the life that dwells within it. Remember that the god is present in the transference of that energy. This is his sacrament. *This is what Dionysos tastes like.* Enjoy it. Share it with him. Immerse yourself in the complete sensual pleasure of eating. Have no thoughts but this.

After that, you may do as you please. Eat more. Drink more. Listen to the music. Dance. Take in everything that surrounds you. Be present in the darkness. Let your thoughts go as they will, but focused on the god and all of the things connected to him. Think about him. Speak to him. Listen in case he has anything to say to you. But above all else, *just be with him.*

That is the Feast of the Senses. Through it you shall learn things about the god that you can never pick up solely by reading books and online articles. Above all, how to experience him and recognize him through the things that belong to him. The Feast can be done on its own or included within a more formal ritual framework. Celebrate the Feast often. Try always to feel his presence around you and use your senses to draw closer to him.

DEVOTIONAL ACTIVITIES FOR DIONYSIANS

For the purpose of this discussion I'm defining "devotional activities" as anything that a person does with the express intent of honoring the god or keeping the mind focused on him outside of formal ritual. Of course these activities can – and should! – be incorporated as part of one's religious observances, especially on specific festival days that are given over entirely to honoring Dionysos, and for many participating in these activities can lead to intense encounters with him. But the point is that they don't have to. They are things you can do any time and in any place, regardless of what else is going on or what sort of headspace you find yourself in. Although it is supremely important to keep Dionysos' festivals and perform regular rituals for him, it is just as important to maintain a relationship in the time between those occasions, to cultivate an awareness of his presence in all parts of our lives, and gain a deeper understanding of his nature and personality through direct engagement with him and his world. These activities – and countless others I probably won't get around to mentioning – are a fine way to do that. They are small things, but collectively they add up to a rich, dynamic and god-saturated life. Keep in mind as well that many of these things can be done simultaneously for greater effect.

Drink wine

Get yourself a nice bottle of wine, especially an expensive variety you may not have tried before, and drink it in the company of Dionysos. Pour him a glass as well and light a candle on his shrine, then sit before it with your own glass, basking in his presence and enjoying the pleasures of the vintage. Pay special attention to how the wine tastes and smells and feels going down. Let each sip take as long as it needs to so that you can get a full sensory experience. Focus on things you might not ordinarily, such as the quality of the light as it interacts with the wine or the glass, how it tastes on your finger or lip versus how it tastes when you drink it straight up. See if you can detect the subtle flavors beneath the surface and compare that to other wines you have had in the past. You can choose to just drink the wine alone or have it with other appropriate foods such as a fine cheese or dark chocolate, but if you do, remain mindful of the unique flavors that these foods bring to the experience and drink plenty of wine all on its own. Also, make sure that you will have enough uninterrupted time to enjoy your sensual feast and put special thought and care into your surroundings. For instance, you may want to light more candles than just the one on his shrine, completely filling the room with their diffuse illumination or you may want to sit in total darkness, blocking out everything except for his shrine. Will you have music playing in the background or total silence? And if so, what will you have playing? Something soft and Classical or something sensual and spiritual? Something that gets your blood going or that has strong Dionysian associations for you? Choose carefully, with the mood you're trying to create foremost in your mind. Sometimes the stuff you normally listen to for him will not convey the precise mood you're going for with this, in which case you should be open to other types of music. After all, enjoying wine is what this is primarily about, so you don't want your music – or anything else – to get in the way. Be open to changing everything with your mood or scrapping it all if that's what's required. Also, you may want to have some nice incense going in the background as well, but make sure that it isn't likely to overpower the bouquet of the wine.

Go to a wine-tasting event

These can be a great deal of fun and an opportunity to learn new ways of appreciating wine, as well as introducing you to varieties of wine you may never have encountered before. Don't be intimidated if you're a rank amateur – very often they'll provide brief instruction at the start of the event or offer classes that you can take beforehand. There's a whole art to wine-tasting based on the cultured appreciation of things that most of us have never even thought about previously. Even if this isn't an activity you're likely to engage in regularly it can be helpful to acquire a new vocabulary and way of looking at things, which can enhance your own private wine-drinking experiences. At the least you should consider reading some of the literature on the subject because there's a great deal more to wine than just how it tastes or how quickly it'll get you drunk. Plus it can be nice to be around other people who are so passionately into wine, even if they do not consciously honor the god who dwells within it. Do not let yourself feel intimidated and outclassed. As a devotee of Dionysos you have as much right to be there as the most wealthy and hoity-toity of the bunch – indeed I'd say you have much more of a right! But if you are a true Dionysian then you will not allow fear and insecurity to get in your way. Pushing through such things, exposing yourself to difficult and unfamiliar situations, transgressing boundaries and triumphing over obstacles is the sign of a true Dionysian, after all, so beyond whatever else you might learn or experience there, this can be a powerful devotional act for these reasons alone.

Visit your local winery and participate in a grape-stomp

If you happen to live in one of our country's wine regions you should avail yourself of the opportunity to see where the magic happens and take part in the process. It's one thing to read about this stuff in old books – quite another to watch it unfolding all around you. Imagine how great it would be to feel the grapes crushed beneath your feet and know that you've helped to create the wine that someone else will one day be drinking! As you are doing so you could even recite a quick prayer blessing the wine and making it *entheos* with the god's spirit. Of course, most wine produced these days isn't in the old style – they have factory lines and machines to do all the crushing and sifting – but it can still be a fun and educational experience to visit and see how it's done. You may even get to tour the facilities and walk among the fields, which can be a powerful thing all on its own. If you aren't able to visit a winery or directly participate in the process you can always take a lovely drive through wine country and wave at the rows of grapes as you pass by.

Homebrewing

This is becoming an increasingly popular pastime and it's something I believe that every Dionysian should do at least once in their life. Think about it: you could make your own alcohol! How awesome would it be to have gone through the whole process, transforming the raw stuff of nature into a sacred beverage that you can drink and offer to the god in ritual? It's a fairly simple process, at that – men have been doing it since the dawn of time, after all – and relatively cheap, considering the yield of alcohol you get. Plus, after the initial expenditure for bottles, fermenting equipment, etc., all you'll have to pay for is the ingredients. Wine-making can be a little tricky, especially if you live in an apartment, but it's not impossible and it's certainly not the only option. After all, important as wine is to Dionysos it's not his only holy beverage. Before wine, honey-mead seems to have been his sacred drink, especially on Crete, and in Phrygia and Egypt beer was drunk by devotees of the god. Mead and beer are probably the easiest to home brew and you can have a lot of fun trying out different recipes, especially the herbal-infused ones. But be careful as this can be a highly addictive hobby. I know folks who started off with a single gallon of mead stored under their sink and before they realized it their whole basement had become transformed into a brewery, with a dozen different kinds going at any given time. These are good friends to have, because they're always calling you over to sample something or to get rid of excess quantities. "Free alcohol" – can there be two more beautiful words for a Dionysian to hear?

Grow

One of the best things that a Dionysian can do is keep a garden for the god, especially if that garden includes grapevines and ivy. These are more than his sacred emblems – indeed, his spirit dwells within the plants – so all the time, energy, and careful attention you put into cultivating them is a very direct and personal way of honoring him. It will also teach you a great deal about the god and his cycles of growth, maturity, decay and rebirth – mysteries you can only truly discover through nature. No matter how many books you read it will never take the place of actually watching the process unfold and being an intimate part of it. Remember as well that Dionysos is not just the god of the grape and ivy – apples, figs, pomegranates and all flowers belong equally to him, so whatever you plant in your garden would be appropriate if cultivated with the god in mind. Furthermore, you could grow herbs and other fragrant items that you normally burn in offering for him. How much better will such things be coming from your own hands and loving labor?

Make your own ritual tools

Likewise, you can create all of the offerings, shrine items and ritual tools that you use in worshiping Dionysos. The act of creation makes them special and uniquely your own, instead of just some cheap crap mass-produced in Chinese sweatshops that you pick up at the mall. "But I have no artistic talent!" you may be objecting right now, to which I reply, "So fucking what?" It's intent that matters, the love and care that goes into it that makes for a true offering, not technical aptitude. Besides, a lot of this stuff isn't all that difficult to make. It requires very little skill to shape a piece of clay into a snake or a phallos or a bunch of grapes – even a child can do it. Sure, it's a little harder to make something that actually resembles a goat or a bull or a human figure – let alone a chalice capable of being drunk from – but they're certainly not impossible, especially if you practice. Maybe it'll take you a while to get the hang of it – and a series of misshapen abominations – but you'll have a great time trying, especially if you open yourself up to the experience, let the creativity flow through you, and don't take anything you do too seriously.

Another fun thing to try your hand at is collage. Collect a bunch of images that remind you of Dionysos or certain things associated with him and paste these together in interesting ways. Make a *papier-mâché* or clay mask, either to wear in ritual or to hang above his shrine. Or you could put together a devotional scrapbook filled with Dionysian imagery and a collection of appropriate quotes, song lyrics and ancient hymns. You could make your own *thyrsos* or weave a garland out of ivy, grapes leaves and fresh flowers. You can decorate store-bought ritual items by repainting them or stenciling appropriate things on them. I highly recommend this practice as it adds character and a personal touch to otherwise fairly anonymous items. Most statues sold these days are blandly lacking in personality. Everyone's got the same ones and their shrines all pretty much look alike. But in ancient times they tended to favor colorful and eccentric decoration, the sacred images painted in bold, gay hues. That white marble isn't Classical – it's what's left after everything chipped off or faded away. So go wild! And when you're done, add other personal touches like draping the statue with necklaces or putting pinecones, ivy and representations of Dionsyiac animals beside it. There are a thousand such projects you could take on – you are limited only by the extent of your imagination.

Collect art

In addition to the art you create with your own hands you can seek out the work of others. I spend a great deal of time on the internet hunting down devotional images for my gods and spirits. I have several large files on my computer full of such things and I set my screensaver to cycle through the appropriate folder on the days I honor them each month. It's fun to just sit there and watch the different images come up while I'm drinking, listening to music or just letting my thoughts wander. I've printed off the best of these and have them prominently displayed around my apartment, especially hanging above my various shrines. When possible I've purchased prints of these works, both to get better quality images and also to support the talented artists who have enriched my life through their craft. It's fascinating to see all the different ways that people have chosen to represent Dionysos over the years, especially noting the common themes that run through them. As I mentioned earlier, you can use these images in your own artistic projects either by making collages or scrapbooks or you can use them as a nice portable shrine if you want to carry the god with you to work or elsewhere.

Glamourbombs

Keeping the theme of creativity going, I highly recommend the practice of leaving Dionysian glamourbombs throughout your city. Basically it's an attempt to inject some weirdness and magic into the lives of ordinary people through beauty, art and randomness, to remind them that the gods still exist and that they're here with us. Such a practice began with the anarchists and street kids and gained popularity among Chaotes and those with a Faerie aesthetic, but there's no reason why we Dionysians can't do it too. You can write scraps of hymns or meaningful quotes on paper and tack them up on a public bulletin board, an electric pole or even tucked inside a book for someone to find. You can make small disposable shrines with a picture of Dionysos, a tea light and some flowers or ivy and leave it somewhere visible and well-trafficked. In the midst of a crowd waiting for a light to change you can start reciting one of the Orphic hymns or a Sufi poem or just shout his name at the top of your lungs. You could go out in full Greek costume to run your errands or better yet wear a crown of ivy with your ordinary clothing. You could spell out his name in flower petals or grain or tiny pebbles or erect a large phallos decorated with pretty ribbons. You could make a flyer with information about Dionysos and links to websites and other valuable resources and distribute them to random passersby or leave them where people will find them. You could make one of those "have you seen me" posters but in place of a lost child, cat or dog put an image of Dionysos and say that the nymphs and satyrs of Nysa are searching for their god. Truly, the possibilities are endless.

Your attire

Although this can certainly be part of an elaborate glamourbomb, it's also good to pay attention to how you dress on a humbler and more purely devotional level. What we wear and surround ourselves with shapes who we are and what we think. Intentionally choosing our clothing and other accoutrements to reflect our status as a Dionysian and to honor him keeps the god fresh in our minds and makes him an integral part of our life, regardless of what else we happen to be doing. Even if no one else recognizes that this is what we're doing – and there's no reason why it has to be flashy and attention-grabbing – we know, and that's what truly matters. So on his holy days or any time that you want to feel close to him, put thought into what you're wearing. It can be as simple as choosing an article of clothing in a color associated with him – purple, green, red or black say – or having a special dress or t-shirt you only wear for him. Accessories are nice as well: pins, brooches, earrings, necklaces or rings that are consecrated to him or have one of his symbols or animals on them. Likewise you can wear a special scent or perfume that will call to mind the god every time you catch a whiff of it. Or you can do your hair in a specific style that you wear only on his days. Though simple and subtle things, they can be immensely powerful over time, especially if you put a lot of thought into it while you're getting ready in the morning. This will enable you to carry Dionysos with you wherever you go and whatever you happen to be doing.

Pretend to be somebody else

Dionysos is the god of fluid nature, of madness, of masks, of the sacred art of drama and transformation in all of its myriad forms. Within his worship we often experience *ekstasis* which means literally to be outside of one's self, and *enthousiasmos* which is to be inspired or filled with a divine spirit. But ritual is not the only context in which we can explore the Protean nature of identity. Such states can come about spontaneously or while drinking or dancing. But we can also bring them about intentionally. Exploring the boundaries of our personality can be a powerfully transformative and liberating act that brings great insight into who and what we are. Is our identity merely the societally conditioned roles we perform? The thoughts in our head? The impulses that drive us – or the ones we choose not to act upon? The name we've been given or assigned to ourselves? The clothes we wear, the contents of our wallet? What happens when you change one of these things? Or all of them? When you give yourself license to act in a manner you'd never normally consider acceptable, go places you'd never ordinarily set foot in? Most people don't even realize the degree to which their personality is an artificial construct, shaped by these seemingly inconsequential factors, until something happens to interrupt the status quo. But what if you don't wait for that catalyst? What if you seek the change out yourself, play around with things? Try on a different persona. Affect an unfamiliar accent. Wear strange clothing. Or clothing of the opposite gender. Do your hair in a novel way. Go out without your wallet. Introduce yourself to strangers with an assumed name and completely fabricated back story. Pretend to be someone else with the people you know – with or without informing them ahead of time that you're going to do so. Note how differently people treat you while you're in this role. Note as well how differently you feel to yourself, and how that awareness can alter the way you act and mentally process things. This can be a fun diversion – or it can be an effective magical operation. Is there something you're afraid of doing, something that feels too big and impossible for you? What happens when you create a "you" that is capable of accomplishing the things you normally can only dream of?

Go to a theater

As fun as it is to experiment with personality, it's even more fun to watch the professionals do it. The dramatic arts arose out of the early agrarian worship of Dionysos and actors have remained sacred to him ever since, even when the roles they performed were no longer a reenactment of his joys and sufferings or even about the mythological figures associated with him. But the stories are still important and the actor's ability to transform himself into something else is a wonder to behold. Though you can watch plays on video in the comfort of your home, absolutely nothing compares to seeing them live and in person, surrounded by a crowd. Indeed the communal aspect is perhaps the most important part, for Dionysian worship has always had a strong collective aspect to it. As part of the crowd you can be swept up in the moment, feel the contagious emotion, the diverse reactions of those around you. Sometimes the audience is far more entertaining than the show put on for its amusement. There is also something primitive and magical about being part of a crowd huddled in the dark, watching a grand spectacle. You lose your sense of self as an individual and take on a corporate identity – or no sense of self at all, save as a spectator of what is transpiring on stage before you. In the same vein you should also attend operas, concerts, movies, protests, sporting events and similar large gatherings with an eye towards perceiving the world through an orgiastic lens.

Watch movies

Watching a movie in your own home, alone or with a small group of family and friends can be a wonderful devotional activity all on its own or as part of a festival observance. I consider this entirely distinct from going to a movie theater or taking in a play, which is why I've given it its own section here. It's much more intimate and inwardly-focused, since you don't have the crowd and their barrage of stimuli. The performance is also forever the same, no matter how many times you watch the movie, whereas an actor on the stage is always going to play his part slightly differently. Even so, multiple viewings of a film can reveal a depth of things one might initially have missed. Because all you've got to focus on is the screen it's easier for your mind to wander, leading to interesting new insights that may or may not have anything to do with what transpires in the movie. I've watched some of my favorite Dionysian films a dozen times or more and I always come away with new things I hadn't noticed before or inspired with new thoughts and understandings. What makes a movie "Dionysian"? That can be difficult to pin down at times. Sometimes it's the atmosphere, a particular scene or piece of dialogue, the themes it explores or even the expressions on an actor's face or the memory of what was going on in one's life when the movie was first viewed. Although I encourage my readers to come up with their own list of Dionysian movies, I figured I'd share some of my own in the hopes that it might get the ball rolling for you.

American Beauty dir. Sam Mendes
The Ballad of Jack and Rose dir. Rebecca Miller
Cleopatra dir. Franc Roddam
Dangerous Beauty dir. Marshall Herskovitz
Dead Poets Society dir. Peter Weir
The Doors dir. Oliver Stone
Fellini's Satyricon dir. Federico Fellini
Fight Club dir. David Fincher

Gothic dir. Ken Russell
The Lair of the White Worm dir. Ken Russell
The Libertine dir. Laurence Dunmore
Labyrinth dir. Jim Henson
Manoushe: A Gypsy Love Story dir. Luis Begazo
Perfume: The Story of a Murderer dir. Tom Tykwer
Stage Beauty dir. Richard Eyre
V for Vendetta dir. James McTeigue
Wicker Man dir. Robin Hardy
The Witches of Eastwick dir. George Miller
And of course the numerous movies about ancient Greece, Rome and Egypt.

Something fun that you can do, especially for old documentaries, trippy experimental films or things you've already seen plenty of times before, is to mute the volume on the movie and play your own music over it. This lends a hallucinatory quality to the whole thing and sometimes it can sync up in eerily appropriate ways.

Go out to a club
Although this can have a very similar effect to some of the things previously mentioned, clubs also have an energy all their own. They are dark and cave-like, with a crowd of dancing, often intoxicated people. Music isn't so much heard as felt, the vibrations pulsing through your whole body. The atmosphere is sensual and wild, the perfect place to feel the spirit of Dionysos moving among and through people. And even if they are not consciously aware of him, they feel the things connected to him, the things he unleashes within them, and they acknowledge that in their own modern, secular fashion. Ask your average club-goer why they attend and they'll likely tell you that it's so they can let go, run free, be wild and uninhibited and burn off all that repressed and anxious pressure that societal conditioning builds up in them. Many want a chance to be someone other than they are in their normal 9 to 5 lives – someone that's sexy and bold and carefree and glamorous. It's a way to show off, to express their individuality, to revel in the sheer carnality of existence. That joyous, exuberant and life-affirming energy is wonderful to be around for a Dionysian, even if you never make it out onto the floor to dance yourself. Unfortunately the music that makes me most want to dance isn't the sort of thing that most clubs play, but I still enjoy going if only to people-watch and soak up the Dionysian ambience.

Dance
Whether you do it in a club, with a group of people in ritual or only in the privacy of your home, dancing is something every Dionysian ought to do as a devotional act. Not only was dancing a prominent part of the god's ancient worship but it's something that he, himself, did even in his mother's womb. Dancing is a way to express one's self, including those things that cannot be communicated through words alone. It's a way to connect with the god, the world around you and the sacred rhythms of life. It makes us

conscious of our bodies, bringing awareness down from the intellectual level to the flesh, the muscle, the bones and blood, which are the things that make us who we are. It is a way to own our bodies, to affirm their beauty and worth, regardless of what fucked up messages society is constantly sending us about them. And dancing is a great way to work through anxiety and negative emotions, purging them by sweat and physical exhaustion. So what if you can't dance well, if there's no grace or elegance to your movement? Stamp and clap and spin about – but move your body, damn it. The god does not command that we dance well, just that we dance! And often, when you get really into it, stop being hyper-conscious and allow your body to find its own rhythm and move as it will, you'll be surprised at how well you actually can dance. It's in you, you've just got to be willing to let it out. And even if the grace never comes, it's still an important thing to do because it's a way to challenge yourself, to push past barriers and go outside of your comfort zone. If you're not willing to look like a fool for him occasionally then what kind of Dionysian are you?

Listen to music

Music should be a huge part of any Dionysian's worship of the god. It certainly was in antiquity. There is scarcely a single mention of his devotees without music somewhere in the background, whether it be the clamorous drums, pipes, cymbals and bull-roarers of the Bacchic ones or the strange, ethereal sounds that accompany the god's epiphany. Music is powerfully evocative stuff. It sets the mood and is capable of changing our whole mental state. I've got the stuff going almost all the time, regardless of whether I'm doing ritual, writing, reading a book, going for a walk or just sitting there meditating. Memory is also deeply enmeshed with music. Things you haven't thought about in years can come flooding back when a song starts to play, which can be extremely useful in a ritual context. When I play certain songs I get all of these powerful associations, images, thoughts and recollections of past experiences with Dionysos, which intermix with what's going on currently, enhancing the moment. Because of that I've created a bunch of different playlists for my various gods and spirits, including several for various aspects of Dionysos. Depending on what I've got playing at the time my whole experience of him can be radically different. Furthermore, these songs can be a wonderful way to get an oracular response from the god. All you've got to do is put your iPod on shuffle, ask a question and wait to see what song comes up next. It's downright spooky at times how accurate a response you can get this way. So spend some time going through your music collection and put together your own devotional playlists. You can include songs that are obviously about him, that have relevant lyrics, that were playing at some pivotal moment or just give you some sort of Dionysian vibe. Then listen to the music either as part of a formal ritual or while hanging out, sipping some good wine. This latter is really important. I don't think people spend nearly enough time just listening to music. They feel like they need to be busy doing something all the time. And while it can certainly be good to have music going in the background while you're being productive, sometimes it's important to just *be* for a couple moments, totally absorbed in the music and letting your thoughts flow freely. Some of the most intense encounters I've had with Dionysos started off in this way. I could include some of the music that I strongly associate with the god but I feel that it's better for you to seek out your own selections and to spend time really thinking about what "Dionysian music" means to you.

Make your own music for the god

It's great to listen to the music that other people have made, especially when you're as untalented as I am, but nothing, absolutely nothing, compares to making your own music for him. All of the instruments traditionally associated with Dionysian worship are thankfully pretty easy to play. As long as you can count to four you can play the drum, shake a rattle or castanet, ring a bell, clash cymbals or all the rest. The bull-roarer is even simpler – you've just got to swing it around over your head until it starts to whir – though it can be tricky to get it going well and you may whack yourself a few times, which really, really hurts. Pipes are also fairly easy, though reed instruments, descendants of the ancient *aulos*, are a little more difficult to master, especially if you want to make something that even remotely sounds like music. But it's well worth it to keep going, even if you're horrible at first. The act of learning the instrument and continually practicing until you gain proficiency can, itself, be a devotional activity, and the music you make can serve as a lovely offering to the god. Plus, at least with the simpler instruments it's even possible to create your own. Just think how awesome that would be! And, again, don't let insecurity or embarrassment get in your way. You're a Dionysian and as such these emotions ought to have no hold on you.

Memorize a hymn

I am a firm believer that ritual scripts are, for the most part, unnecessary. Our prayers should come from the heart, spontaneous expressions of joy, love, reverence and kindred emotions. Your mind should be on the god and what you're experiencing, not checking off items on a list. You need to be free to move and dance and be filled with the spirit of the god – not stuck there holding a bunch of papers in your hands. The steps that constitute your average ritual are fairly simple and flow organically from each other, so there's no need to rigidly adhere to a script unless you are performing an especially complex rite – and even then such things are best kept to a minimum.

Sometimes, however, we want a little something extra or we feel moved to include pieces beyond our own spontaneous creations. In such instances I feel that it's best to memorize the words one intends to use beforehand, especially if we're talking about one of the ancient Greek hymns that have come down to us. Most of these are fairly short and simple pieces, often comprised of strings of epithets one is probably already familiar with. There's something special, even magical, about addressing the god in the same words – especially if you can manage the Greek – that were used by his devotees two thousand years ago. It can be difficult to memorize these lines at first, but it's certainly not impossible. After all people used to memorize whole books of Homeric epics and there are Moslems today walking around with the entire Qur'an in their heads. Compared to that, what's a half dozen lines of Greek? And the great thing about this exercise is that you can do it anywhere and at any time. Print off the passage and carry it around with you wherever you go for a couple weeks. You can work on it while you're waiting for a bus, at your desk at work, standing in line at the bank, preparing dinner, doing the dishes, before you go to bed, etc. Perhaps you could do this instead of watching that episode of *Jersey Shore* or updating your Facebook or spending countless hours playing *World of Warcraft* or all the other mind-numbing activities that suck up so much of our time these days. All the time and effort you put into memorization is a devotional act as well as the actual recitation itself. Plus it's a nifty trick with which to impress folks at parties!

Read

Another great way to spend your time is by reading things relevant to the world of Dionysos, both on devotional days and at other times. Obviously this includes things like ancient sources on him, plays and poetry, collections of his myths, books on his history and cult, scholarly articles, fiction, stuff written by his contemporary worshipers, etc. But you can also broaden your reading to include things like the history of wine-making and theater, ecstatic cults from around the world, dance, the ritual use of masks and entheogens, gender and queer theory and so on and so forth. The more you know about the things associated with Dionysos the greater will be your understanding of the god and how he manifests in the world.

Write

Even if you don't really think of yourself as an author it can be a great devotional activity to write for Dionysos. You can compose your own hymns for use in ritual, poems to communicate experiences you've had with him or insights you've gained about his personality, fictional stories and modern retellings of myth, things you'd like to experience and do in the future or straight up stream-of-consciousness stuff. It doesn't have to be great, and you certainly don't have to share it with anyone other than the god, but Dionysos is a creative deity so any form of creativity brings us closer to him. Who knows, he may even bless you with divine inspiration! Also, it seems that he deeply appreciates things of this nature, especially when we share our efforts with him, in and out of a ritual setting.

Seek Dionysos in unexpected places

I've talked at length elsewhere about the necessity of worshiping Dionysos outdoors, especially in wild places like forests, mountains, caves or even unfamiliar parts of one's own city, so I'm not going to repeat myself here. But I would like to mention some places that one can visit as a devotional excursion which might not be immediately apparent.

The first of these is a museum or art gallery. You may naturally be wondering what a stuffy, high-class establishment like that has got to do with our god, but pause for a moment and reflect on the fact that Dionysos has been one of the most popular of all the Greek gods with artists from the very beginning. Indeed, Keremaikos, the hero of the potter's quarter in Athens, was descended from the god and most of the vases, plates and drinking cups that have come down to us were manufactured for use in a Dionysian context and thus feature a significant number of representations of him, his retinue and the various mythological scenes associated with them. These works of art – to say nothing of ancient Dionysian statues, frescoes, murals, tapestries, etc. – are so plentiful that there's a very good chance that your local museum has got at least a couple pieces worth seeing. And that only takes into consideration the Dionysian artifacts produced during the Classical, Hellenistic, Roman and Byzantine eras. As I've discussed elsewhere Dionysian iconography maintained an incredible vitality up through modern times. Initially copied by the Christians and used in representations of Jesus, beginning in the Late Middle Ages artists once again began depicting the god and his myths and haven't stopped since. It'd be a Herculean labor to attempt to catalogue all of the Renaissance, Baroque, Romantic and more contemporary depictions of Dionysos and his retinue. I'm willing to wager that even if your museum or gallery somehow lacks ancient Dionysian artifacts it will probably have at least something more recent. It is truly amazing to visit these works of art up close and in person, to see how powerful and enduring a figure our god has remained, inspiring all of these great artists down through the centuries. By worshiping the god today we are making ourselves a part of this grand tradition and ensuring that it survives into the future. So why not see what has come before? Be sure to give yourself plenty of time to soak up the history and really examine and appreciate each unique piece of art. Meditate on the context of the artifact: when was it made, why and for whom? What novel elements does it possess as well as what themes are faithfully repeated? What resonance does it have with you and is this how you, personally, view the god? If not, what's different about it and why do you think the artist chose to represent him in this fashion?

Another great place to visit on a Dionysian pilgrimage is a zoo. Although it can be difficult to see the wild creatures in captivity, we must remember that this is the only chance many of them have for continued survival since human habitation and our mad, greedy consumption has destroyed a large percentage of their natural territory. Furthermore a zoo is probably the only place you're likely to see most of the animals associated with Dionysos since they are, for the most part, not indigenous to North America. As you visit the lions, lynxes, panthers, tigers, elephants, gazelles, peacocks, goats, donkeys, deer, dolphins and similar beasts, remain mindful that these are his dear creatures and constant companions in the revel. Call to mind all of the stories and artistic representations that explain why these animals belong to the god. Meditate deeply on their individual characteristics and see if you can discern why the ancients may have associated them with him beyond what the myths tell us.

Participate in communal activities

Although it is certainly possible to be a solitary devotee of the god – and indeed our most important encounters with Dionysos always take place when we're alone with him, even if that happens in the midst of a huge crowd – his worship has a strong communal aspect to it, whether you're talking about the host of nymphs, satyrs and mainades who constantly surround him or the epidemics of collective frenzy and dancing-madness that can suddenly take hold of a city or nation. Few of us today are lucky enough to be able to worship the god as part of a group larger than a dozen people – and most of us make do with considerably less or just ourselves. But with the advent of new technologies, especially the internet, it is now possible to reach out to Dionysians across the globe. There are a great many lists, forums, websites and blogs devoted to discussing the god, his myths, history and contemporary worship. Participating in these discussions can be both a great way to find fellowship with other Dionysians and a powerful devotional activity in its own right. Answer the questions of those new to the god. Share your own insights and experiences with him. Talk about your upcoming festival plans and other devotional activities you intend to do for him. Comment on the blogs of fellow Dionysians, especially if they've shared something that deeply touched or inspired you. You may even want to start up your own blog or website to detail the things you discover in the course of your studies, poems, prayers and other things you have written for him, or just beautiful and inspiring quotes and pieces of Dionysian art you come across. At the end of this book I've included a list of some of the best online Dionysian resources. It would please me immensely to have to substantially revise that list at a future date to reflect a whole new wave of passionate and creative Dionysians out there.

Donate time and money to worthy causes in his name

I have saved this one for last because it is one of the most important devotional activities that we Dionysians can do. There are so many problems in the world that it can leave us feeling impotent and hopeless. We look around us and think that we'll never be able to fix the world or make any kind of meaningful difference. And it's true. Alone, we can't. Thankfully we don't have to do it alone. There are a lot of generous and motivated folks out there doing their part and if you pool your resources with theirs, together you can make even more of a difference. Maybe not on a global level, but locally or in regard to a specific issue, it's more than possible. If you value Dionysos then you should value the things associated with him, and that ought to be manifest through your actions and not just your words. Offerings are a gift to the gods, a return of a portion of the wealth and other blessings they have so generously bestowed upon us, and a tangible sign of our gratitude for such blessings. Donating time and money can be another form of offering. Of course even doing so in the name of the gods does not take the place of actual sacrifices to them, but it can be a thing done in addition to what we rightfully owe them. So think deeply about where you could donate your time and money. First, this should be a cause connected with the god: a group dedicated to protecting the environment or caring for wild animals; a group that preserves indigenous tribal and polytheistic cultures; a group fighting HIV or domestic violence; a group that defends the rights of homosexuals and gender variants; a group that promotes the arts, especially the dramatic arts; a group that helps recovering alcoholics or those suffering from mental illness. One could extend the list considerably for ours is an immense god with a great many concerns and there are also a lot of people out there doing wonderful, important things. But before you start writing that check or setting up an appointment to stop by and help out, be sure to do plenty of research first. How much of the money actually gets spent on the cause in question versus how much of it goes to bureaucratic hierarchies and funding further donation requests? Unfortunately I've learned this lesson the hard way. Shortly after I made one donation news broke that the organizers of the charity had been found guilty of lining their pockets with donations. More innocuously, but no less annoyingly, I made a one-time donation to a conservation group – and made it clear that that was the only time I planned to write them a check. Well, for the next year and a half I received a huge packet of promotional materials, newsletters, flyers, postcards, etc., every couple weeks or so requesting further donations from me. I contacted their offices several times requesting that they stop sending me this stuff but it didn't make any difference. In fact, I'm *still* getting that crap. My donation hadn't been very large to begin with, so clearly instead of saving trees all of it went towards advertisement. I shudder to think how many trees died needlessly all because I was trying to help out. Thankfully, though, these egregious examples are the exception and most charities are fiscally responsible and concerned solely with doing good works. But that's why it's important to do some research first.

And if possible look for charities that are locally based and doing things to benefit your own immediate community. Beyond the axiom that it's best to help those closest to you first there are very solid reasons for this approach. Such charities tend to be smaller, with less administrative overhead, less of an environmental impact by not being spread out across the country, your dollar will go further and being local it'll be easier to determine what sort of impact they're having, where the money is going, and what their reputation is truly like. Additionally there will be a greater opportunity for you to directly help out by volunteering your services, which is infinitely preferable to just writing a check. After all, if you're just giving your time you know it's actually doing some good instead of your money going to advertising or less desirable ends. Plus this gives you the chance to get out and meet people, as well as having interesting experiences.

And with that I bring to a close this discussion of Dionysian devotional activities. Of course this doesn't even begin to exhaust the possibilities, but hopefully it's given you some fresh ideas and pointed you in a direction so that you come up with some of your own. The relationship each of has with Dionysos must, of necessity, be unique to us and shaped by our interests, understandings and aspirations. (Not to mention what Dionysos, himself, expects out of it.) As with all things in life what we receive is commensurate to what we put into it. Having a meaningful relationship with a god like Dionysos requires a great deal of dedication and hard work – but the rewards are immense and well worth whatever effort is required to do so.

THE MIRACLES OF DIONYSOS

There are moments when the ordinary and the uncanny overlap. When the divine and the temporal merge. When the gods break through and touch our lives in some unexpected manner. These moments, rare and beautiful and full of incredible personal meaning, are by definition, miracles. Dionysos, both today and in antiquity, is the god most closely associated with epiphanies and miracles. Here are some of the ways in which Dionysos, the god who appears, has made himself known in the past.

Wine miracles

Wine is so closely associated with Dionysos that for most, Dionysos is simply the god of wine and drunkenness, the lord of the vine's sweet harvest. Anyone who will bother to scratch the surface will see that there is more to him than this, but it is important to remember too that no matter how far he wanders, how great the extent of his power, the god always has the wine-cup in his hand. Therefore it's not surprising to note the great number of Dionysian miracles that involve wine.

Perhaps the earliest of these involves the origin of the vine and grapes. According to the Orphics when the young Dionysos was torn apart by the ferocious Titans his blood splattered on the ground and from that spot rose the vine, thick with clusters of red grapes resembling the drops of blood that had been shed. The grapes, then, contain a part of Dionysos within them, and whenever we crush the grapes and drink their juice, we are drinking the god. It was Dionysos who taught man the art of fermenting the juice of the vine, and how to pour libations during festivals (Ovid's *Fasti* 3.727). As Euripides puts it in the *Bakchai*, "Himself a god, he is poured out to the other gods, so that from him we mortals have what's good in life." (332-35)

In myth, the wine of Dionysos figures prominently. It calms the angry Hephaistos, allowing Dionysos to talk sense into him (the *Caeretan vase*, as well as others), it overcomes the unstoppable hermaphrodite monster Agdistis (Pausanias 7.17.9-12), and Dionysos' mainad companions often bring up springs of wine and milk simply by striking the ground with their thyrsoi (Euripides' *Bakchai* 708).

Achilles Tatius, in his delightful romance *The Adventures of Leucippe and Clitophon* (2.2-3) recounts the story of how Dionysos first introduced wine to mankind. Ikarios was a kindly farmer and herdsman, and one day Dionysos came to visit him. He set before the god a fine meal, but in those days men had no great refreshments – they drank the same water as their oxen. Dionysos thanked the herdsman for his hospitality and pledged him in a friendly cup. But instead of water Ikarios found the god's own wine. He was very excited and begged the god to know how such fine drink was made. Dionysos told him where it came from, and how to ferment the grapes and make wine. The manufacture of wine spread from there, and a festival was established to honor the god's gift to man.

A number of miracles are associated with wine and grape harvests. Pausanias recounts (6. 26.1-2) a curious occurrence in Elis, which happened during the Dionysian festival of the Thyia:

> "The place where they hold the Thyia is about eight stades from the city. Three pots are brought into the building and set down empty in the presence of citizens and of any strangers who may chance to be in the country. The doors of the building are sealed by the priests themselves and by any others who may be so inclined. On the morrow they are allowed to examine the seals, and on going into the building they find the pots filled with wine. I did not myself arrive at the time of the festival, but the most respected Elean citizens, and with them strangers also, swore that what I have said is the truth. The Andrians too assert that every other year at their feast of Dionysos wine flows of its own accord from the sanctuary."

Both Diodoros Sikeliotes and Pliny the Elder talk of fountains of wine that flowed by themselves from the ground, and of spring water from his temple which had the flavor of wine on festival days (*Library of History*, 3.66.1-2; *Natural History*, 2.106, 31.13).

Later, when the Christians wished to lend their god legitimacy they would claim that his first miracle mimicked those of Dionysos by turning water into wine (*John 2-3*). Although they would also claim that Jesus was the "True vine" (*John 15*) the people knew otherwise, and continued calling out the name of Dionysos during the treading of the grapes, even after a Council of Constantinople in 691 CE forbade them to do so, or to wear satyr masks while they worked (Carl Kerenyi, *Dionysos* pg 67).

Miracles of growth

According to Carl Kerenyi, it was not intoxication that was the essential element of the religion of Dionysos but the "quiet, powerful, vegetative element which ultimately engulfed even the ancient theaters, as at Cumae" (*Dionysos*, pg xxiv). For Jane Ellen Harrison, Dionysos was more than just the god of the vine; he was "Dendrites, Tree-god, and a plant god in a far wider sense. He is god of the fig-tree, Sykites; he is Kissos, god of the ivy; he is Anthios, god of all blossoming things; he is Phytalmios, god of growth" (*Prolegomena* pg 426). In short, he is the god of the impulse of life in nature, a god of growth and the green earth. And there are a whole range of miracles associated with this aspect of his being.

Whenever Dionysos appears he does so attended by wild vegetation, whether it is with the vines of ivy and lush grapes he wears in his hair (*Orphic Hymn* 30) or that entwines itself around pillars and altars (Euripides' *Antiope* 203), a face appearing in a plane tree that has been split asunder

(Kern's *Inschr. von M.* 215), or in a burst of beautiful flowers (Pindar fr.75). When Dionysos finally reveals himself in fullness to the Tyrrhenian pirates it is through vegetation:

> "Then in an instant a vine, running along the topmost edge of the sail, sprang up and sent out its branches in every direction heavy with thick-hanging clusters of grapes, and around the mast cloud dark-leaved ivy, rich in blossoms and bright with ripe berries, and garlands crowned every tholepin." (*Homeric Hymn* 7)

In a number of places, but most famously at Parnassos, miracles of the "one-day vines" occurred. These vines "flowered and bore fruit in the course of a few hours during the festivals of the epiphany of the god" (Walter Otto, *Dionysus* pg 98). Sophokles in his *Thyestes* records that in Euboea, one could watch the holy vine grow green in the early morning. By noon the grapes were already forming, and by evening the dark and heavy fruit could be cut down, and a drink made from them (fr. 234). Euphorion tells us that this miracle was related to the performance of cultic dances and the singing of choral hymns by the god's followers in Aigia – that it was their celebration which caused the vines to grow (*Euphorionis Fragmenta* 118).

Ovid recounts a wonderful story that reveals Dionysos' power not only over the vine and ivy, but over all vegetation. Anius was the king of Delos, and he had three daughters who served Dionysos well as priestesses. During a famine, the god appeared to them, and gave them the power to produce corn, oil, and wine for their people, simply by touching the ground. This wonderful gift almost proved their downfall, as Agamemnon tried to abduct the girls to feed his men at Troy, but they called out to Dionysos in prayer, and he turned them into white doves, so that they could escape (*Metamorphoses* 13.628-704).

Other miracles

There are a number of Dionysian miracles which are not connected to the natural or vegetative aspects of the god. Such miracles would be those connected with Dionysos as a supernatural and supremely powerful being, or with the sphere of madness and ecstasy which are uniquely his.

For Walter Otto it is impossible to understand Dionysos except through madness. Madness is a state of intense emotional overflowing, when our small rational minds are swallowed up by a far greater thing – the beautiful but terrible mad god himself, Dionysos – and for a brief moment, we see the world and ourselves as we truly are. In this sublime state of ecstasy, when we feel our soul to be touched by the hand of god, the most amazing things are possible. Euripides in the *Bakchai* describes some of the miracles that the mainades or mad women accomplished, while possessed by Dionysos. They raise up fountains of wine, milk, and honey (710). They gird themselves with snakes, and give suck to fawns and wolf cubs as if they were infants at the breast (699). Fire, swords, and rocks fail to harm them (767). They can tear live bulls apart with their bare hands (743). And they can uproot sturdy, full-grown trees (1109).

Dionysos revealed his supreme divinity through a number of signs. He descended into the underworld to raise up the spirit of his beloved mother (*Homeric Hymn* 2). He transformed Ariadne into a goddess, and put her bridal crown in the heavens as the *Corona Borealis* (*Odyssey* 11.324). He slew giants and monsters (numerous passages in Nonnos' *Dionysiaka*). After conquering and civilizing the peoples of the East, he founded a temple to the Great Mother of the Gods (Lucian's *De Dea Syria* 16). And he moved the very heavens to create the constellations *Asellus Borealis, Lyra, Aries, Boötes, Virgo,* and the dog-star *Sirius* (Hyginus' *Poetica Astronomica* 2.17; 2.23; 2.4; 2.7).

Such are the many wonderful things that Dionysos did in the past. But do not think that that is all that he did, or that his miracles ceased at some point in his history. Indeed, he still acts in the world, and I have felt his gentle touch on many an occasion. The purpose of this essay has been to make you aware of how he has acted in the past, that you might better be able to see when he makes his appearance in your life.

A WINE-FUELED RANT

It's been a while since I've let loose with a good blood-pressure raising diatribe, but some things I've seen recently have me in a mood to borrow the threadbare cloak, leather wallet and gnarled walking-stick of that old dog Diogenes. What's got this devotee of Dionysos all riled up, you're asking? Statements to the effect of:

"Wine tastes gross so I libate grape juice instead."

"I like the idea of what Dionysius represents, but I hate being drunk, don't go to parties, can't dance, and am terrified of letting go. But I'm totally a Dionysian cause I believe in FREEDOM!!!"

"Intoxication has no place in ritual. If I saw somebody drinking at an event I was attending, I'd call the cops."

"We didn't have wine at Anthesteria. We brought some, but then I heard that one of the other guests who came last minute was an alcoholic, and I didn't want them to feel awkward so we just left that part of the ritual out."

And, unfortunately, there have been many, many other instances like this that I could cite.

I find this attitude so profoundly wrong and offensive that it takes everything in my power not to fly into an incoherent rage.

If somebody feels this way they have no business worshiping the gods, least of all Dionysos. This is pretty much a textbook case of *hubris*, folks – and that's saying something because I don't throw that term around lightly. Too many people use it casually, without really understanding what it means. *Hubris* isn't just something you dislike. It isn't synonymous with impiety, either. For the ancients *hubris* had a very specific definition: abusive language or action; complete disregard for another's social standing; placing one's self above others; public humiliation. And whether that's their intent or not, that is precisely what these people are doing.

Religion – especially Hellenic religion – is about honoring the gods. It's a way of concretely demonstrating our gratitude for the multitude of blessings that they have seen fit to bestow upon us. We acknowledge the awesomeness of their divinity, praising their particular qualities and accomplishments. Everything we do in worship should be geared towards pleasing the gods, which is why we conduct our rites in the traditional manner in the first place. We know from past experience – both our own and the accumulated lore that has been passed down to us through the centuries – that the gods look favorably upon certain offerings and respond accordingly. When we come before the gods it should be in a humble and gracious spirit, with the intent to please them above all else.

That is not what happens when you place your own preferences before theirs. It shouldn't matter whether you like wine or not. The gods – and Dionysos in particular – *do*. In fact, if you are worshiping in the proper Hellenic style then it really shouldn't matter since libations are supposed to be poured out upon the altar or ground. The worshiper may take a sip before it's spilled out, or even drink some in the company of the divine, but this is totally separate from the libation itself. So, really, if you don't care for wine or don't feel like getting drunk then *don't drink*. But you should still give to the gods what rightfully belongs to them. In fact, if the person feels this way I think it's even more of a sacrifice since they are doing it solely for the pleasure of the gods without any direct personal benefit aside from the knowledge that they have just made a proper offering.

What really gets me is that I seriously doubt that these people would be so inhospitable to a human guest. Would they invite a vegetarian friend over for a special dinner in their honor and then serve them a big old juicy steak because that's what they themselves happened to be hungry for that night? Hopefully the answer to that is no. So then why is this attitude acceptable when one's guest happens to be a god? And how much more insulting is it when that god happens to be the one responsible for wine? In fact, in some accounts Dionysos didn't just discover the method for cultivating wine – he *is* the wine itself. His spirit lives in the grape; the juice pressed from it is his blood, and the intoxication we feel from drinking is the god's presence within us. So to denigrate wine is to denigrate the wine-god himself.

Does that mean that you can't be a Dionysian if you don't drink? Certainly not. Though he has a very special relationship with the vine, Dionysos is the god of all vegetative and animal life and his spirit can be felt in many different ways. He is one of the most complex and mysterious of all the gods that man has ever known and there are many, many paths that lead back to him. There is nothing wrong with honoring him in a wineless fashion. Indeed, some people are unable to drink for any number of perfectly valid reasons – an unfortunate history, a genetic predisposition towards alcoholism, some sort of medical condition – and yet they still have an intimate relationship with the god. However, even if wine does not enter into that relationship, the true Dionysian will still respect the grape and its social and religious significance. Knowing yourself and your boundaries is an essential part of being a Dionysian. Drinking when you know you shouldn't does no honor to him. But on the other hand, it's not right to impose your limitations on others, particularly the gods.

There are numerous things that I give to my divinities that I wouldn't necessarily partake of on my own. But they enjoy it so I provide it for them. And if, for some reason, I was opposed to doing something traditional, I just wouldn't do it. I find it particularly vexing to hear people talk about celebrating a festival like Anthesteria but with so many adaptations, substitutions and the like that it's hardly even recognizable as the festival any longer. Either do it right or don't do it at all. I think it would be infinitely preferable for one to come up with one's own completely new festival than to compromise that much.

And before people accuse me of being an impractical stickler let me clarify that I'm not talking about things like getting your meat from a store instead of butchering the animal yourself, failing to wear appropriate "period" attire, using English instead of Greek, or not being able to process through the city streets with a crowd of thousands. We live in different times. Many of us are solitaries or worship in small groups. Even in religions with an unbroken lineage and masses of adherents there is bound to be innovation, particularly when circumstances are altered drastically. That's what having a living religion is all about. But we must remain faithful to the spirit of our practice or else what's the point? And I'm no longer just talking about abstaining from wine here, though that's certainly a big one. I've witnessed people assert that they don't see the point of celebrating Anthesteria on three consecutive days, that they moved it to the nearest convenient time even if that was the better part of a month away, that they aren't comfortable with the eroticism or pollution that pervades the festival, that they don't want anything to do with the dead, or that they just don't understand how all these different elements fit together so they'll simply leave out what doesn't speak to them personally. When you've changed it around that much how can you honestly still claim to be celebrating the same festival that the ancients did or that everyone else in the community will be? It's Anthesteria in name only.

I hate to break it to you, folks, but it's not about you and if you can't get that through your thick skull you're in the wrong religion. Hell, you probably shouldn't even bother pretending to be religious at all. Cause you aren't going to get anywhere if you don't know how to leave your ego at the door.

Now if you'll excuse me, I've got some serious drinking to do.

CAN A DIONYSIAN DRINK BEER?

After I got past my initial reaction – which was something along the lines of "Hell yeah! A Dionysian can do whatever the fuck they want – that's kinda the point!" – I realized that this is actually a profound question with some interesting implications.

Because Dionysos *does* have a very special relationship with the grape. More than any other plant it is associated with him. He wears its leaves as a crown, its vines twine his *thyrsos*, he was said to travel the earth teaching men the art of viniculture and the drink made from it is used to banish cares and elevate our spirits through joyful intoxication. The first thing that people usually say when they're describing Dionysos is that he is the wine-god. And this hints at his true relationship with it for he is not just the god *of* wine – he is the god *in* wine, the god who lives in the plant, who suffers as the grape is crushed, pressed and made to ferment into an alcoholic beverage. The Orphics said that grapes first appeared as drops of blood shed when Dionysos was slain by the Titans. When we consume wine we are consuming the god and the intoxication we feel is his spirit moving within us.

So yeah, I get it. And I get that there's this whole separate cultural mythology that has developed around beer and beer-drinkers – a mythology that puts it in opposition to wine and oenophiles. Beer is solid, comfortable, a workingman's beverage. Wine is decadent, sensual, the choice of romantics and aesthetes. Wine is for special occasions and people who know the difference between aroma and bouquet. Beer is for getting drunk with your friends while you watch the big game.

Hopefully we all realize how silly and simplistic this is. There are exotic specialist beers – in fact here in the Pacific Northwest we're famed for our artisan microbrews with no less than four companies operating out of my beloved Eugene alone. Also, there's nothing inherently elitist about drinking wine. I rarely buy a bottle over $15 – unless it's for a festival – and I couldn't begin to tell you what the different properties, tastes and smells of a wine are. I'm sure a connoisseur would say I've got rather plebian tastes but I know what I like and that's good enough for me.

Sometimes what I like is a nice beer. It's different from wine but it's in no way inferior. In fact, on a warm summer night there's nothing better than sitting out in the shade with a cigarette and a pilsner and watching the sun slowly begin its descent through the sky. I also sometimes use beer in ritual with Dionysos and he's never objected. Why should he?

The ancient Greeks made it clear that all vegetative life belongs to him.

Yes, the grape is his – but so is the ivy, the fig, the apple, the pine, all flowers and leafy trees and even the golden-headed wheat and barley.

Although the Greeks looked down on beer-drinkers – as well as those who consumed wine unmixed with water or drank anything to excess – they recognized that Dionysos was being honored by such people as well. In fact devotees of the god under the name of Sabazios drank a sacred beverage called *saba* or beer, instead of wine. Julian remarked that in Celtic lands they drank a barley-beer in honor of Bacchus and you could tell it belonged to him because it smelled strongly of goats. Carl Kerenyi says that in Crete men got drunk for Dionysos-Zagreus on honey-mead which was the primary form of alcohol before the introduction of wine. Egypt had a long history of beer-drinking which did not cease when the Ptolemies planted numerous lush vineyards through the reclaimed swamp-lands of the Faiyum; what's interesting, however, is that we have a dedication from a beer-monger honoring Dionysos after a lifetime of service. And Diodoros recounts that although Dionysos traveled the world planting vines and teaching man how to make wine in lands where the climate was inhospitable or the people's temperament was such that they could not appreciate his gift, he taught them other ways to make alcohol using what they had at hand.

Clearly then all alcohol has something of Dionysos about it and is fit for use in his worship. Who am I to argue with tradition and such venerable authorities? Wine will always be my favorite and first choice – but beer comes in as a close second and whiskey, rum, tequila, absinthe, sake, vodka and all the rest aren't too shabby either. Hell, I've never met an alcohol I didn't like. So raise a toast of whatever you're drinking and let's hail the god who came to quench our thirst!

LAMPTERIA

The days are getting shorter and the nights colder. There's frost on the windows most mornings and fog that doesn't really burn off until mid-day or later. Dead, fire-hued leaves litter the ground, often concealing patches of oddly-shaped mushrooms that weren't there the day before and will be completely gone the day after tomorrow. The squirrels in the park are plumping up. Crows congregate in the skeletal branches of trees. Spiders are an increasingly rare sight. And most of the flowers have closed in upon themselves or hunkered down beneath the earth to wait out the chill, wet months. When winter comes to Eugene it will not be as drastic as in other places. The little bit of snow we're likely to get won't last for more than a couple days at most. Because of the constant rains the trees go back to green after the brief red and yellow interlude, and everything – branches, rocks, the sidewalk, slow-moving creatures – get covered in a thin coating of moss, soft as an animal's pelt. But in the time between fall's end and the winter rains, you feel death and stillness all about. The air is thick with the smell of damp soil and decaying leaves. The branches of the vine are empty, little more than barren twigs. You can't help but wonder if they'll ever bear fruit again.

It's time for Lampteria.

Lampteria has become one of my all-time favorite festivals, although we know about it solely through a handful of random quotes:

> "Opposite the grove is a sanctuary of Dionysos Lampter. In his honor they celebrate a festival called the Feast of Torches, when they bring by night firebrands into the sanctuary and set up bowls of wine throughout the whole city." – Pausanias 7.27.3

> "Surrounded by the light of torches, he stands high on the twin summits of Parnassos, while the Korykian nymphs dance around as Bacchantes, and the waters of Castalia sound from the depths below. Up there in the snow and winter darkness Dionysos rules in the long night, while troops of mainades swarm around him, himself the choir leader for the dance of the stars and quick of hearing for every sound in the waster of the night." – Sophokles, Choral ode from *Antigone*

> "Why Homer speaks of the beautiful dancing-floors of Panopeus I could not understand until I was taught by the women whom the Athenians call Thyiades. The Thyiades are Attic women, who with

the Delphian women go to Parnassos and celebrate orgies in honor of Dionysos. It is the custom for these Thyiades to hold dances at places, including Panopeus, along the road from Athens. The epithet Homer applies to Panopeus is thought to refer to the dance of the Thyiades." – Pausanias 10.4.3

"When the despots in Phocis had seized Delphi, and the Thebans were waging war against them in what has been called the Sacred War, the women devotees of Dionysos, to whom they give the name Thyiades, in Bacchic frenzy wandering at night unwittingly arrived at Amphissa. As they were tired out, and sober reason had not yet returned to them, they flung themselves down in the market-place, and were lying asleep, some here, some there. The wives of the men of Amphissa, fearing, because their city had become allied with the Phocians, and numerous soldiers of the despots were present there, that the Thyiades might be treated with indignity, all ran out into the market-place, and, taking their stand round about in silence, did not go up to them while they were sleeping, but when they arose from their slumber, one devoted herself to one of the strangers and another to another, bestowing attentions on them and offering them food. Finally, the women of Amphissa, after winning the consent of their husbands, accompanied the strangers, who were safely escorted as far as the frontier." – Plutarch, *On the Bravery of Women* 13

For me this festival is all about *heat*. The heat of our bodies after climbing to the top of Skinner's Butte. The heat of the bull-roarer as it spins, making its eerie, otherworldly sound. The heat of our breath as we speak the ancient words of longing and invocation. The heat of the wine as it passes into our bellies. The heat of the god as his spirit moves through us. The heat of the fire as we light the candles in the dark. The heat that drives us on madly through the city streets, pouring out cups of wine on behalf of the community. The heat of the spicy food we share at the close of the festival. The heat of my beloved as we lay together afterwards.

The heat reminds us of what is truly important: life, comfort, love and all the blessings of Dionysos. We appreciate them more for being out in the cold and the dark this night. Before you can have Lenaia there must be Lampteria.

ANTHESTERIA FOR THE LONELY SOUL

One of the sad facts that most of us who worship the Greek gods today have had to resolve ourselves to is the solitariness of that worship. We're lucky if there's another Hellenist in our state, and even if that proves to be the case it's no guarantee that we'll be able to participate in communal worship. After all, they may be too far away to meet regularly, or even if they are close by that doesn't mean that they're going to worship the same gods as you, or do so in the same manner since Hellenismos embraces a wide spectrum of personal practice. Reading accounts of ancient worship with lavish rituals and processionals including hundreds of people can be discouraging, but you shouldn't let that stop you from doing something anyway. After all, true worship is carried out in the heart – and for that you need only yourself and the gods.

Anthesteria is one of my favorite Dionysian festivals, and I would like to encourage more people to celebrate it. To that effect, I've compiled information on how one can observe this festival on their own or within a small group setting. Most of the suggestions that follow consist of small devotional activities that can be performed throughout the three days of the festival. If you're looking for a simple fill-in-the-blanks ritual template that can be done in all of twenty minutes over a single night, I'm afraid you're going to have to look elsewhere. I don't believe that that kind of thing makes for good ritual under normal circumstances, and that holds doubly true for this festival. Each of the days of Anthesteria are unique and possess a powerful poetic language of their own. Lumping them together blurs their meaning and saps the festival of its power.

So, let's begin with some background information.

Anthesteria was one of the most important of the Attic festivals for Dionysos and lent its name to the month Anthesterion. It was also one the oldest, and was common to all of the Ionians, as Thucydides informs us (2.15). Anthesteria derives its name from the Greek word *anthes* meaning "blossoming" or "flowering" and thus is a festival of new beginnings, of rebirth and vegetation. It was a time when the impulse of life was felt to stir throughout all of nature, when the ripe buds began to unfold on the branch and the shoots were springing up from the barren earth after the long, cold winter months. But there is no life without death. The earth from which the plants arise is nourished by the dead bodies placed into it; the souls of the deceased dwell under the earth, thirsty and bitter over their loss. The passages by which life flows into our world, once opened, could also permit other things to escape, and during this festival they did.

So Anthesteria is a strange festival, one of many conflicting layers that flow into each other. It is a time of joy, when we celebrate life triumphant and broach the casks of new wine, letting children get their first taste of the sweet vintage; it is also a time of gloom and pollution, when the dead walk the sunlit paths of the upper world and strange, unnatural things are observed. Uniting these two poles, life and death (which are really just two sides of the same coin), there is also a stream of sensuality, sex as a primal, liberating force – at once the ultimate affirmation of animal existence and the closest we can come to obliteration while still breathing. In this single festival lies the essence of the mysteries of Dionysos.

Apollodoros of Athens informs us that the festival of Anthesteria consisted of three parts: *Pithoigia* "Opening of the Wine Jars," *Khoes* "Pitchers," and *Khutroi* or "Pots" (Scholia to Aristophanes' *Acharnians* 961).

From Phanodemos (cited in Athenaios' *Deipnosophistai* 11.465a) we learn that, "At the temple of Dionysos in Lemnai ("the Marshes") the Athenians bring the new wine from the jars and mix it in honor of the god and then they drink it themselves. Because of this custom Dionysos is called Limnaios, because the wine was mixed with water and then for the first time drunk diluted."

To observe this day of the festival you should set up an image of the god, especially one that is masked and draped with ivy or grape leaves, as we see from representations of this festival on drinking vessels. (Consult Carl Kerenyi's *Dionysos: Archetypal Image of Indestructible Life* for examples.) If you don't have an image, print one off of the internet and frame it, or else use your creativity and make one yourself. The vegetation can either be harvested naturally or you can use the silk ones found at craft stores. Personally I feel that natural is better, but you may not have access to it where you live, and the silk stuff works fine in a pinch. Decorate the altar with all sorts of vegetation and fruit (especially grapes, pomegranates, figs, and whatever produce is in season where you live), since we are honoring Dionysos as the embodiment of the life force. You can also buy flowers to set on his altar, or plait a wreath of wildflowers to garland his image with.

Next set up a bowl in front of the image where you will pour libations, and any other ritual items you wish to have such as candles or incense burners, etc. You may also wish to have a bowl of fresh water to mix with the wine, since this was part of the ritual in antiquity. But not everyone likes their wine mixed that way, and Dionysos himself doesn't seem to care one way or the other. You will need to acquire lots of wine, however. Ideally, this would be wine local to your area, but that's not necessary. It should also be of a fairly recent vintage since we're celebrating the tasting of the new wine. I prefer red wines for all of my Dionysian festivities, but if you like whites, go with that. You may also choose to use sweeter wines, such as the Greek Mavrodaphne, but that's not at all necessary.

At this point you may choose to follow the standard Hellenic ritual formula, or you can just do an informal rite of your own devising. You should, however, invite the god to be present, since the purpose of this part of the festival is to open the wine in front of him, and it never hurts to recite poetry or hymns appropriate to the occasion. Once that's completed, open the wine and pour a large amount of it into his bowl. Then, if you are going to mix the wine you intend to drink with water, do so – perhaps with a blessing and thanks to Dionysos the Savior who instituted the custom for our safety and to fend off madness – and then take a big sip of it. Afterwards express gratitude to the god for his gift to mankind, and an affirmation of the goodness of the season's bounty. Spend the rest of the evening in his company, drinking and otherwise celebrating. Play music that you feel is appropriate to the god. This would also be a good time to dance or sing for him, especially if this is something you're not normally comfortable doing. You can also tell jokes and play lighthearted games. But whatever you do this evening, be aware of doing it *in the presence of the god*. Meditate on his image, on who he is, on what he's done for you over the last year. Think about what wine signifies, about life and the abundance of nature. Really try to feel the god around you and to respond to him in joy and friendship. Close the ritual in whatever way you feel appropriate, or just say good-night and collapse in a drunken stupor.

The second day of Anthesteria is *Khoes* or "Pitchers." The main part of this observance was celebrated in the sanctuary of Dionysos in the Marshes too, though it spilled over into the city and there were numerous private revels on that night.

Certain special rituals were performed in secret by a college of priestesses called the *Gerarai*, and while we have some clue as to what was done, and even the oath which they had to swear, a great deal of it has remained hidden to us. Apparently it involved a *hieros gamos* between the Basilinna or wife of the Arkhon Basileos who was seen as representing the land of Attica and was wedded to Dionysos in the Boukoleion (or cowshed). There has been some speculation about how this rite was carried out. Some have conjectured that the part of Dionysos was performed by the Arkhon Basileos or a priest of Dionysos, who may only have represented him, or may have actually been possessed by the god in a form similar to those who "horse" the *lwa* in Afro-Caribbean religions. Others have conjectured that a phallic idol of the god was used instead or that he possessed her and they engaged in some type of spiritual sex. Others still postulate that the mating was only symbolic or metaphorical, but this is doubtful considering the terminology that Aristotle used in his discussion of the ritual in the *Constitution of the Athenians* 3.5 which has a very carnal context to it.

While the Basilinna was being wedded to Dionysos, a great deal of ribald celebration was being carried on throughout the city. Aristophanes tells us in the *Acharnians*, a play whose theme was the rural celebration of *Khoes*, that rude phallic songs were sung on the occasion, penis-shaped cakes were eaten, and prostitutes were in attendance. We have a number of drinking vessels that were made for the celebration which depict matrons sneaking off in the company of satyrs and people celebrating torchlit orgies (in the lurid sense of the word). (Again, Carl Kerenyi has gathered most of these for us.)

While all of this naughtiness was going on, a somewhat more sedate observance was also being held. Phanodemos (Athenaios 10.437c-d) informs us of this part of *Khoes* and the alleged origins of the festival.

"Demophon the King instituted the festival of the Pitchers at Athens. When Orestes arrived at Athens after killing his mother Demophon wanted to receive him, but was not willing to let him approach the sacred rites nor share the libations, since he had not yet been put on trial. So he ordered the sacred things to be locked up and a separate pitcher of wine to be set beside each person, saying that a flat cake would be given as a prize to the one who drained his first. He also ordered them, when they had stopped drinking, not to put the wreaths with which they were crowned on the sacred objects, because they had been under the same roof with Orestes. Rather each one was to twine them around his own pitcher and take the wreaths to the priestess at the precinct in Limnai, and then to perform the rest of the sacrifices in the sanctuary. The festival has been called *Khoes* ever since."

So, for this part of the festival you should cover up any shrines that you might have for other gods, lest they become defiled by the pollution of the day. Simple white or black pieces of cloth or shawls should suffice, and if possible perform your ritual outside of your normal temple space. Make yourself a garland, either of flowers or vines or something similarly appropriate. You can either choose to wear the garland during the ritual or drape it around the wine pitcher or bottle. A nice way to accentuate the solemnity and abnormality of the day is to speak as little as possible. Obviously if you work in a job where you have to interact with customers this may not be possible, but otherwise try to keep to yourself and remain silent as much as you can. Later on, when you perform your ritual, do it in total silence. Process to the altar, light your incense, pour out your libations, greet the god – all without saying a single word. Believe me, this is an eerie experience and one that will trigger in your mind an awareness that something strange is going on.

Throughout the day think about gloomy and depressing things, especially those related to death and murder. Then, during the ritual, set out several cups of wine, one for yourself, one for Orestes, and one for the people of Athens. Drink your wine in silence. You may choose to make a game of it and challenge yourself to finish the glass in a single draught or to drink X amount of wine throughout the night.

When that part of the ritual is finished, sit for a while in front of the image of Dionysos. Imagine in your mind the god approaching your city, coming as a stranger in the night. Everything is shrouded in darkness and gloom – but here he is, beautiful and radiant and bursting with vibrant life, the king of the vine, the mighty bull, the one who intoxicates the world. Envision him entering the cowshed and bursting in upon the Basilinna and her ladies in waiting, their eyes fearful and yet brimming with lust for him. Feel her joy as he takes her, as his presence awakens the warmth in her body and in the land. And let out an exultant yell, praising Dionysos, the god who comes!

At this time you may begin to speak again. You can recite poetry or sing for him. You can dance and perform joyous, ecstatic worship for the god. If you have a partner, now would be a wonderful time to make love, feeling the presence of the god surround and enfold you. Even if you are by yourself you may choose to experience the bliss of sexual release. But of course, do not feel that this is something that you *have* to do. Some people may be uncomfortable mixing sex and the gods, and that's perfectly alright. (It's not an attitude that I particularly understand, but Dionysos would have each worship him in their own way, and as Teiresias says in Euripides' *Bakchai*, a chaste maiden will come to no harm in the rites of Dionysos.)

After everything is finished, you may choose to take your garland and leave it somewhere outside. The best place to leave it, of course, would be in a wetlands or on the shore of a river or lake. But if such places are not available to you, find somewhere desolate or strange to leave it. You may choose not to discard it if it's non-biodegradable, but you should keep it somewhere where it won't come into contact with your other religious items.

The final day of Anthesteria is *Khutroi*, "Pots." While *Pithoigia* is a day of total exuberance, and *Khoes* a mixture of joy and melancholy, *Khutroi* is given over entirely to solemnity and the uncanny, for it is on this day that the dead walk the earth.

During *Khutroi* we do not see the face of Dionysos as the god of life and light; here he is entirely the dark god of the underworld, the lord of souls, the son of Persephone and the companion of the underworld Hermes. We barely see him at all on this day. In fact, all of the ritual activity of *Khutroi* is consecrated to his brother.

Theopompos, in the Scholia to Aristophanes' *Acharnians* 1076 describes *Khutroi* is the following way:

> "Those who had survived the great deluge of Deukalion boiled pots of every kind of seed, and from this the festival gets its name. It is their custom to sacrifice to Hermes Khthonios. No one tastes the pot. The survivors did this in propitiation to Hermes on behalf of those who had died."

According to Photius it was on this day that the Keres or spirits of the dead walked the earth and they had to be driven off with the ritual exclamation, "To the doors, ye Keres, it is no longer Anthesteria!" Photius also informs us that they used to chew buckthorn and anointed their doors with pitch in order to ward off the dead.

You should keep your shrines covered, since the temples in Athens were closed on this day. Spend the day thinking about your deceased and tell them anything you wish that you could have while they were alive. Make a meal for them. The most appropriate meal would of course be the *panspermia* which is a mixture of beans, grains, and seeds. To this some people add honey, oil and milk since these were the traditional libations to the dead, and additionally it fills the kitchen with a strong, unsettling aroma. Do not taste any of it since this is dead people food, and if you eat it you may soon join them. Leave your offering for them outside and recite a prayer to Hermes while you do so. Later on, expel the spirits and purify your home in whatever you consider to be the customary manner and only after all of that is finished should you unveil your shrines.

There is another practice which is connected to the Anthesteria, though the date on which it was observed is contested. According to the story when Dionysos first came to Attica to share his wine with the people there he was shown hospitality by the kindly farmer Ikarios. In return, Dionysos gave him the vine, and taught him how to make wine. The first people with whom Ikarios shared the gift of the god became drunk and their families thought that they had been poisoned. So they killed Ikarios and stuffed his body in a well. When Ikarios' daughter Erigone came upon the well and saw her father, she was overcome with grief and hanged herself. In punishment for their crime (and because he had fallen in love with Erigone) Dionysos cursed the land of Attica with barrenness and inflicted a plague of madness upon their daughters so that they hanged themselves. The people sought help from Delphi, and Apollon informed them that they needed to pay respects to Erigone and her father. So they gave them a proper burial and instituted the festival of *Aiora* in their honor. In return, Dionysos stopped the girls from killing themselves and made the land fruitful once more. At the *Aiora* young girls would hang ribbons, little cups, and dolls from the branches of trees and let themselves be pushed on a swing. Some hold that this took place on *Khoes*, others on *Khutroi*, but the way I see it, either day works, and the theme of that myth and ritual fit nicely within the context of the Anthesteria.

On whichever night you choose to observe it you can sneak into a park and hang things from trees. (The strangeness of the surroundings and the danger of getting caught will only heighten the experience for you.) In addition to the ribbons, cups and dolls, you could always use bells or strips of paper with Erigone's name written on them, or anything along those lines. Then go to the playground and swing for Erigone, thinking the whole time about her story and the mysteries hidden within it.

And with that, I bring my account of private Anthesteria observances to a close. I hope that this has helped give you some idea of the things you can do, and I would encourage you to come up with your own ideas inspired by the themes of the festival.

Addendum: Primary Sources on Anthesteria

"For they announce with a herald the Dionysia, the Lenaia, the Khutroi and the Gephyrismoi." – Aelian, *On Animals* 4.43

"Not all the magistrates lived together. The King kept what is now called the Boukoleion [cow-shed] near the Prytaneion. The evidence is that even now the mating and marriage of the wife of the King with Dionysos takes place there." – Aristotle, *Constitution of the Athenians* 3.5

"In my Alexandria a festival called Lagunophoria was celebrated, concerning which Eratosthenes has some discussion in his book on Arsinoë. He says as follows: While Ptolemy was celebrating all sorts of festivals and sacrifices, especially ones for Dionysos, Arsinoë asked the one who was carrying branches what day he was celebrating and what the festival was. He replied, It is Lagunophoria and they feast on food brought to them as they recline on rustic couches and each drinks from his own flask or lagunos, which they all bring with them. When he had gone she looked at us and said, 'These are dirty feasts, for it means that there is a gathering of an undifferentiated crowd, offering stale and unattractive food.' If, however, the type of food had pleased her, the queen would not have become irritated, since they were doing the very same things as are done during the Khoes. For during that festival they feast in private and the one who invited them to the feast provides these things." – Athenaios, *Deipnosophistai* 7.276a

"Timaios says that the tyrant Dionysios at the festival of the Khoes set a golden crown as a prize for the one who first drank up his khous and that Xenocrates the philosopher finished first and, taking the golden crown and departing, placed it on the herm set up in his courtyard, the one on which he customarily placed flower crowns as he was going back home in the evening, and for this he was marveled at. Phanodemos says that Demophon the King instituted the festival of the Pitchers at Athens. When Orestes arrived at Athens after killing his mother Demophon wanted to receive him, but was not willing to let him approach the sacred rites nor share the libations, since he had not yet been put on trial. So he ordered the sacred things to be locked up and a separate pitcher of wine to be set beside each person, saying that a flat cake would be given as a prize to the one who drained his first. He also ordered them, when they had stopped drinking, not to put the wreathes with which they were crowned on the sacred objects, because they had been under the same roof with Orestes. Rather each one was to twine them around his own pitcher and take the wreathes to the priestess at the precinct in Limnai, and then to perform the rest of the sacrifices in the sanctuary. The festival has been called Khoes ever since. It is the custom at the festival of the Khoes at Athens that gifts and then pay be sent to teachers, the very ones who themselves invited their close friends to dinner in this way: 'you play the teacher, you bum, and you have need of the pay-giving Khoes, dining not without luxury.'" – Athenaios, *Deipnosophistai* 10.437b-e

"Possis in his third book of *Magnesian Things* says that Themistokles when taking up the office of crownbearer in Magnesia sacrificed to Athene and called the festival the Panathenaia and when sacrificing to Dionysos the Khous-drinker also introduced the festival of the Khoes there." – Athenaios, *Deipnosophistai* 12.533d

"*There are certain Khutroi.* A festival in Athens so named, in which it was possible to mock both the others and especially those in government." – Bekker, *Anecdota* 1.316

"And this woman offered for you on behalf of the city the unspeakably holy rites, and she saw what it was inappropriate for her, being a foreigner, to see;

and being a foreigner she entered where no other of all the Athenians except the wife of the king enters; she administered the oath to the *gerarai* who serve at the rites, and she was given to Dionysos as his bride, and she performed on behalf of the city the traditional acts, many sacred and ineffable ones, towards the gods. In ancient times, Athenians, there was a monarchy in our city, and the kingship belonged to those who in turn were outstanding because of being indigenous. The king used to make all of the sacrifices, and his wife used to perform those which were most holy and ineffable – and appropriately since she was queen. But when Theseus centralized the city and created a democracy, and the city became populace, the people continued no less than before to select the king, electing him from among the most distinguished in noble qualities. And they passed a law that his wife should be an Athenian who has never had intercourse with another man, but that he should marry a virgin, in order that according to ancestral custom she might offer the ineffably holy rites on behalf of the city, and that the customary observances might be done for the gods piously, and that nothing might be neglected or altered. They inscribed this law on a stele and set it beside the altar in the sanctuary of Dionysos En Limnais. This stele is still standing today, displaying the inscription in worn Attic letters. Thus the people bore witness about their own piety toward the god and left a testament for their successors that we require her who will be given to the god as his bride and will perform the sacred rites to be that kind of woman. For these reasons they set in the most ancient and holy temple of Dionysos in Limnai, so that most people could not see the inscription. For it is opened once each year, on the twelfth of the month Anthesterion. These sacred and holy rites for the celebration of which your ancestors provided so well and so magnificently, it is your duty, men of Athens, to maintain with devotion, and likewise to punish those who insolently defy your laws and have been guilty of shameless impiety toward the gods; and this for two reasons: first, that they may pay the penalty for their crimes; and, secondly, that others may take warning, and may fear to commit any sin against the gods and against the state. I wish now to call before you the sacred herald who waits upon the wife of the king, when she administers the oath to the venerable priestesses as they carry their baskets in front of the altar before they touch the victims, in order that you may hear the oath and the words that are pronounced, at least as far as it is permitted you to hear them; and that you may understand how august and holy and ancient the rites are. *I live a holy life and am pure and unstained by all else that pollutes and by commerce with man and I will celebrate the feast of the wine god and the Iobacchic feast in honor of Dionysos in accordance with custom and at the appointed times.* You have heard the oath and the accepted rites handed down by our fathers, as far as it is permitted to speak of them, and how this woman, whom Stephanos betrothed to Theogenes when the latter was king, as his own daughter, performed these rites, and administered the oath to the venerable priestesses; and you know that even the women who behold these rites are not permitted to speak of them to anyone else. Let me now bring before you a piece of evidence which was, to be sure, given in secret, but which I shall show by the facts themselves to be clear and true." – Demosthenes, *Against Neaira* 73; 74-79

"It is commanded to those bringing back the victory spoils that they revile and make jokes about the most famous men along with their generals, like those escorts on wagons during the Athenian festival who used to carry on with jokes but now sing improvisational poems." – Dionysios Halikarnassos, *Roman Antiquities* 7.72.11

"Among the Athenians holy women whom the king appoints in number equal to the altars of Dionysos to honor the god." – *Etymologicum Magnum* s.v. *gerarai*

"(Orestes speaking) At first none of my hosts willingly received me, on the grounds that I was hated by the gods, but those who had scruples supplied me provisions at a single table since we were under the same roof, and by their silence they made me shunned so that I might be separated from them at food and drink, and filling for all an equal amount of wine in individual pitchers, they took pleasure. I did not think it right to question my hosts and grieved in silence and pretended not to know, sorrowing deeply because I was my mother's murderer. I hear that my misfortunes have become a rite for the Athenians and that the custom still remains that the people of Athena honor the khoes-pitcher." – Euripides, *Iphigenia in Tauris* 947ff

"A festival done among the Athenians on the twelfth of Anthesterion. The whole feast for Dionysos is jointly called Anthesteria, but its parts are Pithoigia, Khoes, Khutroi." – Harpokration s.v. *Khoes*

"Instead of reproach and reproaching. Demosthenes in the speech *For Ktesiphon*. He takes the metaphor from those in the Dionysiac processions on wagons being reproached by each other." – Harpokration s.v. *processions and processing*

"Generally priestesses, in particular those completing the sacrifices to Dionysos in Limnai, fourteen in number." – Hesychius s.v. *gerarai*

"A marriage occurs between the wife of the king and the god." – Hesychius s.v. *marriage of Dionysos*

"A festival in Athens." – Hesychius s.v. *Pithoigia*

"A festival in Athens which they called Khoes." – Hesychius s.v. *twelfth*

"Bear Watcher. Some have said that he is Icarius, father of Erigone, to whom, on account of his justice and piety, Father Liber gave wine, the vine, and the grape, so that he could show men how to plant the vine, what would grow from it, and how to use what was produced. When he had planted the vine, and by careful tending with a pruning-knife had made it flourish, a goat is said to have broken into the vineyard, and nibbled the tenderest leaves he saw there. Icarius, angered by this, took him and killed him and from his skin made a sack, and blowing it up, bound it tight, and cast it among his friends, directing them to dance around it. And so Eratosthenes says: Around the goat of Icarius they first danced. Others say that Icarius, when he had received the wine from Father Liber, straightway put full wineskins on a wagon. For this he was called Boötes. When he showed it to the shepherds on going round through the Attic country, some of them, greedy and attracted by the new kind of drink, became stupefied, and sprawling here and there, as if half-dead, kept uttering unseemly things. The others, thinking poison had been given the shepherds by Icarius, so that he could drive their flocks into his own territory, killed him, and threw him into a well, or, as others say, buried him near a certain tree. However, when those who had fallen asleep, woke up, saying that they had never rested better, and kept asking for Icarius in order to reward him, his murderers, stirred by conscience, at once took to flight and came to the island of the Ceans. Received there as guests, they established homes for themselves. But when Erigone, the daughter of Icarius, moved by longing for her father, saw he did not return and was on the point of going out to hunt for him, the dog of Icarius, Maera by name, returned to her, howling as if lamenting the death of its master. It gave her no slight suspicion of murder, for the timid girl would naturally suspect her father had been killed since he had been gone so many months and days. But the dog, taking hold of her dress with its teeth, led her to the body. As soon as the girl saw it, abandoning hope, and overcome with loneliness and poverty, with many tearful lamentations she brought death on herself by hanging from the very tree beneath which her father was buried. And the dog made atonement for her death by its own life. Some say that it cast itself into the well, Anigrus by name. For this reason they repeat the story that no one afterward drank from that well. Jupiter, pitying their misfortune, represented their forms among the stars. And so many have called Icarius, Boötes, and Erigone, the Virgin, about whom we shall speak later. The dog, however, from its own name and likeness, they have called Canicula. It is called Procyon by the Greeks, because it rises before the greater Dog. Others say these were pictured among the stars by Father Liber. In the meantime in the district of the Athenians many girls without cause committed suicide by hanging, because Erigone, in dying, had prayed that Athenian girls should meet the same kind of death she was to suffer if the Athenians did not investigate the death of Icarius and avenge it. And so when these things happened as described, Apollo gave oracular response to them when they consulted him, saying that they should appease Erigone if they wanted to be free from the affliction. So since she hanged herself, they instituted a practice of swinging themselves on ropes with bars of wood attached, so that the one hanging could be moved by the wind. They instituted this as a solemn ceremony, and they perform it both privately and publicly, and call it alétis, aptly terming her mendicant who, unknown and lonely, sought for her father with the god. The Greeks call such people alétides." – Hyginus, *Astronomica* 2.2

"For the Khoes, for the public slaves: victim, 23 drachmae; pots, 5; two measures of wine, 16." – *IG* ii 1672.204

"He was of an age for 'Khoic' things, but Fate anticipated the Khoes." – *IG* ii 13139.71

"Whoever of the Iobacchoi receives an allotment or office or position, let him make a libation to the Iobacchoi worthy of his position – marriage, birth, Khoes, ephebia, civil service, staff-bearing, council …" – *IG* ii 1368 127-31

"For the Limnaian one they held festivals with choruses." – Kallimakhos, *Hekale* fr. 305

"Nor did the morn of the Broaching of the Jars pass unheeded, nor that whereon the Pitchers of Orestes bring a white day for slaves. And when he kept the yearly festival of Ikarios' child, thy day, Erigone, lady most sorrowful of Attic women, he invited to a banquet his familiars, and among them a stranger who was newly visiting Egypt, whither he had come on some private business." – Kallimakhos, *Aitia* 1.1

"Khoes were once called pilikai. The type of pitcher earlier was like the Panathenaic amphorae, but later it took on the form of an oinochoe, like those put out at the festival, a sort that they once called olpai, using them for the pouring of wine just as Ion of Chios says in the *Eurutidai*. But now such a pitcher, having been sanctified in some manner, is used only in the festival, and the one for daily use has changed its form." – Krates, *Attic Dialect* Book Two as cited in Athenaios, *Deipnosophistai* 11.495a-c

"Let the priest have the robe he wishes and a golden crown in the month Lenaion and Anthesterion so that he may lead those bringing home Dionysos in the proper way." – *LSAM* 37.19-24

"At the festival the priests and priestesses of Bacchic Dionysos will bring the god home from dawn to dusk." – *LSAM* 48.21-23

"As for their cups made by Therikles and their goblets and their gold and all the gods produced among them and envied in their courts, I would not take them in exchange for our yearly Khoes and the Lenaia in the theater and yesterday's talk and the schools in the Lyceum and the holy Academy, I swear by Dionysos and his bacchic ivy, with which I wish to be crowned more than with Ptolemaic diadems, for where in Egypt will I see an assembly, a vote taken? Where the democratic throng speaking its mind? Where the law-givers with ivy in their holy hair? What roped enclosure? What election? What Khutroi? What potter's quarter, agora, courts, beautiful acropolis, mysteries, nearby Salamis, the Narrows, Psyttalia, Marathon?" – Menander, *Epistles* 4.18.10

"Anthesteria is for three days, the eleventh, twelfth and thirteenth – but the twelfth day is most special." – *P. Oxy.* VI 853

"At the temple of Dionysos in Lemnai the Athenians bring the new wine from the jars and mix it in honor of the god and then they drink it themselves. Because of this custom Dionysos is called Limnaios, because the wine was mixed with water and then for the first time drunk diluted. Therefore the streams were called Nymphs and Nurses of Dionysos because mixed-in water increases the wine. Then having taken pleasure in the mixture they hymned Dionysos in songs, dancing and addressing him as Euanthes and Dithyrambos and the Bacchic One and Bromios." – Phanodemos, cited in Athenaios' *Deipnosophistai* 11.465a

"Children in Athens during the month of Anthesterion are crowned with flowers on the third year from birth." – Philostratos, *Heroikos* 12.2

"Apollonios said he was amazed at the Athenians regarding the Dionysia, which they celebrate in the season of Anthesterion, for he thought they visited the theater to hear monodies and songs from the parabasis and all the other lyrics belonging to comedy and tragedy, but when he heard that they dance twists to the sound of the aulos and that amid both Orphic epics and theologies they act, sometimes as Seasons sometimes as Nymphs and sometimes as Bacchai, he was amazed at this." – Philostratos, *Life of Apollonios of Tyana* 4.21

"For in the month Anthesterion a trireme raised into the air is escorted into the agora which the priest of Dionysos steers like a helmsman with its lines loose from the sea." – Philostratos, *Lives of the Sophists* 1.25.1

"A plant that at the Khoes they chewed from dawn as a preventative medicine. They also smeared their houses with pitch for this is unpollutable. Therefore also at the birth of children they smear their houses to drive away daimones." – Photius s.v. *buckthorn*

"On the day of the month Anthesterion at which the souls of the departed are thought to come up, they chewed buckthorn beginning at dawn and smeared the doors with pitch." – Photius s.v. *polluted days*

"This is about those mocking openly. For in Athens at the festival of the Khoes those reveling on the wagons mocked and reviled those they met and they did the same also at the Lenaia." – Photius s.v. *that from the wagons*

"Some say this proverb was said because of the number of Karian slaves, since they were feasting at the Anthesteria and not working. When the festival ended they said, sending them out to work, 'to the door, Kares; it's no longer Anthesteria.' But some have the proverb as follows: 'to the door, Keres; Anthesteria is not inside,' since the souls were going throughout the city in the Anthesteria." – Photius s.v. *To the door Kares, it's no longer Anthesteria*

"Once when it was the festival of the Khoes the two of them were feasting by themselves, and Apemantos said, 'What a nice symposium the two of us are having, Timon,' and Timon replied, 'Indeed, if only you weren't here.'" – Plutarch, *Life of Antony* 70

"And yet what difference does it make if one puts a kylix down before each of the guests and a khous, having filled it with wine, and an individual table just as the sons of Demophon are said to have done for Orestes, and orders him to drink ignoring the others, as opposed to what now happens where, putting out meat and bread, each feasts as if from his private manger except that we are not compelled to be silent as were those feasting Orestes." – Plutarch, *Questiones Convivales* 2.10.1

"At Athens on the eleventh of the month of Anthesterion they begin drinking new wine, calling the day Pithoigia. And in the old days, it is likely, they poured a libation of wine before drinking, and prayed that the use of the drug be harmless and healthful or saving for them. Among us Boiotians the month is called Prostaterios and it is customary, sacrificing on the sixth to the Agathos Daimon, to taste the wine after a west wind. This wind of all the winds especially moves and changes the wine and wine that has already avoided it seems to remain stable." – Plutarch, *Questiones Convivales* 3.7.1

"And those drinking the new wine first drink it in the month Anthesterion after winter. We call that day the day belonging to the Agathos Daimon; the Athenians call it Pithoigia." – Plutarch, *Questiones Convivales* 8.10.3

"During the month of Anthesterion they have many memorial ceremonies for the destruction and ruin brought about by rain, since around that time the Flood happened." – Plutarch, *Life of Sulla* 14

"They also introduced laws concerning the comic actors, that there should be a contest in the theater during the Khutroi and that the winner be chosen for the city." – Plutarch, *Life of the Ten Orators* 841

"*Khous* is an Attic measure, holding eight kotylai. For those inviting people to a feast used to put out crowns and perfume and hors d'oeuvres and other such things while those who were invited brought stews and a basket and a khous." – Scholium on Aristophanes' *Acharnians* 961

"For at the Khoes there was a contest about drinking a khous first, and the winner was crowned with a leafy crown and got a sack of wine. They drink at the sound of a trumpet. An inflated sack was set as a prize in the festival of Khoes, on which those drinking for the contest stood, and the one drinking first as victor got the winesack. They drank a quantity like a khous." – Scholium on Aristophanes' *Acharnians* 1002

"The Khutroi and Khoes are celebrated in Athens, at which, boiling panspermia in a pot, they sacrifice to Dionysos alone and Hermes." – Scholium on Aristophanes' *Acharnians* 1076

"The King had care of the contest of the khous and gave the prize to the victor, the winesack." – Scholium on Aristophanes' *Acharnians* 1224f

"*Limnai*. A sacred place of Dionysos in which there is a house and shrine of the god." – Scholium on Aristophanes' *Frogs* 216

"*At the beginning and the end of the pithos.* And among the ancestral customs there is a festival Pithoigia, in accord with which it was not proper to keep slave or hired hand from the enjoyment of wine but, having sacrificed, to give all a share of Dionysos' gift." – Scholium to Hesiod's *Works and Days* 368

"Anthesterion: It is the eighth month amongst the Athenians, sacred to Dionysos. It is so called because most things bloom (*anthein*) from the earth at that time." – Suidas s.v. *Anthesterion*

"And again: Orestes arrived in Athens – it was a festival of Dionysos Lenaios, and since, having murdered his mother, he might not be able to drink with them, something along the following lines was contrived. Having set up pitchers of wine for each of the celebrants he ordered them to drink from it, with no common sharing between them; thus Orestes would not drink from the same bowl [as anyone else] but neither would be vexed by drinking alone. Hence the origin of the Athenian festival of the Pitchers." – Suidas s.v. *Khoes*

"Those who had survived the great deluge of Deukalion boiled pots of every kind of seed, and from this the festival gets its name. It is their custom to sacrifice to Hermes Khthonios. No one tastes the pot. The survivors did this in propitiation to Hermes on behalf of those who had died." – Theopompos, in the Scholia to Aristophanes' *Acharnians* 1076

"The Athenians have the custom of sacrificing to none of the Olympians on Khutroi, but to Chthonic Hermes alone. None of the priests may taste the pot which all throughout the city make. With this offering they beseech Hermes on behalf of the dead." – Theopompos, in the Scholia to Aristophanes' *Frogs* 218

"Outside the Acropolis ... is the sanctuary of Dionysos in Limnai, for whom the older Dionysia are celebrated on the twelfth in the month Anthesterion, just as also the Ionians descended from the Athenians still customarily do so." – Thucydides 2.15.4

"In the ancestral festivals of the Greeks askolia and pithoigia were performed in honor of Dionysos, that is, his wine. The askolia happened as followed: placing wine-skins blown up and filled with air on the ground they leapt on them from above with one foot and were carried and they often slipped down and fell to the ground. They did this, as I said, honoring Dionysos, for the wineskin is the skin of a goat and the goat disgraces himself by eating the shoots of the grapevine. The pithoigia was a public symposium for, opening the pithoi, they gave a share of the gift of Dionysos to all." – Tzetzes on Hesiod's *Works and Days* 368

"Some say this proverb was said because of the number of Karian slaves, since they were feasting at the Anthesteria and not working. When the festival ended they said this, sending them out to work. Others maintain that the proverb came about because the Kares once held a part of Attica, and whenever the Athenians held the festival of Anthesteria, they gave them a share of the libations and received them in the city and in their houses, but after the festival, when some of the Kares were left behind in Athens, those who came upon them said the proverb as a joke to them." – Zenobius s.v. *To the door Kares, it's no longer Anthesteria*

THE LASTING VALUE OF THE GOAT SONG

Every Greek *polis* worthy of the name – whether located on the Hellenic mainland or in Italy, Asia Minor, North Africa and even further afield – possessed four things: an *agora* or marketplace, a *gymnasion* or training-ground for athletes, a *bouleuterion* or democratic assembly-hall, and a *theatron* for the performance of sacred dramas on festival days. The theater was a holy structure belonging to the god Dionysos. His priests were granted the choicest seats and the masked actors consecrated their craft to the god, regarding him as their divine patron. During the Hellenistic period guilds called *technitai Dionusou* or "the artisans of Dionysos" developed into powerful, international bodies whose favor was cultivated by kings and emperors, were given large endowments by the state and permitted to travel freely through hostile territories (even during times of intense conflict). The festivals of Dionysos, during which dramatic shows were put on for a week at a time, were occasions of national importance. People traveled from all parts of the country under a sacred truce to attend. Numerous troupes competed – sponsored and trained by influential individuals – spending half the year in preparation with only the prestige of winning for their reward. (Well, that and free meals at state expense.) Since so many were in attendance these festivals were used as opportunities to demonstrate a *polis'* conspicuous wealth and power: officials gave long-winded speeches, the *ephebate* was granted citizen status, civil servants, veterans and the orphans of those who had died in defense of their city were paraded about and awarded high honors, weighty matters were heatedly debated by the citizenry and important proclamations read out.

Nor was this simply an opportunity for civic grandstanding and popular entertainment – these dramas had a strong religious function as well. The dramatic arts had arisen from the early agrarian worship of Dionysos. In addition to being the god of actors, Dionysos is also the god of vegetation – and especially of the vintage. His spirit dwells in the grape on the vine. Therefore when the vintners harvested the crop, plucking the ripe fruit and then stomping the grapes and pressing them to make wine, they were actually enacting a savage rite whereby the god was murdered and dismembered. At the end of the harvest men would smear their faces with the lees and sing a mournful dirge in his memory to placate his spirit and ensure that the god was not vengeful since he lived on in the drink made from his flesh. This disguise – either to hide their true identities or to give expression to the feeling of intoxicating *enthousiasmos* brought on by the consumption of alcohol, with the god's spirit rising up within them and taking hold of their bodies, making them move and speak in ways they never would otherwise – grew more elaborate until men began fashioning intricate masks out of the different kinds of wood sacred to the god. At the same time the harvest-songs became more formal, with choruses of men singing and dancing and miming incidents from the life and death of Dionysos. Out of this eventually arose the art of drama, with the performances no longer just about the sufferings and triumphs of the god. In time the actor came to impersonate other figures such as famous kings and heroes who had endured similar torments and transformations.

By the time that the triad of great Athenian playwrights (Aiskhylos, Sophokles and Euripides) came on the scene, much about the art-form had changed, and under their skilled hands it would undergo even greater transformation. These men and their lesser-known contemporaries were responsible for introducing more roles so that it was no longer just a single actor accompanied by a chorus up on the stage. They also broadened the themes of tragedy so that they could tell a much wider assortment of stories. They brought in props and mechanical devices, including a contraption of levers and pulleys whereby an actor could be lowered down from on high at a pivotal moment in the plot, usually an improbable rescue of the seemingly doomed hero – the famous *deus ex machina*. Some conservatives resented these innovations, giving rise to the saying "What has this to do with Dionysos?"

For many, the theater was where religion came alive. Not everyone was capable of reading Homer and Hesiod, but the theater was open to anyone including women, slaves, and foreigners. During the performance they could witness the traditional gods and heroes walking about on stage, see the ancient stories given new life and vitality. Here they learned about concepts such as fate and justice, saw wicked deeds punished and pious sacrifice rewarded. Good men endured hardship with courage and strength; brave women (played by male actors, of course) forfeited their lives rather than relinquish the principles they held dear. One can see how important drama was in instilling the virtues of Greek culture by how frequently philosophers, theologians, and scholar-historians made allusions to the plays or employed dramatic terminology in their writing. Nor was drama merely a tool of the *status quo* – often the playwrights would use their stories to challenge the common assumptions of their society. Shortly after the Persian War, for instance, Aiskhylos wrote a play in which the Persians, the ancient enemies of the Greeks, were presented in a noble and sympathetic light:

> "Grief swarms, but worst of all it stings to hear how my son, my prince, wears tattered rags." – *Persai*, 845-849

Can you imagine an American play in which the humanity of the terrorists was emphasized coming right on the heels of 9/11?

Similarly, slavery was decried as an unnatural evil and Euripides had this to say about the alleged second-class status of women:

"Men's criticism of women is worthless twanging of a bowstring and evil talk. Women are better than men, as I will show …. Women run households and protect within their homes what has been carried across the sea, and without a woman no home is clean or prosperous. Consider their role in religion, for that, in my opinion, comes first. We women play the most important part, because women prophesy the will of Loxias in the oracles of Phoibos. And at the holy site of Dodona near the Sacred Oak, females convey the will of Zeus to inquirers from Greece. As for the sacred rites of the Fates and the Nameless Goddesses, all these would not be holy if performed by men, but prosper in women's hands. In this way women have a rightful share in the service of the gods. Why is it then, that women must have a bad reputation? Won't men's worthless criticism stop, and men who insist on blaming all women alike, if one woman turns out to be evil? Let me make the following distinctions: there is nothing worse than a bad woman, and nothing better in any way than a good one." – *Melanippe Captive* fr. 13

Such an argument could have been written by any modern feminist. Instead, these are the words of a 5th century Athenian male, meant to be recited at one of the city's largest festivals where all of his contemporaries would have been in attendance. They did not find such views shocking and offensive; instead they applauded his clear vision and eloquence.

This is heady, revolutionary stuff – and they were no less vigorous in their examination of the traditional myths. Difficult and at times unflattering stories about the gods were put on stage – one thinks of Sophokles' *Prometheus Bound,* for instance, where Zeus' arrogance and violence is condemned and the Titan is presented as a noble, suffering friend of humanity. Probably the most striking line from a Greek play comes from the pen of Euripides (*Belepheron* Fragment): "If the gods do ought that is shameful, they are no gods."

Of course, what makes Greek tragedy so compelling is its unflinching honesty, its recognition that the world is not black and white, that there are not always easy answers to our questions. Our quest for truth, our longing for justice can lead us to commit grave sins. It was Oedipus' desire to see the perpetrators of murder punished that led to his own downfall and the revelation of the sins he had unwittingly committed. It is no easy thing to tell which side Euripides wants us to be on in the *Bakchai*; both Pentheus and Dionysos are sympathetic characters in their own way, and both, in the end, go too far in the pursuit of their cherished ideals. There is virtue in freedom *and* restraint, evil in wildness *and* civilization. If you come away from these plays with a simple answer you are not thinking deeply enough about them. Greek drama challenges us in the way that all great literature does. (And most of the themes of that great literature are taken wholesale from the Greeks.) That is why it still has relevance two thousand years later, why these plays are still being read and performed meaningfully and shall continue to be so as long as man struggles to understand what it is to be human and how the divine intersects with our own world.

DANCING WITH DIONYSOS

When asked by the pagan publication *Thorn* to write about celebration (the impetus for this essay), the first thing that came to mind was the god Dionysos – and the second was dancing in his honor. This is, perhaps, only natural, for when you look back to the earliest sources that discuss the god – the Mycenaean inscriptions at Pylos and Phaistos, Homer's *Iliad* – we already find mainadic activity, dancing, mountain-roving, drinking, and sex connected with him.

Dionysos is a highly visceral god. Although he could inspire lofty spiritual visions, his worshipers never lost sight of the importance of the body or the things of this world. He teaches us that matter and spirit are not enemies, but united in a holy bond. He comes to cleanse the doors of perception – as Blake and Huxley would say – to help us perceive the whole world and ourselves through divine eyes, to stir the radiant life in all until it bursts forth in an explosion of boundless joy. And that is the spirit in which we should worship him.

Dance is probably the oldest means of worshiping the divine, and the most effective way to bring us into direct communion with Dionysos. The hymn that Philodamos of Skarpheia composed for Delphi tells us that Semele, while pregnant with Dionysos, was seized by an irrepressible desire to dance whenever she heard the flute and that Dionysos himself danced in the womb. He is hailed by Sophokles in the lovely choral ode of *Antigone* as the "leader in the dance of the fire-pulsing stars, overseer of the voices of night." When the mainades fled their homes to honor Dionysos they came to the hills and forests to dance all night long. Through dancing they would enter states of ecstasy and become possessed by the god, until overcome with exhaustion they'd collapse and pass into blissful slumber. So Euripides describes them in his *Bakchai* (198-215):

> "'On Bacchants, on!
> With the glitter of Tmolus,
> which flows with gold,
> chant songs to Dionysus,
> to the loud beat of our drums.
> Celebrate the god of joy
> with your own joy,
> with Phrygian cries and shouts!
> When sweet sacred pipes
> play out their rhythmic holy song,

in time to the dancing wanderers,
then to the mountains,
on, on to the mountains.'
Then the bacchanalian woman
is filled with total joy—
like a foal in pasture
right beside her mother—
her swift feet skip in playful dance."

You don't have to be a mainad to dance for the god. The mainades performed specific types of wild, frenzied dances which often included the tossing of the head and contorting of the body. I've seen it first hand and let me tell you, the way these modern mainades moved would have been dangerous if they weren't experienced and already in an altered state. But Dionysos can be honored through any type of dancing, and the more you do it, especially within the context of Dionysian ritual, the more comfortable you'll become, and the easier it will be to attain such a state.

In addition to the joy that our dancing provides for the god (and he definitely enjoys watching his mainades dance!), this physical activity helps us grow more aware of our bodies and more open to our own sensuality. We live in a world that is sarcophobic (body-hating), which teaches us that we are spirits trapped in husks of flesh, that anything we do with that flesh is morally suspect and dangerous to the norms of society. The more we buy into that crap, the more repressed we become, damming up the vital energies of creativity and life until they become deformed. Dionysos is Lusios, he who liberates us from false perceptions and loosens the snares which bind our spirits. Dionysian worship, therefore, must contain an element of transgression and reclaiming, a breaking of all the taboos we accept from others or build up within ourselves so that we can be whole and worthy vehicles through which the god manifests.

And all of this isn't just pretty philosophy. I've been challenged by the god and felt his terrible, transformative grace personally. A couple years back I attended Pantheacon, a major Pagan gathering in San Jose, to help put on a ritual in honor of Dionysos. My good friend Phillupus was doing a similar ritual for Antinous, the deified lover of the Emperor Hadrian. At the last minute I was asked if I'd help out by acting as a Lupercal priest. The Lupercalia was a festival in Rome where young men would run about in the nude (or pretty damn close) and whip maidens with strips of hide to drive off harmful spirits and promote fertility. I asked my friend if he'd be keeping that aspect of the festival intact and he said yes, but it was up to me how much skin I wanted to show. I immediately recognized this as a challenge from Dionysos.

Let's be totally frank here. I'm a big guy and although I don't obsess over it, I do have some body-image issues. The thought of prancing around in the buff petrified me. But I also knew that I needed to do it because there was no way I was going to let fear rule my life. I am a priest of Dionysos and that means embracing life to its fullest and meeting challenges head on.

I agreed and the rest of the convention until we gathered for the Antinous ritual passed by in a blur. I only vaguely remember standing in front of the mirror, examining my nude frame in the surface, wondering how the hell I was going to do this. I could see every imperfection in my body, all the extra weight I was carrying around, and I felt fear and shame rise up in me. But I refused to let it control me. So I wrapped myself in the purple cloth of my make-shift *khiton* (which covered precious little) and descended down through the hotel to the ritual space.

Phillupus led a marvelous rite. It was ornate and beautiful, a mixture of Greek, Egyptian and Roman religious practices. As the words of Phillupus' inspired Latin washed over me I could feel the presence of Dionysos and Antinous in the room, different and yet similar. Up until then I had been uncomfortable, carrying myself stiffly, rearranging the *khiton* so that it concealed everything. I didn't feel like a proud and confident priest of my god; I was the fat and ugly little boy I had been all those years ago, afraid to let anyone too close for fear that they might hurt me. But then, I felt myself enveloped in the warmth and loving care of those gods. I began to see myself through the eyes of the divine: I was frail and imperfect, but so are all creatures. Inside of that imperfection arises perfection and beauty, the beauty of the lotus that sprang up from the droplets of Antinous' blood. I was flesh and flesh is the form through which the divine manifests; I was blood and blood is the source of life; I was spirit and spirit is eternal and expansive. I understood the words that Phillupus had spoken so beautifully in Latin: *Haec est unde vita venit*, "This is where life comes from!" All the cares fell away and I danced for my god.

And when it comes down to it, that's what celebration means for me. It's about feeling the presence of the gods around you, being flooded by an overwhelming sense of gratitude, and letting yourself rise up to join them in joyous exultation.

NOT ALWAYS AN ORGIASTIC GOD

Sex is such a pervasive part of the Dionysian spirit that many have falsely assumed that it is always to be found in his rites. In Euripides' *Bakchai*, for instance, Pentheus was so convinced that the Theban women had fled to the hills to get drunk and have illicit sex that he ignored the testimony of his own spies who returned and told him that they had found no wrong-doing. In fact, to their complete surprise, the women weren't even drunk but were sleeping, or weaving ivy onto their thyrsoi, or nursing the wild animals of the forest. Pentheus, preferring to believe his own perverse fantasies, snuck into their camp dressed as a woman, saw what he should not, and got torn apart by his own mother and aunts in punishment for his transgression. This should serve as a warning to all who would see Dionysian worship simply as an excuse to get drunk and have orgies!

Additionally, there are numerous depictions on vases and drinking vessels of Dionysian women fending off the unwanted advances of the god's lusty satyr companions, accounts of festivals that were open to women only, and depictions of Dionysos which are sexually ambivalent. In Athenian representations of Dionysos the god is frequently at the center of a flurry of wild erotic and religious ecstasy, but remains himself entirely untouched by it. He is never depicted chasing after nymphs or goddesses or participating in the rapes so prevalent among his family, and there are even some hints that he was thought of as castrated or emasculated. Note, however, that all of these representations come from Attica and date to only a couple hundred years. In other places – especially in Southern Italy and Asia Minor – a totally different aspect of the god comes to the fore, one where his followers experience erotic union with him, and where death is seen as a marriage to the god. And even at Athens a sacred marriage between Dionysos and the wife of the Arkhon Basileos was celebrated during Anthesteria – so one should avoid simplistic theories whenever Dionysos is involved. He is the most complex and paradoxical of all the gods, simultaneously embracing all opposites. The sagest advice that one can offer in regards to this aspect of his worship are the words that Euripides puts into the mouth of the wise seer Teiresias:

> "On women, where Aphrodite is concerned, Dionysos will not enforce restraint – such modesty you must seek in nature, where it already dwells. But for any woman whose character is chaste she won't be defiled by Bacchic revelry." (*Bakchai* 314-317)

Or, in other words, whether there is an erotic element to your worship of him or not is really up to you. The best – and only – worship that he finds pleasing is what lies in our hearts. Doing something you don't feel like, and which goes against your nature is wrong, especially if someone else is pressuring you to do it. On the other hand, if this is something you feel comfortable doing it can prove a powerful element in your worship and relationship with him.

THE QUEERNESS OF DIONYSOS

Dionysos is a queer god. It's certainly not all that there is to him – in fact, when I think about Dionysos it's usually stuff like his wildness, his connection to the earth, the dead, animals, masks, dancing, drunkenness, madness, spiritual intoxication, liberation, transformation, fertility and sensuality that come to mind. But queerness is a big part of who he is, and it runs through all of the other stuff as well.

And by queer I don't just mean that he's got a thing for handsome young boys, of which there were certainly plenty:

> "Beardless Ampelos, they say was the child of a nymph and a satyr and loved by Bacchus on Ismarian hills. He trusted him with a vine hanging from the leaves of an elm; it is now named for the boy. The reckless youth fell picking gaudy grapes on a branch. Liber lifted the lost boy to the stars." – Ovid, *Fasti* 3.407ff

> "Dionysos was loved by Chiron, from whom he learned chants and dances, the bacchic rites and initiations." – Ptolemy Chennos, as quoted in Photius' *Bibliotheka* 190

> "Plato, in *Adonis*, says that an oracle was given to Cinyras concerning his son Adonis which read: 'O Cinyras, king of the Cyprians, those men with hairy rumps, the son that is born to thee is fairest and most admirable of all men, yet two divinities shall destroy him, the goddess driven with secret oars, the god driving.' He means Aphrodite and Dionysos; for both were in love with Adonis." – Athenaios, *Deipnosophistai* X.456a

> "Others will have Adonis to be Bacchus' paramour; and Phanocles an amorous love-poet writes thus, *Bacchus on hills the fair Adonis saw, and ravished him, and reaped a wondrous joy.*" – Plutarch, *Symposiacs*, 5

> "Phalloi are consecrated to Dionysos, and this is the origin of those phalloi. Dionysos was anxious to descend into Haides, but did not know the way. Thereupon a certain man, Prosymnos by name, promises to tell him; though not without reward. The rewards was not a seemly one, though to Dionysos it was seemly enough. It was a favor of lust, this reward which Dionysos was asked for. The god is willing to grant the request; and so he promises, in the event of his return, to fulfill the wish of Prosymnos, confirming the promise with

> an oath. Having learnt the way he set out, and came back again. He does not find Prosymnos, for he was dead. In fulfillment of the vow to his lover Dionysos hastens to the tomb and indulges his unnatural lust. Cutting off a branch from a fig-tree which was at hand, he shaped it into the likeness of a phallos, and then made a show of fulfilling his promise to the dead man. As a mystic memorial of this passion phalloi are set up to Dionysos in cities. 'For if it were not to Dionysos that they held solemn procession and sang the phallic hymn, they would be acting most shamefully,' says Herakleitos." – Clement of Alexandria, *Exhortation to the Greeks* 2.30

> "*Appapai* (Oh god!): An expression of affirmation. For when Herakles asks Dionysos 'Were you physically loved by a man?', this is his response." – Suidas s.v. *Appapai* (quoting Aristophanes, *Frogs* 57)

To this list we might add Akhilles, Akoites, Hermaphroditos, Hymenaios, and Laonis according to *Cassell's Encyclopedia of Queer Myth, Symbol, and Spirit*. Unfortunately the editors didn't see fit to provide proper references or citations for us to follow-up with, but it's a fairly reliable work so I'm willing to leave it at that.

After all, Aesop credited Dionysos with the invention of homosexuality so it's not surprising that he'd have a sizable "black book":

> "The answer lies once again with Prometheus, the original creator of our common clay. All day long, Prometheus had been separately shaping those natural members which modesty conceals beneath our clothes, and when he was about to apply these private parts to the appropriate bodies Liber unexpectedly invited him to dinner. Prometheus came home late, unsteady on his feet and with a good deal of heavenly nectar flowing through his veins. With his wits half asleep in a drunken haze he stuck the female genitalia on male bodies and male members on the ladies. This is why modern lust revels in perverted pleasures." – Phaidros' collection 4.16

But these "perverted pleasures" aren't what makes Dionysos queer; plenty of other Greek gods had their *erômenoi*, but I wouldn't think to characterize them in such a fashion.

Dionysos' queerness derives from his blurring of lines, his combining of disparate qualities within himself and his ability to throw everything into a state of utter confusion. It began even before he was born, when Zeus salvaged the fetus of Dionysos from the flames of his mother's womb and sewed him into his thigh in order to carry the child to term. Imagine that – big old butch Zeus, the quintessence of manly vigor and patriarchal authority transformed into an expectant mother by baby Dionysos! And according to the Orphics that wasn't even the first time that it happened. In the *Derveni Papyrus* (COL. 13) Zeus is said to gain his potency and kingship of the world by swallowing the phallos of Dionysos-Eros-Phanês. Nor would this be the last time that we encounter such a role-reversal in a Dionysian context.

After he was born Dionysos was carried off by Hermes, who placed him in the care of his aunt Ino who raised him in the *gynaikon* or women's quarter of her home in an effort to avoid the wrath of Hera, the original "evil stepmother." The ruse went much further than that, however, as the 5th century poet Nonnos of Panopolis (*Dionysiaka* 14.143) informs us:

> "He would show himself like a young girl in saffron robes and take on the feigned shape of a woman; to mislead the mind of spiteful Hera, he molded his lips to speak in a girlish voice, tied a scented veil on his hair. He put on all a woman's manycoloured garments: fastened a maiden's vest about his chest and the firm circle of his bosom, and fitted a purple girdle over his hips like a band of maidenhood."

This, perhaps, began his close association with women and all things feminine. Throughout his life Dionysos was always surrounded by women. They were his nurses, his lovers, his hunting companions and most passionate devotees. Nymphs, goddesses and mainades formed his train, joined only by the pleasure-loving satyrs. It was Rheia or Kybele who cured him of madness (Apollodoros, *Bibliotheka* 2.29) and instructed him in the mystic rites that he would go on to teach the world, a god proselytizing for a goddess. He raised his mortal mother and wife to divine status (Apollodoros 3.38; Hesiod, *Theogony* 947ff) demonstrating a devotion to them unique among other gods. And he was above all else a woman's god, freeing his female followers from the shackles of domestic drudgery and societal convention. All the most important sacred functions in the cult of Dionysos were carried out by women, whether it was the Basilinna who ritually married him at Anthesteria (Aristotle, *Athenaion Politeia* 28-9), the Gerarai who assisted her (Demosthenes, *Against Neaira* 74ff), the Lenai who broached the casks of new wine in the swamp (*Scholion* on Aristophanes' *Akharnians* 202), the Elean women who invoked him in his bull form (Plutarch, *Quaestiones Graecae* 36), the Argive women who called him up out of the underworld through the lake (Plutarch, *On Isis and Osiris* 364f), the mountain-roving Thyiades who danced with him on Parnassos (Plutarch, *Mulierum virtutes* 249e-f) or the savage mainades who tore the god to pieces so that he could be reborn. Women and only women could do these things for him, however important the other roles of Dionysian men might be.

And so it's not surprising that Dionysos often resembles those whom he was closest to. He could be depicted with long flowing hair, a slender, almost androgynous figure and a delicate, beardless youthful beauty. His luxurious robes were described either as those of a woman or an Eastern foreigner, which pretty much amounted to the same thing for the Greeks and Romans:

> "But dainty Bacchus does not blush to sprinkle with perfume his flowing locks, nor in his soft hand to brandish the slender thrysus, when with mincing gait he trails his robe gay with barbaric gold." – Seneca, *Hercules Furens* 472

Not content with a merely effeminate god, there were rumors of what lay concealed beneath all those flowing robes. Some said that he had been emasculated like one of the Great Mother's *gallae* or that he possessed female breasts and a vagina, a detail discussed more thoroughly in Carl Kerenyi's *Dionysos: Archetypal Image of Indestructible Life*. Aiskhylos called him *gynnis* "the womanly one," (Fragment 61), Euripides called him the "womanly stranger," (*Bakchai* 353) and Orphic Hymn 42 *To Mise* invokes him as the "ineffably pure and sacred queen, two-fold Iacchus seen as male and female alike." All of this, of course, was in stark contrast to the other, hyper-masculine and ithyphallic representations of the god, but his fluid nature meant that he could embody either point on the spectrum – or both of them simultaneously. In fact that fluidity is key to understanding Dionysian sexuality, for he is constantly flowing between the gendered poles. One moment he could be effeminate and fearful, escaping the wrath of Lykourgos into the sea and the sheltering arms of Thetis only to return with savage frenzy to punish his enemy with unimaginable cruelty. He could be the peaceful lover, sipping wine and eating grapes in the lap of Ariadne or marching triumphantly at the head of a great army having subjugated all the lands of the East.

There's an almost campy quality to Dionysos' myths. He's never just masculine – he's the baddest, toughest, biggest-dicked guy around. And he's never just a little effeminate – it's all limp-wristed flounce, girly-girly drag. Everything is exaggerated to the point of absurdity to show how artificial and limiting our cultural constructs of gender are. He likes to play with us, to tweak our expectations. So, for instance, he takes the misogynistic Pentheus who's convinced that women are sex-craved irrational creatures up to no good in the forest, and he turns him into one by giving him a wig and make-up, a veil and the full feminine attire as Euripides so humorously put it:

> PENTHEUS: How do I look? Am I holding myself
> just like Ino or my mother, Agave?
> DIONYSUS: When I look at you, I think I see them.
> But here, this strand of hair is out of place.
> It's not under the headband where I fixed it.
> PENTHEUS: [demonstrating his dancing steps]
> I must have worked it loose inside the house,
> shaking my head when I moved here and there,
> practicing my Bacchanalian dance.
> DIONYSUS: I'll rearrange it for you. It's only right
> that I should serve you. Straighten up your head.
> [Dionysus begins adjusting Pentheus' hair and clothing]
> PENTHEUS: All right then. You can be my dresser,
> now that I've transformed myself for you.
> DIONYSUS: Your girdle's loose. And these pleats in your dress
> are crooked, too, down at your ankle here.
> PENTHEUS: [examining the back of his legs]
> Yes, that seems to be true for my right leg,

but on this side the dress hangs perfectly,
down the full length of my limb.
DIONYSUS: Once you see
those Bacchic women acting modestly,
once you confront something you don't expect,
you'll consider me your dearest friend.

Once everything is properly in place Dionysos leads the poor unfortunate into the woods, delirious and hallucinating, to witness a bunch of women that the god has transformed into men. Women who brandish their *thyrsoi* like weapons, hunt wild beasts, repel armed forces from neighboring cities and perform martial dances around the bonfire while drunk. Here is how a previous witness described the mainades to Pentheus:

MESSENGER:
So we set up
an ambush, hiding in the bushes,
lying down there. At the appointed time,
the women started their Bacchic ritual,
brandishing the thyrsos and calling out
to the god they cry to, Bromius, Zeus' son.
The entire mountain and its wild animals
were, like them, in one Bacchic ecstasy.
As these women moved, they made all things dance.
Agave, by chance, was dancing close to me.
Leaving the ambush where I'd been concealed,
I jumped out, hoping to grab hold of her.
But she screamed out, "Oh, my quick hounds,
men are hunting us. Come, follow me.
Come on, armed with that thyrsos in your hand."
We ran off, and so escaped being torn apart.
But then those Bacchic women, all unarmed,
went at the heifers browsing on the turf,
using their bare hands. You should have seen one
ripping a fat, young, lowing calf apart—
others tearing cows in pieces with their hands.
You could've seen ribs and cloven hooves
tossed everywhere—some hung up in branches
dripping blood and gore. And bulls, proud beasts till then,
with angry horns, collapsed there on the ground,
dragged down by the hands of a thousand girls.
Hides covering their bodies were stripped off
faster than you could wink your royal eye.
Then, like birds carried up by their own speed,
they rushed along the lower level ground,
beside Asopus' streams, that fertile land
which yields its crops to Thebes. Like fighting troops,
they raided Hysiae and Erythrae,

>   below rocky Cithaeron, smashing
>   everything, snatching children from their homes.
>   Whatever they carried their shoulders,
>   even bronze or iron, never tumbled off
>   onto the dark earth, though nothing was tied down.
>   They carried fire in their hair, but those flames
>   never singed them. Some of the villagers,
>   enraged at being plundered by the Bacchae,
>   seized weapons. The sight of what happened next,
>   my lord, was dreadful. For their pointed spears
>   did not draw blood. But when those women
>   threw the thrysoi in their hands, they wounded them
>   and drove them back in flight. The women did this
>   to men, but not without some god's assistance.

Though Pentheus didn't live long enough to appreciate the irony, we certainly can. Of course the irony is even greater when you remember that all of the parts in ancient Greek drama were performed by men, regardless if it was a male or female character. So there is something appropriately Dionysian to have an actor playing Pentheus dressing up as a woman to go out and see women that are acting like men while being played by male actors. Of course, it'd be just as appropriate to see a show in which all those parts were performed by women. Because in the realm of Dionysos gender isn't real. It's a grand, theatrical illusion: something that is fluid and playful, something that you can put on or take off as the situation demands or hell, just because you feel like it. We aren't our genitals or the roles that society assigns us based on them. We are something more, something deeper. Do you know the face you wore before you were born, before you had a body? Dionysos does, and he'll show it to you if you truly wish to see. But don't be surprised if it ends up being something strange, something you never could have imagined – for everything in the realm of Dionysos is a little bit queer.

STRONGER THAN DIRT

I talk with a lot of drunk people, which I suppose is only appropriate given my devotion to Dionysos. You see, I do the majority of my writing outdoors in the various parks around town. I like being surrounded by the wildness and the natural beauty. It helps loosen up my thoughts and even when the inspiration doesn't come there are animals to watch, trees to admire and the grand pageantry of the changing seasons to take in. There are also interesting people to meet.

They'll often come sit at the picnic table with me, whether invited or not. Most of the time I don't mind, even if it interrupts the flow of words. After all I'm usually camped out under the overpass and they need shelter from the rain much more than I do. They usually ask for a smoke or spare change and when I've got it I gladly share with them. The gods have given me much over the years and it's only proper to pay it forward as the saying goes. Sometimes they want more. Attention, a kind face, someone to acknowledge them as a person, to offer them friendly words and more importantly – much more importantly – to listen to their stories.

These are usually very broken people, the discarded dregs of our society. They suffer from poverty, hunger and disease, mental illness and assorted addictions. It's not enough to say clean yourself up, get off the drugs and drink, find a job and lead a better life. Without a stable residence employment is impossible. Very often the trauma of their past and their various psychological disorders make functionality beyond their reach. That's often why they turn to intoxicants in the first place, to cope with the bad shit in their brains and dull the pain they're feeling. It doesn't make things better. They know that, most of the time, but they don't know how to get beyond it. Even if they somehow managed to get themselves together enough to apply for a job most people wouldn't give them a shot. Most people won't even directly look at them passing on the street. I've seen it far too often myself. Who am I kidding, I've done it to them plenty of times before. We put our heads down or cross the street to avoid them or just walk by doing our damndest to pretend they don't exist. They are invisible, forgotten, rejected and annoying. We can't deal with their misery and what their existence says about our society. Perhaps on some superstitious level we even fear that if they get too close to us, talk to us for too long, their bad luck will rub off on us.

Well, it's not true. I've spent more hours than I can count talking with these people and it's never done me any harm. Indeed, it's actually done me a great deal of good. It's opened my eyes to a whole other world that's out there on the margins and in the shadows. There's an unwritten code governing their conduct, a set of rules and etiquette for how to act, how to get by, how to treat each other which is different from how they treat people who aren't living on the streets. Though they possess little they are often incredibly generous. Many times they've offered me cigarettes, food or swigs of their beer, told me where I could find free food and shelter for the night, warned me to watch out for certain abusive cops that were patrolling the parks. And they were never offended when I declined their generosity. That just meant more for them.

Their stories are the things I appreciate the most. They are sad and funny and inspiring and horrifying – often all at the same time. I am frequently awed by the courageous spirit they've shown in the face of such overwhelming adversity. You don't end up on the streets as a lark or because you're bored working a nine to five. Many of them have histories of severe childhood sexual and physical abuse. Many have lost loved ones, before and after ending up there. Many have endured a series of horrendous events that would crush a lesser person. But they don't want pity and most don't pity themselves. With an unflinching resolve that Marcus Aurelius or Epictetus would envy, they confess that this just the way the world is and you've got to make the most of what life hands you. They find joy in the simple things, a reason to go on and keep hoping for another and better day. Often they find humor in their situation and love to share a funny anecdote or carefully crafted joke. One fellow has told me the same ribald tale three times without realizing that he's already done so. I sincerely hope to hear it a fourth time.

I cannot help but feel that these rejects on the margins of society are Dionysos' own holy people. Their insanity and alcoholism certainly mark them as his, but it runs much deeper than that. Of all the gods, Dionysos is the closest to mankind. He alone of the Olympians was born of a mortal mother and that mortality is a big part of what makes him uniquely Dionysos. Because of it he has suffered as no proper god ever could. He has experienced death and savage dismemberment and things far worse than that. His jealous stepmother pursued him across the face of the earth, destroying everyone who got too close to him or that he ever loved. She even inflicted a terrible madness on Dionysos and would have succeeded in destroying him as well but for the intervention of the other gods.

Nor should we think that this suffering is just mythological. Consider what the grape must go through in order to become wine. In winter the vine is pruned back until it resembles nothing more than a barren twig. And yet this makes possible the budding of the fruit which ripens in the sweltering heat of summer. In fall the grapes are plucked from the vine, torn from the only life they've known, and then crushed, stomped and pressed until their blood flows out to be collected in vats. Then they are left to rot and ferment until their miraculous transformation into the sacred alcoholic beverage. When we drink that wine we are taking the god into us, his spirit moving within our minds and bodies, producing intoxicated visions both glorious and horrible. Out of the primitive celebrations of the vintners developed the tragic arts, the first actors commemorating the joys and sorrows of the god through their ritual dances and songs. The mask they wore was the face of the god and drunk on his wine they spoke with his voice. In time the actors came to perform other roles beyond that of the harvested god, kings and heroes and great historical figures. But always people who faced adversity and suffered terribly. In other words, art is born out of pain.

So when I see the faces of these vagrants it is tragic Dionysos that looks back at me. I listen carefully to their stories, for it is the stuff of mythology, raw and ugly and sublime. Though it hurts sometimes to be so close to the suffering, I cannot look away, cannot pretend that it doesn't exist, that they are invisible and what they're going through doesn't matter. It does, deeply. And in the midst of it is joy and pleasure, wisdom and beauty. The triumph over adversity and the transformation that lies at the heart of all mysteries. These people are more than their suffering, more than the bad things that have happened to them. They are people. Human. And sometimes, if you're lucky, you'll catch a glimpse of something more than human about them.

THE LAND OF THE FREE AND THE HOME OF DIONYSOS

I agree with the flag-waving patriots that America is god's own land – I just happen to believe that that god is Dionysos.

This thought occurred to me a couple months back while the rest of the country was celebrating the birth of freedom in our land with fireworks and alcohol. We have always intuitively understood that this is the way it happens. The ancient Greeks said that Dionysos came into the world out of the wreckage of his mother's womb amid thunder and fire and savage celebration. He, the youngest of the gods, an outcast and stranger with all the imperfections of a human, earned his way onto Mount Olympos after accomplishing a host of noble deeds. He fought to put down tyrannies and establish peace and civilization throughout the world, he freed slaves, exalted women and taught his mysteries to Greek and barbarian alike.

America, at its best, has often followed the mythical pattern of Dionysos. She was the youngest of the great nations, formed of the cast-off and despised dregs of the old world. Though originally looked down upon she came to lead the way through industry and the arts until World War II cemented her position as the dominant global super power. Most of the wars she fought over the last two centuries have been to ensure the freedom and stability of other countries and she's been in the forefront of the civil rights and equality movements. Refugees from all parts of the globe have sought dreams of freedom and prosperity on her shores and though she has often strayed from her own noble principles – shamefully so at times – America still stands as a shining beacon to many, inspiring their own highest aspirations.

From the beginning there has been something Dionysian about this land. When the first Viking settlers came here centuries before Columbus, they called it Vinland after the lush vegetation they found. The vine is, of course, the supreme symbol of Dionysos, but it's interesting to note that there are only a few indigenous species of wild grape on the continent, the rest having been transplanted from the old world. Dionysos' myths are all about the bringing of the grape to new lands, so our country is a part of that grand process.

Along with the grape Dionysos brought many other gifts to this continent. America is a democratic republic founded on the principle that the common man is capable of governing himself without recourse to King or Pope. All men are created equal and have certain inalienable rights that are not dependent on wealth, race, creed, gender, etc. When these rights are threatened the American will defend them with the savagery of a mainad. These very ideas emerged out of the orgiastic worship of Dionysos back in Greece. Through his sacred art of drama, men challenged the power structures and traditional notions of their society and argued for the fundamental dignity and common brotherhood of man. It was Spartacus, a Thracian devotee of Dionysos, who led the famous slave revolt in Rome and later served as a great inspiration to our founding fathers when they cast off the oppressive yoke of England. This same spirit was at work during the Civil War and again during Martin Luther King Jr.'s march on Washington. America doesn't have a perfect political system by any stretch of the imagination. But what it does have within it are the tools necessary to remedy problems when they arise.

That we live in a fundamentally Dionysian country can be seen in much more than just our political system. It is perhaps most evident in the art-forms that our hallowed shores have given birth to. We have bequeathed to the world three completely new types of music, each of them bearing a strong Dionysian imprint.

Jazz is our modern version of the ancient dithyramb: wild, improvisational, breaking boundaries and even challenging our conventional notions of what constitutes "music." These days it's difficult to imagine what kind of impact jazz had when it burst onto the scene in the early decades of the 20th century. People thought it was crazy, decadent and dangerously revolutionary – and it was! To ears who had only ever heard Mozart and Mahler, folk-ballads and work-songs, ballroom dances and polka, jazz was like the gates of hell blasting open, a pandemonium of jungle rhythms and primal screams capable of shattering the very foundations of society. It's no wonder that the Nazis banned this "deranged Negro music" and had they been around they'd have done the same for its brother rock 'n' roll.

Born out of the South with deep roots extending through Blues and Negro spirituals all the way back to the traditional music of the African continent, rock 'n' roll only gained popularity in the 1950's once it was adapted by White musicians for suburban-dwelling bobby-soxers. But no matter how much they tried to whitewash it and make it safe and palatable, there has always been something dangerous and revolutionary about rock. The danger comes primarily from its obsession with sex. Rock is saturated in the stuff. Rock is the sound of violent lovemaking, of deep, subconscious drives bursting through the walls of repressed inhibition. Rock stars are sex-gods, from Elvis' writhing hips to Jim Morrison whipping out the king snake on stage in Miami to Prince strutting around in assless chaps. All the screaming little girls knew it and so did their fathers who tried to shut the concerts down and ban those records from ever being played on the radio. But you can't control the spirit of Dionysos once he's been unleashed, as Pentheus so painfully discovered.

Rock isn't just about sex, of course, any more than Dionysos' ancient worship was. And that's what scares people the most about it. Rock is about giving vent to all those dark, primal drives, about destroying the old world in order to create a new one. It's about freedom and self-expression and the best rock has always been visionary, transcendent, a violent confrontation with societal norms. This is something that it shares with that other great American music style, rap.

In the early days rap was the music of the streets, a way for people who had grown up in abject poverty and the hopelessness that it breeds to give voice to their dreams and aspirations, to tell their stories and ask why things are the way they are. Early rap had a strong political conscience, infused with the activism and community consciousness of the Black Panthers and similar liberation movements. Rap was an outgrowth of the poets of the street like Langston Hughes and James Baldwin. It's hard to tell that these days since it's all hyper-commercialized and overproduced, would-be gangstas talking about their shiny bling and bundles of cash, their hot hoes and smoking rides. But even the most derivative and clichéd of the bunch still represent the dream of a better life and a challenge to the lie that urban Black youth can't accomplish anything.

In the same vein, dream plays an important role in the other American arts that we either pioneered or came to dominate. And it's no accident that these American arts are also Dionysian arts.

The whole world looks to America for its entertainment, especially when it comes to movies and television. Even when they've got burgeoning industries of their own they still go mad for big-budget Hollywood blockbusters. Many of these industries, in fact, are dedicated to making cheap imitations of our movies or translating the basic concepts into styles more suitable to their own audiences, as we see in India and Nigeria, the second and third largest film-producing countries in the world. For better or worse – and I'm inclined to see it as a negative – American actors and actresses are treated like royalty the world over. We've turned them into gods and people are mad to know even the most mundane details of their lives. Can you imagine actors – actors! – being treated like this at any other time in history? They may have been highly esteemed in ancient Rome or Shakespeare's England, but nothing like they are today. We stand in awe of their ability to take on different personae, chameleon-like, to give our hopes and dreams living flesh, to tell the stories of our hearts – and we lavish unimaginable wealth and power on them for it. There are actors who earn the equivalent of a small nation's GNP for a *single* film! But there is also something primitive and sinister about our relationship with these idols. We elevate them beyond the bounds of ordinary humanity and then wait, hungry, for the inevitable fall. We know that no one can sustain that kind of life for long; it distorts and consumes them, then spits them out broken and bloody for us to gloat over as we sift through the wreckage of their lives. We don't just want people to take up the craft of Dionysos; we want them to impersonate him, to *become* him, the victim on the altar who suffers terribly for our amusement. No other nation treats its celebrities in this way, at least not to the extent that we do, because no other nation is as thoroughly Dionysian in its soul as we Americans are.

Nor is it just actors and musicians that we do this to (though we do seem to have a special fondness for them). Any politician or public figure will do, so long as they squirm and squeal and bleed and put on a good show for us.

Why do we worship Lincoln and Kennedy but forget most of their contemporaries? Nixon and Clinton got off light; their death and dismemberment was symbolic but real enough to etch them into our collective memory. Martin Luther King Jr. and Malcolm X weren't the most important men in the Civil Rights movement, but their assassinations earned them eternal fame.

Of course America isn't *just* about sex and dream and death, though it might seem that way sometimes. There's another part of us that is equally Dionysian, and that's our love of nature. Early in our nation's history we recognized the importance of wilderness and the divinity that is manifest in forest and streams, mountains and caves and all the rest. And when we are too timid to call it "divinity" we instead name the thing that stirs these intense emotions within us "beauty" which, as any Greek will tell you, is pretty much the same thing anyway. Our greatest poets – Emerson and Whitman, Longfellow and Theroux – sang the praises of Nature and reminded us that it was something worth cherishing and preserving for future generations. Even though this was a time of great expansion and conquest we set aside huge swaths of land as pristine and protected nature preserves. This we counted as our greatest national treasure and unlike previous countries we ensured that this was something that all of us could enjoy and use instead of keeping it for the wealthy and elite alone. That is a huge and important thing that makes me proud to be an American every time I visit our public lands. I feel pride, too, when I read our environmental laws and see the steps we're taking to care for this land, to make sure that it doesn't all become polluted and over-used. Yes, absolutely, we've got a long way to go in this regard. We aren't perfect and the planet has suffered intolerably for the mistakes of the past. But so much worse could have happened if our forebears hadn't been as far-sighted as they were. We mustn't stop there. We should take that example and carry it forward into the future, make the hard, tough choices that are necessary if life on this planet is going to continue.

But it's not just our preservation of wilderness that's Dionysian – much of how we think about the land and relate to it honors his spirit. Americans have always had a profound love for the land and an inherent distrust of sedentary city life and the evils of civilization. Our forefathers and -mothers were pilgrims, pioneers, explorers, mountain men, homesteaders and the like. People who left behind the safety of the big cities to travel beyond the horizon and carve out a new life for themselves in strange places. People who shunned the company of others in favor of wild beasts and unspoiled forest, people who wanted their own parcel of land and the freedom to do with it as they pleased.

The legends that arose on the frontier reflect this love of wide open spaces and the men it calls to: Paul Bunyan and his giant blue ox roaming the wilderness; John Henry the steel-driving man that couldn't be beat by technology and spiritless progress; the heroes of the Alamo who died for freedom's sake; and good old Johnny Appleseed who traveled the country planting trees. Though all of these men in different ways can be seen as heroes of a Dionysian mold, none comes as close as Johnny. Especially when you consider that all those orchards he planted were for the sole purpose of brewing alcoholic applejack. Johnny was a real man, a disciple of Swedenborg who held strongly mystical and pantheistic beliefs and felt an abhorrence for modern civilization. He disliked the company of other people, preferring animals and trees, and as soon as settlements encroached on his territory he'd pick up and move on to the next site, leaving his orchards behind for the settlers. A fascinating and unjustly neglected figure of American history – but one that shows how Dionysian our collective spirit can be.

Another important Dionysian "saint" that shows just how far back his presence can be felt in our country is the early colonist Thomas Morton. He arrived in New England in 1622 and created his own colony called Merrymount, but it shared little in common with the other grey and dour settlements of the time. Puritan governor William Bradford wrote concerning the curious religious practices of his neighbors: "They set up a May-pole, drinking and dancing about it many days together, inviting the Indian women for their consorts, dancing and frisking together (like so many fairies, or furies rather) and worse practices. As if they had anew revived & celebrated the feasts of ye Roman Goddess Flora, or ye beastly practices of ye mad Bacchanalians." (*History Of Plymouth Plantation*)

You can probably guess the fate of Thomas Morton and the Merrymount colonists but the spirit of Dionysos has been much harder to drive from the land, resisting every effort of the latter-day puritans to extinguish the flame of liberty. Every time the bastards think they've crushed the heart of America in their iron glove it has come back again, reborn and stronger. Slavery gave rise to the Civil War. Prohibition birthed the flappers and the jazz age. McCarthyism begat the psychedelic sixties. Vietnam was met with the Civil Rights and Anti-war movements. Stonewall created gay liberation. The "Me" generation of Reagan's 80's gave way to environmentalism and anti-globalization. The resurgence of the Moral Majority was beaten back by the optimism and prosperity of the Clinton years. And though Bush and Cheney tried to remake America in their distorted, imperialist image, freedom-loving patriotic souls fought against them every step of the way. We've come close to losing sight of the American Dream, of what makes us unique and special, many times now. And when that happens we let ourselves do some truly horrible things. But the great thing about us is that eventually we always remember and find our way back. And that gives me great hope for the future. May Dionysos continue to guide and bless us as we stumble along the path to greatness.

NYMPHOLEPSY ON THE MCKENZIE

I'm sure that everyone knows that Dionysos has got a strong relationship with the nymphai – they are his nurses, his companions in the revel, his lovers and so much more. This pairing has been a popular theme with artists down through the centuries. There have been so many vases and paintings and statues and hymns and poems that one would be hard pressed to list even the most significant examples. And it's easy to understand the ubiquity of this theme for it is as natural as can be. After all Dionysos is the god of nature, the lord of all animal and plant life and he is to be found primarily in wild places such as forests and mountains, caves and grottoes – the same places traditionally haunted by nymphai. It makes perfect sense that there would be this closeness between them. And yet something happened a while back that helped me to understand their relationship in a much better light.

Several friends and I went hiking along the McKenzie River. Because Eugene is such an awesome place we were able to catch one of the regular city buses and ride it all the way up to a ranger station, paying only the regular nominal fee. Once we crossed the highway and walked the trail for a couple minutes we found ourselves alone in the heart of a primeval old growth forest, the only signs that we were still in this modern world the occasional friendly mountain-bikers who whizzed past us. I can't even begin to describe how breath-takingly beautiful this place is – trees as tall as buildings and so wide across that several men could not link hands around their trunks; moss and lichen draped over everything; the constant sound of the river rushing by us; little stream-fed shady grottoes just a few steps off the path and fire-hued mushrooms everywhere you looked. Words fail me and even the gorgeous pictures my partner took do not do the place justice.

By the end of the day I felt intoxicated and overwhelmed by so much natural beauty. My eyes were worn out from everything I had seen and marveled at. Part of my soul craved stillness and simplicity after the baroque extravagance of the forest, even as part of me wished never to leave it behind. Although we saw many wonderful sights, found many wonderful treasures and had many wonderful conversations between the four of us that day, the thing that sticks out in my mind the most is a rather humble encounter I had with Dionysos and the nymphai. It was so humble, in fact, that I doubt any of the others sensed it was happening although they were just a couple feet away from me at the time.

We had gone off the trail and into this little clearing by the river strewn with large, moss-covered rocks. We had just finished having lunch and the others were busy discussing their religious practice and plans for upcoming festivals. I moved a couple rocks over so that I could have a private smoke and enjoy the sight of the white-capped rapids, when it happened.

It crept up on me slowly, a gradual shifting of focus that I barely noticed until it was fully upon me. My vision grew more clear, more intense, until I was seeing things that had been little more than a grey and green blur only moments before. The light quality changed as well – everything became brighter, purer, lit up from within. And I felt this tingling, prickly sensation all along my skin, but especially at the top of my head and along the nape of my neck. By that point I started to realize what was going on: *nympholepsy*. I had become possessed by the nymphs of this place. I turned to look at something and it was as if the whole world had gone fluid and time no longer functioned the same way. Everything slowed to a crawl and it seemed that the rushing river was just inching along. I felt as if I was floating in the water as well, even as I remained conscious of sitting there on the rock. It didn't matter, though, because I could feel the movement beneath the hard surface, the pulse of life within the rock, within the moss, within the trees and the earth. Everything was alive and moving, everything was fluid beneath the surface. And in that moment I understood that *this* was the essence of both Dionysos and the nymphai, that this is the reason why they're always found so closely together. Moisture and flow, nature and life; the raw, elemental stuff of creation. That's them.

The whole thing lasted for only a couple moments and then I came back to myself and the ordinary way of seeing the world. As I said, I doubt anyone else even noticed what was going on with me and I didn't bother trying to put it into words in order to share the experience with them. I told them something had happened, that I'd felt the presence of Dionysos and the nymphai and that's all that needed to be said. It's all, really, that could be said. Even now, looking over what I've just written, I don't think I've truly captured what that experience was like. I've suggested and provided hints, but that's all. I'm not sure that more is even needed. It's not like this was a huge, life-changing epiphany or even the most intense encounter I've had, either with Dionysos or the nymphai. But there was also a wonder and a magic to the experience that is present in all true encounters with the divine and that, more than anything else, is what I wanted to share here.

THE GEESE AND THE GOD

Today I was at the park writing when something rather strange happened. There was a flock of geese who had been scavenging for food down by the river for a while. Suddenly and without any warning they turned, as one, and came charging towards my table. I watched the imminent approach of these two or three dozen creatures with mild bewilderment. Truth be told, there was a little fear as well. I mean, there were a *lot* of them, they weren't small, and they could have done some serious damage had it entered their heads to do so!

Of course, therein lies the source of my amusement, because rational thought had nothing to do with this. Maybe one or two of the leading geese made a kind of conscious decision to explore over my way, but it was pretty clear that the rest were just swept along for the ride. I doubt any of them, granted the gift of speech, could have said why. It was instinctual, a strong compulsion, overriding individual thought and impossible to ignore.

All of nature obeys this primal drive: herds, flocks, swarms, etc. We humans are not impervious to it, either. Think of crowds, riots, mass political movements, tribal dances, religious hysteria, shrieking young girls at rock concerts. For all the pride we feel in our technological advancement, our social progress, our intellect and individuality – it is a fragile thing that easily gives way before the overwhelming power of the collective. In fact, deep down, I think we yearn for this. The purity of being that is found only in the dissolution of self. Because consciousness, born out of an awareness of our own finite and imperfect mortality, is painful.

The Orphics told a story about the origins of mankind. Zagreus, the child of Zeus and Persephone, was torn apart by the Titans who consumed his flesh. Zeus punished them with fire for their terrible crimes and out of the ashes we humans were formed. Once we were whole. Once we were Zagreus. But then we were torn apart and scattered to the winds. From unity we became multiplicity; in multiplicity is pain, incompleteness, and a memory of a time when things were different.

That is the story, at any rate. I don't know that I believe it, any more than I believe in the Garden of Eden or Freud's theories of the longing for the womb.

But I do know this: there is a healing that comes about through the dissolution of ego. The ancients recognized this, and further recognized that Dionysos had a large part to play in it. Through wine, through music, through group dances, through the mask and the phallos his grace is accomplished. In his worship we are lifted out of ourselves, made strangers to ourselves. We forget our fears, our pains, the banalities of our everyday existence. We behold a world transformed or rather revealed as it truly is: fluid, shifting, dreamlike, and magical – and we are invited to revel in it. We lose ourselves in the rush, the rhythm, the pulse of life that lies beneath all things.

CLEANSING THE DOORS OF PERCEPTION

In Plato's *Phaidros* Sokrates is made to say that "our greatest blessings come to us by way of madness." The madness that he is speaking of is telestic, initiatory and prophetic madness, where one is lifted out of their normal self and filled with something higher, diviner. The Greeks had a number of words to describe these states. *Ekstasis* meant literally to be taken out of one's self, a state similar to *ekphron* meaning "out of one's senses." *Katokoche* was their word for possession, a concept closely allied with *enthousiasmos*, which meant to be filled with a god, or literally "a god is within." When someone is *theoleptos*, they are "seized by a god," which can also be described as being *mainomenos*, or enmaddened, a title shared by Dionysos and his worshipers alike. All of this could also be called simply *epipnoia* or inspiration.

A helpful way to understand this is to imagine yourself as a pool of water. Usually the water is murky and dark so that all you can see within is the grime and detritus that has floated up to the surface. But at other times the water clears and upon its crystal surface one can see the wonders of heaven revealed – or mysterious things peering up from the depths. The murkiness of the water is caused by our ego-consciousness, our fears and anxieties, our wants and needs, the trivial concerns of our daily lives such as what we're going to fix for dinner tonight or anger at the asshole who cut us off on the way into work this morning, our societal conditioning, the expectations that both we and others have for us – the white noise that's constantly going on in the back of our heads. For the average person this is what constitutes their self, the face which they present to the world and the part of their being which takes up so much of their time that they may not even be aware that there is anything more. But Dionysos teaches us otherwise, shows us the immensity of our spirits and offers us a path to reconnection with those hidden, shadowy parts of ourselves. To do so, we must simply let go – stop associating ourselves with that ego-consciousness and come into contact with a more vital, authentic, and powerful level of being, transforming ourselves into a vessel through which beautiful visions can flow.

These visions can come from one of two directions. In the first instance they can come from within, or to return to our original metaphor of the pool, from below. Such things consist of symbols, dreams, fantasies, other aspects of our personalities and even our higher selves, our Agathos Daimon in Greek thought. Each of us has a complex internal world woven of images, memories, desires, dreams, etc. When we have access to this dark, nourishing realm of the imagination we find ourselves creative, whole and vital individuals. But this world can be uncomfortable for many, and society does its best to close off access to it by telling us that it is frightening, dirty, violent, irrational and impractical. All of which it most certainly can be. But it is a part of us and if we are to become whole people we must not be afraid to walk within this world, to give voice to that part of ourselves, to manifest the numinous within our lives, to heed what messages it may have for us – regardless of how "crazy" this may make us appear in the eyes of outsiders.

But the phenomena that we're discussing are not simply internal and psychological. In such states we can open ourselves to influences that lay outside of ourselves, to beings that are normally quite distinct from us such as spirits, natural forces, daimones, gods, etc., all of which can influence, merge with, speak to and through us. There are varying levels of contact and communion with these external beings during trance states – the lowest, perhaps being inspiration, wherein one experiences themselves in conversation with the being but is still in full possession of their faculties and conscious self. At the other end of the spectrum the conscious self is fully submerged and the spirit or god takes complete possession of one's body, compelling its movement and speaking through one like an actor wearing a mask. Between these two poles are a whole range of phenomena, with varying degrees of awareness and bodily control.

Now, while it is convenient to draw a distinction between these two types of trance – the inner and outer – there are also times when they seem to overlap, when the lines blur and we cannot tell if a dream might have originated outside of ourselves, or if a spirit may be speaking from somewhere deep within us. Mystics from many traditions would have us believe that such a distinction serves only a limited, pragmatic purpose anyway, and that upper and lower worlds penetrate and bleed through each other until all is united in the harmony of creation. But you know how untrustworthy those mystics can be.

The ancient Greeks recognized a number of different methods for triggering and achieving these altered states of consciousness, all of which relate in some way to the world of Dionysos. Perhaps the most characteristically Dionysian of these was through dance and music. In the *Ion* Plato informs us that the mainades had special dances and responded only to particular types of music: "they have a sharp ear for one tune only, the one which belongs to the god by whom they are possessed, and to that tune they respond freely in gesture and speech, while they ignore all others." What information we have about this special mainadic type of dance indicates that it is very similar to the dances performed by modern-day Vodouisants – wild, rhythmic, with a strong backward tossing of the head. Euripides in *The Bakchai* describes them as dancing "with head tossed high to the dewy air," and has Pentheus say, "I was tossing my head up and down like a Bacchic dancer." Of Dionysos it is said that he will "bring his whirling mainades, with dancing and with feasts." We have evidence of this particular type of dancing not just from literature but depicted on a great number of vase paintings. Always the mainad is shown with a strong backward bend to her head. Whipping one's head about like this can cause disorientation in the inner ear and vertigo-like dizziness. It can also lead to a powerful shift in consciousness and possession by the god.

When attempting to induce a trance state it is important to pay attention to your surroundings. These can play a very important role, either making it a lot easier or stopping it outright. For instance a setting which is away from the city in some wild place like a desert or forested mountain – under the open night-time sky, with a crackling bonfire, the scent of pine and incense strong in the air, the droning sound of cicadas surrounding you – is going to make entering a trance very easy. Sitting on the couch in your overly hot living room while your husband watches wrestling and your daughter slams her juice cup repeatedly into the wall will make trancing very difficult. Not impossible, of course – sometimes trance-states can come upon us spontaneously, regardless of our surroundings or what we're doing – but it's certainly not conducive to such states either. Another important aid would be austerities – sleep deprivation, fasting, physical exertion, etc which all help loosen the rational mind's control and assists our souls in attaining *ekstasis*. Additionally, alcohol and drugs, particularly entheogens, have a longstanding history with ecstatic trance states.

One tool that is very helpful in attaining a trance state and has no side-effects whatsoever is meditation and visualization. Meditation may seem like a practice that is completely antithetical to the Dionysian *bios*. It probably conjures images of New Age hippies doing strange things with crystals as they chant meaningless syllables or Buddhist monks in rigid *zazen* postures, quietly contemplating the nothingness that lies behind their navels. And yeah, that doesn't really fit in with the realm of the wild and rapturous god of life who is hailed by the dancing, singing, maddened crowd passionately crying "Euoi!" – or what he teaches about how we must be engaged in life, active, fiercely claiming our joy from the world. And yet, we must not forget that Dionysos is always a paradox and that stillness is as much characteristic of him as motion. Remember, Dionysos' supreme symbol is the mask which hangs serenely from the pillar, peering out onto the world around him. Before Dionysos manifests in the riot of colorful new growth he is the empty vine branch, pruned almost to the point of death, slumbering in the world below. He is the calmness at the center of the storm and the silence between notes in a song. He is also Zagreus, the Great Hunter, which requires action to catch his prey – but also great concentration and focus. And so meditation can indeed play an important role in your relationship with the god, serving as a way to quiet your raging emotions, to connect you with his somber, still, quiet vegetative aspects, to give you focus generally, to ground you and bring about awareness of the moment and of our bodies and as a means of opening the doors within us.

There is no one right way to meditate. The important thing is to bring about calmness within yourself and a growing awareness of things, both internally and in the world around you. If you are so caught up in how you're meditating that you can never find this serenity you're just wasting your time. I recommend that you find a quiet place that you will be undisturbed. Sit in a relaxing posture – don't even try yoga postures unless this is something that you've been working on – and start to breathe rhythmically and deeply. Focus on your breathing, how your breath circulates through your body and the effect this has on you. Direct your thoughts to a specific end so that they don't chase themselves around in your head or add to the cluttered white noise of your mind. This may be contemplation of one of Dionysos' names or myths, a particular idea, image, color, scent, etc., music you have playing in the background, or just stillness and emptiness if you wish. Stay like this for as long as you feel necessary, alternating focused thoughts with free-flowing mental tangents. Play around in your head. Try directing your thoughts, creating scenarios and images, thinking of only one thing – and absolutely nothing else – for as long as you can and then stretching that time further and further until you are completely absorbed by that single thought for 24 hours or longer. (Aleister Crowley couldn't even do this, so don't get discouraged if you fail at it. It's still a very helpful practice.) Try not thinking at all, but just *being*, soaking in the sensations around you. Anything and everything, as long as you're not ruminating over your problems for the millionth time that day or contemplating what color you want to paint the kitchen come spring. Regular meditation will make it easier to enter trance states and expand your consciousness, just as it's easier to navigate through a forest when you've been there plenty of times before.

There is, of course, one thing that we haven't really discussed so far: and that's why trance and meditation are important. And it's definitely not for shits and giggles, to see pretty lights and bullshit with the spirits, or because you're looking for some kind of badge of honor for doing it, as if you are somehow a better mainad than your sisters because it's easier for you to enter trance than it is for them. Simply put, not everyone can do it. Some people's psyches aren't elastic enough, they're too grounded in the material world or something in the past caused them so much trauma that they aren't able to relinquish control. That doesn't mean that they love Dionysos any less, that they lack devotion in the performance of their religious duties or that they haven't fully integrated the Dionysian philosophy into their lives. It simply means that they can't trance. So, if these aren't the reasons that we should do it – what are?

Simply put, Dionysian trance brings healing, wholeness, integration, and revitalization. The ancients were most emphatic about this. Plato describes the bacchants as *ekphrones*, out of their senses, and says that it is the combined action of music and dance that restores them to their senses so that they are *emphrones*. In other words, Dionysian trance heals the mainades, taking them from a dangerous madness to a gentler, divine madness. It allows us to access those parts of ourselves that are normally submerged, hidden, and repressed, so that we can access the vital, creative, ecstatic energy that lies at our center, burning bright as the stars in heaven. When we cannot access our internal world, when the ideas, images, and fantasies that make up that world lay dormant, untouched and repressed they stagnate, grow hard and dead, and bleed through into our waking world in the form of unhealthy psychoses, destructive drives, violent madness. But when we immerse ourselves in them, learn to manipulate them, listen to their wisdom, we transform them, transform ourselves – and find wholeness through them. We also – and this is important – become a means through which the divine can act in our world, giving voice to that which has no voice, form to that which is formless.

THIS GOD IS A PROPHET

The Dionysian spirit is one of expansion. He lifts us out of our everyday confines, broadens our horizons, opens us to the fullness of life and dissolves whatever obstacle may be impeding our path. With all of this we should not be surprised to discover that prophecy was closely linked with Dionysos by the ancients – for it is only our limited sight which perceives past, present, and future as three distinct categories instead of merely parts of a single stream, as it becomes when viewed through divine eyes. Plutarch called Dionysian madness a secret knowledge, and Euripides explicitly called the god *mantis*, or seer and "prophet of the Thracians." Herodotos tells us that Dionysos shared the oracle at Delphi while Pausanias testifies to one at Amphikleia and Aristotle tells us that just as the Apollonian seers prophesied at Klaros after drinking from a sacred spring, so Thracian prophets gained inspiration from Dionysos after drinking large quantities of wine.

What sort of prophecy did Dionysos preside over? We have evidence of a number of different types. First, there are what have been called "mechanical" forms of divination, since they required a tool of some sort to communicate the divine will. This is the sort of divination that we see employed at the Villa of the Mysteries. In one of the scenes a young satyr, assisted by two companions, is gazing into the depths of a vessel. This sort of divination or scrying had a long history and is found in numerous places in the Greek Magical Papyri. This may be what is indicated in the Orphic myth when the Titans creep up on the child Zagreus who is lost in meditation on his reflection in a mirror. The cup or bowl would be filled with water, wine, oil or some other substance, and the diviner would gaze into its depths to behold visions. The shimmering reflection of light and shadows on the surface (this operation was usually performed in a darkened room lit only by lamps) would distract the conscious portions of his mind, allowing the images and a deeper, intuitive knowledge to rise to the surface. The visions that the diviner beheld could be symbolic (e.g., if he beheld a flowering tree it meant renewal), more concrete (such as an actual scene from the future), or more along the lines of a monition, as we see from the Greek Magical Papyri which describe the magician actually holding conversations with a spirit inside a bowl. Another form of mechanical divination associated with Dionysos was the interpretation of the lees left in a glass of wine. Unfortunately, we have no evidence of how these were interpreted, although we can surmise that the process was probably not unlike that used by modern readers of tea leaves or coffee grounds. We have evidence of a third form of mechanical divination associated with Dionysos from the *Alexander Romance* of Pseudo-Kallisthenes and the *Indika* of Arrian. According to the tradition represented in these texts, when Alexander the Great visited India he met with and spoke to the god Dionysos who lived in a pair of sacred trees. This brings to mind the oracle of Zeus at Dodona, where the barefoot priests discerned his will through the rustling of leaves. Unfortunately, history has provided us with no clues as to how the priests interpreted the rustling of leaves or how Alexander spoke with Dionysos.

The most common form of Dionysian divination, however, required no tools and was actually possession and prophecy in the proper sense of the term. At the height of Dionysian worship the spirit of the god can enfold and entwine with that of the worshiper, the two uniting in the most intimate form of communion. The Greeks called this *enthousiasmos* or literally "a god is within" and the individual was thereafter known as a Bacchos (m) or Bacches (f) signifying their unity with Bacchus. In addition to being filled with the god's spirit, made whole and new, they were granted prophetic gifts, imperviousness to pain and extreme conditions such as heat and cold as well as the ability to perform miraculous deeds such as the mainades who caused wine, milk, and oil to flow, or Akoites being able to loose the chains that bound him. (We find similar phenomena in Haiti where Vodouisants are "ridden" by the *lwa*.) In such a state it is not the individual's personality that is foremost but the god's. They have greater understanding and speak things that they would not otherwise know, in words they would not normally use. Often there is not just a change in personality but also in voice – as we see from the Greek tradition of "belly-talkers," women who in trance spoke with deep, gravelly voices that seemed to emanate from somewhere deep inside their bellies.

Of course, Dionysos could also inspire visions and prophetic understanding without fully possessing an individual. We see this in Euripides' *Bakchai* when Kadmos utters wise speech which Teiresias attributes to the god and even proclaims an oracle at the end of the play, without ever having experienced direct *enthousiasmos*. The Athenian playwright Aiskhylos attributed his poetry to Dionysos' inspiration after the god visited him and commanded him to compose dramas in his honor. Alexander the Great was visited by Dionysos in a dream, who gave him advice regarding the military engagement that was to take the place the following day. Alexander followed his unlikely advice and saved his army, which would have been soundly defeated had he followed his original course of action. So clearly as Plutarch so astutely observed, Dionysos had an equal share in the prophetic arts which guided the ancient Greeks.

THE ORACLE OF THE LEAVES

I have been interested in divination for as long as I can remember. Even as a child, well before I found Dionysos or thought of myself as a practicing Pagan, I would interpret the shapes formed by dripping hot wax into water, open the Bible at random for guidance, count the seconds between thunderclaps, consult a Magic 8-Ball and pay attention to dreams as well as numerous other folk customs I'd managed to collect. Eventually I progressed to things like palmistry, I Ching, the Runes and geomancy – though I only gained true proficiency with the Tarot, eventually forgetting most everything I'd learned about the other systems. I got so good with Tarot cards, in fact, that during high school I usually had a large group of classmates gathered around me at lunch, eager to have their fortunes told. Often there were teachers, custodians, administrative personnel and sometimes even the principal in the crowd as well.

When my relationship with Dionysos deepened and I came to practice Hellenic reconstructionism I became dissatisfied with the Tarot, wanting to practice a more authentic form of ancient Greek divination. So I set myself to learning scrying, bird omens, the Limyran alphabet oracle and a form of bibliomancy found in the Greek Magical Papyri that utilizes verses from Homer's *Iliad* and *Odyssey*. I proved just as adept with these methods as I had the Tarot and the other systems I'd studied in my youth, gaining a reputation as a well-respected *mantis* or diviner in the Hellenic community. Many people sought my advice on a wide range of topics, religious and otherwise. I came to view the work I did as a holy vocation under the auspices of my god Dionysos. It was a way to serve both him and the community and I felt that much of what came out through my readings was inspired by the god's prophetic spirit. As I've discussed elsewhere, the ancients believed that Dionysos had a great deal to do with the mantic arts. Not only was prophecy one of the side effects of Dionysian *enthousiasmos* but he shared Delphi with Apollon and possessed several oracle centers of his own in Greece and abroad.

I was not content, however, with the tools at my disposal. While it was certainly possible to get good results with Dionysos employing the ancient Greek methods, and even Tarot and systems developed in cultures and time periods completely unrelated to him, there was nothing particularly Dionysian about any of them. I wanted something that belonged wholly to him, which spoke his language through his symbols and associations. So I asked the god for his assistance in devising such a method of divination.

Working closely with Dionysos it took me the better part of a year to flesh out the details of the system. The heart of it had been revealed in a flash of sudden divine inspiration but then I had to sort out what each of the elements meant and how the system would actually function in practice. There were a couple of false starts, some things that had to be revised or omitted altogether, but considering how long it took for the Tarot to be codified into the system we recognize today – to say nothing of the I Ching or Runes – a year is scarcely any time at all.

I tried the system out for the first time on July 10th, 2006 and got stunningly accurate results. It had been effective in readings I'd done for myself and a handful of others before that, but I had no idea if it would work on strangers and especially people with no prior Dionysian history. It worked so well, in fact, that I immediately had people requesting further readings. In particular people were impressed – and shocked – by the intimacy and private nature of the information that came through. Things that they hadn't confessed to anyone else, ever, were laid bare by the god through his oracular leaves. And thus was born the monthly Dionysos Day oracles that I have faithfully performed for the community on behalf of Dionysos ever since.

However, I stopped utilizing the oracular leaves about a year into it and stopped relying solely on them after the fourth or fifth session. You see, the leaves served as an introduction to other oracular techniques, a more direct and intimate form of communion and communication with the god that employed trance, possession and other methods of initiating altered states of consciousness which did not involve mechanical tools. I haven't completely abandoned the leaves, of course. Not only are there some questions better suited to being answered through them but there are plenty of situations where one needs a fast and simple answer or can't undergo the complex procedures necessary to attain the proper spiritual state that makes direct communication with the god possible. So while I generally don't use the leaves any longer in my oracular sessions – unless Dionysos specifically advises that I do so – I keep them around and use them in situations where it's warranted, such as my divination business where I set up a table on the street corner and do readings for curious pedestrians.

When Dionysos revealed this system to me back in late 2004 he informed me that I would one day share his gift with the world, although I had to fully master it before I could do so. Starting around 2007, when I had progressed to the possessionary oracles, I began asking if I could share the system with others. To each inquiry he would respond, "The time is not yet right." I would wait another five or six months to ask again, but always I got the same response. Then in late 2010 while I was putting the final touches on this collection I thought to ask one more time and he surprised me by saying, "Now it is ready."

So, with the god's blessing, I present to you The Oracular Leaves from the Tree of Dionysos. Before we delve into the system itself I would like to provide some of its background.

The genesis of this system lies in a pair of anecdotes found in Pseudo-Kallisthenes' *Alexander Romance*.

"Then came some of the towns-people who said, 'We have to show thee something passing strange, O King, and worth thy visiting; for we can show thee trees that talk with human speech.' So they led me to a certain park full of priests. And in the midst of the park stood the two trees of which they had spoken, like unto cypress trees; and round about them were trees like the myroliolans of Egypt, and with similar fruit. And I addressed the two trees that were in the midst of the park, which were clothed with the skins of animals. And at the setting of the sun, a voice speaking in the Indian tongue came forth from the tree; and I ordered the Indians who were with me to interpret it. But they were afraid and would not." (3.17)

And Philostratos' *Life of Apollonios of Tyana*:

"They were now in the country in which the mountain of Nysa rises, covered to its very top with plantations [...], and you can ascend it, because paths have been made by cultivators. They say then that when they ascended it, they found the shrine of Dionysos, which it is said Dionysos founded in honor of himself, planting round it a circle of laurel trees which encloses just as much ground as suffices to contain a moderate sized temple. He also surrounded the laurels with a border of ivy and vines; and he set up inside an image of himself, knowing that in time the trees would grow together and make themselves into a kind of roof; and this had now formed itself, so that neither rain can wet nor wind blow upon the shrine. And there were sickles and wine-presses and their dedications to Dionysos, as if to one who gathers grapes, all made of gold and silver. And the image resembled a youthful Indian, and was carved out of polished white stone." (2.8)

I had a vision in which these two incidents were combined. I saw Alexander the Great enter the verdant temple of Dionysos, a structure made entirely out of leaves, vines and ivy encircling a crude, primitive wooden idol of the god. Alexander approached the image and sacrificed to Dionysos by pouring out a libation of wine at his feet. The image then came to life and addressed Alexander, telling him to ask the question he had traveled so far to learn the answer to. When Alexander did so a multitude of leaves from the canopy overhead rained down upon him. He caught several of these in his hand and the god ordered him to read them for his answer was written upon the leaves. And that is the essence of the system as it was revealed to me and as I now share it with you.

There are 28 different leaves, each of which references a figure from the myths of Dionysos, a symbol or attribute or something else associated with the god. 28 is a number of deep mystical significance for Dionysos as well as his Egyptian counterpart Osiris. I leave it to you to unravel why this number of leaves was chosen, but know that there can be no more or less than 28 in this system. Likewise there is a great density of meaning behind each of the leaves, things that only a devout Dionysian who has worked very closely with the god for a great length of time and is well-versed in his myths and lore could ever fully hope to comprehend. One could fill a volume many times the size of this present collection with speculation on their nuances. I have presented only the most basic and superficial level of interpretation for each of the leaves in the following commentary. If you are going to use this system effectively you must consider this only a starting point. It is incumbent upon you to search out their true and deeper meaning, to let the god guide you in understanding their mysteries and to open your ears to what each leaf has to say. Keep in mind that the meaning can change significantly depending on the context of the question as well as what leaves are drawn with it. You should spend many hours meditating on the complexities inherent in the leaves before you begin to use them in a divinatory capacity for yourself, let alone others.

In the beginning the only place where the leaves may be consulted is the verdant temple of Dionysos. (Later on, when you've established a relationship with them, you can use them less formally.) Every time that you wish to seek their wisdom you must visit this place. Whether or not it once existed in the distant land of India and was actually visited by Alexander and Apollonios, know that it is a real place and dwells on the periphery between this and other worlds. Those whom the god wishes to use his oracle will be able to find their way to the temple. The path begins in the mind but it leads to a land far from there. Let your imagination form an image of the temple based on the accounts I have provided and what the god himself shows you. Carefully dwell on every branch and vine and leaf that forms the structure, the light shining through the lattice, the smell of damp earth and vegetation, the shadows covering the ancient idol of the god, the fragrant incense and offerings left by past visitors and all of the other sense perceptions that flood your mind. But never forget that the image you construct is only a replica, a phantom of the true temple of the god. It is a real place and the image you construct is the door that leads into it. To properly consult the oracle of the leaves you must pass from illusion into reality – but illusion is how you find your way there.

When you have arrived, make the proper offerings to Dionysos and spend time basking in his presence. The words spoken and the offerings presented to the god will differ from person to person, and necessarily so for this is a highly personal operation. But one thing that must always be present is the sacrifice of wine. You must share the wine with Dionysos, pouring a cup for him to drink and consuming some yourself as well. You need not drink to intoxication, although that can help loosen your mind and allow you to hear the words of the god more clearly, but there can be no true oracle without first exchanging the gift of wine and taking the god's spirit, through the wine, into yourself. This may only be a token sip, but it still has to be done, just as the Pythia had to drink the pure spring water before she could experience the prophetic inspiration of the Lord Apollon.

After you have done this, spend time letting the god's wine settle into you, freeing your mind for the holy work ahead of you. When you feel yourself ready to proceed, ask Dionysos if he is willing to give answer to your questions. You must not rush this part or blurt out your request until he has granted you permission. It is rude and disrespectful and the god may well have good reasons of his own for not wanting to proceed. If he declines your request ask if there is something more you need to do in preparation or if the consultation is better reserved for another time. Sometimes, no matter how ready we think we are for his revelation, the god knows that we are not. The god always knows best and if you cannot trust him utterly then you should not be seeking his oracular guidance. If he says that he will not answer your question under any circumstances take him at his word and do not try it again, no matter how important and pressing the circumstances may seem to you.

Should the god grant you his blessing to proceed then ask your question and await Dionysos' sign to continue. This may manifest in him telling you to draw the leaves, a nod of his head or smile, or the image of leaves falling around you. At that point you may then draw out the leaves.

There is no set number required to answer a question. Sometimes a single leaf will suffice. Sometimes you will need three or five or even a dozen. Allow the god to inspire you with the proper number. Meditate on what each leaf means alone and in connection with the others. Although each leaf has a specific meaning – or rather layers upon layers of meaning – do not limit yourself just to what is there. Sometimes the true meaning is not immediately apparent but only arrived at intuitively, through suggestion and analogy and irrational leaps of connection. Open yourself up to the story the leaves have to tell, mindful of the broad network of associations they possess, the myths they allude to, and your past history with them. Sometimes once we've been working with the system for awhile, a leaf will become an indicator of a person, a particular situation or feeling, regardless of what it originally may have meant. Understanding it in this way is far more important than a literal reading. If you cannot properly interpret the leaves do not hesitate to draw more of them or shuffle the set and start again by drawing a new batch. Also, if it seems like more than the initially indicated number of leaves wish to be present – for instance you draw out four instead of three or a couple extras fall into the pile – include them as part of the reading and give them special consideration for the god may be indicating something important through them. Likewise pay attention to the spatial relationship of the leaves. If two or more of them are touching or laid down closely together in contrast to the rest of the leaves that are scattered about this can be significant. Also, pay attention to how they fall. If a leaf is upside down or reversed this can have a very different meaning than when it is regular side up. It can, for instance, indicate a blockage in this area or that the worst aspects of the leaf are dominant or even that its negativity is diminished or counteracted by one of the other leaves. The only exception to this is the wine leaf. Belonging to Dionysos in a way that none of the others do, it has no negative aspects. Indeed it transforms everything around it into a positive and indicates the ultimate success of a situation. There are other tips and tricks involved with this system, but you'll learn them the more you practice and develop the ability to hear what the leaves have to tell you. This system isn't for everyone and it requires hard work and dedication – as well as a strong relationship with Dionysos – to master.

Here are the leaves:

Ακοιτης (Akoites)
You're on the right path, a divine calling or higher purpose, commitment, fidelity, doing what's necessary to attain one's goals even when one has to make tough choices and sacrifices, clarity, honesty, seeing through deception.
Reversed: blindness, aimless wandering, uncertainty, lack of dedication, shirking one's responsibilities, willful ignorance, pursuing things that are bad for you even when you realize it, letting fear get the better of you.

Αμπελος (Ampelos: The Vine)
Growth, unfolding, the process of a thing, connection, binding together, strength, nature and everything related to earthiness, cultivating the gifts of the gods, having a solid foundation, heat and passion.
Reversed: Entanglement, unhealthy relationships, being smothered or overpowered by something, decay, a need to cut things out of one's life or minimize obligations.

Αριαδνη (Ariadne)
Love, marriage, unity, redemption, wholeness, fulfillment, mysterious feminine power, help from an unexpected source, the unraveling of understanding, a journey through the maze, transformation to a higher state.
Reversed: Loneliness, abandonment, being lost in the dark, unable to find one's way, cruelty, a need to discover one's own power and purpose, denigration of the feminine.

Αστρον (Astron: The Star)
Illumination, revelation, guidance, destiny, insight from a heavenly or unexpected source, hidden things brought to light, have patience and the answer will present itself to you.
Reversed: Doubt, uncertainty, losing one's way, ulterior motives, deception, caution before proceeding and a call to introspection.

Ἑρμης (Hermes)
Friendship, divine assistance, communication, luck, magic, thinking your way out of a tight spot, seek the aid of this god.
Reversed: A misunderstanding, a breakdown in communication, bad luck, trouble, someone is conspiring against you, you *really* need the aid of this god.

Ἡρα (Hera)
Relationships, marriage, the home, wealth, concern with material or domestic matters, a powerful, domineering woman, conflict arising from these sources.
Reversed: You've pissed off a woman in your life and now she's out to get you, unfair persecution, vengeance pursued beyond justifiable measure, a serious problem involving relationships and the home.

Ἠριγονη (Erigone)
Loyalty, faithfulness, devotion to others even at the cost of one's own self, trials, ultimate vindication even if opinion is currently against you, a difficult or melancholy atmosphere.
Reversed: Failure, depression, a situation outside of one's control, a tendency for morbid thoughts and self-harming, seeing things as worse than they actually are, a cry for help, the need for outside intervention.

Ἥφαιστος (Hephaistos)
Work, doing what's necessary to get the job done, attention to detail, absorption in one's calling, beauty found in unexpected places or coming from unlikely sources, the workplace and everything related to it.
Reversed: Laziness, lack of skill, more effort is required of you, the failure of something you were trying to accomplish, problems in the workplace, holding on to a grudge even when it hurts everyone around you.

Θυρσος (Thyrsos)
Tools, resources, raw potential, the focusing of the will, directing energy towards a specific goal, virility, authority, the conduit through which the miraculous manifests in our lives.
Reversed: Impotency, interruption of flow, lacking what it necessary to accomplish one's goals, not knowing how to use what one has, being cut off from the source.

Κισσος (Kissos: The Ivy)
Protection, nurturing, vitality, the ability to thrive under any conditions, expansion, being emotionally cool and aloof, caring only for one's own self.
Reversed: Selfishness, difficulty dealing with others, too much of a good thing, feeling strangled or smothered, co-dependent relationships, indifference to the suffering of others including when you're the cause of it, a cold-hearted bastard.

Κρατηρ (Krater: The Mixing Bowl)
Balance, synthesis, powerful forces coming together, mixing things up, agitation, fullness, bounty, receptacle for divine blessings, flow, pouring into.
Reversed: Too much of a good thing, imbalance, a need to seek out a complimentary opposite, feeling shaken up or overwhelmed by constant stress, a need to stir the pot and see what happens when things become too settled or stagnant, emptiness, poverty, a lack of divine blessing or presence.

Μαιναδες (Mainades)
Passion, devotion, freedom, throwing off the shackles to follow the desire of one's heart, inability to cope with the daily grind, breaking taboos and conventional roles, doing the unexpected and seemingly impossible, being one's own person regardless of the consequences, an unstable woman.
Reversed: If you don't change your situation right now you're going to go mad – and not in a good way, feeling trapped and overwhelmed, living an

inauthentic life, beset on all sides by a host of problems that chase you down and tear you apart mercilessly.

Μαινας (Mainas: Madness)
Intense emotional states, an alternation of consciousness is needed, inspiration, breaking down boundaries, the imagination, disconnect from reality, strange and disturbing behavior, access to wisdom and spiritual gifts unattainable by ordinary means.
Reversed: Delusions, harmful impulses, addiction, paranoia, inability to function, everything you are thinking about the situation is wrong and going to lead to unpleasant consequences, failure of the imagination, healing is called for.

Μιδας (Midas)
Wealth, blessing, the material realm, getting what you want. However, those familiar with the story of Midas will understand that what we want isn't always what's best for us. As such it can also signify lack of understanding, the misuse of what's been given to us, greed, selfishness, being overly concerned with finances and a failure to see the big picture.
Reversed: Money troubles, anxiety, neglecting what's important in life, lack of control and stability, and a warning to stop looking for the easy fix.

Μινυαδες (Minyades)
Arrogance, extremism, control issues, being too driven, a workaholic, failure to enjoy the good things in life, expecting too much out of others, an unfair situation.
Reversed: A crisis is looming because of the above – it may even be too late. Change or dine if it's about you; get out of the way if it's not. Don't even bother trying to talk sense into them, as they won't listen.

Μουσαι (Mousai: The Muses)
Creativity, inspiration, the arts, culture, beauty, charm, fresh ideas, a new way of looking at things, the gifts of the gods.
Reversed: Frustration, the source of creativity is blocked, stagnation, stupidity, brute force, a need to rekindle the flame or look at things in a different way.

Νηος (Neos: Ship)
A journey which can be physical or metaphorical, transformation, a change of scenery and with it a new perspective on things, strangeness, the unexpected, bounty, divine gifts, cutting ties, the start of a new phase of life.
Reversed: Stagnation, going nowhere, set adrift without moorings, feeling trapped, a desperate need for the positive qualities of the lead in one's life.

'Οινος (Oinos: Wine)
Success, abundance, joy, the gift of Dionysos – it makes everything better. It cannot be reversed and cancels out any negativity in the other leaves that are drawn with it.

'Οινοτρόποι (Oinotropoi: The Winegrowers)
Cultivating the gifts you have, doing the seemingly impossible, utilizing your resources to help others, generosity, actively working to improve a situation, the favor of the gods provided you hold up your end of the bargain.
Reversed: Squandering your gifts, negligence, being taken advantage of, failing to live up to your potential or doing what you know is right.

'Ορος (Oros: The Mountain)
Ascending the heights, a goal, success after a difficult struggle, resolution, superiority, gaining a better perspective on an issue, solitude, separating oneself from the crowd and ordinary life.
Reversed: You haven't gone far enough or done enough, difficult work lies ahead, being down in the dumps, matter triumphing over the spiritual, failure because of a lack of effort or vision, inability to get away from one's problems.

'Ορφεύς (Orpheus)
Creativity, inspiration, hidden wisdom, initiation, descent, depths, a heroic quest, journeys both literal and metaphorical, overcoming obstacles, a time of testing to see what one is made of, introspection and transformation, maturity and power gained through suffering.
Reversed: The journey is incomplete. One must go back down and truly face their fears. Brashness and foolishness, egotism masquerading as concern for others, being cut off from the source of creativity.

'Οφις (Ophis: The Snake)
Transformation, shedding one's skin, adopting a new identity or perspective on things, subtlety, secret wisdom, chthonic forces, cold, alien, a lack of emotion, doing what's necessary regardless of what others think, the unknown and unfamiliar.
Reversed: Danger, deception, unexpected problems seemingly arising out of nowhere, a need to go deeper and cultivate the positive qualities of this leaf.

Πενθεύς (Pentheus)
Conflict, overbearing personality, failure to understand nuance, stubbornness, control freak, refusal to listen to other sides in an argument, haughty or abusive language, delusion, spiritual blindness, blundering into situations you aren't prepared to deal with, holding onto outmoded ideas even when they bring you nothing but trouble, unthinkingly perpetuating cycles of violence.
Reversed: Can either mean that the person is beginning to see the error of their ways and is leaving all that behind them or else it's a dire warning of immanent doom.

Πρόσωπον (Prosopon: The Mask)
Mystery, a hint that things may not be what they seem and one should continue peeling back the layers, an indication that the issues has to do with

perception, identity and psychology; it may also indicate that the gods are behind an encounter or situation, even if one does not fully understand how or why.
Reversed: Delusion, active deception, be wary of a person or situation, dissonance between what one does and feels, being trapped in a false and unfulfilling role.

Σατυροι (Satyroi: Satyrs)
Mirth, freedom, sexual rapaciousness, connection with the vital forces of existence, instincts, animality, a reminder to enjoy life and spend less time worrying about what others think and the roles they try to force us into, a crude, rude and uncivilized person.
Reversed: Overindulgence, lack of discipline, misfortune caused by an inability to take things seriously, a call to change one's ways before that happens. Alternately, sterility, being too much in one's head, a need to cultivate one's more foolish qualities.

Σεμελη (Semele)
Maternal, nurturing, self-sacrifice, intensity, being consumed by something, closeness to the gods regardless of the cost, destruction brought about by foolish choices.
Reversed: Being smothered, holding back too much, emotional entanglements, a martyr complex, being taken advantage of or deceived.

Ταυρος (Tauros: The Bull)
Fertility, masculinity, power, rushing headlong into a situation, trampling the obstacles in one's path, stubborn commitment to a cause or idea.
Reversed: Being too focused on the material, refusal to listen to others or give a situation the thought it deserves, lack of virility or passion.

Τιτανοι (Titanoi: The Titans)
Obstacles, conflict, destructive forces whether internal or external, the odds are stacked against you, feeling trapped or persecuted no matter what you attempt to do to fix the situation, being torn apart or pulled in different directions.
Reversed: Most of the time it has the same meaning only to a much worse extent. However if all of the accompanying leaves are positive it can mean triumphing over obstacles or a crisis is coming to an end. However one should still be cautious as the negative influence may linger on undetected for a while.

You will need to make your own set. You can do this a number of different ways. You can inscribe the words on tiles or pieces of wood or pebbles or even actual leaves. You can make cards with them by printing the words or collaging images and other representations of the symbols and concepts onto paper or board. You could also assign numerical values to each of the leaves and use dice to get your answers, though I don't really recommend this course of action.

Once you have created your set of leaves you should consecrate them to Dionysos and treat them with the utmost respect and reverence. The more you use them the more energy and life and Dionysian spirit they will acquire. Merely handling them can become a powerful way to connect with the god. And you may find other uses for them beyond just divination. They can be great for meditation, magical operations, devotional activities and even aids to the creative process. Several times now I've been working on a story and run into writer's block, unsure of how to proceed. I asked the leaves for help, dug a couple out and sure enough they provided me with the answer. In fact a couple of the pieces in this collection were finished that way.

I believe that that is everything you need to know to get started with them. Hopefully they will be as beneficial to you as they have been for me.

DIONYSOS THE MAGICAL GOD

It is almost axiomatic to say that magic and Dionysos are connected. After all, magic at its core is about transformation: the alchemist turning lead into gold; the Wiccan chanting over her candle to attract love into her life; the Roman Catholic priest performing the Rite of Exorcism to drive a demon out of a child. Each of these is but a different form of transformation, and that is the essence of our god: change, blending, releasing, mutation, revealing what is hidden – a whirlwind of manifestation.

Historically, a number of different types of magic were closely associated with him. Plutarch and Plato attribute all of the telestitic arts to him: divination, prophecy, visions, ecstatic trance, and kathartic healing or cleansing. Further, Dionysos is a mediumistic divinity, a gateway between the world of the living and that of the dead. At his festivals the world of the spirits blends with our own. At Anthesteria the dead walk around and must be placated; at the Rural Dionysia they possess actors who give them voices and bodies with which to move. In a fragment of Herakleitos, magoi and Bakchoi were linked, and many of the descriptions traditionally used of witches – eerie powers, imagined sexual voraciousness, shunning traditional gender roles, nocturnal rites out of doors, etc. – would also apply to mainades.

Dionysos is scarcely mentioned, however, in the extant literature on Greek magic, the *defixiones* and lead curse tablets that are found everywhere from Thessaly to Athens, as well as the later Greek Magical Papyri of Egypt. (The only mention of Dionysos there is in theophorics or people who were named after him.) This is especially odd considering the fact that there are numerous references to Orphic priests possessing magical powers (in a Satyr play of Euripides one of the satyrs brags of knowing a charm taught by Orpheus that'll ignite a piece of wood which he then threatens to cast into the Cyclops' eye). There are a number of remaining Orphic magical charms and formulae which do mention Dionysos – the most famous being the bone pieces from Olbia which confirmed a tie between Orphic and Bacchic groups, and the lamellae found throughout Southern Italy and other parts of the Greek world, both of which apparently guaranteed the wearers protection against underworld spirits. The later Neoplatonists and Theurgists were very interested in Dionysos. The Neoplatonic author Olympiodoros associated him with Phanês, and called him the present ruler of the world, while others interpreted his dismemberment at the hands of the Titans as symbolizing the original unity of creation being split into its constituent parts in the primal elements. Another interesting strain of thought was in associating him with foreign deities such as Osiris and the Jewish god Iao/Ialdobaoth, both of whom had strong connections with magic and are perhaps the best represented gods in the Magical Papyri.

This cursory glance at the history of Greek magic should be enough to confirm Dionysos' connection with it and while it justifies the practice of magic by religious Dionysians, it certainly doesn't answer how one might integrate the two. The obvious answer is that you integrate the two by practicing them. The festivals and routine practices represent only one end of the spectrum of your relationship with the god. They are formal, fixed, devotional activities which provide us with opportunities to know and honor the god and to feel his presence in recurring patterns. The other end of the spectrum is a more intimate immersion in the Dionysian – activities such as drinking, dancing, sex, creativity, philosophizing, etc., which we consecrate to him, which reveal the fullness of his presence in our lives and help us to know him as he is, not just as he was in antiquity or as the festivals reveal him to be. That still leaves a great deal on the continuum, activities not quite as passive and devotional as the festivals – whose purpose is to know the god – or consecration, which is about filling our lives with the sacred and experiencing Dionysos.

Magic can be a dynamic, hands-on, willed approach: the practical application of that knowledge and experience within our lives in order to bring about desired changes. Because Dionysos as the *goes* or magician has something important to say even to those who will never pick up a book on magic, never undertake to plum the secrets of the universe and work with the natural energies of creation – and that is this: everything in the world is constantly changing and you have a part to play in shaping how your life comes out. If you are unsatisfied with how things are, change them. Dionysos is a powerful ally in this, for he helps dissolve boundaries and limitations, helps give us the courage and strength to make those changes, even if they are not easy, and shows us that our neat categories aren't quite so solid as we might expect. Under his influence the world becomes magical, filled with possibility and unfolding manifestation. Studying magic – learning how to work with those energies, how to communicate with spirits, how to use divination and incantations – can be a very profound way to honor that aspect of him.

They also augment the more purely religious aspects of worship. For instance, there are a number of steps within the traditional Greek religious ceremony which are decidedly magical in nature, but which tend to get overlooked and hence only poorly performed by those in the anti-magic camp. The first of these is the purification and banishing of *keres* or evil spirits/influences. This is done with the scattering of barley and the recitation of a line of Greek by many. But they do this as if they think that will be enough, as if simply tossing some granules and reciting words will properly banish these forces. Is it any wonder that their rituals are often sub-par and have many things go wrong throughout? You have to fill your words with power, you have to be very conscious of driving those spirits out, of consecrating pure, true, and powerful sacred space. And you can't really do that unless you have some idea of how this works, of what magic entails. The same applies to divination, which traditionally should take place during every sacrifice. But unless the *mantis* truly understands his office and how to trigger the altered state necessary to perceive the divine will – he's pretty much just talking out of his ass, projecting what his conscious mind wants onto the phenomena.

And lastly, in some rituals actual spiritual transformation must take place – the single grain of wheat at the Eleusinia and the animal carcass at the *omophagia* both must become filled with the divine presence – and if you don't understand how this comes about, what the priests must do to enact this change then there is bound to be an emptiness within the rite which will eventually lead to a spiritual emptiness within those who take part in it. So while it is not necessary to be a practicing magician, one must have an understanding and appreciation of magic to do the rituals in their proper manner.

NOTHING TO DO WITH DIONYSOS?

I've long pondered the near complete absence of Dionysos from the Greek Magical Papyri, especially in light of his prominence within the society of Greco-Roman Egypt. As far as I can tell there are only a couple theophoric names belonging to individuals mentioned in the spells, as well as words for madness that in other contexts have a strong Dionysian association. And that's pretty much it. No direct invocation of the god, no allusion to his myths and symbols, and seemingly no awareness of his presence in the land. Even those names are hardly significant since Dionysian nomenclature was about as commonplace back then as James and Sarah are for us.

One might assume that his absence could be explained by the fact that the dominant religious paradigm and milieu of the papyri was thoroughly Egyptian despite the language in which they were written, but this doesn't really hold up. Not only can we find traces of contemporary philosophical thought as well as extensive quotations from Homer and other Classical authors, but there is a wealth of Hellenic religious ideas, mythological material, hymns to the Greek gods and the like mixed into them. In fact we don't just find references to the major Greek gods who made a home in Egypt for themselves (such as Zeus, Apollon, Hermes, Aphrodite and Hekate), as one might expect, but a whole host of minor divinities that must have been fairly obscure even back in their homeland. In fact the Greco-Egyptian magicians prided themselves on an exhaustive and ecumenical knowledge of the divine forces that inhabited the world, and their invocations often read like a Who's Who of the *oikonomos*. It's not uncommon to find Greek, Egyptian, Persian, Levantine and Judeo-Christian divinities rubbing shoulders with each other in the PGM – so the fact that they didn't bother to call upon Dionysos stands out as fairly significant.

Of course Dionysos isn't abundantly represented in the magical literature of Greece and Rome either, so that may have something to do with it. Of the thousands of spells and *defixiones* that have so far been discovered, Dionysos can be found in only a handful of them and that number decreases significantly if you reject his equation with Euboulios and similar shadowy, ill-defined chthonic figures. Most of the references to Dionysos and magic are literary and Orphic. Herakleitos mentions magicians alongside bacchantes, lenai, night-walkers and other Dionysian figures. Herodotos discusses the similarities between Magi and Orphic-Bacchic initiates, as does the anonymous commentator of the Derveni papyrus (although they may have been referring to the Persian priestly caste and not conventional magic-users.) Euripides has his satyrs mention that they know a magical charm of Orpheus that would be effective against the Cyclops and Plato speaks of Orphic begging-priests who go door to door promising to cast out angry ghosts through their secret rites. Likewise Theophrastos lumps together Orphics, devotees of Sabazios and those who employ magic charms in his analysis of the superstitious man. The golden Orphic-Bacchic lamellae with their occult invocations and elaborate guides to the underworld are not substantially different from much that we find in the corpus of Greco-Egyptian magical papyri. In Italy I can think of even less evidence: only Livy's false priest and singer of charms from Magna Graecia who was responsible for the introduction of the Bacchanalia comes to mind. That isn't a whole lot in support of Dionysos' connection to the magical arts, but it's a lot more than many gods we find in the PGM have, especially in light of Dionysos' immense popularity in that time and place.

I've actually considered that as a possible explanation. After all magic is traditionally a counter-cultural, peripheral phenomenon and Dionysos was undeniably a god of the elite and upper class, especially during the reign of the Ptolemies – though his cult was also favored by the Imperial authorities who gave special benefits and tax exemption to the Dionysian priests and artistic guilds. Although this could explain the reluctance of the Greco-Egyptian magicians to call upon him, I find it less than convincing for three primary reasons.

1) Not all Greco-Egyptian magicians were rebellious outsiders. Indeed, many of the magicians came from the upper class of Egyptian society and served in the temples, which is where they acquired their esoteric lore and magical proficiency.

2) Plenty of other gods in the PGM have even more of a claim to being prominent cultural figures favored by the ruling establishment. I'm thinking in particular of Zeus, Apollon, Aphrodite and Helios on the Greek side and Osiris, Isis, Ptah and Re on the Egyptian, although this number could be increased almost indefinitely. Certainly if they had no qualms about including these other gods they wouldn't have been too bothered by Dionysos' royal pedigree. Indeed, it is power above all else that is reverenced in the PGM so I'd think that Dionysos' connections would be a point in his favor.

3) Dionysos' cult was hardly limited to the elite. Not only was he popular among the poor and residents outside the capital – especially in the Faiyum where several small villages were named after him and every third person seems to have a Dionysian theophoric – his cult could also inspire dangerous, seditious notions. That's why Ptolemy Philopator took action to standardize the Dionysian cults in the *khora* and bring them under the control of a central authority. Later on Dionysios Petoserapis led a popular uprising against the crown, almost succeeding in deposing the Ptolemies. He appears to have had some connections to the cult beyond just his name, although precise details are elusive. Most strikingly, however, in the early years of Roman occupation a group of armed brigands calling themselves Boukoloi – a term we find often in Dionysos' cult – were led by a priest in a savage conflict with the invaders, involving guerrilla tactics that sometimes included

human sacrifice and ritualized cannibalism, if our Roman sources are to be believed. So clearly Dionysos' cult was just as popular among the oppressed and disenfranchised as it was among the ruling elite.

Another possible explanation is that the Greco-Egyptian magicians may simply have felt that Dionysos was redundant since Osiris featured so prominently in their spells and rituals already. As far back as Herodotos the identity of these two had seemed a foregone conclusion. Under the Ptolemies the process of syncretic fusion was heightened until Dionysian iconography was indistinguishable from that of Osiris. Not only did they come to share the same visual traits, but epithets and even mythological tales were swapped as well, so that in the end they truly seemed to be one and the same god. This is how most authors of the Hellenistic and early Roman period regard them and so, perhaps, did the composers of the magical papyri. The only problem here is that the authors of the magical papyri tend to glory in listing all of the different forms and culturally shaped expressions that a particular god may have, even when they feel there is some sort of underlying unity there. It's a way of saying you are so great that you are known by all these different names in different lands and my wisdom is so great because I possess an intimate knowledge of such things. It seems unlikely, then, that they would have left out such an important piece of information if that was indeed what they were thinking.

A final possibility is that the Greco-Egyptian magicians just didn't feel that Dionysos' interests and powers were relevant to their own magical operations and thus didn't bother to invoke him. Except that Dionysos wasn't viewed predominantly as the joyful, fun-loving god of wine and theater in Greco-Roman Egypt. More often he was seen as a terrifying and powerful chthonic figure, a god of the dead and the underworld – hence his identification with Osiris. Alternately they viewed him as a god of abundant vegetative life or the triumphant conqueror of the world. These are precisely the themes that we find repeated throughout the PGM. Even the sunny Olympians became transformed into shadowy underworld forces and nasty chthonic daimones are found in love spells, threatening violence, disease, madness and death on the unresponsive intended paramour. If Dionysos would be at home anywhere it'd be the crepuscular, schizophrenic realm of the magicians' subconscious.

And yet he's not, which really only leaves us with two viable options. Either the Greco-Egyptian magicians completely ignored the god for reasons that we may never fully understand – or else they didn't and that evidence just hasn't come to light yet. After all the PGM is not a single, self-contained piece of literature. It was compiled in the 19th and 20th centuries by scholars from a variety of random scraps of papyrus and pottery shards upon which spells, formulas, ritual procedures, and magical recipe books had been inscribed. This material was found all over Egypt and dated from the 1st to 6th centuries of the common era. Although the PGM is a large volume, including several hundred different sources, it would be foolish to assume that it represented the sum total of the magical literature produced in Greco-Roman Egypt. Indeed, several supplementary volumes have been published and new texts are being discovered all the time. There are even a great number of fragmentary sources that scholars haven't gotten around to translating yet and who knows what may still lie hidden in the sands? Maybe Dionysos' name will crop up in some of these – or already has though the general populace is not yet aware of it. Who knows, maybe we'll even find a hitherto unknown body of Dionysian myths, the *hieroi logoi* that Philopator referenced in his decree or something else that will radically alter our conception of things. You never know what will happen in the wild world of archaeology – but until such a time I will continue to ponder this apparent enigma of the absence of a magical Greco-Egyptian Dionysos.

THE SYMBOLS OF DIONYSOS

Communication is not always verbal or written. Indeed, for most of the long history of humanity we were illiterate and had to make do with oral accounts, painting and plastic representations of our thoughts. An intricate system of symbolic language arose, especially surrounding the divine forces which we call gods. This rich, dynamic language conveys truth far better, in my opinion, than oral accounts and especially written accounts. So much is lost in writing things down. The nuance and impression of a statue can never be captured in words, no matter how great the poet. It's a different language, a different world altogether. Even so, I am going to discuss some of the symbols associated with Dionysos, those things which we find repeatedly represented in art and myth and the cult of the god. The symbolic language is an important one – and it is also a specific one. Generally, the things associated with one god will not be found among others. And if there is overlap in some areas (for instance both Athene and Zeus share the aegis) they will not share all of their symbols. This is how we distinguish one god from another in artwork: Zeus carries the lightning-bolt and has an eagle while Poseidon has the trident and a conch-shell; Athene wears a helmet and aegis, Aphrodite has a mirror and doves.

These are the things sacred to Dionysos.

Boots

Dionysos was often depicted wearing the *cothurnus* or high-heeled buskin, which was adopted by the actors who performed on stage at his feast days. Robert Graves maintains that Dionysos was a "lame" god and that this special boot was either meant to disguise or support his wounded heel or thigh. He says that the priests of Dionysos were likewise maimed and so wore the special shoe for this reason. On the other hand the Greeks themselves claimed actors wore them simply because high-heeled boots made them appear taller.

Bull

Of all of the animals that man has domesticated few of them possess the power and virility of the bull. Despite its intimidating size the bull moves with a startling agility. The lethal potential of its horns are difficult to forget if you have ever been witness to a goring. In ancient Crete a beautiful yet deadly sport arose as part of their religious festivals: bull-vaulting, where athletic young men and women would run towards the charging creature, take hold of its horns, and lift themselves up and over the beast's hurtling frame. This sport is attested in stunning frescoes and statues that survive to this day. The bull was also offered in sacrifices, the *hekatomb* or slaughter of a hundred bulls being the Homeric ideal, though the standard sacrifice was generally much smaller. It is no wonder that Dionysos, the god of masculine power and sudden violence would be associated with this animal and this connection is well attested. Dionysos was frequently called the horned god, and specifically the bull-horned god. In *The Bakchai* of Euripides Pentheus comes to gloat over his captive, only to find the beautiful stranger vanished and in his place a raging bull. The women of Elis asked him to come "rushing with thy bull-foot" and chanted "Come, worthy bull, worthy bull!" Plutarch recounts how the Argives called him the bull-born and roused him from the deep waters with trumpets hidden in their thyrsoi. In several vase decorations Dionysos is depicted either standing beside a bull or riding atop one. And the mainades only confirm this connection through their ritual of *omophagia* or the eating of raw flesh. In myth the wild women would fall upon the bull, tearing it apart with their bare hands and teeth. They would bite into the bull while the creature still lived and tear off chunks of its raw flesh, which they would then consume. This was viewed as a sacramental feast, consumption of the god in his animal form for the purpose of integrating his power and virility into their own bodies. Although the ritual of *omophagia* is attested outside of myth as well it is doubtful that women actually fell upon live bulls and consumed them in that manner. In late Roman times the ritual had been diluted almost to the point of losing its original potency and meaning altogether. An initiate, of either gender, would take a piece of raw flesh, put it in their mouth and then spit it out.

Drama

Drama apparently originated with the annual rites of Dionysos; tragedy commemorating the terrible suffering and dismemberment of the god, comedy the joyous and riotous exuberance surrounding his triumph over death and return to the living world. At first the rites were simple affairs consisting of small choruses who sang special songs such as the *dithyramb*. Eventually the choruses grew more complex and individual parts developed. Even after the plays ceased to be directly about the joys and sorrows of Dionysos, they were still performed at his festivals: new dramatic presentations were debuted at the City Dionysia and there were competitions with prizes awarded for the best plays; the Rural Dionysia would see repeat performances of the plays in areas outside of Athens. The Greeks loved their dramas, so much so that people would travel from all over to witness the competitions. They lasted for almost six days and included processions, songs, dances and feasts as well. During the Hellenistic Age, after Alexander had brought Greek culture to the places he conquered, no city was complete without its Greek theater. Special seats of honor were reserved for priests of Dionysos.

Flute

The flute or *aulos* was said to be invented by Athene, who promptly discarded it because it distorted the features of the player. Marsyas, a satyr companion of Dionysos, found the flute and became so skilled at playing it that he dared to challenge Apollon on his lyre. He lost and was flayed for his arrogance. The flute was generally not favored by the Olympians or used in their worship — but it became a central instrument in that of Dionysos and the Phrygian Magna Mater Kybele. There were a number of different kinds of flutes — single and double — made of a variety of materials including reed, box, bay, ivory, or bone. The double flute consisted of two flutes connected by a band fastened around the head. Flute music stirs the passions and was even thought to incite madness. Hence, it is the perfect music for Dionysos.

Goat

Common perception holds that goats are lazy, ugly, stubborn and the very image of lustfulness. For Christians the goat is dark, sinful, and earthy — as opposed to the pure lambs of Jesus' parable — and was early associated with Satan and his followers. The Jews used to symbolically place all of the sins of the tribe upon the goat and send him off into the desert wilderness — the origin of the term "scapegoat." All of this makes him uniquely associated with Dionysos, who represents all of those things and was himself called *Eriphos* or "the kid," as well as *Melanaigis* "the black-skinned goat" when he was honored in the feast of Apaturia. Goats frequently appear in iconography or on amphorae with Dionysos and tragedy, which means the "goat-song," has its name either because of this connection or because a goat was given as the prize for the best presentation. But their relationship is not entirely a pleasant one. Dionysos was known as *Aigobolos* or "slayer of goats" and goats were commonly sacrificed on his altars. The reason for their enmity seems to be the fondness the goat has for eating wild vine, a plant sacred to Dionysos. For eating the vine he punished the goat and thereafter the goat was killed to make amends to the god.

Grapes

The grape is the fruit *par excellence* of the god. It is his special gift to gods and men alike and he was felt mystically to be present within them. Bunches of grapes were a common symbol of the god and were often depicted in his hair, hanging from his thyrsos or being held up as an offering. One of his children was even called *Staphylos,* the Grape.

Ivy

Dionysos was called *Kissos,* "the ivy" and with the vine it is his most common symbol. Ivy is a plant that, like Dionysos, has two births. The first birth is when it sends out its shade-seeking shoots with their distinctive leaves. But after the dormant months of winter, when the god himself is reborn it sends out another shoot, one that grows upright and towards the light, thus honoring the return of the vibrant god. When the fire of Zeus' lightning consumed Semele — with Dionysos still in her womb — it was the cool ivy that surrounded and protected him. Perhaps this was why ivy was allowed within the sanctuary of Dionysos, though it was forbidden everywhere else. When the satyrs were first given wine they were driven mad by its effects. Dionysos placed ivy around them and the plant extinguished the heat of the wine, allowing them to regain their senses – though ivy itself produces a strong poison which has intoxicating properties. The ivy leaf was tattooed on the hand of Dionysian initiates. And Dionysos and his mainades are always pictured wearing crowns of ivy. Sometimes it is a simple crown with only a few leaves to let you know that it's not just a fillet of some sort while other times Dionysos has a full foliate head, with flowering leaves and bunches of grapes hanging down.

Kantharos

The *kantharos* was a special drinking cup said to be invented by the god himself. Unlike the *skyphos* which was round with small handles, the *kantharos* had a high base and projecting handles that stretched from the rim to the foot of the cup. Dionysos' own *kantharos* was always full and could never be drained – even by the great and lusty Herakles himself. The wine that it produced was unrivaled in all the world. One drop from it would make a man drunk – though without any of the negative side-effects that alcohol often produces.

Liknon

Dionysos was called *Liknites* meaning "He of the *Liknon.*" Odysseus was told to travel until he met a people who would mistake the oar he carried for a *liknon*, which is a winnowing fan used to sift the chaff from the wheat. It has an open end in which things can be stored and it was to this use that it was put in the mysteries of Dionysos and of the Two Goddesses at Eleusis. Fruit, grain and a phallos were stored within the *liknon*, and then covered over to be displayed at the height of the ceremony. The *liknon* was said to be the cradle of Dionysos, and he was thought to be truly present within the fruits and grain and phallos, symbol of the masculine force of creation. The *liknon* itself was used for purification. The person seeking to be purified would be veiled and the *liknon* would be passed over their heads. The purifier would speak certain words and then gently touch the *liknon* to their heads, thus making them pure through contagion.

Mask

Masks were used in the rituals of Dionysos, both those that led to the creation of drama and after. Sometimes individuals would don masks of the god or of his satyr companions and would either act out parts, or become possessed by the god or a spirit. Another way that they were used was by affixing the mask of Dionysos to a pillar or herm and then dressing it up and draping it with vines and ivy. This statue was very crude, without arms or legs, and just the human features of the mask. Libations were offered and dances performed around it. The mask suggests something profound and inhuman about the god. Even when we experience communion with the god and are filled completely with him – he is still not us. He is within us. We are a part of him. But he is still the Other. He will always remain the Other, no matter how hard we try to understand him. That is his nature. Tersteegen said, "A god who is understood is no god." And it is only when we accept this that the god lifts his mask and allows us a glimpse of himself. That we are viewing yet another mask when he does this is incidental – it is true revelation nonetheless.

Nebrex

Like shamans the world over, the ecstatic female worshipers of Dionysos had a special animal-skin cloak that they put on when reveling in his honor. It was made out of fawnskin and was called a *nebrex*. With the ivy crown and thyrsos it comprised the "outfit" of the mainad. Saffron robes were also worn by celebrants.

Panther

All wild animals are connected to Dionysos, but none more so than the lion or panther. The supple, feline elegance of its body, the ferocious and easily provoked temper, the boundless appetite and uncanny intelligence of the creature make it uniquely and inevitably linked to the Dionysiac sphere – and indeed, the wild cat is frequently depicted in the company of the wild god. Like the Magna Mater, Dionysos' cart was drawn by lions and panthers. The cats freely accompanied him at other times, sitting tamely at his feet like puppies, or dancing enraptured with the rest of creation during the Bacchic revel. When Dionysos sought to punish someone – Lykourgos for instance – the wild cat was often the agent of the god's awful chastisement.

Phallus

For the ancients the phallos represented the source of life and was a symbol of virility, courage, and power. The *Shiva Purana* says that the phallos is the "sole means of obtaining earthly pleasure and salvation. By looking at it, touching it, and meditating on it, living beings are capable of freeing themselves from the cycle of future lives." (1.9.20) According to Greek tradition, it was Dionysos who carved the first phallos out of fig-wood to commemorate Prosymnos, who had rendered a great service to him. After that the phallos was ubiquitous in the realm of Dionysos – it was carried in processions, herms and other phallic monuments were erected in his honor and a phallos was concealed inside the *liknon*. With Aphrodite, Dionysos had a son, Priapos, a hideous being whose penis was so large that he had to support it by means of a pulley and strings. Representations of Priapos were installed in gardens, both to encourage fertility and the growth of their fruit, but also to protect the garden from thieves. Those who were caught trespassing were punished by being placed on the garden god's erect member. Priapos warned, "si fur veneris, impudicus exis" ("In a thief and out a faggot").

Ship

In *Homeric Hymn* 7 Dionysos is abducted by pirates who – thinking him a young, beautiful prince – intend to ransom him off to his father. They soon discover that he is actually a god when the ship begins to flow with wine, vines cover the mast and wild animals appear, tearing the captain apart. The rest of the pirates jump overboard – only to be turned into dolphins – except for the helmsman Akoites, who had tried to warn them about their captive.

This became a popular theme and was repeated by poets and vase-painters many times over – most exceptionally in the Exekias vase. Dionysos also had a ship that was dragged through the streets on his festival day at the head of a grand procession, the origins of latter-day Carnival floats according to many scholars.

Thyrsus

The thyrsos is the staff of Dionysos and his mainades, a fennel stalk wrapped with ivy-leaves and vines and topped by a pine-cone. In the *Bakchai* of Euripides the mainades are able to bring up wine, water, milk and honey by touching the thyrsos to the ground or tapping it against a rock, and when they make an expedition against the people who live near Kithairon they use their thyrsoi as deadly weapons, casting them like spears, which puncture the armor of their enemies. In Homer Lykourgos boasts of having made the mainades drop their thyrsoi as they fled from him.

Toga virilis

On March 17 during the Roman festival of *Liberalia*, held in honor of Liber (Dionysos), Libera (Ariadne or Persephone) and Ceres (Demeter), the *toga virilis* or *toga libera* was donned. This was a white toga symbolizing that the boy (usually around 14) had passed from childhood and was now *iuvenis*, a young man. The purple-edged *toga praetexta* of childhood was put away and sacrifices were offered to Juventas, goddess of childhood in the temple of Jupiter Optimus Maximus. This was an important step in the ritual life of the individual, comparable to our rites of handing over the car keys to teenagers. Ovid says that Dionysos is associated with the *toga virilis* either because he is depicted as a young man, midway between childhood and adulthood or because he is a father, and it is into his care that fathers place their sons.

Toys

According to the Orphic poets, Dionysos-Zagreus, while still a child, was torn apart by the jealous Titans. To distract the powerful child they offered him a series of toys – knucklebones, a little ball, a lump of wool, a jointed doll that bent at the knee, a bull-roarer, a multi-colored spinning top, fair golden apples from the clear-voiced Hesperides, some pomegranates in honey and finally a mirror, which succeeded in capturing the child's attention. While he was distracted they fell upon him and tore him apart with their murderous knives. They boiled his flesh and ate it, but were interrupted during their feast by Zeus who burned them up with his lightning bolts. From the steam that rose from the ash mankind was formed, so that we possess a half-divine and half-titanic nature which we must strive to purify. The Orphic mysteries sought to accomplish this and according to Clement of Alexandria, these toys were kept in the home as tokens or symbolic reminders of the mysteries. The "toys" probably had some esoteric meaning to the initiates – for instance, Dionysos being mesmerized by the mirror suggests the unrepentant soul caught up in itself – though some have suggested that they were just common, everyday toys that any child would play with.

Trees

Some of Dionysos' other names are: *Anthios* "god of all blossoming things," *Kissos* "the ivy," *Phytalmios* "god of growth," *Setenaios* "god of the new crops," *Staphylos* "the grape," *Sykites* "god of fig-trees," *Euanthes* "the blossomer," *Dendrites* "tree-god." Dionysos is intimately connected with the vegetative world and is actually felt in the growth of all green things in the ripening of fruit on the vine and in the shade of a tree on a heated day. Jane Ellen Harrison said that he is present in "every tree and plant and natural product." An important aspect of Dionysos is the bridger of gaps, the uniter. He brings together the animal, divine, human, and vegetable worlds and shows their essential unity. Nietzsche describes it this way: under the inspiration of Dionysos "alienated, hostile or subjugated nature, too, celebrates her reconciliation with her lost son, man. The earth gladly offers up her gifts, and the ferocious creatures of the cliffs and deserts peacefully draw near. The chariot of Dionysos is piled high with flowers and garlands, and the earth yields up milk and honey."

Tympanon

The *tympanon* was a hand-drum used especially in the rites of Dionysos and the Magna Mater Kybele. The monotonous rhythm of the drumming – along with the sound of the flute, singing, dancing, the fire and darkness, and wine – contributed to an overpowering situation that we would call an altered state of consciousness but which the Greeks themselves called *ekstasis* or "stepping out of oneself" and *enthousiasmos* or "a god is within." While in these states people would experience visions, prophesize and undergo communion with or possession by the gods. This is further suggested by the *symbolon* of the Mysteries of Kybele mentioned by Eusebius of Caesarea (wrongly attributed to the Eleusinian Mysteries) which says, "I have eaten from the drum, I have drunk from the cymbal, I have learned the secrets of religion, I have entered the inner chamber." (This "inner chamber" was *pastos*, a wedding chamber, suggesting some kind of *hieros gamos*.) The mainades are almost always shown rapturously playing the *tympanon*.

Wine

Homer says that Semele bore Dionysos as a "joy to mankind" and Hesiod agreed, calling him "filled with joy." Euripides says that he is, with Demeter, the greatest of gods, and the most beneficial to mankind. The reason that Dionysos is so well-loved is that he has brought to us wearisome mortals an "end to all sorrows" which is "life-giving, healing every ill." Horace, in addressing the god, says, "You move with soft compulsion the mind that is often so dull, you restore hope to hearts distressed, give strength and horns to the poor man. Filled with you he trembles not as the truculence of kings or the soldiers' weapons." This gift to men and gods that Dionysos has brought is the fruit of the vine, care-stealing wine. Wine brings with it convivial happiness, it makes our speech flow eloquently, it allows us to be open and sharing, and spurs the timid youth to approach the beautiful matron he would never dare talk to, were he sober. It makes us forget our sorry lot, and shows us a world that is softer, brighter, just a little more beautiful than the world we usually inhabit. And it brings gentle sleep to us, and wonderful dreams. But nothing in the world is ever simply black or white – and the Greeks, being keen-minded and perceptive were well aware of the darker, and troubling aspects of wine. Too much wine made a man quarrelsome, rough, and headstrong. It unleashed terrible passions which could find expression in violence, madness, or death. The Greeks called wine a terrible conqueror and said that even other gods and the kentaurs fell victim to its baneful effects. Hence, moderation was suggested even by the wine-god himself, who time and again taught people to mix his gift with water to dilute its power. Only the headstrong or barbarians such as the Thracians and Celts drank wine unmixed.

ON THE RITUAL CRY

I haven't a clue what the famous ritual cry of the ancient Dionysians actually means. Although I've read more about the god and the history of his worship than is probably healthy, I haven't really come across scholarly consensus on the matter. A few brave souls have hazarded a guess, but the most honest amongst them readily admit that it's pure conjecture. The ancients themselves seem to have been equally baffled by its origins and ultimate meaning, which is rather peculiar considering its ubiquity. There is scarcely an account of the god's ecstatic votaries that does not repeat the cry. Indeed several of Dionysos' epithets directly derive from it. The cry in Greek is "Io euoi" though in Latin it becomes "Io evohe," with numerous variations for both of these.

As best we can tell it was simply a proclamation of intense emotion, triumphant joy, startled excitement, reverent awe and religious fervor all in one. As such it is comparable to the Christian exclamations "Amen!" or "Hallelujah!" or "Selah!" except that each of these has a discernable etymology within the Hebrew language, whether or not your average charismatic is conscious of this when he makes the cry. Some early Christian apologists attempted to trace the Dionysian exclamation back to Hebrew as well, suggesting that it enshrined a memory of Eve's temptation by the Devil in the garden of Eden. As "proof" of this they pointed out that Dionysos' ecstatic votaries handled serpents, the very form Old Scratch took when he tricked the Mother of All.

More profitably we might compare this cry to similar ritual exclamations found in other ancient Greek cults. The first part of it – "Io" – is actually quite popular and used for gods as diverse as Hermes, Zeus, Asklepios and Apollon. In the slightly modified forms "Ia" or "Ie" we find it used for female divinities, most prominently Aphrodite and Artemis. In this form we also find it attached to Apollon, though it can appear as "Hie" or "Hye" as well. These cries are most commonly accompanied by the epithet "Paian." Paian was originally an independent god of healing who is attested as Paion or Paieon or the even older Pa-ja-wo which is found in Cretan Linear B texts. Later on this epithet and ritual shout took on two separate but related connotations. First it retained its associations with healing and was used specifically of Apollon in his capacity as averter of plagues and other diseases. Secondly it was used as a rallying cry by soldiers – particularly among the Spartans and other Dorians – when they marched off to war. It was used to invoke the blessings of Apollon on behalf of the army, asking him to be near and protect those loyal to him, especially from disease and other evils common on the battlefield. In time this ritual cry became associated with other actions, particularly martial displays so that our sources speak of those who "danced the paian." The paean itself came to refer to hymns in praise of Apollon, especially in an epiphanic role or extolling his triumph over adversaries such as the Delphic serpent. Interestingly, at Delphi the paean was also associated with Dionysos, as in the syncretic hymn of Philodamos who equates the two deities and uses their epithets interchangeably.

A common theme running through all of these instances is, of course, the epiphany or manifestation of a divinity. We find it used most often for those gods who are closest to and most likely to appear to their followers in a cultic setting, while we generally do not find it attached to the more remote deities. Indeed it appears to be a mortal response to the sudden and commanding presence of his or her god, which is perhaps why it is so ubiquitously found in a Dionysian context, Dionysos being the epiphanic deity *par excellence.*

Of course that really only accounts for the first part of the exclamation. What are we to make of euoi/evohe?

Some have suggested that it is an example of *voces magicae*, an incomprehensible string of letters or barbaric sounds meant to induce an altered state through repetitive chanting or even a brief magical spell. In keeping with this some have conjectured that it's got elemental associations corresponding to the primary Greek vowels. I find this unlikely for a number of reasons.

First off, the Greeks had seven vowels while this word is comprised only of five (epsilon, upsilon, omicron and iota) so why doesn't it include the rest? Secondly, and more importantly, Dionysos is not generally one of the gods associated with magical practices in Greece. Indeed he appears to be wholly absent from the Greek Magical Papyri and earlier *defixiones*, etc., which is rather striking considering his prominent place in Hellenistic and Greco-Roman Egypt, as I've remarked on elsewhere. Thirdly, Dionysos only becomes associated with elemental speculation in late Neoplatonic sources which interpret his Zagrean dismemberment as the dissolution of primeval unity into its elemental parts. While this is a profound and fascinating way to look at things, it is also an artificially philosophical interpretation that has no basis in the earlier cult of the god. I rather doubt that your average housewife turned Bacchant ever conceived of the god in this fashion. Most likely she chanted these words with the others as a way to express the intense emotion she felt at the sudden nearness of her beloved god, without requiring that it meant anything deeper or more profound than that. And if it was good enough for them back then, I feel that it ought to be good enough for us today.

So join me in the rousing cry, mysterious yet enshrined by ancient tradition, as we shout to the heavens, "Io euoi! Io io evohe!"

HE MAKES ME WET

"God is in the rain." – Evey, *V for Vendetta*

It was a dark and stormy night.
I've always wanted to start a story that way, but in truth it was an overcast afternoon towards the end of summer. I was walking home after a long day at work, covered in a thin sheen of sweat from the heat and humidity. That summer had been a real scorcher: the earth was baked dry, the trees drooped down almost panting, and the grass, when there weren't just patches of blighted soil, was a sickly yellow-gold color like straw. The whole city was ready for the rainy season to start, but so far we hadn't gotten a drop. There was this mad desperation to everything, made worse by the fact that we could sense the rain was near. Thick grey clouds had hung low in the sky for the better part of a week, making the air moist and thick on top of the sweltering heat. But that's as far as it went. The clouds seemed almost to be taunting us, withholding the relief we so eagerly craved. As I reached up to wipe the sweat from my brow I felt a drop of water hit my hand. Then another, and another. By the time I reached the end of the block it was pouring.

I lifted my face up to the heavens, smiling as big as I could, relishing the sensation of cool rain on my flushed cheeks. Rapturously I called out to Zeus Ombrios, thanking him for this much-needed gift. I stood there for several long minutes, soaking up the moisture through my skin. I wasn't the only one. I could feel the parched earth and the poor plants around me taking it in as well. The sullen, listless spirit that had permeated everything for so long lifted, replaced by exuberant joy and celebration. Before I even realized what was happening I found myself caught up in the glad excitement. I raced down the street, arms stretched wide, laughing and shouting like a madman. I didn't care that I was making a spectacle of myself, my clothes plastered to my body, hair a mess, water streaming down my face and nearly blinding me. I felt free and alive and drunk on the joy of the natural world.

This spontaneous *ekstasis* was incredibly familiar to me. I had experienced it often with Dionysos, but never before with his father. I had had epiphanic encounters with Zeus but nothing like what I was feeling now. As if the stray thought had conjured him I suddenly began to feel Dionysos all around me, dancing in the rain, his spirit moving through the earth and trees and plants, stirring up the life within them, filling all of us with joy and excitement. I heard his pulse in the falling rain, like the distant echo of the hooves of a running bull. And then I was surprised by a clap of thunder through the heavens, the bull-god's booming voice. I screamed "Io Bromios!" at the top of my lungs, right there in the middle of downtown Eugene with cars whizzing by me, "Io loud-thundering Dionysos, born in fire and water, wind and rain! Io io!"

And then I was startled back to myself. No, my mind insisted. This has nothing to do with Dionysos. The rain belongs to Zeus, lord of the storm. Don't try to edge him out and put Dionysos in his place. Dionysos rules over a great deal already. You're practically a henotheist as it is. Experience what is there and give thanks to Zeus.

Properly chastened I turned my mind back to Zeus, said another quick prayer and continued my walk through the rain. But I soon slipped back into that state of Bacchic frenzy and no matter how hard I tried to remain focused on Zeus and keep Dionysos out, he kept intruding into my thoughts. Especially when the thunder came more frequently.

Each time it sounded I cried out in joyous exclamation. The thunder made everything strange, wild and savage. At times it felt like I was surrounded by this mad throng of noisy spirits, shadow-faced and dancing, leaping, howling in the downpour. I gave myself over to them, let them carry me the rest of the way home.

Afterwards I wasn't sure what to make of the experience. I felt powerfully that it had been some sort of authentic encounter with Dionysos and that he did, indeed, have something to do with the rain. But my rational brain fought against it, hard, insisting that such things were solely the preserve of his father Zeus.

But then a couple days later I got confirmation that this was more than just a random UPG. I was on the bus on my way into work, listening to my iPod and reading a book I'd checked out of the university library a couple weeks before. Unfortunately I'm not sure whether it was one of the volumes of the Greek Anthology or a collection of fragments from the Hellenistic poets. But as I was reading the Doors started up with "Riders on the Storm" and the whole incident suddenly came flooding back. The song perfectly captured everything I had thought and felt as if it was a hymn to this particular aspect of Dionysos. I sat there letting it all soak in for a while until the next song came on. Then I returned to my book and read...a poem praising Dionysos as the rain-bringer.

The breath left my body and the book tumbled from my nerveless fingers, making a thunderous noise. I sat there stunned for a while, wondering if I'd hallucinated the whole thing. I picked the book back up, feverishly searched for the passage once more – half expecting not to find it – but indeed it was there. I'd never seen anything like it before. This proved, at least, that if it was a UPG it was something shared by at least one other. Foolishly I neglected to write the poem down and haven't come across it since. But I discovered that the poet and I weren't the only ones who saw Dionysos in this light. Not by a long shot.

The *Etymolicum Magnum*, for instance, records that Dionysos was worshiped under the name *Huês* or "rainy" because "according to Kleidêmos we perform sacrifices to him during the time when the god sends rain."

Demosthenes (*On the Crown* 260) mentions this word as part of the ritual cries of the Dionysian initiates:

> "You led your lovely band of revelers through the streets, crowned as they were with fennel and leaves of white poplar. As you went, you squeezed the snakes and brandished them above your heads while dancing and shouting cries of *Euoi Saboi* and *Huês Attes, Attes Huês!*"

A good deal of Dionysos' mythology points to a connection with rain as well. In fact, Nonnos (*Dionysiaka* 10.290 ff) specifically states that the first Dionysos – Zagreus – was given control of rain and thunder before the Titans destroyed him:

> "O Father Zeus, I have heard how you gave Zagreus your fiery lance and rattling thunder and showers of rain out of the sky, and he was like another Rainy Zeus while yet a babbling baby."

Then his second birth took place during a tempestuous storm, as Diodoros Sikeliotes (4.2.1) informs us:

> "Zeus visited Semele in a way befitting a god, accompanied by thunder and lightning, revealing himself to her as he embraced her; but Semele, who was pregnant and unable to endure the majesty of the divine presence, brought forth the babe untimely and was herself slain by the fire."

Afterwards Dionysos was delivered into the care of the nymphai, specifically the Hyades who, according to Hyginus (*Fabulae* 192), "are so called because they bring rain when they rise, for to rain is *huein* in Greek."

Ovid's *Fasti* (5.164ff) evokes the rising of the Hyades in this beautifully poetic passage:

> "When darkening twilight ushers in the night, the whole flock of Hyades is revealed. The Bull's face gleams with seven rays of fire, which Greek sailors call Hyades from their rain-word."

Hyginus tells us a little more of the back story of these star-maidens at *Astronomica* 2. 21:

> "The constellation Taurus faces towards the East, and the stars which outline the face are called Hyades. These, Pherecydes the Athenian says, are the nurses of Liber, seven in number, who earlier were nymphae called Dodonidae. Their names are as follows: Ambrosia, Eudora, Pedile, Coronis, Polyxo, Phyto, and Thyone. They are said to have been put to flight by Lycurgus and all except Ambrosia took refuge with Thetis, as Asclepiades says. But according to Pherecydes they brought Liber to Thebes and delivered

him to Ino, and for this reason Jove expressed his thanks to them by putting them among the constellations."

So here we have the nurses of the god, who fled into the water with him and later were transported into the sky near the constellation of the heavenly bull, and their rising signals the coming of the rain. It's all so elegant and perfect, really. But it's by no means the only instance of Dionysos being associated with moist and fertile ladies. There were also the Horai or Seasons:

> "Philokhoros has this: Amphiktyon, king of Athens, learned from Dionysos the art of mixing wine, and was the first to mix it. So it was that men came to stand upright, drinking wine mixed, whereas before they were bent double by the use of unmixed. Hence he founded an altar of Dionysos Orthos or the Upright in the shrine of the Horai; for these make ripe the fruit of the vine. Near it he also built an altar to the Nymphai to remind devotees of the mixing; for the Nymphai are said to be the nurses of Dionysos. He also instituted the custom of taking just a sip of unmixed wine after meat, as a proof of the power of the Good God, but after that he might drink mixed wine, as much as each man chose. They were also to repeat over this cup the name of Zeus Soter as a warning and reminder to drinkers that only when they drank in this fashion would they surely be safe." – Athenaios, *Deipnosophistai* 2.38c-d

In another fragment of Philokhoros' work *On Sacrifices*, also preserved in Athenaios (14.656a), the link between the Horai and rain is made even more explicit:

> "When the Athenians sacrifice to the Horai they do not roast the meat but boil it. They petition the goddesses to avert lasting heat and drought and pray to them to ripen everything that grows by favorable warmth and timely rain."

A big part of the reason why Dionysos keeps such company, I'm sure, is because in the words of the Pythagorean Philolaus (as preserved in Proclus' *Commentary on Euclid* 167), "Dionysos supervises moist and warm generation, of which wine, being moist and warm, is a symbol."

A thought shared by Plutarch (*Symposiacs* 5.3) as well, "Dionysos presides over the moist and generative principle," who also (*On Isis and Osiris* 365e) wrote:

> "To show that the Greeks regard Dionysos as the lord and master not only of wine, but of the nature of every sort of moisture, it is enough that Pindar be our witness, when he says 'May gladsome Dionysos swell the fruit upon the trees, the hallowed splendor of harvest time.' For this reason all who reverence the god are

prohibited from destroying a cultivated tree or blocking up a spring of water."

All of which has profound implications for my worship of Dionysos here in the Pacific Northwest, since as I'm sure everyone is aware this is one of the wettest parts of the country. Oregon can get as much as 200 inches of precipitation a year, and our rainy season pretty much extends from the end of fall to the early part of summer (though we get most of it between December and February). There are times when it rains nonstop, every day, for six to eight weeks straight. As a result of that Oregon – and the Willamette Valley in particular – is one of the greenest, richest, most fertile places on earth. Everywhere you look there is an indescribable abundance of vegetation, the gift of our great lord Dionysos *Huês*!

THAT'S HOT

Above all – and I say this with every aspect of the god, for each is supremely important in the instance where they make their appearance – Dionysos is the god of heat. Fireborn, master of the beverage that warms our bodies and excites the mind, worshiped with the dance and torch-lit processions through the forest at night, the friction of bodies in sex, bodies at rest and in motion, the fevers of madness, the frenzy of the crowd watching the actor on stage, the king on display, the sacrificial victim (all the same thing, really) – seen in this light, how could he be otherwise?

What is fire but the friction of molecules, impelled in motion through the eternal dance of life and destruction. Consumption of other living things, the transmutation of trees into ethereal substances, the fragrant, smoky sacrifices of the gods. Fire is also light and life and warmth and safety. The thing we huddle round to keep our primitive fears at bay, the thing that prepares our food, the very basis of civilization and what we use to harm those who would harm us. A corpse is cold, dead, because it has no heat in it, no fire moving the blood about, forcing the unfolding of *nous*.

Is not all this true of the god as well? Indeed it is so, otherwise Sophokles would not have said:

> "Seen in the glaring flame, high on the double mount,
> with the nymphs of Parnassos at play on the hill ...
> Leader in the dance of the fire-pulsing stars
> overseer of the voices of night
> child of Zeus, be manifest,
> with due companionship of mainad maids
> whose cry is but your name."

Nor Aristophanes:

> "Wake the fiery torches which you brandish in your hands,
> – Iakchos, O Iakchos! –
> brilliant star of the all-night celebration!
> The meadow is aflame with light.
> Hold your light aloft
> and lead the youthful chorus, Lord,
> to the lush flowers of the sacred ground!"

Nor Pausanias:

> "When Hera sat down she was held fast and Hephaistos refused to listen to any other of the gods save Dionysos - in him he reposed the fullest trust - and after making him drunk Dionysos brought him to heaven."

Nor again:

> "Opposite the grove is a sanctuary of Dionysos Lampter. In his honor they celebrate a festival called the Feast of Torches, when they bring by night firebrands into the sanctuary and set up bowls of wine throughout the whole city."

Nor Kallixeinos:

> "And first of all went the procession of the Morning Star."

So let us hail Dionysos Phanês, Dionysos Lampter, great Iakchos who leads the initiates at Eleusis on the way to behold the great mystery shining out of the darkness. Hail!

THE PUSSY-LOVING GOD

It's pretty obvious why Dionysos has such a strong connection to the members of the *felidae* family – you'd have to be blind not to see it. Lions, tigers, lynxes, panthers and all the rest are to the animal kingdom what mainades are to us humans. Think about it for a moment.

Like the great cats mainades are wild creatures, the god's companions in the hunt. They are graceful and beautiful and frightening in their lethal potential. They are also unpredictable – one moment lounging about, the next leaping upon their prey with savage teeth and blood-curdling howls. You take your life in your hands if you want to get close to one of them.

But it runs deeper than that. In fact, it's rather enlightening to look at what the ancient Greeks said about these majestic animals. They often compared their effortlessly flowing movement to a dance and claimed that they were inordinately fond of music. They responded particularly to the pipe and drum – the instruments traditionally used in the worship of Dionysos – which could excite them to a terrible frenzy or soothe them into docility depending on the mode employed (also like the mainades, incidentally). And the panther in particular was said to love wine. A number of authors relate how a panther stalked and killed some shepherds until they set out bowls of wine for it; while drunk it was tame as any house-cat and allowed people to come up and stroke it affectionately. Unfortunately this trick doesn't seem to have the same effect on mainades. In my experience the more wine you put in them the more likely they are to bite you.

Although cats are ubiquitous in artistic representations of Dionysos – reclining at his feet, dancing with satyrs, yoked to the god's chariot, serving as a mount for him to ride or as fashion accessories – they don't play a prominent role in his myths. They make an appearance in the *Homeric Hymn* where Dionysos sets them loose on his would-be pirate captors; they stalk the halls of the puritanical Minyades and exact a savage vengeance upon the mad King Lykourgos once he has been blinded and banished to Pangion. A late *aition* explains that the Mesopotamian river was named after one of Dionysos' tigers who ferried him across and it's said that a tame panther was found in Armenia with a collar around its neck identifying it as belonging to Dionysos' temple in Indian Nysa. There are a few other myths – primarily coming from Pliny and Aelian who specialized in animal lore – but not many. Certainly not as many as we find for the other animals associated with Dionysos such as the bull, the goat, the fox or the snake.

And perhaps the reason why is to be found in the nature of these animals, which is so fundamentally different from our own. There is something alien and inscrutable about the feline – something mysterious and in a way feminine. It is difficult to read their emotions, to understand what they are thinking, and it's near impossible to predict their behavior. They can never be truly civilized – even the most pampered house cat has the heart of a hunter beating in its chest. All you can do is watch them and marvel at their eccentricity. No matter how much affection a cat shows you it always remains its own creature, fiercely independent and aloof. Dogs are famed for their friendship and slavish loyalty – but a cat won't necessarily come when you call it and woe to the one who tries to train them to do tricks! It may endure much, but there is always an element of proud disdain there. We think we're their masters but to the cat we are just the one who provides food and shelter, proper tributes that they are entitled to by right of birth. Of course even that is a misguided attempt to anthropomorphize them – something we humans seem desperate to do because we sense their profound Otherness and it makes us uneasy. A cat is a cat and it will never be anything else.

And that makes them, in many ways, the supremely Dionysian animal. All of the qualities that they possess – raw sensuality, superb predatory instincts, strangeness, remoteness, fierce individuality – are his qualities as well. The god walks with the grace of a cat and foolish is anyone who thinks he can be bound or tamed.

The title of this essay is, of course, a reference to cats although Dionysos does have the colorful epithet "khoiropsalas" which scholars blush to translate.

FOXES IN THE VINEYARD

Within the bestiary of Dionysos the fox is perhaps the animal most likely to be overlooked. When we think of Dionysos and his animal companions most people instantly flash to the bull and the snake, the goat and the fawn, all the different types of big cats – and perhaps if they are familiar with Hellenistic iconography they'll include the peacock and the elephant as well. But the fox belongs in Nysa just as much as the others, and for good reason.

After all, the fox lent its name to a whole tribe of Dionysian women – the Bassarai – who wore fox-skin cloaks during their ecstatic dances (Athenaios 5.199) and hailed Lykourgos as Bassarios, the fox-god. Aiskhylos named one of the plays in his *Lykourgos Trilogy* after the Bassarai, though unfortunately only suggestive fragments have come down to us. When Dionysos wished to punish the Thebans he loosed a giant, murderous fox upon them which even the greatest heroes of the age were powerless to stop from devastating the land. It was only by the intervention of Artemis that the beast was finally put down (Pausanias 9.19.1). More humorously, the fox features in one of the Aesopic fables within a Dionysian context (Phaedrus 4.3):

> "Driven by hunger a fox tried to reach some grapes hanging high on the vine but was unable to, although she lept with all her strength. As she went away the fox remarked, 'Oh, you aren't even ripe yet! I don't need any sour grapes.'"

Some may feel that it was just the fox's fondness for wild grapes that brought the animal into association with Dionysos, but I believe that there's a lot more to it than that. Consider the traditional attributes of this animal. It is famed for its beauty and cunning, it's a wild creature never fully domesticated, it's a great hunter and graceful, and it is fiercely loyal to its young. These are all the qualities that we find in the other Dionysian animals – as well as the god himself. But more than that there is something strange and magical about the fox, with a sinister undertone as well.

The fox is the protagonist in a whole series of European folk-tales that have continued down to the present day in the form of Beatrix Potter's Mr. Tod who made his first appearance in *The Tale of Jemima Puddle-Duck*. This "foxy whiskered gentleman" – whose name happens to be the German word for death – is very much in keeping with the spirit of the earlier tales, for he is a suave and clever thief who has no compunction against eating the other animals in Ms. Potter's world, though they're all sentient, capable of speech, dress in human clothing and mimic human behavior. (Shades of Dionysos Omadios, anyone?) In many of those European folk-tales the fox is also a romantic figure, seducing beautiful young maidens and carrying them away to magical other worlds, just as Dionysos whisked Ariadne off to Nysa. This sort of tale isn't limited just to Celtic and Germanic literature – one finds it as well in Japan where an elaborate mythology has developed around a race of mystic fox-spirits called *kitsune*, which are mischievous shape-changers that possess an abundance of tails to signify their awesome power.

Like Dionysos, the fox is also associated with royalty and the enduring traditions of the genteel class. Granted, this tradition has faded somewhat over the last couple centuries so that it is found primarily in heraldry and the dying sport of the fox-hunt, which is carried out for the most part these days by people with no inkling of what this act once symbolized. In ancient times the hunt was the prerogative and indeed the obligation of the King, for it demonstrated his physical prowess, his connection to the vital forces of nature, his ability to impose order on a chaotic world by ridding the land of dangerous threats and providing sustenance for his people. It was not just a sport but a primitive and supremely important rite, which is why the Egyptians depicted hunting-scenes on their temples, Greek and early European monarchs had themselves represented with hunting attire on their coins, and why even Catholic saints are shown in the act of slaying wild beasts. Today fox-hunting has all but disappeared from the world, properly derided as a cruel and barbaric pastime. (Though apparently there are rumors that it persists in a modified form with England's elite dressed in traditional clothing as they hunt the homeless and crazy on the labyrinthine streets of London on certain moonless nights. Then again, Grant Morrison – who recorded this curious bit of contemporary folklore in *The Invisibles* – also believes that we are larval creatures cultivated as food by aliens from beyond space and time, so one can certainly be forgiven their skepticism.)

But we should not be skeptical of the fox's relationship to Dionysos. Indeed, not only do they share all of the traits that I have enumerated above, but the fox wears the god's mark in its very fur which is often a brilliant orange and red. Does this not suggest the flames out of which the god emerged at his birth? Clearly he has a great fondness for this species since he has placed in no other animal such a clear memorial of himself. Therefore, whenever you look at a fox let your mind be carried back to Dionysos, the god who wears the face of a fox.

BACCHUS AND DIONYSOS: MORE THAN JUST GOOD DRINKING BUDDIES

Every now and then I come across people who insist that the Greek and Roman gods are completely separate beings. Not only do they possess totally different names, have different forms of worship attached to them, and perform different functions within their respective pantheons, but they feel different to those who worship them.

Such are the most logical arguments brought to the discussion, though I must confess that most of the discourse isn't carried out on this level. In fact, I've seen people get downright rude and hostile over questions of this sort, which I've never quite understood. I mean, what's the point of getting upset over what some anonymous person online happens to think? Of course, it's especially amusing when the indignant party doesn't actually know what they're talking about. For instance, one frequently sees the assertion that the ancients themselves never accepted the identification of the respective pantheons, and that the only reason that some people do today is because of the popularity of the early 20th century children's handbooks on mythology by the likes of Thomas Bullfinch and Edith Hamilton. I can only assume that such people haven't bothered to crack open a copy of Ovid, Vergil, Horace, or even Plutarch for that matter, but I suppose expecting literacy among people on the internet is asking for too much.

While the equation of deities such as Diana and Artemis or Mars and Ares could be problematic (though not impossible, since there is still a good deal of common ground between them) when it comes to Bacchus and Dionysos, there's really no question about it.

To begin with, there isn't even a difference of names. Bacchus is merely the Latinized form of the Greek name Bakchos, which itself derives from the Lydian Baki, a word used to designate both the wine-god and his ecstatic votaries, the *bakilles*. Baki- became a common element in Lydian personal names and is attested from at least the 7th century BCE.

In Greek it can be found in a number of words denoting ritual ecstasy and madness, such as *Bakche* or *Bakchai* (female votaries of the god), *Bakcheia* (ecstatic rituals for him), and *bebakcheumenos* (inspired by frenzy with Dionysos). We find it in numerous personal names, such as the fifth century dithyrambic poet Bacchylides, and it was used to designate those who had undergone preliminary rituals and reached the stage of full initiation and identification with the god, as we see in the fragment of Euripides' *Cretans*.

Further, it could serve as a name for the god (Euripides, *Bakchai* 85-90) or as a modifying epithet such as Bakchios (Pausanias 2.2.7).

Dionysos-Bacchus had strong, early ties to Italy. According to certain Orphics, Kore-Persephone had actually given birth to the god on Sicily. Sophokles, the fifth century Athenian playwright, hailed Dionysos as the "lord of Italy" in the choral ode of *Antigone*. The 7th *Homeric Hymn* told of the god's encounter with Etruscan pirates. And Dositheüs in the third book of his *Sikiliaka* related several other legends connected to Dionysos dating from a very primitive period in the island's history. And then there is the Roman historian Livy's account of the famous introduction of Bacchus' cult into Italy during the 2nd century BCE:

> "A Greek of mean condition came, first, into Etruria, not with one of the many trades which his nation, of all others the most skillful in the cultivation of the mind and body, has introduced among us, but a low operator in sacrifices, and a soothsayer; nor was he one who, by open religious rites, and by publicly professing his calling and teaching, imbued the minds of his followers with terror, but a priest of secret and nocturnal rites. These mysterious rites were, at first, imparted to a few, but afterwards communicated to great numbers, both men and women." – *History of Rome* 34.8

So clearly Bacchus was not an indigenous deity, but a Greek import.

There were a number of native gods in Italy such as Liber and Fufluns with whom Dionysos-Bacchus soon became equated. But even when people recognized the identity of these gods they observed some distinctions between them. Liber was primarily a god of vegetation and growth, and had only secondary connections to wine. There was no element of ecstasy or transgression associated with him. Further, Liber is a name usually found in a cultic context, while Bacchus became associated with poetry and mysteries. (There were many exceptions to this, but as a general rule it holds fairly solid.) The Romans tended to be uncomfortable with the more Bacchic aspects of the god – especially in light of how immensely popular the deity had become – and thus mercilessly suppressed his cult in the second century BCE. (According to Livy, several thousands were killed or enslaved as a result.) It was allowed to continue, especially in the context of ancestral worship, but only in a very watered-down, straitjacketed form. Julius Caesar repealed the laws against his worship and he became a popular god in Rome, but primarily as a god of drunkenness and sexuality. In the Greek East, Dionysos' cult continued in a purer form, and was immensely popular well into the 6th and 7th centuries of the common era, long after the fall of the Western Roman empire. In fact a council at Trullo was convened to condemn the worship of Dionysos which was still a potent force in many ways:

> "The so-called Kalends, and what are called Bota and Brumalia, and the full assembly which takes place on the first of March, we wish to be abolished from the life of the faithful. And also the public dances

of women, which may do so much harm and mischief. Moreover we drive away from the life of Christians the dances given in the names of those falsely called gods by the Greeks whether of men or women, and which are preformed after an ancient and un-Christian fashion; decreeing that no man from this time forth shall be dressed as a woman, nor any woman in the garb suitable to men. Nor shall he assume comic, satyric, or tragic masks; nor may men invoke the name of the execrable Dionysos when they squeeze out the wine in the presses; nor when pouring out wine into jars to cause a laugh, practicing in ignorance and vanity the things which proceed from the deceit of insanity. Therefore those who in the future attempt any of these things which are written, having obtained knowledge of them, if they be clerics we order them to be deposed, and if laymen to be cut off." (*Canon* LXII)

Thus, although I tend to think of and refer to my god as Dionysos, I do not have a problem when someone hails him as Bacchus. After all, it's better that he be honored than not!

THE GODS SEEN THROUGH THE EYES OF DIONYSOS

When I first began to study Greek religion and mythology I was only interested in Dionysos. He was the most exciting of the gods and he was the only one I felt a call to worship. In fact, I had a rather dim view of the other gods, buying into the whole "The Olympians represent the patriarchal oppression of the agrarian Mother-worshiping people who were indigenous to Greece" nonsense.

I wanted no part of that, so I took Dionysos out of that context and attempted to revive his cult all on its own. Though nominally acknowledging the other gods, it definitely had the spirit of monotheism about it. As part of this endeavor I was trying to put together a grand collection of all of the god's myths and it really wasn't working out very well. I was getting increasingly frustrated. I mean I hate writer's block – and this was a *really* bad one. Finally, in desperation, I clicked off my computer and went to bed.

That night I had an incredible dream where Dionysos actually came and visited me. In the dream, he sat on the edge of my bed and we talked. I remember his words very clearly. He said, "Why do you hate me?"

"I don't," I said, shocked and a little horrified by what he said.

He continued, "You hate my family and friends, who are dear to me. How can you say you love me when you hate them?"

"I don't hate them. It's just....well, I love you so much that there's no place in my heart for them. Aren't you enough?"

He smiled and said, "But I am not alone. I exist in connection with all of the other gods. You can't really know me unless you know them too." He got up and started to walk away but paused at the door and said, "Try getting to know them. See if it helps your writing." Then he was gone.

Well, when I woke up the dream was still fresh in my memory, which is rare since I don't usually remember my dreams. I have kept that wisdom with me and it is a large part of why I have remained a die-hard polytheist ever since. Here's some insight into who Dionysos is through his connections with the other gods.

Aphrodite

The Paphian, Aphrodite, is one of the most powerful, beautiful and omnipresent of the gods. She is the mistress of love and beauty and inspiration and passion and is felt in everything from the draw that brings cells together to the cosmic dance of the heavens. (In fact, the word *kosmos* means beauty, order, adornment – all things Aphrodite is connected with.) Aphrodite and Dionysos were frequently linked as the old proverb shows: "Where wine flows, Aphrodite is sure to follow." The *symposia* or drinking banquets of Dionysos were places for poetry, song, and dance as well as wine, with *hetairai* or courtesans dedicated to Aphrodite in attendance. As Plato demonstrated the theme of such occasions was often the lofty subject of Love. Both gods share the heat of lust, the power of connection and the deep primal rhythms of nature, and together they produced the ithyphallic god Priapos.

Apollon

Apollon is a god of healing, wisdom, prophecy, order and light, the son of Zeus and twin brother of Artemis. Ever since Nietzsche it has been commonplace – almost clichéd – to speak of Apollon and Dionysos as being two sides of the same coin. Apollon is supposed to represent the disciplined, ordered, and realistic within art, Dionysos the wild, overwhelming and fantastic. Apollon the light, rational and heavenly, Dionysos the dark, emotional and earthly. Apollon the masculine and Greek, Dionysos the feminine and foreign. There is a lot of truth to this but it is also too neat a theory, and ignores the areas where the lines blur. Dionysos can be seen as the force of order that arises from the midst of chaos, the pattern that appears in randomness. Nothing with Dionysos is ever clear cut, either/or. Always there is overlap and fluid shifts from one thing to another. Even in antitheses, this is the case.

Ares

Ares is the god of war, courage and physical prowess. Accompanied by Fear and Panic he can be a terrible god, inciting bloodlust and mindless destruction. But he is also a god who gives strength and helps the flagging courage of men on the field of battle. He is in the midst of battle with the blood and fire and the dying soldiers, whereas Athene is the cold, calculating strategy of the generals. Dionysos has his martial aspects, which put him close to Ares. The madness that overtakes nations and drives men to make war on their neighbors is not all that different than the epidemics of mania that Dionysos inspires. The many followers of Dionysos on his conquest of India were called an army, and according to Nonnos, arrayed along military lines, with battalions and such. Both gods had important cults in Thrace which no doubt influenced each other, and there is the myth about how both gods tried to bring Hephaistos back to Olympos, Ares being driven back by molten brands of iron flung by the smith, while Dionysos succeeded, using his charm and his best wine.

Ariadne

Ariadne is the daughter of Minos, the King of Crete, who fell in love with the hero Theseus and betrayed her step-brother, the half man/half bull Asterios, because of her love. After slaying the Minotaur and burning the sea-port of Crete, Theseus took Ariadne with him only to abandon her on the desolate island of Naxos. Lonely and heart-sick, she lay there willing herself to die, until Dionysos came upon her, and fell in love with her. He made her his bride and the Queen of the Bacchants. At their wedding feast, however, Artemis grew angered by something that was said and later hunted the young girl down and shot her through with arrows. Dionysos found the body and in desperation pleaded with his father to bring her back. He consented and Ariadne became a goddess, worshiped on Cyprus and Lemnos as Aphrodite-Ariadne, a goddess who presided over the redemptive qualities of love. In her story we see the hopes and aspirations of the faithful who yearn to be noticed and experience the ecstasy of touching the divine – especially Dionysos.

Artemis

The twin sister of Apollon, Artemis is one of the Three Virgins of Olympos. Her sphere of influence is wild nature and animals. She is both patron of hunters and of the hunted, and though she knows nothing of love and sex she is the protector of pregnant women and newborn children. Dionysos was called Zagreus, the Great Hunter, and from his infancy among the Nymphs of Nysa spent his time running wild in the woods like Artemis. He was, himself, associated with the animals that were hunted, and was torn apart just as his mainades tore live animals apart. In the two myths that the they share it is difficult to tell what the nature of their relationship is. In the first myth, one of Artemis' attendants grows proud and mocks the Virgin Huntress and is punished by the goddess by having her own virginity taken by Dionysos. No longer a virgin, the young girl is spurned by the wild animals and their goddess. In the second myth Artemis slays the woman Dionysos loves – the princess Ariadne – because of some indiscretion on her part. Dionysos is distraught and pleads with his father to bring her back. In some accounts this caused a great breach between the two, and Dionysos caused the death of Orion, the one man the goddess might have loved. In another account, however, it was at Dionysos' own request that Ariadne was struck dead. So, it is difficult to say how these two interact.

Athene

Athene and Dionysos are truly polar opposites. Athene is a strong, hard, war-like goddess, the patron of crafts and of all intellectual endeavors. She values cunning and restraint and is at home in the cities, whom she is the protector of. Dionysos is soft, fluid, effeminate, the patron of exuberance and excess and the shifting world of emotion. He prefers the wild mountains and forests, and upsets the order that Athene works so hard to establish. And yet, when Dionysos was torn apart it was Athene who preserved his heart (or phallos) so that he could be reborn. Obviously she sees the important role he plays in things, for indeed it is passion and exuberance in the heart that make for the best scholars.

Demeter

Demeter is the goddess of the cultivated earth, whose special concern is grain. She has power over all crops and when her daughter was stolen from her she was cast into a terrible grief and she stopped all things from growing, leaving the earth barren and the animals to starve and die.

Euripides said that she and Dionysos were the two most important gods to man, for she gave us bread to eat and he gave us sweet wine to quench our thirst. Dionysos had a role in the Lesser Mysteries, which was a preliminary requirement for involvement in the Greater Eleusinian Mysteries. Dionysos, under his name Iakchos, guided the initiates along the Sacred Way to Eleusis, and may have had a role in the ritual itself.

Eros

Eros is the roguish child of Aphrodite, a god of love who used his arrows of lust to wreak havoc in the lives of gods and mortals alike. According to the Orphics both Dionysos and Eros are the same god – Phanês, the primal generative force that brought creation into being by sundering the cosmic egg. He was a god of light and love, of immense power and beauty, who existed through a series of incarnations the final being that of Dionysos. These gods are connected in a less occult fashion as well, for anyone who has ever experienced love knows that it is a kind of madness. Eros is the god who brings things together – the force of gravity, if you will – while Dionysos is that moment of synthesis when the two opposites are reconciled. Dionysos is liberation, freedom, the tearing down of boundaries – so that we may love, free of all that stands in the way of that love.

Gaia

Gaia is both the earth and the earth-goddess. She is the material foundation upon which all things are based, whose essence all living things partake of. She is the oldest of the gods, who with her husband Ouranos produced the first generation of Titans, and then aided the gods in their war of succession. She was a prophetic goddess and had many oracle centers, including her most famous, Delphi, before it was adopted by a succession of gods, the final being Apollon. Dionysos presided at Delphi during the winter months and his grave was said to be located there. As a god of the natural rhythms of life, intimately linked with the cycles of growth and decay, the very force that causes fruit to ripen on the branch, Dionysos is very closely linked to Gaia.

Haides

Haides is the ruler of the underworld, which is named after him. He is brother of Zeus and Poseidon, who gambled to see what portion of the world each would rule. Zeus received heaven, Poseidon the sea and Haides the underworld as well as all those who come to it. He is a dark, saturnine god who rules over a gloomy world of despair, where souls continue on as mere shades of their former selves – though without the torments and eternal hellfire of the Christian underworld. His wife is Persephone, whom he went up to the world of the living to claim. Whatever she thought of him at first, she soon came to love him and made the underworld her home as co-regent. Dionysos, while a god of joy and vibrant life, also has chthonic aspects. His most famous festival – the Anthesteria – is a time when the ghosts walk among us. He descended into the underworld on several occasions, including when he brought up the spirit of his mother and made her a goddess. And as the spirit of vegetation, he slumbers under the earth for a number of months each year. The connections between these two were so great that they led Herakleitos to suggest that they were really the same god – Dionysos above ground, Haides below. When you consider that it was on the plain of Nysa where Haides took his bride and that Demeter abstained from wine during her grief, one gets the feeling he might not have been so off the mark.

Hephaistos

Hephaistos was rejected by his mother Hera, and cast down from Olympos, which resulted in his laming. There, he was raised by the nymphs of the sea who taught him to work with metal and the forge. He was so skilled that all the gods marveled at his creations. Using deception he created a beautiful throne for Hera which trapped the goddess and would not let her go. He went back to his undersea home and refused to return, even when Ares threatened him. It was Dionysos who succeeded in getting the god to change his mind, which he did by getting him drunk and then listening to his grievances. The god was too drunk to walk back, so Dionysos put him on the back of a donkey and led him up to Olympos. After that they were the greatest of friends. Within their relationship one sees the necessity for passion and inspiration to be combined with technical skill to produce the greatest works.

Hera

Hera is the long-suffering but jealous wife of Zeus who presides over marriage, maternity, the home and cows, from which she gained the name Boophis or "cow-eyed." Although Zeus stepped out on his wife many times, none incurred the wrath of his wife more than when he begot a son through the mortal Semele. She conspired to have the princess slain and then pursued the child with a vengeance when he escaped the flames that consumed his mother. Hera drove Ino and her husband, who were sheltering the infant Dionysos, crazy so that they murdered their own children. Dionysos was transformed into a kid, and raised on Nysa by the Nymphs, who became his nurses. He was safe there, but as soon as he began his journeys Hera pursued him again. She caused the pirates to try and abduct him, but he proved too powerful for them and stole their ship, turning them into dolphins. Finally, the goddess moved directly against him and drove Dionysos mad. He killed the tribe of Amazons, flaying them alive as well as other horrible things. Desperate to escape the madness, he fled to the sanctuary of Kybele where he received purification. Hera and Dionysos became reconciled when her son Hephaistos trapped her in a golden throne, which none of the Gods could release her from. Hephaistos refused to relent, even when Ares threatened him. But Dionysos succeeded in convincing the smith, and after that the enmity between Hera and Dionysos vanished.

Herakles

Like Dionysos, Herakles was half mortal and half divine and like Dionysos, he ascended to Olympos to take his place among the Blessed Immortals once he had performed a great service for mankind. The cult of Herakles was widespread in the ancient world, and all manner of people called upon him for any number of things. In fact, his name became a common exclamation to drive away evil, much the way that even secular people use the name Jesus Christ when they are startled or angry. Herakles is a strong, lusty god, given to drink – so it is not surprising that he was linked with Dionysos. There is an extant fresco which depicts a drinking contest between the two gods – it is difficult to tell who is winning, since they both look quite sloshed. Nonnos is our only literary source for this encounter. Beyond that, there is very little connecting the two, though some have suggested that Herakles was a *kouros* or divine youth connected with Hera (his name means Glory of Hera) which would put him in a similar position as Dionysos and Kybele.

Hermes

Hermes is probably one of the busiest gods. He's the messenger of the gods, patron of thieves, travelers, magicians, communication and he is the psychopomp or guide of the souls to Haides. Hermes saved the infant Dionysos from the wrath of Hera, and conveyed him to Nysa, where he placed him in the care of the Nymphs. He is honored on the third day of the great Dionysian festival Anthesteria. They are both gods who travel between the worlds, spending equal time in Olympos, on earth and in the underworld.

Hestia

Hestia perhaps had the most widespread cult among the gods, for every hearth in every house was her altar, not just the great central hearth of the city. Her concerns are domestic tranquility and concord. It is interesting to note how deeply connected these two gods are, since one would naturally assume that they would be antagonistic towards each other. After all, Dionysos represents freedom and liberation and upturns normal standards. He causes mothers, wives, and daughters to leave their homes and dance wild in the hills, completely abandoning the traditional roles that they have been assigned. But this is only a temporary madness, and is in fact, kathartic, a means of releasing passion and tension that if left untapped, would build up within the individual until it became an unhealthy mania. (Think the Stepford Wives or Martha Stewart.) When this release is over, the women return to their normal roles, better able to cope with the stresses of domestic life. So Dionysos and Hestia have much in common.

Kybele

Kybele, the Great Mother of Gods and Men, is a powerful, intimidating figure, a goddess of mountains and fertility, of blood and lions, of madness and blessed release. She was a Phrygian goddess, early associated with the Greek Rheia, mother of Zeus, who was adopted by the Romans as their patron, bringing them to prominence as a world-ruling nation. She was served by *galli* or eunuch priests who danced and entered trance states, from which they would prophecy and perform miracles. Dionysos himself served this goddess, and like a *gallus* helped to spread her worship. When Dionysos was driven mad by Hera, it was in a sanctuary of Kybele that he found release. She shared with him the secrets of her mysteries and the *tympanum* which figured in both of their rites. There is a curious myth linking the two. Pappas, a sky-god similar to Zeus, once raped the earth. From this union came Agdistis, a terrible hermaphroditic creature that raged and destroyed cities. None of the gods could stop it, except for Dionysos, who got the creature drunk and then castrated it, eliminating its power and releasing it from its madness. Henceforth she was known as Kybele.

The Muses

The Muses are nymphs of oracular springs and mountains, who inspire creative types and are patrons of the arts. The Muses of Mount Helicon were nine in number, and said to be led by Apollon. They sang and danced on Mount Olympos for the enjoyment of the gods, and either took part in or judged many musical and poetic competitions. They were said to cause a poetic madness, similar to that of Dionysos, and they were frequently in his company. Thalia and Melpomene are the Muses who have the strongest connection with Dionysos. Thalia is the Muse of comedy and bucolic poetry, and was depicted with a comic mask, an ivy wreath and the shepherd's staff. Melpomene was the Muse of tragedy and was depicted with a tragic mask, ivy wreath, and the attributes of the hero she is inspiring a song about (e.g., the club for Herakles or sword for Perseus).

The Nymphs

The Nymphs are a class of nature spirits, always depicted as female and categorized into different groups depending upon the element that they are found in. For instance there are naiads or nymphs of springs, okeanids for rivers, dryads for oak trees, meliads for ash trees, hamadryads for any kind of tree, oreiads for mountains, heleads for fens, leimoniades for meadows. Dionysos was raised by the Nymphs of Mount Nysa, who then became part of his *thiasos*. They picked up Nymphs everywhere they went, for these goddesses were very much attracted to Dionysos.

Pan

Pan is a rough, uncivilized god of hills and meadows first worshiped by Arcadian shepherds. It was said that he could instill panic in those who disturbed his noon-time naps, but he was mostly a joyous and fun-loving god who was always chasing after the nymphs or celebrating with his goat-hoofed and horned cousins, the satyrs. Pan was one of the many gods in the *thiasos* of Dionysos, and traveled with him to India where he frightened an enemy army with his raucous shouts.

Persephone

Persephone is the daughter of Zeus and Demeter and the wife of Haides, with whom she rules the underworld. She was abducted by her husband one day as she was out picking flowers, and her mother was so distressed that she made the earth barren with her tears, refusing to allow anything to grow in the absence of her daughter. Finally Zeus relented and allowed the girl to return, but she had eaten pomegranate seeds and so had to remain below the world for one part of the year. Apparently she took to life in the underworld, because in other myths she's the Queen of the Dead and when Theseus tries to rescue her she makes it quite evident she has no intention of leaving her husband. Aside from the chthonic associations (discussed elsewhere) of Dionysos, Persephone and Dionysos are linked through a myth which suggests that she was actually his mother. Zeus came in the form of a snake and seduced her, begetting the bull-horned child, Zagreus. Later he was torn apart by the Titans, except his heart which was preserved and used to create Dionysos.

Poseidon

Poseidon is one of the oldest gods, who governs the watery depths as Zeus rules heaven and Haides the underworld. He is also a god of horses and earthquakes and had several oracular shrines, Cape Tainaron being his most famous. Poseidon had many children with many nymphs and okeanids and goddesses – including, some say, Demeter in the guise of a stallion. The most famous of his offspring was the hero Theseus who was constantly encountering Dionysos in his many bull forms. Poseidon and Dionysos do not share any myths, and in fact, there might have been some unspoken antagonism between them. Homer frequently describes the ocean as a place "where there is no wine." Dionysos was the son of Zeus, and Zeus and Poseidon certainly didn't get along, and above all Dionysos' home was the earth, whereas Poseidon's was the sea. But there are also things which suggest a connection between them – Dionysos' magic ship, his relationship with Thetis and the okeanids and his power over fluid nature – the sap in the trees, running water, wine. From a modern psychological perspective, they are both associated with depths and fluid emotional states.

Priapos

Priapos is the hideous child of Dionysos and Aphrodite, whose penis was so large that he had to support it by means of a pulley and strings. Representations of Priapos were installed in gardens, both to encourage fertility and the growth of their fruit, but also to protect the garden from thieves. Those who were caught trespassing were punished by being placed on the garden god's erect member. Dionysos shares with his son both a concern for the ripe young fruit and their connection with the phallos – visual representation of the erect male member. Dionysos is often felt in the stirring of the sexual organs, in the yearning for connection and lust. He is a god of intense sexual craving, of deep passions, power, heat, and release. In short, he is a god of sex, as Priapos is – though with a difference. Whereas Dionysos is mostly successful in his conquests – indeed, he has women throwing themselves at him – his son is never successful, having to resort to masturbation or farm animals or lusty old women who take advantage of his statue, for his release. Priapos is a mockery of lust and the fools that it makes of men – while Dionysos is a celebration of it.

The Satyrs

Satyrs are the wild spirits of the woodland – human-like, but with animal characteristics. Often they are depicted with hairy goat legs, horns and pointed ears – but some have horse tails and ears, and others are shown with only nominal zoomorphic characteristics. The satyrs formed part of the noisy throng or *thiasos* that attended Dionysos, and they were always drinking or reveling or chasing after the lusty nymphs. In mythology the satyrs almost always appear together as a group – two exceptions being Marsyas and Seilenos. Marsyas was an excellent flute player who challenged Apollon to a contest. He lost and was flayed alive. Seilenos was the tutor of Dionysos who was captured by King Midas and forced to prophecy for him. This, perhaps, explains why they stuck together. The satyrs frequently boasted of their strength and courage, but when it came time to fight, such as in the conquest of India or the Battle of the Gods and Giants, they tucked tail and ran away.

Seilenos

Seilenos is an old satyr, the wise tutor of Dionysos during his boyhood. After the god left Nysa, both Seilenos and the Nymphs who raised him came with, forming the original *thiasos* of the god. At one point Seilenos got separated from the group and was attracted to a bowl of wine that had been set out for him. When he got down to drink from it King Midas jumped out of hiding and grabbed the aged satyr. When a satyr has been captured he must prophesy for you, and that is what Midas compelled him to do. Afterwards the King gave him all of his hospitality, entertaining the satyr with fine food and drink and dancing girls until Dionysos came back to retrieve him. As a boon for taking care of his beloved tutor, Dionysos agreed to grant whatever Midas wished – which, unfortunately was to have everything he touch turn to gold. He soon relented of his hasty wish, and Dionysos took mercy upon him, and took back his gift.

Thetis

Thetis is an Okeanid, one of the daughters of Nereus who had power over rivers and oceans. She was sometimes depicted as a mermaid, and other times as a slim-ankled young woman. She was the mother of Akhilles by an unnamed mortal, and tried to render her son immortal by dipping him in the river Styx, but failed because the heel by which she held him remained dry, and thus vulnerable. Thetis gave Dionysos and his followers sanctuary in her underwater home when they were pursued by the mad king Lykourgos. Before the god left she gave him the crown of Amphitrite, which Dionysos used as the bridal crown for his beloved, Ariadne. Since Dionysos has associations with fluid nature and depths of all sorts, it is not surprising that he would count an Okeanid amongst his companions.

Thyone

"Thyone" is the name that Dionysos gave to his mother once he had raised her up from the dead and established her among the gods. Semele, the mortal daughter of Kadmos, was visited by Zeus and became pregnant with his child, Dionysos. This angered Hera, and before the princess could give birth, she was struck by lightning instigated by the jealous Hera. Once Dionysos was fully established as a god he harrowed the depths of Haides to rescue his mother, making her a goddess. Some have suggested that "Semele" is a corrupt form of Zemelo, a Phrygian earth goddess and therefore Dionysos can be seen as helping to fight against the patriarchal oppression which turns goddesses into mortals, denying the innate power of the feminine. If you don't mind feminist revisionism without any factual basis, it's a very nice thought.

Zeus

Zeus is the King of Heaven, the ruler of gods and men, god of storms, wind, and rain, god of kings, law and justice, god of the home, family, and strangers. Zeus is the brother or father of most of the other gods, and had many mortal children. But above all of them he loved his son Dionysos, which is what caused Hera to hate him above all others. Although Zeus did not directly interfere with Hera, he did intervene on his son's behalf, catching up the fetus and sewing it into his thigh or sending down Hermes to save the boy when Hera drove Ino mad. Zeus allowed Dionysos to bring his mother up out of Haides and he even went against the Fates and brought Ariadne back from the dead. When Zeus was himself a boy, he was hid on Crete where he hunted in the forests, learned the war dances of the Daktyloi and grew strong and wise. Zeus at this time is very much like his son, a wild god of vegetation and sex and freedom. It is no wonder he loved him so, for Dionysos reminded him of himself or what he was before the mantle of leadership weighed heavily upon his shoulders.

WILD CHILD FULL OF GRACE

One of the most unique features of the cult of Dionysos is that at different times and places he could be worshiped as a child. Other gods, of course, had important stories told about their infancy: Hermes establishing a place for himself among the Olympians through cunning deception and the theft of Apollon's cattle; Artemis assisting at the birth of her brother a day after her own; Apollon slaying the Delphic serpent to avenge its insult of his mother; Zeus being sheltered on Mount Ida by the Kouretes whose noisy, armed dances kept his cries from reaching the ears of ravenous Kronos. But with the possible exception of the last instance – and then only on Crete – these remained myths, entirely separate from the cultic reality of the gods and how their votaries conceived and interacted with them. To the Greeks a god's prestige was determined by its power and ability to affect the material world. Cult-hymns pile on awe-inspiring epithets and accounts of the deity's past accomplishments, virtues and powers. Likewise their iconography was carefully chosen to instill a feeling of immensity, grandeur and at times even reverent fear in the heart of all who beheld it. It's hardly surprising, then, that the Greeks tended not to depict their gods as children except in poetry where it was permissible to explore a wider range of ideas – though even then it's usually meant to emphasize the extraordinariness of the divine infant – because who feels awesome fear at the sight of a child? (Utter horror, perhaps, if you're me but that's an entirely different emotion.)

And then there's Dionysos. Not only did he have a host of myths associated with his infancy – myths of greater abundance and diversity than any of the others – but he was also worshiped in this form by his votaries. There are numerous statues and artistic representations of the baby Dionysos; the *liknon*, a common feature in Dionysiac rites and initiations, was emblematic of the basket in which he was carried as a babe; festivals of his birth were celebrated in various locations including Tenedos where a young calf was dressed up in the attributes and attire of the god before being sacrificed; and flesh and blood mainades acted the part of the god's mythical nurses, suckling wild animals at the breast. Unique as well was the Dionysian cult's concern with all young life. Though abortion and the exposure of unwanted children were commonplace in the ancient world and generally treated as matters of indifference even in the realm of religion, several inscriptions from Dionysian temples expressly prohibit the practices, regarding them as a source of miasma equivalent to murder. This, perhaps, explains why in the myths of Dionysos punishment so often falls to the children of the transgressors, the sinful parents forced to dismember and devour the flesh of their babies. In a cult that valued life so highly – and young life in particular – nothing could be worse than its destruction.

Even when Dionysos did not appear in the form of a child there is often a child's youthfulness and immaturity about him. Numerous poets remark on this aspect of his appearance, describing him as beardless, plump, soft, effeminate and long-haired. One of the things that marked the transition into adulthood was the cutting of one's hair and the donning of new clothing, which took place in a Dionysian context. Indeed, the festivals of Dionysos often marked important transitions in the life of a person: during Anthesteria a child got its first taste of wine; during the Greater or City Dionysia children were enrolled in the *ephebate* and orphans of those who died in defense of their *polis* were paraded through the streets to worshipful applause; during the Roman Liberalia young boys put on the *toga virilis* or toga of manhood for the first time. The passage into adulthood also meant the segregation of the sexes and initiation into the mysteries of manhood. Before then boys weren't really boys. They lived with their mothers and sisters in the *gynaikon* or women's quarter of the house and did and learned the things that belonged to womanhood. Afterwards they came to live with their fathers and were given a proper Greek education, trained for athletics, war and statecraft.

This, however, was a journey that Dionysos himself would never follow them on. He remained primarily a woman's god, surrounded by female devotees, nymphs and goddesses. His is the realm of fluid emotion, of nature, of the ontological Other – all things deeply associated with the feminine for the Greeks. Dionysos never grows up. He doesn't cut his hair, wear the right clothing, get a respectable job, buy a home, start a family or any of the other things adult males are supposed to do. He spends all his time lounging about, getting drunk, dancing in the woods with the wild creatures and the women he's called out of their homes and respectable lives, away from their fathers and husbands and children and all the drudgery of their daily chores. His worship is a break from routine and respectability, a chance to blow off a little steam and explore life to its fullest outside our ordinary expectations and obligations. He is the divine source which Peter Pan is patterned after.

But there's more to his childlike nature than just this, important as it is. Children, as anyone who has spent any time with them can attest, are mad creatures. They cannot tell reality from imagination. They speak with things invisible to the adult eye. The whole way they look at the world is strange and dreamlike. The world is whatever occurs to them at that particular moment. They have no concept of what is possible and what isn't, because they haven't been trained to look outside of themselves. They don't understand limits and rules. They are driven purely by their own hungers and desires. As such they are completely amoral. Not necessarily cruel – though it can certainly come across that way at times – but they just don't understand why they can't have what they want, when they want it, or that there might be consequences for their actions. They'll tear apart a butterfly not because they want to hurt it, but because they're curious to find out what happens when they do or simply because they thought it was pretty and wanted to take it home to show mother. Try as they might they cannot comprehend why the mangled creature fails to fly away afterwards. Truly children live in a world entirely their own, in a state of innocence both beautiful and horrifying. Those who glamorize childhood and espouse a return to it I suspect do not fully remember what it was like or what such a state actually means, so far removed from it have they become and so thoroughly indoctrinated in the ways of adulthood as they are. But with Dionysos we are able to see, though few are they who can fully endure his blessings.

That there is something perpetually childlike about Dionysos we can learn easily enough from nature. As with so much about the god all we need do is consider his sacred plant, the grape, and the beverage made from it. As the great German theologian Paul Tillich once remarked, this plant is unlike most other plants in that it has such a dependent, symbiotic relationship with us humans. We care for it the way we care for a child and the grape has a life-cycle that mimics our own. Here it is in his own words:

> "First, it is necessary to understand what wine really is. Truly it is the nectar of the gods. There is no other drink like it known to humanity. Only wine is used in religions as a sacramental drink. In fact, wine is like the incarnation – it is both divine and human. It is a gift of God. Where did the vines come from? From God – we did not make them. But the vines need a very special soil. That is the gift of the gods. Also, the soil must lay just right – in some places steep, in others flat. That is the gift of the gods. And, there must be just the right amount of rain at just the proper time – not too much, not too little, not too early, not too late. That is a divine gift. And above all, the sunshine – again, not too cold, not too hot, all at just the right time. This, too, is a divine gift. But wine is both divine and human. The vines and grapes are from the gods. But only humans learn which grapes to use – through human knowledge alone – and improve the stock; humans carefully tend the vines, learn when to pick the grapes – all this is human. It is human experience that prepares the grapes to become wine – they stomp out the juice with their feet, they prepare the juice to ferment, but the fermenting itself is divine. Humans place wine in barrels that humans make of just the right wood, and at just the right time put it in bottles they make. Now you see that wine is special. Only wine of all drinks continues to grow in the bottle. First, it is a baby, then it is a child, then it enters puberty and becomes a teenager, then a young adult, then wine reaches its full maturity, and slowly it enters old age – some wines gracefully, some harshly, then it dies. Of all drinks wine alone recapitulates life. This is why wine is a sacrament." (A personal conversation quoted by Jerald C. Brauer in his foreword to Robert C. Fuller's *Religion and Wine: A Cultural History of Wine Drinking in the United States.*)

Truer words have never been spoken! So let us praise the *puer aeternus*, the divine child in the basket, the bull-horned infant sitting on the throne of his father Zeus!

MUCH ADO ABOUT NOTHING

Of all the ancient Greek myths the story of how Hestia gave up her seat among the Twelve for Dionysos when he ascended Mount Olympos is probably the best-loved and most frequently cited by contemporary Hellenic polytheists.

The only problem is that there's no such ancient Greek myth.

A couple years back I went through the entire Classics section of the University of Oregon Library – including their full collection of Loebs – jotting down every reference to Dionysos I could find. I've got a huge computer file, a drawer full of photocopied papers and something along the lines of six notebooks' worth of material that's still in need of transcription. And yet I didn't find a single reference to this myth. Don't believe me? Go onto Theoi.com and look at both the Dionysos and Hestia entries. I'll wait here while you do so.

Shocking, isn't it? The myth has become so commonplace that everyone repeats it as Gospel Truth™ – including folks who pride themselves on their book-smarts and go out of their way to show up all the ignorant n00bs. If I was feeling more contrary I'd provide examples of this, but well, I figure you can Google it for yourself if you're curious to see their gaff-in-action. Plus there was a time when I believed this was part of the authentic tradition as well, so it's hardly fair to castigate someone for something I fell victim to myself.

You see, part of the problem is that this isn't just an online phenomenon. There are a lot of popular handbooks on mythology that tell the story. Of course, none of them provide an ancient source for it – but then again most folks these days don't even bother to read the footnotes on the infrequent occasion that they're included, which I suspect is how all of this got started in the first place.

The earliest reference to this myth is Robert Graves' *Greek Myths*. You won't find it in either Bullfinch or Edith Hamilton, pretty much the standard popular texts on mythology before Graves supplanted them – which suggests that, as with a lot of what he wrote, he seems to have pulled this entirely out of his ass. (Or the ass of his "Muse" the White Goddess, if one is feeling generous.)

Here's what he wrote (27.12):

> "Finally, having established his worship throughout the world, Dionysus ascended into Heaven, and now sits at the right hand of Zeus as one of the Twelve Great Gods. The self-effacing goddess

> Hestia resigned her seat at the high table in his favour; glad of any excuse to escape the jealous wranglings of her family, and knowing that she could always count on a quiet welcome in any Greek city which it might please her to visit."

He goes on to recount a rather convoluted version of Dionysos' descent into Haides to retrieve the soul of his mother through the assistance of Artemis.

Graves provided citations in support of this myth, so let's have a look at them:

> "And wishing to be ferried across from Ikaria to Naxos he hired a pirate ship of Tyrrhenians. But when they had put him on board, they sailed past Naxos and made for Asia, intending to sell him. Miraculously he turned the mast and oars into snakes, and filled the vessel with ivy and the sound of flutes. And the pirates went mad, and leaped into the sea, and were turned into dolphins. Thus men perceived that he was a god and honored him; and having brought up his mother from Haides and named her Thyone, he ascended up with her to heaven" – Apollodoros' *Bibliotheka* 3.5.3

> "In this temple are altars to the gods said to rule under the earth. It is here that they say Semele was brought out of Haides by Dionysos, and that Herakles dragged up the Hound of Hell. But I cannot bring myself to believe even that Semele died at all, seeing that she was the wife of Zeus; while, as for the so-called Hound of Hell, I will give my views in another place" – Pausanias' *Hellados Periegesis* 2.31.2

Not a hint of Hestia and the myth of the musical chairs. In fact, there's nothing in those quotes to support *any* of his assertions. Respected authorities on ancient Greek religion and mythology have long recognized the dubiousness of this myth. Carl Kerenyi in *The Gods of the Greeks* wrote, "there is no story of Hestia's ever having taken a husband or ever having been removed from her fixed abode" (pg. 92).

And yet stubbornly, defiantly, there are those who cling to this myth and desperately try to find some vindication for it. In vain they often trot out a passage from Plato's *Phaidros* as if it supported the assertion that Hestia gave up her place on Olympos to Dionysos and now resides on earth.

Again, the passage says no such thing. Here it is in full:

> "Zeus, the mighty lord, holding the reins of a winged chariot, leads the way in heaven, ordering all and taking care of all; and there follows him the array of gods and demigods, marshaled in eleven bands; Hestia alone abides at home in the house of heaven; of the rest they who are reckoned among the princely Twelve march in their appointed order." (246 e-f)

Although Plato does suggest that Hestia remains behind he certainly doesn't claim that she is no longer one of the Twelve – nor is there any mention of her giving way for Dionysos.

But – I'm sure some are asking at this point – since there are numerous references to Dionysos as an Olympian and he's represented among the Twelve on the Parthenon Frieze, how can both he and Hestia be there? Does that mean that someone else was booted out?

Absolutely not. First off, there are dozens if not hundreds of gods, goddesses and assorted other divinities who dwell on Olympos, and furthermore, as anyone who has done even a cursory study of Greek primary sources knows, it was the idea of "Twelve Gods" that mattered, not who those Twelve happened to be. In fact membership in this illustrious body was rather fluid and changed depending upon location and time period. For instance, Plato in the *Laws* 828 connected the Twelve Gods with the twelve months, and proposed that the final month be devoted to rites in honor of Plouton and the spirits of the dead, implying that he considered Haides to be one of the Twelve. At Kos, Ares and Hephaistos are left behind, replaced by Herakles and Dionysos (Gratia Berger-Doer, "Dodekatheoi," in *Lexicon Iconographicum Mythologiae Classicae* (LIMC), vol. 3 (1986), 646-58). Herodotos (2:43-44) agrees with this and counts Herakles as one of the Twelve, while Lucian adds Asklepios to Herakles as a member of the Twelve, without explaining which two had to give way for them. Pindar (*Olympian Odes* 10.49) and Apollodoros (1.251), however, disagree with this. For them Herakles is not one of the Twelve Gods, but the one who established the cult of the Twelve by setting up a series of six altars honoring pairs of deities and performing sacrifices to them by the banks of the Alpheios river at Olympia. Thankfully we do not have to guess who comprised the Dodekatheon in this form, for information has come to light at Olympia itself. According to Wilamowitz (*Der Glaube* 1.329) the Twelve Gods included Zeus Olympios, Poseidon, Hera, Athene, Hermes, Apollon, the Kharites, Dionysos, Artemis, the Alpheios River, and the Titans Kronos and Rheia. That's over half of the 'canonical' gods swapped out with other divinities!

It is not necessary to fabricate a myth to explain this – one need only accept that ancient Greek religion differed regionally. So why, then, did Robert Graves invent this myth? Was he divinely inspired as some claim – or is it another example of his attempts to foist his self-loathing and politically-motivated ideology onto an unsuspecting audience? I think it's pretty clear when you read the full chapter on Dionysos.

Graves hated Christianity and everything about the rational, patriarchal Western world. Throughout *The Greek Myths* he is constantly making derogatory comments about the male deities and claiming that they usurped the position of their female counterparts or are nothing more than artificial constructs to justify the violence and oppression that the invading Greeks committed on the peaceful Pelasgians. No matter how improbable his explanation he always finds a way to turn a familiar story on its head and present the male characters in the worst possible light. Of course, as venomous as his attacks on Zeus, Poseidon, Herakles and all the rest are that's nothing compared to the scathing remarks he reserves for Dionysos. I suspect this is because he bought into the whole Dionysos-as-prototype-of-Jesus thing and because Dionysos is, well, perhaps one of the most unapologetically phallic of all the gods. Of course, he's also the god who's most concerned with women – be they his female votaries or the goddesses, nymphs, and assorted other divine beings that constantly surround him – and also had an effeminate and even androgynous streak of his own. But to Graves Dionysos is an illegitimate interloper, aggressively forcing the great mother goddess out and claiming her powers and accomplishments as his own. The displacement of Hestia myth is just one more example of this – though *The Greek Myths*, *The White Goddess*, *King Jesus* and numerous others of his works are riddled with that kind of thing. (In fact, *King Jesus* is probably the worst of the bunch since he makes Dionysos – and his mortal vessel Jesus – both impotent and lame.)

So, if somebody wants to continue believing this dreck – for which there is *absolutely no support in the ancient lore* – they can go right ahead, it's no skin off my nose. But personally I'm not comfortable with the implications of the story or the source from which it comes.

LACUNAE

If there is any deficiency in my worship of Dionysos it's probably the lack of attention I pay to his wife and mother. Back when I ran Thiasos Dionysos I came up with the following festival proposals:

Ariadneia - A three-day festival for Ariadne. "Finding" to commemorate her exposure on the island, and the triumphal appearance of Dionysos; "Union" to commemorate their love and passion, her status of Queen of the Bacchantes, etc.; "Separation and Final Joining" commemorates her death at the hands of Artemis, Dionysos' anguish at her loss, his descent, and her apotheosis.

Semeleia - Honors Semele, the mother of Dionysos. Both her pregnancy and her ascension to Olympos. Activities include: prayers and sacrifices; dancing, as Semele was said to dance while pregnant with Dionysos; a feast to commemorate her apotheosis.

Unfortunately I never got around to celebrating either of them, nor have I come up with anything to replace them. The closest I get to actually honoring Ariadne through cultus is during Anthesteria where I view her as the divine prototype of the wife of the Arkhon Basileos who is wedded to the god on Khoes. I readily admit, however, that this is more conceptual than cultic. Likewise I'm interested in the similarities between Ariadne and the other female figures with whom Dionysos is romantically linked – Arakhne, Erigone, Althaía and Aphrodite – but I'm rarely moved to worship her on her own. When I do it tends to be a humble and spontaneous affair, albeit one that is deeply moving. Because I do, in fact, consider her to be a supremely important figure – her story is probably one of the most beautiful and sublime that the ancient Greeks ever told – but this rarely translates into actual cultic activity on my part. The same is true of Semele. I feel great fondness for her as the mother of Dionysos and I consider his willingness to face the horrors of the underworld and confront its ruler in order to retrieve the soul of Semele to be one of the noblest things he ever did. But she might as well be a character in a comic book for all I've done anything religiously on her behalf.

I'm well aware that there is ample precedent for worshiping the both of them. They possessed several festivals each in antiquity as well as being the recipients of monthly sacrifices in different locales. Even if they didn't have this history of cultus they would be worthy of it today through their connection to Dionysos. It's no small thing to be counted as the mother and wife of a god, respectively, and Dionysos demonstrated his great fondness for them by transforming his mother into a goddess and placing the bridal crown of Ariadne in the heavens for all to see. Furthermore, although Dionysos had many lovers of either sex he had only one wife, his dear Ariadne, with whom he is represented on countless works of art. This motif was especially prominent in Greco-Roman Egypt where we find it on everything from wine-pitchers to articles of clothing. It is most prominent, however, in funerary contexts including some very lovely sarcophagi from Alexandria.

And understandably so, for theirs is a story of the awesome power of love and its ability to triumph over all things, including the grave. The god came to her, abandoned and grieving on her desolate island, and he healed her suffering, claiming her as his exalted bride. No doubt many Dionysian devotees saw Ariadne as symbolic of the human soul redeemed through love and joined in erotic union with the divine. Death, they hoped, would similarly transform them, bringing them inseparably close to the god they had adored so deeply in life. This, too, is my deepest longing and so I will always have a fond place in my heart for Ariadne, the Mistress of Dionysos' heart and Queen of the Bacchantes.

That ought to be enough to translate into actual cultus, but for some reason it hasn't. I've often wondered why that is. Even leaving aside the eschatological interpretation I give to her myth Ariadne is a powerful and fascinating figure. The Mistress of the Labyrinth who holds life and death in her hands, the clever spinner of the web of fate, the noble queen of a great land, the mortal double of the goddess of love and beauty, the one that Dionysos adored above all others and gave a portion of his followers to rule over. These are all compelling reasons to honor her and yet, for the most part, I feel no call to do so. It's not that I think her unworthy of such honors – not by a long shot! – it's more that she just doesn't resonate with me in a manner that tends to inspire religious devotion within my breast. And, perhaps most significantly of all, I've never felt her as a divine personality outside of her association with Dionysos. A couple times now I've encountered her at his side, leading a host of Dionysian spirits. It was a wonderful, awe-inspiring vision and I acknowledged her to the best of my ability. But aside from that…nothing. Even when I've prayed to her and made offerings I've received no response. I certainly don't demand that the gods come at my beck and call and I've persisted with others for a time without getting any response because worship is about honoring the divine, period, and it's the proper thing to do regardless of what we may happen to get out of it in return. But on the other hand I think it's important to pay attention to the results of our worship and what we experience in the midst of it. If there is never a response, well, that can be telling. Perhaps you're just not meant to have a relationship with this deity or at least not at this time.

And that is generally how I feel about Ariadne. I am open to things changing between us – my spiritual life has undergone so many transformations over the years I'd be a fool to assume anything is writ in stone – but on the other hand until she indicates that she expects more out of me I'm not going to be too concerned if the only time I encounter her is on the lap of her husband Dionysos. And if possible, things are even more ephemeral with regard to Semele. I've never had even so much as a single encounter with her, in the company of Dionysos or on her own. Which is a shame because I gather that she's quite a remarkable lady, which I suppose you'd have to be to give birth to a god.

A NEO-ORPHIC INTERPRETATION OF THE MYTH OF ARIADNE

To understand Ariadne is to understand an important piece in how we relate to Dionysos. This understanding is also central to the mysteries as revealed by Orpheus. You see, the disciples of Orpheus taught that in the beginning there was only the cosmic egg, undifferentiated being, unity, the potential for all that is or could be. Then, something began to stir within the heart of the egg: motion, light, heat. This movement grew in such intensity that the egg shattered apart, and the first thing to emerge from it was Phanês, Eros, the primeval Dionysos. Afterwards, all that is spilled forth, a rushing wave of creation. It would have continued to flow forth, endlessly, a mass of chaos, a gaping void of matter, but Love united the Earth and Sky, making stable material existence possible. Since that time, things have been separate, yet with the memory of a primal unity. That memory, that longing, is Love.

There is a problem with material existence, however. It is so dense that we often forget. We forget who we are, where we came from, that spark of primal creative power that exists within each and every one of us. It isn't so much the world itself that is bad – it is our notions about the world that are the hindrance. Our false perceptions. Our fears, our projections. Our societal conditioning. All the stuff that makes us conform and fail to live up to our full potential. The more we listen to this shit, the more that primal creative power within us gets lulled to sleep – but a sleep without dreams, an empty, half-existence. And in some people, this sleep turns into death. The death of their spirit.

But there are those who do not entirely fall asleep. Some little part of them wakes up, coaxed by a tender lover's hand who comes to them in the darkness and whispers of the possibilities of true existence. The lover is Dionysos. They are filled with such longing for him that their chains and shackles, which before they hadn't even noticed, become unbearable, and they begin to break free and spurn the false existence that so many mistake for true existence. They are awake and alive; they remember who they are, where they came from, what they are capable of. They kindle the flame that burns within them, and they long to feel the embrace of god once more. And so they seek him out in the darkness, in the labyrinth, they follow his laughing voice, and as they draw nearer their hearts leap with ecstasy, their steps are spritely with dance, they burn and ache and love and create.

Many obstacles rise up in their path, especially the nearer they get to their Lord. Frightening monsters, terrible fears, situations that are seemingly beyond their control. And some give in, turn back, and rush to the safety of their chains. But those who press on, who are so filled with love, who have such a clear conception of themselves that nothing can dissuade them, find their path through the labyrinth and out into the open air, into reality, the real reality beyond illusion, where the grass is green, and there are flowers of every hue, and the sky is a most beautiful blue, and there, waiting on the beach, is their beloved, Dionysos, in his crown of ivy. And he rushes to embrace the lover, and in their union is the union of primal existence reborn, and it transforms the spirit into one of the stars in heaven, which shine beautiful and fiery and in a constant state of bliss, an eternal reminder for all those still lost in the labyrinth of the abyss.

SOME THOUGHTS ON ARAKHNE AND ERIGONE

I find the story of Arakhne as told in Ovid's *Metamorphoses* a lot more profound than many people do. What I get out of the story, that a lot of others don't, isn't necessarily the moral about avoiding hubris, but the hints about the relationship between Arakhne and Dionysos that Ovid slipped in there. First off, Ovid sets the story in Lydia, specifically around Mount Tmolos. Lydia is a very early center of Dionysian worship – some even claim that it was the original center of his cult, though equal claims have been made for countless other places. In Euripides' *Bakchai* Dionysos is disguised as a Lydian stranger who has come from Mount Tmolos itself. Arakhne's father is a wool-dyer who specializes in purple. Purple, aside from its connotations of royalty – a point that will be more important later on – has a strong connection to Dionysos. Ovid mentions that the nymphs love to watch Arakhne weave – but not just any nymphs, mind you, he specifically says that they are the nymphs of the vineyard. That is a significant point since vineyard-nymphs are not common in legendary poetry.

Next he goes on to say that Arakhne is so talented that she draws the attention of Athene. When Arakhne will not credit the goddess for her skill Athene is angered and contrives to compete with the girl to show her up. How does she do so? By disguising herself as an old woman. When Athene goes among mortals, she often dons a disguise – for instance appearing as an old friend or mentor to Odysseus. But in this instance she disguises herself as an aged woman, a nurse. Why, you might ask, is that important? Well, also in his great epic, Ovid has Hera disguise herself as Semele's nurse, which leads to the destruction of Dionysos' mother. Ovid never does anything haphazardly; he loves repeating themes and playing them off of each other. And the Greek goddesses are always depicted as youthful and vigorous – to deviate from that is important, especially when you have the scenario 'goddess disguised as crone causes death of upstart or bragging young woman.' In both instances, Dionysos is in the background.

The next overt reference comes in the theme that Arakhne uses for her tapestry during the competition. She creates love scenes: Europa being turned into a bull; Zeus begetting the demigods Dioskouroi and Herakles; the serpent and Persephone. While none of these explicitly mention Dionysos, except for the last, all conjure an atmosphere suggesting the god's presence. And then, finally, she comes to the most important part of her tapestry: Dionysos seducing Erigone with the grape.

Now, why would she include that? It's a marginal story, certainly not the most famous of Dionysos' love escapades, or considered as canonical as the others she depicts. Most accounts of Erigone pass over her seduction by Dionysos, giving her only an accidental role in the story; but Ovid explicitly mentions a love affair between them. Why? Because it foreshadows the fate of Arakhne herself.

Athene is threatened by the talent of Arakhne, so before it's even done she beats the girl, destroys her tapestry, and mocks her. Arakhne, crestfallen, commits suicide by hanging herself. Athene relents, raises her soul from Haides, and transforms her into a spider.

Many of these themes are found in the tale of Erigone. In that myth Dionysos gives his wine to Ikarios (either in return for the man's hospitality, or as a bride-gift for seducing his daughter). Ikarios shares the wine with his neighbors, who never having tasted wine drink it undiluted and pass out. Their families mistakenly think that they have been poisoned and murder Ikarios, dumping his body in a well. Erigone searches for her father, discovers his body in the well, and hangs herself in despair. Dionysos is enraged by the treatment of his people and curses the Athenians with a plague and madness. All of their wives and daughters start hanging themselves like Erigone. They go to Apollon, who tells them to institute a festival of swings where young maidens will swing in trees to commemorate Erigone, who is transported into the heavens along with her dog.

This festival, the Aiora, takes place during Anthesteria, which is quite appropriate considering that Anthesteria deals with death, pollution, sensuality, the dangerous properties of wine, and the fertility of the underworld. During Anthesteria the wife of the Arkhon Basileos is given to Dionysos and they consummate a holy marriage. The Basilinna represents both Erigone and Ariadne – as well as the land of Attica which is mystically fertilized through the union. Like Arakhne, both of these women suffered terrible heartache – Ariadne was abandoned by Theseus after destroying her family; Erigone saw her family destroyed and then killed herself in anguish – but like them, both were transformed through the love of Dionysos and made immortal. The date of all of this is significant. Anthesteria took place on the 11th through the 13th of the month Anthesterion. The sacred marriage is thought to have been on the 12th – so was the Aiora according to Kallimakhos and certain scholia. And, interestingly, Hesiod (*Works and Days* ll. 770-779) says "but the twelfth is much better than the eleventh, for on it the airy-swinging spider spins its web in full day."

There are further connections. First, of course, there's the hanging and weaving: Erigone, Ariadne and Arakhne all hang themselves; Ariadne gives a ball of thread to Theseus to wind his way through the labyrinth; countless instances in poetry and myth mention the mainades refusing to weave, or temporarily leaving behind their loom and shuttle to run wild with the god, and Dionysos punishes the Minyades for refusing either to do this or to permit their slaves to. Secondly, Ariadne can be seen as a spider-like figure. She is Mistress of the Labyrinth, and the Labyrinth is a complex web of winding passages in which the victim gets lost and stuck and waits to be devoured by a ferocious creature. Dionysos himself possesses spider-like qualities. He is a hunter, but also patient. In Euripides' *Bakchai* he teases and coaxes Pentheus, setting a trap for him and waiting for the foolish king to spring it upon himself. He taunts him, he gives him the rope to hang himself with – but he does not directly act against Pentheus, waiting for the king's own base desires and self-destructive madness to surface. According to Aelian, when deer or other creatures are bitten by certain spiders, the only antidote that can cure the poison is wine. Why? Because like the spider's venom, wine is a dangerous poison, a *pharmakon* with the power to heal or to kill.

Another interesting fact is that Dionysos' cult was popular in Magna Graecia. Livy describes how it was introduced into Italy by a Greek prophet and how it involved ecstatic group dances and collective orgiastic rites. We have a good deal of information on the cult of Dionysos-Bacchus there (see Kerenyi's *Dionysos* for a powerful evocation of this cult and its understanding of the god), including some lovely Apulian vases which depict young women who are either being initiated into his cult or are passing into the world of the dead. They have expressions of joy and sensuality; they are dressed up as if for a wedding, taken by hand by winged Erotes and guided to Dionysos in his role as lord of the dead. They are experiencing a marriage to death, at once sensual and ecstatic, full of life and full of death. They must leave behind this world and all of the limitations associated with it to experience a fullness of being that transcends our dualistic conceptions. This phrase 'married to death' is found countless times in poetry in connection to Dionysos – it is also, if I may be so bold, a large part of the theme of Anthesteria and of his mysteries generally. And it is also part of the folklore of the spider, especially the black widow who consumes her mate after having sex with him. He passes from the little death of orgasm into the bigger death of finality – and by so doing ensures the continuance of their species. The same holds true for Dionysos – his mainades play a vital role in his existence. They are his nurses, his hunting companions, his brides – and in time, also his murderers, falling upon him and tearing him to pieces. But that is not the end, for they are also the ones who call him up from death back into life as the young god, that the cycle (and with it the vegetative fertility of the earth) may begin anew.

But that is not all. During the Middle Ages there was an outbreak of collective frenzy and uncontrollable ecstatic dancing. The cause of this was said to be the bite of the tarantula. People afflicted with this disease would become morose and depressed. They might even hang themselves, if they did not dance. And once they began dancing nothing could stop them until they heard one song, the song of the spider that had bit them. This mirrors something that Plato said: he mentions that the mainades are in a state of frenzy until they hear a particular tone, and that tone is the song of Dionysos. No other song will set them free.

Interestingly, outbreaks of tarantism occurred in *exactly* the same localities that Dionysos had previously been worshiped in: Southern Italy, Tarento, Apulia. I don't believe that is simply an accident.

THOUGHTS ON ORESTES AND ANTHESTERIA

Orestes is one of the great figures of Greek tragedy, part of the doomed house of Atreus. His story goes like this:

After his return from the Trojan War Agamemnon, the father of Orestes, was murdered in cold blood. Orestes was obligated by ancient custom, of course, to avenge his father by killing his murderer – but the catch is that Agamemnon's murderer was his wife Clytemnestra, the mother of Orestes. Orestes fled Thebes as a matricide and was pursued by the Erinyes, who punished him with grievous madness for shedding his mother's blood, a violation of the most ancient law of all.

In time Orestes came to Athens where the King received him as a suppliant, as was the ancient custom. However, Orestes was polluted from the murder and had not yet been purified of the crime, so he could not enter any temple or house in the city without inflicting his pollution on them as well. And yet the King could not turn away a suppliant, since that would be a violation of *xenia* or hospitality and almost as horrible as matricide. (All of these conflicting codes of honor are what make Greek thought so engaging: if Orestes does not avenge his father, he has sinned against him – but if he does, he has sinned against his mother; if the King accepts Orestes he risks polluting his kingdom and angering the gods – but if he *doesn't* accept him, he also risks angering the gods, possibly even worse.)

Well, as it happened Orestes came to Athens during a Dionysian festival. (Lucky him. Imagine if it had been Athene?) Dionysos is sort of the one who navigates these complexities, these irreconcilable codes. The solution: lock all the doors to the temple, and have the people come outside so no pollution will gather in their homes. Set up a tent and have a drinking contest there, that way Orestes can be given food, shelter and drink, the minimal obligations of *xenia*. And so it was.

Afterwards this was done in memory of the event. All the temples were closed. The men came out and had this drinking contest under the tent. But it was strange; it was observed in total silence. They left their garlands around the cups, instead of taking them home, so that the pollution would remain behind.

Some people feel this is an accidental addition to Anthesteria, but it isn't. The new wine is opened and tasted, the dead walk the earth – especially those dead who drowned in Deukalion's flood – the earth is barren from the long winter months. Everything is polluted: physically, spiritually, emotionally. But on Khoes, Dionysos comes to awaken the earth, to take the wife of the King as his bride for the night. (Meanwhile, everyone else is having their own nocturnal orgies, women going off with strangers, satyrs cavorting in the streets, young girls swinging in trees to commemorate the young lover of Dionysos who hanged herself in grief.) Their union washes away the pollution, makes everything fresh and new, gives the world a second chance: the new wine, the fresh flowers, the flood of Deukalion, the reception of Orestes, which finds a viable and novel solution to the irreconcilable ancient codes – it's all there, it's all about Dionysos. It's all about creating a new beginning.

Dionysos is a purifying god. But he purifies us by having us pass through the pollution, not avoid it, not clearly mark it off, but immerse ourselves in it as completely as we can – integrating it, giving it its place – and then emerge from it, through it, purification as rebirth, recreation.

NONNOS OF PANOPOLIS: LAST OF THE GREEK EPIC POETS

Nonnos is one of the most interesting authors included in the Library of the Ancients. Homer stands at the head of the line, being the first great poet of ancient Greece, who all subsequent authors must be compared to – and Nonnos, almost eleven hundred years later, stands at the end of the line, the last flowering of the epic tradition. Nonnos is an enigma. His fame rests on two substantial works – the *Dionysiaka* and the *Paraphrasis*. Beyond the fact that he authored these two works, precious little is known about this great man's life.

Here are the solid facts that we possess: He grew up in Panopolis and probably studied in Alexandria. Panopolis was the ancient Egyptian Khemmis or Akhmin, and in addition to being a center of the worship of Min or Pan (the two were syncretized as early as the sixth century BCE as we see from the second book of Herodotos' *Histories*) it was also sacred to Dionysos. We know that mysteries were performed for the god there. We know that its cult of Dionysos had surprising vitality, as Christian authors remark that the rites are still being carried out in the region well into the fifth-sixth century. Panopolis was also famed for its weaving and tapestries, lovely examples of which have come down to us intact. Guess what's a prominent theme in them? Dionysos, scenes from his mythology, and later – once the populace has become ostensibly Christianized – we find grapes, ivy, panthers, lions, and wine still prominent. Considering that, it's not surprising that Nonnos would compose a work on the god who was so popular in his home region.

Nonnos was a respected scholar and teacher. He had a small group of students and writers who gathered around him, and one of the things that they did was revive ancient forms of poetry, most prominently the hexameter. As early as the time of Kallimakhos and Apollonios it had already begun to fall into decline. Poets tended to favor simpler poetic forms such as Bucolic and Iambic verse, with themes centered on domestic things like love, shepherds in the wild, and the origins of obscure words and customs. Apollonios wrote his epic about the Argonauts to prove that it could still be done. And in the centuries between him and Nonnos there were a few more major epics composed, but not many and they tended to lack the vitality of earlier pieces, being the work of dusty antiquarians. Nonnos and his circle attempted single-handedly to revive this ancient poetic form – and Nonnos' work was the shining example of it.

His *Dionysiaka* is huge, about the size of the *Iliad* and *Odyssey* combined. His *Paraphrasis* is also quite large. One of the striking features of the *Dionysiaka* is that he sought to collect every single obscure myth or legend told about the god and weave them into a single narrative. His story also encompasses a vision of the world as an epiphany of the forces of self-generation, of nature as a divine force continually recreating itself through endless transformations. Although the spirit of Dionysos courses through every word of the epic, he doesn't actually introduce the god until about halfway through. Then, once he details the god's birth, youth, and early career he sets the stage for his masterpiece by relating the account of the god's conquest of India, which allows him to tell all of the other stories through complex and lengthy anecdotal narratives. This theme, the conquest of India, was very important after the career of Alexander the Great, who was said to model his exploits after those of his divine ancestor Dionysos. The Ptolemies also made use of the myth, claiming descent from the god, and at times asserting that they embodied his vital essence. (Hence the several Ptolemies' and Marcus Antonius' adoption of the title 'Neos Dionysos.') The Ptolemaiea festival, which celebrated the foundation of their dynasty, had a strong Dionysian element to it, as I have discussed elsewhere.

Now, some of the myths that Nonnos recounts are obscure, and do not come down to us in any other author, though they are represented in works of art and thus we know that they were current at the time, and may have been treated by poets whose work has been lost to us. (For instance, there was another Dionysian epic written around the 3rd century CE which also dealt with the Indian conquest and even preserves Nonnos' name for the evil Indian king that Dionysos fights, a feature attested nowhere else. This, at least, proves that Nonnos isn't completely making it up. Sadly, however, only a handful of lines of this earlier epic survive: a rather gruesome scene where Dionysos' forces have captured an Indian spy, dressed him up in a deer carcass, and sent the fellow back to his king, whom Dionysos is going to compel to butcher and eat!) The legends that Nonnos tells that do have cognates in other poets aren't always consistent with their versions, though again that doesn't mean he's making it up. The Greeks and Romans saw myth as a fluid thing, and there was an almost infinite elasticity to it, with many places having profound local variations on a tale. Nonnos can be trusted as an important source of information – but no poet or writer, not even Homer or Plutarch, should be perceived as the infallible gospel truth. If you strip myth of its complexity and fluidity and turn it into something more along the lines of a nightly newscast, you lose its timeless value, making it mean one thing and one thing only, whereas myth must be allowed to supply many levels of interpretation simultaneously, however contradictory they may seem.

We don't know when Nonnos became a Christian and a Bishop, since so little of his life has come down to us. It's suspected that that his other great work, the *Paraphrasis* or translation of the *Gospel of John* was written after he became a Bishop. But here's the clincher: from internal evidence it seems likely that the *Paraphrasis* was written *before* the *Dionysiaka*. Now, this is controversial, and some scholars maintain that he wrote the *Dionysiaka* in his youth, then converted, and some have even speculated – though this seems unlikely – that he wrote the *Paraphrasis*, but then later apostatized from Christianity and wrote the *Dionysiaka* in his old age! These theories arise from the unlikelihood that a Christian author would compose such a large and favorable work for a Pagan divinity, the seeming antithesis of Jesus, while maintaining his orthodox beliefs. There is, however, a number of examples of Christians from that period who had an entirely favorable view of Pagan culture, art, philosophy, and religion, who didn't feel that one needed to give these up to embrace a belief in Christ, and consequently wrote poetry in honor of Pagan divinities or texts extolling Platonic philosophy while still maintaining their Christian faith. Richard Garnett has written a truly wonderful, if speculative, tale about Nonnos' conversion. In it, Nonnos is about to be confirmed as Bishop when the god Apollon comes before him and makes him choose between Poetry and Acceptability. I won't give away the ending, but I adore this story which captures the spirit of the times better than anything else I've seen. (You can find the story online at the following address: http://www.horrormasters.com/Text/a2641.pdf.)

But the fact is, we will never really know. We also don't know how much Nonnos actually believed in the Dionysos he wrote about. While there is definitely this beautiful undercurrent of Dionysian epiphany and revelation through nature that runs through the whole epic the actual character of Dionysos is quite different. Nonnos' Dionysos isn't very likeable: he's vain, cruel, petty (though that needn't imply a lack of faith, since I definitely believe in the god, but recognize that he has some less than positive character traits), and time and time again triumphs against insurmountable odds, killing a host of transparent cardboard cut-out villains. The battle scenes – while beautifully rendered, with lots of attention to detail and some truly remarkable poetic phrases – get tiresome to read because there's no real dramatic tension. He's a hero – but one who is never in danger of losing. His Dionysos is pretty much the ancient equivalent of Arnold Schwarzenegger or Sylvester Stallone, though not nearly as charming.

That said, the *Dionysiaka* is still a great work, the last flowering of the Classical epic tradition. It provides us with a multitude of obscure or lost stories; there are some amazingly beautiful scenes; and if you go beneath the surface and see the stuff on creation, nature, and epiphany as a revelation of the god, it is a very powerful work indeed. Unfortunately, the *Dionysiaka* has only been translated into English in a very poor, almost unreadable paraphrase by W. H. D. Rouse. I really can't stand it – for one thing, it's actually in prose, when it's supposed to be poetry, and a lot of its beauty and innovation is lost in translation.

As you can tell, Nonnos is pretty dear to my heart. I've gone through periods of intensely disliking his work. But in the end he devoted the single largest Greek poem to my god and that goes a long way towards redeeming him in my eyes.

THE LUSIADS

I recommend that every Dionysian read *Os Lusíadas* by Luís Vaz de Camões. It's often described as the national epic of Portugal, comparable in that respect to the Indian *Mahabharata*, the Finnish *Kalevala* or the Irish *Táin Bó Cúailnge*. And with good cause, for *The Lusiads* (as it is known in English) is the story of how Vasco da Gama led the Portuguese Armada to India with the intent to set up a base of operations from which they could control the seas and all the wealth and natural resources of the country. Along the way our poet tells the whole history of his people beginning with their descent from Lusus (a companion of Bacchus) on up to events that took place in his own lifetime, with an interesting digression on the life and martyrdom of St. Thomas who was sent to convert the Indians and serves as a legendary prototype for Vasco's own missionary efforts.

And at this point most of you are probably scratching your heads, going "So, uh...why on earth would you bother recommending some obscure epic where the principal character is a violent, greedy bastard out to convert the natives to Christianity?"

Simple, really. Although the protagonists are Christian and their major enemies Moslem, the story takes place in a world still controlled by the old gods of Mount Olympos. After some preliminary material where Camões sets the stage and flatters his wealthy benefactor King Sebastião, we are transported to an assembly of the gods who have gathered to debate the fortunes of Portugal as they watch Vasco and his men set sail for India. Jupiter makes a laudatory speech on behalf of the Portuguese who are destined to accomplish great things, but the gods are hardly of one mind concerning the matter. Venus is their primary advocate because the Portuguese remind her so much of her own beloved Romans and Vasco in particular, who could be the very twin of Aeneas. Bacchus leads the party opposed to the Portuguese because the Indian people are dear to him and he does not wish to see them enslaved. He's also concerned that Vasco's accomplishments could belittle his own, as the land has remained unconquered since he first led his triumphant army through it. The gods quarrel, despite Jupiter's best efforts to reconcile them, and eventually they go their separate ways, each party vowing to support or oppose the Portuguese fleet.

All the action is determined by the activities of the gods. So, for instance, when the fleet is caught in a ferocious storm at sea and nearly destroyed it is because of the machinations of Neptune who has sided with Bacchus. Vasco's men pray to Jesus for help – but it's actually Venus who answers by sending

Nymphs to seduce the Winds and calm their fury. Later on Bacchus appears in a dream to a Moslem cleric and convinces him that the foreigners pose a threat to his people. The cleric in turn convinces his king to destroy the invaders and they almost succeed. But then, at the last moment, and with the aid of Venus once more, they narrowly escape with their lives and property intact!

The exclamation mark is to show how *dramatic* it's supposed to be. Unfortunately, by that point, it isn't really any longer. There have been a few too many *dii ex machina* to keep up a pretense of excitement.

As a reward for their bravery Venus creates a beautiful island for Vasco and his men and urges Cupid to fill the Nereides with desire for them. This provides a pleasurable interlude during which a series of stories are told, including prophecies of things to come. Good stuff, over all, especially the bit with the monster and the disease-bringing demon (a less poetically-minded person would call it "scurvy.") The best part is seeing how our gods have continued to inspire folks down through the centuries and even better than that is Camões' acknowledgement that despite the superficial appearance of Christian dominion, the old gods remain the ones who wield true power in the world.

THE IVY-COVERED CROSS: A COMPARISON OF DIONYSOS AND THE JUDEO-CHRISTIAN GOD

Dionysos in Palestine

Although the nature of the soil, the climate, and other factors made farming difficult, the people of Palestine have always made their living off of the land. One of the earliest crops to be introduced into the area was the vine, which grew both wild and cultivated along Palestine's many hills. There are numerous references to wine in the Hebrew Bible — including *yayin* 'wine,' *sekar* 'strong drink,' and *tiros* 'sweet or new wine,' showing its importance to the people (*New Bible Dictionary* 'wine'). The god of wine, Mesopotamian Siras or Ugaritic Tirsu, was also worshiped here from a very early time. (This provides an interesting linguistic connection — *tiros* > *Tirsu* > *thyrsos*, the magical wand carried by Dionysos that made wine flow.) The Levitical Hebrews tried to mask this god's presence by claiming that Noah had invented viniculture (*Genesis* 9:20).

Plutarch of Chaeronea held that the god of the Jews was none other than Dionysos:

> "First the time and character of the greatest, most sacred holiday of the Jews clearly befit Dionysos. When they celebrate their so-called *Fast*, at the height of the vintage, they set out tables of all sorts of fruit under tents and huts plaited for the most part of vines and ivy. They call the first of the two days *Tabernacles*. A few days later they celebrate another festival, this time identified with Bacchos not through obscure hints but plainly called by his name, a festival that is a sort of 'Procession of Branches' or 'Thyrsos Procession' in which they enter the Temple each carrying a thyrsos. What they do after entering we do not know, but it is probable that the rite is a Bacchic revelry, for in fact they use little trumpets to invoke their god as do the Argives at their Dionysia. Others of them advance playing harps; these players are called in their language Levites, either from 'Lysios' or better, from 'Euois.'
>
> "I believe that even the feast of the Sabbath is not completely unrelated to Dionysos. Many even now call the Bacchantes 'Saboi' and utter the cry when celebrating the God. Testimony of this can be found in Demosthenes and Menander. The Jews themselves testify to a connection with Dionysos when they keep the Sabbath by

inviting each other to drink and enjoy wine; when more important business interferes with this custom, they regularly take at least a sip of neat wine. Now thus far one might call the argument only probable; but the opposition is quite demolished, in the first place by the High Priest, who leads the procession at their festival wearing a miter and clad in a gold-embroidered fawnskin, a robe reaching to the ankles, and buskins, with many bells attached to his clothes and ringing below him as he walks. All this corresponds to our custom. In the second place, they also have noise as an element in their nocturnal festivals, and call the nurses of the God 'bronze rattlers.' The carved thyrsos in the relief on the pediment of the Temple and the drums provide other parallels. All this surely befits no divinity but Dionysos." (*Quaestiones Convivales* 4.6.1-2)

Tacitus said that Dionysos Liber was the god of Jerusalem in former times, but a different god had replaced him, a god with less attractive characteristics:

"Liber established a festive and cheerful worship, while the Jewish religion is tasteless and mean." (660)

Antiochos IV Epiphanes tried to Hellenize the Jews, which he almost accomplished through the very popular Greek gymnasia and theaters that he erected. The people liked them so much that they began to neglect their traditions, adopted Greek customs and names, and even refrained from circumcising their sons. There was a considerable backlash led by the Temple to which Antiochos was forced to respond by taking over the Temple and rededicating it to Olympian Zeus. To bring peace to the warring factions, he compelled the Jews to celebrate the Dionysia with a procession of ivy (*2 Maccabees* 6:7). When Demetrios I Soter wished to take Judas Maccabee, a brigand who lived in the hills outside Jerusalem and who had much support from the Temple authorities, his governor threatened to destroy the Temple and build a sanctuary of Dionysos in its place (*2 Maccabees* 14:33). Another King, Ptolemy IV, threatened to have the Jews branded with the ivy-leaf sign of Dionysos (*3 Maccabees* 2:29). When one considers the number of potential gods that were out there it is interesting that he should choose Dionysos for this. It is also interesting that Jesus was accused by Talmudic authority Rabbi Eliezer of having magical tattoos carved into his flesh (Morton Smith's *Jesus the Magician* pg 62).

Other names

Dionysos actually shared a number of names with the Jewish god. As mentioned by Plutarch, there was Sabazios and Sabaoth, Euoi and Eloah. The Greek form of Yahweh is Iao, which is similar to both the Dionysian cry "Io!" (Euripides' *Bakchai* 671) and Iakchos, the name by which he was known at Eleusis (Herodotos' *Histories* 65). Yahweh was called El, Lord, just as Dionysos was called Anax, Lord. In *Exodus* 17:15 Moses erected an altar to Jehovah-Nissi – which sounds like the god from Nysa, a possible etymology of Dionysos found in *Homeric Hymn* 1 and elsewhere. In *Isaiah* god is addressed as the Holy One, just as Dionysos is called Hosioter 'He Who Makes Holy' by Pausanias and Plutarch. Yahweh-salom 'The Lord of Peace' is paralleled in Dionysos Eleutherios 'Dionysos Who Frees.' Even God of the Jews – Theos Ioudaioi – has been compared to Oudaios, a follower of Dionysos (Cladius Iolaus FGrH 788 F4).

These parallels continue with the names of Jesus. According to *Matthew* 1:23 Jesus' name is Emmanuel, meaning 'god is with us.' This is like Dionysos' title Theos Epiphanes – 'god manifest.' *Revelation* 22:16 names Jesus as the 'bright Morning Star' just as Dionysos is Phanês, the Illuminator. In John 15:1 Jesus is called "the true vine" in an obvious attempt to connect him to Dionysos Ampelios, the god of the vine.

Logos and Nous

John opens his Gospel with a beautiful hymn to the *Logos*, the creative power through which "all things were made; and without him was not any thing made that was made" (*John* 1:3). Herakleitos was the first philosopher to speak of the *Logos*, a formative and shaping power in the world. The concept was taken up by a series of Greek philosophers, finding its most devoted advocates among the Stoics. For them *Logos* was not just god acting upon the material world; it was identical with him. This pantheistic fusion of god and *Logos* anticipates the line of John, "In the beginning was the Word, and the Word was with God, and the Word was God" (1:1). John goes on to say that the Logos was "made flesh, and dwelt among us" as the man Jesus Christ (1:13) – something that no Stoic would have conceived of.

As early as Homer, another ordering principle was suggested: *Nous*, or Mind. Anaxagoras speaks of *Nous* in terms very similar to that of the *Logos*, for he calls it the "efficient cause of the general order in the universe" (Aristotle, *Physics* 203). Parmenides affirmed that all things are contained within *Nous* as within a membrane (*On Nature*) but Basilides tells us that *Logos* sprang from *Nous*, the first born of the Unborn Father (Irenaeus, *Against Heresies* 1.24:3). What makes that especially interesting is that Macrobius says that Dionysos is the Material Mind or *Nous* itself, which he discerns from the god's name: Dionusos, he says, comes from *Dios nous* "the Mind of Zeus" (*Saturnalia* 1:18). This is bolstered by Plato in the *Timaios* when he says that there is a goblet of Dionysos which the souls are given to drink from, in order that they may imbibe the intelligence (*noes*) of all things. Yet more evidence that Jesus (Logos) may have sprung from Dionysos (Nous).

Birth and persecution

Mary, the mother of Jesus, was a young virgin, betrothed to wed Joseph. She was sitting in the temple weaving when the angel Gabriel "came in unto her" (*Luke* 1:28) and shortly thereafter she was with child. Joseph was going to put her away when another angel visited him and said, "fear not to take unto thee Mary thy wife: for that which is conceived in her is of the Holy Ghost" (*Matthew* 1:20). Because a worldwide census was announced, Joseph and his family had to travel to the home of his people, Bethlehem in Judea (*Luke* 2:2). There was no room at the inn, so Jesus was born in the animal quarters. He was visited by Magi (*Matthew* 2:1) and shepherds (*Luke* 2:16). Herod the King, when he heard about the birth of Christ, plotted to kill him. At first he tried to get the Magi to lead him to the boy, but they caught on and warned the family so that Joseph and Mary had to flee to Egypt (*Matthew* 2:13).

> "Then Herod, when he saw that he was mocked of the wise men, was exceeding wroth, and sent forth, and slew all the children that were in Bethlehem, and in all the coasts thereof, from two years old and under, according to the time which he had diligently enquired of the wise men." (*Matthew* 2:16)

This has striking parallels with the Orphic story of Dionysos' birth. According to Diodoros Sikeliotes, the virgin Persephone sat in a holy cave and wove a great tapestry on which was depicted the cosmos. Zeus, disguised as a serpent, appeared to her and begat the horned god Zagreus (5.75.4). His birth was witnessed by Kouretes or Korybantes, armed spirits who loved to dance. Hera was furious upon seeing the baby, so Rheia carried him off and hid the baby in a Cretan cave, with the Kouretes to keep watch over him (Nonnos' *Dionysiaka* 6.296). They danced and banged their spears to cover the sound of Zagreus' crying, but still Hera found him. She raised the Titans up from Tartaros and, faces whitened like ghosts, they waited until the Kouretes had fallen asleep. Then they lured Dionysos away with fabulous toys: a cone, a bull-roarer, golden apples, knucklebones, a tuft of wool, and finally a mirror (Kern's *Orphic Fragments* 34). Hypnotized by his image in the mirror, baby Zagreus was grabbed by the Titans but he slipped away, turning himself into many different shapes: a lion, a horse, a man, and finally a bull. But all this was for naught, for the Titans eventually caught the child, holding him by hoof and horn, and fulfilled their obligation to Hera by tearing him to pieces. These pieces they cooked in a stew of milk, and then roasted over a fire, before they commenced their awful feast. The smell of roasting flesh drew the boy's father, and Zeus, upon discovering what happened, hurled his mighty lightning bolts at the Titans, burning them up where they stood. From the steam that rose from their burning flesh came an ash, and it was out of this ash, the Orphics claimed, that man arose. Therefore we have within us both a divine element (Dionysos) and an infernal element (the Titans) and we must strive to separate the divine from the infernal – only then will we be free.

Athena managed to save the heart of the child, and with this Zeus was able to conceive the god again. He did this either by eating the heart himself, or by giving it in a potion to Semele, the daughter of King Cadmus. In this manner, Semele became pregnant without having sexual relations (Euanthes' *On Homer* 2.735). Hera tricked the girl into asking Zeus to reveal himself fully to her, which resulted in Semele being burned up. But Dionysos was saved from the flames that consumed his mother's body by lush vines and ivy which grew up to protect him. Zeus plucked the fetus up from the ashes, sewed it into his thigh, and kept it there until it came to term (Ovid's *Metamorphoses* 3:253-272).

Dionysos was then taken by Hermes to his aunt Ino, where he was dressed as a little girl and raised in the women's quarters (Apollodoros' *Library* 3.4.3). This plot, however, failed to protect him from Hera's wrath. Hera drove Ino and her husband Athamas insane, and they murdered their own children – Athamas shooting Learchus, Ino boiling Melicertes, and then jumping into the Saronic Gulf with him (Homer's *Odyssey* 5.333-353, 5.458-462). Dionysos was saved from this by turning himself into a baby goat and fleeing. Hermes later found him, and carried him to Mount Nysa, where he was raised by Nymphs and the Goddess Rheia (Nonnos' *Dionysiaka* 14.159).

Mission

As early as his twelfth year, Jesus recognized that he had a special mission. It was then, while on a family trip to Jerusalem, that he became lost. His parents frantically searched for him, only to find him in the temple, debating with the learned scholars. Jesus replied, "Why did you seek me? Did you not know that I must be about my Father's business?" (*Luke* 2:49). His public ministry began when John the Baptist, an ascetic desert preacher, recognized him as the righteous judge that he had prophesized and baptized him in the Jordan River (*Matthew* 3:11). He preached for about three years (John mentions three Passovers during Jesus' teaching ministry) all throughout the Galilee, Jerusalem, Caesarea Philippi, the Decapolis and even as far as Mount Hermon. He taught in synagogues (*Mark* 1:21) and to crowds in the open air (*Matthew* 14:15-21).

His message seems to have been a mix of homey good wisdom (*Matthew* 5:3-10) and radical politics (*Matthew* 10:34). He believed that he was the Messiah (*Luke* 9:20), appointed by god to overthrow the Roman occupiers, and re-establish the Kingdom of Israel. But this wouldn't just be David's Kingdom reborn – it would be the Messianic Kingdom of God. The establishment of this Kingdom would herald the coming of the Lord (*Micah* 1:3), whereupon he would judge the righteous (Israel) and the impure nations (Rome). To do this, he had to make the way clear, and to purify Israel to make it ready to receive god as its Bridegroom (*Isaiah* 62:5). This was both a spiritual cleansing and a moral one. Jesus felt that he was doing god's work by this – "My teaching is not my own, but his that sent me" (*John* 7:16); "I and the Father are one" (*John* 10:30).

Similarly, Dionysos' greatest accomplishments were done for another. The death of Semele wasn't enough to quench Hera's anger (Nonnos' *Dionysiaka* 9.206). She pursued him in his infancy – with deadly effect – and finally caught up with him, whereupon she drove him mad (Plato's *Laws* 672b). Dionysos wandered through Egypt, Syria, and other lands committing atrocities, until he came upon a sanctuary of Kybele, the Great Mother of Pessinus. "There he was purified by Rheia (Kybele) and taught the mystic rites of initiation, after which he received from her his gear and set out eagerly through Thrace" (Apollodoros' *Library* 3.33).

With a missionary zeal, he traveled through the East establishing their joint cult, which included mysteries, nocturnal orgies, ecstatic trances, wild dances, and "brass-backed drums, the instruments of Kybelid Rheia" (Nonnos' *Dionysiaka* 14.214). He even created a temple for the Great Mother.

> "For without a doubt, Dionysos came to Syria on that journey during which he went to Ethiopia. And in the temple are many indications that Dionysos is the founder, namely foreign garments and gems of India and elephants' tusks which Dionysos brought from Ethiopia. In addition, two phalloi, or pillars, stand in the entrance, quite high, on which is written this inscription: 'I Dionysos dedicated these phalloi to the Great Mother.'" (Lucian's *De Dea Syria* 16)

Dionysos asserted the supremacy of Kybele:

> "Happy he who, initiated in the mystic rites, is pure in his life... who, preserving the righteous orgies of the great mother Kybele, and brandishing the thyrsos on high, and wreathed with ivy, doth worship her. Come, ye Bakchai, come ye Bakchai, bringing down Bromios, god the child of god, out of the Phrygian mountains into the broad highways of Greece." (Euripides' *Bakchai* 72-90)

Message of peace, love and freedom

According to Nonnos, the god Aion complained to Zeus about the laborious, care-ridden life of mortals. Zeus declared that he would beget a son who was to dispel the cares of the human race, and bring them a message of joy (*Dionysiaka* 7:7). This was Dionysos, who according to Euripides in the *Bakchai*, "ends our worries" (450), "keeps the household safe and whole though the other gods dwell far off in the air of heaven" (466-67) and is a "lover of peace" (500). For, as Horace said, "Who prates of war or want after taking wine?" (*Carmina* 1).

Wine is the tangible symbol and fluid vehicle of the god. When people wish to speak of his blessings, they use wine to symbolize it. Hence we have, "Wine is mighty to inspire new hopes and wash away bitter tears of care" (Horace, *Carmina* 4). "Wine frees the soul of subservience, fear, and insincerity; it teaches men how to be truthful and candid with one another" (Plutarch's *Symposia* 7.10.2). And Aristophanes adds, "When men drink wine they are rich, they are busy, they push lawsuits, they are happy, they help their friends" (*The Knights*). Dionysos' blessing is for everyone – male and female, young and old (Euripides' *Bakchai* 205). And it is very important – for "where Dionysos is not, love perishes, and everything else that is pleasant to man" (*The Bakchai* 769).

According to John, "God so loved the world that he gave his only begotten son" (3:16). Jesus preached a constant message of peace, love and freedom. He said, "This is my commandment, that ye love one another, as I have loved you" (*John* 15:12). "Love ye your enemies, and do good, hoping for nothing again; and your reward shall be great" (*Luke* 6:35). "Peace I leave with you, my peace I give unto you. Let not your heart be troubled, neither let it be afraid" (*John* 14:27). "The peace of god which passeth all understanding, shall keep your hearts and minds through Christ Jesus" (*Philemon* 4:7). "If the Son therefore shall make you free, ye shall be free indeed" (*John* 8:32). And "There is neither Jew nor Greek, there is neither bond nor free, there is neither male nor female: for ye are all one in Christ Jesus" (*Galatians* 3:28).

Beatitudes

Both gods had a set of beatitudes associated with them. Dionysos' were:

> "Blessed, blessed are those who know the Mysteries of god. Blessed is he who hallows his life in the worship of god, he whom the spirit of god possesseth, who is one with those who belong to the holy body of god. Blessed are the dancers and those who are purified, who dance on the hill in the holy dance of god. Blessed are they who keep the rites of Kybele the Mother. Blessed are the thyrsos-bearers, those who wield in their hands the holy wand of god. Blessed are those who wear the crown of the ivy of god. Blessed, blessed are they: Dionysos is their god!" (Euripides' *Bakchai* 72-82)

While Jesus' were:

> "Blessed are the poor in spirit: for theirs is the kingdom of heaven. Blessed are the meek: for they shall posses the land. Blessed are they who mourn: for they shall be comforted. Blessed are they that hunger and thirst after justice: for they shall have their fill. Blessed are the merciful: for they shall obtain mercy. Blessed are the clean of heart: for they shall see god. Blessed are the peacemakers: for they shall be called the children of god. Blessed are they that suffer persecution for justice' sake, for theirs is the kingdom of heaven." (*Matthew* 5:3-10)

Lord of the Dance

In *Antigone* Sophokles called Dionysos the "Leader in the dance of the fire-pulsing stars." Euripides said that those who "dance on the hill in the holy dance of god" were blessed (*Bakchai* 75). Orpheus has him "dancing through the forest in a frenzy" (*Hymn* 46). He was said to have danced already as a child in his mother's womb. And Horace has him teaching the nymphs how to sing and dance (*Carmina* 2.19). He was received by the Muses as their leader in Pieria, where they draped him with ivy and danced in his honor (Philodamos of Skarpheia).

Jesus said that the Son of Man would come "piping and dancing" (*Matthew* 11:17). And in the *Apocryphal Acts of John* there is a beautiful scene just before Jesus goes to be crucified. Joseph Campbell paraphrased it in *The Power of Myth*, page 109:

Just before going out into the garden at the end of the Last Supper, Jesus says to the company, "Let us dance!" And they all hold hands in a circle, and as they circle around him, Jesus sings, "Glory be to thee, Father!"

To which the circling company responds, "Amen."
"Glory be to thee, Word!"
And again, "Amen."
"I would be born and I would bear!"
"Amen."
"I would eat, and I would be eaten!"
"Amen."
"I would be united, and I would unite!"
"Amen."
"A door am I to thee that knocketh at me .... A way am I to thee, a wayfarer." And when the dance is ended, he walks into the garden to be taken and crucified.

Attended by a throng

Large groups regularly formed to hear Jesus preach. Sometimes these got to be so bad that he would have to flee, at least once taking a boat across a lake to get away from them (*Matthew* 8:24). At one point they numbered 5,000 (*Matthew* 14:15-21). Another large group gathered as Jesus made his triumphal procession into Jerusalem on Palm Sunday (*John* 12:14). Even when Jesus was not surrounded by masses of people he had his Twelve Apostles and an unspecified number of assistants, including women (*Luke* 8:1-3).

Dionysos is rarely alone. He has his *thiasos* of satyrs, nymphs, goddesses, daimones, and wild animals (Nonnos' *Dionysiaka* 14.67). He also has his human followers: women called Mainades, Thyiades, Bakchai, Bassarai, Leucippides, Klodones, Dysmainai, and many other groups. He even has male followers, called Bakchoes (Euripides' *Bakchai* 115). According to Walter Burkert, mainades aren't just figures of myth, but are "well-attested in real life too" (*Greek Religion* 3.2).

Wherever he goes, he attracts large crowds. Whether it be the revelers in the street, celebrating as his procession passes by, or the women leaving a city in major exodus to worship in the hills. He is the god of mass movements, who spreads like an epidemic. Erwin Rohde wrote:

"In his moments of greatest exaltation man does not wish to face the more than human vital power he feels surging around and over him by locking himself up in his own private existence and following his normal practice of worshiping it timidly. Rather, he wishes at these moments to throw all restraint to the winds and with passionate exuberance achieve complete 'oneness' with the god." (quoted in Walter Otto's *Dionysus*, page 122)

Women

Dionysos is primarily a woman's god. Aiskhylos called him *gynnis* "the womanly one" (*Fragment* 61). And Euripides called him the "womanly stranger" (*Bakchai* 353). As a child he was taken by Hermes to his aunt Ino, where he was dressed as a little girl and raised in the women's quarters (Apollodoros 3.4.3). When Hera's wrath caught up to him, he was taken to Mount Nysa, where he was raised entirely in the company of Nymphs and Goddesses (Nonnos' *Dionysiaka* 14.159). Later in his travels he's accompanied by women who are called his 'nurses' (Homer's *Iliad* 6.132). His nurses then become lovers and devoted mainades, the ideal image of which is his beautiful bride, Ariadne. There are also the many women to whom he appears, and drives them mad. And the women who summoned the God to Elis (Plutarch *Mor. De mul. virt.* 13). Or the fourteen *gerarai* in Athens, sworn in by the Queen who was given in marriage to Dionysos (Walter Otto's *Dionysus*, page 175).

His realm is that of release and wild nature. At his celebrations, women would leave behind their homes, husbands, and children – all of the familial and societal obligations that were so important to the Greeks – to dance and drink and revel in his honor. They would hasten to a mountain or secluded wood and there commune with wild nature, driven by religious frenzy intensified by music, dance, and wine to states of ecstasy where they experienced possession by and union with the god.

Jesus had a number of women in his inner circle. *Luke* 8:1-3 describes the inner circle of Jesus' followers as 12 male disciples and an unspecified number of female supporters. In *Luke* 10:38-42, he taught Mary, even though Jewish tradition at the time forbade women to be taught. (Rabbi Eliezer wrote in the 1st century CE: "Rather should the words of the *Torah* be burned than entrusted to a woman...Whoever teaches his daughter the *Torah* is like one who teaches her obscenity.") In the *Gospel of Mary*, Jesus gives a special teaching to the Magdalene, which he had not shared with Peter or Andrew (*Mary* 1-9, 15). He expressed concern for widows, and repeatedly stressed the importance of supporting them throughout his ministry. The *Gospel of Luke* alone contains six references to widows (*Luke* 2:36, 4:26, 7:11, 18:1, 20:47 and 21:1). *Mark* 15:40-41 describes many women who followed Jesus from Galilee and were present at his crucifixion. He appeared first to a woman after his resurrection (*Matthew* 28:9-10). And according to Paul, "There is neither Jew nor Greek, there is neither bond nor free, there is neither male nor female: for ye are all one in Christ Jesus" (*Galatians* 3:28).

Upon this rock

Jesus and his followers came to Caesarea Philippi, when he asked them, "Who do people say that I am?" The disciples gave several answers, but it was Simon Peter who answered, "Thou art the Christ, the Son of the living God." To which Jesus replied, "Blessed art thou, Simon Barjona: for flesh and blood hath not revealed it unto thee, but my Father which is in heaven. And I say also unto thee, That thou art Peter, and upon this rock I will build my church; and the gates of hell shall not prevail against it" (*Matthew* 16:13-18).

After that, Peter became the chief of the Apostles, and leader of the early Church. He was with Jesus at the transfiguration and in the Garden of Gethsemane just before his death. After Jesus' arrest Peter was afraid and denied his Lord three times. But at once he was bitterly sorrow. Jesus appeared and reassured him, and after that he had resolute faith. He preached boldly on the day of Pentecost. After Joppa, he began spreading the Gospel to non-Jews as well. He was arrested by King Herod, but the Christians prayed and he escaped. He wasn't so lucky in Rome, where he was killed during the persecution of Nero – crucified like Jesus, but upside down.

Akoites was the helmsman of the Etruscan pirate ship that tried to abduct Dionysos. The god was disguised as a beautiful youth, and the pirates all conspired to kidnap him and ransom him back to his wealthy father. Only Akoites recognized him as a god incognito, and tried to warn his fellows, but they wouldn't listen. When the pirates tried to put chains on Dionysos, he caused wine to flow on the deck, vines to climb up the mast, and terrible creatures to appear and maul the captain. The other pirates dove into the sea, whereupon they turned into dolphins, but Akoites was spared and became a priest of the god on the island of Naxos (*Homeric Hymn* 7). According to Ovid, he was a prophet of the god too, who carried his worship to many distant places, including Thebes, where he was imprisoned by the god's cousin, Pentheus, only to escape when the mainades prayed for his release (*Metamorphoses* 3:572-596).

Counter-culture

Greek festivals usually occurred during the day – Dionysos' at night (see, for instance, Anthesteria, Lampteria, and Pannykhis). Greek festivals were held in the cities – Dionysos' in the hills (called *oreibasia*), forest, or swamp. Traditional sacrifices were burned on the altar of the god – Dionysos ate his raw (the practice of *omophagia*). Dionysian worship often reversed sex roles – the women became warriors and hunters (Pausanias' *Guide to Greece* 2.20.4, Euripides' *Bakchai* 1236-37) and the men engaged in homosexuality (Livy's *History of Rome* 39:8) and transvestitism (Euripides' *Bakchai* 939-960). Dionysos' worship was open to slaves, women, and foreigners – groups of people who could be excluded in some of the Athenian civic cults. Festivals such as the Anthesteria, the Rustic Dionysia, the Haloa, and the orgiastic *komoi* were times of license, when societal restrictions were loosened, and people drank, feasted, and had sex to excess.

Similarly, Jesus was accused of being fond of eating and drinking (*Matthew* 11:19) and was even called a "drunkard" (*Luke* 7:34). He broke the Sabbath law (*Mark* 2:26). He ignored ritual impurity laws (*Mark* 5:25-34). He spoke with foreigners (*John* 4:7). He spoke and even ate with sinners (*Luke* 15:1-2). He taught women, even though it was forbidden (*Luke* 10:38-42). He committed blasphemy (*John* 5:18). He stormed the temple, and physically assaulted people (*Mark* 11:15-19). And he preached open rebellion against Rome by saying, "Render therefore unto Caesar the things which are Caesar's; and unto God the things that are God's" (*Matthew*, 22:21).

(Consider this in light of the absolute dominion of god that Jesus preached through his message of the 'Kingdom of God.')

Some of Jesus' followers, apparently, were quite sexually libertine. According to *Ephesians* 2:15, through Jesus' death on the cross he "abolished the law of commandments contained in ordinances." To many, this gave them license to do pretty much what they wanted since they were saved by grace and faith. Paul had to write to the Church in Thessaly to rein them in (*1 Thessalonians* 4:3-8). But some went far beyond what he discovered there. According to Minucius Felix, a third-century Latin apologist, who was quoting Marcus Cornelius Fronto, a Latin *rhetor* and tutor of Marcus Aurelius:

> "[Christians] on a special day gather in a feast with all their children, sisters, mothers – all sexes and all ages. There, flushed with the banquet after such feasting and drinking, they begin to burn with incestuous passions. They provoke a dog tied to the lampstead to leap and bound towards a scrap of food which they have tossed outside the reach of his chain. By this means the light is overturned and extinguished, and with it common knowledge of their actions; in the shameless dark with unspeakable lust they copulate in random unions, all equally being guilty of incest, some by deed, but everyone by complicity." (*Octavius* 9.6)

Epiphanius of Cyprus, a Christian himself, wrote that a Christian group called the Phibionites used semen and menstrual blood for the Eucharist and wine, and had ritual sex afterwards (*Panarion* 26.4-5).

Wine miracles

In myth, the wine of Dionysos figures prominently. It calms the angry Hephaistos, allowing Dionysos to talk sense into him (the *Caeretan vase*, as well as others), it overcomes the unstoppable hermaphrodite monster Agdistis (Pausanias' *Guide to Greece* 7.17.9-12), and Dionysos' mainad companions often bring up springs of wine and milk simply by striking the ground with their thyrsoi (Euripides' *Bakchai* 708).

Pausanias recounts a curious occurrence in Elis, which happened during the Dionysian festival of the Thyia, which the god was thought to attend regularly.

> "The place where they hold the Thyia is about eight *stades* from the city. Three pots are brought into the building and set down empty in the presence of citizens and of any strangers who may chance to be in the country. The doors of the building are sealed by the priests themselves and by any others who may be so inclined. On the morrow they are allowed to examine the seals, and on going into the building they find the pots filled with wine. I did not myself arrive at the time of the festival, but the most respected Elean citizens, and with them strangers also, swore that what I have said is the truth. The Andrians too assert that every other year at their feast of

Dionysos wine flows of its own accord from the sanctuary." (*Description of Greece*, 6. 26.1-2)

Both Diodoros and Pliny the Elder talk of fountains of wine that flowed by themselves from the ground, and of spring water from his temple which had the flavor of wine on festival days (*Library of History*, 3.66.1-2; *Natural History*, 2.106, 31.13).

John tells the story of Jesus' first public miracle:

> "And the third day there was a marriage in Cana of Galilee; and the mother of Jesus was there: And both Jesus was called, and his disciples, to the marriage. And when they wanted wine, the mother of Jesus saith unto him, They have no wine. Jesus saith unto her, Woman, what have I to do with thee? mine hour is not yet come. His mother saith unto the servants, Whatsoever he saith unto you, do it. And there were set there six waterpots of stone, after the manner of the purifying of the Jews, containing two or three firkins apiece. Jesus saith unto them, Fill the waterpots with water. And they filled them up to the brim. And he saith unto them, Draw out now, and bear unto the governor of the feast. And they bare it. When the ruler of the feast had tasted the water that was made wine, and knew not whence it was: (but the servants which drew the water knew;) the governor of the feast called the bridegroom, And saith unto him, Every man at the beginning doth set forth good wine; and when men have well drunk, then that which is worse: but thou hast kept the good wine until now. This beginning of miracles did Jesus in Cana of Galilee, and manifested forth his glory; and his disciples believed on him." (*John* 2:1-11).

Later on, he has Jesus call himself the "true vine" (*John* 15).

For Christians, a miracle occurs at every Communion service when the wine turns into the blood of Christ, and bread becomes his flesh in memory of the Last Supper (*John* 13:21-30).

Makes food multiply

Matthew 14:15-21 reads:

> "As evening approached, the disciples came to him and said, 'This is a remote place, and it's already getting late. Send the crowds away, so they can go to the villages and buy themselves some food.' Jesus replied, 'They do not need to go away. You give them something to eat.' We have here only five loaves of bread and two fish," they answered. 'Bring them here to me,' he said. And he directed the people to sit down on the grass. Taking the five loaves and the two fish and looking up to heaven, he gave thanks and broke the loaves. Then he gave them to the disciples, and the disciples gave them to the people. They all ate and were satisfied, and the disciples picked up twelve basketfuls of broken pieces that were left over. The

number of those who ate was about five thousand men, besides women and children."

Ovid tells a similar story. Anius was the king of Delos, and he had three daughters who served Dionysos well as priestesses. During a famine, the god appeared to them, and gave them the power to produce corn, oil, and wine for their people, simply by touching the ground. This wonderful gift almost proved their downfall, as Agamemnon tried to abduct the girls to feed his men at Troy, but they called out to Dionysos in prayer, and he turned them into white doves, so that they could escape (*Metamorphoses* 13.628-704).

Control over vegetation

According to Carl Kerenyi, it was not intoxication which was the essential element of the religion of Dionysos, but the "quiet, powerful, vegetative element which ultimately engulfed even the ancient theaters, as at Cumae" (*Dionysos*, page xxiv). For Jane Ellen Harrison, Dionysos was more than just the god of the vine, he was "Dendrites, Tree-god, and a plant god in a far wider sense. He is god of the fig-tree, Sykites; he is Kissos, god of the ivy; he is Anthios, god of all blossoming things; he is Phytalmios, god of growth" (*Prolegomena* page 426). In short, he is the god of the impulse of life in nature, a god of growth and the green earth. And there are a whole range of miracles associated with this aspect of his being.

Whenever Dionysos appears, he does so attended by wild vegetation, whether it is with the vines of ivy and lush grapes he wears in his hair (*Orphic Hymn* 30), or that entwines itself around pillars and altars (Euripides' *Antiope* 203), a face appearing in a plane tree that has been split asunder (Kern's *Inschr. von M.* 215), or in a burst of beautiful flowers (Pindar fr.75). When Dionysos finally reveals himself in fullness to the Tyrrhenian pirates, it is through vegetation.

> "Then in an instant a vine, running along the topmost edge of the sail, sprang up and sent out its branches in every direction heavy with thick-hanging clusters of grapes, and around the mast cloud dark-leaved ivy, rich in blossoms and bright with ripe berries, and garlands crowned every tholepin." (*Homeric Hymn* 7)

In a number of places, but most famously at Parnassos, miracles of the "one-day vines" occurred. These vines "flowered and bore fruit in the course of a few hours during the festivals of the epiphany of the god" (Walter Otto, *Dionysus* page 98). Sophokles in his *Thyestes* records that in Euboea, one could watch the holy vine grow green in the early morning. By noon the grapes were already forming, and by evening the dark and heavy fruit could be cut down, and a drink made from them (fr. 234). Euphorion tells us that this miracle was related to the performance of cultic dances and the singing of choral hymns by the god's followers in Aigia – that it was their celebration which caused the vines to grow (*Euphorionis Fragmenta* 118).

This is echoed in a curious story about Jesus which Mark told.

"And on the morrow, when they were come from Bethany, he was hungry: And seeing a fig tree afar off having leaves, he came, if haply he might find any thing thereon: and when he came to it, he found nothing but leaves; for the time of figs was not yet. And Jesus answered and said unto it, No man eat fruit of thee hereafter for ever. And his disciples heard it." (*Mark* 11:12-14)

Jesus is connected with nature by another saying: "Split a piece of wood and I am there" (*Gospel of Thomas* 77).

On the boat

Jesus performed two miracles while in a boat. Matthew tells how Jesus was preaching one day, when the group of people got to be too much for him. So he got into a boat with his disciples, and went out to take in a little sun and solitude. However, this didn't last long, for:

"behold, there arose a great tempest in the sea, insomuch that the ship was covered with the waves: but he was asleep. And his disciples came to him, and awoke him, saying, Lord, save us: we perish. And he saith unto them, Why are ye fearful, O ye of little faith? Then he arose, and rebuked the winds and the sea; and there was a great calm. But the men marveled, saying, What manner of man is this, that even the winds and the sea obey him!" (*Matthew* 8:24-27)

John relates a similar story: Jesus saw that they were ready to take him by force and make him King, so he went higher into the hills alone. That evening his disciples went down to the shore to wait for him. But as darkness fell and Jesus still hadn't come back, they got into the boat and headed out across the lake toward Capernaum. Soon a gale swept down upon them as they rowed, and the sea grew very rough. They were three or four miles out when suddenly they saw Jesus walking on the water toward the boat. They were terrified, but he called out to them, "I am here! Don't be afraid." Then they were eager to let him in, and immediately the boat arrived at their destination (*John* 6:15-21).

Dionysos had his miracle on a boat too. Disguised as a beautiful young man in rich purple robes, Dionysos was captured by some Etruscan pirates. Only the helmsman Akoites recognized him for what he was – the others thought him a rich prince, whom they intended to ransom. When they tried to put chains on him, Dionysos changed their oars into serpents, made wine flow on the deck, and filled their vessel with clinging ivy. He had wild animals maul the captain, and turned the rest of the fearful pirates into dolphins as they threw themselves overboard (*Homeric Hymn* 7).

Riding an ass

According to John, before Jesus could make his triumphal entry into Jerusalem, he first had to collect a donkey on which to ride (*John* 12:14). He gave precise instructions on how to attain it, and what to say to the person when they collected it (*Matthew* 21:2). He wouldn't enter the city until he had the donkey, that he might fulfill some obscure prophecy: "Tell ye the daughter of Sion, Behold, thy King cometh unto thee, meek, and sitting upon an ass, and a colt the foal of an ass" (*Matthew* 21:5).

This sounds very much like the description of Hephaistos being led up to Mount Olympos on the back of a donkey by Dionysos (Pausanias' *Guide to Greece* 1.20.3). According to the myth, Hera begot Hephaistos without recourse to another. But when he was born, he was lame, so she cast him out of her presence, and he fell for days to earth, whereupon he was taken in by Okeanids who raised him. He became a master artisan, making many fine gifts envied by the other gods. He got his revenge on Hera by crafting a beautiful golden chair from which the Queen of the gods could not rise. Hephaistos returned to his underwater home, quite content to let her languish, despite the pleading of the other gods. Ares tried to compel him by force, but was driven back by firing brands flung by Hephaistos. Dionysos alone succeeded, by getting Hephaistos drunk, and talking with him. His rage tamed, the meek and happy god was led back up to Olympos on the back of a donkey, amid much celebration by the immortals.

There is another story that connects the ass with Dionysos. During the war of the gods and giants, Dionysos and his satyrs rode into the fray on the backs of donkeys. At first the other gods laughed at the humble creatures, but when their braying frightened the fearsome giants, the gods immortalized them by turning them into the constellation *Asellus Borealis* (Hyginus *Poetica Astronomica* 2.23).

Disdains money

Ovid told the following story in the *Metamorphoses* (11.90). One day the thiasos of Dionysos was traveling through Phrygia, when Seilenos, the god's old teacher, disappeared and no one could find him. Finally, escorted by an honor guard sent along by Midas, king of the Mygdonians, the old satyr returned. The king, or some of his peasants, had easily captured the ever-thirsty old satyr by setting out some wine bowls, and once he had prophesized for him – that was what satyrs were supposed to do when they were captured – Midas entertained him with splendid hospitality, giving him his best men as an escort when the old satyr wished to return to the god. Dionysos rewarded the king for his kindness by agreeing to grant whatever Midas wished – and Midas foolishly asked that everything he touch turn to gold. Reluctantly – for once a god has given his word, he cannot turn back – Dionysos did so, and the god was not surprised when the king sought him out the next day, begging that his gift be withdrawn. It had worked too well, and he was starving since his very food turned to gold as well. Dionysos gladly told the king how he might banish his "golden touch" by bathing in the icy waters of the river Pactolus, a river rich with gold to this day. This shows the foolishness of avarice and money-lust.

Something that Jesus frequently derided as well: "It is easier for a camel to pass through the eye of a needle, than for a rich man to enter the kingdom of god" (*Matthew* 19:24). "Woe to the rich, for you have received your consolation" (*Luke* 6:24). "You cannot serve god and mammon both" (*Luke*

16:13). "Lay not up for yourselves treasures upon earth, where moth and rust doth corrupt, and where thieves break through and steal: but lay up for yourselves treasures in heaven" (*Matthew* 6:19-20).

Fallen woman redeemed
Ariadne was the daughter of King Midas of Crete, and sister of the mighty half-man/half-bull Minotaur called Aristios (Hesiod's *Catalogues of Women* 76, Homer's *Odyssey* 11.321-325). When Theseus came to Crete, she fell madly in love with him, and conspired to help him win free of the labyrinth. She also helped him kill her brother, and burn the port of Crete, crippling her father's navy (Plutarch's *Theseus*). Abandoning her home and family, she fled with Theseus until he tired of her, and left her to die on the isle of Naxos. Desperate, she was about to toss herself onto the jagged rocks in the ocean, when Dionysos appeared to her out of nowhere. Redeemed by his love for her, Ariadne became the Queen of the Bacchantes, and her bridal crown was placed in the heavens as a reminder of the transformative power of love (Apollodoros' *Library* 3.1.2).

When we first meet Mary Magdalene, she is a prostitute caught in sin (*John* 8:7). Jesus stops her from being stoned, and then casts seven devils out of her (*Mark* 16:9). After that, she was a devoted follower of Jesus, anointing his feet (*Luke* 7) and traveling with the disciples. According to John, she was the first to arrive at the empty tomb of Christ (*John* 20:1), the one to tell Peter and the beloved disciple (*John* 20:2) and the first to actually see the risen Jesus (*John* 20:14). Clearly, she had an important position within Jesus' circle of followers.

Though this was questioned by Peter in the *Apocryphal Gospel of Mary*. After she relayed certain teachings that the Savior had given especially to her, Peter objected, saying, "Did he really speak with a woman without our knowledge (and) not openly? Are we to turn about and all listen to her? Did he prefer her to us?" Levi answered and said to Peter, "Peter, you have always been hot-tempered. Now I see you contending against the woman like the adversaries. But if the Savior made her worthy, who are you indeed to reject her?" (*Gospel of Mary* 15, 1-19,2). This has led some to suspect that Jesus and Mary had a deep, perhaps even sexual relationship. A number of recent books – some good, some terrible – have been written detailing the supposed bloodline that sprang from the union of Christ and Mary Magdalene.

Bisexuality
Livy says that the Bacchanalia came under suppression in Rome in part because of the homosexual initiation rite that was practiced (*History of Rome* 39:8). Dionysos was explicitly called "bisexual" by Orpheus (Hymn 42 *To Mise*) and "the womanly one" by Aiskhylos (*Fragment* 61). He was connected in romantic liaisons with at least two young men – Prosymnos (Pausanias' *Guide to Greece* 2.37.5) and Ampelos (Nonnos *Dionysiaka* 10:175).

According to the Canonical Gospels, Jesus never married, though he had a beloved disciple – probably John – who often lay upon his bosom and whispered things in his ear (*John* 13:23). This may shed some light on what's contained in the "secret" *Gospel of Mark*. This is a section of the book that Clement of Alexandria claimed was authentic, but hidden because it was liable to be mistaken. According to him, after the resurrection of Lazarus, Mark is supposed to continue as follows:

> "'And going in immediately where the young man was, he stretched out a hand and raised him up, holding his hand. Then, the man looked at him and loved him and he began to call him to his side, that he might be with him. And going from the tomb, they went to the house of the young man. For he was rich. And after six days, Jesus instructed him. And when it was late, the young man went to him. He had put a linen around his naked body, and he remained with him through that night. For Jesus taught him the mystery of the kingdom of God. After he got up from there, he turned to the region of the Jordan.' And after these things, this follows: 'James and John go to him," and that whole section. But the 'naked man with naked man' and the other things you wrote about are not found."
> (*Clement to Theodore*)

Anger

Jesus often accused the Pharisees of being "vipers" or "hypocrites" (*Matthew* 12:34, 15:7, 22:18; *Mark* 7:6). He even went so far as to call some of them "fools" after having specifically admonished others not to use this term, warning that to do so would make them liable to the "fire of hell" (*Matthew* 5:22, 23:17). He looked upon his enemies with anger (*Mark* 3:5). In a rage he "cleansed" the temple – going so far as to attack merchants with a whip (*John* 2:15). He angrily cursed a fig tree when it failed to yield fruit out of season (*Mark* 11:12-14). When accused of being "demon possessed" and crazy he reacted with hostility (*Matthew* 12:22-31; *Mark* 3:20-30). Many of his statements were wrathful, such as:

> "Think not that I am come to send peace: I came not to send peace but a sword." (*Matthew* 10:34)

> "He that hath no sword, let him sell his garment, and buy one." (*Luke* 22:36)

> "But those mine enemies, which would not that I should reign over them, bring hither, and slay them before me." (*Luke* 19:27)

> "If a man abide not in me, he is cast forth as a branch, and is withered; and men gather them, and cast them into the fire, and they are burned." (*John* 15:6)

And he even cursed the inhabitants of several cities, because a few individuals failed to be sufficiently impressed with his "mighty works" to believe what he taught (*Matthew* 11:22-24; *Luke* 10:13-15).

Similarly, Orpheus called Dionysos "loud-roaring" (*Hymn* 30) and "wrathful in the extreme" (*Hymn* 45). He could be especially harsh in punishing his enemies. Dionysos had Pentheus torn apart by his mother and aunts for trying to suppress his worship (Euripides' *Bakchai*). Lycurgus broke up a group of mainades, and chased them with an ox-goad. In retaliation, Dionysos caused him to kill his beloved son, struck him blind, and eventually had him torn apart by a pack of panthers on Mount Rhodope where he had been exposed by his people as a blight (Apollodoros' *Library* 3.5.1; Hyginus' *Fabulae* 132, 192, 242). He made the daughters of Minyas tear apart their infant sons, and then had them transformed into screeching bats (Hesiod's *Catalogues of Women* 84). The daughters of Proteus were driven mad, and made to think they were cattle roaming the hills (Hesiod's *Catalogues of Women* 18). He brought a plague and madness to the people of Attika because they had sheltered the murderers of his friend Ikarios (Hyginus' *Fabulae* 130). And when a group of pirates tried to abduct him, he turned them into dolphins, and had wild animals maul the captain (*Homeric Hymn* 7).

Following him more important than familial obligations

Jesus never used the word "family" in a positive manner. According to the Canonical Gospels, he never married or fathered children, and to his own mother he said, "Woman, what have I to do with thee?" (*John* 2:4). Some of his pronouncements about familial relations seem downright harsh. For instance:

> "If any man come to me, and hate not his father, and mother, and wife, and children, and brethren, and sisters, yea, and his own life also, he cannot be my disciple." (*Luke* 14:26)

> "I am come to set a man at variance against his father, and the daughter against her mother, and the daughter in law against her mother in law. And a man's foes shall be they of his own household." (*Matthew* 10:35-36)

> "But those mine enemies, which would not that I should reign over them, bring hither, and slay them before me." (*Luke* 19:27)

And when one of his disciples requested time off for his father's funeral, Jesus rebuked him: "Let the dead bury their dead" (*Matthew* 8:22).

Dionysos represents freedom and the liberation of the individual. He upturns normal standards, and causes mothers, wives, and daughters to leave their homes and dance wild in the hills, completely abandoning the traditional roles that they have been assigned. Those who do not heed his call often suffer for it. His aunts had refused to acknowledge his divinity after Semele's death, so he drove them, and all the women of Thebes, mad into the hills where they joined the mainades in their wild rites. The culmination of their punishment occurred when Agave, the mother of the new king who also resisted the god's worship, was forced to tear her child limb from limb, and parade with his severed head (Euripides' *Bakchai*). The daughters of Minyas in nearby Orchomenus also refused to worship him, staying in their homes to weave while the women of the city danced in the streets in his honor. In a fit of madness, they tore apart one of their infant sons, and then were transformed into bats (Hesiod's *Catalogues of Women* 84). The daughters of Proteus also found Dionysos' worship distasteful, preferring to remain at home instead of taking part in the wild celebration. So he drove them mad, making them think that they were cattle, and they ate the children they had suckled at their breasts. It took the seer Melampus to clear the plague of madness from Argos (Hesiod's *Catalogues of Women* 18).

Great army

When the temple authorities came to take Jesus, he boasted, "Thinkest thou that I cannot now pray to my Father, and he shall presently give me more than twelve legions of angels?" (*Matthew* 26:53). Apparently after being crucified, he wanted a more tangible army, so he commanded his disciples:

> "Go ye therefore, and teach all nations, baptizing them in the name of the Father, and of the Son, and of the Holy Ghost. Teaching them to observe all things whatsoever I have commanded you: and, lo, I am with you always, even unto the end of the world. Amen." (*Matthew* 28:19-20)

Dionysos had a large army (Nonnos' *Dionysiaka* 14.247). It was comprised of satyrs, sileni, pans, mainades, nymphs, goddesses, and throngs of mortals that he picked up in his various travels. With this army, he conquered the East including Syria, Egypt, Bactria, and as far as India (Euripides' *Bakchai* 13, Pausanias' *Guide to Greece* 10:29, Arrian's *Indika* 5).

Betrayal

Originally, Orpheus started out as a devoted follower of the god Dionysos. He sang beautiful hymns in the god's honor, and was even said to have invented mysteries or secret religious rites for him (Aristophanes' *Frogs* 1032; Plato's *Republic* 2.365e-366a; Pausanias' *Description of Greece* 2.30.2, 9.30.4, 10.7.2). However, after the death of his beautiful wife Eurydice, he had no use for the god of life and the exuberant, lusty world he presided over (Ovid's *Metamorphoses* 10.1-85). He began to worship Helios (Eratosthenes, *Cat.* 24), taught severe asceticism such as abstention from wine and animal sacrifice, and introduced homosexuality (Ovid's *Metamorphoses* 11.1-84). For this, he incurred the wrath of the Thracian women, who tore him apart in a frenzy (Pausanias' *Description of Greece* 9:30.5, Aiskhylos' *Bassarids*). His head, ripped from his neck, was tossed into a river where it floated out to Lesbos. Miraculously, it continued to sing, and the Lesbians erected a temple in his honor, from which the head prophesied for them. Angry, Dionysos turned the Thracian mainades into trees for what they had done to his one-time friend. He placed the poet's lyre in the heavens as the constellation Lyra (Hyginus' *Poetica Astronomica* 2.7).

Similarly, Jesus was betrayed by one of his disciples, Judas Iscariot. For thirty pieces of silver (*Matthew* 26:14-15) he led the chief priests and their guards to the Garden of Gethsemane, where they took and crucified his Lord (*Matthew* 26:47).

Transfiguration

About a week after his sojourn in Cæsarea Philippi, Jesus took with him Peter and James and John and led them to a high mountain apart, where he was transfigured before their ravished eyes. Matthew says "his face did shine as the sun: and his garments became white as snow" (*Matthew* 17:1-6). The *Catholic Encyclopedia* says, "This dazzling brightness which emanated from his whole body was produced by an interior shining of his Divinity." The *Bakchai* ends with a similar scene, with Dionysos appearing on the wall of Pentheus' palace "in the glory of his godhead."

Trial

One may compare the scene in the *Bakchai* (510-670) where King Pentheus arrests, berates, and condemns Dionysos, who has passively allowed himself to be caught and imprisoned, with Jesus' appearance before Pontius Pilate (*Matthew* 27:1-31). In both cases they make evasive responses to the questions.

> "Pentheus: 'The god – you claim to you saw him clearly – what was he like?' Dionysos: 'Whatever he wished – I did not order him about.'" (563-64)

> "Pilate therefore said unto him, Art thou a king then? Jesus answered, Thou sayest that I am a king." (*John* 18:37)

Another similarity occurs when Jesus says to Pilate, "You would have no authority at all over me, had it not been granted you from above" (*John* 19:11). Earlier, Dionysos had said, "Nothing can touch me that is not ordained" (*Bakchai* 602).

Jesus said of his persecutors, "They know not what they are doing," (*Luke* 23:34) just as Dionysos had said to Pentheus, "You know not what you are doing, nor what you are saying, nor even who you are" (*Bakchai* 592).

Death

Mark relates the death of Jesus as follows:

> "And so Pilate, willing to content the people, released Barabbas unto them, and delivered Jesus, when he had scourged him, to be crucified. And the soldiers led him away into the hall, called Praetorium; and they call together the whole band. And they clothed him with purple, and platted a crown of thorns, and put it about his head, And began to salute him, Hail, King of the Jews! And they smote him on the head with a reed, and did spit upon him, and bowing their knees worshiped him. And when they had mocked him, they took off the purple from him, and put his own clothes on him, and led him out to crucify him. And they compel one Simon a

Cyrenian, who passed by, coming out of the country, the father of Alexander and Rufus, to bear his cross. And they bring him unto the place Golgotha, which is, being interpreted, The place of a skull. And they gave him to drink wine mingled with myrrh: but he received it not. And when they had crucified him, they parted his garments, casting lots upon them, what every man should take. And it was the third hour, and they crucified him. And the superscription of his accusation was written over, THE KING OF THE JEWS. And with him they crucify two thieves; the one on his right hand, and the other on his left. And the scripture was fulfilled, which saith, And he was numbered with the transgressors. And they that passed by railed on him, wagging their heads, and saying, Ah, thou that destroyest the temple, and buildest it in three days, Save thyself, and come down from the cross. Likewise also the chief priests mocking said among themselves with the scribes, He saved others; himself he cannot save. Let Christ the King of Israel descend now from the cross, that we may see and believe. And they that were crucified with him reviled him. And when the sixth hour was come, there was darkness over the whole land until the ninth hour. And at the ninth hour Jesus cried with a loud voice, saying, *Eloi, Eloi, lama sabachthani?* which is, being interpreted, My God, my God, why hast thou forsaken me? And some of them that stood by, when they heard it, said, Behold, he calleth Elias. And one ran and filled a sponge full of vinegar, and put it on a reed, and gave him to drink, saying, Let alone; let us see whether Elias will come to take him down. And Jesus cried with a loud voice, and gave up the ghost." (*Mark* 15:15-37)

The Greeks knew several deaths for the god Dionysos. The best known occurred while he was still an infant. Jealous Hera sought to slay the beloved son of Zeus, so she raised the Titans up from Tartaros, and they set upon the young god. He evaded their clutches by taking on different forms – a lion, a horse, a man, and finally a bull, but all his effort was for naught, for the Titans eventually caught the child, holding him by hoof and horn, and fulfilled their obligation to Hera by tearing the child to pieces. These pieces they cooked in a stew of milk, and then roasted over a fire, before they commenced their awful feast. The smell of roasting flesh drew the boy's father, and Zeus upon discovering what happened, hurled his mighty lightning bolts at the Titans, burning them up where they stood. From the steam that rose from their burning flesh came an ash, and it was out of this ash, the Orphics claimed, that man arose. Therefore we have within us both a divine element (Dionysos) and an infernal element (the Titans) and we must strive to separate the divine from the infernal – only then will we be free. Athena managed to save the heart or phallos of the child, and with this Zeus was able to recreate his son. He did this either by eating the heart himself, or by giving it in a potion to Semele, the daughter of King Kadmos (Pausanias' *Guide to Greece* 8.37.3; Diodoros Sikeliotes 3:62; *Orphic Hymn* 14:6, Clement of Alexandria's *Address to the Greeks* 2.16).

There is also a lesser known death, recorded by Pausanias. He said that when Dionysos came to Argos with the *Haliai* or "the sea women" they were resisted by Perseus, and a terrible bloody battle ensued. Afterwards, there was a mass grave, which was still shown in his day (*Guide to Greece* 2:20.4; 22.1). The *Scholion* on Iliad 19.319 adds that Perseus killed Dionysos by hanging, and then threw his body into the lake at Lerna.

Sought but not found
After the crucifixion, Jesus was placed in a tomb with a heavy boulder rolled in front of the entrance. A guard was placed outside, and yet when Mary Magdalene came to view the body, she found the tomb empty, Jesus miraculously having risen (*John* 20:1).

After interrogating Dionysos, Pentheus had him bound and imprisoned. But the god easily slipped out, and when Pentheus came back to taunt him, he found the cell empty (Euripides' *Bakchai* 746).

Descent into Hell and ascent to Heaven
After Dionysos had succeeded in conquering the Indians, and performing many great things here on Earth, he was ready to take his place among the immortals on Olympos. But before he did that, he had one last thing to accomplish: raising up his mother from Hades. The most popular account has him go down through the bottomless lake at Lerna (Pausanias 2.32.2). He either wrestled Hades, the Lord of the Dead, or offered the beautiful myrtle in place of his mother's shade. Dionysos led her up to the world of the living, and gave her the new name Thyone – which means "boisterous one." After that, he led her up to Olympos where she was given divine honors, (Apollodoros' *Library* 3.5.3) and was even reconciled with the jealous Hera (Nonnos' *Dionysiaka* 9.206).

After Jesus was killed, he descended into Hades, and "the third day he rose again, and ascended into heaven" (*The Nicene Creed*). Luke in Acts also asserts that Jesus went down into hell (*Acts* 2:31) as does *1 Peter* 3:18, which reads, "being put to death in the flesh, but quickened by the spirit, by which also he went and preached unto the spirits in prison (hell)." Clement of Alexandria agrees, saying, "The Lord preached the gospel to those in Hades, as well as to all in earth, In order that all might believe and be saved, wherever they were." According to the *Gospel of Nicodemus*, Jesus raised the righteous dead with him while he was in hell.

Intercessor between god and man
In Christianity, Jesus is the mediator between a perfect, wrathful god and weak, fallen humanity. John says that god sent his son to be a bridge (*John* 3:16). And Paul taught that there was "one god, and one mediator of god and men, the man Christ Jesus" (*I Timothy* 2:6). He goes on to praise god:

> "who hath delivered us from the power of darkness, and hath translated us into the kingdom of the son of his love, In whom we have redemption through his blood, the remission of sins; who is the image of the invisible god, the firstborn of every creature...all things

were created by him and in him. And he is before all and by him all things consist. And he is the head of the body, the church, who is the beginning the firstborn from the dead; that in all things he may hold the primacy: Because in him, it hath well pleased the father, that all fullness should dwell; And through him to reconcile all things unto himself, making peace through the blood of his cross, both as to the things that are on earth, and the things that are in heaven." (*Colossians* 1:13-20)

Dionysos occupies a similar position. He mediates between the angry gods, bringing reconciliation to Hera and Hephaistos (Pausanias' 1.20.3). Dionysos taught man how to pour libations during festivals – the principal means of intercourse between gods and men (Ovid's *Fasti* 3.727). And in fact, "Himself a god, he is poured out to the other gods, so that from him we mortals have what's good in life" (Euripides' *Bakchai* 332-35).

Pentecost

According to Luke in *Acts*, about 50 days after the resurrection the followers of Jesus were gathered together, when the spirit of God descended from Heaven and took possession of them (*Acts* 2:1-4). They began making strange noises (7) and the people thought that they were drunk on new wine (13). Paul himself worried that strangers, seeing these spiritual gifts, might think the members of the Church mad (*1 Corinthians* 14:23).

There's a long tradition of religious madness within the Greek religion. According to Plato, "the greatest of blessings come to us through madness, when it is sent as a gift of the gods" (*Phaidros*). In madness, we are taken out of ourselves (*ekstasis*) and filled with a god or spirit (*enthousiasmos*). In this state, we see clearer than we ever could normally, speak things we could never normally know. Dionysos was uniquely associated with madness, *mania*. He was called *Mainomenos* "the maddened one" and was attended by *mainades* the "mad-women." And of course, a person drunk on his wine looks both mad and beatific.

Assorted information

John the Baptist claimed that the one who would follow him – Jesus – would take winnowing-fan in hand and separate wheat from the chaff. (*Luke* 3:18) Dionysos was called Liknites ("he of the winnowing fan") because this tool was used for a "baptism by air," as one can see in the vase paintings which show initiates veiled and seated with a winnowing fan being waved above their heads (Jane Ellen Harrison's *Prolegomena to the Study of Greek Religion*, pages 401-2).

In the *Bakchai*, Dionysos comes to earth in human form. He says that he has "veiled his godhead in a mortal shape" in order to make it "manifest to mortal men" (5). This is similar to John's statement that Jesus became "the Word made flesh" (*John* 1:14) and Paul's statement that Jesus appeared "in the likeness of sinful flesh" (*Romans* 8:3).

Jesus instituted the Eucharist with the words, "Do this in remembrance of me" (*Luke* 22:7-23). It is thought that drama developed out of the worship of Dionysos: tragedy in remembrance of his death and suffering at the hands of the Titans, comedy to commemorate the joyous time of his return or of his marriage to Ariadne.

According to *Revelation* 4:7 a lion sits before the throne of Christ. Dionysos was constantly attended by lions and panthers and lynxes (Nonnos' *Dionysiaka* 6:296, Ovid's *Metamorphoses* 9:391-417). Which, perhaps, has something to do with Celsus' claims about Jesus' father. He found the Virgin Birth story absurd, and quoted a Jewish tradition which held that Jesus had fabricated the story to cover up the fact that his real father was a Greek soldier by the name of Panthera (*Contra Celsum* 1.32).

At one point Jesus was dressed to look like Dionysos, with a purple robe, a plaited crown, and a reed in his hand like a thyrsos (*Matthew* 27:28-29).

A council at Constantinople in 691 CE forbade people to wear satyr masks while treading the grapes, or to call out the name of Dionysos. They were supposed to substitute Jesus' name instead (Carl Kerenyi, *Dionysos* page 67).

Justin Martyr wrote: "The devils, accordingly, when they heard these prophetic words about Christ, said that Bacchus was the son of Jupiter, and having been torn in pieces, he ascended into heaven" (*First Apology*, 54).

A twelfth-century Byzantine play about the Passion of Christ (*Christus Patiens*), once attributed to Gregory the Great, makes ample use of material from Euripides' *Bakchai* – so much so that we can piece together lacunae in the text from that work (Reginald Gibbons' *Appendix* to Euripides' *Bakchai*, page 135).

Nonnos of Panopolis (c. 400) was a Bishop of the Egyptian Church. He is remembered primarily for his two major works – one, a Paraphrase of the Gospel of John into hexameter verse, and the *Dionysiaka*, a huge work detailing the many myths of Dionysos. It is unknown which work he write first, but from internal evidence, it would seem that the Paraphrase was the earlier work, meaning that he wrote the lusty *Dionysiaka* while a Christian – and perhaps even as a Bishop.

Many of the early Popes had names related to Dionysos. For instance, there was: St. Linus (67-76), St. Soter (166-175), St. Eleutherius (175-189), St. Victor I (189-199), St. Anterus (235-36), St. Dionysius (260-268), Liberius (352-66), and Sabinian (604-606) (*The Catholic Encyclopedia*).

There were an exceptional number of Dionysian saints as well:

> Ss Sergius and Bacchus – feast day: October 7. Syrian soldiers and lovers who were tortured for refusing to participate in State sacrifices. Paraded through the streets dressed as women, they persevered because, as St. Bacchus reassured his partner, "the delights of heaven were greater than any suffering, and that part of their reward would be to be re-united in heaven as lovers."
>
> St. Denys – feast day: October 9. Patron of France. After having his head cut off, he carried it to France. Vines grew up on the spot where he finally came to rest.

St Dionysia – feast day: December 6. A beautiful woman scourged to death in the forum by Arian Christians in 484.

St Dionysia – feast day: May 15. A 16 girl who rebuked a Christian when he recanted, took his place.

St Dionysius – feast day: July 27. One of the 'seven sleepers' who were walled up, and then awoke about two hundred years later.

St Dionysius – feast day: February 8. Armenian monk and martyr.

St Dionysius – feast day: September 20. Martyred in Asia Minor. No account remains.

St Dionysius – feast day: February 14. Martyred in Alexandria, when his head was cut off.

St Dionysius the Aeropagite – feast day: October 9. Converted by St Paul. First Bishop of Athens.

St Dionysius – feast day: May 8. Bishop of Vienne, in Dauphine, France, successor of St. Justus.

St Dionysius – feast day: October 3. Martyred in Alexandria in 250

St Dionysius – feast day: May 12 Martyred in Rome in 304

Blessed Dionysius – feast day: November 29. A Carmelite martyr called Dionysius of the Nativity. Slain in Sumatra, Indonesia in 1638

Blessed Dionysius Fugishima – feast day: March 5. A Japanese-born Jesuit novice, slain at Shimabara in 1622.

St Dionysius of Alexandria – feast day: November 17. Called 'the Great' because he comforted plague victims, and the "Teacher of the Catholic Church" because of his learning.

St. Dionysius of Augsburg – feast day: February 26. Martyred in Germany in 303.

St. Dionysius of Corinth – feast day: April 8. Famed for his letters.

St. Dionysius of Milan – feast day: May 25. Banished for defending St. Athanasius; died in exile.

St. Pope Dionysius – feast day: December 26. Rebuilt the Church after the persecutions of Emperor Valerian.

St. Dionysius Sebuggwao – feast day: June 3. Martyred in Uganda, Africa by King Mwanga in 1885.

St. Eleutherius – feast day: August 4. Martyr of Tarsus, Turkey.

St. Eleutherius – feast day: August 16 Bishop of Auxerre, France. He was a patron of the monastic movement and known for his care of the poor.

St. Eleutherius feast day: October 2. A soldier in the army of Emperor Diocletian in Nicomedia. He was accused of setting fire to the emperor's palace and was burned to death after being tortured with companions. (*Catholic Saints Online* http://www.catholic.org/)

Conclusion

So what does this all mean? Are Dionysos and Jesus actually the same god or just incredibly similar? Did the early Christians borrow extensively from the myths and cult of Dionysos when creating their god? Or are there similarities only because we want to see them? Perhaps I am pulling the wool over your eyes, weaving together random, unconnected information in order to "make the weaker argument appear the stronger?" As Pontius Pilate asked when presented with Jesus – what is the truth? (*John* 18:38). That, my dear reader, I leave up to you to decide.

THE BULL-LOVING KINGS: A BRIEF STUDY OF THE PTOLEMAIC PATRONAGE OF THE APIS CULT

The Ptolemies were, unquestionably, a deeply religious family. This only makes sense since they governed a people whom Herodotos (*The Histories* 2.37) characterized as the most conspicuously religious of all the nations of the earth and for whom the role of Pharaoh was first and foremost a sacred office. At one time or another, the Ptolemies had dealings with almost all of the gods of the Greek and Egyptian pantheons. In fact, my compendium listing sources on the Gods of the Ptolemies really just scratches the surface and is in need of substantial revision and addition. However, incomplete as it is, it ought to make apparent to even the most casual reader how seriously the Ptolemies took their responsibilities as Greco-Egyptian monarchs, building temples, funding festivals, maintaining strong contacts with the native priesthoods, and having intense personal encounters with the gods of their adopted homeland. In fact, most of the impressive ruins which tourists visit today – and which shape our very conception of the religious life of Egypt – date from the Ptolemaic or early Roman period. Without the Ptolemies Egypt's religion might not have lasted as long as it did – and our knowledge of it would certainly be greatly impoverished. In fact, most of the complete ritual texts that we possess come from Ptolemaic-era temples and the Egyptian language might never have been deciphered without the trilingual decrees which the Ptolemies had made and set up throughout the country in Greek, Demotic, and Hieroglyphs. Clearly, then, the Ptolemies did much for the gods.

One could argue which of these gods were most important to the dynasty. An obvious candidate for this position would have to be Dionysos. They claimed direct descent from him, modeled their kingship after his mythic role as culture-bringer and peaceful conqueror, they personally oversaw his cult and promoted it abroad, and several were even thought to be mortal incarnations of the god on earth.

Another candidate would have to be Isis. In fact, the Ptolemies were largely responsible for the transformation of the Kemetic Aset into the more familiar Hellenistic "goddess of ten thousand names," playing up her connections with the Greek Demeter and developing proper mysteries for her along the lines of those from Eleusis. This universal mother-goddess was exported to Rome from Alexandria and went on to become one of the most popular deities of late antiquity, her worship found in places as far apart as the British Isles and Afghanistan. Without the influence of the Ptolemies this likely never would have happened.

Other significant deities that we might add to this list are Serapis, Zeus, Aphrodite, Agathos Daimon, Re, Hathor and Ptah. In fact, this last god and his powerful priesthood at Memphis played a pivotal role in shaping the royal ideology of the Ptolemies. When Soter first took control of the country he resided at Memphis, the ancient capital of the country and the place where, according to myth, Upper and Lower Egypt were first unified. The High Priest of Ptah at Memphis served as the *de facto* "Pope" of Egypt, and advised Ptolemy Soter of the duties expected of him as acting Pharaoh. The Memphite priesthood helped bring the rest of the country in line, accommodating them to foreign rule. This priesthood was a hereditary one and its holders maintained a close working relationship with the successive generations of Ptolemies (including presiding over their coronation) accumulating great power and wealth in the process. They functioned as a native nobility and may even have intermarried with the Ptolemies. At least, they are the likeliest candidate to fill the unknown position of Kleopatra VII's mysterious grandmother – though that is a topic of much heated academic debate, especially in recent years with the rise of the "Afrocentric" school of Egyptology.

The god who deserves an even more honored place in the Ptolemaic "pantheon," however, would have to be Ptah's neighbor at Memphis, the Apis bull. According to the official Memphite doctrine Apis *was* Ptah, or at least an incarnation of him, for it is said that the *ba* or soul of Ptah was resident in the bull and Ptah was often claimed as his father. Egyptian religion being what it is, a dreamlike, constantly shifting, polyvalent system of complex and often contradictory associations, this role could also be claimed for Osiris and other deities as well. In fact, the Greeks saw a connection between Apis and their own Dionysos, a syncretism that I will explore more fully in another essay.

The Ptolemaic fondness for Apis was natural (considering the important role he played in legitimizing the Pharaoh) and was established early in the reign of the dynasty. In fact, it began even before Ptolemy Soter claimed the title of Satrap of Egypt. Arrian (*Campaigns of Alexander* 3.1.1-4) claims that after Alexander liberated the country from Persian rule he traveled to Memphis and had himself crowned as Pharaoh in the customary Egyptian manner. His first act after coronation was to make offerings to the Apis bull. This, of course, had a twofold purpose. First, this was one of the duties of the Pharaoh since the Apis bull was intimately linked with the kingship. The Apis bull was the embodiment of the land's fertility and partly responsible for the life-giving inundation of the Nile. (Though there was also a great deal more to the association, the similarities between the names Hapy, the river and Hapi, the bull may have contributed to this.) Part of the coronation rites involved the yoking of the bull and leading him down the processional route. This ceremony needed to be repeated every thirty years as part of the *Heb Sed* or Jubilee Festival, which proved the King's physical and spiritual fitness to rule the country.

But there was also another reason why Alexander went out of his way to honor the Apis bull in such a conspicuous fashion, and that was to create a marked contrast between his rule and that of the Persians which he had come to replace. Although Persian rule was generally tolerant of its conquered peoples' religious customs (think of the position of the Jews during the Babylonian captivity and afterward, as described in the books of *Ezra* and *Nehemiah*) in both Egypt and Greece they had committed grievous sins against the gods. In Athens, Khios, Lesbos, Tenedos and Euboia the Persians under Xerxes had burned down temples to the gods (Herodotos 5.102, 6.101) and Kambyses had murdered the Apis bull in Egypt, running him through with his own sword and mocking the people for their superstitious reverence for animals (Herodotos 3.28). Further, Kambyses ransacked the treasures from the temples – including the statues of the gods he mocked – confiscated temple lands and imposed heavy taxes on the priests. Needless to say, this did not endear the Egyptian people to their Persian overlords and there were frequent rebellions, put down with excessive cruelty. When Alexander came on the scene he was greeted with wild celebration, the long-awaited redeemer, the earthly embodiment of Horus the Avenger of his father who would drive evil out of the land and establish the country on a firm foundation of Ma'at. Alexander exploited this popular support by conforming his actions to Egyptian expectations, observing all of the proper protocols and allowing himself to be declared the son of Ammon at Siwah (Diodoros Sikeliotes, *Historical Library* 17.51.1-4).

Years later when Ptolemy came to power in Egypt he made sure to follow in the footsteps of Alexander. Even as a mere Satrap he campaigned in Asia to retrieve the statues and temple treasures from foreign possession (*The Satrap Stele*). He abolished the unjust laws and crushing taxes which had remained in place under Alexander's corrupt official Kleomenes of Naukratis and he returned temple properties and power to the various priesthoods. But one of the most notable actions that he undertook early in his rule concerned the sacred Apis bull.

Shortly after he took over the satrapy, the Apis bull known as the son of the Cow *Ta-nt-Aset II* (all Apis bulls were named after their mothers), whom Alexander had worshiped in Memphis, died. It was now time to bury the bull, which needed to be done before his successor could be found. This was a long, complicated process lasting over 70 days – and it was also extremely expensive. An ornate sarcophagus had to be constructed, along with a monumental vault in the Serapeion. A seemingly endless series of ceremonies would need to be performed, with costly offerings and elaborate displays of mourning by the community conducted at every step. People from all parts of the country would make the pilgrimage to Memphis and follow the procession to the burial grounds of Saqqara where all of the previous Apis bulls were interred. But the country was in a state of abject poverty after the Persians, and the financial reforms that Ptolemy had instituted had yet to fully take effect with the people still waiting for the benefits to trickle down.

So Ptolemy did the proper thing and made a substantial donation out of his own personal treasury – 50 talents of silver according to Diodoros 1.84.8 – to fund the burial of the Apis. With this generous bequeathment Soter established a precedent which all of his descendants were to follow to a greater or lesser extent. Though Ptolemaic benefactions extended far and wide, Apis retained a significant place in the dynasty's affections. Numerous priestly decrees and royal prescriptions cite the Ptolemies' patronage of the cults of the Apis and Mnevis bulls as being worthy of outstanding honor:

> "King Ptolemy and Queen Berenike his sister and wife, the Benevolent Gods, have made benefits many and great to the temples of Egypt for all time: since they have taken perpetual care of the things of the glorious Apis, Mnevis, and all animals of the temple which are protected in Egypt, for whom they assigned great things supplying numerous things." – *The Kanopos Decree*

> "And whereas he bestowed many gifts upon Apis and Mnevis and upon the other sacred animals in Egypt, because he was much more considerate than the kings before him of all that belonged to the gods; and for their burials he gave what was suitable lavishly and splendidly, and what was regularly paid to their special shrines, with sacrifices and festivals and other customary observances; and he maintained the honors of the temples and of Egypt according to the laws; and he adorned the temple of Apis with rich work, spending upon it gold and silver and precious stones, no small amount; and whereas he has founded temples and shrines and altars, and has repaired those requiring it, having the spirit of a beneficent god in matters pertaining to religion." – *The Rosetta Stone*

> "And King Ptolemy and Kleopatra have decreed that the expenses for the burial of Apis and Mnevis shall be met from the royal treasury, as with those of the royal family who are deified after death. Similarly with the sums for the other sacred animals." – *P. Teb.* 5.75-80

I could go on but, well, you probably get the picture. It is interesting to note, however, that some of the Ptolemies even included the god in their royal titulary or made an exceptional effort to align themselves with the deity. Ptolemy IX Soter II, for instance, was described as "shining out in Egypt at the same time as the living Apis" or "distinguished in his birth together with that of the living Apis" since his birth had coincided with that of the Apis bull, an auspicious omen to be sure. (Though Soter II's reign was not as felicitous as one might expect from this, as we shall presently discover.) Kleopatra VII's reign was also defined by the lifecycle of the Apis bulls. Early in her rule, when she was still co-regent with her elder brother Ptolemy XIII, the Apis bull of the Cow *Ta-nt-Bastet* died, and the Queen made a personal contribution to its burial (*Louvre Stele* 24). Towards the end of her reign she interred the Apis bull of the Cow *Ta-nt-Leby* – generally speaking, an Apis could be expected to live around 22-25 years – who is the bull that Octavian refused to visit after conquering Egypt, claiming that he "worshiped gods, not cattle" (Diodoros 51.16.5).

Unfortunately, not all of the Ptolemies were so favorably inclined towards the cult of the Apis bull. Ptolemy X Alexander I had a tumultuous relationship with his elder brother, Soter II, the two young men competing with each other for many years for the throne of Egypt. At one point Alexander I ousted Soter II, exiling him to Kypros. During his reign the Apis bull of the Cow *Gerget Mut-iyti* died. Work on his vault had begun as far back as 96 BCE but came to an abrupt halt under Alexander I, who not only despised his brother but despised the god whom his brother loved. In fact, without royal support the bull of *Gerget Mut-iyti* lay uninterred until the eleventh year of the next Apis, when Soter II was finally restored to power and could properly lay the bull to rest (*Louvre Stele* 113). Thankfully the Egyptians were exceptionally skilled at the art of embalming — because I can't imagine that that would have been a particularly pleasant situation otherwise!

And don't worry, dear reader, Alexander I got his just reward for treating the Apis bull in such a disgraceful manner. You see, Alexander I was immensely unpopular with his subjects. He was also monstrously obese. So fat, in fact, that he was unable to walk about on his own and needed an assistant on either arm to help him move. That is, when he was sober. Drunk, he could display extraordinary agility in indecent dances (Athenaios, *Deipnosophistai* 12.550b). When the Egyptian army turned against him he was forced to flee to Syria, but before he left the country he stopped off at the *Sema* and stole the golden sarcophagus which contained the mummified remains of his namesake Alexander the Great, so that he would have the wealth necessary to recruit a new mercenary force and regain the country (Strabo, *Geography* 17). Predictably enough, this enraged the Alexandrians and he was hunted down. While at sea, attempting to escape his rabid pursuers, his men mutinied and pushed his corpulent frame into the sea off Kypros to drown. No one, not even his daughter, was said to mourn his passing. Moral of the story: you don't fuck with the Apis bull, something that Kambyses could have told him since Kambyses ended up stabbed in the same place, and with the same weapon that he had used to kill the Apis bull.

Having briefly examined the history of the relationship between the Ptolemies and the Apis bull one may naturally wonder why they chose to patronize this cult so extensively. Apis was not the only deity connected with the ideology of Sacred Kingship in Egypt. Nor was he necessarily the only — or even the most important — god of the Nile flood. Obviously no one at this time, so far removed from their era, can say with certainty *why* they favored this cult, nor am I sure that many of the Ptolemies could have even given us a satisfactory answer. Often, it seems, they did things because they were expected to, because they were told that this is how it had always been done, and must be done for the continuation of Egypt. But I think there may also have been other motivations as well, more personal ones which made this cult especially appealing to them, often above alternative and competing cults. There are two broad reasons for this — one having to do with the living Apis bull, the other having to do with the Apis in death. I shall save the mysteries of the dead bull for another time, and instead focus on those points relevant to his cult as a living deity.

Apis is a fairly unique god, even among the dynamic divinities of the Egyptian pantheon. His uniqueness lies in his immediacy, his epiphanal nature if you will. He is a god who is present, who appears manifest in a physical form which can be experienced directly.

> "About the time when Kambyses arrived at Memphis, Apis appeared to the Egyptians. Now Apis is the god whom the Greeks call Epaphos. As soon as he appeared, straightway all the Egyptians arrayed themselves in their gayest garments, and fell to feasting and jollity: which when Kambyses saw, making sure that these rejoicings were on account of his own ill success, he called before him the officers who had charge of Memphis, and demanded of them – 'Why, when he was in Memphis before, the Egyptians had done nothing of this kind, but waited until now, when he had returned with the loss of so many of his troops?' The officers made answer, 'That one of their gods had appeared to them, a god who at long intervals of time had been accustomed to show himself in Egypt – and that always on his appearance the whole of Egypt feasted and kept jubilee.'" – Herodotos 3.28

> "As soon as a report is circulated that the Egyptian god has manifested himself, certain of the sacred scribes, well versed in the mystical marks, known to them by tradition, approach the spot where the divine cow has deposited her calf, and there, following the ancient ordinance of Hermes, feed it with milk during four months, in a house facing the rising sun. When this period has passed, the sacred scribes and prophets resort to the dwelling of Apis, at the time of the new moon, and, placing him in a boat prepared for the purpose, convey him to Memphis, where he has a convenient and agreeable abode, with pleasure-grounds, and ample space for wholesome exercise. Female companions of his own species are provided for him, the most beautiful that can be found, kept in apartments, to which he has access when he wishes. He drinks out of a well or fountain of clear water; for it is not thought right to give him the water of the Nile, which is considered too fattening. It would be tedious to relate what pompous processions and sacred ceremonies the Egyptians perform on the celebration of the rising of the Nile, at the fete of the Theophania, in honor of this god, or what dances, festivities, and joyful assemblies are appointed on the occasion, in the towns and in the country. The man from whose herd the divine beast has sprung, is the happiest of mortals, and is looked upon with admiration by all people. Apis is an excellent interpretation of futurity. He does not employ virgins or old women sitting on a tripod, like some other gods, nor require that they should be intoxicated with the sacred potion; but inspires boys who

play around his stable with a divine impulse, enabling them to pour out predictions in perfect rhythm." – Aelian, 18.10

Other gods are more distant, abstract or cosmic forces which may only indirectly intersect with our world. Ammon's name means "hidden" and he personified the invisible realm of the upper reaches of the heavens. Thoth and Seshat are deities of the intellect, of wisdom and creative inspiration. Ma'at is more a concept than a goddess. Re's true name – and thus his full nature – is a secret even to the other gods. And time and time again we are told that this or that deity's likeness has been seen and understood by no man. The gods might descend and inhabit their cult images – but these were merely the physical vessels that temporarily housed their *ba* or *ka* (spirits or souls, respectively), while they existed elsewhere, far off in lightland. They could choose to reveal themselves to a special devotee through dreams or visions, but this was nothing more than what the Greeks called a *phantasma*, an *eidolon* – a fabricated spiritual image. Even when the oracular god Ammon of Siwah chose to communicate with people, he did so via ecstatic priests carrying his idol on a portable shrine, its movements the medium through which his message was conveyed. (And yes, I know that there are plenty of sources that completely contradict this – but I'm on a roll and have an interesting point to make, so don't interrupt me!)

But Apis was different. He really was the bull in which he incarnated. Obviously there was more to him than that, hence his ability to manifest in successive bulls. But there was only one Apis bull at any given time, and he had to wait until the death of his previous host to be born again. That bull, however, was a living god, and unlike the other gods, he was here on earth in every sense of the word. He could be seen, touched, smelled and heard. There were no intermediaries between the god and his votaries; anyone could approach him and receive his blessing of fertility or benefit from his oracular guidance. In him all that was divine, transcendent, and powerful had been brought down into the physical realm; simultaneously, all that was material, frail, mutable and transient became imbued with divinity.

This was, in many respects, the single dominant theme of the Ptolemies' religiosity. We see it, of course, in their strong association with Dionysos – who himself united mortal and divine elements and was also "the god who comes." But it is there as well in the emphasis on apotheosis (e.g., Soter, Arsinoë, Berenike), on acquiring divine personae and acting out mythical roles on the human stage (e.g., the Pharaoh as Horus incarnate, or Neos Dionysos or Nea Isis) on being living gods who interceded on behalf of their subjects with the divine world, a way for their people to experience the gods here on earth more directly, more intimately than anything previously possible.

Here are a couple of fascinating quotes that shed light on this aspect of Hellenistic monarchy:

> "Demetrios is present, joyful and beautiful, as a god ought to be, with smiling face showering his blessings round. How noble does he look! his friends around, himself the center. His friends resemble the

bright lesser stars, himself is the sun. Hail, ever-mighty Poseidon's mightier son; hail, son of Aphrodite. For other gods do at a distance keep, or have no ears, or no existence; and they heed us not – but you are present, not made of wood or stone, a genuine god. We pray to you. First of all give us peace, O dearest god – for you are lord of peace – and crush for us yourself, for you've the power, this odious Sphinx; which now destroys not Thebes alone, but Greece – the whole of Greece." – Athenaios 6.253d-e

"Though Kleopatra received many letters of summons both from Antony himself and from his friends, she was so bold as to sail up the river Kydnos in a barge with gilded poop, its sails spread purple, its rowers urging it on with silver oars to the sound of the flute blended with pipes and lutes. She herself reclined beneath a canopy spangled with gold, adorned like Venus in a painting, while boys like Loves in paintings stood on either side and fanned her. Likewise also the fairest of her serving-maidens, attired like Nereïds and Graces, were stationed, some at the rudder-sweeps, and others at the reefing-ropes. Wondrous odors from countless incense-offerings diffused themselves along the river-banks. Of the inhabitants, some accompanied her on either bank of the river from its very mouth, while others went down from the city to behold the sight. The throng in the market-place gradually streamed away, until at last Antony himself, seated on his tribunal, was left alone. And a rumor spread on every hand that Venus was come to revel with Bacchus for the good of Asia." – Plutarch, *Life of Antony* 26.1-3

This was not just about personal aggrandizement, an ego-trip on a monumental scale. (Okay, in the case of Demetrios it was – the guy was a total dick, and had his ass handed to him by both Dionysos and Ptolemy Soter on separate occasions.) They took this very seriously, strived to live up to the exalted expectations that came with embodying such powerful forces. Their whole lives became about personifying these gods, bringing them down to the mortal sphere and lifting the world, and the lives of their people, up so that it would intersect with the divine. Kleopatra VII selflessly sought this type of cultural, religious, and political renewal for her country – and almost succeeded on a grand scale. Others, such as Philopator and Auletes, and even, to some extent, Marcus Antonius, found the burden of the role too great and succumbed under the pressure of incarnating the god Dionysos. This is, perhaps, not too surprising. There is a flawed, tragic streak that runs deeply through the god. It is difficult to harness that awesome fertile, creative, liberating and mysterious power without also falling victim to its self-destructive and madness-inducing excesses. One has only to look at modern avatars of the god such as Jim Morrison to see the dangers that come with being a New Dionysos. Perhaps there is even an inevitability and necessity to it: the god himself was mad and torn to pieces, after all.

But with Apis, there was no such danger. In life his vessel was the bull, not a man. (In death, things could be very different indeed.) However, he was still a god in mortal flesh, a god whose cult was steeped in the same ideas of incarnation and appearance. And likewise, Apis embodied that same masculine potency, that procreative force that made the world fresh and green and vibrant with life, just as Dionysos and his human avatars sought to do. It therefore doesn't surprise me in the least that the Ptolemies favored this cult above all others: it was merely a different way of looking at and articulating ideas so central to their whole way of being Greco-Egyptian kings.

THE MIGHTY BULL OF THE TWO LANDS

There is a startling array of evidence which suggests some kind of link between the Egyptian Osiris and the Greek Dionysos. What I have done with this essay is to collect as much of that evidence as I could, so that the reader can determine what sort of connection there may be between the two. I have no theological axe to grind, no hidden agenda in presenting this information, nor do I intend to persuade my audience one way or another. It may be, as certain ancient authors felt, that the two of them are in fact the same God, perceived through slightly different cultural lenses. Then again, it may also be that they are only Gods who share similar roles, myths, histories, and spheres of influence while remaining completely separate, autonomous individuals. And then again, it may be that their similarities are highly inflated, perceived only because the reader desires to see a connection between them, and conveniently disregards those areas where they differ. Although I have my own personal theories, I have tried to keep these out as much as possible, for I do not feel that it is my place to dictate such an important matter for the reader. I have simply provided the information for you to draw your own conclusions – and would recommend that if this is a pressing issue for you, that you go directly to the Gods and ask them themselves. I think the answers you receive will be most interesting indeed.

The testimony of ancient authors

There are numerous ancient authors who assert the essential unity of these two Gods.

> "There is only the difference in names between the festivals of Dionysos and those of Osiris, between the Mysteries of Isis and those of Demeter." – Diodoros Sikeliotes, *The Library of History*, 1.13

> "Osiris, they say, was reared in Nysa, a city of Arabia Felix near Egypt, being a son of Zeus; and the name which he bears among the Greeks is derived both from his father and from the birthplace, since he is called Dionysos." – Diodoros Sikeliotes 1.15

> "Osiris has been given the name Serapis by some, Dionysos by others, Pluto by others, Ammon by others, Zeus by some, and many have considered Pan to be the same God; and some say that Serapis is the God whom the Greeks call Pluto." – Diodoros Sikeliotes 1.25

"That Osiris is identical with Dionysos who could more fittingly know than yourself, Clea? For you are at the head of the Thyiades of Delphi, and have been consecrated by your father and mother in the holy rites of Osiris." – Plutarch, *On Isis and Osiris*, 35

"It is proper to identify Osiris with Dionysos." – Plutarch, *On Isis and Osiris*, 28

"Dionysos was the first to bring from India into Egypt two bulls, one named Apis and the other Osiris." – Phylarchus

"Dionysos and Osiris are the same, who are called *Epaphos*" – Mnaseas

"For no Gods are worshiped by all Egyptians in common except Isis and Osiris, who they say is Dionysos; these are worshiped by all alike." – Herodotos, *The Histories*, 2.42

"Osiris is he who is called Dionysos in the Greek tongue." – Herodotos 2.144

Cicero included Osiris among the many Gods equated with Dionysos by the Greeks. (*De Natura Deorum* 3.21)

"He [Kadmos future king of Thebes in Greece and grandfather of Dionysos] showed forth the Euian secrets of Osiris the wanderer, the Egyptian Dionysos. He learned the nightly celebration of their mystic art, and declaimed the magic hymn in the wild secret language, intoning a shrill *alleluia*. While a boy in the temple full of stone images, he had come to know the inscriptions carved by artists deep into the wall." – Nonnos, *The Dionysiaka* 4.268

Under the entry for 'Osiris' in Suidas' *Lexicon* we read the following: "Some say he was Dionysos, others say another – who was dismembered by the *daimon* Typhon and became a great sorrow for the Egyptians, they kept the memory of his dismemberment for all time."

In a dedicatory stela erected by a Ptolemaic-era prophet of Chnubis, Dionysos is called *Petempamenti*, "He who is in Amenti," a title usually reserved for Osiris. (E. R. Bevan, *The House of Ptolemy*, 295)

Whether as a result of this equation, or on his own and through his own name, Dionysos has long been associated with Egypt and her neighbors. For instance, Hesychius located Nysa, the mythical birthplace of Dionysos, variously in Egypt, Ethiopia, or Arabia. (*Lexicon* 742) Hesiod locates the mysterious city of Nysa "near the streams of Aigyptos" (*Frag.* 287) as do the author of the first *Homeric Hymn to Dionysos* and Apollonios Rhodios (*Argonautika* 2.1214). Herodotos placed Nysa alternately in Egypt (3.97) or Arabia (3.111) with which Diodoros Sikeliotes was in agreement (1.15).

According to Apollodoros (*Library* 1.6.3), Ovid (*Metamorphoses* 5.319ff), and Hyginus (*Fabulae* 152) among others, during the battle of Zeus and Typhon, the Gods were forced to flee Mount Olympos and take up residence in Egypt, where they took on the shapes of animals in order to conceal themselves. Hermes became an ibis, Aphrodite a dove, Apollo a hawk, and Dionysos a goat. This myth was, in all likelihood, an attempt by the Greeks to explain the predominance of zoomorphic Gods in Egypt, as the ancient author Lucian shrewdly perceived (*On Sacrifices*, 14).

Later on, Dionysos was said to return to Egypt during his wanderings, where he was kindly received by King Proteus (Apollodoros 2.29), and founded the oracle of Zeus-Ammon. (Statius' *Thebaid* 3.476) Hyginus tells the story in greater detail:

> "When Liber was hunting for water in Egypt, and hadn't succeeded, a ram is said to have sprung suddenly from the ground, and with this as guide he found water. So he asked Jupiter to put the ram among the stars, and to this day it is called the equinoctial ram. Moreover, in the place where he found water he established a temple which is called the temple of Jupiter-Ammon." (*Fabulae* 133)

Herodotos insisted that Dionysos and his worship had been brought from Egypt into Greece:

> "Melampos was the one who taught the Greeks the name of Dionysos and the way of sacrificing to him and the phallic procession; he did not exactly unveil the subject taking all its details into consideration, for the teachers who came after him made a fuller revelation; but it was from him that the Greeks learned to bear the phallos along in honor of Dionysos, and they got their present practice from his teaching. I say, then, that Melampos acquired the prophetic art, being a discerning man, and that, besides many other things which he learned from Egypt, he also taught the Greeks things concerning Dionysos, altering few of them; for I will not say that what is done in Egypt in connection with the God and what is done among the Greeks originated independently: for they would then be of an Hellenic character and not recently introduced." (2.49)

Herodotos claimed that the people of Meroe, in Ethiopia, "worship no other Gods but Zeus and Dionysos," (2.29) while the Arabians believed only in Dionysos and Aphrodite Ourania, whom, he informs us, they called "Dionysos, Orotalt; and Aphrodite, Alilat." (3.8) In Libya they celebrated a festival called the Astydromia or "Town-running," which was sacred to Dionysos and the Nymphs and was, Suidas informs us, "like the birthday celebration of the city, and a Theodaisia festival." [An ancient Dionysos festival connected with wine] And Anacreon says that one of the titles of Dionysos was *Aithiopais*, meaning "The Ethiopian."

After the Ptolemies came to power in Egypt, Dionysos was one of the most popular Gods. He was the tutelary deity of their Dynasty – Ptolemy IV even adopted the title "Neos Dionysos" (*Oxyrhynchus*, ii No. 236b) – and under their reign, numerous temples and theaters were erected to him, including a few that are still standing, despite the best efforts of Christians and Moslems over the centuries. It was the destruction of Dionysos' temple in Alexandria by a mob of insane, violent Christians instigated by the Bishop Theophilus which inspired the remaining Pagans of the city to rise to the defense of the Serapeion. (Gibbon's *The Decline and Fall of the Roman Empire*, XXVIII) Under Ptolemy IV Philopator, Egypt became a center of Dionysian mysteries. This King sent out an edict decreeing that "those who perform initiations for Dionysos" should travel to Alexandria and register there, declaring "from whom they have received the sacred things, up to three generations, and to hand in the *hieros logos* in a sealed exemplar." Additionally, he required that the Egyptian Jews in the *nomos* of Arsinoë be initiated into the mysteries of Dionysos in order to "receive the same civic rights as the Alexandrians" (3 *Maccabees* 2.30).

Dionysos and his myths were a favorite subject of Egyptian artists – especially scenes depicting his courtship of Ariadne and his sojourn under the sea with Thetis – and many lovely murals, frescoes, and tapestries have been preserved. The Egyptian Nonnos of Panopolis wrote his monumental collection of the god's myths the *Dionysiaka* – preserving some in the only form that has come down to us – in the 5th century CE.

Almost not born

According to Plutarch:

> "They say that the Sun, when he became aware of Rheia's intercourse with Kronos, invoked a curse upon her that she should not give birth to a child in any month or year; but Hermes, being enamored of the Goddess, consorted with her. Later, playing at draughts with the moon, he won from her the seventieth part of each of her periods of illumination, and from all the winnings he composed five days, and intercalated them as an addition to the three hundred and sixty days. The Egyptians even now call these five days intercalated and celebrate them as the birthdays of the Gods. They relate that on the first of these days Osiris was born, and at the hour of his birth a voice issued forth saying, 'The Lord of All advances to the light.'" (*On Isis and Osiris*, 12)

While Apollodoros relates the following story about Hera's attempts to thwart the birth of Dionysos:

> "But Zeus loved Semele and bedded with her unknown to Hera. Now Zeus had agreed to do for her whatever she asked, and deceived by Hera she asked that he would come to her as he came when he was wooing Hera. Unable to refuse, Zeus came to her bridal chamber in a chariot, with lightnings and thunderings, and launched a thunderbolt. But Semele expired of fright, and Zeus, snatching the sixth-month abortive child from the fire, sewed it in his thigh. On

the death of Semele the other daughters of Kadmos spread a report that Semele had bedded with a mortal man, and had falsely accused Zeus, and that therefore she had been blasted by thunder. But at the proper time Zeus undid the stitches and gave birth to Dionysos, and entrusted him to Hermes. And he conveyed him to Ino and Athamas, and persuaded them to rear him as a girl. But Hera indignantly drove them mad, and Athamas hunted his elder son Learchus as a deer and killed him, and Ino threw Melicertes into a boiling cauldron, then carrying it with the dead child she sprang into the deep. And she herself is called Leucothea, and the boy is called Palaemon, such being the names they get from sailors; for they succor storm-tossed mariners. And the Isthmian games were instituted by Sisyphus in honor of Melicertes. But Zeus eluded the wrath of Hera by turning Dionysos into a kid, and Hermes took him and brought him to the Nymphs who dwelt at Nysa in Asia, whom Zeus afterwards changed into stars and named them the Hyades." (3.4.3)

Culture bringer

Concerning Osiris, Diodoros Sikeliotes wrote:

"Osiris was the first, they record, to make mankind give up cannibalism; for after Isis had discovered the fruit of both wheat and barley which grew wild over the land along with the other plants but was still unknown to man, and Osiris had also devised the cultivation of these fruits, all men were glad to change their food, both because of the pleasing nature of the newly-discovered grains and because it seemed to their advantage to refrain from their butchery of one another." (1.14)

Similarly, he wrote the following concerning Dionysos:

"Some writers of myth, however, relate that there was a second Dionysos who was much earlier in time than the one we have just mentioned. For according to them there was born of Zeus and Persephone a Dionysos who is called by some Sabazios and whose birth and sacrifices and honors are celebrated at night and in secret, because of the disgraceful conduct which is a consequence of the gatherings. They state also that he excelled in sagacity and was the first to attempt the yoking of oxen and by their aid to effect the sowing of the seed, this being the reason why they also represent him as wearing a horn." (4.4.1)

Teiresias, in Euripides' *Bakchai* says Dionysos "discovered and bestowed on humankind the service of drink, the juice that streams from the vine clusters; humans have but to take their fill of wine, and the sufferings of an unhappy race are banished." (279-82)

Hyginus in his *Fabulae* writes, "When Father Liber [Dionysos] went out to visit men in order to demonstrate the sweetness and pleasantness of his fruit, he came to the generous hospitality of Ikarios and Erigone. To them he gave a skin full of wine as a gift and bade them spread the use of it in all the other lands." (130)

Philokhoros wrote, "Amphiktyon, King of Athens, learned from Dionysos the art of mixing wine and was the first to mix it. So it was that men came to stand upright, drinking wine mixed, whereas before they were bent double by use of unmixed wine." (*FGrH* 328 F 173)

And there are numerous references – too many to recount here – to Dionysos instituting the cultivation of the vine in various localities within the Greek world. (Apollodoros and Pausanias recount most of these in a fairly coherent order.)

Peaceful conquest of the world

> "Of Osiris they say that, being of a beneficent turn of mind, and eager for glory, he gathered together a great army, with the intention of visiting all the inhabited earth and teaching the race of men how to cultivate the vine and sow wheat and barley; for he supposed that if he made men give up their savagery and adopt a gentle manner of life he would receive immortal honors because of the magnitude of his benefactions. And this did in fact take place, since not only the men of his time who received this gift, but all succeeding generations as well, because of the delight which they take in the foods which were discovered, have honored those who introduced them as Gods most illustrious." – Diodoros Sikeliotes I.17

Dionysos also gathered together a great army, comprised of his nurses, satyrs, Panes, Seilenoi, mainades, nymphs, and mortals who came to join him. (Nonnos' *Dionysiaka*) They set out to "visit men in order to demonstrate the sweetness and pleasantness of his fruit...he gave a skin full of wine as a gift and bade them spread the use of it in all the other lands" (Hyginus *Fabulae* 130) and also to spread the worship of the Meter Kybele which included mysteries, nocturnal orgies, ecstatic trances, and wild dances. Dionysos "travelled over the whole earth civilizing it without the slightest need of arms, but most of the peoples he won over to his way by the charm of his persuasive discourse combined with song and all manner of music." (Plutarch, *On Isis and Osiris,* 13) When confronted by the Indian army, the Goat-God Pan who travelled in Dionysos' train gave a great shout, filling them with *panic*, and the army dropped their weapons and fled, thus allowing Dionysos to conquer India without even having to shed a drop of blood. (Nonnos, however, tells a different story, and glories in the bloodthirstiness of Dionysos' battle with the Indians.)

Wine

Diodoros Sikeliotes wrote:

"And the discovery of the vine, they say, was made by Osiris and that, having further devised the proper treatment of its fruit, he was the first to drink wine and taught mankind at large the culture of the vine and the use of wine, as well as the way to harvest the grape and to store the wine." (1.15)

Osiris was called "Lord of Drunkenness at the *Wag*-festival," which took place during the season of the grape harvest, shortly before the inundation. (Sigfrid Hoedel-Hoenes, *Life and Death in Ancient Egypt*, pg. 114) And wine was frequently offered to him, for instance, in the stela of Thutmose the doorkeeper, from the 18th Dynasty, we find that "water, a cool breeze and wine" are to be given to "the spirit of the inundation" and Horemheb offers Osiris wine in order to be granted the "gift of life, each day, like Ra." Vines could be depicted in funerary monuments associated with Osiris, the most famous example belonging to the 18th Dynasty Mayor of Thebes Sennefer, whose tomb was known for its stunningly beautiful depiction of a grape arbor as the "tombeau des vignes." The ceiling of his tomb is covered in vines and grapes painted with utmost care, reaching down into the shrine of Osiris within the burial chamber, as if originating from the realm of the God of life and vegetation.

Wine offers a clear connection between Crete, the earliest home of Dionysos, and Egypt, as Carl Kerenyi observes, "The Minoan hieroglyph for wine, an ideogram in Linear B, is similar to the Egyptian hieroglyph of the same meaning. It recalls that form of grape arbor which is represented on a picture of the wine harvest at the time of the Eighteenth Dynasty" (*Dionysos: Archetypal Image of Indestructible Life*, pg. 56).

Wine is so intimately linked with Dionysos that scarcely anyone speaks of the God without mentioning it. It shares his nature, for like the God it is "fiery" (Euripides *Alkestis* 757), "wild" (Aeschylus *Persians* 614), and "madness-inspiring" (Plato *Laws* 7.773 d), and yet it brings "great joy to mankind" (Homer *Iliad* 14.325). Perhaps the best description of the powers of wine are to be found in a hymn of the Roman poet Horace, "You move with soft compulsion the mind that is so often dull; you restore hope to hearts distressed, give strength and horns to the poor man. Filled with you he trembles not at the truculence of kings or the soldiers' weapons." (3.21) Like the God, it is not complete without a second birth, and suffers immeasurably before it attains its final form. Achilles Tatius called wine "the blood of the God" (*The Adventures of Leucippe and Clitophon* 2.2) and Nonnos compared it to the tears of the God. (7.367) Wine was said to spring up miraculously whenever the God approached (*Homeric Hymn* 7) and the female followers of Dionysos caused "the earth to flow with milk, with wine, with the nectar of bees," (Euripides' *Bakchai* 708). Wine was poured out in libations to the Gods, drunk at *symposia*, and used by initiates to attain a mystical union with Dionysos. Euripides equated Dionysos with wine itself, saying, "As a God Dionysos himself is poured out to the Gods" (*Bakchai*, 284).

Beer

Strabo believed that barley beer was a drink peculiar to the Egyptians, and the cultivation of beer was attributed to Osiris by Diodoros Sikeliotes. An inscription dating from 2200 BCE says, "The mouth of a perfectly contented man is filled with beer." And beer formed part of the traditional Egyptian offering formula, "O you who give bread and beer to beneficent souls in the house of Osiris, do you give bread and beer at the two periods to the soul of N who is with you." We read that the bread and the beer of Osiris make the eater immortal, (*Book of the Dead*, 40) an idea which is frequently elaborated. In the *Pyramid Text* of Teta, Osiris Teta "receives thy bread which decayeth not, and thy beer which perisheth not." In the *Text* of Pepi II, the aspirant prays for "thy bread of eternity, and thy beer of everlastingness" (390).

Although wine is the drink usually associated with Dionysos, we find beer connected with him as well through his allonyms Sabazios and Bromios. Sabazios was the Thracian-Phrygian form of Dionysos, a wild, bearded God of fertility, snakes, and ritual ecstasy, whose followers attained union with him by drinking *seba*, beer, much as Dionysos' followers drank wine. Additionally, the Emperor Julian wrote a rather witty epigram upon discovering 'wine made from barley,' that is beer, found in Gaul:

> "Who are you, and whence, Dionysos? For by the true Bacchus, I do not recognize you: I know only the son of Zeus. He smells of nectar, you smell of the goat. Truly the Celts must have made you from grain only for lack of grapes. Therefore we should call you Demetrios, not Dionysos, rather born of grain [than of fire], and Bromos, not Bromios" (*Epigram* IX, 638 *Greek Anthology*)

Ivy, vines, and grapes

In the papyrus of Nebseni, written about 1550 BCE, Osiris is depicted sitting in a shrine, from the roof of which hang clusters of grapes; and in the papyrus of the royal scribe Nakht we see the God enthroned in front of a pool, from the banks of which a luxuriant vine, with many bunches of grapes, grows towards the green face of the seated deity. Hellanikos maintains that the vine was discovered first in Plithine, a city of Egypt and the physician Philomides says that the vine had been brought from the Red Sea into Greece (Athenaios 1.34a, 15.675).

According to Diodoros Sikeliotes, "The discovery of ivy is also attributed to Osiris by the Egyptians and made sacred to this God, just as the Greeks also do in the case of Dionysos. And in the Egyptian language, they say, the ivy is called *khenosiris*, the 'plant of Osiris' and for purposes of dedication is preferred to the vine, since the latter sheds its leaves while the former ever remains green" (1.17.4.).

These two plants are especially sacred to Dionysos.

Homer calls Dionysos *Kissokomes* or "ivy-crowned" (*Hymn* 26) and Pindar calls him *Kissophoros* or "Ivy-bearing" (*Olympian Ode* 2.50). The Acharnian *deme*, which was supposedly the first place where the plant grew up, was more explicit, and simply called him *Kissos* or "Ivy" (Pausanias 1.31.6). The plant was wrapped around the *thyrsoi* of the God and his followers, and draped around the life-size mask of Dionysos in Icaria. According to the *scholion* on Euripides' *Phoenician Women* 65, ivy appeared simultaneously with the birth of Dionysos in order to protect the infant from the flames of lightning which consumed his mother. Arrian in his *Anabasis* says that there was no ivy to be found in all of Asia, except for Mount Meros and Nysa in India as a token that the God had been there (5.1.6). In the Hellenistic period, Initiates in his Mysteries had themselves tattooed with ivy-leaves (3 *Maccabees* 2.29) and decorated their tombstones with it.

According to Plutarch, ivy had the power to insight madness:

> "For women possessed by Bacchic frenzies rush straightway for ivy and tear it to pieces, clutching it in their hands and biting it with their teeth; so that not altogether without plausibility are they who assert that ivy, possessing as it does an exciting and distracting breath of madness, deranges persons and agitates them, and in general brings on a wineless drunkenness and joyousness in those that are precariously disposed towards spiritual exaltation." (*Roman Questions*, 112)

Vines are a prominent feature in the iconography of Dionysos. His statues were frequently draped in it, and the mainades twined vines as well as ivy around their fennel stalks in order to create the sacred wand of Dionysos, the *thyrsos*. Homer describes how the plant creeped up the mast of the pirate ship as Dionysos' wrath was made manifest. (*Homeric Hymn* 7) Alcaeus said that no plant should be planted in preference to vine, and both Horace (*Carmine* 1.18.1) and Ennius (*Trag.* 124.5) called the vine sacred.

But the most famous association of the vine with Dionysos are the miraculous "one-day vines" which Walter Otto describes as follows:

> "These flowered and bore fruit in the course of a few hours during the festivals of the epiphany of the God. A choral song in Euripides' *Phoenissae* ... sings of the twin peaks lit up by the fire of the Bacchic festival and the vine which 'daily bears its yield of juicy thick grape clusters.' As Sophokles tells us in his *Thyestes*, on Euboea one could watch the holy vine grow green in the morning. By noon the grapes were already forming, they grew heavy and dark in color, and by evening the ripe fruit could be cut down, and the drink could be mixed. We discover from the scholia of the *Iliad* that this occurred in Aigai at the annual rite in honor of Dionysos, as the women dedicated to the God performed the holy rites. And finally Euphorion knew of a festival of Dionysos in Achaean Aigai in which the sacred vines blossomed and ripened during the cult dances of the chorus so that already by evening considerable quantities of wine could be pressed." (*Dionysos: Myth and Cult*, pg. 98-99)

The ivied rod

The *thyrsos* is the supreme symbol of Dionysos, carried by all of his devotees. It is a stalk of fennel or other wood, topped by a pine-cone, and wreathed with ivy. It is a powerful tool, through which the God's coursing, vibrant, ecstatic sexuality manifests.

> "The mainades, followers of Dionysos, pound the ground with the *thyrsos*, which drips honey and causes milk and wine to gush up from the earth; a phenomenon into which it is not difficult to read sexual symbolism." (Delia Morgan, *Ivied Rod: Gender and the Phallos in Dionysian Religion*)

The *thyrsos*, also, is found in possession of Osiris. Before Lucius is initiated into the mysteries of Osiris, the God visits him in a dream, prefaced by an encounter with one of the God's devotees. He was "clad in linen and bearing an ivied *thyrsos* and other objects, which I may not name" (Apuleius' *Metamorphoses*, 27).

Plutarch also attests to *thyrsoi* connected with Osiris. "For they fasten skins of fawns about themselves, and carry *thyrsoi*, and indulge in shoutings and movements exactly as do those who are under the spell of the Dionysiac ecstasies" (*On Isis and Osiris*, 35).

And Lewis Spence informs us that, "A pine cone often appears on monuments as an offering presented to Osiris" (*Ancient Egyptian Myths and Legends* p. 72).

Barley and corn

John Ferguson describes a common practice associated with Osiris:

> "Effigies made of vegetable mould and stuffed with corn were buried in graves or placed between the legs of mummies. In a representation at Philae we see the dead body of Osiris with stalks of corn springing from it, watered by a priest. There is an inscription: 'This is the form of him whom one may not name, Osiris of the mysteries, who springs from the returning waters.'" – *An Illustrated Encyclopaedia of Mysticism and the Mystery Religions*

This is given a poignant meaning by *Coffin Text* 330, where it says, "For I live and grow in the corn....I cover the earth, whether I live or die I am Barley."

Diodoros Sikeliotes describes how Osiris was associated with the grain, and how its harvesting was attended by rites of mourning:

> "As proof of the discovery of these fruits they offer the following ancient custom which they still observe: Even yet at harvest time the people make a dedication of the first heads of the grain to be cut, and standing beside the sheaf beat themselves and call upon Isis, by this act rendering honor to the Goddess for the fruits which she discovered, at the season when she first did this. Moreover in some

cities, during the Festival of Isis as well, stalks of wheat and barley are carried among the other objects in the procession, as a memorial of what the Goddess so ingeniously discovered at the beginning." (1.14)

And in the *Contendings of Horus and Seth*, Osiris declares, "It is I who created the barley and wheat to make the Gods live, and after the Gods, the herd of man" (1.14.12).

Grain and barley are not the usual plants associated with Dionysos, but they have their place within his realm as well. For instance, Apollodoros says that Dionysos granted the daughters of Anius, the King of Delos, the power to cause wine, olive oil, and corn to rise up from the earth (E 3.10). Additionally, grain, barley, and corn were connected with him in cult. The *liknon*, the fan-shaped winnowing basket in which the God resided, was often shown filled with grain in addition to grapes, other first-fruits, and the phallos. Bacchus' image was drawn round the fields in a chariot and crowned by the matrons (Augustine, *De civitate Dei*, VII. 21). Pausanias records that in honor of Dionysos *Aisumnetes*, a group of children would go down to the river Meilikhios "wearing on their heads garlands of corn-ears" (7.20.1). At the Haloa, a festival he shared with Demeter, phallic cakes were made out of the grain to honor him, and at Eleusis, when the single sheaf of wheat was harvested in silence (Hippolytos 5.8.39) there were those who saw in it a manifestation of Dionysos-Iakchos, "Hail the green ear that is harvested.... Bacchos, the shepherd of the shining stars" (9.8).

Trees, and vegetation in general

Robert Graves observed that the character of Osiris as a tree-spirit was represented very graphically in a ceremony described by Firmicus Maternus. A pine-tree having been cut down, the centre was hollowed out, and with the wood thus excavated an image of Osiris was made, which was then buried like a corpse in the hollow of the tree. Further connections with vegetation can be enumerated:

> "O thou lord of food, thou prince of green herbs," – *The Lamentations of Isis and Nephthys*

> "Through thee the world waxeth green in triumph." – *Papyrus of Ani*, 2.

> Osiris is hailed as "the Lord of the Acacia Tree" – *Papyrus of Ani*, 19.

The body of Osiris becomes enclosed in the trunk of a tree and is associated with the *Djed* pillar in Utterance 574.

Similarly, Dionysos was connected with all vegetation and green growth, not just the vine and its alcohol-producing fruit.

A fragment of Pindar's preserved in Plutarch reads, "May gladsome Dionysos swell the fruit upon the trees, the hallowed splendor of harvest-time." Plutarch also informs us that Dionysos is worshiped "almost everywhere in Greece" as *Dendrites* "Tree God" (*On Isis and Osiris*, 34). Dionysos' image was found inside of a plane tree which had been split asunder in Magnesia, and the Corinthians were given an oracle by Apollo at Delphi to worship the pine tree "as the God" whereupon they had a statue of Dionysos carved out of its wood (Pausanias 2.27). Dionysos was called *Sykites*, "Fig-God," the wood from which phalloi were carved. The scholiast to Aristophanes' *Frogs* mentions that the myrtle was sacred to Dionysos, and Ovid says that "Bacchus loves flowers," (*Fasti* 5.345) specifically roses and violets, according to Pindar (Frag. 75) This is not surprising considering his epithets *Anthios* "Blossoming" and *Euanthes* "He Who Makes Grow" or his festival the Anthesteria which celebrated the return of life to the earth.

Water

Aristotle observed that everything nourishing is moist, that warmth arises out of moisture, and that the seeds of all living things have a moist nature (*Metaphysics* 1.983 B). So it is not surprising to find Dionysos associated with this element. According to Plutarch Dionysos was "the lord and master not only of wine, but of the nature of every sort of moisture" (*On Isis and Osiris*, 35). And he calls him outright *Huês* "Moisture" (34). Philolaos said that Dionysos held sway over moist and warm creation, whose symbol was wine, it being a moist and warm element, and Varro declared that the sovereignty of Dionysos was not only to be recognized in the juice of fruits whose crowning glory was wine, but also in the sperms of living creatures.

Tradition furnishes us with many connections to water. Dionysos was attended by the Haliai or "sea women" who assisted him in his battle against Perseus at Argos. Nonnos relates how, "In the Erythraian Sea, the daughters of Nereus cherished Dionysos at their table, in their halls deep down under the waves. So he remained in the hall deep down in the waves under the waters, and he lay sprawled among the seaweed in Thetis' bosom" (*Dionysiaka* 21.170). At Brasia, it was said that Dionysos had washed ashore in a chest and at Methymna on Lesbos, fishermen found a *prosopon* "face" or "mask" of olive wood in their nets, which was afterwards worshiped in a procession to honor Dionysos *Phallen* (Pausanias 3.24.3-4, 10.19.3). Dionysos was said to come to Athens "from across the sea" on a dark ship on the second day of the Anthesteria, and Homer tells the story of Dionysos' attempted kidnapping by the pirates, and his turning them into dolphins (*Homeric Hymn* 7). In Pagasae he was worshiped as *Pelagios* "God of the sea," in Chios, Sparta, and Sicyon as *Aktaios* "God of the Seacoast." He also had his grottoes, as at Euboea (Pausanias 2.23.1) and his temple *En Limnais* "in the marshes" (Athenaios 11.465 A).

Osiris, too, was connected with water, as Plutarch observed in his *On Isis and Osiris*: "all kinds of moisture are called the 'efflux of Osiris.' Therefore a water-pitcher is always carried first in his processions, and the leaf of a fir-tree represents both Osiris and Egypt" (36).

He was especially connected with the Nile, whose cyclic rise and fall found parallels in the God's own life: "As to what they relate of the shutting up of Osiris in a box, this appears to mean the withdrawal of the Nile to its own bed. This is the more probable as this misfortune is said to have happened to Osiris in the month of Hathor, precisely at that season of the year when, upon the cessation of the Etesian or north winds the Nile returns to its own bed, and leaves the country everywhere bare and naked" (Plutarch *On Isis and Osiris*, 39).

Herodotos called the Nile the "gift of Osiris" and Pausanias related that, "When the Nile begins to rise, the Egyptians have a tradition that it is the tears of Isis which make the river rise and irrigate the fields" (10.32).

The *Pyramid Texts* also speak of the Nile in connection with Osiris:

> "They come, the waters of life which are in the sky. They come, the waters of life which are in the earth. The sky is aflame for you, the earth trembles for you, before the divine birth of Osiris. The two mountains are split apart. The God comes into being, the God has power in his body. The month is born, the fields live." (2063) And "O Osiris! The inundation is coming; abundance surges in. The flood-season is coming, arising from the torrent issuing from Osiris, O King may Heaven give birth to thee as Orion!" (2113-2117) And in a hymn to Osiris, Rameses IV says "You are the Nile, Gods and men live from your outflow."

Bull

In Egypt, there were a number of sacred bulls who were associated with Osiris. Perhaps the most famous of all of these was the bull God known to the Egyptians as Hapi and to the Greeks as Apis. According to Aelian, Hapi was held in the greatest of honor from the time of the first Pharaoh (*De Natura* 11.10) while in all probability his cult stretched back to Predynastic times.

According to Herodotos, the Apis bull was conceived by lightning and was recognized by the following signs: "it is black, and has a square spot of white on its forehead, and on the back the figure of an eagle, and in the tail double hairs, and on the tongue a beetle" (3.28). Plutarch said that "on account of the great resemblance which the Egyptians imagine between Osiris and the moon, its more bright and shining parts being shadowed and obscured by those that are of darker hue, they call the Apis the living image of Osiris" (*On Isis and Osiris*, 43). The bull, Herodotos says, was "a fair and beautiful image of the soul of Osiris." Diodoros similarly states that Osiris manifested himself to men through successive ages as Apis. "The soul of Osiris migrated into this animal," he explains.

The fusion of Osiris and Apis was known as Asar-Apis, which became in Greek Serapis or Serapis. It is often claimed that the cult of Serapis was invented by Ptolemy I in order to provide a deity which both his Greek and Egyptian subjects could worship in common. However, the union of Asar-Api is found in an inscription from the 18th Dynasty where he is hailed as "the great God, Khent-Amentet, the lord of life forever," – an equation which predates Alexander's conquest of Egypt by almost a thousand years. However, it wasn't until Ptolemaic times that the cult of this syncretic deity truly came to prominence. According to Plutarch (*On Isis and Osiris*, 28),

Ptolemy Soter had a dream in which he beheld a huge statue. Afterwards he communicated his dream to certain close associates of his, who remembered seeing a statue exactly like it at Sinope. The King sent for the statue, and when it was shown to Timotheos, an Eleusinian priest, and Manetho an Egyptian, they said that it resembled the Greek Haides, because of the three-headed dog Kerberos which attended it, but also that it resembled Asar-Api. Ptolemy established the cult of Serapis at Alexandria, building a huge temple for him there which also possessed a library that was said to contain over 300,000 volumes. Serapis' worship was successful, in that both Greeks and Egyptians felt that they were worshiping their own native deity, but his cult really took off once it spread West into Rome, where it became one of the ancient world's most popular religions, patronized by Emperors such as Otho, Caligula (under whom the first Serapeion was built at Rome), and Gaius Julius Verus Maximinus, as well as people from all ranks of society. Serapis acquired the attributes and symbols of a number of Greek and Roman Gods – he was depicted in the traditional form of Zeus/Iuppiter, complete with long beard and lightning-bolts, from Asklepios he gained the power to heal and his serpent companions, from Helios he took the solar-crown and dominion of the heavens, from Haides he became Lord of the Underworld and gained Kerberos as a companion, and from Dionysos he was given a *thyrsos*, ivy, and the *kantharos*, as well as rule over nature. A number of authors came to equate Dionysos and Serapis, most notably Diodoros Sikeliotes (1.25) and Plutarch (*On Isis and Osiris*, 28). However, Serapis and his origins in the Apis bull were not Osiris's only connection with this most holy and powerful of creatures.

Plutarch informs us that the Mnevis Bull, which was kept at Heliopolis was "second only to the Apis" and that "like Osiris, it was black in color," (*On Isis and Osiris*, 34). In temple inscriptions the two are actually identified through the names "Mnevis-Osiris" and "Mnevis-Wennefer" (Richard H. Wilkinson, *The Complete Gods and Goddesses of Ancient Egypt*, 174). Ammianus Marcellinus claimed that the Mnevis was sacred to the Sun as Apis was sacred to the Moon, and in the *Pyramid Texts* he was regarded as the *ba* of Re and linked with Re-Atum, not unlike Osiris himself. In Utterance 307 we read, "I am the wild bull of the grassland, the bull with the great head who comes from Heliopolis. I come to you the wild bull of the grassland, for it is I who generates you, and continuously generates you."

In the vignettes of Chapter 148 of the *Book of the Dead*, Osiris is connected with *Kai Imentet*, the Bull of the West, or Heavenly Bull, who was said to be the husband of seven cows, which accompanied him in his travels.

Another bull connected with Osiris (and which suggests a strong link with Dionysos as well) was the sacred bull of Hermonthis, whose name was variously given as Pacis, Bacchis, Bakha and Onuphis. (The last, found in Aelian 8.11, was in all likelihood a corruption of Osiris Un-nefer, according to Budge.) The Bacchis bull was said to change its color every hour of the day (Macrobius *Saturnalia* 1.26), and was regarded as "an image of the sun shining on the other side of the world, i.e., the Underworld" (E. A. Wallis Budge, *Gods of the Egyptians* vol II, pg 352). He was further styled "Bull of the

Mountain of the Sunrise, and the Lion of the Mountain of Sunset" providing an interesting link with Dionysos which runs deeper than the similarity of their names.

Dionysos was represented as having bull horns (Sophokles Fragment 959) and Ion of Khios refers to him as the "indomitable bull-faced boy" (Athenaios 2.35 d-e) like the author of *Orphic Hymn* 45 who invokes Dionysos as the "bull-faced God conceived in fire." The women of Elis sought Dionysos to come "storming on your bull's foot" and hailed him as the *Axie Taure* "Worthy Bull." In Euripides' *Bakchai*, the Theban mainades ask him to appear as a bull (1017) and Pentheus discovers that in place of the effeminate stranger he had thought he'd imprisoned in the palace, there is a mighty and ferocious bull in his place. At Pergamon and elsewhere, priests of Dionysos were called *boukoloi* and *arkhiboukoloi* (*IPergamon* nos. 485-88) and the sacred marriage of Dionysos and the *Basilinna* was celebrated in the *boukoleion* or sacred cow-shed at Athens (Aristotle *Constitution of the Athenians* 3.5).

Cats

The panther is perhaps Dionysos' favorite animal. It is almost universally depicted in his train, pulling his chariot, ferociously tearing apart his enemies such as Lykourgos, lying docilely at his feet, or as Philostratos tells us, "leaping as gracefully as the Bacchantes" (*Imag.* 1.19.4). The panther was even said to have a fondness for wine (Oppian *Cynegetica* 3.80). Its intractable savagery was compared to that of Dionysos' own (Athenaios 2.38e).

However, Dionysos was also connected with the lion, in whose guise he appears to frighten the pirates in the 7th *Homeric Hymn* and the daughters of Minyas. In this form, he fought in the battle against the Giants (Horace *Carmina* 2.19.23) and it was as a lion that the Theban women sought him in Euripides' *Bakchai*, "Appear as a bull, or as a many-headed dragon, or as a lion breathing fire!" (1017). In Roman times, both the lynx and tiger were added to his train.

There aren't many references linking Osiris to wild cats, though the Egyptians knew lion-Goddesses such as Sekhmet and Menhit. However, Osiris is depicted as having a lion-shaped sarcophagus at Denderah, and Plutarch linked him with this animal, "The Sun is consecrated to Osiris, and the lion is worshiped, and temples are ornamented with figures of this animal, because the Nile rises when the sun is in the constellation of the Lion." (*On Isis and Osiris*, 38) And in the *Contendings of Horus and Seth*, Osiris is hailed as the "lion who hunts for himself" (1.14. 7).

The sun

Jan Bergman observed that:

> "The most decisive divine confrontation encountered in Egyptian religious thought is without doubt that between Ra and Osiris. As the principal representation of sky and earth, life and death, light and darkness, day and night, they constitute one another's necessary compliment. Without some form of union between them, the

Egyptian world view would have been hopelessly divided and the rhythm of life broken."

In the *Book of the Dead* (clxxxi), we find the following lines, "Homage to thee, O Governor of Amentet, Un-Nefer, lord of Ta-tchesert, O thou who art diademed like Re, verily I come to see thee and rejoice at thy beauties. His disk is thy disk; his rays of light are thy rays of light; his *Ureret* crown is thy *Ureret* crown; his majesty is thy majesty, his risings are thy risings..." and continues in that vein for quite some time.

Osiris was considered to be the *ba* or soul of Ra, as we see from the inscription in the tomb of Nefertari, "Osiris who rests in Ra and Ra that rests in Osiris" and he was also connected with the Sun through its nightly journey in the *Duat* or Underworld. This was often depicted quite beautifully on coffins. For instance, we frequently find on the bottom of coffins and in the center of the lid pictures of Nut, Goddess of the sky and mother of Osiris. The images of Nut encircled the entire coffin, and the coffin probably represented the womb of the Goddess. Being buried in the womb of the Goddess implied being reborn in the underworld as Osiris. The sun myths also contain the idea that the Sun God's journey through the underworld occurs through the body of Nut. Thus the deceased is identified with the Sun God because both are reborn through Nut. Osiris was also thought to be the mummy of the Sun God. In the same way that the soul of the dead had to return to the body every night to be revived for a new day, the Sun God had to be united with Osiris every night. Thus the deceased, Osiris, and the Sun God merged.

Diodoros Sikeliotes said that the sun was often identified with Osiris and the moon with Isis (1.11) and Plutarch observed, "Furthermore they everywhere show an anthropomorphic statue of Osiris with erect phallos because of his procreative and nourishing nature. They adorn his statues with flame-colored clothes, regarding the sun as the body of the power of good and as the visible light of a substance which can only be spiritually felt," (*On Isis and Osiris*, 201).

Dionysos has his solar associations as well. The most explicit statement of this comes from the Roman author Macrobius, who outright calls Dionysos-Liber the sun (*Saturnalia*, I, 17-23). More subtly, you find Dionysos and his brother Apollon, who from the 5th century BCE had been connected with the sun, linked, and even equated at times. Plutarch said that they had equal shares at Delphi, and Aiskhylos speaks of "Ivy-Apollo, Bakchios, the sooth-sayer" (Fragment 86) while Euripides in his *Lykymnios* speaks of "Lord, laurel-loving Bakchios, Paean Apollo, player on the lyre" (Fragment 480). Perhaps the earliest point of contact, however, comes from the Thracian prophet and musician, Orpheus.

The following, which I have always found terribly beautiful, was posted to the *Thiasos Dionysos* e-list by Lysiodorus, a Dionysian priest:

> "The inspired scholar Peter Kingsley, who has traced the idea of the Chthonic Sun among the Greeks as far back as Parmenides, makes the profound suggestion (I scent the trace of a Dionysiac Muse in

this inspiration) that when Orpheus, servant of Apollon and Dionysos and Helios-- a triple dedication that has confused many from antiquity to the present day (but which doesn't seem strange or conflicting if They can all be identified as Aspects of each other)-- climbed to the peak of Mount Pangaion every morning to be the first to greet the Sun rising from the Eastern Gates of the Underworld, it was because the Solar shaman-priest wished to be illuminated by hearing His God whisper in the ecstatic beauty of dawn what mysteries He had learned on His nocturnal journey through the Underworld (Mysteries the Sun/ Dionysos/ Apollon could share with the Thracian mystic because it was a Chthonic initiatory journey, let us not forget, that Orpheus himself had made)."

Black is beautiful

For the ancient Egyptians, the color black symbolized both death and the underworld on the one hand, and fertility, resurrection, and the fullness of life on the other. (April McDevitt *Color in Ancient Egyptian Mythology*) Likely, this association derived from the rich black, alluvial soil left after the flooding of the Nile. Herodotos (2.12) observed that the Egyptians drew a distinction between the habitable area of the Nile Valley, and the dry, barren wastes of the desert which surrounded them, calling the first *Kemet* "The Black Land," and the latter *Deshret* or the "Red Land," and Plutarch attests that this was the name that they used in referring to their land: "Egypt, moreover, which has the blackest of soils, they call by the same name as the black portion of the eye, *Khemia*" (*On Isis and Osiris* 33).

Because Osiris was connected with the flooding of the Nile and the rich black soil that it left behind, he was naturally depicted with a dark complexion (*On Isis and Osiris* 22) as we often see in funerary monuments, for instance that of Rameses IX or the basalt statue from the tomb of Psamtik. Further, he was called *Kem* "The Black One," *Kem Ho* "He of the Black Face," and *Kem Wer* "The Great Black One" (E. A. Wallis Budge, *An Egyptian Hieroglyphic Dictionary*).

Dionysos could also be depicted in a similar manner. For instance, at Eleutherai, Dionysos was said to have appeared to the daughters of the King in the guise of a dark goat, after which he was called *Melanaigis* "He of the Black Goat Skin" (Suidas, *Lexicon* s.v. *Melan*). Additionally, Dionysos was known as *Khthonios* or "He Who is Beneath the Earth" as well as *Nyktelios* "The Nocturnal One," and *Nyktipolos* "The Night-Stalker." Additionally, Polemon speaks of a Dionysos *Morychos* or "Dark Dionysos" worshiped at Syracuse.

What green skin you have

In the *Book of the Dead*, as translated by E. A. Wallis Budge, there are a number of references to Osiris's green color. He is described as "Golden of limbs, blue of head, emerald upon both of his sides" (pg. 10) and said to be "encircled by an emerald light" (pg. 254). The earth is said to "Becometh green through thee...in triumph before the hand of *Neberter*," (pg. 253) and

"Thou hast come with thy splendors, and thou hast made heaven and earth bright with thy rays of pure emerald light" (pg. 250).

Dionysos was called *Anthios* "The Blossoming One," *Kissokomes* "Crowned with Ivy," *Perikionios* "He Who is Entwined Around the Pillars," and *Korymbophoros* "The Cluster-laden." He made his appearance amid the ripening of fruit and the vibrant hues of spring, and was always depicted with a crown of ivy or laurel, and ivy dripping off of him.

Sexuality

Sex saturates the Dionysian world-view. The Samians worshiped Dionysos *Enorkhes* "the Betesticled" or "In the Balls" (Hesychius s.v. *Enorkhes*). And at Sicyon the God's lustiness was honored by the title Dionysos *Khoiropsalas* "Cunt-Plucker" (Polemon Historicus, *FHG* 3.135.42). We see this side of the God manifest in the uncomplicated and unapologetic phallicism of his male companions, the satyrs. Hesiod calls the satyrs a "race of lazy, good-for-nothings," (*Catalogue of Women* Fragment 123) and in Attic vase-paintings they are almost always depicted in a state sexual arousal, frolicking in phallic dances to the accompaniment of pipes and drums, chasing after nymphs, or attempting (unsuccessfully) to initiate romantic liaisons with the female votaries of Dionysos. Their eroticism is exaggerated, comical, and rarely finds satisfaction. Nor does their sexuality necessarily need the presence of women for arousal – satyrs are depicted as resorting to masturbation, strange contrivances, bestiality, etc., for release – and sometimes they are simply there with their large, erect members (as opposed to traditional Greek aesthetics which seemed to prefer small, unerect penises) as if the act of sex was an afterthought. It is horniness for the sake of horniness, reveling in the presence and excitement of the phallos, in the thrill and chase and wild exuberance of sensuality, a celebration of the body, of pleasure, in and of itself, whether it ever reaches completion in the act of coitus.

The phallos is ubiquitous in the worship of Dionysos. According to Plutarch, the things carried in the earliest rites of Dionysos were: "A wine jar, a vine, a basket of figs, and then the phallos" (*Moralia* 527D). According to Aristophanes, Phales, the phallos personified, was the "friend and constant companion" of Dionysos, and accompanied him in processions and sacred dances (*Acharnians* 263). Herodotos says that Melampos, who supposedly introduced Dionysos' worship into Greece, instituted phallic processions in his honor (2.49). At Methymna on Lesbos there was a cult of Dionysos *Phallen* in which a wooden trunk with a face on it was carried in procession (Pausanias 10.19.3). Each colony sent a phallos regularly to the Athenian Dionysia, and at Delos large wooden phalloi were carried in processions. And Herakleitos speaks of the phallic songs which would be shameful if they were not sung in honor of Dionysos (Fragment 15). We even have a fragment of one of those songs from the Delian poet Semos, who sings of Dionysos, "Give way, make room for the God! For it is his will to stride exuberantly erect through the middle."

Dionysos' sexual rapaciousness is well attested in mythology. His most famous lover was the Cretan princess Ariadne, with whom he had numerous children – at one count, almost twelve of them (Homer *Iliad* 18.590-92, Apollodoros 1.9.17). But she was by no means his only lover. By Aphrodite he was said to have sired Priapos (Pausanias 9.31.2), by Nikaia, Telete (*Dionysiaka* 16.392), by Aura, Iakchos (*Dionysiaka* 48.887), by Koronis, the Younger Charities (*Dionysiaka* 15.87), by Althaía, Deïaneira (Apollodoros 1.64), by Physkoa, Narkaios (Pausanias 5.16.6). Additionally, he was said to have wooed Beroe, after whom the city in Lebanon was named (*Dionysiaka* 42.1f) and Pallene, who had wrestled and slain all previous suitors. Nor were his amorous encounters limited only to women – Dionysos was also said to have loved the young satyr Ampelos (Ovid *Fasti* 3.407), the sentry to the underworld Prosymnos (Clement of Alexandria *Protreceptic* 2.34.5) and the poet Phanocles even wrote, "Bacchus on hills the fair Adonis saw, and ravished him, and reaped a wondrous joy."

Orgiastic rites were frequently attributed to Dionysos. For instance, Livy recounts the allegations of the Roman Senate in their suppression of the Bacchanalia as follows, "When wine had inflamed their feelings, and night and the mingling of the sexes and of different ages had extinguished all power of moral judgment, all sorts of corruption began to be practiced, since each person had ready to hand the chance of gratifying the particular desire to which he was naturally inclined...no sort of crime, no kind of immorality, was left unattempted. There were more obscenities practiced between men than between men and women" (*Roman History* 39.8, 13). In the *Akharnians*, Aristophanes has Dikaiopolis jokingly refer to his daughter's involvement in Dionysian revels, "Happy he who shall be your possessor and embrace you so firmly at dawn that you fart like a weasel." The chorus of Sophokles' *Oedipus the King* (1105-9) wonders if the King may have been conceived during a Dionysian orgy on mount Helicon, and Plutarch asserts that Alexander the Great was likely conceived during one of Queen Olympias' Bacchic orgies, for which she had a great fondness, where the God appeared in the form of a giant snake (*Alexander* 2-3). And Augustine speaks of a high degree of licentiousness carried on at Dionysos' festivals (*The City of God* 7.21). In Euripides' *Bakchai*, Dionysos is said to "have the charm of Aphrodite in his eyes" (236), and Pentheus suspects that the mainades "prefer Aphrodite to Bacchus in their rites" (215), although the messenger who has come back from observing the rites of the mainades flatly denies any such allegation, saying that they worship "in all modesty. They weren't as you described – all drunk on wine or on the music of their flutes, hunting for Aphrodite in the woods alone" (685-87).

Sexuality is just as important in the realm of Osiris. He is called, "the Lord of the Phallos and the ravisher of women" (*The Book of the Dead*, CLXVIII, 15) and "the mummy with a long member," in which form he is frequently depicted in funerary art. The phallos was even carried in processions to honor Osiris, according to Plutarch. "Moreover, when they celebrate the festival of the Pamylia which, as has been said, is of a phallic nature, they expose and carry about a statue of which the male member is triple; for the God is the Source, and every source, by its fecundity, multiplies what proceeds from it" (*On Isis and Osiris*, 36). In the *Pyramid Texts*, it is said,

"Your sister Isis comes to you rejoicing for love of you. You have placed her on your phallos and your seed issues into her." (Utt. 366, sect 632) Nor was it just Isis with whom Osiris was said to have erotic encounters. Plutarch recounts a secret liaison that Osiris had with his sister Nephthys, "Isis found that Osiris had loved and been intimate with her sister while mistaking her for herself, and saw a proof of this in the garland of melilote which he had left with Nephthys" (*On Isis and Osiris*). This scene is hinted at in the *Great Magical Papyrus of Paris*, where we find the following line, "I have discovered a secret: Yes, Nephthys is having intercourse with Osiris" (*PGM* 4.100-02). It is often suggested that this myth was a later invention, perhaps inspired by Greek stories of infidelities among the Gods – however, in the 183rd Chapter of the *Book of the Dead* a quarrel between Nephthys and Isis is recorded, which clearly predates the Greek presence in Egypt, and for which there is no other mythological explanation.

God of joy

Firmicus Maternus records the *symbolon* of Osiris' Roman initiates (*mystai*) as "Be of good cheer, O *mystai*, for the God is saved, and we shall have salvation from our woes" (*The Error of the Pagan Religions*, 2.21). According to Plutarch, Osiris is "laughter-loving," (*On Isis and Osiris*, 18) and in The *Great Hymn to Osiris*, the following is proclaimed: "There is joy everywhere, all hearts are glad, every face is happy, and everyone adoreth his beauty."

According to Nonnos, the God Aion complained to Zeus about the laborious, care-ridden life of mortals. Zeus declared that he would beget a son who was to dispel the cares of the human race, and bring them a message of joy (*Dionysiaka* 7:7). This was Dionysos, who according to Euripides in the *Bakchai*, "ends our worries" (450), "keeps the household safe and whole though the other Gods dwell far off in the air of heaven" (466-67) and is a "lover of peace" (500). For, as Horace said, "Who prates of war or want after taking wine?" (*Carmina* 1). Wine is the tangible symbol and fluid vehicle of the God. When people wish to speak of his blessings, they use wine to symbolize it. Hence we have, "Wine is mighty to inspire new hopes and wash away bitter tears of care" (Horace, *Carmina* 4). "Wine frees the soul of subservience, fear, and insincerity; it teaches men how to be truthful and candid with one another" (Plutarch's *Symposia* 7.10.2). And Aristophanes adds, "When men drink wine they are rich, they are busy, they push lawsuits, they are happy, they help their friends" (*The Knights*). Dionysos' blessing is for everyone – male and female, young and old (Euripides' *Bakchai* 205). And it is very important – for "where Dionysos is not, love perishes, and everything else that is pleasant to man" (*Bakchai* 769).

Drama

"[Osiris] was the subject of what was known as the Abydos passion play, a yearly ritual performed during the period of the Old Kingdom and until about AD 400. The Abydos passion play depicts the slaying of Osiris and his followers by his brother Seth, the enactment of which apparently resulted in many real deaths. The figure of Osiris, symbolically represented in the play, is then torn to pieces by Seth, after which his remains are gathered by his wife Isis and son Horus, who subsequently restore him to life. The play thus follows the pattern of birth, death, and resurrection, and it also echoes the cycle of the seasons." – *Encyclopaedia Britannica*

"The world's earliest report of a dramatic production comes from the banks of the Nile. It is in the form of a stone tablet preserved in a German museum and contains the sketchy description of one, I-kher-nefert (or Ikhernofret), a representative of the Egyptian king, of the parts he played in a performance of the world's first recorded "Passion" Play somewhere around the year 2000 BCE" (Alice B. Fort & Herbert S. Kates, *Minute History of the Drama*, p. 4).

Similarly, drama in Greece was thought to have developed out of early rituals commemorating the death and dismemberment of Dionysos. Long after the plays enacted ceased to be about Dionysos directly, the theater was still considered sacred to him, new productions were debuted at the Dionysias, and his priests were always given the choicest of seats.

John M. Allegro notes:

"At the beginning of the fifth century BC tragedy formed part of the Great Dionysia, the Spring festival of Dionysos Eluethereus. Three poets competed, each contributing three tragedies and one satyric play. The latter was performed by choruses of fifty singers in a circle, dressed as satyrs, part human, part bestial, and bearing before them huge replicas of the erect penis, as they sang *dithyrambs*." (*The Sacred Mushroom and the Cross*)

Mysteries and initiation

Both Gods had Mysteries associated with them, and *mystai* who sought initiation into a special relationship with the God.

Marvin W. Meyer describes the Hellenistic mysteries as follows:

"[They] were secret religious groups composed of individuals who decided, through personal choice, to be initiated into the profound realities of one deity or another. Unlike the official religions, in which a person was expected to show outward, public allegiance to the local gods of the *polis* or state, the mysteries emphasized an inwardness and privacy of worship within closed groups. The person who chose to be initiated joined an association of people united in their quest for personal salvation." (*The Ancient Mysteries: A Sourcebook*, pg. 4)

The term "initiation" comes from the Latin word *initiare*, which is a late Hellenistic translation of the Greek verb *myein*, whence our word mystery comes from. The main Greek term for initiation, myesis, is also derived from the verb *myein*, which means "to close." It refers to the closing of the eyes which was possibly symbolic of entering into darkness prior to reemerging and receiving light and to the closing the lips which was possibly a reference to the vow of silence taken by all initiates. Another Greek term for initiation was *telete*. In his *Immortality of the Soul* Plutarch writes that "the soul at the moment of death, goes through the same experiences as those who are initiated into the great mysteries. The word and the act are similar: we say *telentai* "to die" and *telestai* "to be initiated"."

Cicero wrote:

> "For by means of mysteries we have been transformed from a rough and savage way of life to a state of humanity, and have been civilized. Just as they are called initiations, so in actual fact we have learned from them the fundamentals of life, and have grasped the basis not only for living with joy but also for dying with a better hope." (*On the Laws* 2.14.36)

Dionysos was the Mystery-God *par excellence* in Greece. Not only did he have mysteries of his own, but he was a central figure in the Eleusinian Mysteries, as well as said to have been the founder and prophet of those belonging to the *Magna Mater* Kybele or Rheia.

Although it was previously thought that Dionysian mysteries only developed in the later Hellenistic and Roman Age, Walter Burkert informs us that, "We find evidence for Bacchic mysteries from the sixth to the fourth century with centers at Miletus and the Black Sea, in Thessaly and in Macedonia, Magna Graecia, and Crete; we find special rituals (*teletai*) performed as private initiations by itinerant charismatics to serve as "cures" for various afflictions, good both for this life and for the Beyond, combined with gatherings of private clubs (*thiasoi*) presenting themselves to the public in procession (*pompe*). The experience of ecstasy, *mania*, is crucial" (Bacchic *Teletai* in *Masks of Dionysus*, pg. 260).

John M. Allegro in *The Sacred Mushroom and the Cross*, writes:

> "The female votaries of the phallos god Bacchus were known as the Bacchants...They were characterized by extreme forms of religious excitement interspersed with periods of intense depression. At one moment whirling in a frenzied dance, tossing their heads, driving one another on with screaming and the wild clamor of musical instruments, at another sunk into the deepest lethargy, and a silence so intense as to become proverbial. The Bacchants both possessed the god and were possessed by him; theirs was a religious enthusiasm in the proper sense of the term, that is, 'god-filled'. Having eaten the Bacchus or Dionysos, they took on his power and character..."

John Ferguson adds:

> "In their ecstasy they would range through the mountains in dizzying dances, and tear some animal apart with their bare hands and ate it raw. There is no doubt that this was a communion in the god's own body and blood; indeed at one center the god was worshiped under the cult-title Raw. The inspiration of the god was believed to confer miraculous power, and, as often, as belief in miracles leads to the performance of miracles. We hear of them caught in a snowstorm so that their clothes were frozen stiff, but rescued unharmed, or falling asleep from sheer exhaustion in an enemy village during wartime, and being protect for their holiness." (*An Illustrated Encyclopaedia of Mysticism and the Mystery Religions*)

Proclus wrote that:

> "The *teletai* cause sympathy of the souls with the ritual in a way that is unintelligible to us, and divine, so that some of the initiands are stricken with panic, being filled with divine awe; others assimilate themselves to the holy symbols, leave their own identity, become at home with the Gods, and experience divine possession."

A Twelfth Dynasty inscription says:

> "Anubis sanctifies the hidden mystery of Osiris, in the sacred valley of the Lord of Life. The mysterious Initiation of the Lord of Abydos." And the teachings of Merikare advise the priest to, "Visit the temple, observe the mysteries, enter the shrine, eat bread in God's house."

The great center for Osirian mysteries in Egypt was Abydos, which was said to hold the tomb of the God, and to which people made annual pilgrimages to take part in the great celebrations. Craig M. Lyons writes about the mysteries as they were celebrated at Abydos:

> "We know that at all the temples of Osiris his Passion was re-enacted at his annual festivals. On a stele at Abydos erected in the XIIth Dynasty by one I-KherNefert, a priest of Osiris during the reign of Usertsen III (Pharaoh Sesostris), about 1875 BCE, we find a description of the principal scenes in the Osiris mystery-drama. I-Kher-Nefert himself played the key role of Horus. In the first scene, Osiris is treacherously slain, and no one knows what has become of his body; thereupon all the onlookers weep, rend their hair, and beat their breasts. Isis and Nephthys recover the remnants, reconstitute the body, and return it to the temple. The next scene, in which Thoth, Horus, and Isis accomplish the revivification, undoubtedly occurs within the sacred precincts, and is therefore not witnessed by the populace. However, in due course the resurrected Osiris emerges at the head of his train; at this glorious consummation, the anguish and sorrow of the people are turned into uncontrollable rejoicing.

Horus thereupon places his father in the solar boat so that he may, since he has already been born a second time, proceed as a living god into the eternal regions. This was the great "coming forth by day" of which we read so often in The Book of the Dead. The climax of the play was the great battle in which Horus defeated Set and which is described so vividly by Herodotos (History, II, 63)."

Although much of the Osirian mysteries was performed openly – in stark contrast to the Greek and Roman mysteries – secrecy attended the holiest portion of them. For instance, Herodotos wrote, "On this lake they enact by night the story of the god's sufferings, a rite which the Egyptians call the Mysteries. I could say more about this, for I know the truth, but let me preserve a discreet silence" (2.171.1). And Plutarch says that he must "leave undisturbed what may not be told" (*On Isis and Osiris*, 35).

The mysteries of Isis and Osiris spread beyond the fertile Nile valley, and found great success in the Roman west. During the reign of Ptolemy Soter, Isis became so popular in Greece that a great temple was built for her at the foot of the Acropolis; and in the ensuing centuries, as we learn from Pausanias, almost every Greek city and village had its Isis-temple. Under the Emperor Caligula, Isis was admitted into Rome, and her worship became so popular that only Christianity and Mithraism rivaled her in number of adherents. Central to her worship was the celebration of the mysteries concerning the death and revivification of her husband, Osiris. The Christian author Firmicus Maternus, describes the Roman mysteries of Osiris as follows:

> "In the sanctuaries of Osiris, his murder and dismemberment are annually commemorated with great lamentations. His worshipers beat their breasts and gash their shoulders. When they pretend that the mutilated remains of the god have been found and rejoined they turn from mourning to rejoicing." (*Error of the Pagan Religions*, 22.1)

The initiate found in the story of the God's suffering, and his transformation by Isis, a hope that he, too, might be reborn and transformed.

Apuleius, an initiate in these mysteries, describes his experience as follows:

> "I approached the confines of death. I trod the threshold of Proserpine; and borne through the elements I returned. At midnight I saw the Sun shining in all his glory. I approached the Gods below and the Gods above, and I stood beside them, and I worshiped them." (*Metamorphoses*, 11.23)

Processions

In Ionia, Katagogia festivals were celebrated to honor the return of Dionysos, whose image was ceremoniously escorted by priests and priestesses. In Athens the image of Dionysos was driven to his sanctuary in a ship on wheels, most probably during the Anthesteria festival on the day of

Khoes. Pausanias describes the procession of Dionysos Eleutherios' image from a little temple in the Academy to his sanctuary before the eve of the City Dionysia (1.29.2).

Carl Kerenyi observes:

> "The core of this ritual procession has its analogies in the religious and cultural history of Egypt, where Gods in their chapels were borne by barks which the gods' servants carried on their backs. What in Greece was an anomaly, limited to the cult of Dionysos, was held to be the most natural thing in the world in Egypt, where the Nile was the main avenue of communication." (*Dionysos: Archetypal Image of Indestructible Life*, pg 167)

Additionally, processions in which representations of the phallos were carried about were quite common for Dionysos. According to Aristophanes, Phales, the phallos personified, was the "friend and constant companion" of Dionysos, and accompanied him in processions and sacred dances (*Akharnians* 263). Herodotos says that Melampos, who supposedly introduced Dionysos' worship into Greece, instituted phallic processions in his honor (2.49). At Methymna on Lesbos there was a cult of Dionysos *Phallen* in which a wooden trunk with a face on it was carried in procession (Pausanias 10.19.3).

Both sorts of processions played an important role in the worship of Osiris, as Emily Teeter observed in *Egypt and the Egyptians*:

> "During festivals the statue of the god was removed from his sanctuary and placed in a portable shrine which was, in turn, placed on a boat. These ritual craft could be quite large; indeed, the texts from Tutankhamun claim that it was carried by eleven pairs of priests. The sacred boat processions might circumambulate the temple or make a pilgrimage from one temple to another, accompanied by temple personnel and local residents who sang, danced, and acclaimed the god." (Chapter 6)

From a Middle Kingdom stela belonging to the high official Ikhernofret, we learn that the second day of the Osirian mysteries at Abydos consisted of a great procession, where a shrine inlaid with gold, lapis lazuli, silver, and bronze was carried on a bark called '*neshmet*' through the funerary complex and to a number of different localities. At Philae, the statue of Osiris was carried in procession from his temple to the neighboring temple of Isis, where a *hieros gamos* or sacred marriage was likely celebrated. Plutarch reports that pitchers carrying water from the Nile were borne at the head of Osiris' processions (*On Isis and Osiris*, 36) and he says that at the Pamylia festivals, "a statue of the god with a triple phallos is carried about" (37). Herodotos attests to phallic processions in honor of Osiris as well (2.49) where women used to go about the villages singing songs in his praise and carrying obscene images of him which they set in motion by means of strings.

Death and dismemberment

E. A. Wallis Budge observed that:

> "the story of Osiris is nowhere found in a connected form in Egyptian literature, but everywhere, and in texts of all periods, the life, sufferings, death, and resurrection of Osiris are accepted as facts universally admitted." (*The Book of the Opening of the Mouth* pg 9)

Despite the seeming prohibition on discussing the death of the God — although the Greek traveler Herodotos had observed the annual mysteries commemorating Osiris' death he felt that he must keep a "discreet silence" regarding their content (2.171.1) — we find many suggestive hints in material such as the *Pyramid* and *Coffin Texts*, and in the *Book of the Dead*. For instance, Utterance 532 from the *Pyramid Texts* mentions that Osiris was struck down by Set. *Pyramid Text* 819a reads, "This Great One had fallen on his side; he had been thrown down." *PT* 1005a-b says, "Osiris had been placed on his side by his brother Set, but the one who is in Nedit will move because his head has been put back in place by Re." *PT* 1255-56a-b reads, "Isis came. Nephthys came. The one of the West, the other of the East, the one as a tern, the other as a kite. They found Osiris as his brother had flung him on the ground in Nedit." *PT* 1007e reads, "Horus struck the one who struck you, bound the one who bound you." *PT* 1544-1545a-b reads, "O Osiris who is here! I hit for you the one who had hit you as an ox. I killed the one who had killed you as a breeding bull. I broke the one who had submitted you to the Red Bull of Upper Egypt. The one who had shot you with an arrow is now shot. The one who stunned you is now stunned." The *Coffin Texts* speak of the drowning of Osiris by Set: "permit me to have water as Set had water when he committed a flight against Osiris on the night of the great storm." (353) *Coffin Text* 4.396a-b speaks of a great cataclysmic storm and the brutal waters of Set which drowned Osiris. And *CT* 184 speaks of Osiris being "put in a box, in a chest, in a bag." And in the *Pyramid Text* of Unas we find perhaps the most explicit mention of Set's attack on Osiris in Egyptian literature, "Unas hath weighted his words with the hidden god who hath no name, on the day of hacking in pieces the firstborn."

However, it was not until the Greek author Plutarch that these various traditions were brought together and given a cohesive form. His narrative on the death and dismemberment of Osiris by Set runs as follows:

> "It is said that Osiris, when he was king, at once freed the Egyptians from their primitive and brutish manner of life; he showed them how to grow crops, established laws for them, and taught them to worship Gods. Later he civilized the whole world as he traversed through it, having very little need of arms, but winning over most of the peoples by beguiling them with persuasive speech together with all manner of song and poetry. That is why the Greeks thought he was the same as Dionysos.
>
> "When he was away Typhon conspired in no way against him since Isis was well on guard and kept careful watch, but on his

return he devised a plot against him, making seventy-two men his fellow-conspirators and having as helper a queen who had come from Ethiopia, whom they name Aso. Typhon secretly measured the body of Osiris and got made to the corresponding size a beautiful chest which was exquisitely decorated. This he brought to the banqueting-hall, and when the guests showed pleasure and admiration at the sight of it, Typhon promised playfully that whoever would lie down in it and show that he fitted it, should have the chest as a gift. They all tried one by one, and since no one fitted into it, Osiris went in and lay down. Then the conspirators ran and slammed the lid on, and after securing it with bolts from the outside and also with molten lead poured on, they took it out to the river and let it go to the sea by way of the Tanitic mouth, which the Egyptians still call, because of this, hateful and abominable. They say that all these events occurred on the seventeenth day of the month of Athyr, when the sun passes through the scorpion, in the twenty-eighth year of the reign of Osiris. But some state that this was the period of his life rather than of his reign.

"The first to hear of the misfortune and to spread the news of its occurrence were the Pans and satyrs who live near Khemmis, and because of this, the sudden disturbance and excitement of a crowd is still referred to as 'panic'. When Isis heard of it she cut off there and then one of her locks and put on a mourning garment; accordingly the city is called Coptos to this day. Others think that the name indicates deprivation; for they use *koptein* to mean 'to deprive', and they suggest that Isis, when she was wandering everywhere in a state of distress, passed by no one without accosting him, and even when she met children, she asked them about the chest. Some of these had happened to see it and they named the river-mouth through which Typhon's friends had pushed the box to the sea. For this reason the Egyptians believe that children have the power of divination, and they take omens especially from children's shouts as they play near the temples and say whatever occurs to them.

"When Isis found that Osiris had loved and been intimate with her sister while mistaking her for herself, and saw a proof of this in the garland of melilote which he had left with Nephthys, she searched for the child (for Nephthys had exposed it instantly upon giving birth to it, in fear of Typhon); and when Isis found it with the help of dogs which had led her on with difficulty and pain, it was reared and became her guard and attendant, being called Anubis. He is said to keep watch over the gods as dogs do over men. They say that she learned as a result of this that the chest had been cast up by the sea in the land of Byblos and that the surf had brought it gently to rest in a heath-tree. Having shot up in a short time into a most lovely and tall young tree, the heath enfolded the chest and grew around it, hiding it within itself. Admiring the size of the tree, the king cut off the part of the trunk which encompassed the coffin, which was not visible, and used it as a pillar to support the roof.

They say that Isis heard of this through the divine breath of rumor and came to Byblos, where she sat down near a fountain, dejected and tearful. She spoke to no one except the queen's maids, whom she greeted and welcomed, plaiting their hair and breathing upon their skin a wonderful fragrance which emanated from herself. when the queen saw her maids she was struck with longing for the stranger's hair and for her skin, which breathed ambrosia; and so Isis was sent for and became friendly with the queen and was made nurse of her child. The king's name, they say, was Malkathros; some say that the queen's name was Astarte, others Saosis, and others Neinanous, whom the Greeks would call Athenais.

"They say that Isis nursed the child, putting her finger in its mouth instead of her breast, but that in the night she burned the mortal parts of its body, while she herself became a swallow, flying around the pillar and making lament until the queen, who had been watching her, gave a shriek when she saw her child on fire, and so deprived it of immortality. The goddess then revealed herself and demanded the pillar under the roof. She took it from beneath with the utmost ease and proceeded to cut away the heath-tree. This she then covered with linen and poured sweet oil on it, after which she gave it into the keeping of the king and queen; to this day the people of Byblos venerate the wood, which is in the temple of Isis. The goddess then fell upon the coffin and gave such a loud wail that the younger of the king's sons died; the elder son she took with her, and placing the coffin in a boat, she set sail. When the river Phaidros produced a somewhat rough wind towards dawn, in a fit of anger she dried up the stream.

"As soon as she happened on a deserted spot, there in solitude she opened the chest and pressing her face to that of Osiris, she embraced him and began to cry. She then noticed that the boy had approached silently from behind and had observed her, whereupon she turned round and full of anger gave him a terrible look. The boy was unable to bear the fright, and dropped dead. Some say that it did not happen so, but, as we said before, that he fell into the sea and is honored because of the goddess, being the same person as the Maneros of whom the Egyptians sing in their banquets. Some say the boy was called [Palaestinus or] Pelousius and that the city founded by the Goddess (Pelusium) was named after him; also that the Maneros of whom they sing was the discoverer of music and poetry. Others again say that it is not the name of a man at all, but an expression such as comes naturally to men as they drink and make merry: 'The best of luck to this and that!' For this sentiment, signified by the word Maneros, is expressed by the Egyptians on all festive occasions. For instance, there is the image of a dead man which is carried round in a chest and shown them: this is not, as some assume, a memorial of the suffering of Osiris, but they say that thus they exhort their inebriated companions to use the present and enjoy it, since everyone will very soon be like the image seen; this is why they bring it into the feast.

"Having journeyed to her son Horus who was being brought up in Buto, Isis put the box aside, and Typhon, when he was hunting by night in the moonlight, came upon it. He recognized the body, and having cut it into fourteen parts, he scattered them. When she heard of this, Isis searched for them in a papyrus boat, sailing through the marshes. That is why people who sail in papyrus skiffs are not harmed by crocodiles, which show either fear or veneration because of the goddess. From this circumstance arises the fact that many tombs of Osiris are said to exist in Egypt, for the goddess, as she came upon each part, held a burial ceremony. Some deny this, saying that she fashioned images and distributed them to each city as though she was giving the whole body, so that he (Osiris) might be honored by more people and that Typhon, if he overcame Horus, when he sought for the true tomb, might be baffled in his search because many tombs would be mentioned and shown. The only part of Osiris which Isis did not find was his male member; for no sooner was it thrown into the river than the lepidotus, phagrus and oxyrhynchus ate of it, fish which they most of all abhor. In its place Isis fashioned a likeness of it and consecrated the phallos, in honor of which the Egyptians even today hold festival." (*On Isis and Osiris*, 13-18)

The commemoration of these events formed the basis for the mysteries of Osiris at Abydos, which Plutarch described as "gloomy, solemn, and mournful sacrifices" (*On Isis and Osiris*, 69) and those of Isis and Osiris in the Roman West. Julius Firmicus Maternus, a Latin Christian writer of the fourth century, declared: "In the sanctuaries of Osiris, his murder and dismemberment are annually commemorated with great lamentations. His worshipers beat their breasts and gash their shoulders. When they pretend that the mutilated remains of the god have been found and rejoined they turn from mourning to rejoicing" (*Error of the Pagan Religions*, 22.1).

Similar stories were told about the death and dismemberment of Dionysos. Plutarch informs us that the "Phrygians believe that the god sleeps in winter and is awake in summer, and with Bacchic frenzy they celebrate in the one season the festival of his being lulled to sleep *Kateunasmous* and in the other his being aroused or awakened *Anegerseis*. The Paphlagonians declare that he is fettered and imprisoned during the winter, but that in the spring he moves and is freed again" (*On Isis and Osiris* 69). More explicitly, an oracle which preceded the founding of the Dionysian colony of Perinthos said, "After Bakchos, who cried 'euhoi' is struck, blood and fire and dust will mix." Himeros speaks of the death of the God in the following manner, "Dionysos lay there struck down, still moaning under the blow. The vine hung down, the wine was disconsolate, the grape as though bathed in tears" (*Orationes* XLV 4).

Pausanias informs us of who the instigators of the God's murder were, "From Homer the name of the Titans was taken by Onomakritos, who in the orgies he composed for Dionysos made the Titans the authors of the God's sufferings" (8.37.5).

Diodoros Sikeliotes adds more detail to the story:

> "The Titans, who are the Sons of Gaia, tore to pieces Dionysos-Zagreus, the child of Zeus and Persephone, and boiled him, but his members were brought together again by Demeter and he experienced a new birth as if for the first time. And with these stories, the teachings agree which are set forth in the Orphic poems and are introduced into their rites, but it is not lawful to recount them in detail to the uninitiated." (3.62)

From Hyginus we get an even more full account:

> "Liber, son of Jove and Proserpina, was dismembered by the Titans, and Jove gave his heart, torn to bits, to Semele in a drink. When she was made pregnant by this, Juno, changing herself to look like Semele's nurse, Beroe, said to her: 'Daughter, ask Jove to come to you as he comes to Juno, so you may know what pleasure it is to sleep with a God.' At her suggestion Semele made this request of Jove, and was smitten by a thunderbolt." (*Fabulae* 167)

But the fullest account of the story was preserved in Nonnos' monumental treatment of the God's myths, the *Dionysiaka*, as follows:

> "[Demeter hid Persephone in a cave in Sicily to try to prevent her mating with any of the Gods] Ah, maiden Persephoneia! You could not find how to escape your mating! No, a *drakon* was your mate, when Zeus changed his face and came, rolling in many a loving coil through the dark to the corner of the maiden's chamber, and shaking his hairy chaps: he lulled to sleep as he crept the eyes of those creatures of his own shape who guarded the door. He licked the girl's form gently with wooing lips. By this marriage with the heavenly *drakon*, the womb of Persephone swelled with living fruit, and she bore Zagreus the horned baby, who by himself climbed upon the heavenly throne of Zeus and brandished lightning in his little hand, and newly born, lifted and carried thunderbolts in his tender fingers.
>
> "But he did not hold the throne of Zeus for long. By the fierce resentment of implacable Hera, the Titans cunningly smeared their round faces with disguising chalk, and while he contemplated his changeling countenance reflected in a mirror they destroyed him with an infernal knife. There where his limbs had been cut piecemeal by the Titan steel, the end of his life was the beginning of a new life as Dionysos. He appeared in another shape, and changed into many forms: now young like crafty Kronides shaking the aegis-cape, now as ancient Kronos heavy-kneed, pouring rain. Sometimes he was a curiously formed baby, sometimes like a mad youth with the flower

of the first down marking his rounded chin with black. Again, a mimic lion he uttered a horrible roar in furious rage from a wild snarling throat, as he lifted a neck shadowed by a thick mane, marking his body on both sides with the self-striking whip of a tail which flickered about over his hairy back. Next, he left the shape of a lion's looks and let out a ringing neigh, now like an unbroken horse that lifts his neck on high to shake out the imperious tooth of the bit, and rubbing, whitened his cheek with hoary foam. Sometimes he poured out a whistling hiss from his mouth, a curling horned serpent covered with scales, darting out his tongue from his gaping throat, and leaping upon the grim head of some Titan encircled his neck in snaky spiral coils. Then he left the shape of the restless crawler and became a tiger with gay stripes on his body; or again like a bull emitting a counterfeit roar from his mouth he butted the Titans with sharp horn. So he fought for his life, until Hera with jealous throat bellowed harshly through the air – that heavy-resentful step-mother! And the gates of Olympos rattled in echo to her jealous throat from high heaven. Then the bold bull collapsed: the murderers each eager for his turn with the knife chopt piecemeal the bull-shaped Dionysos.

"After the first Dionysos had been slaughtered, Father Zeus learnt the trick of the mirror with its reflected image. He attacked the mother of the Titans with avenging brand, and shut up the murderers of horned Dionysos within the gate of Tartaros: the trees blazed, the hair of suffering Gaia was scorched with heat. He kindled the East: the dawnlands of Baktria blazed under blazing bolts, the Assyrian wavesest afire the neighboring Kaspion Sea and the Indian mountains, the Red Sea rolled billows of flame and warmed Arabian Nereus. The opposite West also fiery Zeus blasted with the thunderbolt in love for his child; and under the foot of Zephyros the western brine half-burn spat out a shining stream; the Northern ridges – even the surface of the frozen Northern Sea bubbled and burned: under the clime of snowy Aigokeros the Southern corner boiled with hotter sparks.

"Now Okeanos poured rivers of tears from his watery eyes, a libation of suppliant prayer. Then Zeus calmed his wrath at the sight of the scorched earth; he pitied her, and wished to wash with water the ashes of ruin and the fiery wounds of the land.

"Then Rainy Zeus·covered the whole sky with clouds and flooded all the earth." (6.155)

According to Philodemos, after Dionysos was torn apart by the Titans, Rheia the mother of the Gods, sought for the dismembered pieces, and then put them back together again (*De pietate* 44). Diodoros Sikeliotes wrote that Demeter (who was often equated with Rheia and Isis) gathered together the pieces, drawing a parallel to the vine which after it has been heavily pruned during the wine harvest, must be restored by the earth in order for it to bear fruit once again in due season (3.62.7-8).

The dismemberment and reconstitution of Dionysos was given deep, eschatological significance in the Bacchic and Orphic mysteries.

The Neoplatonic philosopher Olympiodoros wrote that when Zeus burned up the Titans with his lightning-bolts a vapor arose, soot formed, and from the soot, a stuff. Of this stuff men were made. "Our body is Dionysian, we are a part of him, since we sprang from the soot of the Titans who ate his flesh" (Olympiodoros *In Platonis Phaedonem comentarii* 61C).

Plato wrote that during Dionysian initiation, the initiates "search eagerly within themselves to find the nature of their God, they are successful, because they have been compelled to keep their eyes fixed upon the God... they are inspired and receive from him character and habits, so far as it is possible for a man to have part in God."

Macrobius in the *Saturnalia* observed that, "In their Mystery-tradition Dionysos is represented as being torn limb from limb by the fury of the Titans, and after the pieces have been buried, as coming together again and whole and one. By offering itself for division from its undivided state, and by returning to the undivided from the divided, this Dionysian process both fulfills the duties of the cosmos and also performs the mysteries of its own nature."

Plutarch, in *On the E at Delphi* 23, wrote:

> "As for his passage and distribution into waves and water, and earth, and stars, and nascent plants and animals, they hint at the actual change undergone as a rending and dismemberment, but name the God himself Dionysos or Zagreus or *Nyktelios* or *Isodaites*. Deaths too and vanishings do they construct, passages out of life and new births, all riddles and tales to match the changes mentioned. So they sing to Dionysos *dithyrambic* strains, charged with sufferings and a change wherein are wanderings and dismemberment. For Aeschylus says, 'In mingled cries the *dithyramb* should ring, With Dionysos reveling, its King.' (Fr. 392) But Apollo has the *Pæan*, a set and sober music. Apollo is ever ageless and young; Dionysos has many forms and many shapes as represented in paintings and sculpture, which attribute to Apollo smoothness and order and a gravity with no admixture, to Dionysos a blend of sport and sauciness with seriousness and frenzy: 'God that sett'st maiden's blood. Dancing in frenzied mood, Blooming with pageantry! Evohe! we cry,' So do they summon him, rightly catching the character of either change. But since the periods of change are not equal, that called "satiety" being longer, that of "stint" shorter, they here preserve a proportion, and use the Pæan with their sacrifice for the rest of the year, but at the beginning of winter revive the *dithyramb*, and stop the Pæan, and invoke this God instead of the other, supposing that this ratio of three to one is that of the 'Arrangement' to the 'Conflagration'."

Put into a chest to be drowned

According to the earliest traditions about the death of Osiris, he was placed in a chest and drowned. (The dismemberment into 14 pieces is quietly passed over.) Plutarch tells the story in the following manner:

> "When he was away Typhon conspired in no way against him since Isis was well on guard and kept careful watch, but on his return he devised a plot against him, making seventy-two men his fellow-conspirators and having as helper a queen who had come from Ethiopia, whom they name Aso. Typhon secretly measured the body of Osiris and got made to the corresponding size a beautiful chest which was exquisitely decorated. This he brought to the banqueting-hall, and when the guests showed pleasure and admiration at the sight of it, Typhon promised playfully that whoever would lie down in it and show that he fitted it, should have the chest as a gift. They all tried one by one, and since no one fitted into it, Osiris went in and lay down. Then the conspirators ran and slammed the lid on, and after securing it with bolts from the outside and also with molten lead poured on, they took it out to the river and let it go to the sea by way of the Tanitic mouth, which the Egyptians still call, because of this, hateful and abominable." (*On Isis and Osiris*, 13)

A similar story is recounted by the Greek traveler Pausanias of Dionysos:

> "The inhabitants of Brasiae have a story, found nowhere else in Greece, that Semele, after giving birth to her son by Zeus, was discovered by Kadmos and put with Dionysos into a chest, which was washed up by the waves in their country. Semele, who was no longer alive when found, received a splendid funeral, but they brought up Dionysos. For this reason the name of their city, hitherto called Oreiatae, was changed to Brasiai after the washing up of the chest to land; so too in our time the common word used of the waves casting things ashore is *ekbrazein*. The people of Brasiae add that Ino in the course of her wanderings came to the country, and agreed to become the nurse of Dionysos. They show the cave where Ino nursed him, and call the plain the garden of Dionysos" (3.24.3-4)

Various localities for their tombs

> "Regarding the shrines of Osiris, whose body is said to have been laid in many different places. For they say that Diochites is the name given to a small town, on the ground that it alone contains the true tomb; and that the prosperous and influential men among the Egyptians are mostly buried in Abydos, since it is the object of their ambition to be buried in the same ground with the body of Osiris. In Memphis, however, they say, the Apis is kept, being the image of the soul of Osiris, whose body also lies there. The name of this city some interpret as 'the haven of the good' and others as meaning properly

the 'tomb of Osiris.' They also say that the sacred island by Philae at all other times is untrodden by man and quite unapproachable, and even birds do not alight on it nor fishes approach it; yet, at one special time, the priests cross over to it, and perform the sacrificial rites for the dead, and lay wreaths upon the tomb, which lies in the encompassing shade of a persea-tree, which surpasses in height any olive. Eudoxos says that, while many tombs of Osiris are spoken of in Egypt, his body lies in Busiris; for this was the place of his birth; moreover, Taphosiris requires no comment, for the name itself means 'the tomb of Osiris.'" – Plutarch, *On Isis and Osiris* 20-21

Likewise, Dionysos was said to have his tomb in various locations. Philokhoros says that his grave was "in Delphi near Golden Apollo." (Fragment 22) Plutarch informs us that at Delphi the remains of Dionysos rested near the place where the oracle was, and that the *Hosioi* made a secret sacrifice in the temple of Apollo at the very same time as the Thyiads were awakening Liknites, the infant Dionysos in the cradle (*On Isis and Osiris* 35). Clement of Alexandria was informed that there was a grave of Dionysos at Thebes (*Recognitions* 10.24) while others believed that he had been buried along with Ariadne at Argos (Pausanias 2.23.8), and at Lerna, it was believed that Dionysos had been cast into the lake and drowned

Sought after

In the Roman mysteries of Isis and Osiris, the initiates (*mystai*) shared the grief and the joy of Isis, who sought for the body of Osiris and finally found and embalmed him (Plutarch, *On Isis and Osiris* 27). According to Firmicus Maternus, the cry of the devotees at the culmination of these mysteries, the *Inventio Osiridis* or "Finding of Osiris," which took place during November in Rome, was *heureamen synchairomen*, "We have found! We rejoice together!" (*The Error of the Pagan Religions*, 2.9).

Over a millennium before that, one finds evidence of this central feature of Osiris's mysteries in the Pyramid texts. For instance, Utterances such as 478, 482, 532, and 535, for example tell of Isis searching for the body of Osiris, while utterance 364 describes the gathering together of the body parts by Nephthys leading to his resurrection. The exclamation of the Roman *mystai* is even echoed in one of these ancient verses: "... says Isis. "I have found!" says Nephthys when they had found Osiris on his side on the river bank (*Pyramid Texts* Utterance 2144a-b).

According to Plutarch (Quaest. Rom. 102), during the Agrionia festival, the women searched for the lost Dionysos, and at last called out to one another that he had escaped to the Muses, and had concealed himself with them. Philodemos informs us that after Dionysos was torn apart by the Titans, Rheia the mother of the Gods, sought for the dismembered pieces, and then put them back together again (*De pietate* 44). While Diodoros Sikeliotes wrote that Demeter (who was often equated with Rheia and Isis) gathered together the pieces, drawing a parallel to the vine which after it has been heavily pruned during the wine harvest, must be restored by the earth in order for it to bear fruit once again in due season (3.62.7-8).

Something bad happens to their penis

> "The Egyptians in their myths say that in ancient times the Titans formed a conspiracy against Osiris and slew him, and then, taking his body and dividing it into equal parts among themselves, the slipped them secretly out of the house, but this organ alone they threw into the river, since no one of them was willing to take it with him. But Isis tracked down the murder of her husband, and after slaying the Titanes and fashioning the several pieces of his body into the shape of a human figure, she gave them to the priests with orders that they pay Osiris the honors of a god, but since the only member she was unable to recover was the organ of sex she commanded them to pay to it the honors of a god and set it up in their temples in an erect position." -Diodoros Sikeliotes 4.6.1

Carl Kerenyi suggests that Dionysos, like Osiris, was a castrated God. He begins his discussion by suggesting that Dionysos' birth from the thigh of Zeus metaphorically referred to this.

> "The logic of the Greek version of the myth is marred only by the substitution of the thigh birth for the God's self-emasculation, a terrible but not meaningless act. The invention of a birth from the thigh of Zeus had its function in Greece: to cover over the God's lavish gift at the expense of his own body. The myth cruelly emphasized the eternally necessary self-sacrifice of male virility to the feminine sex, and hence to the human race as a whole. One account of the concrete mission of the Dionysian religion – in its more masculine form, the mysteries of the Kabeiroi – tells us that the murderers of the God brought his male organ in a basket from northern Greece to Italy. 'For this reason,' Clement of Alexandria, our Christian source concludes, 'certain persons, not inappropriately, equate Dionysos with Attis, because he too was separated from his reproductive organ.' (*Protrepticus* 2.19.4) Eunuchism was as characteristic of Dionysos as Attis. It was one of the secret components of the Dionysian religion, but to the connoisseurs of the Dionysos cult cited by Clement it was an open secret." (*Dionysos: Archetypal Image of Indestructible Life*, pg 276-77)

Lord of the underworld

The Lamentations of Isis and Nephthys hail Osiris as "Thou Lord of the Underworld," and Plutarch wrote, "There is a doctrine which modern priests hint at, but only in veiled terms and with caution: namely that this god (Osiris) rules and reigns over the dead, being none other than he whom the Greeks call Haides and Pluto" (*On Isis and Osiris*, 78).

Vincent Bridges observed that:

> "As early as 3,000 BCE, Osirian funeral artifacts appeared at Abydos. Within a few hundred years, the 1st Dynasty kings of a unified Egypt

built tombs and cenotaphs at Abydos in order to be near the tomb of Osiris and the gateway to the Land of the Dead. From then on, Abydos was the center of the Osirian mysteries." (*Abydos, the Osireion and Egyptian Sacred Science*)

Jaromir Malek observed:

"The dead king is...in the Pyramid Texts also identified with the God Osiris. Osiris was originally a chthonic deity. At first, he perhaps assimilated the God Anedjti, and became connected with the town of Djedu (Busiris) in the central Delta, and very early on also Iunu (Heliopolis). His importance grew rapidly, and he may have, as early as the Fourth Dynasty, influenced the changes in the royal pyramid-complexes. In private tombs Osiris began to be mentioned in the Fifth Dynasty, which is also the earliest date at which he was represented in human form. He quickly acquired the status of the universal God of the nether-world, with Djedu (Busiris) and Abdju (Abydos) as his main cult centers. In Abdju, he assimilated the original God Khentiamentiu." (*In the Shadow of the Pyramids*)

Osiris as Lord of the Underworld is so well-known, that it hardly bears delving into here. (Especially when this is dealt with more extensively under the God's demise and the individual's identification with him in the afterlife.) However, what is not so commonly known is Dionysos' associations with the Underworld, despite the extensive material on the subject.

An Apulian volute crater of the Darius Painter depicts Dionysos at the head of his thiasos, joining hands with Haides who is enthroned in his *aedicula* opposite a standing Persephone. This could be interpreted a number of different ways – a visual representation of the mystery that Herakleitos revealed in his oft-quoted but little understood line "Haides and Dionysos, for whom they go mad and rage, are one and the same" (Fragment 115), or, as Fritz Graf writes in *Dionysian and Orphic Eschatology*, "Dionysos interceding with the powers beyond on behalf of his initiates" (pg. 256 in *Masks of Dionysus*).

As Walter Otto observed, tradition has much to say about Dionysos the God who visits or even lives in the world of the dead. Horace described how the fearsome Kerberos, guardian of the Underworld quietly watched as Dionysos entered with his golden horn, and even licked his feet as he left (*Carmine* 2.19). Numerous authors tell the story of how Dionysos descended into the underworld to bring his mother Semele back to the world of the living. In Aristophanes' *The Frogs*, Dionysos goes down to the Underworld and joins the Eleusinian *mystai* in their sacred songs and dances. According to *Orphic Hymn* 46, he himself grew up in Persephone's home, and *Hymn* 53 says that he sleeps in the house of Persephone during the long intervals before his reappearances. Clement of Alexandria (*Protreptikos* 2.16) cites the ancient myth whereby Persephone is the mother of the first Dionysos, the Horned Child Zagreus, and there are hints in the *Homeric Hymn to Demeter* that the God who ravishes Kore and steals her away to his underworld realm is actually Dionysos. (The abduction occurs at Nysa, and later when Demeter in her wandering is offered a drink of wine she angrily refuses.) Both Haides and Dionysos share a number of epithets. Dionysos is called *Khthonios* or "Underworld" as well as *Nyktelios* "The Nocturnal One," *Melanaigis* "Of the Black Goat Skin," and *Polygethes* "Giver of Riches" – all titles traditionally belonging to Haides. Euripides speaks of "Bacchantes of Haides" (*Hecuba* 1077) and Aeschylus calls the Erinyes "mainades" (*Eumenides*, 500). Euripides compared the mainades to ghosts, calling them both *nyktipoloi* "night-stalkers," since both became active only after sunset (*Ion* 717, 10458-49). And when we turn to actual cult and funerary practices, we see that this connection remains just as strong.

The Neoplatonic Olympiodoros preserves a hexametrical fragment of Orpheus concerning Dionysos' power over the dead, "Men send perfect hecatombs in all hours during the year, and they perform rites, striving after deliverance from unlawful ancestors. But thou having power over them, you will deliver whomever you wish from difficult suffering and limitless frenzy" (*OF* 232).

Additionally, the Orphics sought Dionysos' intercessory power over Persephone, the Queen and Judge of the Dead. They believed that by undergoing initiation and learning certain secret phrases, they could pass unscathed through the Underworld and find a better existence there. "And then, you will go a long way, a holy one, where also the others – the *mystai* and *Bakchoi* – walk in fame" (Hipponium lamella, 15-16). Numerous texts such as this, inscribed on gold leaves, were buried with the dead to help them find their way through the Underworld. Others believed that in becoming a Bakchos or Bakches, they would not have to face the pangs of death, but live on eternally in a Bacchic state. According to Plato, the Orphics believed that in death they would partake in an eternal *symposium* with ever-flowing wine. "Still grander are the gifts of heaven which Mousaios and his son vouchsafe to the just; they take them down into the world below, where they have the saints lying on couches at a feast, everlastingly drunk, crowned with garlands; their idea seems to be that an immortality of drunkenness is the highest meed of virtue" (*Republic* 2.6). And others still found solace in the face of death through Dionysian imagery, whether they held to the eschatological beliefs of the Orphics and similar groups or not. At any rate, Dionysos played an important role in death and funerary practices for the Greeks and Romans.

Susan Guettel Cole informs us that his symbolism connected with death and life is found everywhere: "in vase paintings, wall and floor decoration, reliefs carved on sarcophagi, and ornamentation on tombs and graves" (*Dionysos and the Dead*, pg. 278 in *Masks of Dionysus*). She goes on to inform us that "There are about seventy-five sepulchral inscriptions that refer to Dionysos, Dionysiac activities, Bacchic organizations, or Bacchic mysteries" (pg. 278). And those are simply the ones that have come to light thus far! She also mentions that "Bacchic organizations took responsibility for the burial of members. They tended the graves of their leaders and officials, but members without rank were also provided with tombstones and rites at the grave" (pg. 285).

We have an inscription from one of these groups, the Iobacchoi of Athens, dating from the second century of our era. It states:

> "And if any Iobacchus die, a wreath shall be provided in his honor not exceeding five denarii in value, and a single jar of wine shall be set before those who have attended the funeral; but anyone who has not attended may not partake of the wine."

A group of devotees of Dionysos (*bebakcheumenos*) at Cumae had their own separate burial ground (LSS no. 120) and a Campnian *Bakche* even had her sarcophagus made in the shape of a mainad (Hern 1972, 82). An initiate from Southern Italy appears entwined with vines on her sarcophagus, presumably symbolizing the intoxicating bliss of the hereafter.

Some of the Dionysian funerary inscriptions are truly beautiful, for instance: At Hermopolis Magna in the second century a father found such comfort in the ripening of the grape and the change of seasons that he decided not to weep for his daughter taken by the nymphs in death (Susan Guettel Cole, *Dionysos and the Dead*, pg. 282 in *Masks of Dionysus*). In Egypt, the vines of Bacchus were said to mourn for a barkeeper who had poured "honey-sweet wine for all mortals, the drops that stop pain" (Susan Guettel Cole, *Dionysos and the Dead*, pg. 282 in *Masks of Dionysus*). And at Philippi we find a Latin funerary inscription that suggests that the dead youth will be restored or refreshed (*repartus*) in the Elysian Fields, dancing as a satyr with the tattooed mystai of Bromios (CIL 3, no. 686).

Revivification

Although both Dionysos and Osiris were said to have been murdered, they both were able to regain their power and life.

An inscription from Thasos describes Dionysos as a God who renews himself and returns each year rejuvenated (Susan Guettel Cole, *Dionysos and the Dead*, pg. 280 in *Masks of Dionysus*). The Christian author Justin Martyr, in his *Dialogue with Trypho the Jew* grudgingly observed that, "Bacchus, son of Jupiter, being torn in pieces, and having died, rose again." Plutarch informs us that the "Phrygians believe that the God sleeps in winter and is awake in summer, and with Bacchic frenzy they celebrate in the one season the festival of his being lulled to sleep *Kateunasmous* and in the other his being aroused or awakened *Anegerseis*. The Paphlagonians declare that he is fettered and imprisoned during the winter, but that in the spring he moves and is freed again" (*On Isis and Osiris* 69). Diodoros Sikeliotes says that after being torn apart by the Titans, Dionysos was pieced back together again by Demeter, and "he experienced a new birth as if for the first time" (3.62). Macrobius in the *Saturnalia* observed that, "In their Mystery-tradition Dionysos is represented as being torn limb from limb by the fury of the Titans, and after the pieces have been buried, as coming together again and whole and one. By offering itself for division from its undivided state, and by returning to the undivided from the divided, this Dionysian process both fulfills the duties of the cosmos and also performs the mysteries of its own nature."

Dirk Obbink observes, "Dionysos is poured out, expended in ritual, yet returns, and is present to be poured again in each new year's vintage. In Dionysos' sanctuaries, fountains flow with wine, vine bloom and produce overnight. In this very domesticated view Dionysos represents the perpetually full cup, from which, when mixed with water in a civilized fashion, humans can drink as much as they like" (*Dionysos Poured Out*, pg. 86, in *Masks of Dionysus*). At Philippi we find a Latin funerary inscription that suggests that the dead youth will be restored or refreshed (*repartus*) in the Elysian Fields, dancing as a satyr with the tattooed mystai of Bromios (CIL 3, no. 686). Another indication of this are the Orphic bone tablets found at Olbia with the words *"bios – thanatos – bios"* inscribed on them – meaning that death (*thanatos*) is a passage between two phases of life (*bios*).

And on the revivification of Dionysos, Walter Otto poetically wrote, "And when he opens his eyes, when he rouses himself, when he grows into glorious maturity, he will fill their hearts with a heavenly terror, their limbs with a maddening desire to dance" (*Dionysos: Myth and Cult*, pg. 81).

While it is true that Osiris, unlike Dionysos, did not return bodily to the earth, but remained a powerful being in the Underworld, he regained his power, strength, and vitality through the ministrations of his sisters Isis and Nephthys, as we see in *Coffin Text* 74:

> "Ah Helpless One! Ah Helpless One Asleep! Ah Helpless One in this place which you know not-yet I know it! Behold, I have found you [lying] on your side the great Listless One. 'Ah, Sister!' says Isis to Nephthys, 'This is our brother, Come, let us lift up his head, Come, let us [rejoin] his bones, Come, let us reassemble his limbs, Come, let us put an end to all his woe, that, as far as we can help, he will weary no more. May the moisture begin to mount for this spirit! May the canals be filled through you! May the names of the rivers be created through you! Osiris, live! Osiris, let the great Listless One arise! I am Isis.' 'I am Nephthys. It shall be that Horus will avenge you, It shall be that Thoth will protect you -your two sons of the Great White Crown- It shall be that you will act against him who acted against you, It shall be that Geb will see, It shall be that the Company will hear. Then will your power be visible in the sky. And you will cause havoc among the [hostile] Gods, for Horus, your son, has seized the Great White Crown, seizing it from him who acted against you. Then will your father Atum call 'Come!' Osiris, live! Osiris, let the great Listless One arise!'"

R. T. Rundle Clark writes:

> "Osiris, however, is imminent. He is the sufferer with all mortality but at the same time he is all the power of revival and fertility in the world. He is the power of growth in plants and of reproduction in animals and human beings. He is both dead and the source of all

living. Hence to become Osiris is to become one with the cosmic cycles of death and rebirth" (*Myth and Symbol of Ancient Egypt*, pg. 97)

Of Osiris it was written, "O you four Gods who stand at the supports of the sky, my father Osiris the King has not died in death, for my father Osiris the King possesses a spirit in the Horizon!" (*Pyramid Text* 556). And in the *Coffin Texts* we find the deceased identified with Osiris proclaiming, "I enter in and reappear through you, I decay in you, I grow in you....I am not destroyed" (330), and "Homage to thee, O my divine father Osiris, thou hast thy being with thy members. Thou didst not decay, thou didst not become worms, thou didst not diminish, thou didst not become corruption, thou didst not putrefy, and thou didst not turn into worms....I shall not decay, and I shall not rot, I shall not putrefy, I shall not turn into worms, and I shall not see corruption before the eye of the god Shu. I shall have my being, I shall have my being; I shall live, I shall live; I shall germinate, I shall germinate, I shad germinate; I shall wake up in peace; I shall not putrefy, my intestines shall not perish; I shall not suffer injury; mine eye shall not decay; the form of my visage shall not disappear. My body shall be established, and it shall neither Lad into ruin nor be destroyed on this earth." The King, again identified with Osiris, is hailed, "O! King, come, you also, tell of this going of yours that you may become a spirit thereby, that you may be great thereby, that you may be strong thereby, that you may be a soul thereby, that you may have power thereby." (*Pyramid Text* 666)

Worshipers become identified with the god

As Dirk Obbink writes in "Dionysos Poured Out":

> "In the worship of Dionysos by private groups the eschatological message of Dionysian ritual (including sacrifice) was the imaginative acquisition of a lasting Dionysiac identity, either as a member of the God's eternal entourage or through identification with one of the God's mythical roles." (*Masks of Dionysus*, pg. 69)

According to Euripides, "He who leads the throng becomes Bacchus," (*Bakchai* 115) and Plato wrote that during the Dionysian initiations, the initiates "search eagerly within themselves to find the nature of their God, they are successful, because they have been compelled to keep their eyes fixed upon the God...they are inspired and receive from him character and habits, so far as it is possible for a man to have part in God." Uniting with God was also an idea shared by the Stoics of that era. Seneca wrote, "God is near you, he is with you, he is within you." We know from the *Inscriptions of the Iobacchoi* that certain members held the title of *Bakchos*, and we find a female devotee who was addressed as a *Bakches*. The Neoplatonic philosopher Olympiodoros wrote, "Our body is Dionysian, we are a part of him, since we sprang from the soot of the Titans who ate his flesh" (*In Platonis Phaedonem comentarii* 61C).

Often, the deceased were depicted in the form of Dionysos. For instance, the statue of M. Marius Trophimus, hierophant at Melos, was shown wearing a panther skin, holding a *thyrsos*, and wreathed with a crown of grape leaves. Two statues of Archelaus in this form have come to light at Lerna – one dedicated by his friends and placed in the sanctuary of Deo, the other by his wife was placed in a temple of Luaios. In Dascylium the thiasoi of *mystai* dedicated a relief "with the figure of Bromius," showing one of their members as Dionysos, carrying a *thyrsos* and standing by a tree. In Rome a mother and father showed the image of Dionysos on the sarcophagus of their child with the inscription, "I am called Saturninus; my mother and father set me up from a child to the representation of Dionysos" (*IGUR* no. 1324). Apuleius describes a widow who had a picture of her dead husband represented in the costume of Dionysos (*Metamorphoses* 8.7). And the Emperor Caligula was even said to have had his likeness made in the guise of Dionysos (Athenaios 4.148b-c).

E. A. Wallis Budge in *The Legend of Osiris* writes:

> "Osiris was the God through whose sufferings and death the Egyptian hoped that his body might rise again in some transformed or glorified shape, and to him who had conquered death and had become the king of the other world the Egyptian appealed in prayer for eternal life through his victory and power. In every funeral inscription known to us, from the Pyramid Texts down to the roughly written prayers upon coffins of the Roman period, what is done for Osiris is done also for the deceased, the state and condition of Osiris are the state and condition of the deceased; in a word, the deceased is identified with Osiris. If Osiris lives forever, the deceased will live for ever; if Osiris dies, then will the deceased perish."

Ancient Egyptian literature furnishes us with many examples of this identification:

> "This King is Osiris, this Pyramid of the King is Osiris, this construction of his is Osiris..." – *Pyramid Texts*, Utterance 600.

> "BECOMING THE COUNTERPART OF OSIRIS. I indeed am Osiris, I indeed am the Lord of All, I am the Radiant One, the brother of the Radiant Lady; I am Osiris, the brother of Isis." – *Coffin Texts*, Spell 227

Being an Osiris, Ani expects a resurrection like that of the God, and therefore addresses himself as follows: "O thou...whose limbs cannot move, like unto those of Osiris! Let not thy limbs be without movement; let them not suffer corruption; let them not pass away; let them not decay; and let them be fashioned for me as if I were myself Osiris" (Ibid., XLV). The same aspirant continues: "The mighty Khu taketh possession of me...Behold, I am the God who is Lord of the *Duat*" (Ibid., X). And again: "I am the Great One, son of the Great One....The head of Osiris was not taken from him, let not the head of Osiris Ani be taken from him. I have knit myself together; I have made myself whole and complete; I have renewed my youth; I am Osiris, the lord of eternity" (Ibid., XLIII).

But perhaps the most beautiful expression of this idea is to be found in *Coffin Text* 330, where we find:

> "Whether I live or die I am Osiris, I enter in and reappear through you, I decay in you, I grow in you, I fall down in you, I fall upon my side. The Gods are living in me for I live and grow in the corn that sustains the Honored Ones. I cover the earth, whether I live or die I am Barley."

Beware of the lake

In the Pyramid Texts, Unas is advised of a challenging situation he will encounter near a lake in the Underworld:

> "O Unas, beware of the Lake ! To say four times : "The messengers of your ka have come to you, the messengers of your father have come to you, the messengers of Re have come to you. Go after your sun ! ... Forget those who shall speak evil against the name of Unas, for when you go up, they are predestined by Geb to be a despised one of his city, he shall flee and falter. You are to purify yourself with the cool water of the stars, and you will climb down upon ropes of brass, on the arms of Horus, in his name He-of-the-Henu-barge." (Utterance 214. 136-38)

A parallel to this is found in the Orphic lamella found at Petelia in Southern Italy:

> "You will find a spring on the left of the halls of Haides, and beside it a white cypress growing. Do not even go near this spring. And you will find another, from the Lake of Memory, flowing forth with cold water. In front of it are guards. You must say, 'I am the child of Ge and starry Ouranos; this you yourselves also know. I am dry with thirst and am perishing. Come, give me at once cold water flowing forth from the Lake of Memory.' And they themselves will give you to drink from the divine spring, and then thereafter you will reign with the other heroes."

Judgment in the afterlife

Chapter 125 of the *Book of the Dead* is entitled, "What is to be said when one reaches this Hall of Truth." This spell was intended to prepare the deceased for his trial in the Hall of Judgment in the Underworld. In the vignette that accompanies the spell, the deceased stands at the far right facing Ma`at, the goddess embodying Truth and Order, as his heart is weighed against the feather of Ma`at by Horus and Anubis. Sitting above the scene are the 42 Gods who judge the dead. Thoth, the ibis-headed scribe of the Gods, records the verdict as Osiris, seated on the throne at left, watches on. The creature Amamet, facing the King of the Dead, would devour the deceased if he were found to be unworthy.

Pindar wrote, "From whom Persephone will accept atonement for ancient grief, their souls she will send forth again into the upper sun in the ninth year" (Frag. 133). This "ancient grief" felt by Persephone likely refers to the death and dismemberment of her child, the first Dionysos who was called by the ancient Orphic poets Zagreus. An Orphic lamella from Thurii reads:

> "Pure I come from the pure, Queen of those below the earth, and Eukles and Eubouleus and the other gods and daimones; For I boast that I am of your blessed race. I have paid the penalty on account of deeds not just; Either Fate mastered me or the Thunderer, striking with his lightning. Now I come, a suppliant, to holy Phersephoneia, that she, gracious, may send me to the seats of the blessed."

Times of their festivals

Rural Dionysia: last half of Poseideon (around December)
Beginning December – 18th Tybi – Going forth of the Netjeru of Abydos
Lenaia: Gamelion 12-15 (around January)
Beginning January – 17th Mechir – Day of keeping the things of Osiris in the hands of Anp
End January – 6th Pamenot – Festival of Jubilation for Osiris in Busiris
Anthesteria: Anthesterion 11-13 (around February)
Middle February – 28th Pamenot – Feast of Osiris in Abydos
Middle February – 30th Pamenot – Feast of Osiris in Busiris; The Doorways of the Horizon are opened
Greater (or City) Dionysia: Elaphebolion 9-13 (around March)
Middle March – 30th Parmutit – Offerings to Ra, Osiris, Heru, Ptah, Sokar and Atum
Oskhophoria: Pyanepsion 7 (around October)
End October – 11th Koiak – Feast of Osiris in Abydos

Omophagia

One of the most disturbing rites associated with Dionysos was that of *sparagmos* "tearing apart" and *omophagia* "eating the raw flesh" of a sacrificial victim. Porphyry reproduced the following from Euripides' *Cretans*, now lost:

> "Pure has my life been since that day when I became an initiate of Idaean Zeus and herdsman of night-wandering Zagreus; and having accomplished the raw feasts and held the torches aloft to the Mountain-Mother, yea torches of the Kouretes, I was raised to the holy estate and called a Bacchus."

Plutarch wrote of "the mysteries....in which the eating of raw flesh, and the tearing in pieces of victims....are in use....and the human sacrifices offered of old" (*On The Cessation of the Oracles*, 14). Clement of Alexandria declares that "the Bacchanals hold their orgies in honor of the frenzied Dionysos....by the eating of raw flesh" (*Exhortation*, 2). And Arnobius describes the feasts of the "wild Bacchanalians, which are named in the Greek *omophagia*....in which with seeming frenzy and the loss of your senses, you twine snakes about you; and to show yourselves full of the divinity and majesty of the god, tear in pieces the flesh with gory mouths" (*Against the Gentiles* 5.19).

In Euripides' *Bakchai* the mainades know "the joy of the red quick fountain, the blood of the hill-goat torn." And they "Quaff the goat's delicious blood, a strange, a rich, a savage food." At other times the sacrificial animal was not a goat as Demosthenes tells us: "spotted fawns were torn in pieces for a certain mystic or mysterious reason" (Fragment preserved in Photius' *Lexicon*). The mainades wore a cloak made from the skin of the fawn, and Dionysos himself is depicted as tearing a fawn apart in several Attic vases. More commonly, however, the Dionysian victim was a bull. This was particularly the case in Crete where, to quote Firmicus Maternus, "the Cretans rend a living bull with their teeth, and they simulate madness of soul as they shriek through the secret places of the forest with discordant clamors."

The devotees tore asunder the slain beast and devoured the dripping flesh in order to assimilate the life of the god resident in it. Raw flesh was living flesh, and haste had to be made lest the divine life within the animal should escape. So the feast became a wild, barbaric, frenzied affair. It could even find expression in cannibalism. Porphyry knew a tradition that in Chios a man was torn to pieces in the worship of Dionysos *Omadios*, the "Raw One." At Potniae, according to Pausanias, a priest of Dionysos was once slain by the inhabitants and a plague was sent upon them in punishment. They sought relief, and the Delphian oracle told them that a beautiful boy must be sacrificed to the deity. Immediately afterward, Dionysos let it be known that he would accept a goat as a substitute. This story records the ancient transition in cult practice from the cannibal to the animal feast. Also in the fearful fate that met Pentheus at the hands of his own mother, as recorded by Euripides, there is a late literary echo of the primitive cannibalistic ritual.

As Harold Willoughby writes in *Pagan Regeneration*:

> "To focus attention on these savage features, however, is to miss entirely the significance of the crude ceremonial. The real meaning of the orgy was that it enabled the devotee to partake of a divine substance and so to enter into direct and realistic communion with his god. The warm blood of the slain goat was "sacred blood," according to Lactantius Placidus. The god Dionysos was believed to be resident temporarily in the animal victim. One of the most remarkable illustrations of this ritual incarnation of the god was described by Aelian. Of the people of Tenedos, he said: "In ancient days they used to keep a cow with calf, the best they had, for Dionysos, and when she calved, they tended her like a woman in childbirth. But they sacrificed the newborn calf, having put cothurni on its feet." The use of the tragic buskins symbolized the conviction that the god was temporarily incarnate in the calf--pious opinion did not doubt that. Primitive logic easily persuaded men that the easiest

way to charge oneself with divine power was to eat the quivering flesh and drink the warm blood of the sacred animal. Some went farther and sought to assimilate themselves to deity by wearing the skin of the animal. The central meaning of the celebration was that it enabled the devotee to enter into direct and realistic communion with his God." (Chapter 3)

We find a similar practice connected with Osiris in the afterlife. In one of the oldest of the *Pyramid Texts*, that belonging to Unas from the 5th Dynasty (cir. 2500 BCE.) we find the famous Cannibal Hymn:

"Unas hath weighted his words with the hidden God who hath no name, on the day of hacking in pieces the firstborn. Unas is the lord of offerings, the untier of the knot, and he himself maketh abundant the offerings of meat and drink. Unas devoureth men and liveth upon the Gods, he is the lord of envoys, whom he sendeth forth on his missions. He who cuteth off hairy scalp, who dwelleth in the fields, tieth the Gods with ropes... The *Akeru* Gods tremble, the *Kenemu* whirl, when they see Unas a risen Soul, in the form of a God who lives upon his fathers and feeds upon his mothers.... He eats men, he feeds on the Gods . . . he cooks them in his fiery cauldrons. He eats their words of power, he swallows their spirits. . . What he finds on his path, he eats eagerly."

As E. A. Wallis Budge wrote in his translation of the *Book of the Dead*:

"Here all creation is represented as being in terror when they see the deceased king rise up as a soul in the form of a God who devours 'his fathers and mothers'; he feeds upon men and also upon Gods. He hunts the Gods in the fields and snares them; and when they are tied up for slaughter he cuts their throats and disembowels them. He roasts and eats the best of them, but the old Gods and Goddesses are used for fuel. By eating them he imbibes both their magical powers, and their Spirit-souls. He becomes the 'Great Power, the Power of Powers, and the God of all the great Gods who exist in Spirit-bodies in heaven. He carries off the hearts of the Gods, and devours the wisdom of every God; therefore the duration of his life is everlasting and he lives to all eternity, for the Heart-souls of the Gods and their Spirit-souls are in him."

Having partaken of this dynamic sacrament, Unas becomes an Osiris and is admitted to the company of the Gods. A parallel passage is found in the Pyramid Text of Pepi II, who, it is said, "seizeth those who are in the following of Set....he breaketh their heads, he cutteth off their haunches, he teareth out their intestines, he diggeth out their hearts, he drinketh copiously of their blood!' (Line, 531 ff.).

Additionally, in the CLXXXI Chapter of the *Book of the Dead* we find the bloody sacrifice of captives and the sacramental rending and eating of the sacred bovine, which symbolized Osiris.

Linked with Isis

Ignoring the equation of Osiris and Dionysos for the moment, there is some interesting evidence linking Dionysos and Isis.

For instance, in Naples, Italy there is a Temple to Isis, which was reconstructed by Numerius Popidius Ampliatus, who also set up a statue of Dionysos there, and had frescoes of Bacchic revelry depicted alongside the more traditional Egyptian motifs. In the late period, when syncretism and the multiplicity of faiths in the Roman Empire had reached a high point, we find a Mithraic *Pater* who was also an Initiate of Isis and an *Archiboukolos* of Dionysos and at Rome a bilingual hexameter text praises a woman who was priestess of Dionysos and attendant of Isis (*ICUR* no. 1150). More to the point, these two deities had been linked by ancients in numerous ways. For instance, Ariston in his *The Foreign Settlements of the Athenians*, tells us that Dionysos is said to be the son of Zeus and Isis and "to be called not Osiris but Arsaphes, the name denoting manliness." Anticleides said that Isis was the daughter of Prometheus and cohabited with Dionysos. And in the Orphic Hymn XLI, Dionysos-Iakchos is said to be "exulting in the fertile plains with thy dark mother Isis, where she reigns, with nurses pure attended, near the flood of sacred Egypt, thy divine abode." And of course, lest we forget, the two were brought together through the tumultuous affairs of Kleopatra VII and Antony – for as Cicero wrote: "Oh yes, he is no longer a worshiper of Dionysos, he *is* Dionysos! And in the East Dionysos is god, not merely of intoxication, but counterpart to their Aphrodite, the wellspring of life itself, in short, Antony is become Bacchus to Kleopatra's Isis!"

Pillar

Alan Gardiner suggests that the *Djed* pillar represents "a column imitating a bundle of stalks tied together," (*Egyptian Grammar*, p. 502) but also suggests that the hieroglyph shows "vertebrae conventionally depicted." It is used in the word *pesed*, meaning "back" or "spine" (Alan Gardiner, *Egyptian Grammar*, p. 566, also Faulkner, *A Concise Dictionary of Middle Egyptian*, p. 95.).

According to E. A. Wallis Budge, the *Djed* is the oldest symbol of Osiris, and symbolizes his backbone and his body in general. He states that originally Osiris was probably represented by the *Djed* alone, and that he had no other form. He regards the *Djed* hieroglyph as a conventional representation of a part of his spinal column and gives its meaning as "to be stable, to be permanent, abiding, established firmly, enduring" (*Egyptian Hieroglyphic Dictionary*, vol. 2, p. 913).

Walter Otto describes a similar item connected with Dionysos and the wine-mixing festival that took part on Khoes during the Anthesteria:

> "The large mask of the God hung on a wooden column, and the wine was not just mixed and ladled up in front of it, but it was also

presented with the first draught. A long robe (or a double robe) extends down from beneath the bearded head, and this gives one the impression of a full-figured idol. Ivy sprigs are brushed up over the mask much like the crown of a tree; and ivy twines around the unobstructed parts of the wooden column or grows up from its base, at times even growing out, like tree branches, from the robe of the god himself." (*Dionysos: Myth and Cult*, pg. 86)

Skin-head priests

Bob Brier observed that:

> "While in temple service, priests purified themselves before they came in contact with the deity. To be pure, or clean in a religious sense, even the most common order of priest, the *wab* priest, had to shave off all the hair on his body. On temple reliefs and tomb paintings, priests are always depicted as shaven-headed." (*Ancient Egyptian Magic*, pg. 37)

Plutarch explained the custom as follows:

> "Most people have failed to notice this very common and small point, why it is that the priests cut off their hair ... some say that they shave their heads as a mark of sorrow, but the real reason is as Plato says, 'It is not right for the impure to touch the pure' (Phaedo, 67B); no surplus matter from food and no dung is holy or pure, and it is from surplus matter that wool, fur, hair and claws arise and grow." (*On Isis and Osiris* 4)

According to Herodotos, some priests of Dionysos also practiced ritual shaving. "And they say that they wear their hair as Dionysos does his, cutting it round the head and shaving the temples" (3.8).

Connection with royalty

According to Diodoros Sikeliotes, Osiris ruled Egypt as an earthly King and gave to them "the greater part of their laws" (3.2). Egyptian tradition offers much in support of this view: a Middle Kingdom Coffin Text reads, "You are crowned Lord of the West after having governed Egypt and the inhabitants of the earth" (CT I 189f-g) and an inscription at the temple of Denderah praises Osiris as the "Lord of Egypt, who governed the inhabitants of the desert, who governed the foreign regions as King, who stopped the massacre of the Two Lands" (X. 240, 2-3). The Pharaoh believed that he had received his crown from Osiris – "Ho! King Neferkere! How beautiful is this! How beautiful is this, which thy father Osiris has done for thee ! He has given thee his throne, thou rulest those of the hidden places (the dead), thou leadest their august ones, all the glorious ones follow thee (Pyr. 2022-3). Whereupon the King was depicted carrying the crook and flail of Osiris as symbols of his appropriateness to rule.

Nebet Mirjam, of the website www.philae.nu, has summarized the Ancient Egyptian views on Kingship as follows:

> "The mediator between humans and gods was the king. At his crowning, a new king became transformed into a living god, a concept which of course went through changes in the more than 3000 year long history of ancient Egypt, but nevertheless was the basis for the prevailing religious, economic and social structure. The theory which this based itself on was that when the king, called the Living Heru, died, he passed over to the Kingdom of Osiris (Osiris) and left the kingship in the hands of his son, just as the myth of Osiris (Osiris), Isis (Isis) and Heru (Horus) describe. The newly ascended king becomes the Living Heru (Horus) at the moment of his coronation, and is thereby transformed into a divine status. So the Divine Kingship rests on mythical precedence and on two generations – a transmission of status from father to son as laid out by the gods in the beginning of time. One important distinction should be made; it is the office of the king which is sacred, the office is eternal but the person holding it is human and of course he changes through time."

Dionysos plays a similar role with Kingship in Greece and Asia Minor. He was, himself, descended from Kadmos, the King of Thebes (Euripides *Bakchai*, 3) and his sons by Ariadne, a Cretan Princess (Homer *Iliad* 18.590-92, Apollodoros 1.9.17), were considered Kings and founders of cities in their own right. (Oenopion ruled Khios, Agrius ruled Calydon, Thoas and Staphylos founded cities after sailing with the Argonauts, etc.). In Sophokles' *Oedipus the King* (1105-9), it is suggested that Oedipus may have been a child of Dionysos and one of the Nymphs of Mount Helicon (though clearly this was not the case). Dionysos took the place of the Calydonian King Oeneus, and bore Deaneira by Althaía (Apollodoros 1.7.10-1.8.2) much the same way that he was annually married to the wife of the *Arkhon Basileos* ("King Ruler") during the Anthesteria festival (Aristotle *Constitution of the Athenians* 3.5). During his travels, Dionysos is said to have visited a number of Kings and their households – Amphiktyon in Athens (Pausanias 1.2.5), the daughters of King Minyas in Orkhomenos (Pausanias 9.26.4-5), Lykourgos in Thrace (Homer's *Iliad* 6.130-140), Proteus of Argos (Apollodoros 3.5.1), Pentheus (Euripides' *Bakchai*) and Polydoros (Pausanias 9.5.3-4) of Thebes, and Perseus of Mycenae (Pausanias 2.23.7) to name only the most famous. (It is worth noting, however, that many of these encounters were hardly felicitous.) And according to Herodotos, the Scythian King Skyles sought to be initiated into the mysteries of Dionysos Bakchios after which his countrymen saw him "playing the Bakchos" (4.72).

According to Plutarch (*Alexander* 2-3) the Makedonian Queen Olympias was "addicted" to Orphic-Bacchic mysteries, and was seen handling winnowing baskets and snakes, hence the story that she was impregnated by a God in the form of a snake to give birth to Alexander the Great. Walter Burkert informs us that "the prominence of Bacchic cults in Macedonia and its surroundings at that time is made clear by archaeological evidence, by remarkable "Bacchic" monuments that have come to light in funerary contexts, such as the gilded krater of Derveni, used as an urn, or tombs painted with Dionysiac scenes, such as the one recently discovered at Potidaea" (Bacchic *Teletai* in *Masks of Dionysus*, pg. 262). According to Herodotos, the Dionysian connection with the Makedonian royal line goes back much further, to the house of the Argeade, who set out in conquest from the Gardens of Midas, where Seilenos dwells, to conquer Makedonia (8.137-38). When Alexander the Great set out to conquer the world, he was, according to Plutarch, simply following in the footsteps of his mythical ancestor, Dionysos. In *On the Fortune of Alexander* Plutarch puts the following words in Alexander's own mouth, "I imitate Herakles, and emulate Perseus, and follow in the footsteps of Dionysos, the divine author and progenitor of my family, and desire that victorious Greeks should dance again in India and revive the memory of the Bacchic revels among the savage mountain tribes beyond the Caucasus." Alexander's mother made sure that during his foreign travels and contact with their religious traditions he did not forget his family cults, "both the *Argadistika* and the *Bakchika*" (Athenaios 15.659-60). It would seem that he did not, for under Alexander's successors, the Ptolemies, Seleukids, and Attalids, Dionysos' worship rose to great prominence in Egypt, Syria, and Pergamon and was intimately linked with their claims to Kingship.

The Ptolemaic Kings in Egypt claimed descent from Dionysos through Arsinoë, whose ancestry branched off from the Makedonian royal house (Satyros *F. H. G.* iii p165). The Makedonians were descendents of Herakles and his wife Deianaira, who was a daughter of Dionysos (Diodoros Sikeliotes 7.15), thus Dionysos came to be their divine ancestor and the tutelary deity of their Dynasty. As early as Ptolemy II this theme was proclaimed in his great procession, where the glory of Dionysos is said to radiate upon the Kings of Egypt (Kallixeinos *FGrH* 627). Ptolemy IV made the most of this connection. I have already discussed how he gave royal patronage to the mysteries of Dionysos, attempting to codify and standardize them, but it was also said that he had himself branded with the ivy-leaf, and played the tympanon in Dionysos' honor at the royal residence (Plutarch *Kleomenes* 33), and even had himself called "Neos Dionysos" and renamed several demes in Alexandria after the God – most notably Bacchias (modern-day Umm-el' Atl) and Dionysias (Kasr Kurun). His work on behalf of the God did not go unnoticed outside of Egypt – *Bakchistai* from Thera passed a decree, about 150 BCE, by which the envoy of the Egyptian King together with his wife and descendants were given divine honors by their thiasos (*OCG* no.735).

The Attalid Kings of Pergamon claimed a similar descent. Pausanias (10.15.3) refers to an oracle of a prophetess called Phaennis, which referred to Attalos as "son of the bull fostered by Zeus" that is Dionysos, and the Delphic oracle made the link even more explicit, referring to the Pergamene King as *Taurokeron*, or "bull-horned." The Attalids issued official coins minted at Pergamon with the *kiste* or mystic basket of the Dionysian mysteries, from which a snake can be seen to emerge. The worship of

Dionysos *Kathegemon* or "The Leader" was installed by the Kings, with the priesthood drawn directly from the royal family (*IPergamon* no. 248). At Teos, near Pergamon, there was a cult of Dionysos *Setaneios* (also meaning "Leader") with its *mystai* and *oregeones*, and in 230-200 BCE the city tried to gain international recognition for its right to sanctuary on behalf of its ancient cult to Dionysos the Leader, claiming that "the city and its land were sacred to the God." It was from Teos that the Dionysian *technitai* or "actors" spread, those crafters of ritual processions which were so intimately linked with the rule of Hellenistic Kings in the East.

Prohibition on wool
Bob Brier observed:

> "Priests were not permitted to wear wool, since wool came from animals, and animals obviously were unclean. They wore only fine linen, stored in special rooms of the temples and cared for by other priests whose function it was to assure their cleanliness." (*Ancient Egyptian Magic*, pg. 38)

Plutarch explained the custom as follows:

> "Most people have failed to notice this very common and small point, why it is that the priests cut off their hair and wear linen clothes; some do not bother at all to understand these practices, while others say that the priests abstain from the use of wool, as from mutton, because they hold the sheep in reverence; that they shave their heads as a mark of sorrow and that they wear linen because of the color produced by the flax in blossom, which is like the sky-blue of the upper air that surrounds the earth. There is only one true reason for all this. 'It is not right', as Plato says (*Phaedo*, 67B), 'for the impure to touch the pure'; no surplus matter from food and no dung is holy or pure, and it is from surplus matter that wool, fur, hair and claws arise and grow. It would therefore be absurd for the priests, while removing their own hair by shaving and making the whole body evenly smooth, to put on and wear the hair of animals." (*On Isis and Osiris* 4)

Herodotos points out a similar tradition connected with Dionysos:

> "But nothing woolen is brought into temples, or buried with them: that is impious. They agree in this with practices called Orphic and Bacchic, but in fact Egyptian and Pythagorean: for it is impious, too, for one partaking of these rites to be buried in woolen wrappings. There is a sacred legend about this." (2.81.1)

Abstention from meat
The Orphics, a reactionary movement which attempted to modify the 'primitive' forms of Dionysian worship, abstained from all animal flesh, as we

see in the following lines from Euripides' play *The Cretans*, which form the 'confession' of one who had been initiated in the mysteries of Orpheus and became a *Bacchos*: "Robed in pure white, I have borne me clean from man's vile birth and coffined clay, and exiled from my lips always touch of all meat where life hath been."

According to Porphyry:

> "The Egyptian priests abstained from eating fish, one-hoofed quadrupeds or such as had more than two divisions in their hoofs and no horns, and all carnivorous birds." (*De Abstinentia* 4.7)

In many places, the prohibition against eating fish – which truly applied only to the priesthood, since fish has always been a staple in the diet of the poor – arose because the fish was said to have eaten the penis of Osiris. Plutarch, in *On Isis and Osiris* testifies to this, "And this is not the least of their reasons for the great dislike which they have for fish, and they even make the fish a symbol of 'hatred'" (*32*).

Crook and flail

Charles York Miller informs us:

> "The crook (*heqa*) was carried by Kings, Gods and high officials. It derived from a shepherd's staff, and in this form, it was carried by Anedijti, the shepherd God. Later, it was depicted as a smaller sceptre, and it came to denote the carrier as a 'ruler'. The crook is often depicted being held with the flail across the chest. Opinions differ regarding the origin of this symbol, it possibly representing a shepherd's whip or a fly-whisk. It was associated with the Gods Osiris and Min, but when carried by kings it symbolized authority, hence the combination with the crook denoting the 'authority and power of the ruler'."

Both of these symbols are part of the repertory of Dionysian imagery. The cowherd's crook (*kalaurops*) was carried by Dionysian priests or *boukoloi* during processions, and were probably used during initiation ceremonies as well. It was even depicted on a funerary plaque for a Dionysian initiate named Herophilus, alongside a switch or flail (Susan Guettel Cole, *Dionysos and the Dead*). The flail is also depicted in the context of an initiation at the Villa of the Mysteries in Pompeii, where the initiate is being flogged by a winged spirit in preparation for receiving the vision of the unveiled *liknon*.

Winged

Although Dionysos is not associated with any birds, the Amyklaians invoked him as *Psilax*, from the Doric word *psila* meaning "winged" (Pausanias 3.19.6).

Similarly, Osiris usually appears as a mummiform being or a bull – but occasionally will be represented with wings, as a hawk, or as the winged solar disc through his syncretism with Re (E. A. Budge, *Gods of the Egyptians*).

Appears in dreams

Dreaming was very important in ancient Egypt. Their word for dream *rswt*, is etymologically connected to the root meaning "to be awake." It was written with a symbol representing an open eye, not unlike the hieroglyph for Osiris's name. It was felt that the dreamer could travel beyond his body and communicate with the Gods and spirits in this state. During Hellenistic times, dream schools flourished in the temples of Serapis. And from the 2nd century BCE we have papyri recording the dream diaries of Ptolemaios, who lived for many years in *katoche*, or sacred retreat, in the temple of Serapis at Memphis. Osiris visited his initiate Lucian in a dream, commanding that he undergo further rites of initiation, and pursue a career as a lawyer in Rome (Apuleius, *Metamorphoses* 27-30). Additionally, according to Robert Moss in *Dreaming Like an Egyptian*, "A rightful king must be able to travel between the worlds. In the *heb sed* festival, conducted in pharaoh's thirtieth year, the king was required to journey beyond the body, and beyond death, to prove his worthiness to continue on the throne. Led by Anubis, pharaoh descended to the Underworld. He was directed to enter death, "touch the four sides of the land," become Osiris, and return in new garments – the robe and the spiritual body of transformation."

Additionally, Dionysos was said to appear in dreams.

> "There is a legend that after the death of Sophokles the Lakedaemonians invaded Attica, and their commander saw in a vision Dionysos, who bade him honor, with all the customary honors of the dead, the new Siren. He interpreted the dream as referring to Sophokles and his poetry, and down to the present day men are wont to liken to a Siren whatever is charming in both poetry and prose.
>
> "The likeness of Aeschylus is, I think, much later than his death and than the painting which depicts the action at Marathon. Aeschylus himself said that when a youth he slept while watching grapes in a field, and that Dionysos appeared and bade him write tragedy. When day came, in obedience to the vision, he made an attempt and hereafter found composing quite easy." (Pausanias 1.21.1-2)

And he was even able to heal people through dream incubation:

> "They celebrate orgies, well worth seeing, in honor of Dionysos, but there is no entrance to the shrine, nor have they any image that can be seen. The people of Amphikleia say that this god is their prophet and their helper in disease. The diseases of the Amphikleans themselves and of their neighbors are cured by means of dreams. The oracles of the god are given by the priest, who utters them when under the divine inspiration." (Pausanias 10.33.11)

Worshiped from time immemorial

> "Up to the present no evidence has been deduced from the hieroglyphic texts which enables us to say specifically when Osiris began to be worshiped, or in what town or city his cult was first established, but the general information which we possess on this subject indicates that this god was adored as the great god of the dead by dynastic Egyptians from first to last." (E. A. Wallis Budge, *The Gods of the Egyptians* pg. 116.)

Dionysos was not a late-comer to Greece, as so many seem to believe. He was clearly known in all of his particulars to the Minoans and Mykenaean, as is attested by the appearance of his name on a clay tablet at Pylos: *di-wo-nu-so-jo*. Another tablet speaks of "Eleuther, son of Zeus" to whom two oxen were sacrificed *jo-i-je-si me-za-na e-re-u-te-re di-wi-je-we qu-o* and even of *wo-no-wa-ti-si* or *oinoatisi* "Women of Oinoa, Place of Wine" showing that already the wine-god had his female attendants in the thirteenth century BCE. Further, as Thoukydides said, the "Old Dionysia" or Anthesteria was common to all the Ionians – hence it must have preceded the migration of the Ionian tribes. The oldest sanctuaries in Athens were to Dionysos of the Swamps. And Dionysos is found even in Homer, where it "speaks of him in the same manner in which it speaks of the deities who have been worshiped since time immemorial, however the poet himself and his audience may feel about him" (Walter Otto, Dionysos pg 54).

Shared epithets and invocations

Referring to Osiris, Richard W. Wilkinson says, "Both the meaning of the God's name and his exact origins are enigmatic" (*The Complete Gods and Goddesses of Ancient Egypt*, 118).

Similarly, there is no agreement about the meaning and origin of the name of Dionysos. It seems not to be a personal name at all, but rather a title – and the ancients offered numerous speculative interpretations. Some suggested that it meant 'The God from Nysa,' (Diodoros Sikeliotes I.15) or 'The Limp of Zeus' (from an obscure Thracian word and on account of the fact that the child had been sewn into Zeus' thigh) or even 'The Divine Intelligence' (from *Dios nous* Macrobius, *Saturnalia* 1:18) – and almost 2,000 years later, we are no closer to understanding the meaning of this most enigmatic of God's names.

Etymologically, Osiris's name may be derived from the Egyptian word *useru* meaning "Mighty One" (Wilkinson, 118) which suggests a connection to Dionysos' Eleusinian epithet *Brimos* also meaning "Strong or Mighty One." As we shall see, this was not the only epithet or cult-title that the two seemed to share.

> "Hail to you Osiris of many names," – *The Great Hymn to Osiris*

> "Come, blessed Dionysos, many-named master of all." – *Orphic Hymn 45*

"... of holy forms, of secret rites in temples." – *The Great Hymn to Osiris*

"... ineffable, secretive, and two-formed ... Lord of triennial feasts." – *Orphic Hymn 30*

"O thou great one of two-fold strength," – *The Great Hymn to Osiris*

"Mighty and many-shaped God," – *Orphic Hymn 50*

"The two lands with one consent cry out unto thee with cries of joy." – *The Great Hymn to Osiris*

"You are honored by all the Gods and by all the men who dwell upon the earth. Come, blessed and leaping God, and bring much joy to all." – *Orphic Hymn 45*

"First-born son" – *The Book of the Dead* Chap. Cxxviii

"O firstborn, thrice begotten," – *Orphic Hymn 30*

"Lord of the two horns" – *The Book of the Dead* Chap. Clxxxi

"Bacchic lord, two-horned and two-shaped." – *Orphic Hymn 30*

"Thou art gentler than the Gods." – *The Lamentations of Isis and Nephthys*

Euripides calls Dionysos the "most gentle" of Gods (*Bakchai*, 860) and at Naxos he was invoked as *Meilikhios*, "the Gentle." "Thou who art of terrible majesty" (*The Lamentations of Isis and Nephthys*).
Additionally, in the Middle Kingdom, there exist in the Coffin Texts descriptions of Osiris that conjure up a picture of a threatening demon. He glories in slaughter, utters malignant spells against a dead person, and runs a 'mafia' consisting of executioners called 'Osiris's butchers painful of fingers' or 'Osiris's fishermen'" (George Hart, *A Dictionary of Egyptian Gods and Goddesses*, pg. 155).
Euripides calls Dionysos "most terrible" (*Bakchai*, 860) and he had numerous horrific and frightening epithets, including *Agrios* "The Wild One," *Anthroporraistes* "The Render of Humans," *Nyktipolos* "The Night-Stalker," *Omadios* "He of the Raw Feast," and *Omestes* "Eater of Raw Flesh."

"Thou Babe of beautiful appearance, come thou to us in peace." – *The Lamentations of Isis and Nephthys*

Dionysos was the Divine Child of Eleusis, the beautiful child in the *Liknon* who was cared for, and later Awakened, by his Nurses.

"O lover of women," – *Lamentations of Isis and Nephthys*

Dionysos is often described as a woman's God. He is constantly surrounded by women – Goddesses, Nymphs, Muses, Mainades, Thyiades, etc. Two of his most important myths revolve around his love for women and their love for him: his marriage to Ariadne, and the raising of his mother from the land of the dead to the realm of the Gods. He was a missionary in the cult of Meter Kybele, and even had many feminine epithets, including *Gynnis* "The Womanly" and *Arsenothelys* "The Bisexual." In Southern Italy, women saw death as an erotic adventure, in which they would be united forever in loving embrace with their God.

Osiris was called *Neb Ankh*, "Lord of Life," while Dionysos was understood to be *Zoe* "Indestructible Life" itself.

Osiris was called Lord of Wholeness, while Dionysos is sought to "come in wholeness to noble Tmolus" (48), Further, the rites of Dionysos have wholeness as their mission – to restore balance to the world, to bring out the hidden, repressed parts of ourselves, and purge unhealthy madness through *katharsis* that we might live lives of wholeness and happiness.

Osiris was the "Lord of All" while Dionysos' worship was open to everyone, from all ranks of society (Euripides' *Bakchai* 205) and he was called *Aisumnetes* "impartial power over all" (Pausanias 7.19.21).

Osiris was called "The Begetter," while Dionysos was called *Auxites*, "Giver of Increase."

Osiris was hailed as "Osiris in Battle" while Dionysos was called *Areion* "War-like" and said to "delight in bloody swords" (*Orphic Hymn 45*).

Osiris was called *Neb* "Lord," and *Ser*, Prince, while Dionysos was called *Anax* "Lord," and was the earthly child of princess Semele, the daughter of the Theban King Kadmos.

Osiris was called "The One in the Tree" just as Dionysos was called *Endendrites* "He in the Tree."

Osiris is called *p3wty n t3wy tm df3 k3w* "Primeval god of the two lands, perfect of nourishment and sustenance," while Dionysos is called, "Primeval ...wrapt in foliage, decked with grape-clusters" (*Orphic Hymn 30*).

Osiris is hailed as *Neb Neheh djet* "Lord of Eternity" while Dionysos is said to "stride the earth forever" (Sophokles, *Oedipus at Colonnus*).

Osiris is the *Nisut Netjeru* or King of the Gods, just as Dionysos, briefly, sat upon the throne of Zeus and ruled over all the Gods and men (Nonnos' *Dionysiaka*, 6.155).

Osiris is called *Neb-er-tcher* "Lord of the Outermost Limit," just as Arrian speaks of Dionysos having traveled to the "furthest reaches of the earth" (*Anabasis* 5.1.1).

Osiris was called *Sa Nut* "Child of Heaven" and *Sa Geb* "Child of Earth," just as the Bacchic initiate was to instruct the Guardians in the underworld that after having become identified with Dionysos he was to be known as a "child of Earth and of starry Heaven."

Osiris is called *Hr st=f m t3 dsr* "Who is upon his throne in the sacred land" just as the Orphics celebrated *Thronismoi Bakchika*, the "Rite of the Enthronement of Bacchus."

Many of Osiris's epithets link him to various cities. For instance, he is called *Khenti Abdju* "Foremost of Abydos," *Khenti Djedu* "Foremost of Busiris," "He Who Dwells in Iunu," and so forth. Similarly, many of Dionysos' epithets were linked to various cult centers belonging to him: *Eleutherios* "Of Eleutherai," *Kalydonion*, "Of Calydon," *Kresios* "The Cretan," and so forth. And of course, both Osiris and Dionysos were connected with Thebes – the one in Boiotia, the other in Egypt.

Utterance 419 speaks of, "the Imperishable Stars, the followers of Osiris," while Sophokles hails Dionysos as, "thou leader of the choral dance of the fire-breathing stars" (*Antigone* 1146).

There is an interesting parallel in the following paradoxical lines. Clement of Alexandria gives the *symbolon* of Dionysos thusly: *tauros drakontos kai pater taurou drakon*, "The bull is father of the serpent, and the serpent father of the bull." In the Pyramid texts we find, "To say the words: "The bull falls because of the sDH-snake, the sDH-snake falls because of the bull. Fall, roll together" (Utt. 289 430).

And that concludes the evidence I've gathered linking these two Gods. It is certainly a considerable amount of material, and suggests more than a casual similarity between them. Does it confirm the equation, however? That, I leave up to you to decide, dear reader!

A STRANGE GOD IN A STRANGE LAND: THE CHANGING FACE OF DIONYSOS IN HELLENISTIC EGYPT

During the Classical period there was a pretty broad repertoire of Dionysiac depictions, many of which cast the god in a hardly favorable light. The comic poet Aristophanes, for instance, made him a bumbling fool in *The Frogs* who has to ask directions to the underworld and pisses all over himself when confronted by Empousa (288 ff).

Certainly this is the sort of thing that one expects from Aristophanes (who regularly included jabs at the audience in his plays, calling them cocksuckers, parricides, and greedy cowards) but Dionysos isn't treated much better by the respectable authors:

> "It was Euripides who created a hungry Herakles, a cowardly Dionysos, a seducer Zeus and a weeping slave in his plays." – Suidas s.v. *Mattontas*

Furthermore, Euripides called him "effeminate" (*Bakchai* 350), Aiskhylos a "womanly man" and a "weakling" (*Edonoi* frag. 30-31). Stories were told of Dionysos being dressed in the clothing of little girls or changed into a goat to escape the wrath of Hera, and he was even said to have been driven insane when she eventually caught up with him (Apollodoros 3.28).

But perhaps the most embarrassing tale of all was the one that Homer told:

> "I will not fight against any god of the heaven, since even the son of Dryas, powerful Lykourgos, did not live long; he who tried to fight with the gods of the bright sky, who once drove the fosterers of Mainomenos Dionysos headlong down the sacred Nyseian hill, and all of them shed and scattered their wands on the ground, stricken with an ox-goad by murderous Lykourgos, while Dionysos in terror dove into the salt surf, and Thetis took him to her bosom, frightened, with the strong shivers upon him at the man's blustering. But the gods who live at their ease were angered with Lykourgos and the son of Kronos struck him to blindness, nor did he live long afterwards, since he was hated by all the immortals." (*Iliad* 6.129)

Nor, unfortunately, was this the only such fable that circulated in the Greek mainland.

Pausanias relates (2.20.4) that in Argos there was a tomb "which they claim belongs to the mainad Khorea saying that she was one of the women who joined Dionysos in his expedition against Argos, and that Perseus, being victorious in the battle, put most of the women to the sword. To the rest they gave a common grave, but to Khorea they gave burial apart because of her high rank." Both Pausanias (2.23.7-8) and Nonnos (25.104) maintain that during this battle Perseus slew the beloved bride of Dionysos who was powerless to save her. A late *scholion* on *Iliad* XIV 319 goes even further, claiming that Perseus drowned Dionysos by dumping him into the supernaturally deep waters of Lake Lerna, one of the traditional entrances to the underworld.

What a different situation we find in Egypt!

Consider the following passage from a 3rd century epic poem about the conflict between Dionysos and Lykourgos. Our fragment picks up in the middle, after Lykourgos and Dionysos have been going at it for some time. The god has just wrought a terrible miracle, transforming the lush countryside into a barren desert wasteland:

> "No longer flowed the spring beside the elm, nor were there ways of watering, nor paths nor fences nor trees, but all had vanished. Only the empty plain was visible. Where a meadow was before, close came Lykourgos, heart-stricken with mighty fear and speechlessness. For irresistibly, beyond mortal defense, all their works were upset and turned about before their eyes. But when Lykourgos knew him for the glorious son of Zeus, pale terror fell upon his spirit; the ox-goad, wherewith he had been at labor smiting, fell from his hand before his feet. He had no will to utter or to ask a word. Now might that poor wretch have escaped his gloomy fate: but he besought not then the divinity to abate his wrath. In his heart he foresaw that doom was nigh to him, when he saw Dionysos come to assail him amid lightnings that flashed manifold with repeated thunderclaps, while Zeus did great honor to his son's destructive deeds.
>
> "So Dionysos urged his ministers, and they together sped against Lykourgos and scourged him with rods of foliage. Unflinching he stood, like a rock that juts into the marble sea and groans when a wind arises and blows, and abides the smiting of the seas: even so abode Lykourgos steadfast, and recked not of their smiting. But ever more unceasing wrath went deep into the heart of Thyone's son: he was minded not at all to take his victim with a sudden death, that still alive he might repay a grievous penalty. He sent madness upon him, and spread about the phantom shapes of serpents, that he might spend the time fending away, til baneful Rumor of his madness should arrive at Thebes on wings and summon Ardys and Astakios, his two sons, and Kytis who married him and was subdued to his embrace.

"Then, when led by Rumor's many tongues they came, found Lykourgos just now released from suffering, worn out by madness. They cast their arms around him as he lay in the dust – fools! They were destined to perish at their father's hand before their mother's eyes! For not long after, madness, at the command of Dionysos, aroused Lykourgos yet again, but this time with real frenzy. He thought that he was smiting serpents; but they were his children from whom he stole the spirit. And now would Kytis have fallen about them, but in compassion Dionysos snatched her forth and set her beyond the reach of doom, because she had warned her lord constantly in his storms of evil passion. Yet she could not persuade her master, too stubborn; he, when his sudden madness was undone, recognized the god through experience of suffering. Still Dionysos abated not his wrath: as Lykourgos stood unflinching, yet frenzied by distress, the god spread vines about him and fettered all his limbs. His neck and both ankles imprisoned, he suffered the most pitiable doom of all men on earth: and now in the land of Sinners his phantom endures that endless labor – drawing water into a broken pitcher: the stream is poured forth into Haides.

"Such is the penalty which the loud-thundering son of Kronos ordained for men that fight against the gods; that retribution may pursue them both while living and again in death."

We aren't dealing with the weak and impotent Dionysos of Homer here, who flees to the bosom of Thetis and can't protect those near and dear to him. The Greco-Egyptian Dionysos is a potent force of nature and master of all vegetative life. He is also harsh and cruel when provoked, and the punishment he metes out to Lykourgos is nothing compared to what he has in store for an Indian spy in the *Bassarika* of the Greco-Egyptian poet Dionysios. There is some speculation that Dionysios may have lived in Panopolis; he certainly influenced the epic school that flourished there a couple centuries later. Not only does Nonnos continue the theme of the Indian War, but he even borrowed the names Deriades and Modaios for his *Dionysiaka*.

In the *Bassarika* fragment that has come down to us, a spy sent into the camp of Dionysos by the Indian king Deriades has just been discovered. The god orders several of his soldiers to go out and hunt a stag. That's when the fun starts.

"They slew it and flayed it, and stripping off the skin, arrayed the wretched man from head and shoulders down. The new-flayed hide clave to his body, molded to the flesh; above, the horns gleamed to be seen afar; to one that beheld him, he wanted nothing of the wild beast's form. Thus had they transformed a man into a counterfeit animal ... The Bacchanal god leapt into the midst of the enemy army, where most of all the Kethaians were rushing to the flame of battle. Standing there he cried aloud to Dereiades and the rest: 'Slaves of women, Indians, consider now this way: to Deriades above

> all I speak this from knowledge. You shall not, in your present straits, withstand the onslaught of the gleaming wine and escape your evil fate, before in the swift night you tear apart the raw flesh of a living animal and eat it. Behold this tall stag straight of horn, the finest that followed us from holy Hellas, a marvel to behold! Come, hasten to rend it in good conflict for its flesh.' So he spoke, and they of their own accord were fain to fall upon human flesh, and to appease their boundless desire, smitten by eager madness. And Deriades answered the son of Zeus, saying: 'Would that I might cut your body limb from limb and swallow the flesh raw....'"

And that, unfortunately, is where the fragment cuts off. You just know that Dionysos had some witty retort, perhaps even revealing the horrendous *sparagmos* and cannibalistic *omophagia* that he had compelled the Indians to unwittingly commit upon their kinsman. Perhaps it even ended with him saying something along the lines of, "Bitch, *this* is what happens when you send spies into my camp. Don't try it again or you will *know* that I am the Lord Dionysos!"

We find this sort of reveling in the raw power and ferocity of the god in other Greco-Egyptian poets as well. One thinks especially of the great Alexandrian Theokritos who composed a poem that told of the conflict between Dionysos and the insolent king Pentheus. I won't bother to cite *The Bacchanals* in full – though it is a lovely poem, subject-matter notwithstanding – and instead cut to the climax, which is very relevant to our discussion:

> "His mother took her son's head and roared like a lioness with cubs; and Ino, setting her foot upon his stomach, tore off the great shoulder with the shoulder-blade, and in like fashion wrought Autonoa, while the other women parted among them piecemeal what was left of him: and to Thebes they came all blood-bedrabbled, bringing from the hill not Pentheus but tribulation. I care not. And let not another care for an enemy of Dionysos – not though he suffer a fate more grievous than this and be in his ninth year or entering on his tenth. But for myself may I be pure and pleasing in the eyes of the pure, like the eagle which is honored by aegis-bearing Zeus. To the children of the righteous, not of the unrighteous, comes the better fate. Farewell to Dionysos, whom Lord Zeus set down on snowy Drakanos when he had opened his mighty thigh. Farewell to comely Semele and her sisters, Kadmean dames honored as heroines, who, at Dionysos' instigation, did this deed, wherein is no blame. At the acts of the gods let no man cavil."

So, how do we account for the Greco-Egyptian authors' apparent divergence from the traditional image of the god?

To begin with, although Aristophanes and Homer can be said to represent *a* traditional view of Dionysos, it was hardly the only one known to antiquity. Dionysos is unquestionably one of the most complex gods that mankind has ever encountered, and that complexity often finds expression through paradox. This becomes abundantly clear when we examine the different ways that Dionysian worship was carried out in the ancient Hellenic world. For instance, in Thrake and Makedonia a primitive and ecstatic type of worship flourished, with Dionysos served by mad-women who savagely tore animals apart and consumed the bloody flesh raw. In Athens this was the stuff of myth. There, the cult of Dionysos was considerably more genteel, consisting of formal drinking parties, civic processions and dramatic competitions held in his honor. At Amphikleia Dionysos was predominantly a healing-god with his own dream-incubation oracle. At Lesbos he was a god associated with poetic inspiration. In Sparta and Magna Graecia he was mostly a chthonic deity, having little to do with wine or theater. In some places he was depicted as a smooth-cheeked *ephebe*, in others as mature and bearded; in still others he appeared as a bull, a black goat, a tree-trunk or a pillar with a mask, draped in ivy.

And even in the Athens of Aristophanes we find a multiplicity of views proliferating. Aristophanes was hardly the only poet writing plays about the god. Euripides, Sophokles, Aiskhylos, and many of their lesser-known contemporaries explored Dionysian themes, and many of their plays centered on conflicts between the god and individuals such as Pentheus, Lykourgos, the Minyades and Proitides, etc., with the god enacting terrible vengeance upon those who opposed him. If anything, the Homeric account of Lykourgos and the later legend concerning Perseus represent an exception to the standard sequence of events in Dionysiac myth. And there were also local traditions that never made their way into the playwrights' repertoire but served as the foundation for a number of important religious festivals such as Oskhophoria, Anthesteria, and Lenaia.

Indeed, some festivals played upon this inherent duality. Athenaios tells us (3.78c) that on Naxos the people worshiped the god through two masks, reflecting his dual and contradictory nature. The first mask was made out of grape vines and represented Dionysos as Bakchios, "the Raving," a dark, destructive god of madness and intense, uncontrollable passions. The other mask, made of fig-wood, represented Meilikhios, "the Gentle," who was the kind and soothing deliverer from madness, the quiet after the storm and invoked to counterbalance the influence of the first mask at the end of the rite.

So, rather than parting with tradition and creating an ostensibly new Greco-Egyptian Dionysos, we should instead think of these poets as selectively choosing to emphasize certain aspects of the god while downplaying others. Of course, this does not solve the important question of why they did this and how they chose which elements to highlight. To answer that I believe that we need to consider several important and interrelated factors.

First we must remember that the dominant culture in Ptolemaic Egypt was not Greek. Nor was it Egyptian or even a hybrid of the two. Not originally, at least, and certainly not in the royal capital of Alexandria. This changed over time as immigrants from different parts of the Greek world came to settle in the land, bringing their native traditions with them and often intermarrying with the indigenous Egyptian population, both of which contributed in important ways to the development of what we today recognize as the distinctive Greco-Egyptian culture. But originally the Ptolemies were Makedonians and so were the high-ranking officials who made up the state bureaucracy. Indeed, Makedonians represented a privileged class within Egyptian society through Roman occupation. Well into the late period we find people boasting of their Makedonian descent, even though their families had lived in Egypt for centuries at that point.

Some may wonder how this is relevant. After all, weren't the Makedonians just another branch of the Greek people? They spoke a similar dialect (albeit with notable differences, e.g., the Makedonians pronounced ph- as a b sound) competed in the Olympics and were largely responsible for the spread of Greek culture during the Hellenistic era.

All of this is certainly true, and the Argead house was not only Philhellenic but strongly Atticizing to boot. Philip II and Archelaus before him were especially keen to emphasize the continuity of Greco-Makedonian culture: they brought artists, philosophers, and tutors to the capital and revised many of their people's institutions and laws to bring them more into line with the Greek mainstream. But in many respects this remained a superficial gloss. There was always a wilder, more primitive strain within the Makedonian soul that could not be done away with by aping Athenian customs and sensibilities. Democracy never took; they always maintained a strong monarchy and an even stronger attachment to their ancestral cults. And though it was asserted that the Herakles, Zeus, Aphrodite and Dionysos that they worshiped were the same gods common to all the Greeks, when you peel away the superficial similarities you find great differences among them. For instance, Makedonian Aphrodite is predominantly a goddess of fertility and the underworld and only secondarily a goddess of love. Likewise, the Makedonian Dionysos – and especially the Dionysos of the royal house – is very much an untamed force of nature: violent, ecstatic, dark and sensual. In fact, the primitive, even barbaric worship that this god inspired was shocking to Athenian sensibilities, familiar as they were with the more watered-down and strait-jacketed version found in their city. Euripides composed his magnum opus *The Bakchai* after a stay at the Makedonian court, and he glories in recounting the shocking and scandalous exploits of the god's female votaries which he saw still being carried out at that time. That such rites continued well into the Hellenistic era is demonstrated by the anecdotes that circulated about Olympias, the mother of Alexander the Great:

> "Moreover, a serpent was once seen lying stretched out by the side of Olympias as she slept, and we are told that this, more than anything else, dulled the ardor of Philip's attentions to his wife, so that he no longer came often to sleep by her side, either because he feared that some spells and enchantments might be practiced upon him by her, or because he shrank from her embraces in the conviction that she was the partner of a superior being. But concerning these matters there is another story to this effect: all the

women of these parts were addicted to the Orphic rites and the orgies of Dionysos from very ancient times (being called Klodones and Mimallones), and imitated in many ways the practices of the Edonian women and the Thracian women about Mount Haemus, from whom, as it would seem, the word *threskeuein* came to be applied to the celebration of extravagant and superstitious ceremonies. Now Olympias, who affected these divine possessions more zealously than other women, and carried out these divine inspirations in wilder fashion, used to provide the reveling companies with great tame serpents, which would often lift their heads from out the ivy and the mystic winnowing baskets, or coil themselves about the wands and garlands of the women, thus terrifying the men." – Plutarch, *Life of Alexander* 2.1.6

And when Dionysos was brought back to Egypt it was in this form, as is made clear in Kallixeinos' account of the Grand Procession of Ptolemy Philadelphos:

"The cart was followed by priests and priestesses and those who had charge of the sacred vestments, sacred guilds of every description, and women carrying the mystic winnowing-fans. Next came Makedonian Bacchants, the so-called 'Mimallones' and 'Bassarai' and 'Lydian women,' with hair streaming down and crowned with wreaths, some of snakes, others of smilax and vine-leaves and ivy; in their hands some held daggers, others snakes."

Also, Poseidippos of Pella, a poet at the court of Philadelphos, wrote the following epitaph for a Makedonian mainad who died in Egypt:

"The Euiades cried, ah! three times in grief, when Fate brought Niko, the youngest of twelve children, lovely in virginity, handmaiden of Dionysos, down from the Bassaric mountains." (VII 20-23)

Indeed, there are numerous references to the ecstatic votaries of the god in Alexandria and the *khora* or Egyptian countryside:

"There was a huge temple in one of the villages which housed a very famous idol, though in reality this image was nothing but a wooden statue. The priests together with the people, working themselves up into a Bacchic frenzy, used to carry it in procession through the villages, no doubt for the ceremony to ensure the flooding of the Nile." – *Historia Monachorum in Aegypto* 8.25

"I want always to dance, I want always to play the lyre. I strike up my lyre to praise the solemn festival with my words. The Bakchai have cast a spell on me." – Dioscorus of Aphrodito, *P.Cair.Masp.* I 67097 v F

"Cast white lilies on the tomb and beat by the stele of Aleximenes the drums he used to love; whirl your long-flowing locks ye Thyiades, free in the city by the river, where people often danced to the tender strain of his flute that breathed so sweetly upon your revels." – Dioscorides, *Greek Anthology* 7.485

"Demophon to Ptolemaios, greeting. Make every effort to send me the flute-player Petoüs with both the Phrygian flutes and the rest; and if any expense is necessary, pay it and you shall recover it from me. Send me also Zenobios the effeminate with a drum and cymbals and castanets, for he is wanted by the women for the sacrifice; and let him wear as fine clothes as possible. Get the kid also from Aristion and send it to me; and if you have arrested the slave, deliver him to Semphtheus to bring to me. Send me as many cheeses as you can, a new jar, vegetables of all kinds, and some delicacies if you have any. Farewell. Put them on board with the guards who will assist in bring the boat. (Address) To Ptolemaios." – *P.Hib.* 54

"Therous and Teos to King Ptolemy. We are wronged by [list of names] and other members of the women's *thiasos* from Kerkethoeris. For Soeris, my sister and wife of the aforementioned Teos, who was a member of the *thiasos* and held the post of priestess for the group for four years, chanced to die. Apart from us she had no close relatives, but when those named were asked for the cost of her burial they would not pay it." – *P. Entreux.* 21

"And Heraiskos the Alexandrian became a Bakchos, as a dream designated him" – Suidas s.v. *Hêraïskos*

"And those called the Boukoloi created a revolt in Egypt and joined with the other Egyptians led by the priest Isidoros. First, in the cloaks of women, they tricked the centurion since they appeared to be the women of the Boukoloi approaching to give him money for their men, and they struck him down. His companion they sacrificed swearing an oath on his entrails and then eating them. Of these men Isidoros was the bravest. Then, when they defeated the Romans in battle, they advanced towards Alexandria and would have reached there had not Cassius been sent against them from Syria and contrived to upset their unity and divide them from each other, for they were too many and too desperate for him to dare to come against them all together. And so he subdued them when they grew divided." – Cassius Dio, *Roman History* LXXII 4

"It is not by the Muses but by a kind of Korybantes that you Alexandrians are possessed; and you make credible the mythmaking of the poets, for they bring on the scene creatures called Bacchantes, maddened by song, and Satyrs too. Though you do not, like the Bacchantes of old, bear lions in your arms, you wear the fawnskin and bear the thyrsos and in every way seem compatible with Nymphs and Satyrs. For you are always in a merry mood, fond of laughing, fond of dancing. If you merely hear a harpstring twang, it's like the call of a bugle, and you can no longer keep the peace." – Dion Chrysostom, *Address to the Alexandrians*

At Gurôb in the Faiyum an interesting document related to the Dionysian mysteries was uncovered:

... having what he finds | ... [Let him] collect the raw pieces | ... on account of the sacrament:

"Accep]t ye my [offering] as the payment [for my lawless] fath[ers].
Save me, gr[eat] Brimo [
And Demeter (and ?) Rheia [
And the armed Kouretes; let us [
                        ] and we will make fine sacrifice.
                        ] a ram and a he-goat
                        ] boundless gifts."

... and pasture by the river | ... [ta]king of the goat | ... Let him eat the rest of the meat | ... Let *x* not watch | ... consecrating it upon the burnt-up | ... Prayer of the [ ]:

"Let [us] invoke [ ] and Eubouleus,
And let [us] call upon [the Queen] of the broad [Earth],
And the dear [ ]s. Thou, having withered the [
[Grant the blessings] of Demeter and Pallas unto us.
O Eubou]leus, Erikepaios,
Save me [Hurler of Light]ning!"

THERE IS ONE DIONYSUS.
Tokens | ..... GOD THROUGH BOSOM | ..... I have drunk. Donkey. Oxherd | ... password: UP AND DOWN to the | .... and what has been given to you, consume it | .... put into the basket | . .. [c]one, bull-roarer, knucklebones | .... mirror.

In fact, Dionysos-worship proliferated to such an extent that it became a common idiom for any type of mystical and ecstatic religious experience, as we see in the work of the staunchly conservative Jewish author Philo of Alexandria.

Most of his references to Greek and Egyptian religion are hardly what you would call favorable:

"Certainly you may see these hybrids of man and woman continually strutting about through the thick of the market, leading the processions at the feasts, appointed to serve as unholy ministers of

> holy things, leading the mysteries and initiations and celebrating the rites of Demeter." (*Spec* 3.40)

> "I mock the bulls and rams and goats which Egypt honors for impressing those who never become men in lofty spirit but are always womanish." (*Post* 165)

And perhaps most damning of all:

> "And if a brother or son or daughter or wife or a housemate or a friend however true, or anyone else who seems to be kindly disposed, urge us to ... fraternize with the multitude, resort to their temples, and join in their libations and sacrifices, we must punish him as a public and general enemy, taking little thought for the ties which bind us to him; and we must send round a report of his proposals to all the lovers of piety, who will rush with a speed which brooks no delay to take vengeance on the unholy man, and deem it a religious duty to seek his death." (*Spec* 1.316)

But he apparently felt quite differently about Dionysos. For instance, he mentions that the female votaries of Dionysos derive their name mainad from *mainas*, a divine madness which is "wineless intoxication" (*methe nephalios*) quite distinct from mere drunkenness (*Plant* 148). He compares this to the Therapeutai, contemplative Jewish mystics living outside Alexandria: "having drunk as in the Bacchic rites of the strong wine of god's love they mix and both together become a single choir" (*Contepl* 85). And in an autobiographical passage in which he is describing a mystic experience he admonishes his soul, "issue forth from thyself. Like persons possessed and corybantic, be filled with inspired frenzy, even as the prophets are inspired" (*Her* 69). These phrases in the original Greek read *korybantian* and *baccheuthesia kai theophorethesia* which clearly attest a Dionysian connection.

But even more striking is this veritable *paian* to the god:

> "Dionysos cultivated the wild vine and drew pouring from it a drink most delicious and at the same time profitable to souls and bodies. The soul he brings into a state of cheerfulness, creating oblivion of evils and hopes of good, while he renders the body healthier and stronger and more agile. In private life he improves each person and converts large households and families from a squalid and toilsome existence to a free and gay mode of living, and for all cities Greek and barbarian he provides a constant succession of banquets, merrymakings, galas, festivals. For all these owe their existence to Dionysos." (*Legat* 82f)

What a strange thing for a devout Jew to say! But then Dionysos' was the spirit of the age, and hardly any level of Greco-Egyptian society remained untouched by him. A big part of his appeal, I suspect, was that Dionysos was more than just a god of *enthousiasmos* and *ekstasis*; in fact, in Hellenistic Egypt he was viewed predominantly as a god of the earth's fertility.

Aelian, drawing on Alexandrian lexicographers, wrote:

> "Note that the ancients used the word *phlyein* (to luxuriate) of an abundant yield of fruit. So they called Dionysos Phleon (the luxuriant), Protrygaios (the first at the vintage), Staphylites (the god of the grape), Omphakites (the god of the unripe grape), and various other epithets." (*Historical Miscellany* 3.41)

A cult-hymn to Dionysos (*Collect. Alex.* 248) dating from the 1st century BCE reads:

> "...lift up your voice to him! We will sing of Dionysos on holy days. Twelve months he was away: now the season is here, and all the flowers...fruit...sacred oak; there grows the corn-ear mixed with barley, all seeds together; there flowers the white-coated wheat together with the dark-haired..."

A theme we find echoed in several passages from the 6th century Byzantine poet Dioscorus of Aphrodito, who wrote in both Greek and Coptic:

> "Under your leadership there has flowed forth the water that surpasses words, the Nile that covers Egypt's fields and is poured out as an offering in the furrows of the earth. You come as Dionysos giving your fellow revelers wine as their companion. As to the farmers...so you come to us with every aid...grain on our threshing floors." (*P.Cair.Masp.* III 67317)

> "They have surrounded the joyful moon with wedding songs, in the furrows of the grain-bearing earth that rejoices with flowers, and granted care-free protection by garlanded Dionysos and the Nile with his many children...the lover of maidens dances before you, Dionysos with his wreathed revelers." (*P.Cair.Masp.* III 67318)

In the *Greek Anthology* there is a poem (9.383) that evokes the Dionysian spirit through the months of the Egyptian year:

> "First Thoth learnt to uplift the hook to prune the grapes; Phaophi brings to fishermen a catch of every variety; Athyr indicated the date of the appearance of the Pleiades; Khoiak shows the birth of the sewn crops; Tybi displays the purple robe; Mecheir bids sailors prepare for a voyage; Phamenoth trains warriors in the use of arms; Pharmouthi is the first herald of the roses of spring; Pakhon keeps for the sickle the ripened corn; Payni is the herald of fruitful autumn; Epephi, who blesses the vine, holds a bunch of grapes; and Mesori brings the vivifying water of the Nile."

The super-abundant fertility of Dionysos was especially manifest in the Grand Procession of Ptolemy Philadelphos, as recorded by Kallixeinos:

> "But in the Dionysiac procession first of all there went the Sileni who keep off the multitude, some clad in purple cloaks, and some in scarlet ones. And these were followed by Satyrs, twenty in each division of the stadium, bearing gilded lamps made of ivy-wood. And after them came images of Nike, having golden wings, and they bore in their hands incense-burners six cubits in height, adorned with branches made of ivy-wood and gold, clad in tunics embroidered with figures of animals, and they themselves also had a great deal of golden ornament about them. And after them there followed an altar of six cubits in height, a double altar, covered all over with ivy-leaves gilded, having a crown of vine-leaves on it all gold, enveloped in bandages with white centres. And that was followed by boys in purple tunics, bearing frankincense, and myrrh, and saffron, on golden dishes. And after them came forty Satyrs, crowned with ivy garlands made of gold. And they were painted as to their bodies, some with purple, some with vermilion, and some with other colors. And these also wore each a golden crown made to imitate vine-leaves and ivy-leaves. And after them came two Sileni in purple cloaks and white fringes to them. And one of them had a petasus and a golden caduceus, and the other had a trumpet. And between them went a man of gigantic size, four cubits high, in a tragical dress and ornaments, bearing the golden horn of Amaltheia. And his name was The Year. And he was followed by a woman of great beauty and of more than ordinary size, adorned with quantities of gold and a superb dress; bearing in one of her hands a garland of peach blossoms, and in her other hand a branch of the palm-tree. And she was called Penteteris. And she was succeeded by the Four Seasons dressed in character, and each of them bearing its appropriate fruits. Next to them came two incense-burners made of ivy-wood, covered with gold, and six cubits in height, and a large square golden altar in the middle of them. And then again Satyrs, having garlands of ivy-leaves made of gold, and clad in purple robes. And some of them bore golden wine-jars, and others bore goblets. After them marched Philiscus the poet, being a priest of Dionysos, and with him all the artisans who were concerned in the service of Dionysos. Next were borne Delphic tripods, being prizes for the managers of the athletics; the one intended for the manager of the boys' class was thirteen and a half feet high, the other, for the manager of the adults' class, was eighteen feet."

And of course we saw this in the Lykourgos epic when the god transforms the lush fields into a barren desert wasteland and binds the malefactor with ivy-ropes. The power of the god is manifest through nature itself, as Greco-Egyptian iconographic representations of Dionysos so often make clear.

Another aspect of the god that gained prominence at this time, and which is closely allied to the above, is his role as a chthonic deity. As Gary Vikan writes in *Catalogue of the Sculpture in the Dumbarton Oaks Collection from the Ptolemaic Period to the Renaissance* (pg. 38):

> "Egypt had a rich tradition of Dionysiac sepulchral art. Dionysos, his symbols, and members of his *thiasos* figure prominently in Egypto-Roman garland sarcophagi, in sculpted and frescoed tomb decoration, and in the niches from Herakleopolis Magna which, like those from Oxyrhynchus, came from tomb chambers. An explicit example is an Alexandrian grave stela of the second or third century whereon the deceased, a three-year-old boy, is portrayed with the attributes of Dionysos. The emphasis on grape vines and relaxed inebriation in the Dumbarton Oaks relief suggests that its eschatological significance was not that of triumph, resurrection, or the regeneration so often associated with Dionysos, but rather the idea that the deceased looked forward to a happy, bacchic afterlife. The general religious context of such a relief is illuminated by an epigram flanking the entrance to a Roman tomb chamber at Tounah el-Gebel. A father addresses his dead daughter Isidora, who has been carried off by the nymphs and deified; he speaks of the yearly libations offered by the Seasons: 'Burning Summer, in its turn, offers drink from the vat of Bacchus, and for you it binds grapes from the branches of a grape vine to make a crown.'"

We know that Anthesteria, one of Dionysos' most important festivals during which he was honored as the Lord of Souls, was celebrated at Alexandria:

> "Nor did the morn of the Broaching of the Jars pass unheeded, nor that whereon the Pitchers of Orestes bring a white day for slaves. And when he kept the yearly festival of Ikarios' child, thy day, Erigone, lady most sorrowful of Attic women, he invited to a banquet his familiars, and among them a stranger who was newly visiting Egypt, whither he had come on some private business." – Kallimakhos, *Aitia* 1.1

And in another Egyptian source the vines of Bacchus were said to mourn for a barkeeper who had poured "honey-sweet wine for all mortals, the drops that stop pain" (Susan Guettel Cole, *Dionysos and the Dead*, pg. 282 in *Masks of Dionysos*).

Dionysos also had a prominent place at Memphis, as P. M. Fraser in his monumental *Ptolemaic Alexandria* writes:

> "The aspect of Dionysus which predominated in the Ptolemaic period was the chthonic...at a very early date, Dionysus had assumed a very important role in the Memphian Serapeum itself. The dromos, about 100 metres long, which at the west end of the whole site linked the 'Temple of Nectanebos' with the main shrine of

Apis, was flanked by a low wall carrying a series of sculptured limestone groups representing the Dionysiac fauna – Cerberus, the panther, the lion and the peacock, and Sirens – and the god himself as a child riding the panther and peacock…It is an indication, once more, of the early development of the 'syncretism' in the religious life of the Greek population of Egypt, that these figures, fashioned to adorn the newly Hellenized shrine of Osor-Hapu, should express not only (through Cerberus) the chthonic, Osirian aspect of Dionysus, but also some essentially Greek features – the conquering child, lion the lion, the panther, and the peacock, reflects not Egyptian beliefs, but the conquering Dionysus from India – and also a fusion with the young Attis." (pg. 206)

This Osirian aspect of Dionysos is amply represented in our sources:

"That Osiris is identical with Dionysos who could more fittingly know than yourself, Klea? For you are at the head of the inspired maidens of Delphi, and have been consecrated by your father and mother in the holy rites of Osiris. If, however, for the benefit of others it is needful to adduce proofs of this identity, let us leave undisturbed what may not be told, but the public ceremonies which the priests perform in the burial of the Apis, when they convey his body on an improvised bier, do not in any way come short of a Bacchic procession; for they fasten skins of fawns about themselves, and carry Bacchic wands and indulge in shoutings and movements exactly as do those who are under the spell of the Dionysiac ecstasies. For the same reason many of the Greeks make statues of Dionysos in the form of a bull; and the women of Elis invoke him, praying that the god may come with the hoof of a bull; and the epithet applied to Dionysos among the Argives is 'Son of the Bull.' They call him up out of the water by the sound of trumpets, at the same time casting into the depths a lamb as an offering to the Keeper of the Gate. The trumpets they conceal in Bacchic wands, as Socrates has stated in his treatise *On The Holy Ones*. Furthermore, the tales regarding the Titans and the rites celebrated by night agree with the accounts of the dismemberment of Osiris and his revivification and regenesis. Similar agreement is found too in the tales about their sepulchres. The Egyptians, as has already been stated, point out tombs of Osiris in many places, and the people of Delphi believe that the remains of Dionysos rest with them close beside the oracle; and the Holy Ones offer a secret sacrifice in the shrine of Apollo whenever the devotees of Dionysos wake the God of the Mystic Basket. To show that the Greeks regard Dionysos as the lord and master not only of wine, but of the nature of every sort of moisture, it is enough that Pindar be our witness, when he says 'May gladsome Dionysos swell the fruit upon the trees, the hallowed splendor of harvest time.' For this reason all who reverence Osiris are prohibited from destroying a cultivated tree or blocking up a spring of water." – Plutarch, *On Isis and Osiris* 364e-365e

"Orpheus, for instance, brought from Egypt most of his mystic ceremonies, the orgiastic rites that accompanied his wanderings, and his fabulous account of his experiences in Haides. For the rite of Osiris is the same as that of Dionysos, and that of Isis very similar to that of Demeter, the names alone having been interchanged; and the punishments in Haides of the unrighteous, the Fields of the Righteous, and the fantastic conceptions, current among the many, which are figments of the imagination – all these were introduced by Orpheus in imitation of Egyptian funeral customs." – Diodoros Sikeliotes, *Historical Library* 1.96

"Demeter has the same meaning among the Greeks as Isis among the Egyptians: and, again, Koré and Dionysos among the Greeks the same as Isis and Osiris among the Egyptians. Isis is that which nourishes and raises up the fruits of the earth; and Osiris among the Egyptians is that which supplies the fructifying power, which they propitiate with lamentations as it disappears into the earth in the sowing, and as it is consumed by us for food. " – Porphyry, *Concerning Images*

Nor was this merely idle speculation about *Interpretatio Graeca*; we find this syncretism borne out in actual cultus of the time. For instance, a Ptolemaic official made a dedication to "...Dionysos, who is called *Petempamenti,*"(*OGIS* 1.130) meaning "He Who is in the West," a title normally attached to Osiris. Many times we find priests and priestesses serving Dionysos and the Egyptian gods jointly:

"Here lies the famous priestess of the god Bacchus the Ancient, chaste *pastophorus* of the Nile goddess, whose name was Alexandria. She had barely attained the bloom of youth when notorious envy of the fates took her away to Dis." – *ILS* 4414

"...he set the people free, and a priest....he splendidly executed the processions and the sacrifices of the Great God Dionysos and gave a share of the meat to the citizens, chosen by lot as the priest of Serapis in the same manner regarding the expenses he turned back nicely and benevolently....The council decreed and the people approved that in honor of all these things Akornio, son of Dionysios, was to be rewarded during the Dionysia a golden crown and a bronze statue and in the future he was to receive during the Dionysia a golden crown every year and among the statues put up in the market-place his ought to have the most prominent place." – *SIRIS* 703

"To Isis and Serapis, Liber and Libera, P. Quinctius Paris having undertaken a vow for the well-being of his son Scapula gladly and deservedly fulfilled his vow." – *SIRIS* 676

Likewise there are several terracotta statues in the Greco-Roman Museum in Alexandria that depict Dionysos with traditional Egyptian iconographic motifs, including the *ankh*, lotus flower, double-plumed crown, and *was*-scepter.

The Ptolemies were happy to exploit this association since Osiris had been a royal deity from the earliest period in the country's history. If Osiris and Dionysos could be seen as the same god, this would lend added legitimacy to their reign since the Ptolemies claimed a special relationship with Dionysos. In fact, the Ptolemies traced their line back to the god:

"Satyros, also giving a history of the Alexandrine families, beginning from Philopator, who was also named Ptolemy, gives out that Bakchos was his progenitor; wherefore also Ptolemy was the founder of this family. Satyros then speaks thus: That Deïaneira was born of Bakchos and Althaía, the daughter of Thestios; and from her and Herakles the son of Zeus there sprang, as I suppose, Hyllos; and from him Kleodemos, and from him Aristomakhos, and from him Temenos, and from him Keisos, and from him Maron, and from him Thestros, and from him Akous, and from him Aristomidas, and from him Karanos, and from him Koinos, and from him Tyrimmas, and from him Perdikkhas, and from him Philippos, and from him Aeropos, and from him Alketas, and from him Amyntas, and from him Bokros, and from him Meleagros, and from him Arsinoë, and from her and Lagos Ptolemy Soter, and from him and Arsinoë Ptolemy Euergetes, and from him and Berenike, daughter of Maga, king of Kyrene, Ptolemy Philopator. Thus, then, stands the relationship of the Alexandrine kings to Bakchos. And therefore in the Dionysian tribe there are distinct families: the Althaían from Althaía, who was the wife of Dionysos and daughter of Thestios; the family of Deïaneira also, from her who was the daughter of Dionysos and Althaía, and wife of Herakles; – whence, too, the families have their names: the family of Ariadne, from Ariadne, daughter of Minos and wife of Dionysos, a dutiful daughter, who had intercourse with Dionysos in another form; the Thestian, from Thestios, the father of Althaía; the Thoantian, from Thoas, son of Dionysos; the Staphylian, from Staphylos, son of Dionysos; the Euainian, from Eunous, son [great-grandson] of Dionysos; the Maronian, from Maron, son [great-grandson] of Ariadne and Dionysos; – for all these are sons of Dionysos." – Theophilus, *To Autolycus* 7

Many of them took an added step and claimed to be the earthly incarnation of Dionysos:

> "The fourth Ptolemy was called the New Dionysos." – Clement of Alexandria, *Protrepticus*. 47

> "And mortals have been kings over Egypt, they say, for a little less than five thousand years down to the One Hundred and Eightieth Olympiad, the time when we visited Egypt and the king was Ptolemy, who took the name of the New Dionysos." – Diodoros Sikeliotes, *Historical Library* 1.44

> "Tryphon, catamite of Ptolemy, the New Dionysos." – *CIG* 4926

They were especially devoted to his worship. Under their reign numerous temples and theaters were erected to honor Dionysos, including a few that are still standing despite the best efforts of Christians and Moslems over the centuries. In fact, centuries later, it was the destruction of Dionysos' temple in Alexandria by a mob of insane, violent Christians instigated by the Bishop Theophilus which inspired the remaining Pagans of the city to rise to the defense of the Serapeion (also of Ptolemaic construction):

> "About this period, the bishop of Alexandria, to whom the temple of Dionysos had, at his own request, been granted by the emperor, converted the edifice into a church. The statues were removed, the *adyta* were exposed; and, in order to cast contumely on the pagan mysteries, he made a procession for the display of these objects; the phalli, and whatever other object had been concealed in the *adyta* which really was, or seemed to be, ridiculous, he made a public exhibition of. The pagans, amazed at so unexpected an exposure, could not suffer it in silence, but conspired together to attack the Christians. They killed many of the Christians, wounded others, and seized the Serapeion, a temple which was conspicuous for beauty and vastness and which was seated on an eminence. This they converted into a temporary citadel." – Hermias Sozomen *The Ecclesiastical History* 7:15

Several *demes* in Alexandria were named after members of Dionysos' extended family, including Thoastis, Staphylis, Euantheus, Maroneus, Deineireus, Althaieus, Ariadnis, and Thestias. Also, Dionysian names were given to a number of villages in the *khora* – most notably Bacchias (modern-day Umm-el' Atl) and Dionysias (Kasr Kurun).

They personally hosted festivals and artistic competitions in his honor:

> "The great Eratosthenes lived on at Alexandria to look with sadness of heart at the outcome of all the teaching he had bestowed upon the son of Ptolemy Euergetes. When the fourth Ptolemy was dead, the old man published a book called *Arsinoë* in memory of the young queen. In this book he described how he had once been with her, when she and certain of her retinue were passing through some place, in or near the palace, and how they had met a man carrying

> green boughs, as for a festival. The queen wondered what festival day it could be — these things were obviously arranged by Ptolemy and his associates without any reference to her — and she inquired of the man. The man said it was the Feast of Flagons (*lagunophoria*), and that it ended up with every one, court and people, getting gloriously drunk in a revel out of doors. Then, Eratosthenes wrote, Arsinoë 'turned her eyes upon us' and broke out in bitter words at the shame of her father's house and the abasement of the royal dignity." – Athenaios 7.276A

> "In the court of the Ptolemy who was called Dionysos there was once a man who accused Demetrios, the Platonic philosopher, of drinking nothing but water and of being the only person who did not wear women's clothes at the Dionysia. He was summoned next morning, and had to drink in public, dress up in gauze, clash and dance to the cymbals, or he would have been put to death for disapproving the King's life, and setting up for a critic of his luxurious ways." – Lucian, *On Slander* 16

> "All these kings, after the third Ptolemy, were corrupted by luxury and effeminacy, and the affairs of government were very badly administered by them; but worst of all by the fourth, the seventh, and the last, Auletes, who, besides other deeds of shamelessness, acted the piper; indeed he gloried so much in the practice, that he scrupled not to appoint trials of skill in his palace ostensibly in honor of Dionysos on which occasions he presented himself as a competitor with other rivals. He was deposed by the Alexandrines; and of his three daughters, one, the eldest, who was legitimate, they proclaimed queen; but his two sons, who were infants, were absolutely excluded from the succession." – Strabo, *Geography* 17.1.11

They gave royal patronage to troupes of actors:

> "Apollonios to Zoilos, greeting. We have released the [teachers] of letters and masters of gymnastic and [performers of] the rites of Dionysos and victors in the [Alexandrian contest] and in the Basileia and Ptolemaia from the tax on salt, them and their (descendants, as the king] has ordered. Farewell." – *P.Hal.* 1

> "Be it resolved by the guild of artists dedicated to Dionysos and the Theoi Adelphoi, and by those who share membership in the guild, that Dionysios, the son of Mousaeus, who is a Prytanis for life, is hereby authorized to adorn himself, in accordance with native custom, with the crown of ivy, in recognition of his generosity to the city of the Ptolemaeans and to the guild of artists dedicated to the great Dionysos and the Theoi Adelphoi. This crowning shall take place publicly at the Dionysia, and this resolution shall be inscribed

upon a stele and set up in front of the temple of Dionysos. The cost of the stele shall be paid by the treasurer Sosibios." – *OGIS* 50

And the fourth Ptolemy directly oversaw the mysteries of Dionysos and even attempted to codify and standardize them:

"By the Order of the King. Those in the country districts who impart initiation into the mysteries of Dionysos are to come down by river to Alexandria, those residing not farther than Naucratis within 10 days after the promulgation of this decree, those beyond Naucratis within 20 days, and register themselves before Aristobulus at the registry office (*katalogeion*) within 3 days of the day of their arrival, and they shall immediately declare from whom they have received the rites for three generations back and give in the Sacred Discourse (*Hieroi Logoi*) sealed, each man writing upon his copy his own name." – *Berlin Papyrus* No. 11774, verso

This Ptolemy was so exceptionally devoted to Dionysos that he had the "ivy-leaf of the Dionysian initiates tattooed on his body" (Etym. Magnum, s.v. *Galloi*) and played the *tympanon* during ceremonies conducted at the royal residence (Plutarch *Kleomenes* 33). According to Jewish sources he was so zealous for the god's worship that he engaged in one of the few instances of religious intolerance in antiquity and attempted to forcibly convert the Jews:

"At the monthly celebration of the King's birthday people were driven by harsh compulsion to partake of the sacrifices, and when a festival of Dionysos was celebrated, they were forced to wear ivy wreaths and walk in the Dionysiac procession. At the suggestion of the people of Ptolemais a decree was issued to the neighboring Greek cities, enforcing the same conduct on the Jews there, obliging them to share in the sacrificial meals, and ordering the execution of those who did not choose to conform to Greek customs." – *2 Maccabees* 6

"Ptolemy set up a stone on the tower in the courtyard with this inscription: 'None of those who do not sacrifice shall enter their sanctuaries, and all Jews shall be subjected to a registration involving poll tax and to the status of slaves. Those who object to this are to be taken by force and put to death; those who are registered are also to be branded on their bodies by fire with the ivy-leaf symbol of Dionysos, and they shall also be reduced to their former limited status.' In order that he might not appear to be an enemy of all, he inscribed below: 'But if any of them prefer to join those who have been initiated into the mysteries, they shall have equal citizenship with the Alexandrians.'" – *3 Maccabees* 2.27-30

Of course, these anecdotes have found no corroborating evidence, are of late composition and likely reflect anti-Roman sentiments disguised as an attack on the Ptolemies. Furthermore, it's completely out of character for the Ptolemies, who were extremely tolerant of the religious diversity of their subjects and in fact showed great Philosemitism – note the translation of the Septuagint carried out at the request of Ptolemy Philadelphos (*Letter of Aristeas*), the promotion of Jews to high-ranking positions in the government and military and the construction of a Jewish temple at Leontopolis (Josephus, *Jewish Antiquities* 13.1-3). But I digress.

One of the reasons why Dionysos held such a strong appeal for the Ptolemies was the example set by the myth of his conquest of the East. From the earliest times Dionysos had been presented as a world-traveler and leader of a great army. Already in Homer Dionysos is located beyond the boundaries of the conventional Hellenic world: he fights against the Edonian king Lykourgos (*Iliad* 6.129), his birthplace is either in Phoenicia or "near the streams of Aigyptos" (*Homeric Hymn* 1), he is abducted by Etruscan pirates while headed for Egypt and Kypros (*Homeric Hymn* 7) and he is said to "wander continually, thickly wreathed with ivy and laurel, and the Nymphs followed in his train with him for their leader" (*Homeric Hymn* 26). Herodotos, likewise, places the god on the periphery: Thrake (5.7), Lydia (1.150), other parts of Asia Minor (4.87), the Ukraine (4.79), Egypt (2.42), North Africa (3.97), Arabia (3.111), Phoenicia (2.49), and elsewhere. In the choral ode of *Antigone*, Sophokles hails Dionysos as "the lord of all Italy" and Plato mentions that festivals are carried out in his honor at Tarenton in Magna Graecia (*Laws* 637b). And for the ancients Dionysos was not merely the sight-seer *par excellence*; he traveled with a mission. Numerous ancient legends speak of his bringing wine and viniculture to various localities. Here are two from Athens alone:

> "Philokhoros has this: Amphiktyon, king of Athens, learned from Dionysos the art of mixing wine, and was the first to mix it. So it was that men came to stand upright, drinking wine mixed, whereas before they were bent double by the use of unmixed. Hence he founded an altar of Dionysos Orthos (Upright) in the shrine of the Horai (Seasons); for these make ripe the fruit of the vine. Near it he also built an altar to the Nymphai to remind devotees of the mixing; for the Nymphai are said to be the nurses of Dionysos. He also instituted the custom of taking just a sip of unmixed wine after meat, as a proof of the power of the Good God, but after that he might drink mixed wine, as much as each man chose. They were also to repeat over this cup the name of Zeus Soter as a warning and reminder to drinkers that only when they drank in this fashion would they surely be safe." – Athenaios, *Deipnosophistai* 2.38c-d

> "When Father Liber went out to visit men in order to demonstrate the sweetness and pleasantness of his fruit, he came to the generous hospitality of Icarius and Erigone. To them he gave a skin full of wine as a gift and bade them spread the use of it in all the other lands. Loading a wagon, Icarius with his daughter Erigone and a dog Maera came to shepherds in the land of Attica, and showed them

the kind of sweetness wine had. The shepherds, made drunk by drinking immoderately, collapsed, and thinking that Icarius had given them some bad medicine, killed him with clubs. The dog Maera, howling over the body of the slain Icarius, showed Erigone where her father lay unburied. When she came there, she killed herself by hanging in a tree over the body of her father. Because of this, Father Liber afflicted the daughters of the Athenians with alike punishment. They asked an oracular response from Apollo concerning this, and he told them they had neglected he deaths of Icarius and Erigone. At this reply they exacted punishment from the shepherds, and in honor of Erigone instituted a festival day of swinging because of the affliction, decreeing that through the grape-harvest they should pour libations to Icarius and Erigone. By the will of the gods they were put among the stars. Erigone is the sign Virgo whom we call Justice; Icarius is called Arcturus among the stars, and the dog Maera is Canicula." – Hyginus, *Fabulae* 130

He collected an army:

"The whole tribe of Satyroi is boldhearted while they are drunken with bumpers of wine; but in battle they are but braggarts who run away from the fight – hares in the battlefield, lions outside, clever dancers, who know better than all the world how to ladle strong drink from the full mixing-bowl. Few of these have been men of war, to whom bold Ares has taught all the practice of the fray and how to manage a battalion. Here when Lyaios prepared for war, some of them covered their bodies with raw oxhides, others fortified themselves with skins of shaggy lions, others put on the grim pelts of panthers, others equipped themselves with long pointed staves, others girt about their chests the skins of long-antlered stags dappled like stars in the sky. With these creatures, the two horns on the temples right and left strengthened their sharp points, and a scanty fluff grew on the top of the pointed skull over the crooked eyes. When they ran, the winged breezes blew back their two ears, stretched out straight and flapping against their hairy cheeks: behind them a horse's tail stuck out straight and lashed round their loins on either side." – Nonnos, *Dionysiaka* 14. 105 ff

"You drive your pair of lynxes with bright colored reigns. Bacchae and Satyri are your followers, and that old drunkard whose stout staff supports his tottering steps, who sits so insecure upon his sagging ass. Wherever your course leads you, young men's shouts and women's cries echo afar with noise of tambourines and clashing bronze and long-bored pipes of box." – Ovid, *Metamorphoses* 4. 25 ff

And led them to the very edge of the world:

"Dionysos was, in my opinion ... the first to invade India, and the first to bridge the river Euphrates. Zeugma was the name given to that part of the country where the Euphrates was bridged, and at the present day the cable is still preserved with which he spanned the river; it is plaited with branches of the vine and ivy. Both the Greeks and the Egyptians have many legends about Dionysos." – Pausanias, 10.29.4

"Destruction feeds, O Bacchus, on that soldiery of thine, thy comrades to farthest India, who dared to ride on the Eastern plains and plant thy banners on the world's first edge. The Arabs, blest with their cinnamon groves, they saw, and fleeing horsemen, the backs of the treacherous Parthians, to be feared for their flying shafts; they pierced to the shores of the ruddy sea, whence Phoebus discloses his rising beams, opens the gates of day, and with nearer torch darkens the naked Indians." – Seneca, Oedipus 112

"Megasthenes says that the Indians were originally nomads, like the non-agricultural Scythians, who wander in their wagons and move from one part of Scythia to another, not dwelling in cities and not reverencing shrines of the gods. Just so the Indians had no cities and built no temples, but were clothed with the skins of wild animals they would kill, and ate the bark of trees; these trees were called in the Indian tongue Tala, and what look like clews of wool grew on them, just as on the tops of palm trees. They also fed on what game they had captured, eating it raw, at least until Dionysos reached India. But when he arrived and became master of India, he founded cities, gave them laws, bestowed wine on the Indians as on the Greeks, and taught them to sow their land, giving them seed. Dionysos first yoked oxen to the plough and made most of the Indians agriculturalists instead of nomads, and equipped them also with the arms of warfare. He also taught them to reverence various gods, but especially of course himself, with clashings of cymbals and beating of drums; he instructed them to dance in the Satyric fashion, the dance called among Greeks the 'cordax', and showed them how to wear long hair in honor of the god with the conical cap, and instructed them in the use of perfumed ointments, so that even against Alexander the Indians came to battle to the sound of cymbals and drums." – Arrian, *Indika* 7.2-9

One of the most beautiful evocations of this can be found in the prologue to Euripides' *Bakchai*:

"I, Dionysos, have left the wealthy lands of the Lydians and Phrygians, the sun-parched plains of the Persians, and the Bactrian walls, and have passed over the wintry land of the Medes, and blessed Arabia, and all of Asia which lies along the coast of the salt sea with its beautifully-towered cities full of Hellenes and barbarians mingled together; and I have come to this Hellenic city first, having already set those other lands to dance and established my mysteries there, so that I might be a deity manifest among men."

The Dionysiac Triumph was particularly popular in Egyptian works of art, as Jack Lindsay points out:

"On a mosaic is represented a procession in his honor; he stands in a car drawn by centaur and centauress. On a Coptic textile he holds a bowl in his right hand and a duck in his left as he stands in a car drawn by spotted panthers. On two other textiles the car is drawn by rampant panthers or lions. Elsewhere mosaics, silver plate, and sarcophagi show lionesses, tigers, panthers, elephants drawing the chariot; and at times lions accompany the god. The child Dionysos is set astride both a lion and a panther on Ptolemaic sculptures at Memphis. A relief on an Alexandrian ivory pyxis depicts Dionysos in a car drawn by panthers, while he fights Indians, a torch in his right hand and a shield in his left. In a mosaic from Acholla in N. Africa he is drawn by galloping centaurs, a kantharos in his right hand, in his left a spear such as was used in hunting. Such spears are shown as carried by bacchantes: on a Coptic textile of a Triumph and in a Pompeian wall-painting of the dismemberment of Pentheus."
(*Leisure and Pleasure in Roman Egypt*, pgs. 225-226)

As you can see, the essential features of this myth had already been firmly established long before Alexander the Great. This is significant since some scholars have sought to dismiss the story as a Hellenistic fabrication. Granted, the myth was given new relevance after Alexander and like all myths it accumulated novel elements through repeated retellings, but the core of it had always been there, and indeed is essential for a proper understanding of Dionysos. Because Dionysos is the epiphanal god, he who appears, who comes from afar. He is the stranger, the embodiment of the Other. He affirms the norms of a society by outlining and transgressing their boundaries. And Dionysos is a culture-bringer in every sense of the word, for you cannot have culture without agriculture. When we learn to till the soil we come to value what is permanent and settled, and most important of all, how to get along with others. Cooperation is essential for this; you cannot sow the seeds, tend the fields, and harvest its produce all on your own. You must rely on others and come up with satisfactory ways to settle disputes. Those who place their own petty desires above the needs of the community bring great suffering to all. So out of agricultural cooperation are born all of our laws and customs. This is the heart of the myth of Dionysos the world-conqueror. He sets out to bring knowledge of the vine to distant lands. In the process he teaches them law and civilization, the tools necessary to properly care for the fields. He puts down evil customs such as cannibalism and opposes those who are haughty and unjust, those who are selfish, violent, and quarrelsome such as Lykourgos and Deriades. And with the advent of agriculture comes the blessings of civilization: prosperity, peace and happiness. Men's bellies are full, their spirits free, and their hearts joyous.

When Alexander sought to put down the tyranny of the Persians he looked back to the glorious accomplishments of his ancestor and consciously sought to follow in his footsteps. In fact, Plutarch even makes Alexander admit as much:

> "I imitate Herakles, and emulate Perseus, and follow in the footsteps of Dionysos, the divine author and progenitor of my family, and desire that victorious Greeks should dance again in India and revive the memory of the Bacchic revels among the savage mountain tribes beyond the Kaukasos." (*On the Fortune of Alexander* 1.332A)

Alexander not only imitated the military accomplishments of his ancestor, but also his theatrical displays which, in a sense, were deeply intertwined:

> "Some writers have recounted a story, which I do not myself credit, that Alexander bound together two war-chariots, and drove through Carmania reclining with his Companions to the sound of the pipes, while his army followed behind, garlanded and sporting; that provisions and everything else that could make for luxury had been brought together along their path by the Carmanians; and that this pageantry was devised by Alexander in imitation of the Bacchic revelry of Dionysos, since there was a story about Dionysos that, after subduing India, he traversed the greater part of Asia in this way, that he himself was surnamed 'Triumph', and that processions after victories in war were for this very reason called 'triumphs'." – Arrian, *Anabasis* VI.28.1-2

> "Therefore, as was said before, rivaling not only the glory of Father Liber which he had carried off from those nations, but also his procession, whether that was a triumph first invented by that god or the sport of drunken revelers, he decided to imitate it, in a spirit raised above the level of human greatness. To this end, he ordered the villages through which his route lay to be strewn with flowers and garlands, mixing-bowls filled with wine, and other vessels of unusual size to be placed everywhere on the thresholds of the houses, then carriages to be spread, so that each might hold many soldiers, and to be equipped like tents, some with white curtains, and others with costly tapestries. At the head marched the king's friends and the royal troop, wreathed with chaplets made of a variety of flowers; on one side was heard the music of flute-players, on another the notes of the lyre; the army also joined the revels in vehicles adorned according to the means of each man and hung around with their most beautiful arms. The king and his companions rode in a chariot loaded down with golden bowls and huge beakers of the same material. In this way the army for seven days marched in riotous procession, an easy prey if the conquered had had any

courage even against revelers; a single thousand, by Heaven! provided they were real men and sober, could have captured in the midst of their triumph those who for seven days had been heavy with drunkenness. But Fortune, who assigns renown and value to actions, turned to glory even this disgrace to an army. Both the age of that time, and afterwards posterity, regarded it as wonderful that they marched drunken through nations not wholly subdued, and that the barbarians took this rash conduct for confidence." – Quintus Curtius Rufus, *Historiae Alexandri Magni* IX.10.24ff

Likewise, when the Ptolemies succeeded Alexander they modeled their rule on that of Dionysos:

"Great King Ptolemy, son of King Ptolemy and Queen Arsinoë the Brother and Sister Gods, the children of King Ptolemy and Queen Berenike the Savior Gods, descendant on the paternal side of Herakles the son of Zeus, on the maternal of Dionysos the son of Zeus, having inherited from his father the kingdom of Egypt and Libya and Syria and Phoenicia and Cyprus and Lycia and Caria and the Cyclades islands led a campaign into Asia with infantry and cavalry and fleet and Troglodytic and Ethiopian elephants, which he and his father were the first to hunt from these lands and, bringing them back into Egypt, to fit out for military service. Having become master of all the land this side of the Euphrates and of Cilicia and Pamphylia and Ionia and the Hellespont and Thrace and of all the forces and Indian elephants in these lands, and having made subject all the princes in the (various) regions, he crossed the Euphrates river and after subjecting to himself Mesopotamia and Babylonia and Sousiane and Persis and Media and all the rest of the land up to Bactriane and having sought out all the temple belongings that had been carried out of Egypt by the Persians and having brought them back with the rest of the treasure from the (various) regions he sent (his) forces to Egypt through the canals that had been dug ...." – *OGIS* 54

"There was a great Viceroy in Egypt, Ptolemaios was he called. A person of youthful energy was he, strong in both arms, prudent of mind, powerful amidst men, of firm courage, steady foot, repelling the raging, not turning his back, striking the face of his foes amidst their combat. When he had seized the bow not a shot is from the opponent, a flourish of his sword in the fight no one could stand his ground, of mighty hand, nor was his hand repulsed, nor repented he of what his mouth utters, none is like him in the stranger's world. He had restored the statues of the gods, found in Asia, and all the furniture and books of the temples of Northern and Southern Egypt, he had restored them to their place. He had made as his residence the fortress of the King, 'Loving the name of Amen the sun-chosen the Son of the Sun, Alexander,' as it is called on the shore of the great sea of the Ionians. Rakotis was its former name. He had gathered many Ionians and their cavalry (and) their numerous ships, with their crew. When he marched with his men to the Syrians' land, who were at war with him, he penetrated its interior, his courage was as mighty as the eagle amongst the young birds. He took them at one stroke, he led their princes, their cavalry, their ships, their works of art, all to Egypt. After this, when he set out for the region of Mermerti, he took it in one time, he brought home their folk, men, women, with their horses, as revenge for what they did to Egypt. When he arrived in Egypt, his heart was rejoicing in what he had done, he solemnized a holiday, (and) this great Viceroy seeking the best for the gods of Upper Egypt (and) Lower Egypt." – *The Satrap Stele*

"Ptolemy rules the land of Egypt, and has added to his empire a part of Phoinikia and Arabia, and of Syria and Libya and the black Aithiopians. He rules all the Pamphylians and Kilikians, the Lykians and the war-loving Karians, and the islands of the Kyklades. For his ships are the best that sail the seas, and all the seas and lands and roaring rivers acknowledge Ptolemy's reign. Many horsemen and many foot-soldiers clad in shining bronze gather round him. In riches he outweighs all kings, so many things come every day to his splendid palace from every side. His people carry on their trades in peace. No enemy from the land crosses the Neilos, teeming with monsters, to raise the battle cry in villages not his own. And none leaps armed from his swift ship upon the shore to harry Egypt's cattle, so great a man is throned in those level plains – Ptolemy, gold-haired, skilled spearman. Like a good king he is determined to hold everything inherited from his fathers and to add something of his own." – Theokritos, 17th *Idyll*

When necessary Dionysos could be a forceful and heroic figure, squashing his enemies. But that was not his main purpose. He was no Ares or Herakles; he was the culture-bringer, the peace-lover, the inaugurator of a new golden era of civilization. And that's what they wished the Ptolemaic Kingdom to be. And in many respects it was:

"In all the qualities which make a good ruler, Ptolemy Philadelphos excelled not only his contemporaries, but all who have arisen in the past and even til today, after so many generations, his praises are sung for the many evidences and monuments of his greatness of mind which he left behind him in different cities and countries, so that, even now, acts of more than ordinary munificence or buildings on a specially great scale are proverbially called Philadelphian after him. ... To put it shortly, as the house of the Ptolemies was highly distinguished, compared with other dynasties, so was Philadelphos among the Ptolemies. The creditable achievements of this one man almost outnumbered those of all the others put together, and, as the head takes the highest place in the living body, so he may be said to head the kings." – Philo, *Life of Moses* 2.29-30

"In Egypt a young man could find everything there is and will be: wealth, the wrestling arena, power, peace, renown, shows, philosophers, money, young men, the temple of the Sibling Gods, the king a good ruler, the Mouseion, wine, all the goods somebody may desire, and more women, by Hades' wife Kore, than the sky boasts of stars, and beautiful like the goddesses who once came to Paris to let him judge their beauty." – Herondas, *Mimes* 1.26ff

"Zeus, the son of Kronos, has in his care all great kings, but especially the one he has loved from birth. Much wealth is his, and he rules many lands and many seas. Ten thousand countries and ten thousand tribes ripen their crops with the help of Zeus' rain, but none is so fertile as Egypt's plain, when overflowing Neilos soaks the soil and loosens it. The piles of gold, like the stores of ever-toiling ants, do not lie useless in the rich house of Ptolemy. The glorious temples of the gods receive much, for he offers first-fruits and many other gifts, and he gives much to mighty kings, and much to cities, and much to his loyal friends. No singer skilled in raising his clear-voiced song comes to Dionysos' sacred contests without the receiving the gift his art deserves. And these interpreters of the Muses sing of Ptolemy for his kindness." – Theokritos, 17th *Idyll*

"The advantages of Alexandria are of various kinds. The site is washed by two seas, on the north by what is called the Egyptian Sea, and on the south, by the sea of the lake Mareia, which is also called Mareotis. This lake is filled by many canals from the Nile, both by those above and those at the sides, through which a greater quantity of merchandise is imported than by those communicating with the sea. Hence the harbor on the lake is richer than the seaside harbor. The exports of Alexandria exceed the imports. This any person can ascertain by watching the arrival and departure of the merchant ships, and observing how much heavier or lighter their cargoes are than when they depart or return. The shape of the city is that of a *chlamys* or military cloak. The whole city is intersected with streets for the passage of horsemen and chariots. Two of these are exceeding broad, over a *plethrum* in breadth, and cut one another at right angles. The city contains also very beautiful public parks and royal palaces, which occupy a fourth or even a third of its whole extent. For as each of the kings was desirous of adding some embellishment to the places dedicated to the public use, so besides the buildings already existing each of them erected a building at his own expense. All the buildings are connected one with another, and these also with what are beyond it. The Mouseion is a part of the palaces. It has a public walk, and a place furnished with seats, and a large hall, in which men of learning, who belong to the Mouseion, take their common meal. This community possesses also property in common; and a priest, formerly appointed by the kings, but at present by Caesar, presides over the Mouseion. In the great harbor at the entrance, on the right hand, are the island and the Pharos tower, on the left are the reef of rocks and the promontory Lochias, with a palace upon it; at the entrance on the other hand are the inner palaces which are continuous with those on the Lochias, and contain many painted apartments and groves. Near by is the theater, then the Poseideion, a kind of elbow projecting out from the merchant harbor with a temple of Poseidon upon it. There follow along the water front a vast succession of docks, military and mercantile harbors, magazines, also canals reaching the lake Mareotis, and many magnificent temples, an amphitheater, stadium, etc. In short, the city of Alexandria abounds with public and sacred buildings. The most beautiful of the former is the Gymnasion, with porticoes exceeding a stadium in extent. In the middle of it are the court of justice and groves. Here, too, is a Paneion, an artificial mound of the shape of a fir cone, resembling a pile of rock, to the top of which there is an ascent by a spiral path. From the summit may be seen the wide city lying all around and beneath it. The Wide Street extends in length along the Gymnasion to the Kanopic gate. Next is the Hippodrome, as it is called, and other buildings. The greatest advantage which the city of Alexandria possesses arises from its being the only place in all Egypt well situated by nature for communication with the sea — by its fine harbor, and with the land, by the river by means of which everything is easily transported to the city, which is the greatest market in the habitable world." – Strabo, *Geography* 12.1.6ff

Egypt under the Ptolemies was the most prosperous nation in the world, and its wealth was utilized to promote culture in ways never imagined before. The specifically Dionysian nature of their Kingship was demonstrated for all to see in the Grand Procession of Ptolemy Philadelphos. Here are some choice excerpts from the account of this spectacle that has come down to us from the pen of Kallixeinos of Rhodes via the anthologist Athenaios of Naukratis:

> "Next there followed another four-wheeler, thirty and more feet long, twenty-four feet wide, drawn by three hundred men; in this was set up a wine-press thirty six feet long, twenty-two and a half wide, full of grapes. And sixty Satyrs trod them while they sang a vintage song to the accompaniment of pipes, and a Seilenos superintended them. The new wine streamed through the whole line of march. Next came a four-wheeled cart thirty-seven and a half feet long, twenty-one feet wide, and drawn by six-hundred men; in it was a wine skin holding thirty thousand gallons, stitched together from leopard pelts; this also trickled over the whole line of march as the wine was slowly let out. Following the skin came a hundred and

twenty crowned Satyrs and Sileni, some carrying wine-pitchers, others shallow cups, still others large deep cups – everything of gold. Immediately next to them passed a silver mixing-bowl holding six thousand gallons, in a cart drawn by six hundred men. It bore, beneath the brim and handles and under the base, figures of beaten metal, and round the middle ran a gold band, like a wreath, studded with jewels. Next were carried two silver stands for drinking-cups, eighteen feet long and nine feet in height; these had end-ornaments on top, and on the swelling sides all round as well as on the legs were carved figures, many in number, two and three feet high. And there were then large basins and sixteen mixing bowls, the larger of which held three hundred gallons, while the smallest held fifty. Then there were twenty-four cauldrons ornamented with an acorn boss, all of them on stands; and two silver wine-presses, on which were twenty-four jars, a table of solid silver eighteen feet long, and thirty more tables nine feet long. Added to these were four tripods, one of which had a circumference of twenty-four feet, plated throughout with silver, while the other three, which were smaller, were studded with jewels in the center. After these were borne along Delphic tripods of silver, eighty in number, but smaller than those just mentioned; at their corners (were figures in beaten metal), and the tripods had a capacity of forty gallons. There were twenty-six water jars, sixteen Panathenaic amphoras, one hundred and sixty wine-coolers; of these the largest contained sixty gallons, the smallest twenty. All of these vessels were of silver."

"Next to these in his catalogue were six-foot tables on which were borne remarkable scenes lavishly represented. Among these was included the bridal chamber of Semele, in which certain characters wear tunics of gold bejeweled with the costliest gems. And it would not be right to omit the following mention of the "four-wheeled cart, in length thirty-three feet, in width twenty-one, drawn by five hundred men; in it was a deep cavern profusely shaded with ivy and yew. From this pigeons, ring-doves, and turtle-doves flew forth along the whole route, with nooses tied to their feet so that they could be easily caught by the spectators. And from it also gushed forth two fountains, one of milk, the other of wine. And all the nymphs standing round him wore crowns of gold, and Hermes had a staff of gold, and all in rich garments. In another cart, which contained 'the return of Dionysos from India,' there was a Dionysos measuring eighteen feet who reclined upon an elephant's back, clad in a purple coat and wearing a gold crown, of ivy and vine pattern; he held in his hands a gold wand-lance, and his feet were shod with shoes fastened by gold straps. Seated in front of him on the elephant's neck was a Satyr measuring seven and a half feet, crowned with a gold pine-wreath, his right hand holding a goat-horn of gold, as though he were signaling with it. The elephant had trappings of gold and round its neck an ivy-crown in gold. This cart was followed by five hundred young girls dressed in purple tunics with gold girdles. Those who were in the lead, numbering one hundred and twenty, wore gold pine-crowns; following them came one hundred and twenty Satyrs, some in gold, some in silver, and some in bronze panoply. After them marched five troops of asses on which were mounted Sileni and Satyrs wearing crowns. Some of the asses had frontlets and harness of gold, others, of silver. After them were sent forth twenty-four elephant chariots, sixty teams of he-goats, twelve of saiga antelopes, seven of beisa antelopes, fifteen of leucoryse, eight teams of ostriches, seven of Pere David deer, four of wild asses, and four four-horse chariots. On all these were mounted little boys wearing the tunics and wide-brimmed hats of charioteers, and beside them stood little girls equipped with small crescent shields and wand-lances, dressed in robes and decked with gold coins. The lads driving the chariots wore pine crowns, the girls wore ivy. Next after them came six teams of camels, three on either side. These were immediately followed by carts drawn by mules. These contained barbaric tents, under which sat Indian and other women dressed as captives. Then came camels, some of which carried three hundred pounds of myrrh, and two hundred of saffron, cassia, cinnamon, oris, and all other spices. Next to these were negro tribute-bearers, some of whom brought six hundred tusks, others two thousand ebony logs, others sixty mixing-bowls full of gold and silver coins and gold dust. After these, in the procession, marched two hunters carrying gilded hunting-spears. Dogs were also led along, numbering two thousand four hundred, some Indian, the others Hyrcanian or Molossian or of other breeds. Next came one hundred and fifty men carrying trees on which were suspended all sorts of animals and birds. Then were brought, in cages, parrots, peacocks, guinea-fowls, and birds from the pheasants and others from Aethiopia, in great quantities. Also, one hundred and thirty Aethiopian sheep, three hundred Arabian, twenty Euboean ; also twenty-six Indian zebus entirely white, eight Aethiopian, one large white she-bear, fourteen leopards, sixteen genets, four caracals, three bear-cubs, one giraffe, one Aethiopian rhinoceros. Next in a four-wheeled cart was Dionysos at the altar of Rheia, having found refuge there while being pursued by Hera; he had on a gold crown, and Priapos stood at his side, with a gold ivy-crown. The statue of Hera had a gold diadem. Then there were statues of Alexander and Ptolemy, crowned with ivy-crowns made of gold. The statue of Goodness which stood beside Ptolemy had a gold olive-crown. Priapos stood beside them also wearing an ivy-crown made of gold. The city of Corinth, standing beside Ptolemy, was crowned with a gold band. Beside all these figures were placed a stand for cups, full of gold vessels, and a gold mixing-bowl of fifty gallons capacity. Following this cart were women who wore very rich robes and ornaments; they bore the names of cities, some from Ionia, while all the rest were Greek cities which occupied Asia and the islands and had been under the rule of the Persians; they all wore gold crowns. In other carts, also, were carried a Bacchic wand of gold, one hundred and thirty-five feet long, and a silver spear ninety feet long; in another was a gold phallos one hundred and eighty feet long, painted in various colors and bound with fillets of gold; it had at the extremity a gold star, the perimeter of which was nine feet."

It is hard not to be awe-struck by such accounts, to marvel at the power and wealth of these great Dionysian Kings. And this was a tradition that continued down to the end of the Dynasty. Kleopatra and her Roman husband Marcus Antonius were no less skilled in the art of pageantry, nor unaware of the importance of Dionysos in maintaining their power.

Marcus Antonius claimed the *epiklesis* "Neos Dionysos" that so many of the Ptolemies had borne before him:

"Marcus Antonius had previously given orders that he should be called the new Father Liber, and indeed in a procession at Alexandria he had impersonated Father Liber, his head bound with the ivy wreath, his person enveloped in the saffron robe of gold, holding in his hand the thyrsos, wearing the buskins, and riding in the Bacchic chariot." – Velleius Paterculus, *Roman History* 2.82

Both he and his followers exploited this connection to dramatic effect:

"At any rate, when Antony made his entry into Ephesus, women arrayed like Bacchanals, and men and boys like Satyrs and Pans, led the way before him, and the city was full of ivy and thyrsos-wands and harps and pipes and flutes, the people hailing him as Dionysos Carnivorous and Savage." – Plutarch, *Life of Antony* 24

And Kleopatra herself used it to win Antony over after the assassination of Julius Caesar:

"Though Kleopatra received many letters of summons both from Antony himself and from his friends, she was so bold as to sail up the river Kydnos in a barge with gilded poop, its sails spread purple, its rowers urging it on with silver oars to the sound of the flute blended with pipes and lutes. She herself reclined beneath a canopy spangled with gold, adorned like Venus in a painting, while boys like Loves in paintings stood on either side and fanned her. Likewise also the fairest of her serving-maidens, attired like Nereïds and Graces, were stationed, some at the rudder-sweeps, and others at the reefing-ropes. Wondrous odors from countless incense-offerings diffused themselves along the river-banks. Of the inhabitants, some accompanied her on either bank of the river from its very mouth, while others went down from the city to behold the sight. The throng in the market-place gradually streamed away, until at last Antony himself, seated on his tribunal, was left alone. And a rumor spread on every hand that Venus was come to revel with Bacchus for the good of Asia." – Plutarch, *Life of Antony* 26.1-3

The two were well-matched, and famed for their luxurious Dionysian celebrations:

"But Cleopatra having met Antony in Cilicia, prepared a royal entertainment, in which every dish was golden and inlaid with precious stones, wonderfully chased and embossed. And the walls were hung with cloths embroidered in gold and purple. And she had twelve triclinia laid; and invited Antony to a banquet, and desired him to bring with him whatever companions he pleased. And he being astonished at the magnificence of the sight, expressed his surprise; and she, smiling, said that she made him a present of everything which he saw, and invited him to sup with her again the next day, and to bring his friends and captains with him. And then she prepared a banquet by far more splendid than the former one, so as to make that first one appear contemptible; and again she presented to him everything that there was on the table; and she desired each of his captains to take for his own the couch on which he lay, and the goblets which were set before each couch. And when they were departing she gave to all those of the highest rank palanquins, with the slaves for palanquin bearers; and to the rest she gave horses, adorned with golden furniture: and to every one she gave Ethiopian boys, to bear torches before them. And on the fourth day she paid more than a talent for roses; and the floor of the chamber for the men was strewed a cubit deep, nets being spread over the blooms. Antony himself, when he was staying at Athens, a short time after this, prepared a very superb scaffold to spread over the theatre, covered with green wood such as is seen in the caves sacred to Bacchus; and from this scaffold he suspended drums and fawn-skins, and all the other toys which one names in connection with Bacchus, and then sat there with his friends, getting drunk from daybreak, a band of musicians, whom he had sent for from Italy, playing to him all the time, and all the Greeks around being collected to see the sight. And presently, he crossed over to the Acropolis, the whole city of Athens being illuminated with lamps suspended from the roof; and after that lie ordered himself to be proclaimed as Bacchus throughout all the cities in that district." – Sokrates the Rhodian, *History of the Civil War* Book 3 [Quoted in Athenaios, 4.29]

Indeed, Antony was so closely linked with the god that after the defeat of the Ptolemaic naval force at Actium there was a legend that Dionysos had abandoned him:

"During this night, it is said, about the middle of it, while the city was quiet and depressed through fear and expectation of what was coming, suddenly certain harmonious sounds from all sorts of instruments were heard, and the shouting of a throng, accompanied by cries of Bacchic revelry and satyric leapings, as if a troop of revelers, making a great tumult, were going forth from the city; and their course seemed to lie about through the middle of the city toward the outer gate which faced the enemy, at which point the tumult became loudest and then dashed out. Those who sought the meaning of the sign were of the opinion that the god to whom Antony always most likened and attached himself was now deserting him." – Plutarch, *Life of Antony* 75

Dionysos was all and everything to the Ptolemies, and that may go a long way towards explaining why we find such a unique focus on the god in the Greco-Egyptian sources that have come down to us. When the power of the King is dependent on the god and the King views himself as the earthly vessel of Dionysos, that is going to change how you see Dionysos or at least how you openly write about him.

In previous times it was acceptable to have a wider range of representations, including some that went beyond satire into the realm of the irreverent and blasphemous. But when royal authority is intertwined with the image of Dionysos, doing so becomes not just a challenge to the foundation of one's society but perilously close to treason. And while the gods may be slow in punishing impiety – or even willing to laugh it off entirely – Kings generally are not. The example of Sotades should suffice to make the point:

> "Sotades of Maroneia was famous for the license of his language: abusing Lysimakhos the king in Alexandria, and, when at the court of Lysimakhos, abusing Ptolemy Philadelphos, and in different cities speaking ill of different sovereigns; on which account, at last, he met with the punishment that he deserved. For he had said many bitter things against Ptolemy the king, and especially this, after he had heard that he had married his sister Arsinoë, 'The king has put his prick in an unholy hole.' But when he had sailed from Alexandria (as Hegesander, in his *Reminiscences*, relates), and thought that he had escaped all danger, Patrokles, the general of Ptolemy, caught him in the island of Caunus. Patrokles shut him up in a leaden vessel, and carried him into the open sea and drowned him." – Athenaios, *Deipnosophistai* 14.621a

In fact, we have a very good example of how politics influenced the conception of Dionysos, albeit in a negative light.

Eratosthenes is perhaps best remembered for codifying the system of geography as we know it – in fact, he was the first to accurately calculate the circumference of the earth – but he was also interested in astronomy and compiled an extensive collection of star-myths called the *Katasterismoi*. In it he told the story of the famous musician and founder of mysteries Orpheus.

Originally Orpheus had been a devoted follower of Dionysos, singing his praises far and wide. But then he had a change of heart:

> "When he descended to the underworld to recover his wife, Orpheus saw things there and ceased to honor Dionysos, through whom he had gained glory. Instead, he considered Helios the greatest of the gods, calling him Apollon." (*Vat. Fragm.* 24)

So, what did he see down there?
I believe that the answer is Dionysos.
Of course, Eratosthenes never explicitly states this. But it could account for the radical conversion: Orpheus, the poet of beauty and life is plunged into darkness and despair at the loss of his beloved. He harrows hell to retrieve her…only to discover that the god he has dedicated his life to serving is also the god of death. It'd be a shock for anyone. Of course, as psychologically compelling as this explanation might be, it's even more probable when you consider Eratosthenes', shall we say, complicated relationship with the Ptolemies.

Earlier I quoted an anecdote about Eratosthenes at the court of Ptolemy Philopator, recounted by Athenaios (7.276A), in which the savant came upon a distraught Arsinoë who was upset over her husband's continuous Dionysian excesses. I suspect his dislike for Philopator – who so strongly associated himself with the god – lies behind the Orpheus story, which is basically a rejection of the chthonic aspect of Dionysos so important to the Greco-Egyptian and Ptolemaic conception of the god. It certainly wouldn't be the only time that Eratosthenes did so.

In fact, whenever Eratosthenes mentions Dionysos in his works – particularly when it overlaps with the Ptolemaic ideology we've been discussing – he tends to treat the god and these subjects in a slyly mocking and dismissive manner.

For instance, in Kallixeinos' account of the Grand Procession which celebrated Dionysos' mythical conquest of the Indians as the basis of Ptolemaic power we find the following:

> "One hundred and twenty Satyrs followed the five hundred girls, some wearing silver armor, others bronze. After them marched five troops of asses on which rode crowned Silenoi and Satyrs. Some of the asses had frontlets and harnesses of gold, others of silver." (quoted in Athenaios 200e)

Eratosthenes was highly critical of this. Not only did he question the whole myth of the Indian Conquest (as Strabo mentions in *Geographika* 11.5.5) but he told a mock-heroic tale about Dionysos and the asses, perhaps with this portion of the Ptolemaic procession in mind:

> "When the Gods were marching against the Giants, it is said that Dionysos, Hephaistos and the Satyrs traveled by donkey. When they were near the Giants, who, however, were not yet visible, the

donkeys brayed and, and the Giants, hearing the noise, fled. For this reason the donkeys were honored, being placed on the western side of the Crab." (*Kat.* 11)

As Jordi Pàmias noted, "this turns the legendary exploits of Dionysos into a satirical and ironic episode, insofar as the god's triumphal and warlike aspects, intensively promoted by the Ptolemies, are overshadowed and neutralized by the donkeys" (*Harvard Studies in Classical Philology*, Vol. 102 (2004), pp. 191-198).

Thus we see the complex relationship between myth and politics. The myth of Dionysos could influence Ptolemaic policy – but the crown could also affect how such myths were told in both a positive and negative light. Nothing with Dionysos is ever simple, so why should we expect this to be?

PRAISES OF THE STRONG FRUITFUL ONE

Perhaps one of the most interesting documents of ancient Greco-Egyptian polytheism is the so-called *Aretalogy of Karpokrates*, which was written in Greek circa 250-300 CE and later found on the island of Khalkis. It is similar in form to the better-known aretalogies of Isis, which are praise poems enumerating the accomplishments or virtue (*arête*) of the goddess, often phrased as first-person statements made by the deity herself. Aretalogies were works of propaganda, intended to exalt the goddess above all others and bring awareness of her to a wider, usually Greek audience. In many instances Isis is equated with well-known divinities from other cultures who are viewed as aspects of this supreme and all-powerful goddess, leading to a kind of quasi-monotheism that appealed to the philosophical tendencies of the late antique Pagan mind. The *Aretalogy of Karpokrates*, however, shows some significant differences.

> "I am Karpokrates, son of Serapis and Isis...of Demeter and Kore and Dionysos and Iacchos...brother of Sleep and Echo. I am every season and take thought for all seasons, the inventor of...I created...I was the first to make *adyta* and sanctuaries for the gods; I devised measures and numbers...I produced the sistrum for Isis; I devised the ways to hunt all kinds of animals...I established rulers for cities at all times; I preside over the upbringing of children; I established hymns...and dances of men and women, the Muses aiding me; I invented the mixing of wine and water;...of flutes and pipes; I am always at the side of litigants in order that nothing unjust may be done; I always share the *thiasoi* of Bakchoi and Bakchai; I caused...to spring up; I cleansed the whole earth; mountain-dwelling, sea-dwelling, river-dwelling, divining by throne, divining by stars...horn-shaped, Agyieus, Bassarios, of the heights, Indian-slaying, thyrsos-shaking, Assyrian hunter, wandering in dreams, giver of sleep...approving...vengeful against those who are unjust in love. I hate the accursed...all the science of drugs... Titanian, Epidaurian. Hail Chalcis, my mother and nurse...Ligyris inscribed this." – trans. by A. D. Nock *Gnomon* XXI.221

This aretalogy makes a radical departure from the standards of the genre in that it is first not about Isis as most of the extant Hellenistic aretalogies are, but instead focuses on her son Har-pa-khered or Horus the Child, whose name in Greek became Harpokrates. Secondly, the syncretic tendency of the age is kept to a minimum, the deity being equated only with Dionysos and to a much lesser extent his brother Apollon. Considering the literally hundreds of goddesses with whom Isis is regularly identified in her aretalogies this feature stands out all the more.

This equation is rather interesting, for while the identification of Horus and Apollon is fairly commonplace, going back to at least the 5th century BCE when Herodotos could speak of it as a well-known fact, Horus = Dionysos is much scarcer, no doubt because Dionysos was usually equated with the father of Horus, Osiris or later Serapis.

A clue as to why the author of this text linked the two can be found in the name that he gives the deity. The usual translation of Har-pa-khered was Harpokrates, but here it is given as Karpokrates. The translator claims that this was a careless mistake on the part of the author – but I wonder if it might signify something deeper. *Karpos* means "fruit," "vegetation," "crops" and *krates* means "strength" or "might." "The Strong Fruitful One" would indeed be an appropriate epithet for the child of Isis, the discoverer of grain and agriculture, whose mysteries centered on the cyclic fertility of the earth, as well as Dionysos, the discoverer of the vine and lord of all vegetative life. Later, our author mentions the Seasons or Horai. The Horai were traditionally regarded as the Nurses of Dionysos who presided over the growth-cycle of the grape and other plant life. However, Greek philosophers such as Plutarch had long noted the similarities between the names *Horos* and *Horai* and maintained that he governed the annual cycles of growth and decay, which makes sense when we consider Horus' solar attributes. Clearly, then, our author was familiar with Greek notions about traditional Egyptian religion – but one wonders if he was familiar with those Egyptian traditions as well, for in Egyptian the Green Eye of Horus was called *irt-Hr W3dt*, and this was used as a metaphor for the wine-offering that was libated during the sacrifice, providing yet another link between Dionysos and Horus.

Another clue as to our author's familiarity with indigenous Egyptian and Greek traditions comes in the references to sleep and dreams. In some versions of the story Osiris comes to his son from the land of the dead and converses with him while he sleeps in the rushes. He instructs Horus in his duties as king and avenger of his father and teaches him the martial art so that he can overthrow the usurper Seth. Likewise, Pausanias informs us that Dionysos presided over an incubation oracle where men could receive healing and visions through dreams and specifically cites a prophetic visitation to the playwright Aiskhylos.

There is much more to be unraveled in this fascinating document, but a final instance I would like to discuss are the references to the Indian War. The story of Dionysos' travels through the East and conquests of those ancient lands go back as far as Homer and Euripides, though originally it was only Asia Minor that he brought under his thrall. After Alexander, who claimed to be following in the footsteps of his divine ancestor, the setting was pushed further and further back until Dionysos' empire came to include the Indian continent as well as Egypt, Afghanistan, Syria, and the rest of the Near and Middle East. The fullest treatment of this myth to come down to us is the *Dionysiaka* of Nonnos of Panopolis, a fifth century Christian Bishop who sought to write a heroic epic to rival the works of Homer. We have fragments of other epics on this theme, as well as references in numerous ancient authors and even frescoes and tapestries depicting scenes from it, attesting to the wild popularity of the myth during the Hellenistic era.

It is not very surprising that this would become one of Dionysos' most popular myths at precisely this time, for almost all of the Hellenistic monarchs, including Alexander, the Ptolemies, the Attalids, Demetrios, as well as many Roman leaders such as Julius Caesar, Marcus Antonius, Caligula and Hadrian, consciously sought to identify themselves with the god and modeled their exploits after his own mythic precedents. From the very beginning Dionysos had been connected with the concept of divine kingship in Greece. His sons were kings; he introduced viniculture first to the royal houses of Athens, Thebes, and Argos; the Arkhon Basileos' wife was wedded to him during Anthesteria, etc. Dionysos embodied the fertility of the land and the charismatic power that the king needed to rule properly; his myths of world conquest, the bringing of culture and the blessings of civilization, and his founding of a new era of peace, prosperity, and creative abundance were potent symbols adopted by the Hellenistic and Roman rulers to solidify and legitimize their position in the eyes of their subjects.

This was especially true for the Ptolemies in Egypt, who came to rule a people with a 3000 year-old tradition of divine kingship of their own, with the Pharaoh acting the part of a living god on earth. That god was Horus, the son of Isis. The Ptolemies were clever monarchs. They were careful to learn the native Egyptian traditions and performed all of the duties and sacred ceremonies that came with the divine office of Pharaoh. But they were also Greeks and kept their people's own traditions alive, welding the two systems together into the syncretic tradition that we call Greco-Egyptian polytheism today. The person of Ptolemy was doubly divine: to his Greek subjects he was the personification of Dionysos while to the Egyptians he was the living Horus. While this identification is usually expressed in Greek and Egyptian sources respectively, here is this aretalogy written several centuries after the last Ptolemy went beneath the earth, and we find them wedded together and expressed in the most beautiful, profound way. Thus the Karpokrates Aretology of Khalkis deserves to be considered one of the most important Greco-Egyptian documents that we possess, even if it is a document with which not many are familiar.

QUID ME NUTRIT ME DESTRUIT

Marcus Antonius was the νέος Διόνυσος; this is one of the cardinal tenets of my faith.

"Neos Dionysos" is perhaps an unfamiliar term to some; it means the young or new Dionysos. Many see it as nothing more than religious-political propaganda, a ruler representing himself as Dionysos so as to communicate something important to his subjects about the nature of his *basileia* which is patterned after the mythical exploits of the god and places a strong emphasis on the triumphantly conquering, world-creating and civilization-bringing aspects of the Lord of Nysa.

But there's more to it than that. Neos Dionysos is the intersection of the mortal and the divine; it is a life lived entirely in the shadow of the god; it is not just the embodiment of his qualities but the acting out of the god's myths. In short, it is the face that Dionysos wears when he wishes to be a man. And I believe that Marcus Antonius was the New Dionysos because there are things about him that fit the pattern even though they aren't obvious, aren't necessarily desirable and in some ways contradict the primary themes that we tend to associate with this concept.

I'm not talking about Marcus Antonius' successful military conquests, his ability to inspire the masses and win over even the most bitter of enemies, his love of luxurious parties and pageantry, his frequent inebriation, his wildly fluctuating mood which was by turns joyfully exuberant, ferociously aggressive and melancholic to the point of being suicidal, or even the final failure and sacrificial destruction. No, these are all important elements of the archetype but what I'm thinking of is something simpler and in some ways more profound. Something deep down in his personality, something subconscious, a quality that no one would intentionally cultivate no matter how much they wished to resemble the god. But it's there and to me it's a sign of the true Neos Dionysos.

You see, Dionysos loves women who belong to other men. He stole Ariadne from Theseus. He weds the wife of the Arkhon Basileos each year at Anthesteria. Oineus discreetly removed himself from his home when he saw that his wife Althaía was attracted to the god. He seduced Erigone who nevertheless slew herself out of devotion to her father. He calls the madwomen out of their homes, away from their fathers, husbands and children – but once the music's over they always go back. His love for all of these women is great – but there is always a part of their heart which cannot be touched by his love because that part of them ultimately belongs to another.

It is the same with all those who have borne the mask of the New Dionysos. Ptolemy Philadelphos was passionately in love with his sister Arsinoë – but she had already been married and bore children to another man, something she could never do for him. Ptolemy Philopator was similarly in love with his own sister Arsinoë – but she was coldly indifferent to him and in fact grew to hate him in later years.

And Marcus, of course, was joined to Kleopatra. Though they were equals in temperament and political ambition and had a fiery love that threatened to consume both Rome and Egypt with its intensity, Marcus always took second place with her. First she had loved Caesar who had given her both her kingdom and a son. Caesar's shadow loomed large over their lives and I suspect that Marcus always felt that he failed to measure up against the man who had once been like a father to him. He had been there when the Roman Dictator and the Egyptian Queen first met, watched as their love blossomed, as their alliance was formed and after his death helped protect the Queen and legitimize the claims of Caesar's son and heir. Though Kleopatra and Marcus' original friendship, born of political expediency, grew into a grand and tragic love affair that was in many ways deeper and more significant than the brief time she had spent with Caesar, his ghost always hovered in the background – to the end she had herself represented as the grieving widow and the vigilant defender of her child, Isis incarnate. Marcus had to have been keenly aware that the only reason he ended up with the great love of his life was by an accident of Fortune. Would she have chosen him had Caesar survived the plot of Brutus? Assuredly not. And yet he loved her with all his heart until his dying day, accepting that her love was not equal to his own, that he could never take the place of this other man and that their affair was leading the both of them down a path of destruction.

How could a man who was a god do otherwise?

I VALUE MY GOD'S COCK

Perhaps the most important value to me as a Greco-Egyptian polytheist is the fact that my gods have really huge dicks. Of course, while size *is* important when you're considering god-cock it's what they do with it that truly matters. And in this regard the Greco-Egyptian gods stand head and shoulders above the rest. (Especially Min and Priapos!)

This point was vigorously thrust home recently while I was watching Alejandro Amenábar's exquisite biopic of Hypatia of Alexandria, *Agora*. Early on in the film there is an exchange between a Pagan intellectual and Ammonios, the fire-walking Christian fanatic from the desert.

We catch Ammonios midway through a frothing-mad rant about the sinful proclivities of the Pagan gods, with the puritan's special wrath reserved for their vile fornication. As anyone who has ever engaged in interfaith dialogue with Christians knows this is their favorite method of discrediting polytheism. They parade the mythological tales which are full of adulteries and violence and say, how can you believe in gods such as these, who are engaging in acts so immodest and so beneath human dignity? If your gods are immoral then you must be incapable of formulating an ethical way of life yourself – despite the fact that the whole field of ethics was pioneered by Pagans such as Sokrates, Plato, and Aristotle.

Since Christians have been harping on this point pretty much from the beginning, Pagans have had a long time to come up with a proper response. Unfortunately that response is usually along the lines of the one championed by the likes of Julian, Sallustius and the Stoics before them – namely the allegorical method. The myths aren't real, such people aver, at least not in a literal sense. Rather they are poetic abstractions, fanciful stories created to convey profound cosmological and philosophical truths about the divine in such a way that even the most simple-minded amongst us can understand them. The marriage of Aphrodite and Hephaistos represents the union of transcendent beauty with technical skill which is the aim of the true artist; Pan doesn't rape the nymphs he chases after, that is just the universal principle seeking embodiment through nature. Go onto pretty much any Hellenic polytheist forum today and you're likely to find the majority expressing views similar to this. They seem embarrassed by the mere thought of the gods having bodies and sexual desires like their own.

But Amenábar has his Pagan intellectual offer a different sort of answer: "If my gods eat and drink and fornicate – good for them!"

This is the answer of a true son of Alexandria.

Although Alexandria was the première intellectual center of the ancient world – famed for her artists, poets, philosophers, mathematicians, scientists, inventors and doctors who all made monumental contributions in their respective fields of study – the Alexandrians keenly understood that the pleasures of the mind were not the only ones worth pursuing. Indeed they gained a notorious reputation for being sensualists of the first order, heroic in their appetites for beauty in all its forms. Herondas, in listing the sights worth seeing on a trip to Alexandria, mentions her courtesans in company with the Mouseion and the Pharos Lighthouse which was considered one of the Seven Wonders of the World. Forgoing accounts of epic battles and tragically suffering kings, the Alexandrian poets wrote about handsome shepherd-boys, scullery-maids, stolen kisses, fragrant flower-garlands and nymph-haunted grottoes. It is said that Kleopatra was such an accomplished lover that men willingly gave up their lives for a single night with her. Her ancestor Ptolemy Philopator famously bedded a brother and sister at the same time – and Soter himself had no less than three wives and nearly a dozen courtesans in his prime. The spirit of Alexandria was masterfully evoked by one of her modern sons, the poet Constantine P. Cavafy in his *The Tomb of Iasis*:

> I, Iasis, lie here—the young man
> famous for his good looks in this great city.
> Men of learning admired me, so did simple, superficial people.
> I took equal pleasure in both.
>
> But from being considered so often a Narcissus and Hermes,
> excess wore me out, killed me. Traveler,
> if you're an Alexandrian, you won't blame me.
> You know the pace of our life—its fever, its unsurpassable
> sensuality.

Of course, sensuality was only part of the story. For the Alexandrians it was always a sensuality mixed with a deep spiritual yearning, a mystic-religious-sensuality that found the divine in the physical.

We see this in the account that the Roman traveler and historian Strabo left us of his visit to Alexandria:

> "Kanopos is a city situated at a distance of one hundred and twenty *stadia* from Alexandria if one goes on foot, and was named after Kanopos, the pilot of Menelaüs, who died there. It contains the temple of Sarapis which is honored with great reverence and effects such cures that even the most reputable men believe in it and sleep in it — themselves on their own behalf or others for them. Some writers go on to record the cures, and others the virtues of the oracles there. But to balance all this is the crowd of revelers who go down from Alexandria by the canal to the public festivals; for every day and every night is crowded with people on the boats who play the flute and dance without restraint and with extreme

licentiousness, both men and women, and also with the people of Kanopos itself, who have resorts situated close to the canal and adapted to relaxation and merry-making of this kind."

Here the pilgrims come to see their god, to gain his wisdom and healing – and to indulge their senses to the fullest, enjoying all the pleasures that come with being incarnate beings. There was no contradiction here, no dichotomy between spirit and flesh. They were just different parts of the same thing, each holy in their own way. The pleasures of the flesh were not an impediment to the spirit; they were seen as a path to a fuller experience of the spirit, a gift from the gods and something that they, themselves, enjoyed.

Consider, for instance, this lovely hymn to Hathor from the Ptolemaic-era temple at Denderah:

> Come, O Golden Goddess, the singers chant
> for it is nourishment for the heart to dance the *iba*,
> to shine over the feast at the hour of retiring
> and to enjoy the *ha*-dance at night.
>
> Come! The procession takes place at the site of drunkenness,
> this area where one wanders in the marshes.
> The royal children satisfy you with their love
> and the lector priest exalts you singing a hymn.
> Ladies rejoice in your honor with garlands
> and girls do the same with wreaths.
> Drunkards play tambourines for you in the cool night,
> and those they wake up bless you.
> The bedouin dance for you in their garments
> and Asiatics dance with their sticks.

This sort of intoxicated dancing was a common feature of ancient Egyptian worship. Herodotos (2.60) relates:

> "When the people are on their way to Boubastis, they go by river, a great number in every boat, men and women together. Some of the women make a noise with rattles, others play flutes all the way, while the rest of the women, and the men, sing and clap their hands. As they travel by river to Boubastis, whenever they come near any other town they bring their boat near the bank; then some of the women do as I have said, while some shout mockery of the women of the town; others dance, and others stand up and lift their skirts. They do this whenever they come alongside any riverside town. But when they have reached Boubastis, they make a festival with great sacrifices, and more wine is drunk at this feast than in the whole year besides. It is customary for men and women (but not children) to assemble there to the number of seven hundred thousand, as the people of the place say."

Another piece of Egyptian literature from the Ptolemaic era makes the eroticism of the gods even more explicit:

> "Oh, great bull, lord of sexual pleasure, burden your sister Isis; then remove the pain of her limbs; so that she can embrace you, without you being far from her; place life upon the forehead of the cow!" – *Songs of Isis and Nephthys* 5.24–6.1

Other characteristic epithets of Osiris from the *Songs of Isis and Nephthys* include "bull of the two sisters" (*k3 n sn.ty* 2.6) and "the bull who ejaculates within cows" (*p3 k3 sty m k.wt* 3.6). In fact, as Plutarch relates, "Isis and Osiris were enamored of each other and consorted together even in the darkness of the womb before their birth" (*On Isis and Osiris* 356a).

Death itself wasn't even able to put an end to their love affair, as Plutarch relates. After Osiris was slain and dismembered Isis sought out the scattered pieces of his body and restored them so that she could have sex with her husband one last time. Their post-mortem union resulted in the conception of Horus who went on to avenge his father and claim the throne of Egypt as Osiris' heir. Interestingly, this was not just the prerogative of the gods. In fact, the ability to continue having sex in the afterlife was one of the most important hopes for the ancient Egyptian, and during the Greco-Roman period there were numerous funerary texts that sought to enable this to happen, as scholar T. G. Wilfong remarked in his review of the recent collection of Greco-Egyptian funerary texts, *Traversing Eternity*:

> "Readers unused to Egyptian funerary texts in general might find the emphasis on post-mortem sexuality to be a surprise. Earlier texts certainly address the afterlife fertility and procreative powers of the deceased, especially the royal dead. But these Graeco-Roman period texts go beyond what one finds in earlier periods—the afterlife is not only a place of procreative sex, but also a place in which the dead experience sexual pleasure."

This is something that we find in the mysteries of Dionysos as well. Carl Kerenyi talks at length in his *Dionysos: Archetypal Image of Indestructible Life* about how in Southern Italy women saw death as an erotic adventure in which they would be united forever in loving embrace with their god. He includes numerous literary sources and vase paintings to this effect – which may help explain the popularity of Dionysian funerary iconography in Egypt, which often depicts Dionysos with his bride Ariadne, whom the devotee may have identified herself with.

We know that something analogous took place during Anthesteria with the wife of the Arkhon Basileos:

> "In ancient times, Athenians, there was a monarchy in our city, and the kingship belonged to those who in turn were outstanding because of being indigenous. The king used to make all of the sacrifices, and his wife used to perform those which were most holy

and ineffable – and appropriately since she was queen. But when Theseus centralized the city and created a democracy, and the city became populace, the people continued no less than before to select the king, electing him from among the most distinguished in noble qualities. And they passed a law that his wife should be an Athenian who has never had intercourse with another man, but that he should marry a virgin, in order that according to ancestral custom she might offer the ineffably holy rites on behalf of the city, and that the customary observances might be done for the gods piously, and that nothing might be neglected or altered. They inscribed this law on a *stele* and set it beside the altar in the sanctuary of Dionysos *En Limnais*. This *stele* is still standing today, displaying the inscription in worn Attic letters. Thus the people bore witness about their own piety toward the god and left a testament for their successors that we require her who will be given to the god as his bride and will perform the sacred rites to be that kind of woman. For these reasons they set in the most ancient and holy temple of Dionysos in Limnai, so that most people could not see the inscription. For it is opened once each year, on the twelfth of the month Anthesterion." – Demosthenes, *Against Neaira* 74-6

These ineffably holy rites, carried out as part of a *hieros gamos* between the queen and the god (who may have used the body of the king for this purpose) was intended to cause the land to be fruitful and prosperous. Fertility and kingship were connected in the minds of the Greeks from the earliest of times, as the poet Homer makes clear:

> "Like that of some flawless king, who, god-fearing, ruling a numerous and doughty people, upholds justice so that the dark earth brings forth wheat and barley, and the trees are heavy with fruit, and the sheep and goats give birth without fail, and the sea provides fish from his good leadership, and the people flourish under him." – Homer, *Odyssey* 19.109-14

Which sheds light on the Dionysian pageantry that took place during the meeting of Kleopatra and Marcus Antonius:

> "Though Kleopatra received many letters of summons both from Antony himself and from his friends, she was so bold as to sail up the river Kydnos in a barge with gilded poop, its sails spread purple, its rowers urging it on with silver oars to the sound of the flute blended with pipes and lutes. She herself reclined beneath a canopy spangled with gold, adorned like Venus in a painting, while boys like Loves in paintings stood on either side and fanned her. Likewise also the fairest of her serving-maidens, attired like Nereïds and Graces, were stationed, some at the rudder-sweeps, and others at the reefing-ropes. Wondrous odors from countless incense-offerings diffused themselves along the river-banks. Of the inhabitants, some

accompanied her on either bank of the river from its very mouth, while others went down from the city to behold the sight. The throng in the market-place gradually streamed away, until at last Antony himself, seated on his tribunal, was left alone. And a rumor spread on every hand that Venus was come to revel with Bacchus for the good of Asia." – Plutarch, *Life of Antony* 26.1-3

It was the sexual potency of the god Dionysos – channeled through a human vessel – that made the land strong.

That is why all the Ptolemies played up their connection to the god – and none more so than Ptolemy Philadelphos whose Grand Procession spectacularly demonstrates the phallic power upon which their rule depended:

"In other carts, also, were carried a Bacchic wand of gold, one hundred and thirty-five feet long, and a silver spear ninety feet long; in another was a gold phallos one hundred and eighty feet long, painted in various colors and bound with fillets of gold; it had at the extremity a gold star, the perimeter of which was nine feet." – Athenaios 5.201

But it's not just mortals who require the potency of the penis to rule – the Orphic author and commentator of the *Derveni Papyrus* maintained that Zeus only became king of the gods after swallowing the phallos of the primordial deity Dionysos-Eros-Phanês:

COL. 13

He swallowed the phallos of [...], who sprang from the aither first.

Since in his [i.e. Orpheus] whole poetry he speaks about facts enigmatically, one has to speak about each word in turn. Seeing that people consider that generation is dependent upon the genitalia, and that without genitals there is no becoming, he used this (word), likening the sun to a phallos. For without the sun the things that are could not have become such ... things that are ... the sun everything ....

COL. 16

It has been made clear above [that] he called the sun a phallos. Since the beings that are now came to be from the already subsistent he says:

**[with?] the phallos of the first-born king, onto which all
the immortals grew (or: clung fast), blessed gods and goddesses
And rivers and lovely springs and everything else
That had been born then; and he himself became solitary**

In these (verses) he indicates that the beings always subsisted, and the beings that are now came to be from (or: out of) subsisting things. And as to (the phrase): 'and he himself became solitary', by saying this, he makes clear that the Mind [Nous] itself, being alone, is worth everything, as if the others were nothing. For it would not be possible for the subsisting things to be such without the Mind. And in the following verse after this he said that Mind is worth everything:

Now he is king of all and will always be

.... Mind and ...

Not only does reverence for the penis honor the gods, have cosmological significance, is important for promoting fertility and martial power and is pleasurable in its own right – but when you look at what happens when people denigrate the phallos and deny their libidos you see just how all-important this value is.

Pretty early on Christianity developed a pronounced anti-sex and even sarcophobic tendency. Virtue was chiefly demonstrated by avoiding sensual temptation and maintaining virginity – even if that meant holy men had to spend all their time out in the desert, torturing their bodies with starvation, flagellation and the most horrendous physical austerities imaginable instead of, you know, preaching the gospel or helping the poor and needy which one tends to think of as more Christ-like activities. Most of the time this proved a fruitless endeavor, bound to fail even before it began. That inevitable failure filled them with guilt and hatred for their human weakness, which in turn polluted their souls and often found an outlet through violence. Eros cannot be banished; it merely becomes deformed, inverted, and diseased. One only has to look at the long centuries since the dimming of the Alexandrian spirit to see what fruit comes from such a twisted tree. The profoundly unhealthy relationship that the Catholic church has with sexuality – insisting that men give up the love of woman and family to serve god, not to mention the debasement and disenfranchisement of women within the church – is coming back to haunt them in the form of rampant child sex abuse scandals, devastating overpopulation and consequent poverty in staunchly Catholic countries, the AIDS pandemic in Africa because people aren't permitted to use life-saving contraception, pregnant nuns, etc.

And that doesn't even begin to touch on the correlation between sexual deprivation and violence. I doubt all those radical Islamic terrorists would be causing so much trouble – or so many witches would have burned at the stake – if these men got a little pussy or ass now and again. A well-fucked man is a mellow and happy man – and also a man that is much harder to control. Which, of course, is why so many of these religions jump on the whole "sex is bad, mmmkay" bandwagon. You keep someone perpetually horny, convince them that their desires are unnatural and ungodly and that maybe, if they do what you say, they will finally find release in the afterlife but only if they are obedient because you hold the keys to the kingdom –

well, you've got yourself a mindless drone right there. Drain him of excess semen and he'll start thinking for himself and asking dangerous questions.

Which is what we need now! For the sake of our planet we have to have golden copulations in the streets, orgies of a sort that even Ptolemy Philopator couldn't have imagined! Phallic processions! Satyrs and nymphs frolicking in the forests! Choirs of beautiful young people singing paeans to the gods of cock and cunt! Io euoi! Hail Dionysos and Aphrodite and all the others! And may the sound of your fucking, dear readers, echo through the halls of eternity!

DO YOU REMEMBER WHEN WE WERE IN AFRICA?

I've never had a problem reconciling my worship of Dionysos with my love for Egypt. Even before I got into Greco-Egyptian syncretism and was trying to go the pure Kemetic route, Dionysos was there alongside the Netjeru and his presence felt both right and natural. In some respects he feels more at home in Africa than in Hellas.

Although there's plenty of evidence for his cult in the Greek mainland going back as far as the Minoan-Mycenaean period – if not earlier – Dionysos was always something of an anomaly to the Greeks, an outsider who was worshiped in a most unhellenic fashion. Greek religious thought is predicated on boundaries: order imposed on chaos, the holy separated from the impure, the insurmountable chasm between the divine and the mortal realms, the distinct masculine and feminine spheres and man elevated above nature and the brute beasts. The Greeks prided themselves on their rationality, their clear and precise thinking – and their gods are a reflection of that, each with its own distinct personality, its carefully articulated attributes and functions.

And then there was Dionysos, who appeared like a whirlwind, throwing everything into a state of excited confusion. He compelled people to flee their homes and run wild in the woods with the animals, unleashing pent-up emotions and reveling in the irrational and absurd. He made women into men and men into women; his ecstasy blurred even the firm line between mortal and divine. His followers were neither beasts nor men, but a strange mixture of the two. His worship inverted the normal sacrificial procedure so that instead of roasting the meat and consigning the gods' portion to the flames the whole thing was devoured raw and bloody by the frenzied god-intoxicated devotee. Dionysos lacked the manly, civilizing virtues of the Hellenic world; he was soft and sensual, decadent and fierce – a womanly god who fled from his enemies, seeking shelter in the bosom of the nymphs. When he exacted vengeance it was from a distance, teasing out the self-destructive tendencies of his enemies through madness and deception instead of directly confronting them. Dionysos represented everything that the Greeks feared and loathed and sought to suppress – everything that was strange, irrational and barbaric. Unhellenic, in a word.

Of course, they grudgingly granted him a place in their world because they were clear-sighted enough to realize that you can't have just one side of the coin and all those primal drives were necessary for the full vitality of life.

But his place was always on the periphery, kept at a safe distance and permitted loose rein only on the rarest of occasions. A society that completely rejects the Dionysian will soon be destroyed by its puritanical sterility – but a society that embraces it too fully cannot abide for long either. This the Greeks knew well and that is why his home was Delphi which taught men both γνωθι σεαυτον and μηδεν 'αγαν.

But although the Greeks made a home for the god in their land they were always keenly aware that he had come to them from some other part of the world. Where, exactly, they were never entirely certain. The place of his birth, the magical Mount Nysa that is commemorated in his name, had no definite geographical location save that it was somewhere far, far away. Some placed it on the edges of the Hellenic world – Thrake or Makedonia, Italy or the Anatolian plateau. Others claimed that it was somewhere in Afghanistan or North Africa, Arabia or Palestine. When Alexander's men marched to the very ends of the earth they reported finding Nysa in India and a tribe of men there who had worshiped the god from the dawn of time. But most people believed that Nysa was in Egypt and that it was from here that Dionysos' worship had spread to Greece.

It is easy to understand why they felt this way. After all, the highest ranking religious officials wore the same leopard-skin pelts as the devotees of the god and carried ceremonial staves that resembled *thyrsoi*. Many of the religious taboos in the cult of Dionysos – particularly its Orphic-Pythagorean form – were the same in Egypt, such as the prohibition of wool in temples, the avoidance of fish, beans and other common foods, a concern with elaborate funerary rites, etc. Egypt had its masked rituals, its mysteries and dramatic performances, its phallic processions through the streets, its massive communal dancing and frenzied intoxication – all like the cult of Dionysos. And like Dionysos their most important deity was a god who suffered death, dismemberment and rebirth along with the vegetation he ruled over. But even more extraordinary than all this was the grand boat-procession.

In Greece during certain festivals the image of Dionysos was carried through the streets mounted on a sacred trireme that was fitted with wheels. It was dragged along to exuberant celebration so that he could visit the temples of his divine kin and spread his blessings throughout the city. No other Greek god had anything quite like this – though Athene later acquired her own vessel, modeled after Dionysos' – and so in order to explain this curious feature the Athenians fabricated the legend of his attempted capture by pirates and arrival in the land by ship. There was just one problem with this: the god couldn't have come to Attica by sea. The introduction of his cult followed the land route down from Phrygia and Thrake through central Greece before taking root in Attic soil, at least if the evidence of his earliest cult centers and the history of viniculture is any indication. Then again, it might not be. Scholars have been heatedly debating this issue for the last hundred and fifty years and I don't pretend to be an authority on it.

What is beyond debate, however, is the existence of an interesting parallel to Dionysos' boat-procession in Egypt. The sacred images of the

Egyptian gods were often loaded onto lavishly decorated barques and sailed down river so that they could visit the temples of allied deities before returning home. As with Dionysos' boat-procession this was thought to distribute the fertile, healing and protective powers of the gods throughout their respective territories and many thousands gathered along the shore to get a glimpse of the sacred vessels and share in the blessing. This became such an important and popular aspect of Egyptian religion that smaller, portable replicas of these vessels were constructed and carried about on the backs of priests in the forecourts of their temples for the benefit of the congregation. This was the medium by which the famous oracle of Ammon was communicated to his devotees.

Another interesting parallel can be found in the visual arts. Early on both the Greeks and the Egyptians tended to portray their deities in profile. Even when they are represented alongside or interacting with their mortal worshipers they are not directly facing them. It is as if the gods are gazing into another world, serenely absorbed in contemplating the perfection of creation and thus blithely unaware of the audience who is observing them. But Dionysos is different. His mask-like countenance is turned directly towards us, forcing an intimate confrontation with the onlooker. A similar exception in Egyptian art is the dancing dwarf Bes who wears animal skins and a mask and was also a stranger who migrated to Egypt. There is something uncanny and unsettling about the way these two gods break with convention and dissolve the fourth wall. These are the gods who are closest to man, who communicate most freely with him, whose wild motion threatens to engulf him and drive him mad with the ecstatic pulse of life that it contains. They are dangerous gods, apotropaic gods who frighten off malevolent spirits with the clamorous raucous they raise and also healing gods who soothe our frenzied emotions.

Another point of contact between Dionysos and Egypt is its cult of zoomorphic deities. Though the Greeks recognized that Dionysos could appear as a bull they were never entirely comfortable with such epiphanies. And understandably so, since all of their other gods with the exception of Pan were uncompromisingly anthropomorphic and even he was human from the waist up. Homer might describe Athene and Hera as owl-eyed and cow-eyed respectively, but no Greek artist ever represented them as such. The crow is the constant companion of Apollon, Hermes carries a sheep on his shoulders, Rheia rides in a chariot drawn by lions, Asklepios' staff is twined with serpents and Aphrodite stands upon a tortoise shell – but no matter how close the gods are to these animals they do not appear in their form. Zeus, of course, is an exception to this for he took on the guise of numerous birds and beasts in order to seduce his young and beautiful conquests. But this was never anything more than a clever ruse. Once the deed was consummated he regained his true form, something analogous to our own.

But not so Dionysos. He was the bull-god and everything that that implies. When Pentheus finally sees through all the illusions he beholds Dionysos as a raging bull. Dionysos was invoked to come on his bull's foot at Elis. He mated with the Basilinna in the ox-shed during Anthesteria. Orphic initiates ate bull's flesh to commune with their god and a young calf was dressed up in Dionysian attire before being sacrificed at Tenedos. Even when Dionysos appeared as a man he had the visible horns of a bull.

Though such things seemed strange and out of place for the Greeks they were perfectly natural for the Egyptians. From the very beginning they had recognized the presence of the divine in the animal world and represented their gods accordingly. There were even a number of distinct godly bulls in their land such as Apis and Mnevis and Buchis as well as their counterparts the Bat, Hesis and Hathor cows, all of whom were given extravagant cultus, with all of their needs from feeding to procreation looked after by the priesthood. What's particularly interesting from a Dionysian perspective is that these sacred bulls didn't just preside over fertility, vegetative and animal life or masculine potency the way one might expect. Like Dionysos they also had royal authority and underworld powers as part of their concern. The Apis bull in particular had a close relationship with the Pharaoh, both when he was alive and ruling and in the underworld. The Pharaoh was often represented with bull's horns, proved his physical fitness and worthiness to rule by yoking the bull and running down the processional route with him as well as a host of other things too numerous to go into here. Huge expense went into the ceremonial burial of the bull and the search and installation of its successor which was often paid for directly by the Pharaoh himself. When the Greeks came on the scene they were struck by the similarity of the rites conducted in honor of the Apis bull and those of Dionysos. Both Plutarch and Diodoros provide lengthy comparisons of the two and it is certainly remarkable how much they've got in common.

But all of this is really just scratching the surface. Even my detailed analysis of the similarities between Dionysos and Osiris doesn't exhaust what could be said on the subject, for Dionysos' roots go deep into the heart of Africa – a subject that deserves its own essay.

EXPERIENCING GRECO-EGYPTIAN DIONYSOS

I've talked a lot about the Greco-Egyptian face of Dionysos in the past, but I haven't necessarily talked about why that has become the dominant form for me. Sure, it's great that he unifies my dual interests in Greece and Egypt, and there's all the cultural, artistic, literary, historical and mythological elements that are fun to play with and keep my mind fresh. But there's more to it than all that. This is the face of Dionysos I respond to because this is the face that he has shown me numerous times through dreams, visions, epiphanies, hallucinations and other experiences in and out of ritual. I would like to talk a little about what that face of the god is actually like. The problem is, it's kind of difficult to put into words. It's easy enough to recognize while it's happening, especially since it's often very intense and richly layered, but like all mysteries it must be experienced directly to be properly understood. But I'll give describing it a shot anyway.

Probably the best place to start is with the elements that are easiest to identify. And that would be the Egyptian iconography. When most people form a mental picture of Dionysos it is usually to some extent influenced by vase paintings, statuary or the work of the Greek poets. This is often how I see the god as well, though there are times when he appears as a more generic "Horned God" or made of vegetation like the Green Man foliate masks. Sometimes he is entirely modern, a cross between Jaye Davidson and Jim Morrison. But Greco-Egyptian Dionysos is different. He's appeared in a variety of ways so far, but there's usually something recognizably "Egyptian" about him. I've seen him with a gold and green pectoral and traditional kilt holding a ceremonial staff; with exotic, flowing robes and this crazy horned and feathered head-dress or attired in a loose-fitting striped or elaborately embroidered Coptic-style tunic. I've seen him dark-skinned and African-featured; like a Middle Eastern man with *kohl*-rimmed eyes and as a more conventional Greek or Italian – though often this is when his dress is most conspicuously Egyptian. But what's really interesting is when I see him as a bull, because it's not just any bull but an Egyptian bull that so strongly resembles Apis that it can be difficult at times to tell them apart. Often his image cycles through all of these and more – including the more familiar Hellenic ones – or several are brought together simultaneously. However, none of this is what really stands out in the visions; it's more their baroque nature.

Actually, baroque is a very good way to describe it, because there's often all this stuff happening at once. It's dense: layers upon layers upon layers coming through simultaneously. So much that I can't really see or process it all, I've just got to sit back and let it wash over me and hope I don't get swallowed up by it. He's often surrounded by this mad flourish of vegetation. Ivy and grape-vines and roses and lotuses and papyrus stalks and everything else you could imagine, swirling around him. Sometimes it grows out of him, sometimes he's holding it or it's wrapped around his body, and sometimes it's just there in the background. But it's alive and moving, swelling and contracting, dancing, pulsing with abundant life and vitality. It's hypnotic to watch, like a kaleidoscope made entirely of different shades of green, and it's never just that. He's often surrounded by animals as well – all the ones you'd normally associate with him such as snakes and panthers and goats and the like, but there's also peacocks and elephants and gazelles. Sometimes he's riding one of them in a procession, sometimes they're just in the background but he's almost never alone. Even when he is I get the feeling that there's this multitude of unseen presences hovering just beyond the periphery.

And animals aren't the only ones who show up with him. He's accompanied by satyrs and nymphs, mainades and madmen, clowns and musicians – this huge troupe of revelers who follow him about on his endless journey. And the music they play! Ah, it's mad and frantic and delirious. It's like nothing I've ever heard before. The closest I've come is Juno Reactor's "God is God,", but even that pales in comparison. The really strange thing, however, is that he is often not the only god who shows up. There are Aphrodite and Hermes, which I suppose is only to be expected – but also Anubis, Horus, Hathor, Nephthys, Sobek and Apis. Horus and Apis are probably the most frequent companions, after Hermes. Sometimes I interact with them directly, but a lot of the time they're just there or he shows me how they're connected and why it's important for me to continue honoring them, regardless of whether I feel a strong connection to them on their own. I've seen whole myths played out before my eyes. Myths that belong to the tradition and myths that no one has ever put down on paper before.

And all of that? It's really just one level of it. There are symbols all over the place. On his clothes, held in his hands, carved into a wall behind him or just floating in space. Sometimes they're present throughout the whole vision, sometimes they shift and change into something else. Sometimes I recognize them as hieroglyphs or geometric patterns or things like that, and I understand what they mean, but a lot of the time it's stuff I've never seen before and can only guess at its significance. There are also shapes and more obvious things like a phallos or an ankh, a heart or a mask, as well as stuff that's completely random but feels deeply meaningful at the time.

The background changes as well. Sometimes he's on a mountain or in a forest or the verdant temple where I do my oracles with him, but often he's come out of the desert or is on the bank of a river or leading his procession through the streets of a great city like Alexandria. The river is very important and crops up frequently. It's the tangible sign of his power, his incomparable abundance. The procession, too, is important for that is how he spreads his blessings to the people.

And that's really what this aspect of Dionysos is all about. Fertility, abundance, making the land fruitful and strong and bringing good things to his people. All the rest is an extension of this or has largely faded into the background for me. Well, that's not entirely true. Greco-Egyptian Dionysos has two faces. The one I've been talking about this whole time is the Dionysos above ground, but there is also the Dionysos below the earth. The still, somber god who receives the souls of the deceased and sheds his blood to fertilize the earth. He's a dead god, dreaming of a life outside the labyrinth that he can never have, dreaming that he is the other, triumphant Dionysos above the ground. Or else this shadowy Dionysos is nothing more than the fearful hallucination of the real Dionysos during one of his bouts of madness. I can't tell which it is, and both ideas horrify me in their own ways. But it's what he continues to show me, over and over again, so clearly there has to be something to it.

SECTION II
Poetry

"I know how to lead off the dithyramb,
the lovely song of the lord Dionysos;
I do it thunderstruck with wine."
— Archilochos, Frag. 107

TO DIONYSOS

Dionysos, I sing, whose head is twined with ivy
and grapes in ripe bunches that tumble to his gentle shoulders,
clad in their fawn-skin cloak.
Swift-moving god racing down the side of Olympos,
or through the wooded coverts of the Nysan plane,
attended by goat-footed satyrs, and the lovely nymphs,
giving out the call, "*Euoi*!"
All-conquering, fierce-eyed one,
who wields his thyrsos like a fiery brand,
striking with madness those who offend him.
Mystery discovered through our bodies,
in dancing round raging fires till exhaustion overtakes us,
and the touching of
trembling flesh against trembling flesh
underneath the all-seeing moon.
I suppose there are older gods, and stronger –
but there has never been a god dearer to my heart
than the son of Semele and Zeus who reigns in heaven!

PRELIMINARY PRAYER

Oh Dionysos,
may my words rise up to you like clouds of fragrant incense,
intoxicating as the rich red wine I pour out for you in libation.
May my thoughts never be far from you
calling to mind your innumerable noble names
and the marvelous things you've done in ages past
and continue to do for your people today.
As Bakchos you free our souls of harmful emotions
driving us wild into the hills to dance and shout.
Bromios we hail you as when sweet slumber takes hold of us
after many cups of good wine have been drained.
Anthios you are when the lovely flowers show their faces come springtime
and as Kissokomes we see you wrapt in the evergreen foliage of the ivy.
You are the bull-faced son of thunder,
the companion of the moisture-loving nymphs,
the giver of many gifts,
the joyous one who makes our hearts glad,
the lord of all vegetation,
master of the wild beasts,
the mad one who loves the frenzied women,
the revealer of mysteries,
all-holy one who has come to set us free!
I could go on and on,
for I never tire of praising you
but my feet long to dance in your worship,
so let these few words suffice and I will show you
just how much you mean to me, O Lord, with this body of mine!

INVOCATION OF DIONYSOS

I summon to this sacrifice
the god who dances through the woods,
who wears the skin of ferocious beasts
and delights in the bloody feast.
Maddened, rapturous, holy in the extreme,
you with bull's horns on your head,
bearing snakes and tossing your long hair about
with the frenzy of a thunderous storm.
Lord of every tree,
with a face lovelier than the first flower of spring,
raving in the night when decent folk are behind doors,
leader of the mad throng down from the mountain
and through the shadowed streets.
Decked with ivy and clusters of bountiful grapes,
he who takes pleasure in the phallos
and the screams of intoxicated maidens
tearing the fawn to pieces
and dancing about,
proudly bearing their trophies of the hunt.
Come to this place,
hallowed in your name,
and bless us with your many gifts
god of Nysa's heights
and the hidden places of our hearts.

HYMN TO DIONYSOS MEILIKHIOS

Come thou, O Lord,
   in thy name of Meilikhios
   gentle and loving master of all,
with the warmth of life in thy ruddy cheeks,
a gracious smile upon thy soft lips,
thy head of flowing locks crowned with a wreath of juicy figs
and thy ivy-wrapt wand held high!
Before thee is set a table overflowing with bread and meats,
heaped with piles of fruit from the vine,
and wine that flows as freely as thy maniform blessings.
Join us in the feast, O Kindly One,
and raise thy voice along with ours,
as we sing of the good things of life
and the joys that thou bringest to us.
Away, away all sorrows!
Take flight depression and thou winged madness,
for Meilikhios is here,
laughter-loving, all-embracing lord of life!
Io Io Meilikhios!

LENAIA

Awaken, O Bacchic One, from your long slumber
and raise yourself up from the earth with loud thunder!
You who wear ripe fruit as your crown
and cause the mad-women to leap and fall down;
they who rave and dance before your ivy-draped idol
praising your power and beauty and all your fine titles.
O Bromios, sweet is the wine we draw from your casks,
and sweet the laughter of the street-marching youths in their masks.
Rude jokes and ribald songs they sing on their way
that none may forget in whose honor we esteem this day.
From death comes life and in dark there is light;
changing sorrow to joy – yea, such are the secrets of your rites.
No god has a festival as great as your Lenaia
not even the ram-bearing feast belonging to the son of Maia!
So join us, Dionysos, as we drink to good cheer
and may all who tip their glass to you be back next year!

HYMN FOR THE WORTHY BULL AND HIS MOTHER

Oh Mother of the Worthy Bull, incline your horned head to our prayers,
you who are the gentlest of all the creatures that tread the broad-bosomed earth,
you who give sweet milk for us to drink and consent to be yoked to the plough
that we might plant our seed in fertile furrows
and watch as the ripe stalks of corn leap up to feed our hungry bellies.
Your heart is cheerful and delights in our lovely songs and spritely dances,
and your boons to man are beyond reckoning.
But the greatest kindness you have shown to us is the bearing of your mighty son!

For all these many months your belly has grown heavy with a joyous burden,
and about you has shown a heavenly light.
We have seen the child of promise stir within you,
dancing in the womb in expectation of the time when he will come
to lead the throng of mainades in rapturous celebration on the hill.

And now, after such a long time,
you have given us the god.
Oh Mistress of wide-pastures and musical lowing,
your son is here!
And how lovely he is to look upon,
with his gleaming golden horns and his wine-dark hide
and his massive frame to bear our sorrows.
When he bellows deep in his throat the whole earth rumbles in echo
and the wild women feel their bodies burn with love for him!
And when the time comes to perform the terrible deed
his blood will wash over the land,
making it new and full of vibrant life once more,
the red drops turning into green grass and black grapes and golden corn.
Oh, Mother, your noble son fills us with awe and wonder,
for here is a mighty god in the mighty form of a bull!

TO DIONYSOS II

Hail to thee Dionysos,
   prince of those beneath the earth,
   wild one who brings liberation and madness,
lord of the vine and the magical drink made from it,
father of kings, lover of mad-women, joyous one
who makes the whole earth turn green with life at his coming.

HYMN TO EGYPTIAN DIONYSOS

The face of Dionysos shines as he strides across the land,
   luminous as the moon in heaven,
   golden as the wings of the Bennu-bird in flight.
Where he steps the earth becomes black,
the trees swell with fruit,
clear water rushes forth,
and the scent of acacia and pine fills the air
like a fine incense.
Dionysos appears as a bull in his strength,
as a young king in his power.
He is terrible and mighty,
filling the hearts of all who behold him with awe.
When he comes forth, there is great rejoicing in the land.
Wine is poured out, tables are piled high with food for feasting,
the maidens sing and dance in the street
and husbands take their wives to them.
The whole world is renewed through its Lord!

HYMN TO DIONYSOS PETEMPAMENTI

While I live may I always kiss the earth before thee
and sing thy praises, O great Ancestral King,
whose face is beautiful in the land of shadows,
whose soul is radiant in the house of the gods,
whose spirit is life-giving to the fruit trees in the orchard.
My heart longs for thee, O Good Brother,
like the barren earth yearns for the floodwaters of the Nile,
like the cow in the field aches to be mounted by the virile bull,
like the poor man desires the coming of a righteous judge who will set things straight.
My mind is inflamed with the memory of thy presence, O Noblest of the Noble Ones,
how thy breath smells of pine and cedar and sweet acacia wood,
how thy eyes are silver, like the moon's reflection in a still pool,
how thy flesh is green like ivy clinging to a wall.
I am overcome with the thought of thee:
it makes my heart tremble in my breast.
For thou art the Lord of the Double Horns,
mightier and more potent than ten thousand bulls.
For thou art the Chief among those in the West
whom even death could not destroy.
For thou art the One whose Word is True,
who gives laws to gods and whose counsels all must obey.
O Dionysos, may these words be pleasing to thy heart
so that when I come before thee thou wilt give me cool water to drink
and permit me to take my bread from the offering table of eternity.

A PRAYER

Dionysos, make me drunk on the wine of life!
   Open me up to every experience
   so that when it is time to stand before the judges in the West
I will be able to say that I wasted not a second of life
and that I ended my days without a single regret.
Cause my spirit to overflow its bounds,
like the Nile spilling over its banks,
and may this inundation make the soil fertile
so that every type of crop and plant can take root in it.
Dionysos, nurture the seed that I plant and guide it until it reaches fruition.
Be just as gentle to me, Lord, as I undergo the journey into wholeness.
Show me the source of true being,
which survives every transformation,
even that of death,
so that I might see
just how small and powerless my fears are.

INVOCATION OF PASSION

Come, my bull-footed god,
   come raving out of the woods,
   maddened, furious, ecstatic, orgasmic.
Take me.
Fill me.
Possess me, god.
Make me drunk, Lord.
Drive away all these hateful thoughts,
trample my fears,
squash my worries,
destroy all limitations!
Make me fall in love with the world.
Make me forget the hateful, boring grey world that men live in.
I want colors.
I want explosions.
I want a depth of feeling that I have never even imagined before.
I want it all,
all at once.
With your flaming brand, drive me on!
Rip the clothes from my body.
Make my flesh hot,
my dick hard.
Take me, take me.
Fuck me hard.
Make me throw my head back,
make me scream out in ecstasy.
Don't stop, not ever!
Fill me with pleasure,
wave after wave of pleasure,
so much pleasure that it melts my head,
sets my feet on fire,
pleasure like no one else has ever felt.
I want to burn with pleasure.
I want to dissolve in the ocean of milk.
I want to be spread out across the face of the earth,
a wave of pleasure washing across the earth,
making people laugh,
making them horny,

making them dance in your honor, god.
Io Dionysos!
Io Evohe!

A HYMN TO THE LORD OF THE WESTERN LANDS

Hail to you
   mask-wearing Dionysos,
   god of grape and grain,
bull of fertile rain,
king of the fruitful delta,
snake of fire and rock
who shapes the earth and dreams;
come with a joyous heart
and accept these holy offerings,
you who have done so much for us.

TO DIONYSOS AT DELPHI

Io euoi! Ie paian!
Let us honor Dionysos the King,
the Lord of Delphi during the cold winter months,
the intoxicating, liberating lover of the ivy,
the vine-clad son of Semele
who sleeps beneath the tripod
and is aroused by the frenzied songs of the mad women
who dance upon the mountainside at night
bearing their bright torches.
Io io Dionysos!

TO DIONYSOS OF THE DESERT

Hail to you Dionysos,
    lord of the Red Lands,
    master of the places far from man.
Yours is the thunder and the winds that smash,
the blinding sand storm and the sudden downpour of rain.
You delight in the hunt and the taste of raw flesh torn by your savage teeth,
in strong wine and the pungent smoke of thick cigars.
You snarl and howl, a sound to make even a strong man tremble,
and your laughter echoes into the stillness of the night,
a sound like crunching metal and shattering glass.
You fear nothing and bend the knee to no one.
You are the one who turns things upside down and rends us apart,
especially when we are stuck in an unhealthy rut and cannot free ourselves
from the self-made snares.
Your purification is painful and without mercy –
but all too often exactly what we need.
Hail to you, world-destroyer, wild one bringing liberation,
the feral god we ignore at our own peril!

TO THE HOLY BULL

Hail to you, bull-formed Dionysos,
    twin of the most holy Apis,
    I sing your praises and ask you to come in peace,
for you are the source of all good things in life.
With your horns you drive off the foe,
keeping the two lands safe, and protecting those who love you.
You are solid, like truth, and your heaviness
speaks of the rich yields that we shall harvest with your blessing.
Your thunderous bellow stirs my soul and sends me into a frenzy of joyous
    ecstasy.
Your hooves are made of the stuff of stars and light my path
as I make my way through life.
Your gentle tongue wipes away my tears and soothes all my cares.
Come, O beautiful bull,
O mighty and majestic one,
that I might place a garland of sweet roses around your fragrant neck,
and rest in the presence of your godhood.

FRAGMENTS OF LENAIA

I.

The earth slumbers and the sky is grey
and we shiver as we walk the cold streets at night.
Winter lies heavy over the land and sadness fills our lonely hearts.
Where have all the flowers gone, and the plump grapes on the vine
and the young girls dancing in the fields with nimble feet?
Ie ie! The god is dead at Delphi, dreaming of summer's long coming.
Oh you mad-women, you wild ones who love Semele's dark child,
put on your fawn-skin and weave crowns of ivy for your hair
and run headlong into the hills to rave and rouse the bull-horned king.
Sing the songs of birth and becoming that will drive the cold winds away.
Stamp your feet in rhythmic dance on the barren earth to break up
the icy chains that bind him.
Feel the god begin to move within you, a frantic frenzy, an
overbearing fullness...

II.

Hey hey Dionysos is near
can't you feel him stir
in the cold wind and the crackling fire
the rotting leaves and the moss-covered trees
Hey hey Dionysos is near
and soon he'll come to drive the barren winter away
dancing down from Delphi
leading his mad women and the wild nymphs at play
Hey hey Dionysos is near
the smiling babe in a bed of ivy
the lover whose touch we've longed to feel
the wild frenzy that drives us to the mountain
Hey hey Dionysos is near
and his song will coax the flowers out of the earth
and make dead vines bear plump red grapes
and the wild things come out of hiding ...

III.

The snake stirs in the belly of the earth.
The bull dances with fiery hooves.
The panther stalks the forest at night.
The mad-woman howls in ecstatic delight.
The god awakens! The god awakens!

ACROSTIC LENAIA POEM FOR DIONYSOS

His spirit moves upon the earth
   a stirring of life into fullness, heady and sensual
   intoxication overwhelming our senses,
liberating us from our cares so that we may dance freely in his
   riotous
throng, wild like the mountain-dwelling beasts,
holy like the stars in heaven.
Euoi drips from every lip like nectar,
calling up the god with everything we have.
He stalks through the night,
invisible to human eyes, yet no one can deny the feeling of his
   presence in their flesh.
Languid like the heavy bunches of grapes hanging plump on the
   vine,
drawing us closer to the edge of insanity, and we not caring one bit.
Into his arms we fall, panting and flushed from the dance, our
   hearts racing,
not able to speak or think or feel anything except
the pounding of the drums, echoing through our bodies, the
heat of the fire lighting up the night, the
exquisite joy of worshipping the god with our bodies!
Blessed are we who dance in frenzy for Lusios,
awakened fully by the call of the god whom we awakened this night.
Sap courses through the trees,
keeping time with our stamping feet.
Earth is soft as it receives those who fall in the dance, a bed of grass
   and ivy
tendrils cushioning their bodies.
Hidden in the forest nearby the animals join in the revelry, leaping
and lifting their brute voices in praise of the god.
In the clearing we can hear them, and are glad, for we know that
   they too worship the
lord of all creation, the living god of Nysa.
Does anything remain apart from the rapturous bliss?
If so, I am not aware of it.
Onward we dance throughout the night,
numb to the pain of aching feet and tired limbs,
yearning to feel his presence deeper and more completely, that

sensual stirring of the god within us
our bodies throbbing and burning in the flames of desire that
   birthed him,
sexual and something more at the same time, his presence
lifting our spirits up until they are
immense as the god's own.
Kaleidoscopic, the world shifts before our eyes, and we see things as
   they are.
Not the dim, shadowy existence that most people sleep-walk
   through –
instead we behold the earth alive, and vibrant, and everything connected.
The pulse of life, the rhythm of the dance, the
ecstasy of Dionysos flows through it all,
surging forth like wine poured from the flask.

Io! Io euoi! Io Dionysos Liknites!

A GARLAND FOR DIONYSOS ON ANTHESTERIA

I. Pithoigia

Fill my cup so that my voice will be full of song
    as we honor the god on his long awaited festival.
    I want to taste the new wine;
none of that old shit we've made do with during these long winter nights,
nights so cold that my wife shivered
even when I tried to kiss her under the covers.
Give me some fresh from the jar with the must still in it,
heady with the aroma of flowers and sunshine.
There's a bite to the new stuff,
before time has had a chance to mellow it.
But I like the sharpness
for it reminds me of my own youth
when the blood flowed hot in my veins
and my limbs were strong still.
How handsome I was then,
with long thick curls and pouty lips the envy of any woman.
When I danced the *cordax* all eyes were upon me
and my bed was never empty afterwards.
I dance still,
under the spell of the god,
but you'd never mistake me for the rose-crowned Adonis these days.
Instead people think me a companion of old tipsy Seilenos,
balding and pot-bellied with my wrinkly sack swinging about.
But at least I still dance in the riotous *komos* of our lord Dionysos.
Through the streets we run,
singing our drunken songs and shouting our lewd jokes
to anyone who remains locked behind doors.
The whole city's gone mad,
clad in ivy and flower-garlands,
celebrating the arrival of the maniac god.
The temples are closed,
no business is done,
for we have more important things to do this day.
By afternoon the streets are crowded with spectators
awaiting the arrival of the ship,

that strange boat mounted on wheels and driven up to the steps of his
   temple.
It bears the god they say,
though I've already felt him all day:
with every cup of wine that passed my lips,
in the joyous faces among the throng,
and everywhere else you look.
Buds on the tree-branch,
and the beautiful flowers pushing up through the soil,
the warmth of the sun on your cheek
and the fire in your loins ready to consume you.
Oh yes, Dionysos is already here!
But it is fit that our officials should welcome him back to our city
in the proper ancestral fashion.
So lift high your cups,
sons of Athens,
and have your first taste of the god.
And lift even higher your skirts,
you Attic daughters,
and show us the mystery we have longed for
these many frigid months.
Let every mouth cry out "euoi"
and let no foot remain still,
shunning the dance that gladdens our god's heart,
so that he in turn may bless our land
with an abundance of flowers
and good new wine come next year!

II. Khoes

How different the city feels today.
Yesterday all was a frenzy as we drank and sang
and watched the grand procession pass us by.
There were stolen kisses and every head crowned with flowers
– but today the garlands lay forgotten,
trampled under our dancing feet.
Today the spirit is subdued,
and everybody goes about with gloomy faces.
Sure, some of that is due to the after-effects of the wine –
my own throat is raw from shouting
and my head feels like it's been split open by an axe –
but there's more to it than that.
We feel the dead walking,
dark shapes caught out of the corner of the eye,
a light caress from an invisible hand,
whispered words when no one else is near.
And the memories are overwhelming.
I haven't thought of Leukos in five years or more,

but there he was in my mind this morning,
looking like he did in our youth,
before the down appeared on his cheeks,
with that great big laugh of his,
that came so freely and was always so infectious.
There wasn't much laughing towards the end,
once he came back from the fighting in Sicily.
It was good to hear him laugh again.
Nor was he the only one.
I saw old Timotheos the sophist speaking in the *agora*,
and Mnasithea beautiful on her wedding day,
and Dion the flute-player,
and Hermogenes covered in soot and sweat,
pounding away at his forge once more ...
And so many others, too many to name in full.
The older I get the more dead people I seem to know.
Some day soon I'll be among their ranks,
and I wonder if anyone will bother to remember
this old scribbler of second-rate verse.
I doubt it, but you never know.
This is a day for the remembrance of all the dead,
not just those who are near
and dear to our hearts.
We honor those from primordial times,
the great souls who perished in the flood-waters
sent by Zeus to rid the world of quarrelsome man,
saving only Deukalion and his blessed family.
And the maidens driven mad by the wine-god
in retribution for the murder of Ikarios,
good steward of the vine.
They say that Dionysos loved his daughter Erigone
and the grape was her father's bride-price after the god lay with her.
Wishing to spread the joy he felt, Ikarios came to Athens
and gave the men of our city their first taste of wine.
Out of their minds with drunkenness they thought themselves poisoned,
and so murdered the vintner and stuffed his body in a well.
Erigone sought her father for many nights
and when she finally found his corpse she was overcome with grief
and hanged herself.
The god's wrath was great and all the women of Athens killed themselves
in imitation of the mournful daughter
until gentle Phoibos soothed his brother
by instituting a festival of commemoration.
And so it is that you see dolls and precious objects hung from trees,
and the young girls in swings,
swaying silently like a spider on the web.
Silent, too, are the feasts of Orestes
which old men like myself observe on this day.

We sit at tables erected outdoors,
each man with his own cup of wine
sharing neither sip nor word with his neighbor.
As he drinks the polluted cup
he broods and thinks back to the day
when Orestes came to our land,
hands stained with mother's blood.
Back then the festival of Dionysos had a more joyous character,
and men drank their fill in the temple with noisy chatter and gay songs.
But the King was caught on the horns of a dilemma:
he could not turn the stranger aside,
for the gods punish those who refuse hospitality to suppliants,
nor could he invite Orestes into the holy house of god
before he had appeased the Kindly Ones who hunt those
that have spilt the blood of kin.
So the wise King locked all the temple doors
and set up a table for his guest
and from that day forth we have feasted in like fashion
on this most solemn of days.
Walking through the city today I have seen many such tables
and old friends quietly sipping their wine.
They did not hail me as I passed,
nor I them,
though there would have been a place for me had I chosen
to sit and share the silent cup with them.
But I had other things on my mind
as I hastened to the house of my friend Sosibios.
Tonight he is throwing a grand celebration
since his matronly aunt has been chosen to assist the venerable Gerarai,
themselves assistants to the wife of the King Arkhon.
This is a great honor for the family of Sosibios,
a sign that they're moving up in the world.
Only the very best of our city
have anything to do with the sacred marriage.
And true, his aunt is merely assisting those who assist the Queen,
but these are the most important rites imaginable,
upon which the fruitfulness of the land
and the safety of our city depend.
All reverence attaches to those who take part in it,
however minimal their role.
His whole family will hold their heads high in the year to come,
 the people whispering in admiration as they pass.
That only the noblest among us can participate in these rites
is shown by the fact that we have retained the office of King
even after becoming a democracy.
The King has no more power among us than any elected official,
and considerably less than most,
but these are rites so old and so awesome

that the gods will recognize them only when they are performed
by those with royal blood.
During the rite the god takes the Queen away from her husband
like he did when he stole the bride of Theseus,
for Dionysos comes mighty as a bull,
and in the bull's shed he mates with her,
spilling his seed in a fertile womb
so that the womb of the earth may bear much fruit
and flowers of every hue.
There is much more to these ancestral rites,
but they are shrouded in mystery
and not for the likes of you and me to know.
But I know what happens after the grave rite is enacted,
and so does anyone who can look out and see our land prospering.
So I give thanks to the wife of the King
and all those who help her conduct the mystery,
and soon I shall give thanks to Sosibios and his family
for their wonderful feast!

III. Khutroi

We've reached the last day
and things are starting to get back to normal.
I've boiled the pot of porridge,
chewed the bitter herb,
and painted my door with pitch
to expel any remaining spirits.
They come up out of the ground
when we broach the jars of new wine,
making a path for the flowers to follow.
It is good to have the dead with us once more,
but nobody wants them around all the time.
So we call upon the Underworld Hermes
to come and collect the souls who linger too long
like drunken guests at a party who have overstayed their welcome.
I had to help Sosibios clear a few of those out last night,
rowdy young things who had had a little too much to drink.
You could hear them shambling about on the street afterwards,
so unsteady on their feet that their friends had to hold them upright,
but still they were thirsty for more
and accosted the slave of a neighbor who wouldn't let them in.
They didn't even know the fellow,
but they heard the laughter and singing through the door
and wished to join the fun.
Hours later when I headed for home
the sounds of revelry were still going on.
The wife of the King wasn't the only one
who took a strange lover into her bed this night.

The whole way back I was serenaded by the sounds of desire
and caught my own slaves going at it in the forecourt.
I watched for a little while,
appreciative of the spectacle.
Neoboule is certainly a fetching lass,
with a backside Aphrodite would be proud of.
If I were just a little younger,
I'd be bending her over all the time myself.
When I sought my bed
I found my wife already fast asleep,
and if she had had a little fun of her own earlier in the evening,
she showed no signs of it.
As long as such things happen only then,
and I don't have to know about it,
it's fine by me.
We look the other way during Anthesteria,
when the world is turned upside down,
everyone is mad with wine,
and nothing is what it seems.
But with the coming of the final day,
normalcy returns
and the dead crawl back into the earth through the empty jars.
All that remains is to clean up the mess we've made,
the broken dishes,
the discarded garlands,
the upturned tables
and remnants of the feast.
Gods, what a tumult this festival is
and how my head hurts from all the wine I've drunk!
But though it's only just now ending
I confess that I'm already looking forward to the next time.

THE THYIA

The crowd has gathered outside the temple
   some milling about impatiently, eager for the solemnities to be over
   so that they can get their free cups of wine.
Others have a look of reverent expectation upon their sleep-deprived faces.
They've been up since before the dawn,
having succumbed to slumber mere hours before.
They crane their necks to catch a glimpse of the priests
and the well-dressed city officials who will come and break the seals
on the temple doors,
revealing a thing of wonder to all.
The miracle of the wine is like a myth of the old days,
when marvelous, impossible things happened all the time.
But now everything is dull and all too familiar,
except here at Elis when the god makes his appearance during the Thyia.
Is that the sweet fragrance of wine they catch upon the breeze,
wafting out of the inner chamber of the temple,
wine that just the night before was water poured into the big clay jugs?
What will it taste like, this heaven-sent beverage?
Like dreams and everything that's good, one man whispers to his neighbor,
a stranger who's come all the way from Athens to take in the spectacle.
He belongs to the school of Diogenes
and has the shabby cloak and beard to prove it.
He's sure the priests are up to no good,
pulling an elaborate scam on the populace.
He examined the seal earlier and it seemed sound,
just the way they'd left it the day before,
but that's no proof of a lack of deception in his eyes.
Maybe the priests snuck in through a back door
and exchanged the water for wine while everyone was sleeping,
though he could find no secret entrance
and it's unlikely they'd be able to smuggle in so many jars
with the crowd outside the whole time.
Maybe they're all in on it then,
the whole city conspiring in the feigned miracle
to attract the curious and superstitious from abroad.
Or maybe it's a case of mass hysteria,
the water unchanged except in the minds of the credulous.
He'll have to have a cup – or three – himself to decide.

Will the wine be enough to transform his doubt into faith,
and if so what will he say to his fellows back in Athens
who scoff at such things?
Time enough to sort that out later.
A cry erupts among the crowd
as they spot the purple-robed priest of Dionysos
marching along the processional route,
flanked by his associates,
the town council,
and all the foreign dignitaries.
It's begun! It's begun!
The Thyia has started
and soon there'll be wine for all!
Oh, joyous day of the god's epiphany
in the thrice-blessed land of Elis!

FRAGMENTS OF AN INITIATE

Wandering in the field of rushes.
... blood up to your ankles ...
... the moans of the unburied dead, the wails of virgins who never beheld the lovely torches of Hymenaios.
... thirst and hunger so great ...
Do not drink the cool water of the pool shaded by the white poplar, for it is Forgetfulness. Nor eat the sacrificial cakes of the Benevolent Ones ... dung and menstrual blood, the flesh of sinners are these ...
... the lake of fire ... shadows ... a mound of skulls piled high.
... and there, the forest of bones where dead girls hang in trees and watch you with sorrowful eyes.
... another road, trod by Initiates in white robes, bearing the holy phallos in the underworld ... the sweet song of Iakchos ever on their lips.
They have drunk the wine of god ...
... run with the bull ...
... crowned with serpents, holding the precious grapes in hand.
Beautiful ...
... radiant light ... the torch ...
... the dancers ...
... the secret tokens of the mysteries, the words to speak to the Sentries.
... banish the tears of sorrowing Persephatta, she who longs ... her child.
I will wear the ivy; I will never take it off.
... the lap of Ariadne ...
... joy beyond measure.
His face ...
... my beloved.
Come again to the banquet hall of Dionysos, where the wine is never exhausted and there is ...
... laughter ... eternal drunkenness.

This holy account belongs to Oinomaos, son of Arete, husband of Aidesia, Initiate and Priest of the god for twenty-three years. Though heaven-sent lightning laid him low, he knows the better fate that awaits his divine race, and carries this golden sheet as a perpetual reminder during his journey through the gloomy House of Haides. But there is no gloom for those who know their god, the Lord Dionysos.

DIONYSOS MAINÓMENOS

We say it so frequently,
    with such casualness,
        that we don't really pause to consider the full implications of it.
And maybe it's better that way.
Not just a god who makes people mad, mind you,
but a god – *a god* – who is himself a madman.
We smile and think of poets caught up in the frenzy of their craft,
charming old eccentric ladies sipping tea with their cats,
anonymous vagrants mumbling to themselves on park benches,
visionaries, dreamers, people who don't conform to society's conventions.
Strange ones, to be sure, but for the most part harmless.
They add some much needed color to our lives
and the world is a better place for having them in it.
But that's just part of the picture,
just one type of madness.
There are 5,642 different flavors of madness
and Dionysos has tasted them all.
The woman who drowns her babies in a bathtub
because she thinks they're demons,
the man who scribbles complex algebraic equations on his wall in feces,
the frail lunatic whose arms are covered in a web of scars
because the only thing that stops the shrieking in her head is the blood…
This is the face of madness. It's not pretty, it's not fun.
Now imagine such a being with the powers of a god
and you've got some idea of what the true Dionysos is like.
Remember that the next time you call upon him
and see his grinning face in the dark.

TO DIONYSOS KHOREIOS

The other gods are depicted in static profile,
   stately and serene in their rigid postures,
   gazing out into eternity.
But not you, Dionysos,
for your face is always turned towards us.
Every glimpse of you is epiphanal,
a direct encounter with the divine
manifest in the expressionless mask.
Your elegant form is perpetually in motion,
a desperate dance to drive away demons,
or the rhythm of life as it unfolds in the frenzy of creation.
It is impossible to look upon you and not hear the
thunder of drums and the trill of pipes,
to feel our own hearts begin to beat faster,
caught in the snare of your delicious delirium.
You move so fast that it all seems a blur,
the world spinning out of control
and one thing blending into another in orgiastic rapture.
Yet in the wild flurry one thing remains still,
your mask staring with empty eyes straight into our hearts,
a silent challenge beckoning us to leave behind our fears
and our foolish inhibitions
to join you in your manic revels.
Hail to you Dionysos, who came to Egypt to teach us how to dance!

TO DIONYSOS ORTHOS

Hail upright god,
   stout one who plows the field,
   lusty one who makes men hard,
joyful one who fills the women with phallic frenzy,
fruitful one, bursting with seed.
Lover of the moist ripe grape
and the delicate, late-blooming flowers,
Bull of His Mother,
who impregnates a thousand cows in a single night!
Come, o potent one, come in peace,
smelling of sweat and the salty sea,
he whom all the gods adore
in the innermost chambers of their temple.
Thou greatest of the great ones,
without whom there would be no life upon the earth!

EPIPHANY

He comes! Great Lord Sabazios comes,
  howling madly as he dances through the dark forest
  wearing snakes for bracelets and bull's horns as his crown.
He tosses his long-haired head about,
graceful as the deer whose blood stains his beard.
He gnashes his savage teeth and stomps his boot-clad feet
to make the sky thunder and light up with brilliant fire.
The little forest-gods cower before him,
and all the beasts have fled far from here.
But we dancers,
drunk on his beer,
remain where we are
for Sabazios has devoured all our fears.
What of it if he should chase us down
and strip the flesh from our bodies?
Has he not already done much worse during initiation?
So we will dance and rave and drink in his presence
until morning light drives us back to our homes
and Sabazios returns beneath the earth
waiting for our drums to raise him up once more.

POSSESSED

When the god comes
he comes dancing leopard-footed,
eyes flashing in the dark,
feral teeth bared in mad laughter.
The fire leaps and crackles
as the air grows thick with wine-scent
and the perfume of damp forest earth.
I hear the sound of savage tympanums far off –
or perhaps it's just the frantic beating of my heart in its chest.
He is everywhere at once,
and nowhere,
moving faster than I can follow.
Faintly I catch glimpses of him:
his dark head crowned with bunches of plump grapes,
the spotted pelt slung across his broad shoulders,
the ivy climbing up the staff he uses
to strike the ground in time with the invisible drummers.
But when I try for more than this,
a vision of his beautiful form in its fullness,
I am thwarted.
My eyes water and my head swims and I am forced to look elsewhere:
the turf altar drenched with libations,
the shadowy trees that surround us,
the clear night sky overhead lit up by the pregnant moon.
He is toying with me,
like an agile cat playing with its prey,
leaping down on it unexpectedly,
batting it into stunned submission with its big paws,
but holding off the lethal bite until amusement wanes.
Unlike the fearful mouse, though,
I have no intention of fleeing.
I am afraid.
What man wouldn't be,
finding himself in the presence of the lord of savage feasts?
But this god is my god
and I have given myself fully to him.
If he should choose to rend my flesh
and drink the warm blood that spills forth

as I have so often drunk his wine,
I will bare my throat and gladly accept my fate.
At this thought the motion ceases,
and I find myself staring straight into his empty eyes.
He smiles
and I smile
and he whispers, "Come!"
Howling, the two of us run into the dark woods,
leaving the familiar world behind.
I am possessed by his spirit,
an alien to myself.
Free and pure I race with the god,
my feet inerrantly finding their way.
It seems to me that I am no longer wholly human
but have become a wild beast,
golden-furred and sharply-fanged,
one of the graceful leopards that belong to the hunting party of Lyaios.
"Euoi!" I cry into the night,
"Io Dionysos!"
And it is the last thing I remember
before waking the next morn far from the sacred grove.

CONFESSION OF A DIONYSIAN MUMMER

I roam where midnight Zagreus roams,
through the maze of empty streets
and homes still with slumbering souls inside.
No other mortal dares venture forth at this late hour,
but I am hardly alone on my desolate way.
The wind whips through skeletal trees made barren by winter's harshness,
and in the distance I hear the awful cry of crows,
shredding the night's silence like a veil torn in two.
Strange things lurk in the shadows,
misshapen and wild-eyed.
The thirsty dead and spirits of the land long forgot,
loosed to revel on this eve
that's stretched across the old and new years,
yet belongs fully to neither.
Dangerous are they,
and eager to snatch the unwary,
dragging them down beneath the loamy soil
never to be heard from again.
All this is true, yet I have no fear
for on this night I am one of them.
I wear a mask of crude animal pelts to conceal my face,
and tattered clothes like a revenant's worm-eaten shroud.
Around my waist are strung noisome bells,
and I beat an old drum and sing a drunken song
taught to me by the ancestors.
My steps are fleet as I dance through the streets,
and the frenzy of Lusios drives me on to unknown places.
Tonight I am a creature of the hunt;
not human, but a wild beast in feigned man-shape
or so it would seem to any unfortunate who strayed across my path.
But I howl and I growl and I stamp my boots
to make sure that that won't happen –
for who would dare approach such a mad thing as I?
This roaming with the ghosts and elder gods
is a rite primordial and full of deep magic.
I could try to explain to you why we do it
and have done it since the dawn of time,
but if you don't already know

and feel it down in your bones and soul,
you never will,
and better by far for you to hide
safe in your snug little bed on this night.
And pray, o gentle man,
that the spirits don't find their way into your dreams,
riding upon the frightful steeds of Nyx,
lest you fail to wake and greet the glorious morn
of our new year.

ENTHEOS

I can hardly see through this mask I wear,
heavy on my face and crudely carved of pine,
the tree on which Pentheus hung for his crimes.
It still smells strongly of sap and smoke and the paint that covers it;
beneath that my own sweat, pouring down my cheeks,
and a powerful animal musk.
From me or the god, I cannot tell.
I notice all this in the back of my mind,
but don't pay much attention to such things.
My feet dance his dances without having to be told what to do.
I spin around and leap like a leaf caught on the breeze,
like a goat bounding over the rocks on the perilous heights of a cliff,
like a bull rushing through a field of flowers and ivy.
I don't need my eyes to tell which way to go;
all I've got to do is let my body follow its own course,
winding through the other god-maddened dancers,
jumping over the tall flames of the raging fire,
twirling round and round until I can't tell which way is up.
I toss my head back and howl to the heavens for all I'm worth,
the sound of my voice carrying beyond the clearing
into the deep forest where others of our kind have fled.
The cry is picked up by them,
sent back to me through a dozen throats and more,
lifting me even higher out of myself.
The god is in me as he's in the others.
Fierce and bull-formed,
a serpent of fire,
wine with the face of a man.
He lifts me up and carries me on his back,
dancing around the clearing with my borrowed body.
I watch him do things I've never dreamed of.
Prance panther-agile,
stomp the glowing coals with his bare feet,
chasing the laughing maidens around
with a hard cock in his hand.
It's not I who does these things;
truly I haven't got it in me,
except when the god had complete control of my body and soul.

Then I can't help myself,
and who would blame me?
The others are just as wild,
a team of horses with Dionysos wielding the reins.
He whips us on,
drives us into a frenzy,
and we couldn't stop even if we wanted to.
But who would ever stop
when the madness is this much fun?
So on we run,
dancing through the night
until the first rays of dawn
creep through the forest
chasing us back to our homes.

TARANTELLA

Uncontrollably we dance,
    driven on by the frenzy of the music
    and the bite of the little *taranta*.
Come Saint Paul,
clutching your snakes,
and dance with us as you danced
on the road to Damascus
when the wine-god appeared
and bid you drink from his sacred cup.
The venom is in our blood
and we'll dance until it comes out in our sweat.
We'll dance all day and dance all night
and dance and dance til the grace is upon us.
It does no good to try and stop us;
this dancing isn't something we want to do.
The *taranta* crawls beneath our skin
and makes us flail our limbs.
Dancing is the only thing that drives it out
and the more we fight the harder she bites
until we're out of our minds with pain.
So get out of our way,
don't block our path.
Let us dance as we will,
for as long as we may.
And if you've any Christian charity left
you'll all take up an instrument and play for us
– saint and sinner alike –
as we dance the little *taranta*'s dance
and dance and dance and dance!

CHTHONIC

A mound of candles, incense and offerings
heaped beneath a crude mask of leaves and twigs
that hangs from a stalactite formed by water
slowly dripping down the side of a cave
carved out of the earth by the flow
of molten rock thousands of years before
the first men settled this land.
The air is cold and moist on your bare skin,
but that isn't why you shiver.
You feel him in the shadows,
dark and still as death,
watching you from the empty eyes of the mask
and elsewhere.
He dances in the lava flame
deep, deep beneath the ground.
You smell him in the pools of condensation,
wet and musty and fungal.
You hear him whisper to you in the silence,
sounds that never quite form into words.
Images half-glimpsed, strange and unfamiliar
invade your mind but leave no lasting impression
except the desire to hold onto them,
to better understand this face of your god.
You open your mouth to call out to him,
to speak his name in this dark, strange place
and an ancient song you've never heard before spills forth,
calling him up into the world,
out of the cave,
through the flowers and the trees,
to feel the sun's warmth once more upon his beautiful face.
You don't know what you're singing;
it isn't words or like any song you've sung before.
It isn't your song at all,
but his,
and it's old, old, old,
a song from the days before man.
Persephone sang this song in her grief;
so did Ariadne and many others after her.

You feel all of them with you there in the cave,
singing through your voice,
and you feel what the song is doing to him
as it brings him up out of the dark.
You don't understand any of it,
but it must be done anyway.
He can't do this without you,
and you can't do anything without him.

A MODERN DIONYSIA

Arms flailing in graceless beauty
heads rolling on limp necks
sweaty bodies pressed close together
desperate to banish the loneliness of space,
aching to find some fleeting connection in the passing moment.
the bass beat vibrates deep within them, rousing the sluggish life in
  their limbs.
the melody controls their movement like an unseen puppeteer
  pulling the strings.
all inhibition falls away,
all worry of the day,
all fear of looking foolish.
even the bashful ones slip from the shadows onto the dance floor,
driven irresistibly on by the daimonic power of the music.
the strobe lights and the impenetrable darkness create another
  world for them,
a safe place where they can lose themselves and become someone
  else for a few moments
someone sexy and agile, someone who does the things
they only dream about in the daylight hours.
the god walks among them,
unseen in the hazy dark,
fed by their sweat and moans,
born again in the flames of human desire.
this is his temple in the modern world,
these his willing worshipers,
and the DJ directing it all, his sanctified priest.

BURSTS OF DRUNKEN POETRY

You
gorgeous
frantic
drunkard
dance
like the stormy sea
soar above the sky
light as a rose petal
smooth like peach honey

***

We live
& dream
recalling
moments of
love
beauty
worship
&
shining playful freedom

***

The ship of Dionysos,
the ship of fools,
the ship of millions of years,
floating on a sea of wine
in unending time,
with a mast of vines,
twining clusters of grapes,
driven by the rain-heavy winds
through endless, red seas.
A dream leads him to distant lands
to find his fortune in the sand,
to meet the woman with the snake
and a cup of poison,
precious to drink.

LUSIOS

The ways of the gods are dark
   and dimly perceived by mortal eyes.
   Who can say whether the path they set before us
will lead to happiness and release
– or to madness and destruction.
(Or whether these may not, in the end, be the same.)
Trying to figure that out only muddies the waters
and makes us like Asterios lost and raving in the labyrinth.
In the end, all we can do is submit to trust,
and have faith that the gods will guide us safely to shore.
To give ferocious assent to all life has to offer,
and echo the ancient Bacchic cheer, "Io euoi! Io Dionysos!"

MEMORIES

Serpentine coils rise from the incense stick
   spiraling images recreating themselves with the slightest breath
   the intoxicating smell of sandalwood and patchouli
fills my head with phantom images of a world I've never known
but remember in feverish dreams and stolen moments

I hear long forgotten chants rise and fall in sonorous rhythm
against the cool marble walls of an ancient temple
I see huge bronze statues of naked gods before whom dance
lithe girls in flowing gowns, their heads crowned with ivy
as young men play Asian songs upon their flutes

the sun – kingly and majestic, the source of all life –
beats down upon the sprawling city and the fertile valley beyond
watches as the city falls to sword and flame and inner decay
mutely watches as the wind and sand and centuries wash over the ruins
until nothing of these people exists
save for in the mind of a fool
who stares too long into the fumes of incense sticks millennia later

WRITTEN IN WINE

You pray to the invisible air
   wondering if anyone is there,
   but my god is wine,
born of heat and earth;
he is dark in every glass I lift,
and when drunk he takes hold of my mind,
compelling my feet to dance.
I do not doubt;
why should I when every store stocks my god
and a cork is all that keeps me from divine communion?
Drunkenness is holy;
I have witnessed things you can only dream of.
The delusions of a poisoned mind, you call it
little realizing how pathetic your sobriety seems
to those of us initiated in the mysteries of god's blood.
I laugh at you
and down another glass,
drawing closer to the sublime
on red, wet wings.
Do not fight against what is good;
even animals desire intoxication.
Everything noble about the human race
came about as a result of the derangement of the senses.
So let us praise Bacchus, the savior of mankind!
All are welcome in his rites,
regardless of birth, virtue or belief:
he cares only that you drain your cup to the last drop
and gladly ask for more.

LONGING FOR DIONYSOS

When I lower my head that final time
 I pray my soul will be carried away
 to that land I've visited so often before.
I've walked through its shady culverts in dream
and tasted the pure water that flows
from the hidden grotto in daylight visions.
I know this place better than any other —
Nysa is more my home than any land I've ever set foot on before.
All I have to do is close my eyes
and the thick smell of pine trees and damp soil fills my nostrils.
If I listen closely enough,
I can hear the soft sounds of bare feet playing through the delicate grasses,
as ancient nymphs collect flowers for garland crowns
and the mad-women dance with snakes in their hands.
Sometimes the memory of the god's own wine
is strong upon my tongue,
so strong that my vision blurs,
my heart begins to race,
and I am fully drunk
just from the thought of him.
Oh my beloved, my king, my god —
I yearn only to be near to you,
to spend eternity in your joyous company,
lift my proud head, crowned with your ivy,
and feel your praises pour out of my mouth in inspired verse,
like the river of wine that spills from the foot of your throne,
flooding the earth and making the world green with new life.
I long to dance beside the lusty satyrs,
to dance the dance of limitless intoxication
which knows no weariness,
that never comes to an end.
I ache to gaze upon the beauty of your well-chosen bride,
Ariadne whose flesh shines more brightly even
than the lovely wedding-crown of stars you placed upon her fair brow.
She knows the singular pleasure of resting her head in your lap,
of feeling your lips pressed to hers in a kiss
whose power was so great that it triumphed over death,
raising her up from the house of shadows and dust

to sit ever by your side as your queen.
O! Just to look upon one so lucky would fill my heart with boundless joy!
So when my time comes, O merciful Dionysos,
do not forget me,
but cause the music of your merry band to play even louder,
so that I can find my way sure-footed to the place of your birth,
the mountain from which you rule the hearts of all
who bear the sign of your mysteries engraved upon their soul.

MY LIFE IN THE LABYRINTH

I can't hide from you no matter how far I travel
or what strange passageways I turn down
for you are always there,
the hunter of my heart,
with your bull's shape lurking in the shadows
and your breath warm upon the back of my neck.
From the first moment that I set foot on this uncertain path
you have pursued me,
the ghostly god who haunts the dark places of my imagination,
my secret seducer.
Boldly I came here to hunt you:
foolish I was then!
For when I finally found you,
my heart was overwhelmed with fear and I fled.
I was not ready for what I saw;
your terrible beauty and the mad mysteries that hid within your eyes.
I knew that you would consume me,
for that is what you do,
and in the process I'd be set free.
That scared me most of all.
And so I ran.
And you, smiling, let me go,
knowing full well that I'd find my way back to you in time.
And why wouldn't I?
For the world is dull and barren
without you to quicken the pulse
and stir the soul to frenzy.
You bring everything into sharp focus
and reveal things as they truly are
brimming with life and magical.
So here I stand at the threshold of your temple
deep beneath the earth,
a willing sacrifice upon your altar,
purged of all my impurities,
my doubts and fears and all the rest,
to use as you see fit
if you would but consent to have me,
O Bull-horned Lord of the House of the Double Axe.

TO MY BELOVED

Now that I've found you, what shall I call you?
God, I think, is what you are,
but not the God of garish Cathedrals
and red-faced Baptist preachers.
Nor the God painted in Imperial hues,
who sits above a fallen world,
and finds fault in everything that man does.
You are the wild and untamed wind that blows across the sun-blasted plain
and the perfect silence upon which nothing can intrude.
A song, a dance, and a merry laugh among good friends,
the unexpected inspiration that drags me out of bed late at night.
You are manifest in the shapely curves of a beautiful woman
in the defiant cries of a new-born baby.
Great books and ribald jokes.
You are an enigma that the mind cannot unravel,
but my flesh knows you.
A Mystery whose only answer is experience,
an absurdity that makes reality seem dim by comparison.
Even contemplating the tiniest part of you makes my head swim
and fills me with excitement.
I can't even sit still when I think of you.
I have to get up and dance.
Dance, dance, dance – and sing!
O how I must sing.
What do I sing?
I don't know, each time it's different.
"Io Bacchus!"
"Alleluia!"
"I am alive!"
"Fucking a!"
Each time I'm singing your name.
Everything that I sing,
everything that I say or think or do –
is just another name for you.
But my favorite name is Dionysos,
the name of my beloved!

OMOPHAGIA

In Samos they worship the Gaping Dionysos
a god with his mouth stretched grotesquely wide,
the better to swallow and consume living things.
This is what it means to be a votary of the god,
one of the sacred mad ones.
For we take everything inside us.
We do not separate the good from the bad,
pleasure from pain,
or other silly dichotomies.
We take it all in, slurping it down,
intoxicated with the taste of life upon our lips.
There is only sensation,
and different grades of it,
and we are greedy for the experience of each in their particulars.
Most people when they are sad wish to be happy,
and when they are happy find a reason to be sad.
But we, we stop and feel the emotion to its fullest,
probing the contours like a tongue stroking an aching tooth,
like an artist enraptured by the nuanced colors of the setting sun.
We are not content until we have sucked the marrow from the moment,
until our souls are satiated,
full to bloat and spilling over the rim.
Others turn from pain,
they shield their delicate hearts,
but we crave the rawness, the frenzy and the horror.
Dionysos is the mouth of the world,
and we the world's tongue, tasting what is swallowed.

THE SONG OF THE FIRE-BORN

"The fire is coming," he whispers,
"Be ready to dance through the flames."
Oh Lord, I am ready!
This life I've built for myself is dry and brittle
and aches for your fiery kiss to set it ablaze.
Burn it all down. I am ready.
I will hold onto nothing but you
and together we will dance in the ashes.
And if you ask I will immolate myself on the pyre of your love
and sing your praises as I burn for you.
Oh, what joy to burn for you!
I do not fear the pain,
for no lasting transformation comes without it.
And if the flames should destroy me, what then?
You have destroyed me before
and remade me, closer to your image.
That is all I ask my Lord.
I am ready.
Bring the flames that will purify me
and provide the substance of my rebirth.
And when the fire has eaten my face
I will see with the eyes of my heart.
And when my heart has been consumed,
then I will be set free.
And in that moment I will rise from the ashes,
reborn like the *bennu*,
a creature of pure fire with wings of flame.

ECSTASY BY MIDNIGHT

I have heard the call of Dionysos late at night,
   as the blood echoed in my ears like wine sloshing against the rim of a
      drinking cup,
and my feet ached to dance the ancient dances in the shadow-haunted hills.
In that moment I felt myself immense,
kin to the fiery stars dancing in the vaulted halls of heaven,
and the wild beasts who roam the desert wastes.
And I knew myself free and flowing, bound by no law, by no limits.
In that moment I could do anything, be anything,
for a god dwelt in me, and I was an ivy-branded priest of Bacchus, beautiful
   and ecstatic!

DIONYSOS TO HIS MAINAD

I have tasted the sweat on your skin after the dance
the fragrant aroma of Ariadne running through the labyrinth
hungry for bull's flesh
and the smoke of torches at night.

The mask hides mysteries,
but it also reveals what lies beneath.
So dance with me,
daughter of ivy,
and hold nothing back.
I know it all anyway,
for I have looked at you with the eyes of eternity,
I have known you before you had a face.

Come and rave among the trees,
and do not be afraid of losing yourself.
How can you lose what does not belong to you anyway?

No matter where you are,
I will find you. This I promise.

The grape is your eternal reward,
to taste eternity every time you swallow.

Hiss like a serpent,
howl like a panther,
and dance like a nymph.

This I command above all else,
to go beyond what you imagine,
to trust even when it makes no sense.
This is the only way you will discover
what is truly possible for you,
and what I desire of you,
my wild one.

THE MASK

My face is a mask;
there is nothing beneath it.
Wear me and you will truly live.
Reject me and none will know your name.

I make miracles happen
through the fire and the vine and the mask.

Put me on like a fine fawn skin
and know the truth that cannot be spoken
but is understood by all the blessed initiates.

I, Dionysos, have spoken these words in wine.
Understand them and live forever,
the sweet fruit of the vine.

THE CROWN

You wear me every time you drink.
What you experience isn't false,
the raving delusion of a drunken mind.
No, it is the gospel of Dionysos,
whispered to you in these ecstatic moments
when you are truly alive.
There is truth only in wine;
all else is dream.
That is why I bid you always be drunk,
for it brings us closer together.
You wear the ivy as a token of our relationship,
like a bridal ring of green.
You want the earth to be fertile,
to bear much fruit. So be it.
This boon I grant to you,
so long,
and only,
when you wear my crown.

PENTHEIAD

I came to Thebes to speak with my cousin, the king.
He did not recognize me, even though we were kin.
I tried to show him the truth,
but he was cunt-hungry,
convinced that the things in his head
were what others cared about.
(And they call *me* mad!)
How absurd.
He bound me in chains,
but I easily slipped out.
He saw me,
eventually,
manifest in the bull and the lightning.
Then,
and only then,
the Suffering One listened to me.
But by then it was too late.
His doom was already upon him.
All that remained was the march to the forest,
and the frenzy of the mad-women.
How I smiled as he hung from the pine.
How sweet his expression
as his mother carried his head about like a trophy.
You don't fuck with the gods,
you foolish mortals,
unless you want to die.
Even then it's outside your hands
for it is we that decide the time and the means.

ANAMNESIS

B lood
      dripping
      dripping
         down my face.
How can I see my own face?
Not my face,
    his.
His face looks like mine,
the same full lips and round cheeks,
that wavy brown hair –
    the only difference is in the eyes.
His eyes,
    full of a child's love and wonder,
        as he sits on my lap, listening to the stories I tell him.
His eyes,
    strong and proud like his father's
        on the day when they placed the crown on his head.
His eyes,
    cruel and mocking,
        as he sees what no man should ever see.
No.
I won't think about that.
I won't remember.
The disdainful words we said to our sister …
The way my son fought against those religious fanatics …
The smiling face of the god …
The hunt,
    oh the joyful hunt!
What *is* this thing I've got in my hands?
It's so familiar – and yet not.
Why can't I recognize it?
And what's that sound?
It's like a distant drum,
    or blood,
        dripping,
        dripping
            down.

ARAKHNEIAD

Twilight gloom in the vineyard
   summer heat laying heavy over the drooping fruit
   everyone's gone home, locked safely behind their doors
except for the spiders, unseen lovers of the grape.
They spin their webs in the field, and crawl
soundlessly over the gnarled vinewood,
hunting the insects that would devour Bacchus' plump children.
The race of spiders has been friend of the wine-god for as long as
   they have lived,
and before that, for the sweet virgin Arakhne
lay with Lyaeus before she competed with the Weaver.
They met in an arbor and danced together while the Nymphai of
   Lydia watched
and sang the Hymenaeus song for them, and Bromios lifted his cup
   to her sweet lips
and poured the holy ecstasy-inducing poison for her to drink.
Drunk on his wine, the young girl rushed through the wood, wild as a
   mainad,
a hunting companion of Lord Zagreus.
Life coursed through her supple limbs
and she grew impetuous under his yoke,
tossing back her head and calling Euoi to the dark vault of heaven.
She gave her body to him beneath the moon,
and he filled her with greater pleasure than any mortal had ever known.
And later, when Arakhne returned to her father's house and loom
she carried the memory of that night into her weaving,
letting the ecstasy she had felt guide her nimble fingers.
And she wove scenes of startling beauty and such realism
that everyone who saw them marveled and thought that the waves
   she wrought
would leap off the loom and that they could almost smell the sweat
   of the dancing girls
or the grapes near to bursting in their ripeness.
And they whispered that her skill was more than mortal,
that she had to have been taught by Pallas herself.
But Arakhne just laughed and said that her skill was her own,
and the inspiration for it came from Dionysos her lord.
She would not give ground to the gods – in fact that stubbornness

was what Dionysos loved so much about her.
Athene was jealous and challenged her to a duel, and the
    headstrong girl accepted
and wove the story of her seduction by Dionysos.
When Athene saw the theme of her rival she grew enraged, for she
thought Arakhne was mocking the gods
by weaving the stories of Zeus' seductions
and of Dionysos bribing Erigone with the grape,
little understanding what the girl was saying with her web.
So she beat the girl and destroyed the mantle she had worked so hard on,
and taunted her work, saying no god could love a foolish, frail mortal –
that they used them for their own pleasure and then quickly forgot them.
And Arakhne was crushed, because that mantle she had meant
to give to Dionysos as a bridal present
and when she saw her hard work destroyed,
and the jealous goddess mocking her love,
Arakhne's heart broke in two and she took a rope and twined it
around the rafters of her father's home
and hung herself, a victim of love.
And when Dionysos came and saw, he was doubled over in grief,
for this girl had been much more than just a trophy to him.
Athene saw her brother's grief and was moved to tears herself,
so she caught up the girl's soul and made a new vessel for it,
giving her a spider's body so that she could continue to weave
and be the grape's lifelong companion.
And Dionysos picked her up and carried her to his vineyard
and set her up there to be Queen of the Fields.
So when you see a spider creeping along the vine,
nestled tightly beneath the green covering of its leaf,
hunting even yet the vermin that would devour the young plant before its
    time,
remember this story and the power that love has to triumph over the grave.

ALTHAÍA

His lips taste of wine as they kiss in a room gone dark.
How long have they been doing this?
The lamps were still going when his hand touched hers
while reaching for the pitcher.
Everything is a blurred memory before now,
before the warmth of his body pressed against hers.
It's a strange body,
soft and slender like a woman's
but full of a man's hunger and force.
It's nothing like her husband's body,
all muscle and hair, garlic-sweat and clumsy groping.
This man moves like a panther
and she fears that he will devour her.
But she cannot pull away.
From the moment her husband let this strange man into their home
she was seized by a terrible longing unlike anything she had felt before.
Her husband had sensed it,
though it was secret and black, hidden deep in her heart;
he must have.
Why else had he gotten up during dinner
claiming that urgent, distant business demanded his attention.
She remembers the hurt, weak look in his eye
and the stranger's gloating smile.
She wanted to chase after him,
to assure him that she loved him,
only him, always him.
But when she tried to rise her head was dizzy from wine,
her flesh too hot,
and there was the stranger's predatory grin,
as he reached to take the pitcher.
By the time their hands touched, it was already too late.
And now,
now she thinks that she should be full of shame,
of regret over the life she's wrecked.
But she can't think of anything except the taste of his kisses,
the taste of wine on his lips.

A LAMENT FOR AMPELOS

Of all the satyrs who made their home on the ivy-covered slopes of
    Mount Nysa,
    fairest by far was that thrice-happy youth,
Ampelos of the curly locks.
Though the bashful nymphs fled whenever his brothers came near,
him they never did run from.
They took great pleasure in stroking his soft skin,
bronze from days of lounging in the sun
listening to the sweet song of the birds nesting in the trees overhead.
The lovely daughters of Nysa would smile as they combed
the boy's dark tresses until his hair shone like the midnight sky
gleaming with jeweled stars.
They never tired of hearing his gentle voice sing
of flower-strewn fields and lowing cattle,
nor the handsome young men that watched them,
playing bucolic tunes on an *aulos* to pass the time.
"What next?" The nymphs would ask, hoping Ampelos would spin a tale of
    love,
introducing some modest maiden
or better yet a tree-dwelling nymph
seduced by the hero in the field,
with the cows watching on.
But Ampelos never sang of such things,
nor had he any interest in the nymphs' considerable charms.
What would they have given for just one kiss from the satyr boy?
The entire world and more,
whatever he asked,
no matter how steep the price.
But he never asked.
His heart belonged wholly to another,
the lord of the mountain and king of the tribe of satyrs,
Dionysos of the joyful dance.
And the reason Ampelos was called thrice-happy youth
by all the denizens of that fabled place
is because his love was returned in full by the master of his heart.
Whenever Dionysos ran in the hunt,
chasing the fawns through the dark woods,
Ampelos was there at his side,

giving out the triumphant cry "Euoi!"
They'd lay entwined upon a single couch
while the rest of the Bacchic company feasted through the night,
dancing to amuse the happy couple,
though often they were too busy kissing
and exchanging tender words even to notice.
To impress his beloved Ampelos competed
in all the athletic contests of the satyrs;
none could throw him to the mat or outrun him in a race;
he leapt over bulls with more grace than the rest
and could swim through the lake faster even than the fish.
There was nothing that Ampelos wouldn't do
to gain glory in the eyes of Dionysos,
and even the nymphs,
though full of longing for the boy,
felt no jealousy since the two were so obviously meant to be together.
I wish I could say that they were still;
oh, it pains my heart to tell the next part,
but if Dionysos can bear the sorrow of his loss,
then certainly I must find the strength to carry on.
An evil day came to Nysa: the perfect joy could not forever last.
Ampelos the fair,
the sweet,
the one whom all could not help but love
– he died.
The page is stained with tears. My pen does not wish to write.
It happened so long ago, but the grief is as raw as if it was just yesterday.
But for his sake I will continue and tell it all.
There are different accounts of how it happened.
I don't know which is the truth, so I'll sketch them all in brief.
Some say it was an accident, that Ampelos' foot slipped
when he was about to leap a bull and instead the beast's savage horns rent
his tender flesh and he expired, bleeding in the arms of his beloved.
Others have it that the boy drowned while swimming at night,
with only white-breasted Selene to witness his sad end.
The nymphs found him washed ashore the following morning,
and their wails brought the grieving god to the scene.
Still others say that it was the vengeance of Hera that did him in.
Since she could not touch Dionysos directly
she destroyed that which he loved most in the world
by afflicting Ampelos with a terrible madness
so that he hung himself from a tree.
Another tradition holds that Ares was jealous of the boy
since Dionysos no longer came to his bed,
and so he turned himself into a wild boar
and gored the satyr when they were out hunting one day.
I know other stories as well, too numerous to mention even in brief;
these I have listed seem the most probable so I will end my account here.

It matters not how or even why, just that Ampelos died
and Dionysos was beyond consoling
when he found the mangled remains of his beloved.
He stroked the curly hair out of the boy's unseeing eyes
and kissed those soft lips, gone cold with death, one last time.
They did not warm, no matter how hard he tried to breathe life back into them.
His soul had already flown to the gloomy shores of Haides,
beyond the reach of even a god to retrieve him.
Dionysos implored his father to have him back,
he begged as no god had begged before,
but Haides was unrelenting, even when confronted by heavenly Zeus,
for he had fallen as deeply under the spell of Ampelos' beauty as everyone else,
and refused to give back what now rightfully belonged to him.
Later he was even willing to part with the shade of Semele,
so much had he gained when Ampelos entered his domain.
So all that Dionysos was left with was his tears
and the boy's lovely name upon his sad lips.
That he might never be forgot,
and celebrated in all the lands of the earth,
Dionysos attached that name to his fairest gift to man,
the grape-bearing vine whose tendrils resemble the dark locks of the boy
who, though mortal, owned the heart of an immortal.
Up until that time the plant had simply been called after Dionysos,
since it had come to be with his birth
and bore the spirit of the god within its green flesh.
But since that sorrowful day men have known it as *ampelos*, the vine,
and a fitting name it is too, honoring the thrice-happy youth who once danced
on the ivy-clad slopes of Mount Nysa
and knew the greatest love that a mortal has ever felt.
So when you see a vine heavy with plump grapes,
or taste the wonderful wine that is made from it,
hail it by its god-chosen name and honor the one
who gave incomparable pleasure
to our joy-loving Dionysos.

DA-PU-RI-TO-JO PO-TI-NI-JA

She bit the grape with her sharp teeth
and smiled as its sweet blood spilled out over her lips.
The sun was warm on her skin as she lay
with her head in his lap and he stroked her dark hair fondly, absently,
watching the blue-green waves beneath
and the spiraling gulls overhead,
as they sailed past Naxos, far away from Crete.
Her thoughts were elsewhere as well,
back in the dank, cool cavern beneath the earth
where the only light came from smoky torches.
The sun hurt her eyes now,
but she would get used to it over time.
That's what he had told her
when he let her eat the fruit from his hand.
"I'll make you my queen,
and set your crown among the stars for all to see."
That's what he said,
but she barely heard his words
over the sound of the strong heart beating in his chest.
The sound was strange to her ears;
mostly it was just dead things that found their way into the labyrinth.
But his eyes were brighter than any flame,
and full of destructive fury;
upon his head were great savage bull horns
for the tearing of flesh,
and there was something dark and mad and dangerous about him,
a spirit not unlike her own.
So the girl accepted his offer,
leaving the name her mother had given her behind in the shadows
to become his all-holy queen,
the mistress of wild things and mad-women,
the bride of the ivy and the grape.
What exquisite pleasures,
what bizarre spectacles she had to look forward to
now that he had set her free.
And the best part was
he'd known exactly what he was doing.
That's why he did it.

It was worth enduring the sun
to see where all this would lead.

THE MARRIAGE OF DIONYSOS AND ARIADNE

They say that on a certain summer night
   when the warm winds drive the waves crashing
   onto the shores of rocky Naxos,
if you listen carefully you can hear an invisible choir singing,
the sound of phantom drums,
and pipers playing a long forgotten tune.

Some fishermen from the *taberna*,
deep in their cups,
have even reported seeing a strange old ship
with green vegetation in place of a sail
and dolphins following close behind –
though when they rowed out to get a better look
the whole thing vanished before their astonished eyes.

A foolish tale to be sure,
told in the hopes of more ouzo –
but if you ask the washerwomen they'll make the sign of the cross,
checking to be sure that none of the locals are listening.
Then, in hushed and nervous tones,
they'll tell you of the demons they've seen.

Shaggy-legged creatures with Satan's horns upon their heads,
shambling over the rocks and dancing in the moonlight
like some drunken *geros*.
They laugh and howl and make obscene gestures,
beckoning the chaste women to join them
in their debauched infernal revels.

These devils aren't alone.
They're joined by beautiful *neráïda* in gowns of white,
shimmering like the moon,
who litter the beach with fragrant-smelling flower petals
that disappear come morning –
though the intoxicating scent lingers on long through the next day.
Wild beasts walk tamely behind them
with gay colored garlands draped about their savage necks.

And other things are present too,
a host of half-glimpsed shapes
who have no faces behind the primitive masks they wear.
They raise such a hellish racket
that it makes the women think they're going out of their minds –
yet the dancing is so lovely that they dare not look away.

Always this is where the story ends;
they'll tell no more nor hazard a guess
as to what brings this fantastic troupe to their island
or what sort of things these spirits get up to
on that certain summer night
when the warm winds drive the waves crashing
onto the shores of rocky Naxos.

ARIADNE AND DIONYSOS IN EGYPT

Ariadne lays with her head in the lap of Dionysos,
her *kohl*-darkened eyes growing heavy with sleep
from the gentle motion of the waves as they sail up-river.
Only the light breeze in from Eunostos and the gauzy sheath dress she wears
makes the summer heat at all bearable.
But she does not mind. She has lived in Alexandria long enough
that she has grown accustomed to linen instead of wool,
palm-sandals on her feet replacing leather buskins,
and the sensuous sound of the *sistron* which is heard more often
than the clamor of the wild *tympanon*.
Now she drinks wine from the vineyards of Panopolis
and hardly remembers the taste of the Lesbian vintage.
These days she holds the *ankh* in one delicate hand and with the other
strokes the head of the temple's tame serpents
– serpents so like the ones she left behind in Crete –
and she smiles as the bald-headed priests kiss the earth before her
and burn the most fragrant incense from *Ta-Netjer* on her altar
reciting the daily liturgy in their odd but musical Egyptian tongue.
She quite enjoys these novelties –
the brightly plumed peacocks that run free in the forecourt of the temple,
the gold and precious stones that decorate everything,
far more ornately than in the Greek style.
The exotic perfumes and lush fabrics from far off places,
brought to Egypt by foreign traders.
The fatted geese they kill for her, and the plump melons and local
honeyed figs they provide her with as offerings.
Not to mention the strong *zythus* that she never got in Hellas!
She is glad that her husband brought her with him to Egypt.
It took some getting used to at first,
especially the other gods with their hawk and cat and crocodile heads.
But it wasn't that strange she supposes.
After all, Dionysos first came to her as a bull in the labyrinth,
long before he found her abandoned and disgraced on Naxos.
And now even her father-in-law wears the ram's horns
and Hermes can be seen haunting the *nekropoleis* disguised as a dog.
This land has been good to her, she thinks.
Its Kings, if you trace them back far enough,
came from her husband's loins,

and they have never forgotten that.
They build ornate temples for the couple,
and put on lavish processions with giant statues made of gold –
so large they have to be wheeled through the streets on carts!
And the statues pour wine like fountains, and dispense bread and coins,
mechanical marvels worthy of Daidalos himself,
whom she knew in her youth.
The Egyptian Kings personally oversee her husband's cult
and have themselves initiated into his mysteries,
proudly bearing his ivy-leaf tattoo.
They fund dramatic competitions in his honor
and have even given over large parts of the fertile farmland to growing grapes.
No other kingdom in all the earth honors Dionysos and his bride
the way that Egypt does, and in return he grants them abundance, and wealth,
and all the sensual pleasures of earthly existence:
tryphe as the Greeks would say.
It is for that very reason that they are now sailing along the Nile,
so that Dionysos may spread his blessings throughout the land,
from glorious Alexandria to the furthest reaches of the *khora*.
Ariadne has come along because she likes the crowds
and enjoys seeing the sights.
But most of all because there is no pleasure greater
than lounging in the lap of her beloved.

PEACOCK BACCHUS

Amused, the tipsy satyrs pause in the midst of their
wine-pressing to watch the plump baby Bacchus ride through
sitting proudly astride his peacock mount,
oblivious to the bird's frantic squawks as it darts
this way and that over the sandy shore,
the young god's delighted squeals lingering long after.
"Ho ho!" laughs Seilenos, "Look at him go!"
in between mouthfuls of juicy grapes fed him
by one of the lovely Kanopic nymphs
dark-haired and dusky-skinned.
They watch the peacock vanish into the distance,
racing off to the western desert wastes
and Zeus only knows where else.
Then Seilenos claps his hands and says,
"Back to work, my boys! Those grapes aren't gonna stomp themselves!"

HYMN TO DIONYSOS, FATHER OF THE PTOLEMIES

Dearest to me of all things in heaven and earth is the Lord of the Vine,
the ivy-draped son of Semele and the Loud-thundering Zeus,
King Dionysos who rides at the head of an army of satyrs and mad-women,
bringing peace to the eastern countries
and joy to the care-worn hearts of mortals everywhere.
His arrival in the land unleashes the floodwaters of the Nile,
transforming barren soil into fields of golden wheat
and orchards of lush fruit to fill the bellies of the hungry multitude.
Likewise he pours out a river of wine to inspire the frenzied poets
and light the fires of lust in the hearts of lovely maidens.
Beside him stands his chosen representatives,
the great ancestral spirits who govern in the underworld
as they once ruled on earth,
the divine sons of Dionysos,
the bull-loving kings of Alexandria.
It is proper to begin with the founder of the dynasty,
Ptolemy whom men called Savior.
Unparalleled in wisdom and courage,
he fought by the side of Alexander and claimed all Egypt
as his spear-won prize.
He set the kingdom to right,
abolishing the rule of the foreign oppressor
and campaigned to retrieve the treasures of the gods from barbarian hands.
In return the gods blessed him with power and wealth and a lengthy, happy life.
None of his contemporaries ruled for as long as he did
or saw their kingdoms prosper as much as his.
If any man could be called blessed by the gods,
surely it was him!
His son carried on in his ways, ruling with justice and wisdom.
He used the wealth of Egypt to good effect,
building fine homes for the gods,
strengthening her armies,
and feeding those who hungered.

He made the House of the Muses to flourish,
winning Alexandria undying fame as a center of learning and a home of the arts.
His dear sister was recognized as a goddess in the flesh,
the very image of Aphrodite,
who protects the lovesick and those lost at sea.
Euergetes is justly famed for his good deeds and prowess in war –
he extended the borders of Egypt beyond what they had ever seen before.
While battling the Syrians for their impious crimes,
his lovely wife dedicated a lock of her hair to the gods
to see him safely returned home.
This gift was transported into the heavens for all to witness,
an immortal monument to the power of love.
The fourth Ptolemy, who loved his father,
was keen to promote the worship of his great ancestor Dionysos,
and gained a reputation for his gentle soul and pleasure-loving ways.
The fifth Ptolemy was like a god manifest,
and dedicated himself to doing the work of the gods.
He built many fine temples and gave much wealth to the priests,
and through the record of his deeds a great miracle was wrought,
making it possible for men to decipher the holy letters of Egypt once more.
The other Ptolemies I honor too,
though their accomplishments were often marred by trouble at home and abroad.
Much blood was shed by them, including blood of kin –
and some fell victim to their own mad excesses.
But not everyone can be as virtuous as Soter or wise as Philadelphos –
and so they found other ways to make their mark in the history books.
The maddening blood of the wine-god flowed through their veins,
and often this proves too much for a mortal man to bear.
Auletes was the most Dionysian of all,
and perhaps should have been a mystic poet instead of king.
But even so, he tried his best to do right by the crown,
and there is an important lesson to be learned in that.
And now I come to the last of the line,
the greatest of the Ptolemaic Queens,
Kleopatra the young goddess who loved her father and loved her homeland.
Unrivaled in beauty and wisdom and courage,
she set out to make Egypt great once more.
The scourge of Rome,
who nearly brought mighty Octavian to his knees,
she is an inspiration to all who have come after.
Beside her in the halls of the gods
stands her loving husband Antony,
who walked in the shadow of Dionysos
and would have made a great Pharaoh,
equal in prestige to Soter, had things gone just a little differently.
He fought like a lion and reveled like a satyr

and at the end he met his fate with gallant indifference.
Their memory shall endure for all time,
those tragic lovers,
and I hold them dear to my heart, noble Kleopatra and passionate Marcus.
Just as you are first,
so are you last in my affection O Lord Dionysos,
whose spirit fills my body on oracular nights,
who urges me to run wild and free and dance until my body is bathed in sweat.
You have torn me to pieces and built me back up in your image,
frenzied my mind with the revelation of your mysteries,
and consumed me in the flames of your passion.
My heart, my mind, my body, my soul —
every part of me belongs to you,
to use as you see fit,
my master, my lover, my god!

A FEAST OF FLAGONS

You wonder why I drink,
    as you sneer at me with contempt.
    Well, woman, I drink to forget,
because remembering is too painful.
Once we were young, and you loved me.
At least I thought you did
– but that was so long ago
and there has been so much wine since then,
who can say anymore?
You were my Ariadne,
more lovely than all the women at court,
and I had eyes only for you.
I longed for nothing but to lay my bull's head in your lap
and feel your soft hands run through my shaggy hair.
I fancy you thought me your Dionysos,
a conquering god in mortal flesh
come to set your soul free like a mainad reveling on the hill.
But you never thought that, did you?
Or if you did, it quickly passed in the face of harsh reality.
Soon all you could see
were my endless faults,
how many fears gripped my soul,
how dull my spirit was when the god was not animating it.
I needed your faith to light the fires within me,
to become what I had the potential to be.
But all I got was your contempt instead,
or worse than that, cold indifference.
So the god remained dead inside me,
unroused by his mad-woman.
I tried to do it myself
through strong drink
through dance
through passionate prayer.
But I am clumsy-footed,
my faith is weak,
and I ended up just a sorrowful drunkard,
drinking now to forget what I might have been,
or that look in your eyes whenever you see me anymore,

or what I've done to this god inside me.
He deserves better than this,
and I want to free him
but I haven't the strength to hang myself
or open up my veins.
So instead,
each night,
I drown myself in wine,
hoping that tomorrow will be the morning I fail to wake.

THE ORACLES OF PTOLEMY PHILOPATOR

L isten closely, for the king has much to say.

I.

It is trauma that leads to greatness.

A mirror is what made Dionysos tumble into many.

Wine is poured into a *skin*.

The king is the one who weaves it all together.

The Many in their time and place.

The empty pocket will be the Recipient.

Will she see me as Dionysos or a drunkard?

The answer is yes. Always.

Trauma is what creates greatness.

II.

A Satyrika.
An oracle.

I have decided on the method of my death: by drowning, at 54, in the Willamette.

The songs of this land are the new holy songs.

I saw the American Dionysos,
Jim Morrison-faced,
dancing like a buffalo across the plains
his birth celebrated with fireworks and booze.

Do you know the land?
The flowers? The Trees?
The River?

The nymphs are responsible for wealth;
Hermes provides the music:
it is Aphrodite who soothes the Bacchic Dionysos.

I wonder if Ptolemy Philadelphos had the Hebrew Scriptures translated into Greek because he believed that the Jewish god is Dionysos?

Dionysos did not come quietly into the world.
A clap of thunder,
the roar of flames,
anguished cries
heralded his arrival.

This is what it's like inside my mind.

Isn't it great that we can hide behind our fictions while we reveal our truths?

III.

When it comes to Dionysos always sacrifice in threes.

Strange smells: the sign of worship.

Tweets are like oracles from the god. Brief, enigmatic and absurd. But it is true: who has not heard of birds of omen?

You cannot properly rave without *oreibasia*.

Descent and ascent: ultimately both ways are the same. *Ultimately.*

The River. The Makedonian star. Flowing forth. Dionysos. Dionysos!

It is not I who says this, but the wine. The Wine!

The ground waits. Wet and waiting for me. From my body will come the flowers and the grapes you eat and drink as wine. Drink up!

Dionysos says that these are my mysteries, for you to see:

The deer torn apart.
The phallos erect.
The goat singing at night.
The bull roaring.
The spider on the grape.
The tomb of the bull, with Egyptian writing on the wall.
The ivy wrapped around the oak tree, struck by lightning.

The mask handed to you by the skeleton.
The crown of stars.
The flowers.
The Queen given to the god by her husband in the ox-shed.
The white snake at the base of the tripod.
The torch in the hand of Hekate, the first mainad, the mistress of the hounds of hell, as she searches for what was lost.
The ghosts gathering about, chalk-faced.
Hermes lifting the goblet of wine to his lips, smiling.
The crows and ravens leading the way of the hunting god.
The mask. It always comes back to the mask. And the dancing panther, in mainad form, to a lesser extent.

Do you understand? Do you, really?

There will never be another one like you, one who can do the things you do.

Open the door and walk within and you will find yourself in the palace of wonders.

Dithyrambos, who entered the door twice. Once, as a god. Then as a king.

Remember: the wine must be poured out in offering, ever and always. This is what keeps the machinery of the world running.

Without Dionysos, what have you got? Nothing. Nothing. Nothing.

Never forget, for the memory is the life.
Except when you must eat from the white tree. The mushroom. Then drink of the cool waters of the well.

Persephone weeps.
Ariadne laughs. Coldly, cruelly.
And Hekate searches.

But where is Aphrodite?
Oh, she's in the garden. Taste the fruit she offers. It is sublime.
The life of the gods, for Dionysos.

The snake wrapt around the giant phallos, the true tree of life.
And the goblet of wine, our redemption.

I'd like to have another kiss, one last kiss before I must go. But have no fear: we will meet again, in the place where your freedom lies.

IV.

We live in a world created by Alexander the Great,
who was possessed by Dionysos.

Do you understand what this means?
Do you?

India, the land of incense and spices and people,
oh, so many people!
But they had ivy. That's one thing they had going for them.
And the dances of Dionysos, the Destroyer. That's another.

The ancient world and the modern are happening simultaneously.

I don't care what you believe; it is true. The god is real. His myths are unfolding, all around us.

Olympias making love to a serpent: this is a mystery.

So, too, Ariadne on the beach of Naxos, ready to kill herself before the Lord comes to save her.

And the spidery Erigone, hanging from the tree.

It's too late, and yet still he tries. That's what he does,
he who is poured out with the wine,
he who makes us mad,
makes us sublime.
The god who wears a mask;
the god who is in the king.

I am the king, the mask worn by Mainomenos Dionysos
who is taking his last breath as he sinks beneath the waves.
In the distance, the sound of Lykourgos' taunts.
Soon he shall get his just reward.
But before then, there is the drowning
and the soothing arms of large-breasted Thetis
who looks so very much like Ariadne,
though I do not know her yet.
In time I will. It is destined.
And her crown will shine in the heavens forever after.

Before then, though, there is the urn in which the bones of Akhilles will be stored,
when it is time for him to taste the sweet waters of Lethe.
No dog will gnaw his bones,
because Aphrodite is there to protect him,
as she protected Hector.
That is her job, as well as love,
she who dances upon the tomb.

Oh, I am dizzy. Bromios spins me round in the revel,
screaming from the top of the mountain as the mainades dance

and tear the fawn to pieces.
I see it all, that is why I am dizzy.
His wine reveals the past, the future,
and what is happening before my face right now.

Oh, Arsinoë, why do you spurn me?
Your ancestor would not have done so.
I know, because I have made love to her while the panther danced
and the hawk cried and the goat capered on the hill,
Banebdjedet.

The wife of the god,
stolen on the festival,
is what makes the grape ripen.
Do you understand this mystery?
If you don't, then the mask is meaningless to you;
likewise the child taking his first sip of wine
and the ghosts dancing,
driven into a frenzy by the bull-voiced drums.

It is all true!

Io euoi!

The god is great!

Dionysos dances forever,
his feet making grape-pulp of his enemies.
The blood nourishes the earth,
the wine tastes of ghosts.

I know these things because I am drunk on the god,
so what I say must be true.
How could it be otherwise?
I wear his mask. I am his son.
Look at my phallos and you will know me.

Will you be my Ariadne?
Will you love me and restore me?
Will you see the bull horns on my head,
I who am the king,
the ruler of the Two Lands?
How can I rule without you by my side,
my Arsinoë?
my Ariadne?
my Aphrodite?

I shall wear many faces over the course of time.
Some of them will seem strange,

hard to recognize.
But I trust that you will.
You always have before.
Without you to rouse the *Liknites* how can I rule?
How can I be who I am meant to be?

I am a proud son of Ptolemy,
with blood of Dionysos in my veins.
Taste me. Do I not remind you of the grape
and the bleeding bull
whose voice is heard on mountain top and blackest cave?

Do not tell me your mysteries, for I will reveal them.
It is what I do,
in the fire and the flesh and the dance that never ends.
I cannot even help myself. I've tried, but it does no good.

Io! I shout, Io euoi!

The goat-skin I wear,
and the horns of consecration.
My blood is what makes the flowers blossom.
Goodbye, my love. I will miss you.

Until I am reborn when the new wine is poured out,
when the maiden copulates with the serpent!
Then I will be reborn, only then.
But it will happen. Do not doubt.
Do not fear. It is meant to be.
Have you not read the ancient books,
written by poets drunk on the god's wine?
They tell you everything you need to know,
especially what you need to know about me.
It is absurd, but it is true.
The wine and the wine-drunk poets tell us so.

V.

The drums! Ah, the drums, they compel me to dance,
to be born again in the fire and the sweat and the blood
that comes from the pomegranate.

What is seed without existence? Existence, without the seed?
Impossible!
Dance, dance, dance!

I write this so that I can find my way back
when it is my time to return,
a gift to my future self.

I write this without knowing any of it.
Will it make sense later on?
Or will it be incomprehensible raving?

I hope so. Desperately, I hope so.

The fire flickers. I dance, intoxicated by god.
The toxic poison is in me.
It is what makes all of this possible.

The snake. The bull. The panther. The mask. The phallos. The dance. The
mad-women.

None of it would be possible without the wine.

Or the one hanging in the tree.
Why just one?
Let all the little girls of Athens hang, the bitches.
My power will be manifest in the atrocity.

What great things the god gives to us. What beauty beyond imagining.

Oh Pentheus, oh daughters of Minyas,
even you Lykourgos of the ox-goad,
do you understand the part you play in this drama,
forever the victims of the god for your impiety?
Do you relent, even now, so much later?
No?
Good. It is the part that matters, after all, not who plays it.
The actor is inconsequential,
as long as the suffering
and the triumph of the god
are visible to all.

Oh! Oh! The wine,
the luscious and beautiful grape on the vine.
Isn't it amazing to behold?
A miracle, I tell you.
I can see it, even here in Egypt.
Why can't you?
Ah, you aren't properly drunk, that's why!
Here, drink the god's wine, his blood,
and everything will make sense to you.

It's better now, isn't it?
You're a Jew with the ivy-tattoo of the god on your flesh.
Lucky you.
I did this. I who am revealed through the wrath of the elephant

and the cheetah.
I, the king of Egypt and whatever new land the god chooses to inhabit.

I have said too much.
And yet, I cannot help myself.
I am impetuous with wine.
I am the great phallos carried in procession through the streets of Alexandria.
I am the revealer of mysteries, the dancer,
the one who loves his father even when he is absent,
the Dionysos in mortal flesh.
All this, I am.

Thank you.

There is more I wanted to say. But this will suffice.
Originally Nine Oracles I had for you, but Five will state all
you need to know to inherit the kingdom.
The other Four you must discover on your own,
when the time is right.
This, I leave for you, child of a future generation.
Continue what I have started.
It is your birthright.
Your time to put on the tragic mask
and dance as king of the mysteries.
Remember, though, it always comes back to the phallos.
ALWAYS.

I did this for you. Never forget that.

Trust me. Trust me. Trust me.

ALEXANDRIA, 1910

He lights another cigarette,
a pretext to get a better look at the boy across the room
who is talking with his friends in thickly accented French,
laughing and illustrating his points with frantic gestures.
His hands are like little doves, the poet thinks,
delicate and eager for flight,
pulsing with the uncontrollable energy of youth.
Those hands brush the dark hair from his dark eyes,
stroke the sensual cheek unmarred by age's down,
rest for a moment on the shoulder of his friend
– and the poet's breath catches in jealousy
wishing that it was his shoulder bearing the weight of those divine digits.
He inhales a puff of smoke and lets it out slowly,
imagining that he's kissing the boy's tender lips,
soft as a woman's but full of ephebic vigor.
Such a vision of beauty seems out of place in this drab modern coffee shop.
He, like the poet, belongs to another age
the Alexandria of ancient days,
when the cultured spoke Greek
and lived by Greek ways.
The boy should be reclining at a symposion
with a crown of ivy for those curly locks,
singing a prayer to Dionysos as the torch-flame flickers
on the surface of cups of dark red wine.
All the men would be competing to win the heart of this voluptuous satyr,
even if his fickle affections lasted only through the night.
They would woo him with their philosophical discourses on love
and exquisite metrical verse composed on the spot.
But he would only choose the one who could dance the best,
for a boy like that needs a man who can match his own athletic prowess.
How striking his own dances would be when he performed in the streets
as the Artisans of Dionysos paraded through Alexandria
on the god's festival day.
He'd leap and spin with effortless grace,
pounding his thyrsos in time with the tympanon,
commanding the attention of all the spectators
so that they'd hardly notice the giant statue of the god pass by

pouring wine through some mechanical contrivance.
The crowd would cheer this lovely satyr and toss their garlands for him to catch,
drunk on his good looks and the vitality of his limbs.
The poet sighs, coming back to himself,
and realizes that he's been staring.
The boy noticed and now his friends are making jokes at the poet's expense.
He stabs out his cigarette and quickly leaves the coffee house,
head hung low, weighted down by shame
and regret that he lives in this dreary, barbaric age.

A HYMN TO HERMES DIONYSODOTOS

Once the god Hermes,
    kind and clever-hearted son of Zeus,
    stooped down to pick up the infant Dionysos,
swaddled in cool leaves of ivy to protect him
from the burning remains of his mother,
lightning-wed Semele,
who met her fiery end at the hands of jealous Hera.
But Hera's anger did not die
with the slim-ankled daughter of Cadmus,
and so to protect the young god,
crafty Hermes whisked him off to Nysa,
the mountain that lies beyond the farthest shore,
where nymphs and satyrs cavort on its misty, tree-shaded slopes.
Hermes appeared in their midst,
with the child cradled in his arms,
and the long-haired goddesses left off their stunning dances;
the lazy satyrs got up from sunning themselves on the rocks;
and all came close to see the wonderful gift
that the messenger of the gods had brought before them.
Little Dionysos cooed and lifted up his fists;
the hearts of the nymphs melted and they argued over who would hold him
    first.
Hermes explained to them
how Hera nursed an unquenchable hatred for the child in her heart,
and would pursue him to the very ends of the earth to cause him torment.
But Father Zeus loved his boy,
and wanted to see him grow up into a strong, handsome young god.
So he had charged Hermes with finding a safe shelter for his dear son.
Nysa was so far away that it had escaped even the sight of cow-eyed Hera,
and so Hermes brought him there.
He asked the nymphs to watch over the boy,
to protect and nurture him,
and the nymphs eagerly agreed.
They fed him with milk from their own breasts,
and later on sweet honey and water from their sacred springs.
They sang to him and taught him their dances
and how to play the pipe and drum.
And when he was older he learned to hunt from the satyrs,

and spent his days roaming through the forests,
a friend to all the animals.
At the feet of Seilenos his tutor he learned many things,
and under the care of the lovely nymphs he grew strong and wise
until he reached the full blush of manhood,
and his adventurous spirit led him away from Nysa,
to seek his destiny in the world
and bring mankind wine and mysteries and limitless joy.
So you who love the Bacchic Lord,
do not neglect to honor Hermes as well,
who did such a kindness to him when he was most in need.

HERMES AND DIONYSOS

You lifted him from the ruin of his mother,
    this infant god in swaddling flames,
    held him close as he trembled,
watched as he took in the world for the first time.
You wrapped your traveler's cloak around his tiny frame,
smiled at Zeus' baby boy,
knowing what joy he would bring to care-worn mortals,
knowing the pranks you'd both play,
knowing that you'd dance with him one day,
surrounded by the buxom nymphs and shades of the lonely dead.
You raised your hand over his head,
looked once more into those innocent purple eyes,
and gave Bacchus a goat's form,
tiny horn nubs and a perky tail,
to hide him from the vengeful gaze of cow-eyed Hera.
Ie Hermes! Good friend of my god, I praise you!

GOLDEN VERSES

Oh foolish Midas,
gold-hungry Midas,
has there ever been a man of less sense than you?
You didn't recognize what you had before you,
a magical creature in your rose-garden,
bound with chains of wine.
Did he seem like a hairy vagrant
muttering incomprehensible oracles to himself
or did you intuit that there was something more
beneath that rough, ugly exterior?
Likely not,
otherwise you would have asked him to share his wisdom,
to tell you the secret things of the forest
and the ways of the god made manifest.
Instead you asked him for wealth,
worthless treasure that brings pleasure to the eyes
and nothing else.
Did you ask him this boon because you didn't really believe
that he was capable of granting you anything more,
or is that all your impoverished imagination could dream of?
Soon enough you repented your greedy ways,
your lack of foresight and wisdom,
for true happiness is found in other things:
the beauty of nature,
the smile and laugh of a loved one,
dancing to exhaustion and drinking good wine.
The accumulation of wealth beyond due measure
breeds a thousand noxious worries,
troubles the poor man need never concern himself with.
Worst of all, it is an insatiable hunger
made worse by attempts to feed it.
The more you acquire the more you want
until you are alone,
surrounded only by your worthless trinkets and gleaming trash,
all your loved ones forgot or kept at arm's reach,
a source of distraction,
of constant anxiety.
Are they plotting to take what rightfully belongs to you?

Do they feign affection in order to gain your wealth?
Would they have anything to do with you if not for your gold?
This is no way to live,
as you learned too late.
But at least your sorrowful tale can serve as a reminder
to the rest of us who will not follow in your gilded footsteps.
We, at least, can see that true value isn't found
in the things you carry in your hands
but what lies hidden in the heart.
And when we find a satyr rummaging around in our yard,
we'll know to ask him for the right sort of blessing,
or better yet to set him free without demanding any price,
considering the experience of meeting one of the god's own
boon enough for us.

A POEM FOR DIONYSOS

Follow the shaggy satyr through secret forest paths
   Until you reach the gathering where the nymphs still dance
   Circling round and round in rapturous worship of
King Lusios, crowned with clusters of ripe grapes and green
Foliage, he the master of men's hearts whose tender touch
Unleashes their hidden spirits, freeing them from ego's
Cruel chains to revel in primal purity, feeling themselves not apart but
Kin to all creation. They dance a dance old as time,
Flowing blissful on waves of wine, their every move
Under the control of their god, whose heartbeat is heard in the
Clangor of drum and pipe and wailing barbarous shouts.
Keep the memory of this moment in your heart, how it
Felt to touch the divine and be touched by him in return, the
Unspeakable ecstasy of dissolving at his feet, your fears and
Concerns, your fragile, broken, imperfect parts melting away in his
Kiss and the way he stroked your cheek, saying:
Follow me, my child, and I will make you whole again,
Unbelievable as it may seem, and teach you to be free.
Child, my path is not easy: it will cost you everything to be mine.
Knowledge of this sort is a heavy burden – though ignorance is heavier – and
Freedom, real freedom, is never easy. But
Unless you walk this path, you will be like a dead man,
Close to living, but not really. How empty the other way seems,
Kept apart from the source of life. Never to
Feel the heart in your breast thunder with excitement,
Ugliness all about instead of the beauty of the mountain -
Crisp snow beneath your feet and the smell of pine in the air -
Knife-sharp pain and transcendent joy, these two sides of one coin.
Feel everything, and feel it intensely!
Understand this above all else: mine is the path of life,
Child, and everything in it. Leave no sensation unexplored;
Kill what holds you back inside and drink your
Fill from my cup, emptying it and asking for more
Until your lips are stained with wine and you
Cannot recall a time when you were sober.
Keep these commandments of mine and I will bless you, o
Friend of mine!
Up you lift your head, proud to be

Counted among the ivy-clad Bakchoi of
Kissokomes, the ivy-crowned god.
From your wine-drenched lips
Unbidden and incomprehensible
Comes a shout like that made by the mighty
Kine in the field, and in that moment you understand the mystery.

THE SATYR'S LIFE FOR ME

You look down your smug noses at us,
    call us ugly and lazy and good for nothing,
    but we, the much-maligned race of Satyrs,
dwellers in the green forest and happy vineyard,
know a thing or two of which we're justly proud.
First, of all the inhabitants of this broad earth,
we accepted the ivy-crown of the Lord Dionysos,
giver of many good things,
and danced in his holy rites,
even before he had set out from Nysa.
There was no need for harsh compulsion,
no fighting against the god until blood stains kingly halls.
We saw clearly his divinity,
and the wonderful things he's capable of.
Before anyone else we tasted the rich wine that soothes all cares,
and our lips have never been dry since.
What virtue is worth boasting of more than this?
I can't think of a single one
and yet I can easily call to mind a great many other things
to the credit of our race.
Certainly we are accomplished sleepers,
especially when our bellies are full of wine
and the sun beats down hot and heavy from the noontime sky.
We have but to close our eyes
and then we're drifting upon the waves of sweet dream.
Show me a man equal to us in this regard,
and him I will highly esteem.
Likewise we are famed for our skill in devouring a feast.
The more food you put before us
– and it doesn't matter what; we are not a discriminating people –
the more we can make it disappear.
Our stomachs are vast as the stupidity of man;
some say they are bottomless, though I find that hard to believe.
But I've never yet met my match at the table,
nor have any of my brethren,
so perhaps there's something to the rumor after all.
If you want a dirty joke
or a song to make maidens blush,

you well know where to come.
I myself have composed a grand epic
– a thousand lines of hexameter verse no less! –
on the lofty subject of heroic farters.
Aye, the crafty Odysseus did it,
and so did the petulant son of Thetis.
But the one who broke wind the best,
was undoubtedly the king of far-famed Argos,
Gorgon-slaying Perseus.
Nor is knowledge of history
and proficiency in the ways of the Muses
our only virtue
– though I challenge you to find one better than us! –
but we have been well-trained in the gymnasium of Eros as well.
All the ladies pant and snort when we come near,
trembling at the sight of our masculine beauty
and incomparable endowments.
(My own is so big that I can wrap it
round my middle like a belt
three times over, with plenty to spare.
Care to see for yourself?)
Sure, they run fleeing into the woods
or gird themselves with serpents
and the savage, pinecone-tipped thyrsos.
But this is just to excite our lust through the chase.
And finally,
when they are worn out from running and collapse,
like the heavily-breathing fawn pursued by blood-hungry Artemis,
placidly giving us consent to do our business,
they are awed by how little time it takes
to commence the great mystery of Aphrodite.
Lesser souls labor long in the affair,
lavishing attention upon their paramour,
but not us!
We're in and out of there
and oftentimes it's over before we've even begun.
Likewise we're quick to run
on the gory, blood-drenched battlefield.
Others may rush towards the bronze-helmed foeman,
but we've actually got brains in our heads
and so go the other way.
They do not follow after us;
indeed, they're often doubled over in laughter
at our fearful stumbling and our womanly screaming,
which takes a great deal of practice to master, I might add.
Some might find such behavior shameful,
but I don't much care.
Glory may come to those who die in defense of their country,

but the poor souls aren't around to enjoy it, now are they?
Me, I'd much rather live
to drink and feast and dance another day.
So go ahead and feel your haughty disdain,
but remember what Sextus said;
your way is not the only way,
and perhaps the things you honor, we reproach.
What good is all your wealth, after all,
if you've got no time to enjoy it?
You certainly can't eat all that shiny gold you pile up.
(It's quite bland, actually: I know, because I've tried it.)
Nor is your home with its broad court
any better at keeping the rain off one's head
than my humble cave
or the thick-leaved boughs of the trees
beneath which I slumber.
You can't leave your job,
no matter how vexing it is to your spirit,
unless you want to be out on the street
and watch your wife and child go hungry.
But me, I've got no attachments,
nor any dependents to speak of.
(Maybe they're out there somewhere,
just let them try and find me.)
I'm free to go where I want
and to do as I please.
So I ask you, fair sir,
which of us is truly better off?
In my opinion there's no real question.
For ever and always,
it's the Satyr's life for me!

SOTADEAN VERSE

What marvelous children Dionysos had:
    Wine-face and Grape, Intoxication and Initiation,
    Madness and Luxury – but the dearest of them all
would have to be old Lampsakene Priapos.
The others went on to become kings over great lands,
agriculturists beyond compare,
daimones honored in the holy rites of their father.
But everyone, mystic or not,
reveres the upstanding, unflagging protector of the garden.
They say that even though you can worship him alone in your room,
it's always much better with a crowd.
Lusty young men salute him when he's near,
and blushing maidens fall to their knees in homage,
for without him our whole race would perish,
and what's more, we'd never have any fun at all!
Granted, he's not much to look at
and pops up when least expected
demanding our immediate, unwavering attention.
And even when you give it
(and especially then!)
he makes a terrible mess.
But he's good in a tight spot
and comes with his own libations in hand,
which is more than you can say for certain other gods.
His favorite birds are the male chicken and members of the *hirundininae*
    family
though anything with a lovely tail will catch his eye,
for he's a pricky not a picky god.
In the dark all flesh is one,
all cries sound alike,
so climb on top and let him take you for a ride.
And if you're lucky he'll do it again in half an hour!

HYMN TO PRIAPOS

I sing of Priapos,
   but without the aid of the Muses,
   for those chaste goddesses turn a blushing cheek as he comes near,
ambling along with that great thing between his legs.
The son of Dionysos is a friend of man,
for he stands firm in the garden,
and under his careful gaze
corn grows ripe on the stalk,
and fruit swells with life's sweet juices.
He watches out for thieves,
half hoping that they try to pluck the fruit in his garden,
for then he'll have a chance to pluck their fruit.
Ass, cunt, mouth – it matters not to him,
so long as his cock finds a home within their warm bodies.
Ha, I told you my verses would be crude,
but what did you expect for an ugly god made of fig-wood?

THE PROPHET OF DIONYSOS

The stranger entered the city at dusk,
    a wild man with madness in his eyes
    and drunk on much wine.
He wore the clothing of a distant land
and his hair fell in unruly tangles to his shoulders
which bore the weight of a massive serpent
that hissed as he danced and shouted strange things.
"I have come among you to teach you the ways of the god!"
He cried, eyes rolling back in some sort of bizarre trance.
"Ask not the land of my birth nor who my illustrious ancestors were.
I know only the forests and mountains of the wild one;
my people are they who go mad in his honor
and dance the sacred dances that bring healing to the land.
I will teach them to you,
and teach you how to throw off the shackles of your slavery.
You do not know who you are.
You do not know what great things you are capable of,
what miracles and more than miracles are possible
through him that gave us wine as a remedy for our sorrows!"
He spoke of many strange things then,
things that the people had never heard of before,
things that scandalized their ears,
and above all he spoke of the wine and the dance that sets you free.
The men laughed and mocked his queer enthusiasm.
They said he was a superstitious fool,
a womanly freak with his long hair and soft garb.
But then they saw the effect he was having on the women
– their own wives and daughters, no less –
and suddenly they changed their tune.
The women watched the stranger shout and dance,
enthralled by the spectacle.
Their eyes grew large, their mouths hung wide,
and their bodies began to sway to the rhythm of his words,
to a music the others could not hear.
There was something uncomfortably sexual about it all.
They flushed and touched their sweating cheeks;
they moaned and shook and rushed to be near him.
Some threw off their veils and modest attire,

trampling these into the dust under their delicate feet.
Others clapped and shouted and sang with a wild frenzy.
When the men saw this happening
they tried to grab the women and hold them down.
It did no good.
With a strength they'd never shown before,
the little things easily knocked down their would-be captors
and ran to join the stranger.
They danced beside him and threw themselves at his feet.
They howled the name of his god so loudly
that he could no longer be heard over the tumult.
Some brave men strode forward to break the shameful dancing up
and beat some sense into this golden-tongued stranger.
They never reached him.
The women fell upon them like ferocious beasts,
shrieking and biting and clawing at those
they had called husband, father and fellow-citizen mere moments before.
All was forgotten in the frenzy of the stranger's god.
Terrified, the men were driven back
to the crowd of mute spectators.
Many could not bring themselves to witness the vile license
that the women had so freely given themselves up to.
They hid in their homes,
hands to ears,
desperate to block out the sounds of savage celebration.
Other men, however, made no effort to stop the women
inspired with the frenzy of the stranger's god.
Indeed, these men gladly joined them in the dance
and were accepted as fellow-revelers.
They cared not for the mockery and disdain of others;
they had learned a better way through the snake-bearing stranger.
Eventually he gave the call,
saying it was time to head for the hills and forest
where the god with bull's horns made his home.
And he led the mass of mad revelers out of the city,
far from their homes and all they had previously known,
never to return.
Where they went and what they saw when they got there
is not for me to say.
It is a mystery which only the mad-ones may know.
But all those called out by the stranger are still there,
dancing the holy dances of their god,
though many centuries have passed
and the cities they once knew
have turned to rubble and dust.
This much you may know and be certain of.
So when the stranger comes to your city,
do not reject or mock him.

Do not try and stop those he calls out,
even if you have no desire to be counted among
the glorious revelers of gladsome Dionysos,
for the god is great
and great too his prophet
who once, so very long ago,
steered a ship on the Etruscan sea.

I COULD NEVER LOVE A WOMAN WHO WASN'T A MAINAD

I could never love a woman who wasn't a mainad,
at least half mad, with a poet's heart.
A woman who would never wear a bridle, even mine – or ask me to.
I want a woman who's drunk on god, who has felt her soul swell like a
pregnant woman's belly at the touch of the divine.
I want a woman who can blow my mind by saying things like,
"I can describe the Mysteries in one word: fuck."
I want a woman whose eyes look back upon ancient days, and whose lips
always taste of wine.
I want a woman who gets up and dances when a good song comes on,
and doesn't care what anyone else thinks.
I want a woman who after long hours of worshiping the god in the hills,
will come back to me smelling of pine trees and damp earth,
sweat and wood smoke, and the crisp night air.
I want a woman who'll push me to the floor, lift up her skirt,
and ride me all night long.
I want a mainad – and no other woman will do.

THE CALL OF THE MAINAD

Will you come to the place where the wild ones are,
away from your home, away from your life,
away from everything that makes you you?
Will you run free with your hair down,
naked feet leaping over rocks and roots
as tree branches whip your skin and you howl into the night?
Will you crawl on your belly like a hissing snake,
like a ferocious leopard;
will you claw the earth and tear the ivy with your teeth?
Will you sit in front of the fire with vacant eyes,
watching the flames leap and dance
until you can see him moving there?
Will you reach out and touch your god without being burned
– will you do it even if it hurts?
Will you dance for him,
with him,
until you can't go on any more,
until your body is covered in sweat, your limbs ache,
your heart is going to burst in your chest,
and your head is too small to contain the madness that swells within:
will you keep dancing anyway?

THE DANCERS ON THE HILL

I dance with my sisters the sacred dance of god. The drum lifts our feet, teaches us the ancient steps which none of us knew, which our bodies have always known. Step lively, sisters, the god is with us. I see him in little Alkesta, the way she stares so intently at nothing, and moves to a rhythm no one else can hear. Oh, and Dika has him too – see her tossing that red mane of hers all about, and the way "Euoi!" rises frequently to her lips. Kleis has him, but with her it's harder to tell. She doesn't step outside the dance, and only makes the ritual shout when the others do. But her dance is a little more graceful than it was before, and the smile on her lips says something's going on. Dionysos is everywhere tonight – in the fire and the darkness beyond, in the drummers and the dancers and the earth beneath our feet. He is that ancient, primal rhythm – older than all the gods, older even than the earth – that brings all things together, together in joy, together in fullness, together in the holy shout of the god! Words do not convey the meaning of god – only motion, that motion given expression in our bodies. Come sisters, let us dance for the god – for it is the best way to honor him!

MAINADES INVOKING THE GOD

What god do we honor here on the mountain? None but Dionysos, the wild and untamed savior who, with his joyous companions, comes bursting over the hill top. He is the bull, can't you see – strong, passionate, fierce, all unbridled power and unconquered spirit. The capering goat is his animal, and the snake in the wicker basket. He is the one who causes the life to quicken, who makes the sap to flow through the branches and the blood to course through our veins. He is the heat of spring, whose gentle touch unfolds the blossom and makes the maidens blush. He is the very spirit of connection, the intimate urge for another warm body, the overpowering need to feel their flesh against yours, their lips pressed against yours, their spirit mingling with yours. He is felt in the rising cock and the heated cunt. Hail god, great is your power! The realm where his power is the greatest is the natural world. He is felt in the rich black earth of crop-lands, and in strong, fruit-bearing trees. He explodes into the world in the riotous colors of the spring flowers, but he is there in the muted hues of fall as well. He looks out at us from the forest, beckoning us to follow him. He is there when trees wave in the breeze and the grass sways under the sun. All the green growth of the earth is his. Though he is in every plant, no plant better represents all his heat and passion than the flowering vine, heavy with bunches of grapes. Take those bunches of grapes in your hands and squeeze them tight, and you will feel the god poured out over your fingers. From those grapes men make wine, and there is no better vehicle for him than that holy drink. Whenever you're drinking wine, you're drinking the god. He jumps into your body with the first sip – by the time you've emptied your cup he's already made his home in your belly. The feeling of warmth and expansiveness, that freedom from restraint, that boldness and flowing speech – all this is the god, all this is Dionysos working within you. But moderation is advised in the drinking, for it is a dangerous draught which often leads to destruction. A little wine brings eloquence, they say, but too much brings madness. But for those willing to expose themselves, god can be found in the madness too. What we mortals consider normal and right and good is so very limited. The earth is wide, and her mysteries deep. Darkness, fear, and suffering – these are the barriers to truth and light and joy, and if we would attain the goal we must first pass through them. But we needn't walk that way alone, for Dionysos can be our guide, a leader through the pathways of madness. He lifts us up, helps us attain freedom, helps us feel joy, helps us experience creativity. Through him our lives are made better, given shape, filled with holiness. He is the goal, the source, the prize that we yearn for all of our lives. He is the bridegroom, and we the bride. Joyous is the wedding of these lost lovers! That, then, is the god that we honor in song on the mountain.

AFTER THE REVEL

My eyelids are heavy, and I feel sleep coming upon me. My limbs are so tired – all night I have danced round the fire in honor of the god, and exhaustion is my sweet reward. Heavy now my limbs and heavy my tongue. Earlier wine loosed my tongue and I chanted the ancient songs with the rest of them – but now it's an effort to speak, and not worth the trouble at that. The world is creeping towards stillness – and we honor the god with quiet during the long hours of the night. Occasionally the fire still crackles as the last embers slowly burn themselves out. Now and then intermittent laughter is heard, and if you listen real hard you can still hear the soft moans as an occasional couple honor the god in Aphrodite's mystery – but these rare noises serve only to remind the rest of us how still and quiet the world is. I find it hard to think anymore – all the wine I drank this evening is catching up with me. My body is awash in the purple waves of Bacchus, a kid I fall into the ocean of milk, I go down tasting the god's sweet honey on my lips. Lord Bromios, carry me away!

EXPERIENCING DIONYSOS

Imagine a moment in your life when you felt most alive, most free, most yourself. When you stopped sleepwalking through things, stopped being in your head all the time, stopped caring what anyone else thought about you. You were aware of every part of yourself: the sweat on your skin, the heat of your body, the hair on your head, the blood pumping through your veins, the soul rising up in your chest. Your heart was thumping so loud you thought it would explode. Your vision was so intense, so clear it was almost painful. You were so full of life it was almost agonizing. You felt like you were seconds away from bursting you were so full. And yet, you didn't care. You wanted more, more, more. Even if it meant your extinction. Because this was the perfect moment. This is what it means to be alive. This is what it's like to experience Dionysos.

AFTER

Pretend no more, my child,
   for you are free now.
      You have drowned your cares in wine
and felt the madness of the god take hold of you.
Having experienced what you've experienced,
how could you ever go back to the way things were
– a life half-lived and dreams unfulfilled?
You crave what only he can give,
your senses aflamed and frenzied by his presence.
You know what's possible and what lies even beyond that.
So don't let yourself go back to sleep,
don't fall for the traps you once escaped.
Take up the thyrsos and dance until your days are done,
and with your final breath howl out his name
so that all will recognize you as one of his own.

QUESTIONS FROM DIONYSOS

Who are you? No, who are you *really*? Not what you do for a living, or how much you make, or what you own, or don't own. Not what religious or political group you belong to, not what hobby you have to take up your time. Not what your parents always wanted you to be, or who your friends think you are, or who you think you have to be when you're around other people. But who you really are, deep in your core, in those dark, hidden parts of your being, those parts made of dream and fantasy and passion. Do you remember who you once were, before it all went wrong, before you made those compromises, before you started pretending to be someone else in order to fit in? Do you remember the way that it could have been, if only? Remember and be who you are.

SECTION III
Stories

"Originally they used to write *satyrika* in honor of Dionysos and stage them for competition. But later on, having progressed to writing tragedies, they turned gradually to myths and historical subjects, no longer with Dionysos in mind. Hence they also exclaimed the proverb *nothing to do with Dionysos.*"
– Suidas s.v. *Ouden pros ton Dionyson*

RUNNING WITH THE APIS

Marcus Antonius pushed open the door to the Queen's private chambers, sending the startled ladies in waiting and guards scurrying off. Even had he not been the Queen's recent husband they wouldn't have opposed him: there was a dangerous, mad quality to his disheveled appearance, and Marcus well knew how to use the sword he carried always belted at his hip.

Marcus stumbled in, slammed the large, ornately wrought door closed and then slumped against it, panting.

Kleopatra glanced up from her work – she was writing a philosophical treatise on the womanly arts of persuasion and cosmetics – and took in his massive frame. Marcus' hair was in disarray, his ivy-crown hanging in tatters from his dark head. His *khiton* – no longer a Roman toga – hung loose about his waist, completely exposing his battle-scarred torso. It was torn and stuffed inside his sword-belt to keep it from falling off of him entirely, and there were plenty of wine stains and muck from the streets covering the once pristine fabric. His chest heaved; he seemed scarcely able to catch his breath. Dark shadows made his face resemble a death's mask. His normal sun-browned flesh seemed pale even in the shadows of her chamber. He frightened her.

Kleopatra rose and rushed to his side. He collapsed into her arms and with great difficulty she managed to walk him over to the bed they now shared as man and wife. He fell back and lay staring up at the ceiling. In a moment of annoyance Kleopatra noted that they would have to get new sheets, because there would be no way to get the filth and sweat out of them now. She lay down beside him, pressing her slender body against his massive frame, and tried not to inhale too deeply.

"Are you okay, my husband? It is late. Where have you been this evening?"

From the looks of him, partying with their friends and then brawls in Alexandria's back alleys. At least he didn't stink of whores. This time. Kleopatra stroked the dark curls out of his eyes; his expression was vacant, haunted. For a moment she worried that he had lost his speech. She sat up and prepared to call for the court physician. Then his gravelly voice boomed in his chest, sounding like a lion's rattling roar.

"I was running with the Apis."

Kleopatra smiled. "No wonder you look exhausted – it is quite a journey from Memphis to Alexandria."

Marcus' lip curled up. "Do not mock me, woman."

Kleopatra went cold at the lethal fury that shown in his eyes.

"I do not understand, my lord," she whispered.

Marcus heaved a sigh. "Neither do I, my love. But it happened nonetheless."

Kleopatra rested her hand on his chest comfortingly, felt its warmth rise and fall beneath her delicate fingers, and then whispered, "Go on. Tell me. I will not laugh."

There was silence for a long while. Neither spoke. The only sound aside from their slow breathing was the guttering of the oil lamp's flame on her writing desk. Then, finally, Marcus spoke, his voice hoarse from thirst.

"I stayed at the dinner-party after you left. The wine was too good, and the conversation even better. We were discussing Dionysos' conquest of India, a topic that has been close to my heart, of course, ever since Ephesos."

"You truly are the New Dionysos, my love." Kleopatra's hand slid down his chest, resting fondly on the swell between his legs. Normally this would have stopped all conversation and ended with them rolling together under the sheets. Instead he seemed not to notice.

"Like your father and Philopator before him."

"Yes." The mention of Auletes brought a sad smile to her lips. She had genuinely loved him, a rare enough occurrence among the Lagides.

"And before them Philadelphos and Soter too?"

"Yes. We are all descendents of Dionysos – his blood has flowed stronger with some than others, however."

"Yes, and that is why you love me – isn't it?"

"It is one of the reasons, yes." Marcus Antonius was not as other men. His passions dwarfed theirs. His spirit loomed larger than other men's, doing things they only dreamed of but lacked the courage to accomplish. Marcus felt things more strongly, was more sensual and decadent than anyone she had ever met – aside from herself. He was given to great kindness and generosity – to all he met, not just his friends – but when provoked to wrath, he was terrible, crueler than anyone had a right to be. If any single mortal exemplified the contradictory excesses of her people's ancestral god – it was this man.

"My whole life has been lived under his shadow. Unconsciously I have acted out his myths through my campaigns, my feasting, my loving, my intense joy – and my volatile wrath. Tonight I finally understand why – and what the Ephesians meant when they gave me that title. I wonder if they even understood how right they were in bestowing that half-mocking epithet."

"I do not understand. What happened?"

"*He* happened – that is what. I met the god tonight, in a way I never have before. During the conversation about the Indian conquest, something stirred within my soul, something dark and ancient. The god within me awoke. I sat there for awhile, drinking, but it was not I who tasted the wine. I watched the drunken revelers, but it was not I who stared out of my eyes – it was the god, and he was wearing my body like a mask. I would speak, but it was not my words that poured out. I was merely an actor, reciting the lines scripted by another mind. The evening passed. More wine was drunk. I could not stop myself; cup after cup was drained by me and I hardly seemed to notice it. The topic changed. They began discussing the charms of the various whores down by the Pharos, and Octavian's intrigues at Rome. I grew bored with their idle chatter. I got up, without so much as a parting word, and fled out into the night, not even stopping to grab my cloak.

"I fled into the darkness, desperate to be alone. Old friends hailed me on the street, asking where I was going. I rushed past, ignoring them. I left the familiar royal quarters of the city, the temples and shops and wealthier districts. I had no idea where I was going; my body carried me along, through dark alleyways and deserted thoroughfares. This city is different at night – it changes as the pimps and thieves and sailors come out. I don't know if they recognized who I was, or if they feared the crazed look in my eye, but none of them hassled me. They stepped out of my way, even when the streets were narrow; they crowded together and whispered as I passed, making warding gestures against the evil that had so clearly taken possession of my soul.

"And they were wise to do so, for I was an animal in human guise, a beast hungry for blood and the crunch of bone beneath my fangs. Had any tarried across my path too long, or tried to give me trouble, I would have been on them in an instant, a ravening beast glorying in the tearing of flesh, the warmth of their blood spraying against my skin, their pitiful shrieks filling the night air. But they knew themselves to be prey and so stayed far from me.

"Finally the dreadful spirit inside me had reached its destination, alone in the night, in an empty quarter of the city, far from the prying eyes of mortals.

"I bent over, trying to catch my breath. At some point I must have been running. I had no idea where I was. Finally I glanced up – and that's when I saw him: the bull. He was huge, his thick black frame blotting out the light around me. He was darker than night, but his eyes glowed more brightly than the moon. His hooves were made of fire, and the earth scorched wherever they touched. Plumes of smoke rose from his nostrils. He was staring directly at me: challenging me. I should have been afraid. He could have easily gored me with his massive horns or trampled me under his mighty weight. I felt no fear; my heart thundered with reckless pride to be in the presence of so majestic a creature. I met his gaze unflinchingly and accepted his challenge.

"I stood up tall, stretching my body out to its fullest. He dwarfed me, and yet I was proud of my masculine frame. I showed my teeth, giving back my own challenge. He snorted once, the sound a rumble I could feel through the earth, accepting my challenge, and then he turned and began to run. I understood immediately: I was to chase him.

"Despite his size, the bull was fast, faster than he should have been. In moments he was almost out of my sight.

"Growling like a wild beast, I gave chase. I had no idea what I would do once I caught him. I was intoxicated with the frenzy of the hunt; it impelled me on, unthinking.

"As I ran, I felt the power of the god stir once more within me. I reveled in the unbridled strength that coursed through my body; the blood pumping through my veins; my muscles stretching as my lithe limbs carried me forward. I knew myself to be a man in that moment, a great man capable of great deeds. I felt alive, in a way that made everything before seem like a pitiful dream. I have had moments where I glimpsed something of what it is to be alive – in battle or while making love – but here it was in its fullness, not just a fleeting image. This all came to me afterwards; at the time there was no room for thought, even thoughts such as these. My mind completely shut down – I was a creature of pure instinct, relying on my body to find its own way through the narrow streets, leaping automatically over rubbish in my way, darting down an alley when the bull changed its course at the last moment. I had no doubts, no troubling questions about my place in the world, I knew exactly why I existed – to catch this bull!

"Everything else fell away, vanished into the darkness, until the world consisted of nothing more than the bull and myself. All I could see was the bull before me, shining brilliantly with life in the shadows. Never before had I seen anything as beautiful as him: not a fleet of ships, not the work of Pheidias, not even you, my beloved. His hulking frame transfixed my gaze. I marveled at how his tautly muscled legs found their way unerringly through the narrow streets with a dancer's agility, those fearful horns which existed for the sole purpose of rending flesh, those glowing eyes in whose depths all the secrets of the world are kept. And I knew that this was no ordinary bull – this was Apis, the god: Apis who contains the abundant fertility of the Nile within him; Apis who makes the grass green, the fruit to swell on the branch, the ripe corn to spring forth that men might have food for their bellies; Apis who fills the women with lust; Apis in whose movement the motion of the cosmos is manifest; Apis, power in its most primal, procreative form. Apis is life itself – and without him, no man rules. Rulership, in fact, is nothing more than harnessing the power of this god and learning to direct it outwards into the world. Without thinking about this, I understood all of it – and I knew that I had to capture the Apis bull. I had to possess him, consume him, *become* him.

"And so, even though my limbs were growing tired from the chase, my heart beating dangerously in my chest, my breath beginning to come with more difficulty, I dug deep and found even further resources of power within myself to continue on. I blocked out the pain. I ignored my aching body. I channeled everything I had into the race – and my focus narrowed even further, thoughts of the race and of my desire to catch Apis falling away until he and I existed alone. Just us. The Apis and I. I and the Apis. As he ran, I ran. As he breathed, I breathed. As he snorted, I too snorted. No longer was there distance between us – we were one soul in two bodies, mirror images of each other.

"And then I understood: Dionysos was the Apis, and I was Dionysos. I was chasing myself, and this race between us was an ancient ceremony, as old as time, and it had been performed many times before, and it would be performed again many times after I had completed it. This is how the King is chosen, how he shows himself worthy to rule. He must race the bull and in the process become the bull himself. The race awakens the sleeping god within him, rouses the bull and all of its bountiful powers into life. Not all who start on the path, however, succeed. They must be able to shut off their minds, trust completely in their bodies, which is where the power of the god resides. If fear or indecision or their doubting mind takes hold, they will fall and be trampled beneath the hooves of the bull. They must permit themselves to exist in the perfect moment of the chase, all else closed off to them. Only then will they discover that they are in actual fact the bull themselves, and understand how to direct the power of the bull into the land to promote fertility and to bring peaceful harmony to the realm. I understood this as I ran without understanding it, and I did not let that knowledge distract me.

"And as I chased the bull I felt the presence of others chasing the bull with me. Your father – and all of your ancestors going back to Ptolemy. And before him Alexander. And before him Theseus and Minos, and the Kings of Egypt, stretching back to the dawn of time. Each had performed this ceremony, some succeeding, others not. And I realized that in some sense, each of us was the same man, running this same race, in the same place, at the same time, and I could feel their thoughts in my head, and knew their experiences to be my own. How many times had I chased this bull, acting out this ancient ceremony? How many times would I do so again, in how many different forms? And then I came to realize that I was no longer chasing the bull through the streets of Alexandria – I was somewhere else, somewhere much older, much darker. I was chasing him through the labyrinth at Crete – and the bull was in reality the Minotaur. Apis was Dionysos and Dionysos was the Minotaur – and I was both the Minotaur and Theseus. And we never got out. We were still in the labyrinth, and always will be. The world is nothing more than the labyrinth and the bull chases himself around in it, dreaming sometimes that he is a monster, sometimes that he is a god, and sometimes that he is a man.

"He dreams himself many different lives, and he lives each one out fully as he dreams it. Some are joyful, some sorrowful, some full of unrivaled glory – others lived in total obscurity. But in every life there is the chasing of the bull, because he desires to know himself. It always comes back to that because all that exists is the labyrinth and the bull. Everything else is just a dream. Everything else except one other – the one who loves the bull, Ariadne, the Mistress of the Labyrinth. She is there dreaming too. And when he is not busy chasing himself through the winding passageways, he seeks her out. And when he finds her, he gives her his crown, places it in the heavens for her, and they love each other, until they fall asleep and forget who they are. But when they awake, they always find each other again, because they are the only two people in existence. Sometimes he wakes first and finds her; sometimes it is she that rouses him from slumber. She was Isis when he was Osiris; he was Haides when she was Kore. As Alexander he found her both as Olympias and Hephaistion. They were brother and sister as Philadelphos and Arsinoë, but that did not stop them from loving each other – and why should it, since they were the only real ones, and all else but a dream? He put her star-crown up in the sky as Berenike's lock. And he has been both Auletes and Caesar – and now me, dear. He has finally reawakened as me – and you are my beloved Ariadne. I would recognize you no matter how much your form has changed. I will love you forever. And when we die and our form changes shape once more, I will seek you out in the labyrinth, no matter what new flesh you wear."

All the while Kleopatra had sat quietly listening to her husband share his mad story at a feverish pitch, the words pouring forth like wine from an upturned vessel. Mad it must be: how could this man be both her father and Caesar, since all three were contemporaries – let alone all the rest of it? She was uncertain what to say to that, but figured that she ought to say *something*, that her continued silence might set him off, and she feared the madness in his eyes. She was trying to find the right words, words that would seem comforting and supportive and not provoke him, when Marcus picked up the thread of his narrative once more, oblivious to her troubled expression.

"It was then that I noticed that the bull was no longer in front of me, leading the chase. He was nowhere to be seen in fact. I was running wild through the streets, alone as I must be alone in the labyrinth. I slowed down to a trot and then a leisurely stroll and finally came to a stop altogether. I found myself somehow in Rhakotis – what winding path or twist of fate had led me here I could not say. I made my way up to the great temple of Serapis there. The forecourt was abandoned, naturally enough since the hour was so late, but I stood outside and stared up at the massive edifice and the ancient statues that lined the path up to the temple doors, a mixture of Greek and Egyptian, as everything in this city is a hybrid of the two.

"I was out of breath, my body exhausted from the run, my clothing torn and falling off of my body from stumbles I do not remember taking. My mind was reeling from all the things I had learned. And yet, despite it all, I had never felt so alive, so full of wild energy, so unabashedly a man. The pulse of life echoed in my ears – not just my life, but all life. I could feel the priests inside the temple, some sleeping, others rousing themselves in preparation for their morning duties in the sanctuary. I felt the lives of all the people nearby, safe asleep in their beds, dreaming or stumbling home from a night of revelry. And I felt you, so far away here in the royal palaces – beautiful and shining more brightly than all the other lives.

"And I felt all these individual lives, thin streams, flowing together into a single great river, and I realized that the Nile is the earthly image of the spiritual river of life. And when the spiritual river wanes or grows sluggish, the earthly Nile recedes – but when the spiritual river is strong, the Nile overflows its banks, flooding the earth and filling it with bountiful life. And it is the duty of the King to make the river strong, through his person, through his power, through his ability to direct and control others. He must do things to promote life, to enhance the lives of his subjects, to make them whole, healthy, and vibrant – communing with the gods of life, the source of life, in order to add to the streams that flow into the great spiritual river, making it bountiful so that the earthly river, too, will become bountiful. This is the sole function of the King – he exists for no other purpose, and no other can perform this duty, for the King stands midway between gods and mortals. He is the bridge between the worlds, uniting the two lands within himself. The running of the Apis is how he proves himself – but it is also how he channels the energy of life, making it flow and move, making the two rivers that are one race along their course and flood the earth, infusing it with life and bringing forth its material bounty in the form of the fruit and grain and newborn animals. Wherever his feet set in the race, life springs up.

"And how is this possible? Why can the King do this – and no other? Because the King is dead. (As he races with the Apis, he is racing with death. The labyrinth is just a dream too: in reality, the bull-god-man is laying in the underworld, a corpse.) The dead, too, reside midway between gods and mortals. The King is a vessel for the dead, who dwell within him. Inside the King are all the thousands upon thousands of the dead – they direct his every thought and action. I understood this as I stood before the great Serapeion. I understood what Serapis is: he is the dead King, the King of all the dead. The spirits of every Apis bull, the spirits of all the Kings that have come before, they are united in Serapis, combined into a single living form, for Serapis is the tomb of the Apis, the living bull in death, the dead bull in life. And Serapis is the current King, whoever that is. (Which is why people's accounts of Serapis are constantly changing – for he shifts depending on who embodies him.) And in that moment, I learned so much more about what it means to be King.

"The King is the door through which the dead can act in this world, of which they are no longer a part. He unites the world of mortals with the dead, the realm of the gods with the material plane. He is the pivot of the wheel, upon which all things depend. Through him the prayers of people pass upwards to the gods; through him the blessings of the gods descend to mortals. He must make the way clear – he himself must be pure and fit – because when things are blocked, there are famines and war and suffering and death. Everything in the world is a reflection of what is going on inside the King – and everything within the King reflects what is in the world.

"And that, my beloved, is all that I can say. There was more – oh, so much more! – but I am sure that I already sound a mad-man raving in his delusion. I am tired, my love. So tired."

He collapsed at that, the manic spirit that kept him animated while he poured out his tale in one long, feverish burst vanishing on the wind. His eyes closed, and moments later his breathing deepened and sleep claimed Marcus.

Kleopatra sat beside him, unmoving. She did not wish to disturb her husband – was unsure what strange thing would be unleashed upon her if she did. She felt herself to be in shock, as if a great violent storm had just passed through, uprooting and destroying everything. She wasn't entirely sure what had just happened, how she was supposed to take the marvelous tale Marcus had just relayed to her. Was there something to it? Was he completely insane? Parts of it felt real to her – some of the things he said only a true King of Egypt might know – and a glimmer of hope stirred within her. Though her brother Ptolemy had been crowned Pharaoh, he had never been King. He was a foolish, power-mad boy, who did not understand what the office entailed. But now...she wondered. Did this strange Roman, this profligate adulterer, this violent brute whom she had seduced for power but come to love over time – did he finally understand? He seemed to. And how glorious that would be, for Egypt to have a true King once more. Together they would make the land strong again, drive out the Romans, re-conquer all the territories that her ancestors had claimed...and perhaps more. And yet...other parts of his story seemed utter foolishness to her, bizarre and jumbled ramblings, like one hears from the beggars on the street or the recluses who have spent too long in the Serapeion at Memphis.

War was brewing with Octavian. It was only a matter of time now – and she wondered how Marcus would stand up. He had proven himself on the field of battle numerous times before, in Gaul, Italy, and the East. He had been Caesar's right hand man and chosen successor before that conniving whelp of Atia had schemed his way into the succession. He was a strong, courageous man – but also a man with great weaknesses which crept up from time to time. And what she had seen tonight made her worry all the more. Was he falling apart? Had he lost his mind? How would he ever compete with Octavian, who for all his failings was a shrewd tactician and a deadly opponent to Egypt's interests?

But what if his visions were real?

What if...?

Kleopatra worried, and morning light filled her chamber before sleep finally found her.

THE SIGN

Alexander turned his eyes to the heavens and caught the flight of crows overhead. The sight was strange at first, unfamiliar after days of endless brown monotony. The desert stretched out like an ocean around his men, the sky hardly distinguishable from the sand dunes and distant cliffs.

They'd been wandering, lost in the Libyan wastes, for longer than he cared to remember. His men would have been mutinous if hunger and thirst and total physical exhaustion had not dulled their spirits. It was all they could do to keep putting one foot in front of the other.

He'd been a fool to trust the local guides, though they'd seemed like good, smart men at the time and had welcomed him as a liberator from the yoke of Persian tyranny. But this land was dangerous and deceptive, especially to strangers. Hadn't Kambyses lost a whole army here, on its way to consult the oracle of Zeus-Ammon? Some said even his noble ancestor Dionysos had nearly suffered the same fate with his troop of satyrs and madwomen until the Libyan god sent them a ram to show them the way to the oasis. Afterwards he built a temple and established the oracle of his benefactor, and that more than anything else was why Alexander had to visit the site. There were oracles aplenty in other lands, and he had visited most of them on his trek to Persepolis. But this one was special, for it had been built by Dionysos' own hands.

His whole life Alexander had lived in the shadow of the god, following in the footsteps he'd left in his journey through foreign lands. Alexander wouldn't be happy until he reached the ends of the earth and traveled beyond even where Dionysos had gone.

What did it matter that he'd already surpassed the accomplishments of all the kings and generals who'd come before him when his own divine ancestor's deeds had yet to be matched? Alexander took no pleasure in his Olympic victories or defeating the nations he marched against. They were men of flesh and blood and shit, with the stink of mortality about them. Nothing they did mattered in the end. To prove his greatness Alexander must compete against the very gods themselves, the only thing in this sorrowful world that came near to being his equal.

"Do you see those black birds upon the horizon?" His general Ptolemy said, intruding upon Alexander's brooding thoughts.

The king nodded, careful not to show surprise. He'd half assumed that they were phantom shapes and invisible to others, a delusion born of thirst and weariness. It wouldn't be the first time that such things had revealed themselves to him, while in the desert or before.

"I think we should follow them."

Alexander cleared his dusty throat. "Sent by the gods, you reckon, to lead us out of this Typhon-blasted land like the ram father Zeus sent to guide my great ancestor Dionysos?"

Ptolemy paused for a moment, choosing his words carefully.

"Assuredly that's the case, my lord, and you are wise to discern the hand of Providence behind things. Myself, I had just thought that the birds would show us the way to a hidden source of water, but your explanation is far superior."

THE INITIATION OF IVY

Dorion clenches his teeth against the pain as the priest's knife cuts deep into his flesh, forming the sacred ivy-leaf mark of the god's *mystai*. The blood wells up over the pattern, spilling down his arm like thick, black droplets of wine from a libation bowl. His breathing comes shallow, the world suddenly spinning before his eyes as the priest works the ink into the wound and whispers his secret prayers over it.

He gladly accepts the pain as a final sacrifice given to Dionysos for his initiation. Even so, Dorion momentarily feels like he's going to faint. He's fasted for three days, preparing himself for his initiation. The only thing in his stomach is the large quantity of wine he's drunk tonight during the ritual. The *rhyton* was continuously passed back and forth between the group of new initiates – yet somehow every time it reached his lips it was just as full as when it had left, thanks to the efforts of the assistant-priests.

On top of that he had danced for what seemed like hours on end, until he reached a delirious ecstasy and collapsed to the ground, certain his heart was about to burst through his chest, panting like a wild beast. It was then that the high priest, draped in animal skins, decked with an ivy crown, and his face daubed red with the lees of the wine, stepped forward and proclaimed, "This one is ready now."

Dorion can still hear his fellow initiates dancing outside the darkened chamber – the sound of their feet slapping against the polished flagstones, the clapping hands, the beat of the drum and trill of the pipes driving them on and on, and periodically, the otherworldly cries of the god's women beckoning him to join them.

Dorion's body finds the rhythm and begins to sway to it uncontrollably, something deep inside him responding to the music, his flesh no longer subservient to his mind. The priest tightens his grip on Dorion's arm and finishes applying the ink. Dorion no longer feels the pain – it's just one of the countless sensations that wash over him. He thinks about the prayers he's chanted that day, the ritual actions he's performed, how the priests led him into the holy chamber and revealed to him wondrous things beyond description – things even now his mind cannot fully articulate, but which have been imprinted on his soul forever.

Dorion is flushed, beyond intoxication. He feels the sweat pour from his body. He feels the heart crash in his chest. He feels the hair on his body stand on end, his skin so sensitive the linen garment he wears is almost unbearable. And underneath the linen he feels his cock proud and swollen.

Oh! He has never felt like this before! Never felt so full of life, so keenly aware of his body – and paradoxically so removed from its petty confines. His soul, like the mighty Nile coursing nearby, has overflowed its bed and threatens to spill forth, fertilizing the ground beneath his feet. He feels too immense to be bound; he aches to leap up and join the dancers once more. This is what it means to be alive – full of life to the point of bursting, like an old sack into which too much wine has been poured. He is awake, and everything before this moment has just been a daydream.

The priest lets go of Dorion's arm, slaps him on the shoulder, and says, "It is finished. The god is in you. You belong to him now and forever more. This ivy shall be your constant reminder of the fact. May the blessings of Dionysos be yours!"

Howling his joy, Dorion leaps to his feet and rushes out into the sultry night air to join the revelers of the god. He is a *mystes* now. A Bakchos. His soul bears testimony to that – and now so does his flesh.

A TRANSLATION OF OINOMAOS OF ALEXANDRIA'S *PHILOPSEUDES* 5.23 FF

On the day when we Romans keep the most ancient Liberalia* many others are busy celebrating the festival of the Holy Patrick. In truth all are doing the same thing and honoring the same god, and not even through different names as when people speculate on the identity of Osiris and Dionysos. For at Delphi is not Dionysos known as the one through whom things are made holy (*hosioter*) and at Rome isn't he called the Father of Freedom (*Liber Pater*) on account of his care-soothing gift to man? Clearly, then, people have just sewn together these two epithets like when Zeus stitched up his thigh after he saved the divine child from the flames.

But there is no need to rely solely on learned etymologies to make our case – one has but to look at the idol which the masses carry through the streets in procession. This Holy Patrick is depicted as a man with a venerable beard much like Dionysos is shown returning from his conquest of India. In his hand he holds a staff shaped either to resemble the crook of the cow-herd who oversees the Bacchic rites or better yet the *thyrsos* carried by the mad-women in their revels. That it's more likely to be the latter is indicated by the numerous serpents draped over the Holy Patrick's arms or resting at his feet. As everyone knows serpents are ubiquitous in the worship of Dionysos but scarcely found on the island from which Holy Patrick is said to come. A further clue as to his identity is the green garb which both the idol and those who carry it through the streets wear. Certainly this is meant to commemorate the vintage and all the lush vegetation of trees and grass and flowers that come about through the agency of Dionysos Anthios.

Now the nature of this festival is also a sure sign that it is carried out in honor of Dionysos alone. First there is the parade through the streets which is modeled after the triumphant processions that the god made on his return from the East. But other gods have processions as well, one might object, and that is certainly true, but when the Owl-Eyed is escorted to her temple during the Panathenaia the crowd is not intoxicated and shouting crude jokes at one another. Such things we find done only for Dionysos. Indeed, the parade of the Holy Patrick lasts for only a couple hours in the morning but the rest of the day is spent in public drunkenness with contests to see who can consume the most alcohol, as we do during our Dionysiac symposia.

And the fact that beer is what most drink on this day, and not the beverage made from the blood of grapes, should not confuse us. When Dionysos traveled about he encountered many lands where the soil and climate were such that they could not support his vines. So to those people he taught the art of making other kinds of alcohol – some from barley or wheat, others from date palm or honey or whatever was at hand, thus allowing them to have a remedy for their cares and a way to experience his blessed intoxication. Recognizing that Dionysos is the giver of many blessings those who honor him as the Holy Patrick dye their beer a dark green so that it will resemble the god's ivy. They do not do so at other times, but since this day is especially sacred to him they feel the extra step is required as a reminder and a form of respect.

The last proof that I wish to bring before you is, to my mind, the most convincing, and that's the claim that the Holy Patrick comes from Ireland. What is this place "Ireland"? Have you ever heard it mentioned in Hesiod or Homer, Orpheus or Vergil – in any of the other inspired, authoritative poets for that matter? In their sacred verse they set down the creation of the world and list all of the countries that comprise the inhabited world, including places so distant that the poets had never traveled there but only heard rumor of them. Yet nowhere can one find mention of a land of Ire. From this it is sensible to deduce that the island came into existence long after the rest of the world took shape, just like that Ortygia which rose from the sea to give solid support to Leto when she was gripped with the birth pangs of Apollon and Artemis. Since it was of so recent origin our poets felt it unworthy of mention. However I have heard a sacred myth about this island which I shall now relate for you.

It is said that Hera had great enmity for Dionysos in his infancy. She tried many times to destroy him and when that failed she inflicted punishment on all who sheltered him, driving them mad, destroying them or giving them bestial forms. And though she could not directly harm Dionysos, she did succeed in putting madness in his mind which drove him across the earth like a gadfly, making him commit many heinous acts before he sought purification at the hands of the Great Mother Rheia. While in this state he came to the country ruled over by Lykourgos, a violent and insolent man. The king repulsed the god and his nurses, driving them into the sea with his cruel ox-goad. (Had Dionysos not been out of his wits he easily could have defeated Lykourgos; as it was he later came back and destroyed him.) Well, Dionysos swam in the sea for a great long while until he grew tired and his hallucinations got the better of him. Where he stopped an island rose up around him, conjured by his mad delusion. It was populated by strange and unnatural creatures – things only an insane god could dream of – and everyone who has ever set foot there has been either a drunkard or a madman, and usually both. That is how this place earned its curious name.

Some say that Ireland is derived from *ara* because Dionysos was *cursed* by Hera and others that it refers to the *irae* or *anger* that Dionysos felt for the many unjust actions his step-mother had taken against him. Still others hold that it comes from *iouernia* on account of the *abundance* of strange things that inhabit that place. Consider as proof the men who live there. Proper humans, since we were molded from the clay of the earth, have brown skin and even darker hair. This is true whether you're talking about Greeks and Latins, the most civilized of all races, or our Egyptian, Assyrian and Indian neighbors, not to mention those from further away. Even the Jews look like normal people, except for the horns on their heads that they must wear hats to conceal. But the men of Ireland look nothing like us. Their skin is white as milk and their hair a fiery red. This is yet another proof that Dionysos created them for their flesh suggests the food he was fed by the nymphs of Nysa, and their hair the torches carried in his nocturnal revels. Their character is also incredibly Dionysian. By temperament they are all quarrelsome and difficult to govern but also gifted poets and capable of seeing things none of the rest of us can. So when it is said that this Holy Patrick is Irish what people really mean is that he has the nature of Dionysos and considering all the rest I think it certain that he *is* Dionysos.

*NOTE: *The ancient Roman festival of Liberalia (honoring Liber Pater, often associated with Bacchus) was held on March 17, also the date of St. Patrick's Day.*

WORSHIP OF THE GODS IS NOT IN VAIN

TO LEUKOS FROM EUNOMIOS: Greetings! I received your letter just the other day, and it could not have come at a better time, old friend. It pleased me to hear how well things are going for you and your community – I just wish things were going as well here.

To begin with, the Christians from the city are spreading out into the countryside and making many converts among the simple and superstitious. Normally this would not matter – after all, who cares what the simple believe, so long as they get their work done – but the conversions are not just among the poor and ignorant, but even my neighbor Timon has accepted that Jew from Galilee; and if there are not better crops this year, I fear he will not be alone. To make things even worse the local Bishop is a cruel and petty man, as nakedly avaricious as any Caesar, for all that he feigns holiness and humility. He preaches conquest and says that good Christians should have nothing to do with *Pagani* (which is what they are calling those of us who hold to the Hellenic way). Already I am having some difficulty with the men who tend my land. I have been good to them in the past – that, I think, is the only reason that they still work the land for me. But if this Bishop Ambrose continues spurring them on, and I am left with no one to work my fields or buy my crops, what will I do?

I fear that dark times lie ahead for us. But is this not what the Egyptian Hermes said when he proclaimed, "Egypt will be forsaken, and the land which was once the home of religion will be left desolate, bereft of the presence of its deities." And again, "The dead will far outnumber the living; and the survivors will be known for Egyptians by their tongue alone, but in their actions they will seem as men of another race. O Egypt, Egypt, of thy religion nothing will remain but an empty tale, which thine own children in time to come will not believe; nothing will be left but graven words, and only the stones will tell of thy piety." These prophecies were not just about Egypt; they concern all the lands wherein the gods were given proper honors. Already we are seeing the prophecies come true: the ancient temples have been given up to rats and spiders, desolate for lack of use; men have forgotten what it means to be men, have forgotten the greatness of their ancestors and care now only for themselves and the lie of personal immortality which the priests of Christ deceive them with; the very gods who once walked the earth now seem to have returned to their home in heaven, abandoning us to our own foolishness.

This is the way that it seems, but as a priest of Bacchus I know that it is not so, and that is the only thing that helps me to continue. For I know that my worship of him is not in vain. Even if all the gods of Olympos and elsewhere withdrew to their divine home, Dionysos would remain here with us in the world below. Truly he is present in the world, in the ripe fruit of my fields and my green pastures. He I feel in the earth and wind and mountains. In my wife and my children and my very own soul. I know he is all about – you would have to be blind not to. It is a niggardly man who does not honor the god of life, the very god that brings him joy and wealth. And so I honor him with the rites that he is due, and consider it a joyous burden at that. These rites that we perform in his honor are old – that is how we know that they are true, for what is false does not last. The performance of these rites makes my life better. Even if I received no outward benefit from them, I would still perform them for there is a great inward benefit which one receives for honoring Dionysos, a purification of one's soul, an immersion in joy. All this the Christians would destroy, claiming theirs is the only way.

When it comes to theology there is no contest. We have Homer, Plato, Plotinos and all the great minds of Greece and Rome on our side. In the short time that they have been around, how many great men have they produced? Few enough, and those that they do produce are eventually considered heretics by their fellows, for they truly despise original thought.

So if the contest is not be intellectual, then let it be spiritual – for we have ecstasy and all the techniques of the theurge at our disposal. Further, we have the Immortal Ones on our side, and whom the gods favor, that one cannot lose.

So I do not fear the dark days ahead, Leukos, even if the Christians beat at my door. Eventually reason will return and the gods will be honored again. And we who remained faithful to them shall be remembered fondly. Herakleitos the Obscure said that all is flux – let us hope that the flux overtaking our world is not overly violent.

ON WHETHER IT IS ACCEPTABLE TO DISCUSS SACRED THINGS

TO THEON FROM EUNOMIOS. I hope this finds you well, dear friend; it has been too long since I have heard anything from you. I received one of your students the other day, Marcus, and he filled me in on all that had transpired up to the point of his departure, but the boy had been on the road for over a month and I know how quickly things can change in these raging times. I am glad to hear that your school is prospering – however else the world goes, there will always be a need for Plato and people to interpret him.

Your Marcus has certainly taken to philosophy – we had a very enjoyable discussion on the immortality of the soul. You know my thoughts on the subject, but I couldn't help needling your pupil, and so I played the Epicurean for him. Very strong, that Marcus; no matter how much I tried to ruffle his feathers he kept his calm and refused to fall for my verbal snares. You should be proud, old friend, for the virtue of the teacher is reflected in his students.

And that is why I have undertaken to write you. Marcus told me about another of your students, Isidoros, and how he has begun to write an epic about the things that Dionysos did. This, as you can well understand, is a subject close to my heart. I have been a follower of Dionysos for almost fifty years, since I was of the age to put on the toga of manhood in his festival. I have held almost every position within his mysteries from Torch-bearer to Bakchos to Chief Herdsman and all the others. I have explored the rites sacred to Dionysos in Greece, Phrygia, Thrace, and Egypt that I might discover how they differ and which are closer to the truth. I have read the books of Orpheus and Mousaios and the accounts made by Timotheos. I am well-versed in these sacred things. And on account of that I was very disturbed to hear that this student of yours intends to put down a holy account of Dionysos, and to deal openly with the mysteries that are sacred to him.

For in the course of study which prepares one to accept the initiations, there are oaths which must be sworn and secrets that can never be revealed. And yet, from what I heard, this Isidoros of yours is throwing out his oaths and trampling on the secrets of god. If this truly is his intention, then he shall pay for it in the world to come, and shall suffer the torments which Orpheus has taught us about. The courts of this world may no longer try blasphemers, but Justice will forever be the concern of the Immortal Ones.

Having said that, I must admit that my thoughts are not entirely against your student. I have not read his epic, and so I cannot say to what degree he has violated his oaths, if in fact he even has. That he is your pupil, and well-liked by Marcus gives me reason to pause, for these are not trifling things, and speak to his good nature. There is a difference, I suppose, between one who reveals sacred things in order to glorify them, and one who brings them out only to mock at them. Isidoros, from my talks with Marcus, does not sound like such a person, and perhaps I am overreacting. But there have been too many attacks on our religion of late, Christians parading the gods before the unworthy public like actors on a stage, making sport of stories and rituals they scarcely understand.

It is, perhaps, because they do not understand that which they ridicule, for no one who knows what lies behind the veil, no one who has ever experienced the holy gods through the mysteries, ever forsakes them. Maybe it is only the secretive nature of our rites which allows the atheists to mock us. Perhaps if, like Isidoros has done, we were to bring the holy things out into the open, where everyone could see and take part in them, then there would be no contest, and the Christians would have no ground to attack us on.

But I do not think that that is even possible, for the mysteries are not stories or tokens to be handled, but rather a communication of souls to souls, of man to man and man to god; therefore what is truly of the mysteries is unspeakable – not because it is forbidden, but because it is not conveyed through mere words alone. In this, the mysteries are not unlike philosophy, as you well know. So I am willing to suspend judgment on this matter, however important it is, until I can get ahold of Isidoros' work.

Maybe I am just an old man, stuck in my ways. Perhaps Isidoros and those like him are the future of our faith. In these dark days, when the whole world seems to be conspiring against us and against the gods, maybe it is time for change. We must save the accomplishments of civilization, or watch as everything that our ancestors fought for is lost.

May the gods continue to watch over you and your students.

THE *HIEROS LOGOS* OF ISIDOROS

Unquestionably it is best to begin our account of the myths of Dionysos at the beginning, with the birth of the god. But there are so many different versions of his birth that this is no simple matter. I shall begin, then, with what Orpheus has taught us regarding this matter. According to him Demeter and her daughter Kore – who one day would be called Persephone – lived on the island of Sicily, where they made their home in a cave near the spring of Kyane. One day, Zeus, the father of the girl, came to the cave when the mother was gone, and in the form of a snake lay with his daughter and conceived by her a child, the bull-horned god Zagreus, the first Dionysos.

Now Zeus took the child back to Olympos with him, and his wife Hera grew jealous, for Zagreus was a most special child. Because of her jealousy Hera plotted against the child, and when the guards who Zeus had placed over the boy were distracted, Hera caused the Titans to rise up from the underworld and set upon the child with their murderous knives. Brave Zagreus sought to evade the Titans by turning himself into a number of different creatures, a lion, a horse, a man, and finally a bull, but all his effort was for naught, for the Titans eventually caught the child, holding him by hoof and horn, and fulfilled their obligation to the goddess by tearing the child to pieces. These pieces they cooked in a stew of milk, and then roasted over a fire, before they commenced their awful feast. The smell of roasting flesh drew the boy's father, and Zeus upon discovering what happened, hurled his mighty lightning-bolts at the Titans, burning them up where they stood. From the steam that rose from their burning flesh came ash, and it was out of this ash, as Orpheus teaches, that man arose. Therefore we have within us both a divine element (Dionysos) and an infernal element (the Titans) and we must strive to separate the divine from the infernal – only then will we be free.

Athena managed to save the heart of the child, and with this Zeus was able to conceive the god again. He did this either by eating the heart himself or by giving it in a potion to the daughter of King Cadmus who, however it was done, soon was with child.

Now when Hera discovered that Semele – as the girl was called – was pregnant with Zeus' child and the child was none other than Zagreus reborn, her wrath knew no limit. Immediately Hera disguised herself as the girl's old nurse, Beroë, and with cunning words began to set doubt in the girl's mind as to whether her lover was a god indeed, or just some rascal out to play a trick on her. The only proof, Hera claimed, was for her lover to reveal himself in his fullness; otherwise Semele would never know if Zeus really was a god. The next time that Zeus came to lay with the girl, for he had fallen in love with her, Semele made him promise to grant her wish, whatever it would be. Impetuous Zeus made his promise, only to regret it when she made her request. Now, once a god has given his word he cannot go back on it, however much he'd like to. So Zeus put off his human form and revealed himself to her in his fullness. The sight of Zeus in this form proved too great for her, and the girl was burned up at once.

The child in her womb would have died too, but for a miracle. Lush foliage wrapped itself round the baby in his mother's womb and kept him safe from the heavenly fire that consumed her. And when Zeus saw that the child was safe, he immediately lifted the fetus up and sewed it into a pocket in his thigh, there to keep him safe until he should come to term. When Zeus got back to Olympos Hermes laughed at the funny way he walked, and so it was that the child was called Dionysos, for one meaning of that name is "the limp of Zeus."

When the child was born Zeus gave him into the care of his aunt, Ino, whose husband was Athamas. To hide him from the wrath of Hera they dressed little Dionysos as a girl, and kept him in the women's quarters of the palace. This only succeeded for a short time, and then Hera's vengeance caught up with the child and his foster parents. Hera sent a madness against them and Ino and Athamas slew their children, thinking that they were killing the boy. Dionysos, however, had turned himself into a kid, and so escaped the terrible trap.

Zeus sent Hermes to retrieve the boy and find a safe place for him. The Messenger of the gods traveled far until he came to the mountain of Nysa, where there were some nymphs into whose care the child was placed. Sources differ as to which Nysa the god was brought to: the one in Egypt, the one in Ethiopia, the one in Thrace, the one in Makedonia, the one in Italy, the one in India or some other Nysa altogether.

Now the nymphs took good care of their charge and loved him dearly. They suckled him on milk from their breasts, and later wild honey from nearby caves, until Dionysos gave them wine to drink, and neither they nor the child ever again tasted that inferior food. The nymphs kept the boy entertained by singing songs to him and playing the drums and pipes for him. Little Dionysos loved the pipes very much and he begged them to teach him how to play. The nymphs could refuse the boy nothing and before long he had mastered the pipes. Animals and birds came to listen to him; trees and rocks too. Never before had the world heard such fine playing as Dionysos on his pipes – it was only the memory of the god's playing that made people respond so to that Thracian and his lyre.

Seilenos, that half-man/half-horse satyr, wisest of the daimones, was the god's own teacher. Every day he sat the boy down and gave him his lessons. It wasn't long before Dionysos had surpassed his teacher in rhetoric and philosophy and then it was the boy who was schooling the satyr in these weighty matters.

For all that, Dionysos preferred to spend his time in the forests surrounding Nysa. He would run through the vales, his joyful songs filling the forest with their gay sound. The nymphs and Seilenos tried to keep up with him but Dionysos knew the forest as if he had spent his whole life there, and they would always fall behind. No part of the forest was unknown to him; all the creatures that dwelt there acknowledged him as their Lord. Frequently the god would hunt in the forest. After chasing down a deer he would catch the creature and tear it apart with his bare hands. Once he had eaten its raw flesh he would bring the deer back to life, that it might run and hunt another day.

This was how the god spent his youth, and while Dionysos loved his Nurses and wise old Seilenos, he nevertheless grew bored at Nysa and longed to travel the world. When he explained this to the nymphs, they tried to dissuade the youth by explaining that he was safe from Hera only on the holy mountain. If he left there would be no protection. Like all youths Dionysos was headstrong and in his heart he did not fear Hera. So Dionysos left his home to explore the world and suffer many great adventures. The nymphs, unwilling to be without their Lord, came too.

The first of these great adventures happened shortly after leaving. Dionysos was sitting on a beach, appearing to all as a handsome youth with rich purple robes and long golden locks, when some pirates came upon him. The Tyrrhenians, for that was their race, spotted the boy and thought him some wealthy king's son who had wandered off. If they caught him, certainly the boy's father would pay a hefty ransom for his return, and so they plotted his capture. When Dionysos hailed the sailors and begged passage to the island of Naxos the Tyrrhenians agreed and took the boy aboard their ship. Now their helmsman was a man named Akoites, and he was good in his heart. When he saw the beautiful youth he immediately recognized him as something more than mortal and begged his fellows to set the boy free, warning them that they had taken some god aboard their ship and that he would not take kindly to their plans. The captain did not listen to this man's wise words and in fact he punished him for speaking them.

Just as his crewmen were about to toss Akoites over the side of the ship a sound of flutes was heard. Though there was a stiff breeze in its sails the ship stood still. Ivy and grapevines twined themselves about the masts and the oars turned into snakes. The ship was flooded with sweet wine and on the deck appeared wild creatures – panthers, lions, and bears, who presently set upon the treacherous crew. The captain was devoured by a lion, or else Dionysos leapt upon him and attacked him with the ferocity of a lion. Those crewmen who were not mauled by the fierce creatures tried to jump to safety over the side of the ship, though when they hit the water they were no longer men, but had become dolphins. Akoites, fearing for his life, tried to jump over the side with his former friends but the god stopped him saying that he had nothing to fear. For the kindness that he had shown the god he would grant Akoites whatever he wished. And so it was that Akoites joined the holy band of the god's followers, for that was his wish. Dionysos placed a dolphin in the sky to commemorate this event, and, no doubt, as a warning to all sailors.

Hera saw this and grew angry. Some claimed that Hera had sent the pirates to catch the young god, others that it made Hera fear for her safety, for in this encounter the power of Dionysos was revealed. Out of her anger

Hera sent a madness to Dionysos and it drove the young god across the face of the earth. He wandered through Egypt, Syria, and other lands, and in his madness did many terrible things. He killed a whole tribe of Amazons, flaying them alive. He made the Argive women think that they were cows and made them eat the children that they had suckled at their breast. And he almost laid waste to the oracle at Delphi and would have succeeded had Apollon, thinking quickly, not offered the god rule of the oracle during the winter months which succeeded in checking the Dionysos' wrath. Finally the god came to Phrygia where in a swamp he collapsed as he tried to cross the marsh. Two asses came along and helped the god across where he found a temple belonging to Kybele. In gratitude, the god placed one of the asses in the sky and gave the other a human voice.

As it happened Kybele was present in her temple and when she spotted her grandson (for this was the same goddess whom the Greeks called Rheia, the Mother of Zeus) she brought him inside and tended to his needs. She purified the god, freeing him from the grip of madness and taught him her ancient rites, which she gave over to Dionysos. It was also in Phrygia that he adopted the oriental costume that he and his followers would wear.

Dionysos met up with his Nurses at Dodona where they had been waiting for him. (In some accounts, this was their original home.) Together they traveled the world, establishing his worship and giving to those who honored him the gifts of wine and ecstasy. In that holy band there were nymphs and satyrs, mortal women called mainades and Thyiades and Bassarides and Mimallones, and mortal men too, who dressed in the same flowing robes as the women, and everyone, whether mortal or immortal, man or woman, wore crowns of ivy, laurel, or myrtle, and carried the god's emblem, the thyrsos-wand topped with a pinecone and twined with ivy or colored ribbons. Through the god, the mainadic women were able to accomplish many great things: they could carry fire unscathed by its flames, speak with animals, conjure milk and wine with the touch of their thyrsic wands, and they possessed the ability to control weather. Mainad rites culminated in states of ecstasy where the god and his followers became one. While in these ecstatic states mainades were impervious to physical harm, gifted with the arts of prophecy, and possessed incredible amounts of strength so that they could lift a full-sized bull over their heads, or tear apart a sacrificial goat with their bare hands. The mainades honored Dionysos with drumming and dances and with the special rite of *omophagia* or the eating of raw flesh. Everywhere they went women left their homes to join the revels of the god. Most returned after fulfilling their duty – but some stayed with the god the whole of their lives, traveling with him across the world, part of the triumphant army of Lord Dionysos.

There were many places that accepted the fabulous gifts of the god and gladly worshipped him. Among them the Laconians, the Delians, the Eleans, the Carians and all the people of the Islands – but their stories are not the most famous ones, for the poets preferred tales of opposition. And the first and greatest of those who opposed the god was Lykourgos, Dryas' son, that violent fool who ruled the Edonians.

Now the Edonians lived on the banks of the river Strymon and their soil was such that it received the grapevines of the god with ease, and before long the vines were everywhere. The people liked this, for they were fond of the god's wine, but Lykourgos detested the plants and the nocturnal rites that Dionysos had established with them. Therefore one night when the followers of the god, and Dionysos with them, had gathered to perform their holy dances outside the city, Lykourgos and his men crept upon the revelers to disrupt the sacred rites. Lykourgos, brandishing an ox-goad, burst upon the group and scattered them, chasing the women to the shores of the river where they, urged on by Dionysos, sought refuge under the waves with the Okeanid Thetis, who kept the girls from drowning out of her love for the god. Now Lykourgos thought that he had won, since he had gotten the mainades to drop their thyrsoi and run, fleeing with their god into the water. This only confirmed the king's contempt for the god, for he had fled from a mere mortal and what sort of god would do that? Little did he understand that it was not fear that drove the god to flee, but concern for his followers, and so once they were safe, the god came back up and confronted the king, who was busy trying to pull up all of the god's vines.

It was an easy thing to beat the king – indeed he was already half-mad to begin with. All that the god did was put before his eyes a vision of endless rows of grapevines, one after the other, grapevines that multiplied as the king and his men tried to pull them up. All through the morning and into the day the king labored in his fields, and still they were full of vines. He bid his servants tear up the hateful plants and when they were too slow or grew tired and begged for rest, the king leapt upon them and beat them with his ox-goad. The king's son began to worry for his father and when the boy approached Lykourgos to beg him to put off this madness, the king picked up an ax and began hacking away at his son, thinking as he did that the boy was covered in vines. When the son's blood splattered on Lykourgos Dionysos made him think that the vines had taken hold of him – and so the king took the ax to his own legs. This seemed to bring the villain's fit to an end – or at least stopped him from harming others with his madness. Fearing the man they had once proclaimed king, the Edonians banished the son of Dryas to a nearby mountain, Pangaeüs where the panthers roamed. Those wild beasts, sacred to the god, hunted down Lykourgos, tearing him apart like a fawn in the hands of a mainad.

Another man who resisted the worship of god, and should have known better, was Pentheus the king of Thebes, whose own mother was the sister of Semele. Dionysos came to the daughters of Cadmus: Agave, Autonoe and Ino who had returned to the city of her father after the evil done in her husband's home. Dionysos sought to convince these women that he was a god and that his mother had indeed conceived him from a god. They would not listen; they persisted in their belief that Semele had only ascribed her pregnancy to Zeus, and that for this lie she had been punished with death. To them, Dionysos had died in his mother's womb – they would not hear Ino's tale of nursing the child, thinking as they did, that it was a delusion born of her madness. They spoke other lies against their sister and spread this falsehood among the women of Thebes, who, on hearing it believed and doubted the god. This was intolerable for the god and so he drove the women of Thebes into the mountains outside their city and there on Kithairon they honored the god whom they had denied, honored him with songs and dances and the red, raw feast which so delights him.

The men of Thebes, Pentheus chief among them, found the situation unbearable, and so the king sent his soldiers into the hills to flush the women out. This got them nothing, for Dionysos was among his followers, and through him they were able to resist the armed men, working wonders before their awe-struck eyes. The women were able to turn aside the soldiers' sharp-bladed swords, and cut through their bronze shields with the ivy-wrapped wands that they carried. Women held fire in their hands and caused milk and wine to flow along the mountain's side. Tiny girls, through the god, found the strength to lift full-grown men over their heads, and wild creatures ran at their sides, sharers in the holy mysteries of god. The women routed Pentheus' finest soldiers; even so, a few Bacchants allowed themselves to be captured, that they might greet the king and show him the ways of god. Among those that Pentheus' men captured was Dionysos himself, disguised as a mortal priest in the robes of god.

Pentheus interrogated him at length, thinking correctly that he was the leader of the Bacchae, and though the god answered his questions in all truth, it made no sense to the king, for his mind was closed to all but the narrowest of truths. As the god continued on, trying to teach Pentheus a better way, the king grew enraged for he thought that the god mocked him. Finally, when Pentheus was near to tears, the god ended the conversation, saying that if Pentheus intended to punish him he should let nothing stand in his way. While Pentheus attempted to do just that, it proved a far more difficult task than he had expected. The chains that he had bound the god with fell from him and his followers at a word from Dionysos. When the king ordered his men to take hold of the prisoners they could not move their limbs till the god gave them leave to, and when Pentheus tried to run the god through with his own sword he found in Dionysos' place one of the tall columns of the palace, the god having set before him a confounding image to do battle with.

The king was powerless to stop him, yet still he would not concede and grant the god that which he deserved, namely to be honored in the city that once housed his mother. Recognizing that Dionysos placed before the king the method of his own demise, and Pentheus, blinded by his own foolishness, grasped for it as a thirsty man grasps for a cup of wine. Dionysos persuaded the king to follow him into the hills where the Bacchae awaited them. He promised an end to this war and the return of peace to Thebes. Pentheus interpreted this as the death of the mainades – but it was his own death that the god offered him.

Dressed as a mainad, in gown and crown and ivy-wrapped wand, the king crept upon the camp of the mainades, eager to see what infernal rites they were up to. When the king couldn't see things as well as he had hoped, he climbed a pine tree to spy on the women in their nocturnal rites. From that vantage point all was revealed to Pentheus – and Pentheus was revealed to all. The mainades saw the intruder, and were upon him in an instant, pulling the king from his tree and tearing him apart once they had him on the ground. Chief among those who mauled the king were Autonoe and Agave, the very aunt and mother of Pentheus. When the deed was done, the women returned to their proper states of mind – only to witness the horrible things that they had done. All who had partaken in the savage rite were banished from Thebes and wandered the world alone until alone they died. This, then, was the fate incurred by those who mocked the god in his own home – to commit an awful crime and die a hideous death.

This should have proved a warning to all those who would deny another's right to honor the god. However, the daughters of Minyas paid no attention to the fate of Pentheus and when the holy band came to their city, and people filled the streets with revelry, the girls remained in their father's bower, busying themselves with the "proper" work of women. Dionysos did not care that they refused to honor him, but when he heard that they would not allow their slaves to join the celebration the god was forced to visit on them the punishment which comes to all those who refuse him – namely the madness which leads to death. The daughters, spurred on by the god, ate each other's children, and then were themselves turned into bats who fled into the hills and the darkness, both of which they had previously felt were unfit places for well-bred women to frequent.

At Tangara they accepted the god, and their women honored him in the proper way. But Tritons, those terrible creatures who live under the sea, sought to disrupt their holy rites, though the god would not let them. He battled the Tritons to keep his votaries safe and drove them far from Tangara once he had vanquished their leader, that they might never harm that holy people again. When Butes and his men tried to rape the Thessalian mainades, the god hunted them down, until every last one of those black-hearts had paid the penalty for assaulting those dear to the god. To the daughters of Anius he gave the gift of growth, that they might produce corn, wine, and oil for their drought-stricken land. And when Agamemnon's men tried to carry the girls off to feed his army, Dionysos kept them safe, turning them into doves that they might fly to freedom. He punished the Thracian bacchants when they killed his chosen prophet, Orpheus of the splendid voice, giving the singer's head into the care of the Lesbians, that it might continue to give oracles in times of great need. Dionysos honored his votary Dirce when she died by causing a holy spring to rise up on the spot. He placed the Haliae in the sky when they were slain by Perseus the king of Argos for bringing wine into his city and getting his soldiers drunk while he was at war with the Aegean islands. (Perseus was well punished for his hastiness, although he eventually repented and established the god's worship in his city.) And he danced up the rains for the people of Limos, an eastern city.

When Dionysos came to Attica it was not a king that greeted the god but a humble shepherd who offered the god his hospitality – modest though it was – and so was rewarded with the gift of wine and the knowledge of its cultivation. Ikarios, for that was the shepherd's name, took such great pleasure in the god's wine – before then, all that he had had to drink was water, the same as his sheep – that he immediately wanted to go off and share this wonderful gift with his neighbors, for he was indeed generous of heart. Erigone, the man's daughter, agreed with her father that they must share that which the god had given to them, and so the girl watched her father's flocks while he went to the neighboring farm to bestow on them the rich wine of Dionysos. Now in his eagerness Ikarios did not cut the wine with water, as the god had taught him to do, and so his neighbor's sons were soon quite drunk, for they liked the wine as much as Ikarios had. When the father came upon his sons in their drunken state he thought that Ikarios had poisoned them for they had passed out and would not waken, or stumbled about in their drunken stupor. The neighbor and his friends sought vengeance against the kindly shepherd, killing him with heavy rocks and sticks plucked from the ground. When the boys awoke, no worse for wear, the father and his friends repented their hasty action, but too late, for Ikarios was already dead. Fearing that others might find out what they had done the men carried Ikarios' body to a nearby well and stuffed it in there, that he might be hidden from the eyes of men and their dark deed go unpunished.

When Erigone's father did not return the girl began to despair. With her faithful dog Maeara, the girl searched out her father and eventually found the well where his body was hidden, directed to the spot by the light of the moon. When the girl saw her father's lifeless body madness took hold of her and the girl hung herself from a tree that grew near the spot. The dog, abandoned by those that he had loved, flung himself into the well where he died.

Now the men did not escape their evil deeds – as always happens, vengeance caught up with them. The Lord sent a madness upon the women of Attica and as Erigone had hung herself from a tree, so too did they hang themselves. Nothing that the men of Attica could do stopped their women from taking their lives – even force of arm failed to stop the maddened women. In desperation the men of Attica consulted the Delphic oracle where they discovered the cause of their plague and the means by which they could remedy it. First, they hunted down the killers of Ikarios, slaying the impetuous men as they had slain the helpless shepherd. Next, they instituted a festival of Dionysos, the Aiora or "swinging festival" which was held during Anthesteria. During the Aiora young girls swung from trees on swings in imitation of Erigone and all sorts of small images were hung on trees and swung, and fruits were brought as an offering to the father and daughter. Dionysos relented and the women regained their sanity, those that had not killed themselves. He further honored his votaries by placing them in the sky as the constellations Boötes, Virgo and Canicula or Procyon.

In Aetolia the god received a hospitable welcome from Oineus, king of Calydon. Not only did he entertain Dionysos and his holy band, but when the king recognized that Dionysos had taken an interest in his wife he arranged it so that he was called away on urgent business that the two might be left alone. For his generosity Dionysos gave him the vine and taught him to make wine. Calydon prospered from its production of wine and became in time one of the richest of nations. By Althaía, the wife of Oineus, the god bore a daughter, Deïaneira, the future bride of Herakles.

Crete had been at war with the nations of the Aegean and because of her greater naval strength and the fact that the gods loved her above every other nation she was able to overcome them. As a result of this, Minos forced Athens to pay tribute in the form of seven youths and seven maids which she was forced to send to Crete on every ninth year. These youths were then sacrificed to the Minotaur, a monstrous creature – half-man and half-bull – that lived in the labyrinth, a giant maze that Minos had constructed under his palace. Despite his father's pleas Theseus volunteered to be one of the fourteen, and came to Crete to slay the beast and topple Minos' rule. When Ariadne met the handsome youth she immediately fell in love with Theseus. She gave the dashing young hero a silver thread, which, unraveled as he wandered through the labyrinth, would help him find his way out again – a thing no one, including the Minotaur, had been able to do before. When Theseus succeeded in killing the beast and overthrowing Minos he left for his home and took Ariadne with him as he had agreed to do. But on their way home, they stopped off on the isle of Naxos where Theseus – who didn't really love Ariadne – abandoned her to die.

Some time later Dionysos arrived at the island and found the princess near to death from exposure and heartbreak. He nursed her back to health and when she recovered her strength, married the god, as they had fallen in love while she was recuperating. Ariadne bore many children for the god and theirs was a most happy marriage. But it was not without sorrow for the goddess Artemis, thinking that Ariadne had betrayed Dionysos with Theseus, killed the princess on the Isle of Dia, which some claimed was the same as Naxos. Devastated, the wine-god placed the bridal crown of Ariadne in the heavens as the Corona Borealis, and unable to bear the loss of his great love, begged his father Zeus to bring Ariadne back to life. Though it went against the very laws of heaven, Zeus consented and Ariadne was made a goddess. Together the two immortals dwelt happily on Olympos and on the world, their love ever flowing.

Dionysos sought to share his mysteries and the gift of wine with all the men of the world, not just the Greeks and Asiatics who clung to the shores of the Mediterranean. Indeed, the god and his army – for that is how the holy band came to be called – carried his message to the very ends of the earth, "through Syria and Arabia and Palestine they traveled, into Egypt and Persia and Bactria they came, and on to India they went, that land of a hundred tongues," as the poets have it. Everywhere he went the god accomplished many wonderful things, teaching men to plant the vine and harvest wine and worship the gods through mysteries. He got the Arabians to stop eating the flesh of men and established among them civilization, with laws and art and worship of the gods. In Egypt the holy band was lost and would have died of thirst, but for the intervention of the god Ammon, who appearing as a ram, led the votaries back to their god and caused a spring to rise up that they might drink and lose their thirst. For this kindness Dionysos established a shrine to the ram-headed god Ammon, and placed a ram in the sky as Aries. Also in Egypt Dionysos won the throne back for its rightful owner, punishing the interloper who had taken it with madness so that he wandered the land thinking himself a cow like Io – only there was no Isis to take pity on the man, and his days were ended as some farmer's dinner.

Dionysos was well loved in India – many of the ascetics' wives fled to him, longing for that which their husbands would not give them, simple love. Dionysos taught the women powerful magics to win back the affections of their husbands and taught the men to see in their wives an image of the Paphian goddess, so that in making love to them they worshipped the divine. Seeing the popularity of the god, an Indian king declared war on him. The two armies met, the king's and the assorted followers of the god, and they prepared to make fierce war. But Pan, who has always been a good friend to Dionysos, was traveling with him at the time and he gave a great show which frightened the enemy and all the king's men fled in a panic, leaving the holy band victorious. This was how they conquered the world without the shedding of blood. In order to cross the Euphrates (some said that it was the mother of rivers, the Ganges) Dionysos constructed a bridge of plaited vines and ivy strands for his followers to cross, and as for the Tigris – how else should he cross that river, but on the back of a tiger?

One day as the holy band was traveling through Phrygia, Seilenos – the god's old teacher – disappeared, and no one could find him. Finally, escorted by an honor guard sent along by Midas, king of the Mygdonians, the old satyr returned. The king, or some of his peasants, had easily captured the ever-thirsty old man by setting out some wine-bowls, and once the old man had prophesied for him – that was what satyrs were supposed to do when they were captured – Midas entertained him with splendid hospitality, giving him his best men as an escort when the old satyr wished to return to the god. Dionysos rewarded the king for his kindness by agreeing to grant whatever Midas wished – and Midas foolishly asked that everything he touch turn to gold. Reluctantly (for once a god has given his word, he cannot turn back) Dionysos did so, and the god was not surprised when the king sought him out the next day, begging that his gift be withdrawn. It had worked too well, and he was starving since his very food turned to gold as well. Dionysos gladly told the king how he might banish his "golden touch" by bathing in the icy waters of the river Pactolus, a river rich with gold to this day.

Now that all the world worshiped him as a god Dionysos took his place with the other immortals on Mount Olympos; but not, however, before he had descended into the underworld to bring up his mother out of that dark land. He took his mother up to Olympos with him where she assumed the name Thyone and lives among the gods to this day.

At some point – when, I cannot say with certainty – Dionysos found himself involved in the war between the gods and the giants. Warlike Dionysos battled the giant Eurythus with his wand, vanquishing his fierce opponent. Next the god took on Alcyoneus who was awed by the god's powers and forsook battle with the Lord. Chthonious was not so wise – Dionysos dug a pit which the giant fell into and then filled the pit with wine, drowning his opponent. Pelorus and Porphyrian attacked the god together – together they were torn apart by the god's fierce panthers. The other giants were routed by the braying of the asses on which Dionysos and his satyr companions rode. And when the gods finally overcame the giants, it was Dionysos' suggestion which brought them victory. The god said that only by taking on their animal forms could they hope to vanquish their foes. The gods feared losing their place in the world by lowering themselves in this way. But as it turned out only by adopting their bestial natures were they able to keep their noble place in heaven. His role in the Gigantomachy had gone a long way towards resolving the enmity between him and Hera – when a giant had threatened to rape the goddess, it had been Dionysos not Zeus who came to her aid. It was the following incident, however, which completely ended it.

Hephaistos had always resented being abandoned as a child by his mother. So one day he hatched a plan to get revenge on her. The Great Artisan crafted for the gods marvelous gifts, each one greater than the last. Finally, he presented to them the greatest gift of all – a marvelous golden throne for his mother, a chair inlaid with gems and precious stones and sculpted with all her favorite things. The queen of the gods sat in her throne and proclaimed it the most comfortable thing she had ever sat upon in all her long lifetime. Hephaistos replied that that was good because she was going to be spending a lot of time in the chair – and when the goddess tried to rise from her seat, she found that she was quite stuck. Many of the strongest gods tried to pull her free – they would have yanked the goddess' arms off before they would have pulled her free. In all the commotion the throne was overturned and that is how it remained, hanging upside down with the goddess still stuck in it. After the gods had all gotten a good laugh, kingly Zeus ordered Hephaistos to free his mother (noting, as he had, the fierce look in her eyes) but the smith-god was nowhere to be found. He had gone down to his home below the waves, where his great smithy was. Now Ares, angry at the rough treatment of his mother, volunteered to go down and bring back the god – but this was a task easier to declare than to fulfill. Hephaistos was waiting for the war-god under the waves, and when Ares approached Hephaistos began to fling fiery brands at his brother and drove him back to the shore, where he fled, nursing his wounds.

Dionysos proved more successful in his attempt. He did not try to bring the artisan back by force, knowing as he did that that path would not succeed. Instead the god brought his best wine and he and the smith began to talk, speaking about Hera and Olympos and the problems that they had had with both. Before long Hephaistos was drunk – this was, after all, Dionysos' best wine – and Dionysos managed to convince the god to relent. But because the god was so drunk he couldn't make it back up to Olympos under his own power. Dionysos placed the heavy god on the back of an ass and led him up the high path to Olympos where the gods were waiting anxiously for their return. Drunk Hephaistos agreed to set Hera free – but only on the condition that she acknowledge him as her child and Zeus grant him the beautiful Aphrodite as his bride. All his demands were met, and Hera was released. Out of gratitude for this service done her, Hera relented in her wrath. Further, she nominated Dionysos to the ruling council of the gods and all agreed that this was a grand idea.

So ends Isidoros' account of the things that Dionysos did, the wonders he wrought, the gifts he shared, the marvel he became. Great is the god Dionysos!

THE TRUE ACCOUNT OF THE DEATH OF DIONYSOS

The Argives show an old, crumbling monument so overgrown with ivy that it's difficult to read the inscription. They say that it was erected by one of their early kings, the hero Perseus whose statue is nearby holding up the bloody head of Medousa. The story of the monument is this. The god Dionysos came through their land on his way to conquer the Indians. He was accompanied by a great army of satyrs, nymphs and madwomen from all the cities he had previously visited. Everywhere they went Dionysos planted his grape-vines and taught men how to make wine as a remedy for their cares. In return he demanded to be acknowledged as a god and worshiped through wild, orgiastic rites. Perseus, who was an accomplished warrior, refused the gifts of Dionysos on the grounds that intoxication was shameful, unmanly and corrosive to proper social order. When his subjects persisted in the licentious worship of the new god Perseus came out and confronted Dionysos directly. The two quarreled and Perseus got the better of him since Dionysos was by nature soft and unaccustomed to the arts of war. Not only did Perseus rout the Dionysian forces, slaying many, but it is even claimed that he killed the god himself. Afterwards Perseus set up three monuments – one to proclaim his victory over Dionysos, who was buried there, the second for Khorea who had shown exceptional valor and skill in battle, particularly since she belonged to the fairer sex, and also a common grave for the followers of Dionysos who fell at his hands. That is the story that the Argives tell and they'll show you what remains of each monument for the right price. But you must know that the Argives are all liars, down to the last one of them. They're worse than the Cretans in this regard for it was a Cretan who said this about his brethren, while you can't even find a single man from Argos who is capable of recognizing the truth.

What a dim-witted, thick-skulled people the Argives are to fall for such nonsense. How could any mortal man contend with the gods, let alone slay one of them? And Dionysos is most assuredly a god. Why the whole world knows his name and his holy rites are carried out in countless different lands. Many see him and speak to him on a frequent basis and many miracles are reported, attesting his awesome power. Do the Argives believe that the gods have bodies of flesh and blood like their own which can be destroyed by mere tempered metal? Even if the gods possessed such forms – a notion that no doubt fills those of a philosophical temperament with abject horror – what is to stop the gods from fashioning new bodies for themselves, they who made the heaven and earth and all things in it and who cause our flocks to increase and our fields to flourish in due season? But why should they even need to go to that length? Do not the gods heal those who are infirm and send purifying dreams and visions to the pious? It is a poor physician indeed who can heal others but not himself. So clearly this story stinks of the worst sort of impiety, namely the belief that the gods are either impotent or incompetent. Better that there be no gods than weak ones who cannot even stop a lone madman from harming them and the ones they love.

Is there, then, no truth at all to the tale? There is – but not the sort that the Argives would ever recognize. I wager that if you dug down deep beneath that faded monument you would indeed find some bones – but they are no bones of a god.

Let me, a man who has researched this and other sacred matters extensively, reveal the truth of the matter to you. For the remains found there – if time has not obliterated them entirely – belong to a man of my own race who went by the Greek name Akoites. This was not the name that his father gave him – that, unfortunately, has been lost to history. He was born of humble stock in the farming region of Tyrrhenia. The land is harsh and unforgiving, blasted by the winds and baked by the sun. But his people managed to scrape out a meager existence by toiling in the fields ever since Demeter had passed through and taught them the ways of agriculture. Though such a life had been good enough for his father and his father's father before him, Akoites dreamed of something better for himself. So he packed up his few belongings and bid his family farewell, heading for the coast. The dream he dreamed was of a life out on the seas, visiting strange lands and amassing a handsome personal fortune. Like many such men with that dream he had no awareness of the realities of life at sea nor how much hard work and danger is truly involved before one even boards a ship. On his first night there in the city on the coast he was mugged and all his possessions stolen. He tried to find work on one of the respectable merchant vessels but none of them would have him since he was so inexperienced. There were plenty of young men just like him, fresh from the farm, ignorant even of how to man an oar. So the merchants had their pick and there was nothing exceptional about Akoites. He lacked even the physical prowess that comes with tilling the soil since he had been a lazy dreamer with his head in the clouds all his youth.

It seemed that Akoites was destined to starve or worse in the city on the coast, but then he fell in with a disreputable lot of vagabonds and trouble-makers. They, too, made their living on the sea, by preying on the poor merchant vessels. Piracy has never been a career with much of a future in it, so they were always on the lookout for fresh blood.

Akoites started out as rower and common brigand and against all odds he managed to survive and work his way up through the ranks. Eventually he even became second-in-command of the pirate crew and served as helmsman. In fact that's what the name we know him by means – it is merely a title, representing his position in the pirate crew.

Over the years they had become quite successful, a force to be reckoned with along the Italian coast. All other ships feared them and many paid tribute to the pirates to ensure that they weren't set upon. Many cities had sent their best men to destroy these wolves of the sea, only to have their ships sent down to Poseidon. They grew fat on stolen goods from Crete and Egypt and Phoenicia or on the ransoms awarded them in return for dignitaries and princes. Others would have been content with such wealth – but not Akoites and his crew-mates.

In fact it was his greed that eventually led to Akoites' change of profession. The pirates had encamped on an island in the Aegean – though it wasn't yet called that then – when a young man approached them seeking passage to Egypt. He had the handsome looks of the well-born and the clothing to go with it, so they took him for some minor prince out for a pleasure cruise. As they had done many times before they planned to bind him once they were out to sea and force him to tell them where he came from so that they could extort a prince's ransom from his wealthy father.

Such was the plan, at any rate, but as soon as Akoites set eyes upon the boy he could tell that something was wrong. It seemed to him that the boy glowed with a heavenly light and there was something strange, something cold and cruel and supernatural about his eyes. This was no ordinary boy, though what he was Akoites could not say. He pleaded with the pirate captain to turn back and let him go. Nothing good would come of dealing with him. The captain laughed and mocked his foolish, superstitious helmsman and ordered him back to his post. He considered refusing right then and there but he feared the unpredictable and violent nature of his captain. Reluctantly he did as ordered and the ship pulled out to sea. His eyes never left the strange young man and his heart went cold when the boy smiled back at him.

A little while later the pirates proceeded to question the boy about his origins and the wealth of his father. When he was not forthcoming they threatened him and got out chains to bind him so that he'd sink even faster when they threw him overboard. Akoites rushed over and warned them against doing so. He feared his captain but he feared the boy even more. The brigands turned on Akoites and beat him until he could barely breathe for his insolent disobedience. Then they proceeded to bind the youth. He laughed at them and the chains fell right off. Then everything turned to madness. Ivy started growing up the mast. Wine washed over the deck like a wave. The sound of strange music could be heard though there were no musicians in sight. And savage beasts appeared out of nowhere, mauling the crew. Many jumped overboard to escape the lion and bear that he had conjured. But as soon as they hit the water they began to transform into dolphins. The shrieks of the dying were matched only by the wails of those who had lost hold of their sanity. The god Dionysos had revealed himself in all his glory. Only Akoites was spared that day, for he alone of all the pirates had seen through the illusion and recognized the true face of the god. Since Akoites had risked his own life to spare Dionysos indignity at the hands of his fellows, the god taught him his mysteries and appointed him to be his messenger.

And Akoites proved himself a faithful servant of his newfound god. He steered the ship wherever Dionysos wished to go – it was rowed by an invisible host – and he traveled all over the earth teaching men how to plant the vine and celebrate Dionysos' sacred rites. He lived so closely with the god, and dedicated himself so fully to his mission, that he entirely lost his previous identity. When people looked at this stranger they could see only the face of his god staring back at them. He collected a great army and marched through Greece and the eastern lands as far as India and Baktria, spreading the message of Dionysos. In many places he was warmly received and the women in particular flocked to him, falling under the charm of his charismatic personality and good looks. In other places he met opposition, but always vanquished his enemies for he had become a ruthless man-killer during his pirate days and he had the favor of Dionysos who watched over and protected him.

Akoites was victorious in all the lands he marched through, save only Argos. By that time he had become an old man, worn out through a lifetime of hard drinking, feasting, fighting and womanizing. On the day that he met Perseus in battle he could barely stand on his own without assistance, through he was able to keep his many mistresses more than happy and there wasn't a man alive who could drink him under the table. Had such feats decided the contest between them Perseus would undoubtedly come out the loser. When he saw that Akoites could barely lift his sword Perseus' pride should have stopped him from accepting the challenge. What honor is there in beating a senile old drunk? But he was cruel and vain and took offense at the lewd comments Akoites had made about his mother. So he ran him through and then turned on Akoites' companions, a group of young women that helped walk him onto the battlefield. These girls – little more than children – he raped and then killed, leaving their bodies for the crows. Such was the noble victory of Perseus over "Dionysos" and his army.

The actual Dionysian army was nowhere near Argos. Akoites had heard that the Argives were a simple-minded people, lovers of luxury even though they didn't yet know of wine and the worship of Dionysos. So he had sent the army on to Epidauros, figuring that he could bring the Argives round with just himself and a small band of beautiful maidens, chosen more for their looks than their skill in battle. By the time that the Dionysian army heard the sorrowful news, it was too late. Perseus and Argos had already fallen to Dionysos – the true Dionysos, and not just his votary. The god came to the king that night and visited horrors unimagined even by the most deranged madman upon Perseus. Before the night was over he was reduced to a blubbering child, pissing himself in fear. Under the cruel goad of Dionysos he perpetrated all manner of vile and sacrilegious outrages upon the members of his household. I won't dare to speak of what the Argives found when they entered the palace the next morning – and neither did they. They were filled with shame and horror at the depravity of their king that they swore a solemn vow never to admit what happened there. They slew Perseus, mercifully ending his misery, and then they fabricated a story that he had gone off to distant lands to continue the adventuring he was justly famed for, knowing full well he would never return. They gave the violated Dionysian girls a proper burial, concocting the legend that they had died valiantly in battle. And Akoites, too, they honored by naming him Dionysos. To many he had been the very image of the god on earth, so it was a fitting way to remember him.

And the reason why they made a separate monument for Khorea is because she was the one who taught them the proper rites for honoring Dionysos. She had been part of Akoites' band but had avoided violation by Perseus because she had been passed out drunk in the camp after an especially vigorous night of celebration and never made it to the palaver. When she roused herself a couple days later and stumbled into town the horror had already passed. The people of Argos begged her to teach them the worship of Dionysos in order to avert further wrath from the god and since she didn't really have anything better to do until the Dionysian army came back to retrieve her, she agreed. They Argives took so readily to her teaching and made her so hospitably welcome, in fact, that Khorea remained with them even when the Dionysian army returned and continued on their march, content that things had been satisfactorily resolved. Years later when she quietly passed, an aged and well-respected member of the community, they buried her alongside her companions, creating a noble if not altogether truthful memorial honoring her tireless service on their behalf. As time passed memories faded and the people of Argos began to believe the lies their ancestors had told out of expediency. Perseus was remembered as a great hero who had accomplished many grand things during his adventurous life – including the slaying of a god. That no one else believed such a patently absurd story did not bother them. After all, by that point, it had become enshrined in tradition and everyone knows that if something is old and traditional, why, it must be true.

ARIADNE'S STORY

Ariadne did not awake until long after Theseus and his Athenians had gone. By then the sun was beginning its decline in the late afternoon sky and winds from an awful storm were blowing huge waves onto the jagged rocks of the beach. At first Ariadne didn't remember where she was, but then visions of her father's harbor burning and the laughing faces of the Greeks filled her head and she knew all too well where she was. Ariadne began searching the island for her companions, but they were nowhere to be found. Only footprints in the sand told the story of their ever having been there.

Her heart gripped with fear, Ariadne began to climb the jagged rocks that projected out into the sea. She cut her hands as she scrambled over them, Ariadne whose hands had never felt harder toil than working a loom. Stepping in shallow water between two boulders, she cut her feet on the black spines of the sea urchin, but she paid no attention to her wounds and let the blood flow as she clambered over the rocks, hoping beyond hope to spot the ship of Theseus. Its black sails had long since passed beyond the horizon. With the certain knowledge of her abandonment Ariadne gave up all hope. Theseus' sweet words had brought her to this fate, but it was her own folly that had caused her to accept their deception. For a pretty-faced hero she had betrayed her father, betrayed her brother, betrayed her people – is it any wonder that she had been betrayed in turn? Ariadne wondered at her father's fate; it was a thing too bitter to contemplate for long. Commending her spirit to Haides, Ariadne passed into a deep sleep from which she hoped never to awaken.

This, then, was how Dionysos found her. Ariadne was slumped against the rock with waves washing up over her naked frame, the ocean having long since torn her delicate dress to shreds. She was covered in innumerable scrapes and bruises, and harsh sand from the beach coated her lovely body. Ariadne barely lived; she longed for the comforting embrace of death, and the sweet oblivion that would come with it.

Dionysos stooped down and picked the girl up in his arms. Careful not to cause her any harm the god carried her out to sea, and the waiting ship from which he had come. The whole of the ship was covered in strands of vine and ivy as if it had been made from these plants, and hundreds of grape clusters hung from the mast like a giant purple sail. For oars it had snakes, its crew were satyrs and nymphs and horse-men like Seilenos, and upon its prow was mounted the head of a bull, Dionysos' symbol, which moved about with life, and spoke many things, especially when it neared land. This was the ship that once had belonged to the pirates of Tyrrhenia, those fools who had conspired to ransom off the god whom they mistook for a lost prince walking aimlessly along the shore. Dionysos confounded them however, slaying many with his wild beasts and turning those that fled into dolphins. He kept alive the good helmsman Akoites, who carried word of the god to many people and continued to steer the pirate ship which Dionysos now claimed as his own.

As Dionysos carried the girl Ariadne roused and, looking up into the god's face, let out a sigh. Never before had she seen one so beautiful. The god's hair was black and curly, for black is the color of youth as white is the color of old age. His eyes were like wine, sweet and deep and full of secrets man will never know. His head was crowned with ivy and his skin was golden as the sun which shines above. He wore long flowing robes from Asia and smelled of Arabian incense and hot desert days. With her gentle hand Ariadne reached out and touched his beautiful face and even then she wasn't sure that all this was really happening, for he was too beautiful to exist in the drab and dismal world she had been plunged into. Dionysos smiled at her touch, kissing her tender fingers and Ariadne felt a wonderful calm come upon her, a peace for which there are no words.

After boarding the ship Dionysos gently set her down on his couch and called for his wine-cup to be brought. Holding the girl's head the Lord bid her drink and the wine was sweet as it passed over Ariadne's lips. The wine washed away the bitterness of her heart and soothed her body's wounds, leaving pleasure where there had been pain and joy where there was sorrow. Finally, when the wine had brought back her voice, Ariadne asked, "You are a god, are you not? For only a god could have carried me across the waves like that."

Dionysos nodded, and said, "Indeed I am. Heavenly Zeus sired me and I was born of Kadmos' virgin daughter Semele. I am a god and the son of a god, the Raving One, Dionysos."

"If you are a god then certainly you know what I've done. Why, then, did you not leave me to my fate, for death is no less than what I deserve."

"In your sorrow you called out to me and I came. What evil you have done you have also repented; further, it was love that motivated your actions, not hate. Love forgives much. The law may call for your death – but I am greater than the law."

Overcome by the love in the god's eyes Ariadne began to weep. Dionysos reached forward and touched her tears, saying, "These are more precious than jewels; their worth is greater than all the treasure in the world. Theseus and the others may not have understood what they meant, but I do."

Ariadne pulled away from the god's touch and cried out, her words full of self-loathing, "See how wicked I am! These tears I shed are not born of repentance, but of lust! Being so close to you is driving me mad with sexual longing. You are a god, yet my body aches to feel you like a man. Truly you should have left me to perish on Dia!"

"I know, my Ariadne, and that is why I said that your tears were precious." And then he leaned forward and kissed her with such ardor that it left no room for further discussion. Madly the couple made love while the nymphs and satyrs busied themselves with other tasks, pretending that they could not hear what was going on.

After much time had passed and Dionysos and Ariadne had finished, the crew decided to throw a feast in her honor, to welcome her among the holy band of the god's followers. Dionysos was very much in favor of this and so he left her in the care of the nymphs to go and help prepare the banquet. The nymphs took every care with the girl, bathing and anointing her flesh, combing out her long hair and arranging it artfully, and finally dressing her in a gown of shimmering silk, such as only goddesses wear. Meanwhile, Dionysos and the satyrs labored to prepare the feast, setting up a huge table on the ship, and many couches. All sorts of food were served – indeed, the satyrs took great pride in their culinary skill, despite what everyone said about their culture being no better than a Skythian's. There were cakes, cheeses, and heaps of roasted flesh; olives and figs and grapes; dates and lettuces and stew; barley-meal, onions, and poached eggs; loaves of bread, fishes, and oat-porridge; exotic dishes from Bactria, Arabia, Egypt and India; and three or four different kinds of wine, mixed with water and unmixed. Indeed, it was a wonderful banquet and several of the satyrs played their flutes to entertain those delighting in the feast. Ariadne sat upon the Lord's lap, resting her shoulder on his raised left knee while he stroked her hair and fed her grapes and olives with his own fingers. When the meal was done several more satyrs joined their fellows and formed a chorus to serenade the princess with lovely songs that they had picked up during their travels through Egypt, India, and Bactria – songs that the nymphs much preferred to the lusty Thrakian tunes that the satyrs usually chanted.

As the satyrs sang Dionysos repositioned Ariadne so that her back rested against his chest and her head lay against his shoulder. He leaned forward and whispered gentle words into her hair as his hands explored the supple curves of her body through the silk of her gown. His poetry had the same effect as wine – it caused her head to swim, and roused a pleasant fire within her belly. Ariadne took the Lord's hand and brought it down between her legs, saying, "This flower is yours. From all time it has been yours. Nourished from the beginning in your love its whole purpose has been this moment. Having plucked it Lord, you may now cast it aside, thinking it of no account. But this flower has already felt the bliss of heaven – what, then, are the torments of hell to it?"

Dionysos tilted her head back and kissed the princess. "Do not fear, Ariadne – I am in no hurry to dispose of you. In fact I was just about to ask if you would have me as your husband."

Ariadne slid from the god's lap and fell to her knees before him. She placed her head on his thigh and began to weep. It was not tears of sorrow that she shed but tears of a joy so profound that few mortals ever experience its like in life. "Yes," she wept, repeating that word many times.

From the empty air Dionysos drew a golden crown for Ariadne, the shining crown of Amphitrite which Aphrodite had given to the sea-goddess on her own wedding day. When Dionysos had gone beneath the waves with the Okeanids he had met Amphitrite there and performed a great service for her. In gratitude Amphitrite gave him her crown, saying that he would one day have need of it. This, then, was to be that day.

Dionysos placed the crown on her head and lifted her up to stand by his side. Addressing the satyrs and nymphs, Dionysos said, "Give ear you all, this one have I made your queen!" And the holy band cheered the god's decision, praising Ariadne and her new husband.

They came to Nysa to perform the ceremony, Nysa which had nursed the god in his youth. Before their approach the earth had slumbered in winter. At the touch of the god's feet she roused herself and put on splendid finery to honor him. Where the land was brown and barren it sprang anew with great green life. Where the fruit-bearing tree had stood pitiful with their naked branches they now hung proudly with heavy fruit. The broad meadows of Nysa took on the wonderful colors of spring, donning flowers of every color and lush green grass as their wedding attire. The air smelled of spring; of unfolding blossoms, and fruit on the tree, of green grass and moist earth, sun and rain. The earth made an altar for the wedding, raising a portion of herself up, a mound covered in white blossoms and decked about with strings of flowering ivy and grape vines – an altar fit for the god. Hundreds of birds came to sing the bridal hymn, perching themselves in the fruit-trees till the time was right. Wild animals from the forest came to watch the ceremony, and the nymphs went among them placing flower-garlands around their wild throats, which the beasts joyfully consented to. Many of his fellow gods came and Zeus, king of all, officiated over his son's wedding and he whose word gives order to the world was very eloquent.

The feast on board Dionysos' ship was fabulous. It was like a Lakonian feast, however, compared to the sumptuous meal that followed the ceremony. Even Homer, the greatest of poets and himself fond of extravagant feasts, could not have done it justice. The gods themselves were even awed at its plenitude, for however much they ate there was still more to eat, and ever finer food set before them. And the wine. Oh, the wine! One drop on the tongue was like heaven – yet there was an ever-flowing source of it.

Dionysos ate more sparingly than his fellows, and only emptied his cup twice before he had finished eating. Instead, he watched his fellow gods and mortal followers cavorting, taking pleasure in their hearty laughs and raucous songs. Even modest Hestia got up and danced, drunk on the god's holy wine. More often than not, however, his gaze was caught by his lovely wife, radiant Ariadne, who was in the midst of a large group that continually drank to her honor and sang songs for her, laughed, and made merry. Dionysos looked with pleasure on that, for so much of his young bride's life had been filled with sorrow and seriousness. Blessed are the merry-makers, thought Dionysos, for they are already half divine!

Artemis, the sister of Apollon, came up and sat beside the god. "Honor to you, Dionysos!" She said, raising a cup of his wine. "Your bride is most beautiful. I hope your time with her is filled with more happiness than sorrow."

"Indeed." Dionysos replied after a moment. "Although I think your toast a most peculiar one to make on such a happy day."

"Peculiar, maybe, but true. This fling of yours is bound to end in sorrow. It can be no other way – for you are a god and she a mortal. She will grow old and die – you will not. These mortals are so small, so fragile...I don't know why you'd ever risk getting involved with one of them."

"Love is a powerful thing, Artemis. Its ways are not rational ways. Love is filled as much with sorrow as with joy – but every moment is worth it in the end. For only in love are we truly alive. And that applies just as much to us gods as to men."

"No. Never. I will never open myself to that...that madness. Love is a loss of self, a criminal abdication of the will. You may call that living, but I call it a death, a death unbearable."

"Oh Artemis, if only you knew what you were missing. But describing love to one that has never felt it is like describing a sunset to one who does not see. It simply cannot be done."

"That's just like you to resort to poetry when you're about to lose the debate."

"All life is poetry, don't you see. The world is a myth in which our lives play themselves out."

"Oh great, now you're a philosopher! Just what we need on Olympos."

Dionysos let out a belly laugh and raised his cup in Artemis' honor. "Too true, too true, Forest Mother."

"Truth is precisely what I came to speak with you about. This love of yours has clouded your sight. I think you do not see the injustice your bride has done you, blind as you have become."

"Those are strong words, Artemis. What do you mean by them?" Dionysos inquired, stroking his beard.

"As I sat dining with the Nereïds the subject of your new bride arose. According to them, it seems, Ariadne is no virgin."

"That is hardly news to me." Dionysos smiled. "I had the pleasure of her as we sailed from Dia."

"Yes, but did you have first pleasure?"

"Well no, she was not a virgin when first we lay together. Nor the second time, nor even the third."

"Do you even know who it was that she betrayed you with?"

"I haven't got a clue. It was probably that gallant Theseus who abandoned her on Dia. But maybe someone else beat him to it. There are plenty of pretty boys on Crete, and plenty of opportunities to honor Aphrodite in that delightful manner. For all I know it could have even been that hairy brute Asterios, Minos' own bull, who did the deed. While I doubt it was her half-brother, you seem to suggest something just as bad."

"You make light of all this, but I tell you it is no laughing matter."

"I think it is. A wife is more than a maidenhead and my Ariadne more than most wives. What I care about is the content of her heart – and on that count she is above reproach. She is full of generosity, compassion, gaiety and most importantly when I look into her eyes I know what it is to be loved – and not just sparingly, but with her whole heart. That is a gift of greater value than her virginity. Maybe she took one man to bed before me – maybe she took one hundred; but in the end it was I that she chose, and I that she gave her heart to."

"A god should not be this blind. Tear yourself from her deceptive eyes and look, brother, look at the wrong that she has done you. Virginity is a precious thing, the most precious thing that a girl has – and as such it shouldn't be squandered like a common coin with just any ruffian in the street. It is a jewel that belongs to the girl's husband and if she does not possess it on her wedding day she has stolen from her lord. It is a terrible crime when it has been committed against a mortal – but when the victim of the theft is a god: that is a crime beyond bearing!"

"Now in my journeys I've had the pleasure of a number of young virgins and I can assure you that you're making altogether too much fuss over a bit of skin and some blood. Besides, the first time's never any good and whoever had Ariadne's is welcome to it. I much prefer my women to be experienced in the art of love – it's always better if they know what to do with their hands and mouth and if that part has already been stretched they whimper and cry for different reasons altogether."

Blushing and furious Artemis rose from the table and left. Dionysos, nonplused, returned to the festivity and his cup of wine. Had the god guessed at the contents of Artemis' heart he would have followed her into the forest and pleaded with her to turn from her path of anger. But her heart remained closed to him, and her offended dignity, fueled as it was by the embarrassment she felt at Dionysos' words, turned to dark rage and deadly vengeance. And as the weeks passed this lethal combination festered in the goddess' heart until she had to act upon it.

Now Ariadne had dreamed of travel her whole youth, and as the bride of Dionysos she was able to fulfill her life-long dream. In his chariot drawn by swift-footed panthers the Lord carried his bride across the earth, showing her all the places that he had gone, the people he had met, the wonders he had performed. Ariadne particularly enjoyed the land of the Egyptians, for many things there resembled her home and being among such familiar settings brought back memories of her life before Theseus. Dionysos knew that he could not take her back to Crete, for Minos had interrogated Daidalos and knew of his daughter's involvement in Theseus' rescue of the Athenian virgins, and so Minos had disowned his daughter. Although Minos' power extended to most of the islands beyond Crete, many were sanctuaries of the Lord, and as such owed allegiance first to god, then to man. One such sanctuary was Naxos, the island that Theseus and his men had called "Dia." Abandoned on the southern part of the island Ariadne had thought herself alone on that great piece of land for there were no people to be found, nor signs of there ever having been any. But had she gone just a little further beyond the forest that covered the middle part of the island at the time she would have found a fabulous city with a temple of Dionysos at its center. The Lord brought his bride to Naxos, and they spent many wonderful days together walking on the beach and making love in his temple.

Every year the Thrakians honor Dionysos with drunken feasts which they call Routs, and it was his custom to attend these feasts. Now the time came for Dionysos to go among the Thrakians and while he offered to bring his wife along Ariadne would have no part of it. Wild and bloody, these drunken feasts lasted many days and it was their custom to share the women of a village in common during the course of a Rout – a prospect Ariadne did not find appealing. So Dionysos left her on Naxos with the promise of returning as soon as the Routs had finished.

One day shortly after Dionysos had left, Ariadne was walking along the beach on the southern part of the island, near where Theseus had abandoned her. She often came to this spot and sat on the rocks where Dionysos had found her, staring out to sea. This day she found no comfort on the spot for she felt baneful eyes upon her back, but whenever she sought out their source she was always alone. This sense of unease kept her from climbing the great rocks on the beach and shortly after she had arrived, Ariadne turned back and started heading towards the temple. That was when Artemis struck.

A shrill sound spilled from the forest and as Ariadne turned to discover its source an arrow plunged into her thigh. The princess screamed and collapsed to the ground and like an avenging Fury the Huntress burst from her forest cover and took aim with her silver bow. "Die you harlot!" the goddess cried and let another arrow fly. Miraculously the arrow went wide and Ariadne struggled to rise. She was on her feet and limping away when Artemis caught up with her. Having missed the prone girl, a thing unthinkable, the goddess was in a rage. Using her indestructible bow like a club she struck the princess over the head and beat her to the ground. Bloody and battered, Ariadne lifted a weak arm to try and fend off the goddess' blows; Artemis broke her arm and then brought the bow down on Ariadne's head, sending her into unconsciousness. Artemis stepped back and drew her bow taut. Her black arrow flew straight and punctured the girl's heart. Blood passed over her lips and Ariadne was dead. Artemis took a moment to oversee the carnage she had wrought. Smiling she said, "Dionysos is avenged," and then took on the shape of a doe, disappearing once more into the forest.

Now Dionysos was among the Thrakians when this happened, partaking of the red, raw feast which they had made a sacrament in his mysteries. The moment Ariadne was struck by the goddess, Dionysos knew. Immediately he left the revelers, flying back to Naxos without bothering to make use of his panther-drawn cart or vine-covered ship. Though he traveled with all speed he was too late to save his beloved wife. He found her on the beach surrounded by the temple assistants who had come to search for the girl when she had not returned at the appointed hour. The sight of lovely Ariadne pierced by those arrows, her flesh bruised and bloody, sent the god into a madness.

"Who did this? Why did you let this happen?" the god bellowed and the priests fell to their knees, cowering in their fear. Angered at their displays Dionysos waved his hands over them and they immediately began to change, shrinking and contorting until their form was that of the worm, basest of creatures which moves only by writhing contemptibly. Dionysos then knelt down and picked the girl up in his arms, holding her lifeless body to his. Shaking with his anger, wracked by his loss, Dionysos wept and the winds came, furious winds that lashed at his flesh and tore the nearby trees from the ground. Huge waves pounded against the shore as Dionysos' fists pounded against his chest. Black clouds like the god's own black rage filled the sky and sheets of rain fell to the ground as his tears fell upon Ariadne's body. Lightning filled the sky and thunder threatened to rip the heavens apart. The earth shook with the Lord's fury and the animals in the forest wept along with their god.

Immortal Zeus in heaven took notice and the sight of his own son wracked by pain moved the exalted god so that he descended to earth to comfort the Lord of Nysa. Zeus, arrayed in his fabulous robes, approached Dionysos on the beach and as the son of Kronos came near the winds quieted, the rains ceased, and thunder was heard no more.

Dionysos, his eyes red from weeping, stared up at his father and in a low, lethal voice said, "That storm was mine. You had no right to stop it."

"But son, if I had permitted it to continue all the people on Naxos would have drowned and the island would have been under water before your anger was slaked."

"What care I for those people? My beloved Ariadne is dead. Why shouldn't they join her in the house of Haides?"

"Because, son, it would not be right."

"Oh, don't you dare speak to me of what is right. Was it not you who drowned the whole human race because of the sleight of a single man, and again you who punished Prometheus for bringing fire to them? These are not 'right' actions, however you wish to justify them."

"Indeed, I have done many things of which I am not proud. But having done both good and evil, I can tell you – the good is by far the better."

"If that is all you have come to say, go back up to Olympos father, for I have no intention of killing these innocents. I have other victims in mind." With that, the Lord pulled the arrow from Ariadne's thigh and held it up for Zeus to see. It obviously belonged to Artemis.

"Will you bring war among the gods for the sake of this mortal?" asked Zeus.

Dionysos broke the arrow in two and cast the halves at his father's feet. "Absolutely!"

"But she was only human. They are like the grass – here today, gone tomorrow. This is a great thing to do over such an insignificant being."

"Ariadne was not insignificant. She was the most wonderful woman I have ever met. I loved her with all my heart – there was not another like her in all the world. Tell me, father – did you not love my mother in the same way?"

Zeus did not reply at first. He looked down at the ground for several long moments, the weight of his crown and his kingly attire all of a sudden extremely heavy. Finally, he looked back up at Dionysos and said, "Yes, I did. Your mother was more special to me than any of the other mortal women that I took to bed. More special than Europa, more special than Leda, even more special than Alkmene. Your mother was more special to me than I would often like to admit – a day does not go by that I do not repent my hasty promise."

"Perhaps, then, you understand something of what I feel. Unlike you, however, I cannot sit by and let the woman that I love go unavenged. You may not be able to stand up against Hera – I will not bow to Artemis. And if that means war, so be it."

There was another stretch of time during which neither god spoke. Zeus' head was bowed once more, deep in thought. Then, abruptly, the king of the gods came to a decision and he addressed his son. "This goes contrary to the natural order and the Fates will not like it. But damn them all, what good is being the Ruler of the Universe if you cannot occasionally bend the rules? Now listen up, son. If I raise your wife to the rank of gods, making her immortal, you will have to put aside this enmity of yours. With Ariadne by your side for all time, there will be no need for you to make war against Artemis – and that is the condition that I set for you. Do you accept my terms?"

Dionysos stared up at his father, scarcely believing what he had heard. Then, when it had set in, the god leapt up and rushed to embrace his father. Kingly Zeus accepted his son, returning the embrace as firmly as Dionysos offered it.

Zeus indeed kept to his word. Together Dionysos and he carried the body of Ariadne to Kypros where they gave it a proper burial and placed her wedding crown in the sky as the Corona Borealis. (One can still see her grave on that island, though so many years have passed.) Next Zeus raised the spirit of Ariadne up out of Haides and transformed her into a goddess, bestowing on her all of the power and the immortality of an Olympian. On earth she was worshipped as Ariadne-Aphrodite and her cult spread from Kypros to all the world, including Crete, her home, where she was honored as an earth goddess, and protector of animals. She continued to be the Queen of the Bacchantes, and together she and Dionysos had many children, among them Staphylos, Phanos, Oinopion, Thoas, Peparethos and Keramos. Their love is a shining example to all who feel Aphrodite's sweet embrace and a promise that love persists, even unto death.

Now my story is not, by any means, completed. For though Dionysos kept his part of the bargain and did not make war against the goddess, he nonetheless had his vengeance on her. Dionysos caused the chaste goddess to fall in love with the handsome hunter Orion who many times had accompanied her on the hunt. Despite her initial reluctance Artemis found herself warming up to the fellow and Orion, winning her confidence, was even allowed to watch her bathe, a thing she had killed a number of mortals for attempting. As the days passed and Artemis grew closer to Orion she began to think of wedding the giant hunter and this was a prospect that much disturbed her brother Apollon, so he conspired to dispose of this man who had gained his beloved sister's affections.

One day as he and his sister were hunting near the shore he noticed Orion swimming far out to sea. Pointing to the black object, which Artemis had not recognized, he wagered her that she could not hit it with an arrow. She won the bet by piercing her lover's head. When Orion's body washed ashore she was horrified by what she had done and so Dionysos' vengeance was complete. Dionysos caused her to love and to lose the one that she had loved, that she might know the bitter suffering that she had caused him.

JUSTICE

"Come away from there," Alkithoe ordered, her voice thin and sharp as the needles she was busily sliding through the length of fabric in her lap.

The young girl sighed heavily – though not loud enough that it would carry to her mistress' ears – and returned to her place with the other slaves. All things considered, she had it pretty good as one of the princesses' handmaidens. Her chores consisted mostly of sewing and readying the daughters of Minyas for court appearances, as well as keeping them company. She didn't even have to fetch their meals or run errands for them – there were plenty of other slaves for such things. But tonight she would have gladly exchanged places with any of the field hands or even those who labored – and very often died – in the mines. They, at least, were free to join in the festivities that had taken hold of Orkhomenos and all Boiotia. Even the other house slaves had slipped away in the night to dance with the mad ones in the forest. Only the daughters of Minyas and their closest attendants were immune to the call of the god Dionysos, and the latter most unwillingly.

Nikaia shuddered at the memory of Klite's pitiful shrieks. The old woman had made it as far as the courtyard before they'd noticed she was gone. Then the King's daughters had chased her down like hounds slathering for the hunt, dragging the poor thing back to their bower where they had the palace guards whip her in front of everyone else to send a clear message to the others. A strong man would have had a difficult time enduring the punishment meted out, but the old crone was already like a frail and trembling bird when they started. By the time they were done with her she was a bloody and broken wreck, hardly recognizable as human any longer. Bad as her cries and the sight of the torture had been, the way the princesses had acted was much worse. They were like Furies, terrifying and inhuman as they goaded the tormentors on. No matter what the men did, it was never enough to quench their thirst for blood and vengeance. Nikaia pitied the poor bastards almost more than the crone. They weren't bad men by nature, just trying to do their duty to King and Country. But their mistresses forced them to destroy the woman, mocking their weakness when they tried to show pity or even when their arms grew tired from wielding the lash. In the end they even forbade the men from finishing her off or getting something to ease her pain. Let nature take its course, they hissed like serpents, or better yet let this false god come and heal his would-be votary if he's got the power to do so. At this moment the woman was lying in the far corner of the room, away from everyone else who carefully tried to ignore her as she moaned and wept to herself.

Nikaia feared she would never get the looks on their faces out of her head. What could this god ever have done to them to fill them with such wrath and disdain? And now they just sat by the fire, sewing and weaving as if nothing had happened. The others, terrified, played along, telling jokes and stories as if it was just another night in the palace. But Nikaia had never been good at pretending. Even if she hadn't wanted to join the others in the forest and see what marvelous things took place during the worship of this strange god who had so recently arrived in their land she now wanted to be as far away from these mad women as possible.

"So what were you looking at through the window, oh little bird? Dreaming of making an escape?"

"Not I," Nikaia said, taking up the roving she'd been working on earlier. "Why would I want to be anywhere but here, with my fine ladies, doing the work that Athene has appointed for those of our sex? You generously provide me with food and safety and a roof over my head. What more could one ask for?"

"Rightly so," Leukippe laughed, a sound like a donkey's dumb braying. "And don't any of you forget it. We treat you better than you rightly deserve. And for all of our generosity we just ask a little respect in return. That's not too much, now is it?"

All the slaves answered, "Certainly not," in unison.

"Do you think you'd be better treated out there?" Arsippe chimed in, setting aside her sewing. "Out there in the wild with all those drunkards and maniacs and lecherous fools? We're protecting your virtue by keeping you safe in here with us. What sort of god takes pleasure in such disgusting rites?"

"He's no true god at all." Alkithoe snorted. "Just an excuse for the rabble to engage in indecent acts under the guise of religion. But we can see through the deception; we know the truth."

"Those foul rites aren't even Greek." Arsippe sneered. "They were brought to this land by dirty foreigners, a pestilence that has spread everywhere but here, infecting minds with a disgraceful madness that is corrosive to morals and our good Greek ways."

"But I heard that the god is a Greek, too." Melia, the nursemaid of Leukippe, said, rocking the child gently in her arms. "Wasn't his mother Semele, the daughter of Kadmos who once ruled nearby Thebes? I heard that she was visited by Zeus in disguise and that he saved the babe from the flames when she perished in a terrible fire that destroyed a portion of the palace."

"All lies!" Leukippe said, "A fable those good for nothing religious fanatics dreamed up to give their false god a respectable pedigree. But even there they have failed, for the story proves his impotence in that he was unable even to save his mother from the flames. And why didn't Zeus himself spare her if he loved the girl so much?"

"You are absolutely correct, my sister." Alkithoe said, picking up a dainty treat with her fat fingers. "The truth behind the tale is assuredly this: Semele learned about the god from some stranger at her father's court and made herself out to be a priestess in his unholy rites. This offended heaven, for we of the royal blood are expected to behave better than the rabble. And so she was struck with lightning sent by Zeus to obliterate the evil before it could be spread to other parts of Greece. Such things may be fine in foreign lands, where the people are degenerate and inferior by nature, and they don't really know any better and couldn't help themselves if they did, but we Greeks are a better lot and so more is expected of us by the gods."

"If that's true then Zeus wasn't very effective. The dances of Dionysos are known in every land, even here." Nikaia whispered under her breath.

"What was that?" Arsippe demanded, brows knit dangerously.

"I was just complimenting my mistress on her exquisite needlework."

Arsippe grinned and held the fabric up. "Why thank you. It is coming along rather nicely, isn't it?"

Nikaia nodded and busied her fingers with the loom. That was close. She'd better learn to keep her mouth shut. And yet she couldn't help herself. Something had come over her and forced the words out of her lips. It had felt indescribably good to speak them, even if they'd gone unheard by her mistresses.

A dark shape stalked the shadowed halls of the house of Minyas. The palace was nearly deserted, except for the women's quarters. Even the King, a kindly old man whom many thought treated his daughters too indulgently, had gone to join the revelers, exchanging his crown for a garland of gay ivy. Only the daughters and their slaves remained behind.

As the shadowy figure walked through the empty hallways the torches on the wall roared to flaming life. An intoxicating aroma of wine and incense trailed behind him. His footsteps grew louder the closer he got to the door. They were heavy and rhythmic, like the sound of a drum beckoning one to dance. Inside the room the women began to respond, though to what they could not say. The motion of their hands as they diligently worked the thread fell into the rhythm of his steps. Their heads nodded and their feet slapped the ground as if they were dancing to a music none of them could hear. Some got so carried away that they rose to their feet and began swirling around the room in graceful strides punctuated by spinning and leaping. The princesses might have protested but they were caught in the same enchantment. Alkithoe kicked over the loom; Arsippe tore apart the fabric she had been working so hard on; Leukippe howled and clapped, surprising even herself with her frantic outburst. But she couldn't control herself – none of the women could stop what they were doing, for another had control of their bodies.

Faster and faster they ran around the room, shrieking like beasts and smashing everything in sight. And when there was nothing left to break they collapsed to the ground and beat their fists upon the floor, writhing like wild animals to free themselves of their clothing. Indecently stripped naked, they convulsed and shrieked and began yanking fistfuls of their hair out and piercing their flesh with the instruments of their craft. Though the slave women were just as much in the grip of the frenzy they did no compulsive damage to themselves. They merely danced and howled and mocked their cruel mistresses.

Then everything stopped.

A deathly still and quiet settled over all and the chamber went blacker than the night-time sky. There wasn't even the sound of a breath being drawn. Just emptiness, total and complete. It stretched on for an eternity, though in truth it was merely seconds. The absence was so unbearable that the women ached to scream, just so that they could know they were still there. But even that was denied them.

Then, suddenly, they were no longer alone.

The darkness was filled with an overwhelming presence coming from everywhere and nowhere at once. They couldn't see it – or anything, for that matter – but they could feel it, watching them. And it saw deeper than just their naked flesh lying upon the ground. It saw to the heart of them and beyond. Every secret thing they had done or thought, all the shameful things they had hid from others. But there was no hiding now, no escaping from the thing that was with them in the darkness, that *was* the darkness. It knew them. Every part of them.

And it laughed.

Had they been able to, they would have shielded their ears from the horrible sound with their hands. It would have done them no good, however, because the laughter came from deep inside them, from their souls and through their lips. They were the ones laughing and they could not stop.

Then the chamber was bathed in light. It came not from the lanterns, which were still smoldering, but from everywhere at once as if a star had suddenly appeared in their midst. And what the light revealed was beyond imagining. The walls were covered in ivy. Vines wrapped around the wreckage of their looms and overturned couches. It blocked the door and all of the windows, leaving no escape for the frightened women. Outside they could hear panthers growling, clawing at the door, desperately trying to get in. The sound almost drowned out the strange music, but nothing would ever truly be able to do that. It was a discordant onslaught of sound, the music of delirium played on instruments no mortal hand had ever touched, accompanied by a choir of voices ululating in triumphant joy or indescribable torment; none could say with certainty which it was. But all felt the melody deeply familiar, for it was the same song their heart sang in times of intense emotion, when the company of others was unbearable and oppressive. Those precious moments when the truths they lived by, the truths that sustained them and defined them as a person dissolved into falsehood, transforming into something older, purer and more primitive. When they felt that there was more to themselves than any other could ever guess at or possibly hope to know, when they seemed a stranger even to themselves, capable of wondrous things and terrible things and things that were wonderful and terrible at once. Most in the room had only felt this fleetingly, rarely, before recoiling in horror and slamming the mask back safely into place, unwilling to acknowledge that it was a part of who they were and even more unwilling to let others get a glimpse of it. But now the music gave them no choice. It was all around them, all they could hear and know, impossible to shut out or deny. And it brought all they feared and hated and wished to keep secret up to the surface.

And worse even than the music was the smell that hung over the strangely lit room. It was the aroma of flowers and damp soil, heavy with the perfume of trees and the fragrant, cloyingly sweet incenses of the East. But that was just the most superficial level of the scent; beneath it, rich and dark, was the heat of animal bodies aroused by lust. The room stank of longing and sweat and the salty brine of the ocean. Each woman recognized her own familiar musk in the mixture and realized that she was damp between her legs, even the ones so old they had nearly forgotten the feel of a man's hand on their bodies, and the ones too young to know what that experience was like. But all of them responded to the intoxicating miasma in the air. They felt their skin flush and their breathing quicken and deepen. Even the air upon their naked skin seemed unbearable, and yet they longed to be stroked, to have the heat in their loins put out through joyous friction. The desire was overwhelming – if they did not find release they would surely die from it, or go out of their minds, yet none of them could move so much as a muscle. All they could do was lay there and ache and smell the palpable desire around them.

And then something joined them in the room. They heard the sounds of its feet as it crossed the floor but none of the women could see a thing even when it passed right by them.

Finally it stopped at the far corner of the room where the old battered crone lay in a heap, as close to death as it's possible for a mortal to come.

"Oh, how beautifully you suffered for my sake, grandmother." At the sound of his voice all the women were freed from their stupor. In unison they rose to get a better look at the intruder.

He was a young boy, not more than nine winters old, with soft lips and large dark eyes. Thick, dark curls spilled down to his nude shoulders with green tendrils and plump red grapes interspersed. He was more beautiful than any boy had a right to be and he carried himself with a strength and predatory, feline grace that belied his apparent youth. There was also something uncomfortably sexual about the way he stood there looking at them. Had he gotten it in his head to act upon it they would have been powerless to resist. Indeed many of them secretly longed for the child to do something to them, anything, provided it was to them. Their own husbands and fathers and children were completely forgotten. Only the child existed and he was the lord of their heart.

He smiled and motioned for the crone to stand. She paused for a second, thinking it impossible to do more than continue breathing, and even that was a chore. But then she did as he asked, because she couldn't do otherwise. To everyone's surprise she found her feet with ease. All the pain and the wear of a lifetime's servitude had vanished. Her flesh showed no sign of the cruel whip; indeed it had grown supple and firm as in the days of her maidenhood, without so much as a wrinkle or grey hair to mar her beauty. Disbelievingly she examined every inch of herself, spinning about with an ease and gaiety she had not known for decades. Then with tearful eyes she turned to the smiling boy and looked him a question, her voice choked by joy.

"I welcome you into my troop to revel for all time in payment for what you endured here this night. Now go and suffer no more."

The vegetation parted and the door flew open of its own power. The woman who was no longer a crone, and would never again taste the bitterness of infirmity and old age, cast a longing glance at the boy and then fled from the chamber into the night and the forest, eager to find the revelers of the god and join them in their holy dances. She had so much to dance for now, and she would never stop.

"You others may go as well."

The slave women got up and howled for joy, chasing after their sister. But when the daughters of Minyas made to follow, the boy raised his hand and the door slammed shut, the vegetation growing back in place.

"Not you three. We have much to discuss before the night is through."

Arsippe fell to her knees at the boy's feet, crying and pounding her fists on the floor in frantic desperation. She implored him to forgive her foolishness and blamed it all on the others. Alkithoe and Leukippe began shouting as well, proclaiming their innocence and trying to pass the blame elsewhere. Eventually words failed them and they started to scream and rage, weep and wail, tear their hair and beat their flesh. The boy stood smiling the whole time, taking in their morbid theatrics with cold indifference. When exhaustion finally overtook them and they collapsed at his feet, he laughed once more and said, "I do enjoy a good show, but I think that's quite enough of that. Unless you three wish to go on, of course. I've got all night."

Silently they looked at each other and then back at him.

"I thought not. And anyway you had your chance to implore me and squandered it."

"How were we to know that you truly are a god?" Alkithoe demanded, wiping the snot and tears from her face.

"What does that matter? I'm not here because you rejected my divinity. I could care less what you think of me and my worship. I have blessings aplenty to give to those who acknowledge me, and those who don't want anything to do with me are no concern of mine."

"Then why are you here?" Leukippe snarled, suddenly indignant.

He turned to look at her with savage eyes and she shrank back before he even spoke a word.

"Simple. You went beyond the bounds of what is acceptable and forbade your slaves from having any part of my worship. You locked them in here with you and forced them to toil all through the night when the rest of the city – and your own father as well – were off in the woods dancing my holy dances."

He sprang forward with the speed of a panther, grabbing her neck with his small hand. He hissed the next words, his lips almost touching her own.

"That I could not abide."

She thought he was going to choke the life from her then; his dark eyes hinted he might. Instead he let go and regained his composure. She fell back, her head hitting the hard floor, limp and trembling.

"Worse yet, you beat your slaves for defying you and would not listen to a thing they said, even when they tried to speak sense into your senseless heads." As he talked he paced around the room, hands folded neatly in front of him, glancing at each in turn.

"Do you think it was right what you did? Kings and Queens are appointed by the gods to rule a land and govern its people. They have an awesome, unviable power from heaven, but that authority only extends so far. It cannot touch the souls of the subject populace, cannot control what is in their hearts and minds. Even the lowliest slave is free inside their head, though their body is bound in chains. This is especially true when it comes to the realm of religion. No one has a right to compel another to worship against their wishes or to stay them from offering what they feel is proper to the gods who are responsible for all the good things in life. Indeed the most important function of royalty is to ensure that the people are able to honor the gods in the proper way, to ensure that the ancient rites that make the land strong and prosperous are dutifully carried out. It's why you've been given such wealth and authority in the first place. Without the gods you would be nothing and less than nothing. But instead of doing what was just you did what was most shameful in the eyes of the gods. You fought against me and against religion itself. You treated your slaves as no one deserves to be treated. You showed yourselves, time and again, to be unworthy of all that had been given to you."

He spread his boyish hands out and smiled.

"So I have come to take it back."

The women all screamed then, a horrible sound as if they were being consumed by fire, though none was visible.

"First I will take your sanity. Then I will take your decency and compel you to do things so horrifying that none have ever before dreamed up such abominations. Then when your father and countrymen learn of the atrocities you have committed they will drive you out of the land, lest your evil breed a true pestilence. Deprived of all you have known and the love of all you hold dear, you will wander the earth, rejected and scorned by all you meet. Should any be foolish or kind enough to take you in in your filthy and maddened state you will turn on them and commit even more heinous and bloody acts, until even a stranger's hospitality is denied you. Nor will it be possible to end your torment. If you try to murder yourselves I will just heal whatever wounds you inflict.

"But do not think that I am entirely without mercy. No, once you have suffered as much as you have made others suffer and become a tale old women tell to frighten children into being good, a warning as well to all tyrants that would attempt to impose their will on the people, forbidding them to worship what is good and true, when your names have become a byword for impiety and universally reviled – then I shall show you mercy by stripping away the last vestiges of your humanity, granting you a disgusting physical form to match your disgusting souls. Then you shall haunt the forests and cry at night, a sound to fill all who hear it with fear. This is the chastisement you have brought upon yourselves. This is what you deserve, and then some. Be glad that I am a merciful god: I could have devised much worse for you."

The boy smiled at the weeping women, then turned to leave, the music and vegetation disappearing with him. When the door closed behind him the women sat for several long seconds in silence. Then they heard the pitiful sounds of Leukippe's child, forgotten in the corner of the room when the slaves fled.

Suddenly the daughters of Minyas realized that they were ravenously hungry.

A DIALOGUE OF THE GODS

Hera enters the celestial court of the gods where she finds Zeus, Hermes and Aphrodite lounging about and enjoying the view of earth thousands of miles below them. Hera is noticeably upset.

Hera: Do you know what that son of yours has gotten up to now?

Zeus: I am almighty Zeus – there is not that transpires upon the broad-bosomed earth or in heaven's starry expanse that escapes my all-seeing eye. And you'd do well to remember that, dear wife of mine.

Hera: [*After a weighty pause*] Well…?

Zeus: Which son are we talking about again? I have so many of them.

[*Hera scowls*]

Zeus: Ah…that one.

Hera: Yes. *That* one. The good-for-nothing whelp of a mortal princess.

Aphrodite: [*Lifting a goblet of wine*] I wouldn't say he's good for nothing…

Hera: Don't you start in, hussy. [*Turning back to her husband*] The house of god-fearing Minyas is no more. They all lay dead in pools of their own blood after a night of unspeakable horrors.

Hermes: Not all of them. The little bitches are flitting about on bat's wings even as we speak. He let them off lightly if you ask me.

Hera: No one asked you, *errand-boy*.

Zeus: Now, now. There's no need for language like that, sister of my heart. Certainly we can discuss this matter with civility.

Hera: Civility? You dare speak to me of *civility* when your son's hands are stained with the gore of innocents?

Hermes: Dionysos' hands are pristine. He didn't dash those babies to the ground and roast their flesh. That was all their mothers' own doing.

Hera: He drove them mad. He put the vile idea into their frenzied brains.

Hermes: Maybe. But it was still their own choice, and their choice to insult him in the first place.

Aphrodite: None of this would have happened if they weren't so insolent and head-strong. Even after they mocked his divinity and refused to take part in his worship he came to them disguised as an old slave woman and begged them to relent. That's more than any of us would have done. No god should have to humble themselves before a mortal.

Hermes: And by that point he wasn't even asking Minyas' daughters to acknowledge his divinity. He came to plead on behalf of the slaves, begging their cruel mistresses to give them license to worship as their hearts bid them. The daughters flew into a rage and ordered their slaves beaten to show that they were the ones in control. That's what provoked his deadly wrath. Granted, the punishment may have been a little extreme…

Hera: They ate the flesh of their own children!

Hermes: And it sent a clear message. I bet everyone who hears the tale will think twice before trying to stop another from worshiping the gods. See, we all benefit from this terrible situation, so why hold it against him?

Hera: Because this isn't the first time it's happened. Lykourgos, Pentheus, the Proitides, Deriades…he's littered the earth with the corpses of his enemies. Will you excuse all the madness and murder he's unleashed?

Hermes: With all due respect, my sovereign lady, I don't think you really want to be taking up the cause of that lot. Every last one of them deserved what they got. Dionysos fled into the sea to avoid conflict with Lykourgos and only emerged with black vengeance in his heart when the mad-man thrashed his defenseless nurses with an ox-goad. Pentheus he gave every opportunity to repent his impiety and in the end it was his own mother who slew him.

Hera: Dionysos made her do it.

Hermes: Yes, and that was justice working itself out. Agave's cruel mockery contributed to her sister's demise. Since she took his mother away from him, Dionysos saw to it that she destroyed her own son so that she'd know the pangs of loss and the bitter consequences of her actions. How could anything be more fair than that?

Aphrodite: And the Proitides are fine now. Sure, they can't show their faces in public and no one'll take them in marriage, but they had enough sex for a lifetime – and then some! Silly cows, that'll teach them to act the prude. If Dionysos hadn't driven them mad I was going to.

Zeus: And I don't really have any pity for Deriades. The man was a tyrant lording it over his people. My boy set them free and because of him our names are known even among the far-off Indians. Sure, a little blood was spilled during the conquest but that's always the case.

Hera: I can't believe you're all on his side.

Aphrodite: What can I say, he's a charmer.

Zeus: Takes after his father, the boy does.

Aphrodite: [*winking*] He sure does.

Hera: You're all incorrigible. I bet the other gods will be able to see through his ruse.

Hermes: That's a bet I'd be glad to take. He and Hephaistos are old drinking buddies. Ares went with him to India. He and Demeter have been brainstorming some new agricultural techniques. Haides thinks of him like a younger brother. Dionysos just took Poseidon out on his new boat. Athene's the one who saved his heart when the Titans got the munchies. Artemis thinks he's the best hunter since Orion. Apollon recently went in on a time-share at Delphi with him. Hestia's got the hots for Dionysos – not that she'll ever act on it, mind you.

Aphrodite: [*snorts*]

Hermes: About the only god you might have on your side is Herakles since he's still smarting after Dionysos drank him under the table. But considering the strained relationship you two have got I'm guessing he'd side with him just to spite you. Face it, Hera. You're the only one who's got it out for Dionysos and this vendetta of yours isn't doing you any good. Let it go would be my advice to you.

Hera shoots a baleful glance at the grinning Hermes as she gets up and leaves the gleaming court of the gods. Zeus gives a smile of paternal pride and then follows after her. Hermes raises his glass in a toast to his dear friend and then Aphrodite joins him in Olympian laughter.

REMORSE

While Hermes nervously glances over his shoulder, eager to get underway, Zeus continues to look down upon the slumbering face of the child he cradles in his hands. They are big, strong hands – hands that have slain giants and made the earth shudder with their might. His rule is supreme: he steers the course of the world with those hands, and every god bows the knee to him. Yet he knows in his heart that he is powerless to protect this little one, this tiny babe that is nearly lost in the folds of his palm. Those innocent eyes, those soft, girlish lips, those delicate curls framing chubby cheeks – how he wants to hold him tight, shelter him from every affliction, raise him up to manhood on Olympos' brilliant heights as his beloved and most honored son.

But Zeus is far-seeing, wiser than any creature on earth or in heaven – though often he wishes that he wasn't. He knows the implacable hatred that his wife harbors for this child. Twice already she has tried to destroy him – and twice failed, which has stoked the flames of her hatred all the more. The boy's life will not be easy. Hera will pursue him wherever he flees, maddening his mind, tormenting everyone who gets too close to him – and that is just the beginning of the evils she has in store for him. Zeus has pleaded with his wife, threatened her, but to no avail. He knows many things, but he cannot comprehend why she hates him with so great a passion.

Zeus has looked into the web of the Fates, seen the other worlds created by his decision to forcefully oppose Hera over this matter. All of them are worse than the one that comes about through the suffering of Dionysos. Wars among the gods, the loss of his throne, the earth laid waste – it's too much to risk, too much to lose, even for the sake of this sweet child. He hates what must happen to him, hates the part he must play in the tragedy, but there is no choice left to him. That is what the responsibility of kingship means, and though it is a burden that weighs heavy upon his heart, it is his and his alone to bear.

So with tears streaming down his great broad cheeks, Zeus hands the sleeping child over to Hermes, the most precious gift he has ever entrusted to the messenger of the gods, and watches silently as they depart for distant lands. He knows that he will see him again, after many adventures and welcomed among the gods even by Hera herself – but it doesn't make what he's done any easier to endure.

LOVE AMONG THE VINES

Even after all this time I can still remember the way she looked that night. Her long black hair had come loose from its braid and hung down over her face, concealing everything except for her small mouth which was spread in a strange, feral grin. Her nipples were erect; I could tell this because the elaborate Greek-style dress she wore had come undone, and she'd casually tossed the fabric over her right shoulder, completely exposing the left side of her body from the waist up. The dress was ruined; it had grass and dirt stains across its whole length from rolling around on the ground, as well as a dark smear at the top that I initially took for blood until I noticed the broken wine bottle beside her. She was on her knees, rocking back and forth, chest heaving and head whipping about in time to a song that none of the rest of us could hear. There was music that night – a bunch of folks back at the house had a drum circle going – but it was clear from the way she moved that she was listening to something else entirely. It was also clear she couldn't see me, even though she was looking right in my direction. She was staring through me, beyond me, seeing the god alone knows what. That made it easier for me to watch her without feeling self-conscious about it.

And watch her I did. Hell, I couldn't take my eyes off her. I was completely mesmerized by the way the shadows played across her pale skin, the way the golden serpent wrapped around her forearm reflected the light of the distant bonfire, the way her fingers shredded the ivy-crown she had been wearing earlier, but most of all by the depth of the ecstatic trance she was in. Right there in front of my eyes was a real, live mainad and it felt like a huge honor just to be in the presence of such an amazing creature. The hair on the back of my neck was standing up and it felt like I had butterflies in my stomach. I'd always heard people describe it that way and wondered what the hell they were talking about. Now I knew.

Yeah, Klea always did know how to make an impression, that's for sure. I probably would have felt that way regardless, but I think part of what made her stand out so much that night was all the other people who were taking part in the ritual. It was a big Dionysian festival put on by one of the local Wiccan covens. It wasn't just Wiccans, of course, but they made up the majority of attendees, as they do at most of the Pagan events here in the city.

I'd been living in the city for about six months at that point, having fled from Bumfuck, Nowhere. Part of what had brought me here was the city's thriving Pagan scene. I was tired of doing all my rituals alone and having my "community" consist entirely of e-mail lists and forums that were mostly populated by argumentative blowhards that were more concerned with debating historical minutiae than actually, you know, worshiping the gods we all claimed to care so much about. So, after settling in I started hanging out at one of the larger occult bookstores and attending open circles, coffee klatches and the annual Pagan Pride event. I'm sure I don't have to tell you how disappointing most of this stuff was and the quality of people it tended to attract. After five months I was pretty much ready to throw in the towel and resign myself to a lifetime of solitary worship. But then Autumn, a sympathetic friend I'd met through a class on Qaballah, told me about the Dionysos festival.

Initially I was excited. What Dionysian wouldn't be? And then it dawned on me who would be there and I did my best to think of a reason to beg off. Autumn wouldn't take no for an answer, and when she set her mind to something she could be quite persistent. And pushy. Eventually I realized it would just be easier to cave in and go, because I knew I'd never hear the end of it otherwise. Besides, she promised it wouldn't be as bad as I feared. Although they were Wiccans, the coven knew their stuff and had a reputation for hosting some of the best rituals in the area. Plus, it wouldn't just be Wiccans there, as some of Autumn's Ceremonial Magician friends were planning to come, as well as a couple Druids, Discordians and even an Asatruar. I mentally wondered why a Heathen would be coming to a festival of Dionysos, but I'd attended plenty of non-Hellenic events for the sake of community outreach, so I supposed it wasn't all that odd. With foreknowledge of the eclectic nature of the guest-list I should have known what I was getting myself into, but somehow I wasn't prepared for the reality of it.

As I got out of my car, a 300 lb. guy in a toga made from a bed sheet and a crown of plastic grapes was chasing a nubile redhead through the parking lot, shouting, "Come to papa Bacchus, you lusty nympho!" at the top of his lungs. I considered getting back into my car and driving off but Autumn was on the porch having a cigarette and she spotted me, waving excitedly. Resigned, I stuffed my keys into the pocket of my shorts beneath my *khiton*, fixed my ivy-crown and walked up the tiki torch-lined steps to greet her.

It pretty much got worse from there. Inside I found a group of people in store-bought "Roman" Halloween costumes eagerly debating whether *Star Wars* or *Star Trek* was the better franchise. I also overheard a woman in t-shirt and jeans holding forth on how the mainades had originally belonged to the primordial Great Mother Goddess until "that phallocentric interloper" stole them away. I was about to ask what business she had coming to a festival of Dionysos if she held such ludicrous and offensive beliefs, but Autumn took me by the arm and guided me into the living room before I had a chance to.

Autumn introduced me to our hosts for the evening as well as the rest of the coven who were sitting on a big couch and some folding chairs that had been brought inside to accommodate the large number of guests. I took an immediate liking to the High Priestess and her husband, who had a warm, friendly energy about them. They were both in their late 40's, worked in the computer industry and had been Pagan of one sort or another their entire adult lives. Their home was truly impressive – a spacious, double level with a large fenced-in backyard and a stunning view of a sprawling forest behind. It was tastefully decorated with lots of Classical art on the walls and assorted deities wherever there was space for them. I drooled over their library which dwarfed my own and contained a number of volumes I would gladly have killed to own. Nor were the books just for display. As we waited for the last of the guests to arrive and settle in we had a very pleasant conversation about Greek religion and the ancient cult of Dionysos in particular. They were excited to learn that I was a fellow Dionysian since they considered him their patron, despite the fact that the coven was ostensibly Celtic. They rattled off a bunch of vocabulary, trying to see whether their Greek pronunciation was proper and in fact it was better than my own, which admittedly is quite atrocious. We commiserated over the various ways that people butcher the god's name, agreeing that the most egregious was, without a doubt, "Dionysius."

This led to an extended diatribe on the part of Gwydion – the husband – concerning popular depictions of him in shows like *Xena* and *True Blood*, particularly the notorious "Lolo Bromius" gaff which elicited belly laughs from him every time he heard it. Sadly, that was sometimes even in ritual space. I found myself relaxing into the conversation and thankful that Autumn had forced me to come. For the first time since moving to the city I'd actually found some Pagans that seemed to be on the same page as me. At least they didn't make me cringe with embarrassment on their behalf and want to run for the hills, desperate to get as far away from them as possible – which is saying something, since that tends to be my normal reaction upon meeting "co-religionists."

That feeling of goodwill lasted through the better part of the ritual, even when they cast a circle complete with an elaborate quarter-calling. They'd warned me ahead of time that it wasn't going to be an authentic Greek ritual, much as they, personally, would have liked to do it that way. The Pagans of our city were staunchly traditional in their eclecticism and expected things to be done a certain way. It was inconceivable to them that one would worship the gods without first consecrating sacred space and inviting the elemental guardians to keep negative forces out. Once, when Gwydion and Lady Larkspur had attempted to do so, one of the coveners blurted the invocation out assuming they'd just plum forgot (even though they'd explained beforehand that they were trying something a little different this time). Though it wasn't really my thing, I politely stood by with the rest while they went through the motions. After all it was their ritual and their home, and we Hellenes are big on the code of hospitality, whether as guest or host.

All things considered, it was a pretty decent ritual, certainly better than I had been expecting. After the nod to Wiccan sensibilities it was pretty much straight out of the Greek playbook. There was a procession around the backyard, a sacrifice and a recitation of one of the Orphic hymns to Dionysos, which Gwydion had impressively memorized instead of just reading it off a script. The idol of Dionysos was impressive as well, a lovely bearded bronze mask mounted on a pole in the middle of their yard and decked with various types of vegetation. After they presented the god with a plate heaped high with fruit and poured out two bottles of wine for him, they led the group in a series of energy-raising chants. I've got to say, there was something indescribably awesome about almost thirty people passionately shouting Dionysos' name at the top of their lungs. Sure, it's entirely possible to have deep and powerful experiences with the god entirely alone. Of necessity most of mine had been like that up to then. But there are parts of him that you can only experience when you're worshiping with a bunch of other people, worshiping as part of a group. That collective frenzy which spreads from person to person, building up as each succumbs to the orgiastic loss of identity, dissolving into the god-intoxicated throng. Granted, it was there on only the most superficial level that night and most had no idea what true *ekstasis* was, let alone had ever experienced it. But I could feel something stirring within me as all of our voices together called the god, and it was different from anything I had known before. Not better, and certainly not deeper, but it was different and there's no denying that.

The chanting led quite nicely – and naturally – into dancing, the whole group joining hands and moving around the idol in a rough circle as a couple of bearded guys drummed slow and steady. It took us a while to get the hang of it, especially since the yard, while spacious, wasn't infinitely so. But in time we did and as the drummers increased their speed and tempo we fell into a pretty good rhythm. Gradually the drums drove us on faster and faster until we were almost running around the circle. I really got into it, so much so that I shouted out "Io evohe!" without really thinking about it. As soon as the cry left my lips I felt intensely self-conscious but then someone else took up the call and before I knew it so was the whole group. That was definitely the high point of the ritual, as far as I was concerned: dizzily racing around the idol of the god, yelling as loud as we could. Shortly afterwards the leaders collapsed to the ground and everyone joined them, dropping where they stood.

I lay there for several long moments, feeling the cool grass and damp earth against my cheek, trying not to get sick as the stars continued rushing round and round overhead. My neighbor's foot struck my chest, but it barely registered. All I could feel was the blood pumping through my veins, the chill night air, and the god all around us and in me. Our dancing and cries had drawn him up out of the earth, out of the idol, and he was everywhere I looked. I felt totally drunk, though I hadn't had so much as a glass of wine that evening.

A couple minutes or an hour later – it could have been either, for all I could tell – the High Priestess and her husband rose to their feet and addressed the crowd. They explained that the remainder of the ritual would be free-form worship where each of us could commune with the god in whatever way we felt moved to. Wine had been set up near the masked idol and at various places throughout the house and yard. We were encouraged to drink as much as we wanted, since it was his gift to mankind, but that we should do so responsibly. There were designated drivers and they'd call a cab for anyone who needed it; otherwise the house was open for anyone who wanted to crash overnight. There was also fruit, meat and bread for any who were hungry or needed help grounding. The drummers would continue for another hour or so, so that people could dance individually or as part of small groups. They were lighting the fire so that folks could hang out by it; alternately we could head to the woods beyond the gate if we wanted some time alone or to commune with the god in the wild. It was natural at festivals like this for people to experience altered states and ecstasy. Usually these were good; sometimes people had bad trips though. Especially appointed members of the coven would be circulating to help people ride it out or ground and center. Above all we should have a good time, enjoy ourselves and honor the great god Dionysos.

Though I was appreciative of all the detailed planning and organization, I was glad when they were done with their explanation. Really, they should have gone over that stuff before we got started. It was a total buzz-kill having to sit there and listen to ramble go on and on for what seemed an eternity. When they were through I picked myself up and staggered over to the idol, getting a large glass of red wine. I immediately dumped half of it out for the god with a quick prayer, downed the rest in a single gulp and then refilled my cup.

Presently I found myself caught on the horns of a dilemma. On the one hand I liked being close to the idol of my god. It was pretty to look at and was giving off this amazing energy. Plus it was within easy reach of the wine. There was a lot of it and I'd just gotten started drinking.

But on the other hand, there were people. A lot of them. They were garish and loud and getting awfully close to me. A couple of them sat down right next to me, actually touching me and trying to engage me in conversation. I didn't want to talk. I couldn't. The primitive, pre-verbal part of my brain had completely taken over and what I was feeling at the moment wasn't the sort of thing you could have put into words anyway. Their chatter was actually painful to my ears. I couldn't understand how they could talk, let alone talk about such banalities, at a time like this. And when some guy clapped me on the back jovially it took everything in my power not to break the fucker's arm off and club him to death with it.

That pretty much decided me. I traded my cup for the rest of the bottle and stumbled off, snorting when the guy's girlfriend asked me to fill her glass. I held the bottle protectively to my chest as I made my way towards the gated fence. I passed a lot of people, a blur of laughing faces and couples making out and lone figures dancing to the drums, which had started to pick up steam once more. They all seemed to be having a great time, and I was happy for them and happy for my god as well, in whose honor they were having such a grand party. But I was also a little nonplussed. That's all this seemed to be for these people, a party. Did they feel nothing else but light-hearted merriment? Even this ritual, which hadn't been terribly deep or profound by the standards of my own observances, had had a noticeable effect on me. My spirit was heavy with *entheos* and I found it difficult to focus my vision or even walk a straight line as a result. From the moment that we had gathered outside I could feel Dionysos moving along the edges of my consciousness, transforming it through his touch so that everything took on a strange, dreamlike quality. By the end of it my thoughts seemed no longer to be entirely my own. They had grown dark and dense and fertile, filled with the things of the earth.

I sensed none of that in the others. They remained much as they had been at the beginning. A little more gay, perhaps, but not substantially different. Some of them played at being in a state of possession, but all you had to do was glance into their eyes to see how deep it went. They danced, but in an intentional, cautious, self-conscious fashion. There was no flow to their movements, no wildness, nothing that did not come entirely from them. The grace of the god was entirely absent. Nor had most of them even given it room to manifest. They were too busy preening in their costumes, showing off their impressive moves or just plain gossiping to bother. And why not? They weren't Bakchoi; calling them wand-bearers would have been overly generous in many cases. But that's the way it always is. No doubt it was like that even in ancient Greece. Dionysos needed to be worshiped by huge crowds, even if most returned to their homes and ordinary lives untouched by his mysterious spirit. Who's to say that they didn't get some benefit from the revel – or that the god himself did not either?

I certainly wouldn't say such a thing. And yet I felt a strong need to be away from them, to commune alone with my god in a truly wild place. And so I wandered as deep as I could into the woods on the edge of Gwydion and Lady Larkspur's property, until I could barely hear the sound of the drummers. At first I was envious of the couple for having access to such a place while I lived in a shitty apartment in the heart of the city. The things I could do with such land! But then the magic of the woods took hold of my heart and I thought no more about such things. I slumped down beneath an ancient pine and drunk in the sights and smells of a forest at night. I dug my fingers deep into the soil and stroked the bark behind my head. I listened to a soft breeze through the branches and the scurrying of some small creature only a few feet away from me. The scent of loam and moss and pine intoxicated me with every breath I took. I poured out some wine for the nymphs of this place, then another libation for Dionysos, and began drinking in earnest until there wasn't a drop left in the bottle. It was good wine, too. Rich and strong, but smooth going down, with a complex, earthy taste that reminded me of vetiver and musk. In fact it was almost like drinking the forest itself and I was sad when it was all gone. I put off going back for as long as I could, but the bottle had done nothing to allay my considerable thirst and there was sadly no wine in the forest. So, regretfully, I bid farewell to the peaceful solitude of the sylvan oasis and started back.

And that's when I came upon Klea. I didn't know that that was her name at the time, of course, and wouldn't learn it until the following morning over breakfast. To me she was just a mainad, a true mainad, and in a way that's what she always remained. Stumbling upon her like that, disheveled and in the throes of ecstasy, was a sublime experience. It was magical. It was like something out of an ancient myth. I immediately recognized what was happening to her and that Dionysos was behind it. This was about as far apart from the things I'd been seeing that evening as it's possible to get. She was doing stuff they'd only ever read about or dreamt of. But it was real, and happening right before my eyes.

And not just my eyes. A trio of would-be Bacchantes came out of the woods where they had been dancing and stopped cold, as if they'd stumbled upon an alien creature. I suppose, in a way, they had. They watched her, open-mouthed, for several moments and then she did something that shocked them out of their stupor. She began to laugh and to cry simultaneously. Her whole body shook with the laughter and it echoed through the chill night sky, louder even than the drums. But her face was red and blotchy and tears streamed down her cheeks so plentifully that she couldn't wipe them away with her arm fast enough, so she just gave up trying.

"Something's wrong," one of the women whispered to her companions. Then louder, to Klea. "Are you okay? Do you need some help?"

There was no response, nothing to acknowledge that she was even aware of their presence. She just kept laughing and crying.

"We've got to help her." The second woman said. "This looks bad. *Real* bad. I've seen this before. We've got to get her to ground and center. Drain some of that energy off into the earth or it could really mess her up."

"I don't know how to do that yet." The third woman, clearly the eldest of the bunch, said. "I just started my 101 classes and we haven't gotten to energy work."

"First thing we've got to do is grab her. Make contact, skin to skin. That'll help bring her back to herself. Then we lay her down on the earth, make her comfortable so the soil can suck up all the negative emotions. I'll do some Reiki to help the process along, but you two need to get her talking about what happened. She may not want to at first, but it's absolutely imperative that she share and process everything. One of us should probably run and get her something to eat. Chocolate maybe. Anyone know where we can get some chocolate?"

"For your own safety, why you don't you ladies just move along, eh?"

While they had been plotting strategy I had quietly moved between them and Klea, making myself a human shield. To drive the point home I crossed my arms over my chest and broadened my stance.

"Are you...*threatening* us?" The second demanded, incredulous.

"Nope. Just trying to protect you from making a serious fucking mistake. I'm the least of the things you've got to worry about right now. Though," I flashed my teeth in a grin. "I wouldn't fuck with me either if I were you."

"What do you mean? Get away from her. Do you know her?"

"Nope. But I know *what* she is: a mainad, and that's not something you want to be messing with, especially when they're in a state like that."

"She needs help," the first interjected. "If we don't bring her down she could suffer permanent damage."

"I'm not so sure she's in any danger, ladies. This comes with the territory, and she looks pretty experienced to me. It's from the god and it's best if she just rides it out and comes down on her own, after doing whatever the two of them are doing right now. And if you do try and force her down, the way you were suggesting, one of two things is going to happen. Either you're going to fuck her up or she's going to do it you. Possibly both."

"How could she hurt us?" The third asked.

"Do you know anything about mainades? They tore live bulls apart with their bare hands. They carried fire without getting burned. They were the hunting companions of Dionysos. Even if she doesn't eviscerate you, do you really think *he's* going to be very happy with you if you interrupt him before he's finished with her?"

"But Dionysius isn't real. He's just a myth, an archetype of the – "

"Don't even finish that fucking sentence. Go. Now. Before *I* do something to you, let alone either of them." I growled, summoning every ounce of power, authority and brute aggression at my disposal. I felt totally bad-ass and they apparently concurred because they scattered, rushing back to the house.

I gave Klea a quick once-over to make sure the little altercation hadn't disturbed her – she'd stopped laughing, but the tears were still flowing and it was clear she had remained in a very deep state of *entheos*, completely oblivious to everything around her – and then took a couple steps back to give her some space. I'd been there before. Well, not precisely *there*. Only a woman can be a mainad, and Dionysos takes his mainades places none of the rest of us can follow. But I was no stranger to trance and possession, so I knew what she needed, which was to be protected from stupid bitches like that. I waited there with her for another twenty minutes or so, and only had to shoo off a couple more well-meaning Wiccans before Klea came out of it and back to herself, or as much as one can after being in such a state. I expected her to be a bit more surprised, hell, even profoundly upset to find some weird guy she'd never met before sitting there watching her trance out. She wasn't. She said she trusted Dionysos to watch over her when she went that far out. Tonight, I'd done it for him. We talked. A while later I helped her up, got her to my car and drove her back to her place. She asked me if I'd stay the night and watch over her some more, in case there were any after-effects. I did. And I've been by her side ever since.

THE BACCHAE 2005

Dramatis Personae
George W. Bush
Dick Cheney
Chorus
White House Page
Secret Service Agents (3)
Dionysos
Anchorwoman

Interior of the Oval Office: *indicated by a chair, a table, and a flag.* George W. Bush *is sitting in the chair,* Dick Cheney *is at his side, and behind them stand the* Chorus.

George W. Bush: So how is the invasion going?

Dick Cheney: Very well, Mr. President. Our troops have already taken Paris, and two-thirds of France has been liberated. Things are still a little shaky in Bordeaux where we met with some unexpected resistance, but that should be mopped up by night's end.

Bush: Have we found any Weapons of Mass Destruction yet?

Cheney: Uh...unfortunately not, Mr. President. And there was some minor protest of our unilateral strike by the international community. But not much. It was France, after all.

Bush: It's truly a shame that France became a rogue nation. Nice people, the French – though that whole Jerry Lewis thing is a little odd. But I like their bread. And their fries!

Cheney: Yes, well now they'll be able to enjoy their baguettes with a side of Freedom and Liberty. Once Haliburton has finished rebuilding France's infrastructure that is.

Chorus:
Zeus' pet eagle no longer sits tamely at the side of the Heavenly Father,
symbol of justice and far-reaching equanimity.
But now is perched upon the shoulder of dread Ares,
who has burst his brazen bonds and strides through the land,

his dark shadow inciting men to madness and war.
The eagle calls out for blood and vengeance,
its shrill cry echoed in that of weeping brides and fatherless sons.
Dark days behind us, and darker days to come.

Bush: So how are the other points on our agenda coming along? I've got a State of the Union address to prepare.

Cheney: Well, there's been a slight bump in the road to progress up in Alaska.

Bush: A bump, you say?

Cheney: Yes. It seems that there was a little spill in the Natural Preserve where we've been drilling. Nothing major, mind you. Won't even be a drop in oil prices. But there are a few dead animals and some black beaches now.

Bush: Just great! This is going to look horrible when it hits the news. My ratings are going to plummet.

Cheney: It won't reach the news, Mr. President. Our trained puppies in the Media say what we tell them to. And as far as they're concerned, nothing's happened up there – and nothing will. We've already got our men picking up the seal and bird carcasses, and who's going to notice a few oily rocks?

Bush: I don't like this. What if all those hippies were right?

Cheney: Mr. President, don't get all emotional on me. Besides, you can't make an omelet without a few cracked eggs; progress and financial stability require sacrifice.

Bush: I suppose. Give me some good news, please!

Cheney: Our 'Defense of Marriage' Act has passed both Houses – without so much as a peep – and is just waiting for your signature to be made Law, Sir.

Bush: That's great news! Such a holy and universally esteemed institution must be protected. Why, if we granted equal recognition to those homos, who knows what would be next. I once saw a man on Jerry Springer who made love to his dog. Should they be allowed to get married too?

Cheney: No Sir, they should not. And nothing, not even the Constitution, will stand in our way of upholding decency and God's own morality.

Bush: Amen! Speaking of which, how are things going on the religious front? What was the response to my declaration to recognize Christianity as our State religion?

Cheney: Well, Sir, it looks promising – I mean, during the elections we did pretty much fill both Houses with loyal men who'll grant you whatever you ask – but there has been some pretty strong opposition to your proposal. In fact, for the first time in centuries, Jews and Moslems are getting along, peacefully united in their hatred for you.

Bush: What do you mean? Aren't they Christian too?

Cheney: Uh…no Sir.

Bush: But Jesus was a Jew. It doesn't matter if they wear those silly little beanies when they do it, we all pray to the same God.

Cheney: They don't seem to see it that way, Mr. President.

Bush: Well, they had better. We're in a time of war, fighting for the future of our country. We need all the support we can get – especially from Almighty God himself. Anybody who disagrees with me is clearly un-American, un-Christian, and siding with the terrorists. If they're not careful, they'll end up being tried as enemy combatants.

Chorus:
O beautiful for spacious skies,
for amber waves of grain,
for purple mountain majesties
above the fruited plain!
America! America!
God shed his grace on thee
and crown thy good with brotherhood
from sea to shining sea!

A White House Page *enters, breathless.*

White House Page: Excuse me, Mr. President. I hope I'm not disturbing you, but I've got urgent news.

Bush: No, ma'am. We were just finishing up here, right Mr. Cheney?

Cheney: Well, there were a few more things I wanted to address – like my proposal to transfer funds from Medicare to Homeland Security so that we can better spy on those pinkos in Hollywood – but it can wait.

Bush: Very well. So what's this urgent news you've brought me?

Page: Well, Sir…it seems like your daughters are up to it again.

Bush: *(holds his head, as if he's got a headache)* What is it this time?

Page: Well, Sir... (*The page looks at the desk, the wall, down at her feet, anywhere but the President.*)

Cheney: Out with it now!

Page: Well, Sir...it seems that your daughters are drunk.

Bush: So what's new?

Page: They're drunk, and running around the streets of Washington...uh...topless, Sir.

Bush and Cheney: What?!?

Page: Yes. It's like something out of one of those 'Girls Gone Wild' videos. They're wearing these odd animal-skin capes and headbands made of ivy and grape-leaves, and other than that, there's not a stitch of clothing on their bodies.

Bush: But it's February, for God's sake! They must be freezing.

Page: They don't appear to be Sir. But maybe the frenzied dancing and singing are keeping them warm.

Bush: Where are they doing this? Please tell me it's somewhere out of sight. Some secluded club, where we can go in and make sure that this story never reaches the light of day.

Page: I wish that were the case, Sir. Your daughters are dancing in the streets down below, right in front of the White House gates for all to see.

Bush and Cheney: What?!?

Page: I'm afraid so, Sir. Mixed in with all the protestors and rabble that usually gather out front.

Bush: Oh Jesus Christ, I can't believe this! How could they do this to me? My enemies are just going to love this. It's going to be all over the papers. Can you imagine what the headlines will be?

Cheney: This is bad.

Page: It gets worse.

Bush: (*bangs his fist on the table*) How? How can it get worse than this?

Page: It seems your daughters have joined some kind of free love hippie cult. They're dancing down there naked at the instigation of a long-haired, bearded cult leader, dressed in strange flowing Arab robes.

Bush: This is too much! I can't believe this. It has to be some kind of joke. It really isn't very funny to say things like that, you know. I'll have your job for this.

Page: Mr. President, I'm telling you the truth. I wish it weren't true. I wish I wasn't the one who had to carry this news to you. But it's my job, and it's not fair to punish the bearer of bad news.

Cheney: You've said enough, now get out of here before we decide to do exactly that.

White House Page *exits*.

Bush: What are we going to do? I simply can't believe this. My daughters, daughters sprung from my very own flesh…hippies. This is an outrage!

Cheney: I'll take care of this for you, Mr. President. We'll send the Secret Service down there and bust heads until we get your daughters back. They aren't in their right minds; they've been brainwashed by this strange cult leader. We'll paint the streets red with their spilled blood and brains if we have to, to get your daughters back – and to take this man into custody.

Dick Cheney *exits*.

Chorus:
Down from the Mountain have we come,
to the banks of the Potomac,
and the shining marble of the Nation's Capitol,
come out of your homes, o people,
dawn the fawnskin and lift high the ivied wand,
and sing with us praises to Bromios, the beautiful and boisterous One,
whose simple worship gladdens the heart.
Sweet it is to lose yourself in the dance,
to feel the juice of the grape course through your body,
tiring your spirit until you toss back your head
and give the ecstatic cry Euoi! Euoi! Io Euoi!
Drunk on the God, we have no care for empty possessions,
and the foolish rantings of angry Kings,
for with Dionysos, we know ourselves free,
and have the Earth's rich bounty as our inheritance.
Ie ie Bacchos! Io io Bromios!

Bush: Oh, shut up.

Dick Cheney *enters, followed by several* Secret Service Agents *who are holding, between them, the* Stranger, *his hands bound*.

Cheney: We caught the rogue, and he didn't even put up a fight. He was standing down there, amid a throng of his followers decked out like it was

Mardis Gras. They were singing and dancing, some of them playing tambourines, others pipes, and others still plaiting garlands of flowers for the spectators to wear. It was like a party was going on down there – not a protest. But when they saw the Secret Service Agents come near, a change came over the crowd. They began screaming for blood, and hurled the foulest of insults at us. They rushed the gates, and would have broken through, but this one just lifted his hands, and said, "Let them pass unharmed. I have business with the President." And the wild, raging crowd quieted, lions become lambs as the gates parted and our men walked up to him. He simply held out his hands, and let us cuff him, then let us escort him away, stopping only to say, "Remain still, my Bacchae, and keep your faith. I will soon return."

Secret Service Agent 1: That's the power of the gun. It turns even the bravest man into a craven coward.

The Stranger: I am no coward; had I wished, your throat would have been torn out, and you'd be choking on your own black blood, and not your stupid words.

SS Agent 1: (*lifts his hand to strike him*) Why I ought to!

Stranger: But you won't.

Bush: Stop! There'll be plenty of time for that later. First I want to find out what this man's done to my daughters.

Stranger: I freed them. I helped them discover who they truly were, and brought that out for the world to see.

Bush: You brainwashed them. You corrupted them. You made them do dirty things.

Stranger: I made them do nothing: that was already in their hearts. I simply removed the restrictions. Had your daughters been truly chaste and modest, then that's what would have come out. But then, you know better than I how your daughters resent the yoke, how wild and sensual their spirits are.

Bush: I don't need you to tell me about my daughters!

Stranger: (*wryly*) No, I imagine you don't.

Bush: Leave us. I want to interrogate this man alone.

SS Agents: Are you sure, Mr. President? What if he…?

Bush: You heard me!

The Secret Service Agents *reluctantly leave.*

Dick Cheney *prepares to leave as well.*

Bush: No, not you. You're my right-hand man.

Cheney: I'm considerably more than that.

Bush: That's why I need you to stay.

George W. Bush *gets up from his chair, and stands in front of the* Stranger *trying to look intimidating.*

Bush: Who are you?

Stranger: I am a Mystery.

Cheney: Don't get smart with us, what's your name?

Stranger: I have many names in many lands.

Bush: Then how shall we call you?

Stranger: You may call me Dionysos.

Bush: Do you lead that cult down there?

Dionysos: I lead them from their homes and dreary lives, lead them to the distant mountain, lead them in their sacred songs, lead them as they dance their holy dances, lead them as they celebrate the ineffable mysteries by moonlight. Yes, I am their leader.

Bush: What sort of mysteries are these?

Dionysos: Something only the initiate may know.

Cheney: This is some strange New Age cult, right?

Dionysos: No. My worship is as old as time.

Bush: It's a scheme. Something you thought up to make yourself rich, and to ruin people's lives.

Dionysos: Only one as venal as you would think such thoughts. No, my worship is what enriches people's lives, not your endless chasing after money.

Cheney: Commie!

Bush: (*touching* Dionysos' *robes*) Look at how's he's dressed. These soft, flowing robes. Why, these are the clothes of a Moslem terrorist. And look at this beard! (*Grabs the ends of his beard.*) What's he hiding under this beard? An evil heart? A sinister nature? A mind plotting against America? No decent man wears a beard. Rasputin, Osama, Saddam – all the villains have got beards.

Dionysos: But you're clean-shaven.

Bush: What's that supposed to mean?

Dionysos: You heard me.

Cheney: How dare you say that to the President of the United States of America?

Dionysos: (*stands fully upright*) How dare *he*? How dare he claim what is not rightfully his? How dare he parade as a just and upright man, while his nature is base and his heart full of sin? How dare he use deception to enflame the lust for unrighteous war in his people? How dare he trample on the rights of the free individual man, censuring his words, policing his thoughts? How dare he show such contempt for his people, letting the poor languish in destitution and sickness, while bestowing even greater wealth upon his friends? How dare he despoil and exploit the resources of the Earth, generous mother of us all? How dare he flout the laws of his land, bending them to his own corrupt uses? How dare he, indeed!

Cheney: Enough! Stifle yourself, or I'll do it for you!

Dionysos: Raise a finger against me, and you'll regret it.

Cheney: What can you do? You're locked in chains.

Dionysos: I remain in chains only because I consent to.

Bush: Oh yeah?

Dionysos: Yeah.

Dionysos *raises his hands and the manacles fall off.*

Cheney: (*stepping between* Dionysos *and* George W. Bush) Don't you dare harm the President. You'll regret it!

Dionysos: I'm not going to harm him. Yet. First he must be given a chance to see the error of his ways and repent. I am a just God, after all.

Bush: There is only one God!

Dionysos: I have met considerably more than that walking through the gilded halls of my Father's palace on Mount Olympos.

Bush: The only true God is Jesus Christ. In his name, I rebuke this insanity of yours.

Dionysos: (*laughs*) You would rebuke me by myself?

Bush: You truly are insane! You think you're Jesus?

Dionysos: I don't think: I know. For I, Dionysos, am the True Vine. It was I who turned the water to wine; I who healed the sick in spirit; I who bade the women leave their homes to follow me no matter the strictures of family and society; I who purified the temple and made the triumphant procession amid ivy and palms into Jerusalem; I who gave the Apostles the gift of prophecy; I who was hung upon the tree for the remission of sins; and I who rose again; I, whose blood is the wine. I, Dionysos, did all this!

Bush: Blasphemy! I won't stand here listening to that. Guards! Guards!

The Secret Service Agents *come running in. They circle around* Dionysos *menacingly.*

Bush: Get this man out of here! Take him down to the basement for interrogation. Summon John Ashcroft. He'll know what to do with a man like this.

Cheney: Not so brave now, are you?

Dionysos: Nothing can happen to me at your hands that I do not allow. I go now, humbly, to make my return all the more conspicuous. Soon it shall be you trembling before my might. Fighting against the Gods is as futile as kicking against a stone; you shall see.

Dionysos *puts up his hands, and lets the* Secret Service Agents *lead him away.*

Cheney: Did you hear that man? How foolish and audacious he was. The very nerve, speaking to you like that, Mr. President!

Bush: Ashcroft will bring about a change of attitude in him, I'm sure – he has his ways.

Cheney: Even I'm a little squeamish around that man. He raises torture to an art form. He has tools that can remove a man's tongue without even leaving a mark. I wouldn't want to be that foolish Dionysos right now.

Chorus:
Rise up, O Lord!
No longer suffer the inequities of this unrighteous King with mildness and restraint,
but like boiling lava flowing down the side of a mountain, come, come!
Mad and raving, to inflict terrible destruction upon this fool and lay him low!

Rise up, O Lord!
As you rose up against Pentheus, who vainly sought to oppose your worship in the city of your birth. You drove him into a frenzy of madness, and beneath a pine-tree, his own mother tore him to pieces.
Rise up, O Lord!
As you rose up against Lykourgos, who put your women to flight. You blinded him, and made him think that his son was made of vines, then opened his eyes that he might witness the bloody spectacle he had wrought.
Rise up, O Lord!
As you rose up against the daughters of Minyas, who shunned your sacred rites. You inflicted such hunger upon them that they cast lots to see which of their children they would boil in a pot.
Come, come night-roving Bacchos, terrible to look upon, roaring like thunder, like a bull in frenzy, shake the earth to its core, and topple this arrogant bastard!

The lights suddenly flicker and go out.

Cheney: Ah! The floor is shaking! We're under attack!

The lights come back on. George W. Bush *is cowering under the table.*

Cheney: Mr. President! Mr. President! Are you okay?

George W. Bush *climbs out from under the table, brushing off his jacket.*

Bush: I...I think so. What happened?

Cheney: I don't know, Mr. President. The whole room shook and then the lights went out. An earthquake, perhaps? Or a bomb going off? Your guess is as good as mine. But at least we've got power back.

The Secret Service Agents *bust through the door.*

SS Agent 1: Oh, thank Heavens, the President is alright!

SS Agent 2: Yes, we got here before he did. Quick! Take up your positions!

The Secret Service Agents *spread out around the room, taking up defensive postures.*

Cheney: What in the hell is going on here?

SS Agent 3: The prisoner got loose!

Cheney: He's just one man. Why all the commotion?

SS Agent 2: He's not a man. Had you seen what we saw, you'd be convinced of that.

Bush: What was the loud boom, and why'd the power go out?

SS Agent 2: The whole earth trembled when he broke his bonds; in death and madness his divinity was made manifest.

SS Agent 3: Shut up, you superstitious fool. It was just a coincidence. There was an earthquake, and in the confusion the prisoner got free. That's all.

SS Agent 2: How can you deny what you saw with your own eyes? You saw the ivy suddenly appear, covering the walls and twining itself around the table on which the stranger sat. You heard the ghostly sound of drums and cymbals and shrill pipes that came from nowhere and everywhere at once. Saw the floor washed with red wine. Smelled the sweet, cloying incense. Heard things walking about the room that were not there. And finally, you saw the fierce beasts fall upon Ashcroft, tearing him to shreds as we fled in fear. How can you deny what we all saw and heard?

SS Agent 3: Hallucinations; nothing more than hallucinations. When the earthquake happened it must have broken open some of Ashcroft's nerve gas, and we all started to hallucinate.

Bush: What's going on? I don't understand. Where's the prisoner?

SS Agent 2: He's on his way here. He's coming for you, Mr. President.

Cheney: Enough of that! Now tell us what happened. How'd you let him escape – he was just one prisoner!

Secret Service Agent 1: We had no trouble bringing him down to Ashcroft's interrogation chamber. Like a lamb being led to the slaughter, he meekly let us take him without complaint. In fact, he didn't say a thing the whole time: he just stood there in eerie silence, his face like an unseeing mask. Even when Ashcroft strapped him to the table and brought out his tools, he uttered not a word. Now Ashcroft's needles and knives have reduced the hardest men to tears; Saddam he had blubbering like a baby in minutes. But this one, he could not reach, no matter what atrocities he performed on his flesh. We would have thought him dead – there was enough blood on the floor to prove it – but his chest still rose, and his eyes continued to stare, and all the while, that hateful, mocking smile remained on his lips. It drove Ashcroft insane! He began stabbing the prisoner, screaming, 'Do something, do something!' And then, the prisoner did something.

Bush: What? What did he do?

SS Agent 1: The earth shook. He sat bolt upright, the straps on the table splitting apart. Ivy, and wine, and music filled the room. And suddenly, we were not alone. Swirling around him as if he were the calm center of a devastating tornado were... things. I can't say what exactly they were. Now they had one shape, and now another. But they were fierce, and bestial, and I,

I who have served my country my whole life, who have faced death in the deserts of Iraq, turned and fled, fear clutching at my heart with its black claws.

Cheney: Your story is preposterous! It's too much to be believed.

SS Agents 1 & 2: Soon, you shall see – and you will believe.

Dionysos *enters. The* Chorus *screams.*

Dionysos: I have come! I am Dionysos, the son of Zeus, Lord of the fruitful Earth, who has given man sweet wine for the enjoyment of life, and blessed mysteries to purify his care-worn soul. Down from the Mountain have I come, snowy Nysa where dance the lovely-ankled nymphs and the shaggy-haired satyrs, my dear companions. I have come to Washington because you are an arrogant King, who hates my ways, and would rather send young men to kill and die in gold-hungry conquest than see them lay in loving embrace, their hair soaked in sweat after long hours of honoring me with their bodies. Many times have I come to you, and you did not recognize me. Even when the voice of your people rose up and pleaded for you to put off this crazy bloodthirstiness of yours, and welcome the Goddess Peace once more into your land – you would not listen. And so now I have come, I who am most gentle and most fierce, and now you will listen to me!

Cheney: Don't just stand there! Get him.

Secret Service Agent *3 steps forward, as if to charge the intruder – but then notices that the other* Agents *are holding back. He loses courage, and falls back.*

SS Agents 1 & 2: No, we won't fight against a God. Listen to him: what he says makes a lot of sense. You are ruining our country; put on the ivy-crown and dance with us in joyful celebration. Great is the God Dionysos! And great his worship! Io euoi!

Chorus: Io euoi! Io io euoi!

Cheney: Cowards and fools! No, I will never honor this liar, falsely claiming to be a God. I fear no one! Aaaarrrgghh!

Dick Cheney *lunges for* Dionysos *but manages only two steps.* Dionysos *holds up his hand.*

Dionysos: I know how to make a dick go soft.

Dick Cheney *clutches his heart, convulses.*

Cheney: No! Not again! Aaaaaggghh!

And collapses to the floor, dead.

Dionysos *turns to* George W. Bush.

Dionysos: O puppet, what will you do, now that your strings have been cut, and your puppet master lies broken?

Bush: I'm not a puppet! I made all the decisions around here.

Dionysos: Then you have a lot to answer for, little man.

Dionysos *advances on* George W. Bush, *who backs up until he bumps into the table.*

Bush: I have nothing to answer for. I made all the right decisions. America was attacked! We had to defend ourselves!

Dionysos: Then you should have gone after those who harmed you. When you spill innocent blood, it calls out to heaven. And how do you answer to the crime of stealing from the coffers, while the poor die in the streets from want?

Bush: Being President is hard work: I deserve some reward. The poor will always be with us.

Dionysos: And the law – you claim it is your sacred duty to uphold it, yet you have corrupted its spirit, and used it as a bludgeon against your enemies. You have overstepped your bounds; you have tried to impose your will in places it has no right to go.

Bush: The State is the father of the people, and I am the State. Like any father, it is my duty to protect and guide my children, to correct them when they do wrong.

Dionysos: And so you answer, and stand condemned by your words. You are hateful to me, and I will not allow your arrogance to go unpunished.

Dionysos *raises his hands, as if to strike him;* George W. Bush *falls to his knees, clutching his head and weeping.*

Dionysos: In times past, I would have brought you down like a stag felled by hounds. I would have torn you to pieces, and took pleasure in your flesh parting beneath my fingers, your warm, red blood gushing out to stain the black earth. I would have delighted in your piteous whelps of pain, would have smiled as you shrieked out your last breath. But these are different times, crueler times, and there are bitches more fierce than my mainades now. I will give you over to them!

The stage clears, replaced by a News Anchorwoman, *seated at the desk.*

Anchorwoman: And in a stunning turn of events today, President George W. Bush called a halt to all foreign involvement by American troops. He called the invasions of France and other countries 'grossly unjust and uncalled for' and said that he 'sincerely apologized for any inconvenience the Imperialistic Military Industrial Complex had caused.' He also disbanded the 'Patriot Act,' the 'Defense of Marriage Act,' and the 'Affirmation of the Christian Religion Act' – saying that this legislature was 'insane' and 'everything that decent Americans should stand against.' He has also promised that he will bring about universal healthcare and give tax breaks to the working poor. And, perhaps most shocking of all, President Bush announced today that he will be seeking a divorce from his wife, and replacing her with his new lover, Raoul Hernandez, a Cuban refugee and exotic dancer, who some sources claim has also worked as a male prostitute. These sudden, sweeping, and drastic changes have met with almost universal condemnation. For special commentary, we now turn to conservative columnist....

THE SATYR OF NEW ORLEANS

The young satyr sat hunched over, his head — with its unkempt mass of tiny bronze curls barely concealing his goat ears and tiny horn nubs — cradled in his hands. His fingernails were chipped, broken to the quick, and covered in blood and grime from digging through rubble like that upon which he was perched all day. Once this had been a grand old French theater, one of the oldest buildings in New Orleans. Now it was just a heap of wood and stone and ashes. His slender young body convulsed with noiseless sobs; he had no more tears to shed, but still he cried.

"Here," a voice said from behind him, soft and gentle like a young bud on the vine. "Drink."

Dionysos pushed the cup into his nerveless fingers and the young satyr just held it, the coolness soothing to his bruised and flushed hands.

"Drink," Dionysos repeated, more insistently. Martes, for that was the boy's name, slowly raised his head and stared at his God. Dionysos' handsome face was covered in dirt and his ivy crown hung lopsided on his head, damaged in places. His long, flowing *himation* was in tatters, soaked and covered in mud waist high. One of his buskins had been damaged and was hanging from his leg in shreds, kept there only by the laces. Dionysos smiled at his young charge, but the gesture didn't quite reach his eyes, which were dark with sadness and suffering. Martes felt the God's hands enclose his own and lift the cup up to his mouth. He let the wine pass over his lips, cold as ice, and swallowed. The wine was sweet and soothed his dry, parched throat. As it entered his body it left a warm, pleasurable sensation in its wake and he took several more mouthfuls before Dionysos let go.

Dionysos sat down beside him on the rubble and sighed heavily. The two sat in silence for several long moments, the warm, humid night air clinging to them wetly. Off in the distance they could hear the buzzing of cicadas, and faintly a person crying.

"Why?" Martes finally asked. "Why did this happen?"

"I don't know," Dionysos confessed, taking up a piece of masonry and exploring it with his fingers. "None of us do. We all thought Typhon was safely imprisoned beneath Aetna, with chains of adamantine forged by Hephaistos. He shouldn't have been able to get loose." Dionysos tossed the stone and it bounced off a neighboring streetlamp that somehow still stood. It skidded a few times and then came to rest in the empty intersection. "Somehow he did."

"Is this the end?"

"No. It only seems that way."

Martes swallowed hard. It was difficult to believe him. Everywhere he looked there was total destruction: ruins of buildings that just a couple days before had stood whole; fires smoldering in burnt-out husks of homes; mountains of filth; houses covered in the thick, brown, brackish water of the river; corpses laying exposed in the streets, floating in the water, hanging from trees; men running around lawless, looting and murdering and raping little children. Certainly if this was not the end, it was the beginning of the end.

Dionysos placed his hand on Martes' shoulder; he hadn't realized that he was shaking.

"I saw the winds toss waves into buildings and knock them flat as if they were made of sand. I saw the levy, which seemed so strong, so invulnerable, begin to crumble, and not even you or Athene standing there holding it up could stop the water from coming. I saw families desperately fleeing overcome by the water, and moments later, they were floating on the surface as corpses. I dug through the wreckage, all the while hearing the desperate pleas for help growing softer and softer, until, by the time I got to them....it was too late. I saw men and women hunched in alleyways, too weak from hunger and thirst to even move. On the bridge I saw young children wandering terrified and alone, toddlers who could only cry out for their mothers, whom they would never see again. I saw..." but Martes' voice faltered, overcome by weeping. Dionysos enfolded him in his arms and held the young satyr as he wept. Finally, Martes broke away and stared up at his God.

"How can you tell me that this isn't the end?"

"Man is a remarkable creature. He is resilient and strong. Somehow, when things seem the worst, and all hope is lost, he finds the courage and resources within himself to come back, to continue in the face of hardship, to rebuild and recreate life anew. Man has faced much worse than this and survived. I promise you, my son, bad as it is, this is not the end."

"But what's the point? Why should he even bother if it can all be swept away in an instant?"

"Because that is the way of life. It is a delicate thread stretched over a gaping chasm, and it can snap at any moment. And it will snap, because that is its *moira*. But, by Zeus, how beautiful that thread is while it lasts – it shines brighter than any star in heaven. And while men live, they are driven to create, to build, to reflect on what it means to be alive, to share their experiences with others, to love and live their lives to the fullest. This is an uncontrollable drive in men, as instinctual as a bird's need for flight or an ant's desire to gather food. And this desire – to reach out across the chasm to touch another, to create and thus to leave a lasting mark on the world that will extend beyond their mortal limits – ensures that this city will not die, that it will be reborn, one brick at a time, one life after another. It will not be easy, and it will not be as it was before, but life here will continue; Typhon shall not prevail, for creation is more powerful than uncreation."

"Are you sure?"

"Yes. This is my city, and my people."

They sat for a while longer in silence, Martes reflecting on the God's words. And then Dionysos stood and brushed some of the dirt from his ragged *himation* and said, "Come, my child. You need your rest. We have much to do tomorrow if we are to help these mortals rebuild. There are lives to be saved, and *psukhai* to be guided, and food to be brought to the hungry survivors. Hermes and Demeter cannot do it alone."

And so Martes stood and took Dionysos' hand in his own and the pair walked into the darkness.

APPENDIX I: SELECT LIST OF DIONYSIAN EPITHETS

Aigobolos (slayer of goats)
Agrios (wild one)
Aisymnetes (elected monarch, judge)
Akratophoros (of unmixed wine)
Aktaios (of the seacoast)
Anax (lord)
Anthios (god of all blossoming things)
Anthroporraistes (slayer of men)
Areion (martial one)
Arretos (ineffable)
Arsenothelys (man-womanly)
Auxites (bringer of growth)
Bassareus (fox god, Thracian)
Botryophoros (bearer of grape clusters)
Briseus (son of the nymphs)
Bromios (boisterous)
Charidotes (giver of grace)
Choreutês (dancer)
Chthonios (subterranean)
Dasullios (of the thicket, wild-wood)
Dendrites (of the tree)
Dikerotes (two-horned)
Diphyes (two-natured)
Dithyrambos (of the dithyrambic hymn)
Diwonusojo (Linear B)
Druphoros (oak-bearer)
Eiraphiotes (insewn)
Eleuthereus (emancipator)
Endendros (tree)
Eriphios (goat kid)
Euanthes (fair blossoming)
Eubouleus (good counselor)
Euios (from the ritual cry)
Hagnos (pure, holy)
Hues (of moisture)
Hugiates (dispenser of health)
Iackhos (crier, caller)

Iatros (healer)
Isodaites (divider of sacrificial meat)
Katharsios (he who releases)
Kissobryos (ivy-wrapped)
Kissokomes (ivy-crowned)
Kissos (ivy)
Korymbophoros (cluster-laden)
Kresios (Cretan)
Kryphios (hidden, secret)
Lampteros (torch-bearer, of lights)
Leibenos (of libations)
Lenaios (of the wine press)
Liknites (in the liknon)
Limnaios (of the marsh)
Luaeus (he who frees)
Lusios (liberator)
Mainomenos (he who makes mad)
Manikos (mad one)
Mantis (prophet, seer)
Meilikhios (mild, gentle)
Melanaigis (he of the black goatskin)
Melpomenos (harp-singer)
Morychos (dark one)
Nyktelios (nocturnal)
Nyktiphaês (night-illuminating)
Nyktipolos (night prowler)
Omadios (of the raw feast)
Omestes (feeds on raw flesh)
Orthos (the erect)
Pelagios (of the sea)
Perikionios (of the column)
Ploutodotês (bestower of riches)
Polyeides (of many images)
Polygethes (bringer of many joys)
Polymorphos (many formed)
Polyonomos (many named)
Polyparthenos (of many maidens)
Protogonos (first born)
Protrugaios (feast before the vintage)
Psilax (winged)
Purigenes (fire born)
Skêptouchos (scepter-bearer)
Soter (savior)
Sphaleotas (he who causes stumbling)
Staphylos (the grape)
Sukites (of the fig tree)
Taurokeros (bull horned)
Taurophagos (bull devourer)

Tauropôn (bull faced)
Teletarches (lord of initiations)
Thriambos (of the triumphal hymn)
Thullophoros (bearer of boughs)
Thuoneus (son of Thyone-Semele)
Thursophoros (thyrsus bearer)
Trigonos (thrice-born)
Zagreus (hunter)

APPENDIX II: A LIST OF GODS WITH WHOM DIONYSOS IS SYNCRETIZED

Adonis: Plutarch, *Symposiacs* 4.6
Agathos Daimon: Philokhoros fragment
An unnamed Gaulish deity: Strabo, *Geography* 4.4.6
An unnamed Indian deity: Philostratos, *Life of Apollonius of Tyana* 2.6-10
Antinous: Pausanias, *Guide to Greece* 8.9.8
Apis: Diodoros Sikeliotes, *The Library of History* 1.85
Apollon: Aiskhylos fr. 86
Ares: *Orphic Hymn* 30
Arsaphes: Plutarch, *On Isis and Osiris* 37
Asklepios: *PL* 498
Attis: Hippolytos, *Refutation of All Heresies* 5.9.9
Chaldaean Demiurge: John Lydus, *De Mensibus*, 83
Dioskouroi: Cicero, *De Natura Deorum* 3.53
Dusares: *ZDMG* 14465
Enyalios: Macrobius, *Saturnalia* 1.19.1
Epaphos: Mnaseas fr. 37
Eros: Diodoros Sikeliotes, *The Library of History* 1.2.3
Eubouleos: *Orphic Hymn* 42
Haides: Herakleitos fr. 115
Helios: Macrobius, *Saturnalia* 1.17
Hermes: Nonnos, *Dionysiaka* 136ff
Horus: *The Karpokrates Aretalogy from Chalcis*
Iakchos: Strabo, *Geography* 10.3.10
Jesus Christ: Justin Martyr, *First Apology* 54
Liber Pater: Plutarch, *Roman Questions* 104
Orotalt: Herodotos, *The Histories* 3.8
Osiris: Herodotos, *The Histories* 2.42
Paian: *The cult-hymn of Philodamos*
Phanês: Orphic fr. 60
Priapos: Athenaios, *Deipnosophistai* 1.30b
Sabazios: Strabo, *Geography* 10.3.18
Serapis: Diodoros Sikeliotes, *The Library of History* 1.25
Tammuz: Lucian, *De Dea Syria* 16
Thracian 'Hero': *CCIS* II D3
Yahweh: Tacitus, *The Histories* 5.2.5
Zagreus: Suidas s.v. *Zagreus*
Zeus: *CIG* 358

BIBLIOGRAPHY

Ancient Sources

There are countless references to Dionysos scattered throughout ancient Greek literature. Among the most important are:

Apollodoros' *Library*
Aristophanes' *The Frogs*
Athenaios' *Deipnosophistai*
Diodoros Sikeliotes' *The Library of History*
Euripides' *Bakchai*
Hesiod's *Theogony*
The Homeric Hymns
Nonnos' *Dionysiaka*
The Orphic Hymns
Ovid's *Metamorphoses*
Pausanias' *Guide to Greece*
Plutarch's *Moralia* (especially *On Isis and Osiris*, *Table Talks*, the *Pythian Dialogues*, and the *Greek and Roman Questions* though there are many references found throughout his other works as well)

Modern Sources

Burkert, Walter. *Greek Religion*. Oxford: Blackwell, 1985.
___ *Ancient Mystery Cults*. Harvard University Press, 2005.
Buxton, Richard, ed. *Oxford Readings in Greek Religion*. Oxford University Press, 2000.
Carpenter, Thomas H. *Dionysian Imagery in Fifth-Century Athens*. Oxford University Press, 1997.
Carpenter, Thomas H., and Christopher A. Faraone. *Masks of Dionysus*. Cornell University Press, 1993.
Codellas, Pan. S. "Modern Greek Folklore: The Smerdaki." *The Journal of American Folklore* 58.229 (1945): 236 - 44.
Cosmopoulos, Michael B., ed. *Greek Mysteries: The Archaeology and Ritual of Ancient Greek Secret Cults*. London: Routledge, 2003.
Dalby, Andrew. *Bacchus: A Biography*. Getty Trust Publications: J. Paul Getty Museum, 2004.
Danielou, Alain *Gods of Love & Ecstasy: The Traditions of Shiva & Dionysus*. Inner Traditions, 1992.
Detienne, Marcel. *Dionysos Slain*. Johns Hopkins, 1979.
___ *Dionysos at Large*. Harvard University Press, 1989.

Dodds, E. R. *The Greeks and the Irrational.* University of California Press; New Edition, 2004.
Elderkin, George. *Kantharos: Studies in Dionysiac and Kindred Cult.*
Evans, Arthur. *The God of Ecstasy: Sex Roles & the Madness of Dionysos.* St. Martin's Press, 1988.
Everett, Percival. *Frenzy.* Graywolf Press 1996.
Fraser, P. M. *Ptolemaic Alexandria*, 3 Volumes. Oxford University Press, 1985.
Garland, Robert. *Religion and the Greeks.* Classical World Series. Ed. Michael Gunningham. London: Bristol Classical Press, 1994.
Graf, Fritz and Sarah Iles Johnston, *Ritual Texts for the Afterlife: Orpheus and the Bacchic Gold Tablets.* London and New York: Routledge, 2007.
Guthrie, W. K. C. *Orpheus & Greek Religion.* Norton, 1966.
Harrison, Jane Ellen. *Prolegomena to the Study of Greek Religion.* Princeton University Press, 1991.
Hazzard, R. A. *Imagination of a Monarchy: Studies in Ptolemaic Propaganda.* University of Toronto Press. 2000
Hölbl, Günther. *History of the Ptolemaic Empire.* Routledge, 2000.
Houser, Caroline. *Dionysos and His Circle : Ancient Through Modern.* Fogg Art Museum, Harvard University, 1979.
Hutchinson, Valerie J. *Bacchus in Roman Britain: The Evidence For His Cult.* Oxford, England: B.A.R., 1986.
Jones, Prudence. *Cleopatra: A Sourcebook.* University of Oklahoma Press, 2006.
Kerenyi, Carl. *Dionysos: Archetypal Image of Indestructible Life.* Trans. Ralph Manheim. Princeton University Press, 1976.
___ *The Gods of the Greeks.* London: Thames and Hudson, 1951.
Kondoleon, Christine. *Domestic and Divine : Roman Mosaics in the House of Dionysos.* Cornell University Press, 1994.
Laquer, Thomas. *Making Sex: Body and Gender from the Greeks to Freud.* Harvard University Press, 1992.
Larson, Jennifer. *Greek Nymphs: Myth, Cult, Lore.* Oxford University Press, 2001.
Lada-Richards, Ismene. *Initiating Dionysus : Ritual and Theatre in Aristophanes' Frogs.* Oxford University Press, 1999.
Lenzen, Victor Fritz. *The Triumph of Dionysus on Textiles of Late Antique Egypt.* Berkeley: University of California Press, 1960.
Lindsay, Jack. *Men and Gods on the Roman Nile.* Barnes & Noble, 1968.
___ *Leisure and Pleasure in Roman Egypt.* Barnes & Noble, 1966.
Little, Bentley. *Dominion.* Signet. 1996.
Lonsdale, Steven H. *Dance and Ritual Play in Greek Religion.* Longon: The Johns Hopkins University Press, 1993.
Lopez-Pedraza, Rafael. *Dionysus in Exile: On the Repression of the Body and Emotion.* Chiron Publications, 2000.
McClure, Laura K., ed. *Sexuality and Gender in the Classical World: Readings and Sources.* Oxford: Blackwell Publishing.

Meyer, Marvin W., ed. *The Ancient Mysteries: A Sourcebook, Sacred Texts of the Mystery Religions of the Ancient Mediterranean World.* University of Pennsylvania Press, 1999.

Mikalson, Jon D. *Ancient Greek Religion.* Oxford: Blackwell Publishing, 2005.

Nietzsche, Friedrich. *The Birth of Tragedy and Other Writings.* Cambridge University Press; 1999.

Otto, Walter. *Dionysus: Myth and Cult.* Indiana University Press, 1995.

Palescandolo, Frank. *Phallos Dionysus.* Writer's Showcase Press, 2000.

Paris, Ginette *Pagan Grace: Dionysos, Hermes, and Goddess Memory in Daily Life.* Spring Publications, 1990.

Porter, James I. *The Invention of Dionysus : an Essay on the Birth of Tragedy.* Stanford University Press, 2000.

Pryse, James Morgan. *The Adorers of Dionysos.* Kessinger Publishing, Facsimile Edition, 1993.

Rice, E. E. *The Grand Procession of Ptolemy Philadelphus.* Oxford University Press, 1983.

Rieger, Branimir. *Dionysus in Literature: Essays on Literary Madness.* Bowling Green University Popular Press, 1994.

Riu, Xavier. *Dionysism and Comedy.* Rowman & Littlefield Publishers, 1993.

Sannion, et al. *Written in Wine: A Devotional Anthology for Dionysos.* Bibliotheca Alexandrina, 2008.

Seaford, Richard. *Dionysos.* Routledge, 2006.

Sissa, Giulia and Marcel Detienne, *The Daily Life of the Greek Gods,* Trans. Janet Lloyd. Stanford University Press, 2000.

Tartt, Donna. *The Secret History.* Knopf Publishing Group Reprint 2004.

Thornton, Bruce S. *Eros: The Myth of Ancient Greek Sexuality.* Westview Press, 1997.

Wetmore, Kevin J. *Black Dionysus : Greek Tragedy and African American Theatre.* McFarland & Co., 2003.

Zaidman, and Pantel. *Religion in the Ancient Greek City.* Trans. P Cartledge, Cambridge University Press, 1992.

Online Resources

Wildivine: *http://www.wildivine.org/dionysos.htm*
Theoi.com: *http://theoi.com/Olympios/Dionysos.html*
The Dionysion: *http://www.hermeticfellowship.org/Dionysion/*
The Dionysos Page: *http://home.earthlink.net/~delia5/pagan/dio/index.htm*
Dionysos Links: *http://www.baubo5.com/dionysos.html*
Neos Alexandria: *http://neosalexandria.org/the-pantheon/dionysus/*
Where Dionysos Dwells: *http://wheredionysosdwells.tumblr.com/*
Thiasos Lusios: *http://groups.yahoo.com/group/ThiasosLusios/*

ABOUT THE AUTHOR

H. Jeremiah Lewis is a writer and a passionate devotee of the god Dionysos. Everything else about him is subject to periodic change. He currently resides in Eugene, Oregon.

Learn more about the author and Nysa Press at www.thehouseofvines.com.

ALSO FROM NYSA PRESS

The Balance of the Two Lands: Writings on Greco-Egyptian Polytheism

This collection of essays explores the long history and contemporary manifestations of Greco-Egyptian polytheism. It provides an overview of the system, information on theology, ethics, the afterlife, and material on domestic worship, ritual forms, and the basics needed to begin practicing today. This is a book for all who have heard the call of the gods of Greece and Egypt and wondered what to do next.

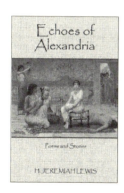

Echoes of Alexandria: Poems and Stories

This volume of poetry and short stories celebrates the author's undying love for the incomparable city of dreamers and the immortal gods and famous historical figures who once walked Alexandria's fabled streets. It offers a unique glimpse into the religious life of a man dedicated to a rich multicultural pantheon drawn from Greece, Egypt, Rome and the Near East. Included are hymns, poetry, imaginative retellings of ancient stories, and modern myths set down for the first time.

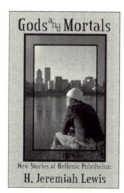

Gods and Mortals: New Stories of Hellenic Polytheism

These are the stories of Hellenismos today. What it feels like to recognize the presence of the gods around you. To discover the mystery of the divine, the joy of love, the struggle with doubt, the loneliness of belonging to a minority faith. You can read about ancient Greek religion in academic tomes, but none will tell you what it's like from the inside. The only way to do that is to hear our stories, in our own words. Stories of gods and mortals.

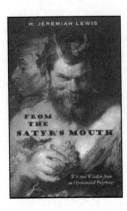

From the Satyr's Mouth: Wit and Wisdom from an Opinionated Polytheist

In ancient Greece, satyrs were famed for their mocking criticism of societal conventions. H. Jeremiah Lewis brings that same spirit to a discussion of contemporary Pagan life and values in this latest collection of essays.

Prepare to be challenged, informed, annoyed and hopefully entertained!

"Bacchus"
Polidoro da Caravaggio (c. 1499 – 1543)

Printed in Great Britain
by Amazon.co.uk, Ltd.,
Marston Gate.